Column headings (left to right): Los Angeles, CA · Louisville, KY · Memphis, TN · Miami, FL · Milwaukee, WI · Minneapolis, MN · Mobile, AL · Montgomery, AL · Nashville, TN · New Orleans, LA · New York City NY · Norfolk, VA · Oakland, CA · Oklahoma City, OK · Omaha, NE · Orlando, FL · Philadelphia, PA · Phoenix, AZ · Pittsburgh, PA · Portland, OR · Providence, RI · Raleigh, NC · Reno, NV · Richmond, VA · Rochester, NY · Saint Louis, MO · Saint Paul, MN · Salt Lake City, UT · San Antonio, TX · San Diego, CA · San Francisco, CA · Seattle, WA · Shreveport, LA · Spokane, WA · Tallahassee, FL · Tampa, FL · Toledo, OH · Tucson, AZ · Tulsa, OK · Washington, DC · West Palm Beach, FL · Youngstown, OH

City	LA	Lou	Mem	Mia	Mil	Min	Mob	Mon	Nas	NOr	NYC	Nor	Oak	OKC	Oma	Orl	Phi	Pho	Pit	Por	Pro	Ral	Ren	Ric	Roc	StL	StP	SLC	SAn	SDg	SFr	Sea	Shr	Spo	Tal	Tam	Tol	Tuc	Tul	Was	WPB	You
Albany, NY	2911	868	1232	1439	933	1215	1322	1178	993	1453	146	505	2982	1523	1308	1249	251	2512	471	2869	178	656	2763	482	219	1028	1215	2290	1986	2855	2966	2855	1599	2652	1249	1281	633	2442	1409	378	1396	462
Albuquerque, NM	823	1332	1021	1994	1443	1256	1265	1345	1232	1187	1995	1905	1134	559	905	1751	1922	446	1654	1378	2156	1759	1056	1833	1857	1054	1362	621	684	787	1135	1500	868	1346	1508	1759	1526	486	674	1864	1938	1646
Amarillo, TX	1095	1041	721	1694	1143	1062	965	1045	932	875	1695	1632	1430	267	754	1451	1622	746	1354	1636	1856	1458	1345	1533	1557	754	1062	917	530	1078	1396	1805	568	1563	1208	1459	1220	656	336	1564	1638	1346
Atlanta, GA	2197	421	397	665	784	1105	340	164	243	493	855	551	2488	863	989	446	766	1810	712	2763	1027	397	2411	572	715	568	1105	1900	965	2174	2511	2656	624	2367	268	476	641	1785	803	636	632	719
Austin, TX	1410	1022	658	1338	1203	1100	656	804	869	535	1728	1403	1786	414	847	1142	1630	1030	1412	2059	1898	1355	1775	1463	1623	806	1120	1301	81	1313	1776	2157	340	1981	899	1150	1315	908	462	1509	1329	1368
Baltimore, MD	2676	680	900	1095	794	1105	990	833	688	1136	201	237	2864	1322	1143	917	97	2311	245	2765	356	324	2562	155	300	827	1095	2051	1646	2714	2765	2686	1229	2417	932	949	454	2246	1208	41	1046	298
Billings, MT	1254	1550	1557	2580	1143	812	1854	1836	1640	1820	1926	2098	1218	1168	904	2271	2051	1220	1681	867	2238	2273	1021	1655	1692	1381	812	579	1600	1309	1239	815	1691	541	2306	2143	2355	1691	945	1041	2065	2736	1632
Birmingham, AL	2067	373	239	788	766	1088	269	93	195	352	1019	711	2321	701	904	545	880	1700	778	2571	1189	557	2363	699	965	539	1188	1895	2034	2371	2475	474	2469	302	553	673	1621	636	781	702	738	
Boise, ID	837	1908	1833	2860	1777	1488	2143	2346	2059	2191	2571	2551	671	1451	1274	2695	2498	1022	2203	439	2701	2560	404	2594	2352	1727	1398	349	1709	1010	595	524	1912	369	2512	2763	2020	1144	1582	2441	2492	2090
Boston, MA	2993	976	1379	1516	1078	1362	1379	1232	1062	1525	203	560	3124	1659	1443	1297	327	2644	584	3149	41	713	2871	544	381	1184	892	2417	2052	2992	3133	2961	1618	2693	1313	1329	742	2571	1532	430	1426	568
Brownsville, TX	1678	1321	957	1580	1530	1456	851	1041	1168	730	2002	1735	2034	680	1249	2034	1954	1289	1713	2468	2222	1506	2068	1646	1891	1216	1565	1609	300	1074	2044	2501	644	2359	1094	1345	1622	1191	835	1787	1542	1695
Buffalo, NY	2521	608	689	630	1032	1316	607	464	576	727	787	454	2788	1176	1303	401	688	2222	777	3018	501	688	2238	772	1379	770	1093	1976	1695	2577	2583	2713	1176	2590	1172	1213	293	2231	1131	410	1181	192
Charleston, SC	2394	258	653	1046	566	874	825	632	458	891	524	369	2600	1031	899	814	517	2045	211	2615	699	297	2407	251	495	544	870	1894	1419	2402	2616	2748	899	2503	868	903	284	2100	941	299	982	251
Charleston, WV	2417	438	592	604	835	1143	575	415	399	721	625	341	2755	1069	1135	552	604	2757	785	162	2570	280	689	1143	2059	1272	2423	2756	2765	885	2505	559	581	1913	989	334	673	502				
Charlotte, NC	1989	300	551	1338	92	405	908	762	474	925	794	851	2098	804	454	1127	757	1776	470	2140	924	802	1897	788	608	292	405	1386	1208	2306	2108	2043	916	1775	957	1143	243	1711	673	697	502	413
Chicago, IL	2164	105	469	1086	388	696	712	561	283	810	628	601	2317	835	721	892	559	1808	790	540	2201	503	502	340	696	1671	1306	2193	2329	2192	813	2066	881	1091	114	1971	933	341	1192	74		
Cincinnati, OH	2392	349	446	445	753	989	815	527	1078	446	493	2498	1047	824	1046	430	2045	128	2416	600	559	2238	583	268	552	753	1727	1443	2384	2408	2336	1070	2068	949	1091	114	1971	933	341	1192	275	
Cleveland, OH	2426	494	612	658	891	1276	555	379	458	701	715	412	2703	1091	1283	440	627	2025	172	2972	888	215	2396	390	789	737	1013	1765	1481	2572	2408		497	683	2080	1018	498	586	561			74
Columbia, SC	2254	211	575	1210	448	753	834	707	389	940	591	450	2646	1159	957	460	597		434		745		1711	1305	2277	2461	2408	592	2115	828	513	1833	795	418	146	170						
Columbus, OH	1401	1908	1013	1013	592	677	666	530	1525	1359	1803	211	693	1078	1427	1013	1209	2059	1695	1152	1731	1313	1420	641	1013	284	1369	1865	2203	196	1978	835	1086	1112	964	259	1306	1265	1193			
Dallas, TX	2407	801	749	259	1180	1458	502	458	639	632	1054	702	2831	1257	1402	81	914	2102	859	3018	1201	959	781	1176	936	548	2283	1157	2418	2827	3070	903	2811	259	141	1063	1999	1156	802	195	986	

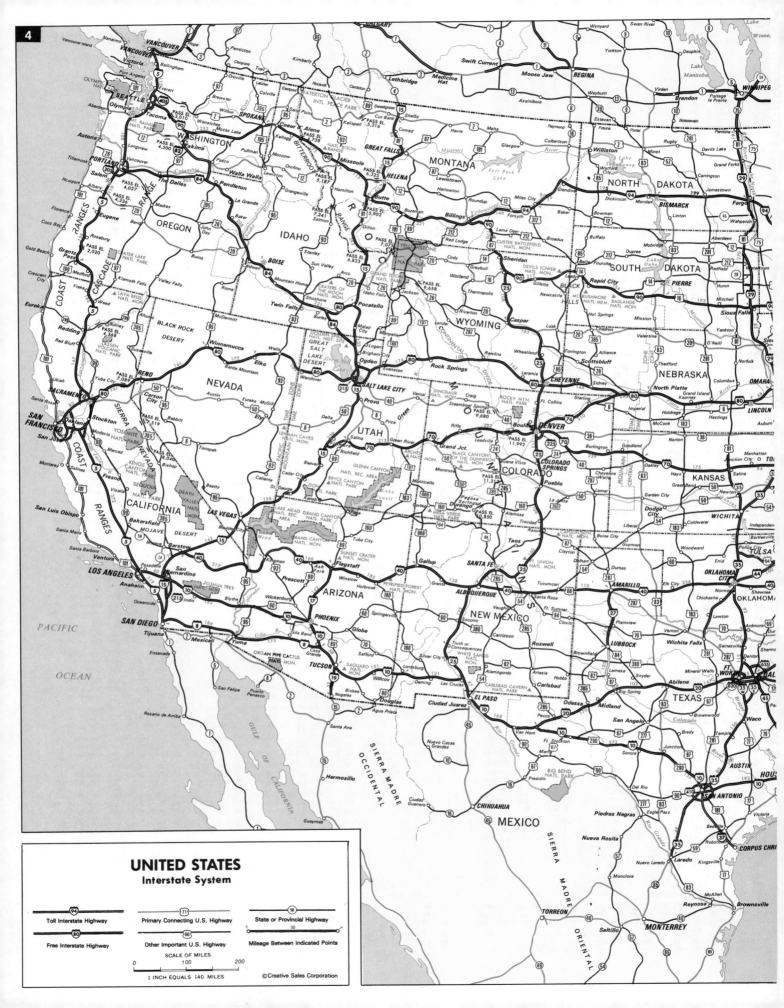

American Map Corporation

UNITED STATES
Road Atlas
Including Canada and Mexico

3 00

Contents

Area Code And Time Zone Map
. . . . Facing Page
Mileage Chart 2-3
U.S. Interstate Highway Map 4-5
National Parks and
    Landmarks Map 6-7

Canada 8-9
Mexico 10-11
State Maps 12-89
City Maps 90-150
Index to Cities and Towns . . . 151-176

State Maps

Alabama 13
Alaska 14
Arizona 16-17
Arkansas 15
California 18-21
Colorado 22-23
Connecticut 24-25
Delaware 43
Florida 26-27
Georgia 28-29
Hawaii 30
Idaho 31
Illinois 32-33
Indiana 34-35
Iowa 36
Kansas 37
Kentucky 38-39
Louisiana 40
Maine 41
Maryland 42-43
Massachusetts 24-25
Michigan 44-45
Minnesota 46-47
Mississippi 50
Missouri 48-49
Montana 51
Nebraska 52-53
Nevada 54
New Hampshire 55

New Jersey 56-57
New Mexico 62
New York 58-61
North Carolina 64-65
North Dakota 63
Ohio 66-67
Oklahoma 68-69
Oregon 70-71
Pennsylvania 72-73
Rhode Island 24-25
South Carolina 64-65
South Dakota 74
Tennessee 38-39
Texas 75-79
Utah 80-81
Vermont 55
Virginia 82-83
Washington 84-85
West Virginia 82-83
Wisconsin 86-87
Wyoming 88-89

City Maps

Atlanta, GA 90
Baltimore, MD 91
Birmingham, AL 92
Boston, MA 93
Buffalo, NY 94
Charlotte, NC 95
Chicago, IL 96-99
Cincinnati, OH 100
Cleveland, OH 101
Columbus, OH 102
Denver, CO 103
Dallas, TX 104-105
Detroit, MI 106-107
Fort Lauderdale, FL 120
Fort Myers, FL 108
Fort Worth, TX 104-105
Houston, TX 109
Indianapolis, IN 110
Jacksonville, FL 111
Kansas City, MO 112
Las Vegas, NV 113
Los Angeles, CA 114-117
Louisville, KY 118
Memphis, TN 119
Miami, FL 120
Milwaukee, WI 121
Minneapolis, MN 122-123
Nashville, TN 124
New Orleans, LA 125

New York, NY 126-129
Norfolk, VA 130
Oakland, CA 144-145
Oklahoma City, OK 131
Omaha, NE 132
Orlando, FL 133
Philadelphia, PA 134
Phoenix, AZ 135
Pittsburgh, PA 136
Portland, OR 137
Raleigh, NC 138
Richmond, VA 139
Rochester, NY 138
Sacramento, CA 141
Saint Louis, MO 140
Saint Paul, MN 122-123
Saint Petersburg, FL 148
Salt Lake City, UT 141
San Antonio, TX 142
San Diego, CA 143
San Francisco, CA 144-145
San Jose, CA 146
Seattle, WA 147
Tampa, FL 148
Tucson, AZ 149
Washington, DC 150
West Palm Beach, FL 120

Columns (left to right): Albany, NY · Albuquerque, NM · Amarillo, TX · Atlanta, GA · Austin, TX · Baltimore, MD · Billings, MT · Birmingham, AL · Boise, ID · Boston, MA · Brownsville, TX · Buffalo, NY · Charleston, SC · Charleston, WV · Charlotte, NC · Chicago, IL · Cincinnati, OH · Cleveland, OH · Columbia, SC · Columbus, OH · Dallas, TX · Daytona Beach, FL · Denver, CO · Des Moines, IA · Detroit, MI · El Paso, TX · Fargo, ND · Fort Lauderdale, FL · Fort Wayne, IN · Fort Worth, TX · Grand Rapids, MI · Greensboro, NC · Hartford, CT · Houston, TX · Indianapolis, IN · Jackson, MS · Jacksonville, FL · Kansas City, MO · Knoxville, TN · Las Vegas, NV · Lincoln, NE · Little Rock, AK

City	Alb NY	Albuq NM	Amar TX	Atl GA	Aus TX	Balt MD	Bill MT	Birm AL	Boise ID	Bos MA	Brnsv TX	Buf NY	Charl SC	Charl WV	Char NC	Chi IL	Cin OH	Clev OH	Col SC	Col OH	Dal TX	Dayt FL	Den CO	Des IA	Det MI	El Paso	Fargo	Ft Laud	Ft Wayne	Ft Worth	Grand R	Grnsb NC	Hart CT	Hous TX	Indpls	Jack MS	Jack FL	KC MO	Knox TN	Las Veg	Linc NE	L Rock
Albany, NY	0	2125	1825	1007	1882	332	2073	1112	2601	170	2007	292	932	639	795	795	729	496	823	657	1679	1209	1853	1193	690	2327	1463	1403	705	1682	710	661	106	1825	836	1320	1111	1279	836	2609	1336	1370
Albuquerque, NM	2125	0	300	1387	716	1881	1022	1260	970	2214	988	1801	1695	1583	1628	1346	1394	1606	1598	1468	673	1716	446	1013	1537	267	1314	1953	1410	632	1491	1677	2084	870	1289	1087	1678	811	1407	576	837	883
Amarillo, TX	1825	300	0	1087	485	1581	1037	965	1235	1914	784	1501	1517	1304	1338	1046	1094	1306	1298	1168	363	1467	454	806	1289	508	999	1670	1109	344	1191	1377	1822	608	989	787	1378	552	1107	876	596	607
Atlanta, GA	1007	1387	1087	0	884	669	1804	160	2252	1068	1175	912	300	495	251	695	438	692	211	543	805	446	1401	924	726	1453	1364	681	612	837	749	348	969	1057	680	383	346	805	199	1873	1053	520
Austin, TX	1882	716	485	884	0	1550	1449	793	1716	1930	331	1566	1247	1251	1237	1100	1127	1371	1095	1233	203	1158	1009	897	1330	583	1333	1326	1200	192	1288	1281	1867	162	1111	519	1057	680	1192	1037	513	405
Baltimore, MD	332	1881	1581	669	1550	0	1875	804	2416	409	1825	352	567	339	430	697	510	355	513	405	1347	877	1610	1101	511	1997	1339	1016	584	1508	710	334	346	308	449	1065	584	1006	770	1078	503	2408	1192	1037
Billings, MT	2073	1022	1037	1804	1449	1875	0	1759	586	2237	1771	1857	2221	1762	2075	1654	1395	2173	579	959	1579	1284	625	2466	1405	1406	1396	1958	2169	1739	1400	1743	2270	1078	1723	1060					836	1439	
Birmingham, AL	1112	1260	965	160	793	804	1759	0	2101	1267	1065	941	460	539	411	669	468	722	359	584	637	505	1370	838	721	1304	1311	764	610	702	739	493	1058	676	497	251	472	724	255	1822	953	394
Boise, ID	2601	970	1235	2252	1716	2416	586	2101	0	2794	1921	2271	2503	2246	2408	1777	1983	2058	2289	2069	1610	2576	870	1402	2020	1241	1245	2820	1871	1598	1917	2408	2652	1854	1890	2091	2579	1476	2022	662	1205	1781
Boston, MA	170	2214	1914	1068	1930	409	2237	1267	2794	0	2255	454	989	728	828	965	875	632	928	738	1727	1257	1953	1305	795	2376	1623	1492	847	1761	908	739	105	1878	933	1395	1167	1435	871	2765	1500	1472
Brownsville, TX	2007	988	784	1175	331	1825	1771	1065	1921	2255	0	1865	1491	1479	1426	1430	1426	1670	1360	1533	526	1353	1251	1184	1694	806	1601	1542	1455	518	1585	1480	2094	357	1427	791	1264	1008	1320	1573	1216	819
Buffalo, NY	292	1801	1501	912	1566	352	1857	941	2271	454	1865	0	947	430	666	543	438	195	822	333	1363	1069	351	726	449	1917	908	1051	397	1492	512	1119	1068	1007	671	2254	1057	1046
Charleston, SC	932	1695	1517	300	1247	567	2221	460	2503	989	1491	947	0	479	203	912	628	750	113	670	1164	351	1743	1185	874	1729	1557	586	740	1116	959	271	867	1027	743	702	248	1135	368	2247	1287	814
Charleston, WV	639	1583	1304	495	339	1762	728	1479	410	276	469	178	284	376	156	1134	726	1377	761	371	1672	1126	1004	284	1056	457	227	662	1246	328	790	676	777	284	2119	960	707
Charlotte, NC	795	1628	1338	251	1237	430	2027	411	2408	828	1426	666	203	276	0	738	446	543	100	453	1054	469	1548	1029	607	1710	1414	721	602	1061	791	89	763	1053	551	640	413	943	1195	1535	1151	743
Chicago, IL	795	1346	1046	695	1100	697	1214	669	1777	965	1430	543	912	469	738	0	291	348	794	340	932	1169	1000	357	284	1435	649	1348	186	1160	186	762	999	543	537	1749	527	675
Cincinnati, OH	729	1394	1094	438	1127	510	1479	468	1983	875	1426	438	628	178	446	291	0	249	502	110	924	861	1199	583	260	1472	940	1086	184	956	357	458	746	1053	105	680	786	591	246	1921	715	608
Cleveland, OH	496	1606	1306	692	1371	355	1662	722	2058	632	1670	195	750	284	543	348	249	0	627	138	1168	952	1407	672	171	1716	997	1232	211	1200	284	486	539	1297	317	924	908	803	489	2059	867	851
Columbia, SC	823	1598	1298	211	1095	513	2075	359	2289	928	1360	822	113	376	100	794	502	627	0	513	1032	381	901	123	745	1668	1446	622	671	1057	858	189	836	1066	625	610	290	1025	267	2162	1199	759
Columbus, OH	657	1469	1168	543	1233	405	1859	584	2069	738	1533	333	670	156	453	340	110	138	513	0	1030	901	1270	657	195	1540	989	1097	100	1030	33	1110	1065	1152	104	1664	243	908	422	1005	511	820	648
Dallas, TX	1679	673	363	805	203	1347	1579	637	1610	1727	526	1363	1164	1134	1054	932	924	1168	1032	1030	0	1123	806	714	1203	648	1131	1097	1030	33	1176	1122	1664	243	908	422	1005	511	820	1249	648	317
Daytona Beach, FL	1209	1716	1467	446	1158	876	2173	505	2576	1257	1353	1069	351	726	469	1096	883	952	381	901	1123	0	1823	1329	1103	1728	1714	227	1006	1126	1143	551	1138	952	880	688	97	1209	603	2316	1401	904
Denver, CO	1853	446	454	1401	1009	1610	625	1370	870	1953	1251	1602	1743	1377	1548	1007	1199	1407	1616	1270	806	1823	0	695	1321	705	915	2067	1186	773	1201	1621	1988	1060	1091	1246	1779	608	1341	743	507	992
Des Moines, IA	1193	1013	806	924	897	1101	2466	838	1402	1305	1184	867	1185	761	1029	357	583	672	1126	657	714	1329	695	0	600	1114	475	1581	516	747	502	1028	1283	930	478	846	1270	203	846	1290	1211	793	562
Detroit, MI	690	1537	1289	726	1330	511	1405	721	2020	795	1694	366	874	371	607	284	260	171	745	195	1203	1103	1321	600	0	1701	922	1346	157	1203	145	648	728	1444	272	1006	1070	748	1460	1070	1626	915	850
El Paso, TX	2327	267	508	1453	583	1997	1406	1304	1241	2376	806	1917	1729	1672	1710	1435	1472	1716	1668	1540	648	1728	705	1114	1701	0	1460	1869	1573	609	1554	1783	2263	743	1460	1070	1626	915	1488	722	946	960
Fargo, ND	1463	1314	999	1364	1333	1339	625	1311	1245	1623	1601	908	1557	1126	1414	649	940	997	1446	989	1131	1714	915	475	922	1460	0	2007	808	1072	827	1412	1531	1334	835	1155	1668	259	1156	1452	1451	451	1091
Fort Lauderdale, FL	1435	1953	1670	681	1326	1016	1958	764	2820	1492	1542	1051	586	1004	721	1348	1086	1232	622	1097	227	1279	2067	1581	1346	1869	2007	0	1271	1129	1342	786	1603	1191	1232	883	332	1459	860	2530	1670	711
Fort Wayne, IN	705	1410	1109	612	1200	584	2169	610	1871	847	1455	381	740	284	602	184	184	211	671	150	1030	1006	1186	516	170	1573	808	1271	0	1053	172	561	768	1176	122	784	929	648	430	1878	686	711
Fort Worth, TX	1682	632	344	837	192	1379	1739	702	1598	1761	518	1395	1116	1056	1061	945	956	1200	1057	1062	33	1126	773	747	1236	609	1072	1129	1053	0	1121	1154	1696	264	914	467	1037	513	853	1203	648	349
Grand Rapids, MI	710	1491	1191	749	1288	624	1396	739	1917	908	1585	512	959	457	791	178	357	284	858	311	1110	1143	1201	502	162	1554	827	1342	172	1121	0	707	794	1196	263	957	1071	638	573	1889	699	799
Greensboro, NC	661	1677	1377	348	1281	348	1743	493	1598	739	1480	271	229	89	457	458	381	486	189	33	1110	551	1621	1028	567	1783	1412	786	561	1154	707	0	650	1167	563	770	483	1013	283	2237	1202	778
Hartford, CT	106	2084	1822	969	1867	308	2169	1058	2652	105	2044	397	867	662	763	875	746	539	836	641	1664	1138	1988	1283	701	2263	1531	1403	768	1696	794	650	0	1773	805	1306	1117	1297	841	2675	1378	1344
Houston, TX	1825	870	608	1057	162	1409	1639	676	1878	357	1042	1246	1053	1160	1053	1197	1066	1159	243	952	806	1004	930	1304	743	1334	1191	1196	264	1196	1167	1773	0	681	867	486	351	1816	892	446
Indianapolis, IN	836	1289	989	680	1111	449	2058	497	1890	933	1427	512	743	371	551	186	105	317	641	104	908	980	1091	497	293	1460	835	1208	122	263	263	563	805	1041	0	591	716	506	350	1650	874	251
Jackson, MS	1320	1087	787	383	519	1065	1743	251	2091	1395	991	1119	702	790	640	762	688	924	610	786	422	857	1287	846	1070	1335	832	784	446	957	770	1306	406	681	591	0	716	506	660	874	251
Jacksonville, FL	1111	1678	1378	329	1057	770	2227	472	2579	1167	1264	1068	248	676	413	999	786	908	290	850	1005	97	1779	1270	1046	1626	1944	332	929	1037	1071	891	867	591	716	0	1110	556	752	1345	211	409
Kansas City, MO	1279	811	552	805	680	1006	1078	724	1476	1435	1008	1027	1135	777	943	527	591	803	1025	665	511	1209	608	203	791	916	609	1459	648	513	638	1013	1297	486	506	1110	0	752	1345	211	843
Knoxville, TN	836	1407	1107	199	1192	770	1789	255	2022	871	1320	671	368	284	219	537	246	489	267	351	820	603	1341	821	506	1483	1195	860	430	872	573	283	841	922	351	506	555	752	0	1983	944	523
Las Vegas, NV	2609	576	876	1947	1297	2408	1060	1822	662	2765	1573	2254	2247	2119	2173	1749	1921	2059	2162	1995	1299	2316	743	1399	2011	722	1535	2530	1878	1203	1889	2230	2675	1468	1650	2230	1345	1983	0	1224	1483
Lincoln, NE	1386	832	596	1053	851	1192	836	953	1205	1500	1216	1057	1287	960	1151	527	802	867	1199	776	648	1401	507	203	819	946	451	1670	686	648	699	1202	1378	892	673	874	1321	211	944	1224	0	616
Little Rock, AK	1370	883	607	520	405	1037	1439	394	1781	1472	819	1046	814	707	743	675	608	851	759	713	317	904	992	562	850	960	1091	1184	711	349	799	778	1344	446	608	251	843	409	523	1483	616	0
Los Angeles, CA	2911	823	1095	2197	1410	2676	1254	2067	833	2993	1678	2593	2394	2617	1989	2394	2617	1989	2554	188	300	105	349	494	211	819	801	1127	591	365	1467	949	1078	222	851	373	462	867	948	129	575	729
Louisville, KY	868	1323	1041	397	1022	608	1550	373	1908	976	1321	543	608	258	430	300	105	344	494	211	819	801	1127	591	365	1467	949	1078	222	851	373	462	867	948	129	575	729	519	246	1861	730	502
Memphis, TN	1232	1021	721	397	658	900	1557	239	1833	1379	957	908	689	653	604	551	469	713	612	575	455	749	1151	599	712	1103	1242	989	592	487	690	640	1209	584	470	211	697	470	385	1581	647	138
Miami, FL	1439	1994	1694	665	1338	1095	2580	788	2860	1516	1580	1514	630	1046	745	1338	1085	1298	745	1159	2131	1582	1386	1958	1896	24	1326	1353	1356	810	1427	1207	1208	907	356	1475	2570	1673	1208
Milwaukee, WI	1443	1143	784	721	1092	794	1143	764	1711	960	1512	492	901	526	769	92	388	445	891	440	1013	1180	1070	365	389	1524	731	1443	208	1266	1059	255	948	1155	283	664	1155	568	643	1752	560	750
Minneapolis, MN	1215	1256	1062	1105	1120	1105	812	1088	1488	1362	1456	948	1316	874	1143	405	696	753	1276	753	1013	1458	951	244	698	526	244	1723	564	1001	583	1135	1257	1266	591	1123	1376	459	932	1630	409	881
Mobile, AL	1322	1265	965	340	656	990	1854	269	2343	1379	911	1185	607	825	575	908	745	989	555	834	592	502	1372	954	988	1236	1415	705	686	701	806	512	1133	709	590	255	379	867	348	2015	975	470
Montgomery, AL	1178	1345	1042	164	804	833	1836	90	2318	1232	1041	1076	464	632	405	762	561	815	379	707	681	448	1412	1311	814	1325	1521	671	686	701	1006	512	1133	709	302	422	592	784	302	1792	770	349
Nashville, TN	993	1232	932	243	869	688	1640	195	2059	1062	1168	722	576	458	399	474	283	527	458	389	666	639	1167	712	536	1314	1136	900	385	698	541	334	976	714	289	465	601	555	174	1792	770	349
New Orleans, LA	1453	1187	875	493	535	1136	1820	347	2571	1526	720	1926	1019	871	821	925	820	446	715	561	1525	1054	1775	1010	620	2173	1450	289	691	1557	706	101	1679	730	1192	957	1192	771	2520	1274	1114	430
New York City, NY	146	1995	1695	855	1729	201	1926	1019	2571	201	2002	390	786	524	625	794	820	446	715	561	1525	1054	1775	1010	620	2173	1450	1289	691	1557	706	519	1071	810	1436	367	857	607	1800	1114	430
Norfolk, VA	505	1905	1632	551	1403	237	2098	711	2551	660	1735	569	454	369	341	851	681	493	412	559	1359	702	1800	1202	711	1998	1536	907	709	1382	802	227	471	1362	669	948	632	1119	412	2534	1354	1025
Oakland, CA	2982	1134	1430	2488	1786	2864	1218	2321	671	3124	2034	2744	2788	2600	2755	2098	2317	2498	2703	2391	1803	2851	1223	1742	2350	1194	1870	3041	2251	1799	2509	582	1604	1984
Oklahoma City, OK	1523	559	267	863	419	1322	1168	701	1451	1659	700	1451	1169	1069	804	835	1047	1091	900	1031	1069	464	721	824	1283	795	693	1402	559	146	726	1256	464	604	634	634	640	1208	1321	969	616	914	1305	195	930	1249	57	690
Omaha, NE	1308	905	754	989	847	1143	904	904	1443	1249	1005	1303	903	1116	464	721	824	1283	795	693	1402	559	146	726	1256	464	604	634	634	640	1208	1321	969	616	914	1305	195	930	1249	57	690
Orlando, FL	1249	1751	1451	446	1142	917	2277	545	2695	1297	2034	1306	401	814	559	1127	892	1046	440	627	460	1427	1078	81	1896	1363	1143	1737	1326	208	1059	1110	1188	648	1208	964	989	697	131	1452	965
Philadelphia, PA	251	1922	1622	766	1630	97	2051	882	2488	321	1954	391	683	637	522	757	522	436	460	395	1460	1007	1760	1160	604	2075	1360	208	1709	1500	2100	1277	1845	284	1236	1379
Phoenix, AZ	2512	446	746	1810	1022	2311	1220	1700	1022	2644	1269	2269	2222	2045	2061	1760	1808	2045	2025	1907	1013	2101	802	1497	2019	438	1791	2244	1831	983	1906	2099	2523	1110	1719	1500	2100	1277	1845	284	1236	1379
Pittsburgh, PA	471	1654	1354	712	1412	245	1681	778	2203	584	1713	219	778	211	504	470	291	128	567	186	1209	859	1475	790	304	1833	1117	436	1345	349	438	486	1345	349	986	882	851	515	2181	965	899
Portland, Or	2869	1352	1637	2805	2765	867	2571	439	3149	2648	2510	2757	2140	2474	2612	2972	2478	2051	3018	1283	1816	2368	1661	1484	3204	2003	2251	2823	2877	2369	2335	2518	3042	1870	935	2683	1451	1395
Providence, RI	178	2156	1856	1027	1898	372	2238	1189	2701	41	2222	454	956	699	815	924	790	600	888	713	1695	1201	1961	956	746	2335	1566	1410	799	1727	859	706	73	1849	892	1362	1127	1378	935	2683	1451	1395
Raleigh, NC	656	1759	1459	397	1355	324	2273	557	2560	713	1506	721	300	297	162	812	540	559	215	453	1152	559	1694	1123	643	1800	1485	794	603	1381	786	73	624	1233	635	316	2143	2716	1606	2363	478	1611	1986
Reno, NV	2763	1056	1345	2411	1775	2562	1021	2383	426	2947	2570	2897	2742	2570	2407	2570	1897	2142	2197	1280	788	356	583	390	498	1313	713	1904	1293	609	2023	1481	946	635	1333	722	191	455	2291	907	946	693	1205	440	2406	1249	962
Richmond, VA	482	1833	1533	527	1463	155	1655	699	2594	544	1646	552	462	251	280	788	356	583	390	498	1313	713	1904	1293	609	2023	1481	946	635	1333	722	191	455	2291	907	946	693	1205	440	2406	1249	962
Rochester, NY	219	1857	1557	1015	1623	300	1922	965	2352	381	1891	81	871	495	689	608	502	268	789	397	1420	1176	1637	932	424	2036	1249	1410	464	1452	499	600	324	1555	1185	1102	1062	710	2371	1135	1111
Saint Louis, MO	1054	754	588	806	827	1381	539	1771	526	1194	1216	747	884	456	292	340	562	737	414	641	956	377	585	1231	208	762	1030	935	291	1185	1063	251	187	738	244	564	987	583	1278	1257	1266	591	1130	376	413	422
Saint Paul, MN	1215	1362	1062	1105	1120	1095	812	1118	1398	892	1555	948	1316	870	1143	405	696	753	1230	745	1013	1458	956	251	698	1541	244	1723	564	987	583	1135	1257	1266	591	1130	1376	459	951	1630	408	881
Salt Lake City, UT	2290	621	1324	1900	1341	2051	579	1825	349	2417	1775	1922	2254	1896	2059	1386	1710	1727	2115	1711	1287	2283	519	1085	1679	892	1172	2578	1357	1184	1556	2059	2238	1460	1552	2286	1095	1158	1742	413	900	1462
San Antonio, TX	1986	684	530	965	81	1646	1600	891	1709	2052	300	1638	1371	1419	1212	1308	1351	1495	1219	1357	276	1314	975	1122	1501	576	1431	1505	1305	203	1200	1965	210	1200	649	1086	795	1150	1273	916	582
San Diego, CA	2855	787	1078	2174	1313	2714	1309	2034	992	2992	1573	2613	2505	2402	2463	2335	2193	2334	2389	1207	1369	2418	1014	1760	2419	721	1934	2621	2189	1332	2269	2457	2944	1484	2067	1783	2329	1627	2269	349	1573	1543
San Francisco, CA	2966	1135	1396	2511	1776	2765	1239	2371	595	3133	2044	2403	2923	2616	2756	2108	2329	2408	2738	2461	1865	2827	1233	1832	2360	1184	1886	3073	2304	1735	2318	2740	3019	1947	2224	2189	2918	2498	2585	3090	1884	2553	1209
Seattle, WA	2855	1500	1805	2656	2157	2685	815	2475	504	2961	2521	2591	2692	2748	2695	2140	2472	2544	1229	1144	909	228	1018	937	1519	271	827	223	814	624	729	1468	727	219
Shreveport, LA	1599	868	568	624	368	1452	1691	474	1912	1616	691	1265	945	945	899	885	916	826	1070	833	592	196	903	1112	827	1069	844	1129	1144	909	228	1018	937	1519	271	827	223	814	624	729	1468	727	219
Spokane, WA	2652	1346	1563	2367	1981	2417	541	2469	369	2693	2359	2263	2700	2503	2505	1775	2066	2068	2572	2115	1978	2811	1095	1556	2020	1686	1166	3014	1921	1978	1941	2503	2650	2222	1977	1818	421	170	1045	584	1068	1227	670
Tallahassee, FL	1249	1508	1208	268	899	932	2306	273	2565	1356	1143	1107	436	647	525	984	735	864	559	744	716	228	1566	1094	1492	1849	268	1092	861	1022	673	1240	1069	672	195	1296	730	2319	1477	542
Tampa, FL	1281	1759	1459	470	1150	949	2143	553	2763	1329	1345	1136	479	746	547	1143	908	1091	497	1013	1086	141	1858	1460	1094	1849	268	1092	1917	673	1240	1069	672	195	1296	730	2319	1477	542
Toledo, OH	633	1526	1220	641	1315	454	1557	673	2020	742	1622	309	973	341	533	243	203	114	683	138	1112	1063	1272	567	65	1699	885	1289	105	1144	170	516	624	1249	243	876	989	716	449	1954	762	863
Tuscon, AZ	2631	267	785	1908	1124	2416	1342	1802	1041	2749	1082	2039	1913	1711	1750	1601	1569	1820	1890	1683	935	1898	718	1325	1921	316	1897	2075	1580	861	1637	1891	2317	1037	1504	616	510	1167	283	782	1224	416
Tulsa, OK	1409	674	336	732	419	1293	636	686	1532	835	1128	1103	945	989	651	733	1018	795	259	1156	714	411	916	972	1409	738	301	818	1037	504	616	510	1167	283	782	1224	416
Washington, DC	378	1864	1564	630	1509	41	2006	781	2441	430	1787	429	559	299	334	697	478	341	498	418	1306	802	1654	1054	506	1954	1322	1062	531	1338	608	309	341	1220	551	965	730	1046	554	2376	1184	832
West Palm Beach, FL	1396	1938	1638	632	1326	1046	2736	702	2942	1426	1524	1443	568	982	673	1265	1063	1192	586	1146	1265	195	2157	1646	1305	1922	2028	41	1157	1297	1476	737	1339	1151	1176	851	284	1052	806	2498	1598	1101
Youngstown, OH	462	1632	1334	719	1368	298	1632	738	2090	568	1695	190	709	251	502	413	275	74	581	170	1193	986	1421	737	230	1804	1038	1129	275	1225	340	482	470	1321	341	949	958	843	521	2124	923	876

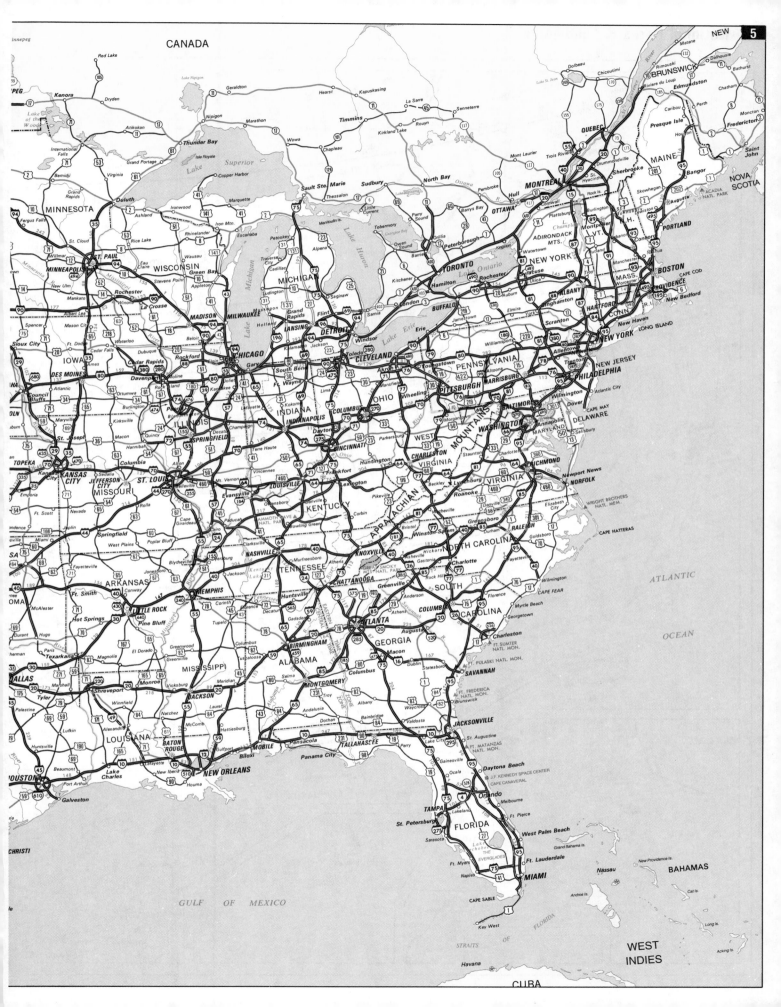

1 • 2 • 3 • 4 • 5 • 6 • 7

A B C D E F G H J K

PACIFIC OCEAN

BRITISH COLUMBIA Vancouver Calgary **ALBERTA** Saskatoon

Pacific Rim Nat'l Park · San Juan Island Nat'l Hist Park · Mt. Baker N. Cascades Nat'l Forest Okanogan · Colville Nat'l Forest · Waterton-Glacier Int'l Peace Park · Glacier Nat'l Park · Rocky Mtns. Forest Preserve · Saskatchewan River · Moose Jaw · Regina **SASKATCHEWAN** · Riding Mountain Nat'l Park · Winnipeg **MANITOBA**

Olympic Nat'l Park · Seattle · Tacoma · Mt. Rainier Nat'l Park · Spokane · **WASHINGTON** · Yakima · Wenatchee Nat'l Forest · Coeur d'Alene · **CANADA** · **UNITED STATES** · Great Falls · Ft. Peck Lake · Ft. Union Nat'l Hist. Site · Williston · Theodore Roosevelt Nat'l Mem. North · Knife River Indian Village Nat'l Hist. Site

Ft. Vancouver Nat'l Hist. Site and Museum · Astoria · Portland · **OREGON** · Walla Walla · Pendleton · Clearwater Nat'l Forest · Lolo · Deerlodge Nat'l Forest · Helena · Butte · **MONTANA** · Billings · Bismarck · **NORTH DAKOTA** · Fargo

Mt. Hood Nat'l Forest · Salem · Eugene · Willamette Nat'l Forest · John Day Fossil Beds Nat'l Mon. · Malheur Nat'l Forest · Payette Nat'l Forest · **IDAHO** · Salmon Nat'l Forest · Gallatin Nat'l Forest · Custer Nat'l Forest · Theodore Roosevelt Nat'l Park South · **SOUTH DAKOTA**

Crater Lake Nat'l Park · Grants Pass · Rogue River Nat'l Forest · Winema Nat'l Forest · Fremont Nat'l Forest · Deschutes Nat'l Forest · Boise Nat'l Forest · Sawtooth Nat'l Forest · Targhee Nat'l Forest · **Yellowstone** Nat'l Park · Shoshone Nat'l Forest · Bighorn Nat'l Forest · Devil's Tower Nat'l Mon. · Thunder Basin Nat'l Grassland · Rapid City · Pierre

Redwood Nat'l Park · Eureka · Six Rivers Nat'l Forest · Klamath Nat'l Forest · Oregon Caves Nat'l Mon. · Lava Beds Nat'l Mon. · Modoc Nat'l Forest · Twin Falls · Craters of the Moon Nat'l Mon. · Pocatello · Caribou Nat'l Forest · Grand Teton Nat'l Park · Jackson · Bridger-Teton Nat'l Forest · Mt. Rushmore Nat'l Mem. · Badlands Nat'l Park · Wind Cave Nat'l Park · Hot Springs · Sioux Falls

Redding · Shasta Nat'l Forest · Trinity Nat'l Forest · Lassen Volcanic Nat'l Park · Plumas Nat'l Forest · Winnemucca · Humboldt · **GREAT SALT LAKE DESERT** · Golden Spike Nat'l Hist. Site · Wasatch Nat'l Forest · Ogden · Fossil Butte Nat'l Mon. · Medicine Bow Nat'l Forest · Laramie · Scottsbluff Nat'l Mon. · Samuel R. McKelvie Nat'l Forest · **NEBRASKA**

Sacramento · Tahoe Nat'l Forest · Reno · Carson City · **NEVADA** · Salt Lake City · Provo · Uinta Nat'l Forest · Dinosaur Nat'l Mon. · Rock Springs · Cheyenne · Roosevelt Nat'l Forest · Pawnee Nat'l Grassland · North Platte · Lincoln

San Francisco · Oakland · San Jose · Eldorado Nat'l Forest · Toiyabe Nat'l Forest · Ely · Lehman Caves Nat'l Mon. · **UTAH** · Manti-La Sal Nat'l Forest · Colorado Nat'l Mon. · Grand Mesa Nat'l Forest · White River Nat'l Forest · Arapaho Nat'l Forest · Boulder · Denver · **COLORADO**

Monterey · Pinnacles Nat'l Mon. · Fresno · Yosemite Nat'l Park · Sierra Nat'l Forest · Kings Canyon Nat'l Park · Inyo Nat'l Forest · Death Valley Nat'l Mon. · Cedar Breaks Nat'l Mon. · Capitol Reef Nat'l Park · Dixie Nat'l Forest · Canyonlands Nat'l Park · Arches Nat'l Park · Black Canyon of the Gunnison Nat'l Mon. · Gunnison Nat'l Forest · Colorado Springs · **KANSAS** · Dodge City · Wichita

San Luis Obispo · Los Padres Nat'l Forest · Bakersfield · Sequoia Nat'l Forest · Sequoia Nat'l Park · Las Vegas · Bryce Canyon Nat'l Park · Lake Powell · Natural Bridges Nat'l Mon. · Mesa Verde Nat'l Park · Durango · San Juan Nat'l Forest · Rio Grande Nat'l Forest · Comanche Nat'l Grassland · Pueblo

Channel Islands Nat'l Park · Ventura · Los Angeles · Anaheim · San Bernardino Nat'l Forest · Angeles Nat'l Forest · Joshua Tree Nat'l Mon. · **MOJAVE DESERT** · Barstow · **CALIFORNIA** · Grand Canyon Nat'l Park · Kaibab Nat'l Forest · Rainbow Bridge Nat'l Mon. · Havasupai Ind. Res. · **ARIZONA** · Canyon De Chelly Nat'l Mon. · Aztec Ruins Nat'l Mon. · Santa Fe · Carson Nat'l Forest · Ft. Union Nat'l Mon. · Capulin Mtn. Nat'l Mon. · Kiowa Nat'l Grasslands · **OKLAHOMA**

San Diego · Cabrillo Nat'l Mon. · Cleveland Nat'l Forest · Tijuana · Mexicali · **BAJA CALIFORNIA** · Prescott · Coconino Nat'l Forest · Flagstaff · Walnut Canyon Nat'l Mon. · Sunset Crater Nat'l Mon. · Wupatki Nat'l Mon. · Petrified Forest Nat'l Park · El Morro Nat'l Mon. · Chaco Canyon Nat'l Mon. · Bandelier Nat'l Mon. · Albuquerque · Amarillo · Oklahoma City

Phoenix · Tonto Nat'l Mon. · Tonto Nat'l Forest · Globe · Coronado Nat'l Forest · Apache Nat'l Forest · Gila Nat'l Forest · Gran Quivira Nat'l Mon. · **NEW MEXICO** · Lubbock · Wichita Falls · Ft. Worth · Dallas

Yuma · Organ Pipe Cactus Nat'l Mon. · Saguaro Nat'l Mon. · Tucson · Casa Grande Ruins · Gila Cliff Dwellings Nat'l Mon. · White Sands Nat'l Mon. · Lincoln Nat'l Forest · Carlsbad Caverns Nat'l Park · Odessa · Midland · San Angelo · **TEXAS** · Waco · Austin

MEXICO · **UNITED STATES** · Nogales · Douglas · Coronado Nat'l Mem. · Chiricahua Nat'l Mon. · Tumacacori Nat'l Mon. · El Paso · Ciudad Juarez · Guadalupe Mtns. Nat'l Park · Abilene

PACIFIC OCEAN · **U.S.S.R.** · Wainwright · Barrow · **Arctic Ocean** · Point Hope · Prudhoe Bay · Noatak Nat'l Preserve · Gates of the Arctic Nat'l Park & Preserve · Santa Ana · Nuevo Casas Grandes · Old Ft. Davis Nat'l Hist. Site · **SONORA** · **CHIHUAHUA** · Big Bend Nat'l Park · San Antonio

Noatak · Nome · Kobuk Valley Nat'l Park · Bering Land Bridge Nat'l Preserve · Norton Sound · Fairbanks · College · Fort Yukon · Yukon-Charley Nat'l Preserve · **YUKON** · Austin

Hooper Bay · Unalakleet · **ALASKA** · Denali Nat'l Park and Preserve · Delta Junction · Tok · **CANADA** · Lihue · Piedras Negras · Nueva Rosita · Corpus Christi

Togiak · Anchorage · Glennallen · Palmer · Valdez · Cordova · Wrangell-St. Elias Nat'l Park · Kluane · Wahiawa · Pearl City · Kaneohe · Honolulu · **COAHUILA** · Laredo

Bristol Bay · Lake Clark Nat'l Park & Preserve · Chugach Nat'l Forest · Katmai Nat'l Park & Preserve · Kenai Fjords Nat'l Park · Seward · Lahaina · Wailuku · Haleakala Nat'l Park · **HAWAII**

Aniakchak Nat'l Mon. & Preserve · Kodiak Island · Gulf of Alaska · Glacier Bay Nat'l Park & Preserve · Juneau · Sitka · Tongass Nat'l Forest · Ketchikan · **B.C.** · City of Refuge Nat'l Hist. Park · Hawaii Volcanoes Nat'l Park · Hilo · **NUEVO LEON** · Monterrey · Brownsville · **TAMAULIPAS**

Aleutian Islands

USE ONLY FOR ORIENTATION TO NATIONAL PARKS AND LANDMARKS. FOR MORE DETAILED HIGHWAY INFORMATION, SEE INTERSTATE HIGHWAY MAP, PAGES 4-5, AND STATE MAP SECTION, PAGES 13-89.

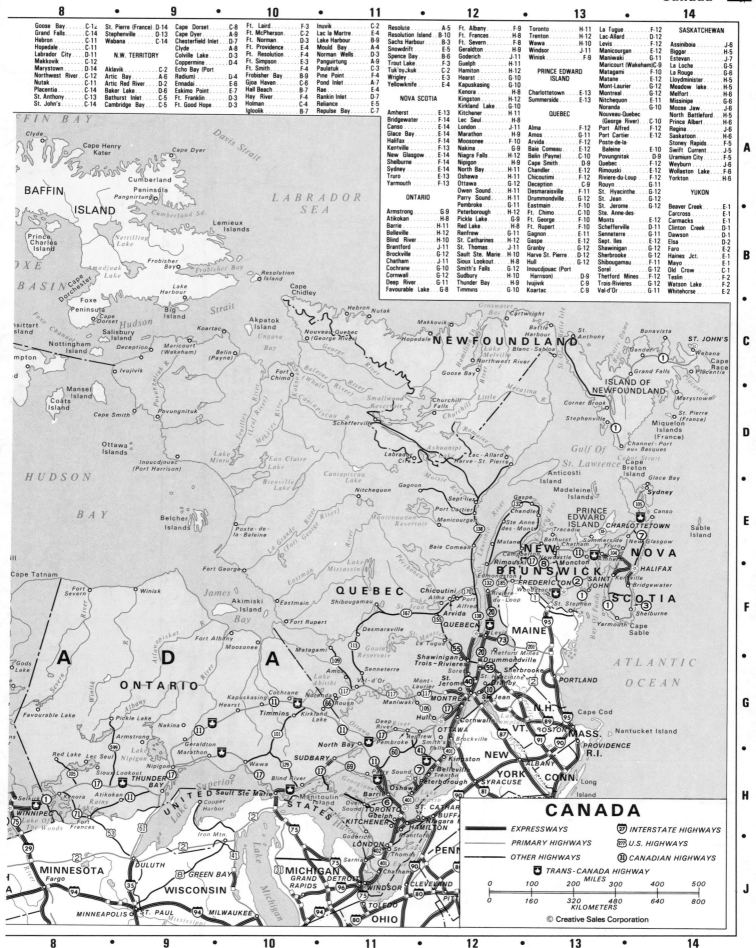

MEXICO

Tijuana · Mexicali · Yuma
Tecate · San Luis
Ensenada
Baja California
196 / 122
5
San Felipe
190 / 119
El Rosario
1
Punta Prieta
519 / 324
Rasarito
Baja California
Baja Calif Sur
1
San Ignacio
72 / 45
Santa Rosalía
198 / 124
Rosarito
217 / 136
65 / 41
Ejido Insurgentes
115 / 72
El Medano
236 / 147
La Paz
108 / 67
190 / 119
9
Todos Santos
1
San Jose del Cabo
90 / 56

Ajo
ARIZONA
Sonorita
85
86
Tucson
19
82
666
80
Nogales · Agua Prieta
Douglas
Cananea
Caborca · Altar
Magdalena
Santa Ana
Bavispe
Puerto de la Libertad
Hermosillo
16
15
Bahia Kino
Sahuaripa
Tonichi
Guaymas · Empalme
Rosario
Ciudad Obregón
Navojoa
El Fuerte
Sinaloa
Tameapa
Los Mochis
Topolobampo
Guasave
Altata
Culiacán
Cosalá
Eldorado
La Cruz
Mazatlán
Villa Union
Rosario
Los Corchos
Las Varas
Puerto Vallarta
El Tuito

UNITED
Silver City · Alamogordo · Artesia
90
25
NEW MEXICO
Las Cruces
Hobbs
82
285
Carlsbad
Big Spring
385
Midland
Odessa
CIUDAD JUAREZ · EL PASO
STATES
54
Pecos
180
Rankin
20
Rio Grande
90
Presidio
67
Ojinaga
COAHUILA
Boquillas del Carmen
La Cuesta
Nacimiento
208 / 130
Sabinas
Ocampo
50 / 31
81 / 51
186 / 116
30
190 / 119
San Pedro de las Colonias
19 / 12
40
206 / 129
Parras
TORREÓN
Concepción del Oro
Camacho
Cuencamé
Durango
El Salto
15
40
Sombrerete
290 / 181
49
227 / 142
Rio Grande
261 / 163
Fresnillo
Zacatecas
Monte Esgobedo
93 / 58
184 / 115
54
45
128 / 80
AGUASCALIENTES
Tuxpan
Jalpa
83 / 52
Moyahua
159 / 99
Lagos de Moreno
43 / 27
Tepic
226 / 141
200 / 125
Tepatitlan
15
GUADALAJARA
Tlaquepaque
Irapuato
Ocotlán
Salamanca
90
Sahuayu
Autlán
Sayula
54
110
Uruapan
75 / 47
Ciudad Guzmán
58 / 36
Tomatlán
Melaque
80
115 / 72
COLIMA
Apatzingán
Manzanillo
200
Colima
156 / 98
37
Arteaga
203 / 127
Playa Azul
200
Ixtapa

SONORA
CHIHUAHUA
2
282 / 176
Janos
10
Nueva Casas Grandes
219 / 137
Villa Ahumada
Moctezuma
196 / 122
10
Gallego
Madera
157 / 98
El Sauz
Ciudad Guerrero
105 / 66
Chihuahua
67 / 42
Cuauhtémoc
La Perla
259 / 162
16
45
154 / 96
Delicias
Ciudad Camargo
67 / 42
79 / 49
Jiménez
Escalón
Hidalgo del Parral
Santa Barbara
233 / 146
49
172 / 107
45
La Cadena
159 / 99
30
Gómez Palacio
109 / 68
Abasolo
39
240 / 150
172 / 108
Canatlán
144 / 90
40
45
318 / 199
40

M E X I C O
CHIHUAHUA / DURANGO
DURANGO
DURANGO / ZACATECAS
NAYARIT
JALISCO
JALISCO
COLIMA

Gulf of California

Pacific Ocean

N
W · E
S

MEXICO

━━━	EXPRESSWAYS	(38)	MEXICAN HIGHWAYS
───	PRIMARY THROUGH ROUTES	(31)	INTERSTATE HIGHWAYS
━━━	OTHER THROUGH ROADS	(83)	U.S. HIGHWAYS
┄┄┄	OTHER ROADS	(31)	STATE HIGHWAYS

Approximate distances are shown between red markers on map.
Red numbers are kilometers, black numbers are miles.

0 ... 100 MILES 200 ... 300
0 ... 160 KILOMETERS 320 ... 480

© Creative Sales Corporation

MEXICO

Cities and Towns

Abasolo	D-5
Acambaro	F-6
Acapulco	G-6
Acatlan	F-7
Acayucan	F-8
Agua Prieta	A-3
Aguascalientes	E-6
Altar	A-3
Altata	D-4
Alvarado	F-8
Apatzingan	F-6
Arcelia	F-6
Arriga	G-9
Arteaga	F-6
Arlixco	F-7
Autlan	F-5
Bahia Kino	B-2
Bavispe	B-4
Becal	E-10
Boquillas de Carmen	B-6
Buenaventura	B-4
Caborca	A-2
Camacho	D-6
Campeche	E-10
Cananea	A-3
Canatlan	D-5
Cardenas	F-9
Celaya	E-6
Celestun	E-10
Champoton	F-10
Chetumal	F-11
Chihuahua	B-5
Chilpancingo	F-7
China	C-7
Ciudad Acuna	B-6
Ciudad Camargo	C-5
Ciudad Guerrero	B-4
Ciudad Guzman	F-5
Ciudad Juarez	A-4
Ciudad Madero	E-7
Ciudad Mante	E-7
Ciudad Victoria	D-7
Ciudad de Carmen	F-9
Ciudad de Valles	E-7

Ciudad del Maiz	E-7
Coatzacoalcos	F-9
Colima	F-5
Comitan	G-9
Conception de Oro	D-6
Cordoba	F-8
Cosala	D-4
Cuauhtemoc	B-4
Cuencame	D-5
Cuernavaca	F-7
Culiacan	D-4
Delicias	B-5
Durango	D-5
Dzilam de Bravo	E-10
Ejido Insurgentes	C-3
Eldorado	D-4
El Fuerte	C-4
El Medana	D-3
El Rosario	A-1
El Sauz	B-4
El Tuito	E-5
Empalme	B-3
Ensanada	A-1
Escalon	C-5
Escarcega	F-10
Fresnillo	D-5
Gallego	B-4
Gomez Palacio	C-5
Guadalajara	E-5
Guasave	C-4
Guaymas	B-3
Hermosillo	B-3
Hidalgo del Parral	C-5
Hopelchen	E-10
Huajuapan de Leon	F-7
Iguala	F-7
Irapuato	E-6
Iturbide	F-10
Jalapa	F-8
Jalpa	E-6
Janos	A-4
Jimenez	C-5
Juchitan	G-8
La Cruz	D-4
La Cadena	C-5
La Cuesta	B-6
Lagos de Morena	E-6
La Paz	D-3
La Perla	B-5

La Pesca	D-7
La Piedad	E-6
Las Varas	E-5
Leon	E-6
Linares	D-7
Los Corchos	E-5
Los Mochis	C-3
Madera	B-4
Magdalena	A-3
Malpaso	G-9
Manuel	E-7
Manzanillo	F-5
Matamoros	C-7
Matehuala	D-6
Matias Romero	G-8
Mazatlan	D-4
Melaque	F-5
Merida	E-10
Mexicali	A-1
Mexico City	F-7
Miahuatlan	G-8
Mier	C-7
Minatitlan	F-8
Moctezuma	B-4
Molango	E-7
Monclova	C-6
Monte Escobedo	E-5
Montemorelos	D-7
Monterrey	C-6
Morelia	F-6
Morelos	B-6
Moyahua	E-5
Nacimiento	C-6
Nautla	E-8
Navojoa	C-3
Nogales	A-3
Nueva Casas Grandes	B-4
Nueva Rosita	C-6
Nuevo Laredo	C-7
Oaxaca	G-8
Ocampo	C-6
Ocotlan	F-6
Ojinaga	B-5
Ometepec	G-7
Orizaba	F-8
Pachuca	E-7
Palenque	F-9
Papantla	E-7

Paraiso	F-9
Parras	C-6
Peto	E-10
Piedras Negras	B-6
Pijijiapan	G-9
Pinotepa Nacional	G-7
Piste	E-11
Playa Azul	F-6
Pochutla	G-8
Poza Pica	E-7
Progreso	E-10
Puebla	F-7
Puerto de la Libertad	B-2
Puerto Escondido	G-8
Puerto Juarez	E-11
Puerto Madero	G-9
Puerto Penasco	A-2
Punta Prieta	B-2
Queretaro	E-6
Rasarito	B-2
Reynosa	C-7
Rio Grande	D-6
Rio Lagartos	E-11
Rosario	C-3
Rosario	D-4
Sabinas	C-6
Sabinas Hidagalo	C-6
Sahuaripa	B-3
Salamanca	E-6
Salinas	C-6
Salina Cruz	G-8
Saltillo	C-6
San Andres Tuxtla	F-8
San Cristobal	G-9
San Felipe	A-2
San Fernando	D-7
San Ignacio	C-2
San Jose del Cabo	D-3
San Luis	A-2
San Luis Potosi	E-6
San Pedro de las Colonias	C-6
Santa Ana	A-3
Santa Barbara	C-5
Santa Rosalia	C-2
Sayula	F-5
Sinaloa	C-4
Sombrerete	D-5

Sonorita	A-2
Soto La Marina	D-7
Tameapa	C-4
Tampico	E-7
Tapachula	G-9
Tapanatepec	G-9
Taxco	F-7
Teapa	F-9
Tecate	A-1
Tehuacan	F-7
Tehuantepec	G-8
Temporal	E-7
Tepatitlan	E-6
Tepehuanes	D-5
Tepic	E-5
Ticul	E-10
Tijuana	A-1
Tiquicheo	F-6
Tlaciaco	G-7
Tlaxcala	F-7
Tlaxiaco	G-7
Todos Santos	D-3
Toluca	F-7
Tomatian	F-5
Tonichi	B-3
Topolobampo	C-3
Torreon	C-5
Totolapan	G-8
Tulancingo	F-7
Tulum	E-11
Tuxpan	E-5
Tuxpan	E-7
Tuxtepec	F-8
Tuxtla Gutierrez	G-9
Uruapan	F-6
Valladolid	E-11
Veracruz	F-8
Villa Ahumada	A-4
Villagran	D-7
Villahermosa	F-9
Villa Union	D-4
Xcan	E-11
Yecora	B-4
Zacatal	F-9
Zacatecas	E-6
Zamora	F-6
Zihuatanejo	F-6
Zimapan	E-7
Zitacuaro	F-6

STATE MAP LEGEND

ROAD CLASSIFICATIONS & RELATED SYMBOLS

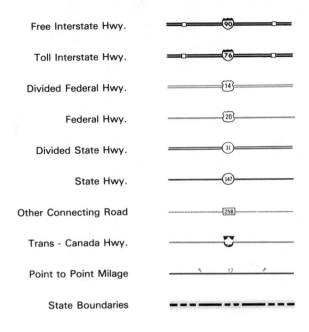

Free Interstate Hwy.	90
Toll Interstate Hwy.	76
Divided Federal Hwy.	14
Federal Hwy.	20
Divided State Hwy.	31
State Hwy.	147
Other Connecting Road	258
Trans - Canada Hwy.	
Point to Point Milage	17
State Boundaries	

LAND MARKS & POINTS OF INTEREST

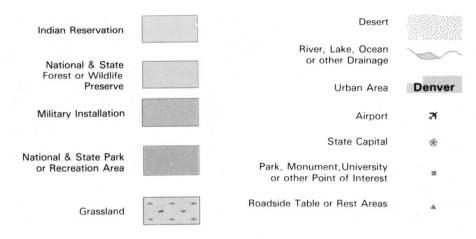

Indian Reservation	
National & State Forest or Wildlife Preserve	
Military Installation	
National & State Park or Recreation Area	
Grassland	

Desert	
River, Lake, Ocean or other Drainage	
Urban Area	**Denver**
Airport	✈
State Capital	✸
Park, Monument, University or other Point of Interest	■
Roadside Table or Rest Areas	▲

ABBREVIATIONS

A.F.B. - Air Force Base
Hist. - Historical
Mem. - Memorial

Mgmt. - Management
Mon. - Monument
Nat. - Natural

Prov. - Province
Rec. - Recreation
Ref. - Refuge

S. F. - State Forest
St. Pk. - State Park
W.M.A. - Wildlife Management Area

CITIES & TOWNS - Type size indicates the relative population of cities and towns

Mapleton	Kenhorst	Somerset	Butler	Auburn	Harrisburg	Madison	Chicago
under 1000	1000-5,000	5,000-10,000	10,000-25,000	25,000-50,000	50,000-100,000	100,000-500,000	500,000 and over

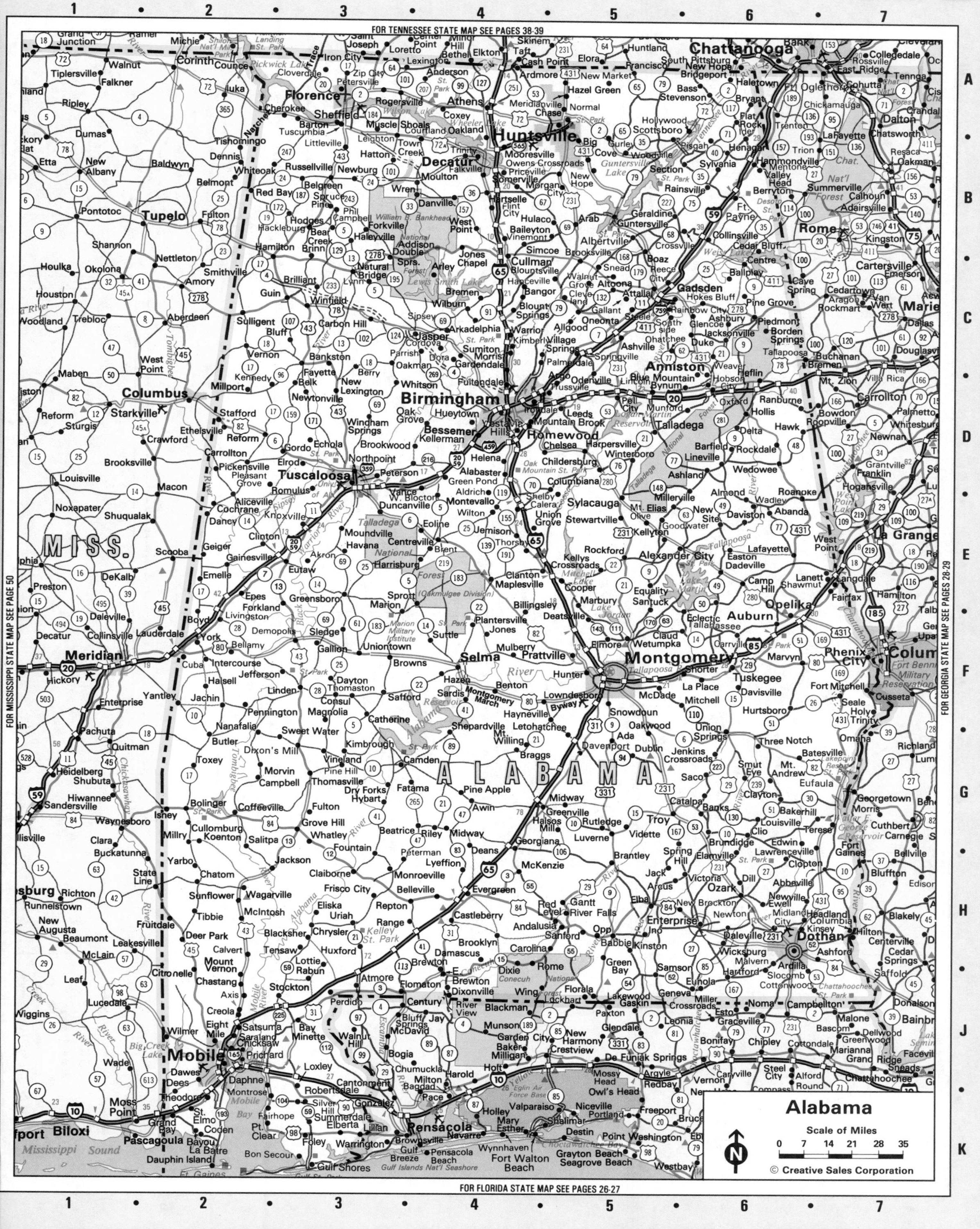

FOR TENNESSEE STATE MAP SEE PAGES 38-39
FOR MISSISSIPPI STATE MAP SEE PAGE 50
FOR GEORGIA STATE MAP SEE PAGES 28-29
FOR FLORIDA STATE MAP SEE PAGES 26-27
ALABAMA
MISS.
Alabama
Scale of Miles
0 7 14 21 28 35
N
© Creative Sales Corporation
Chattanooga
Florence
Sheffield
Huntsville
Decatur
Athens
Cullman
Gadsden
Anniston
Birmingham
Bessemer
Homewood
Tuscaloosa
Talladega
Sylacauga
Alexander City
Auburn
Opelika
Phenix City
Montgomery
Selma
Prattville
Tuskegee
Troy
Enterprise
Ozark
Dothan
Andalusia
Evergreen
Brewton
Atmore
Mobile
Prichard
Pensacola
Meridian
Columbus
Starkville
Tupelo
Rome
Dalton
Corinth
Biloxi
Pascagoula
Mississippi Sound
Gulf Shores
Gulf Islands Nat'l Seashore

FOR CANADA MAP SEE PAGES 8-9

SEE MAIN MAP F1

SEE MAIN MAP E6

SEE MAIN MAP E6

RUSSIA USA

Alaska
Scale of Miles
0 40 80 120 160 200

© Creative Sales Corporation

Arctic Ocean

Beaufort Sea

Chukchi Sea

Bering Sea

Gulf of Alaska

Pacific Ocean

Bering Sea

N.W. TERR.

YUKON

B.C.

Canada
United States

ALASKA

Aleutian Islands

Near Islands

Anchorage

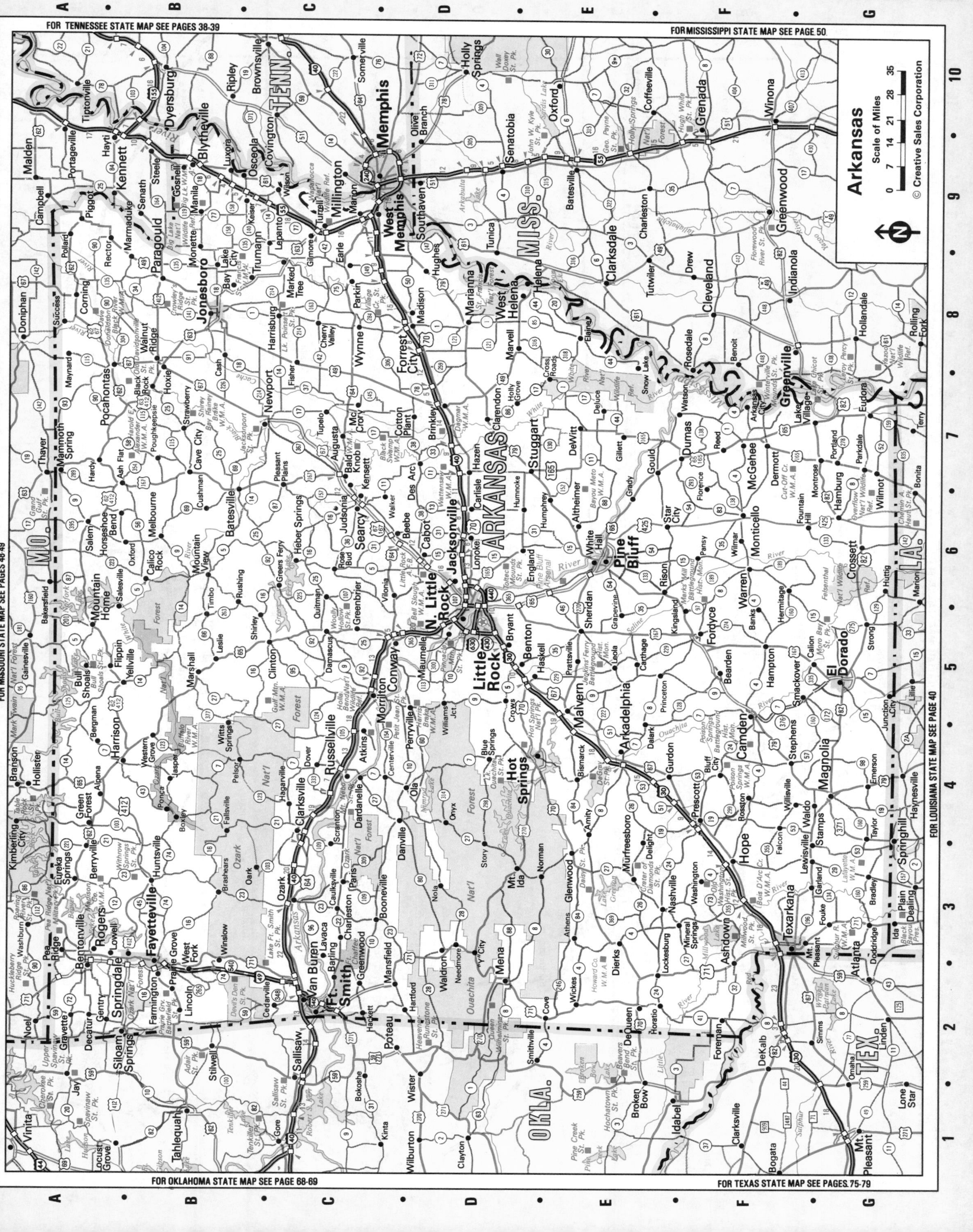

FOR TENNESSEE STATE MAP SEE PAGES 38-39
FOR MISSISSIPPI STATE MAP SEE PAGE 50
FOR MISSOURI STATE MAP SEE PAGES 48-49
FOR LOUISIANA STATE MAP SEE PAGE 40
FOR OKLAHOMA STATE MAP SEE PAGE 68-69
FOR TEXAS STATE MAP SEE PAGES 75-79
Arkansas
Scale of Miles
0 7 14 21 28 35
© Creative Sales Corporation
N
ARKANSAS
TENN.
MISS.
MO.
OKLA.
TEX.
LA.
Little Rock
N. Little Rock
Memphis
West Memphis
Pine Bluff
Hot Springs
Fort Smith
Fayetteville
Springdale
Rogers
Jonesboro
Texarkana
El Dorado
Camden
Conway
Russellville
Searcy
Batesville
Harrison
Mountain Home
Blytheville
Helena
Greenville
Jacksonville
Stuttgart
Arkadelphia
Malvern
Hope
Magnolia
Monticello
Forrest City
Dyersburg
Oxford
Clarksdale
Greenwood
Grenada
Mena
Van Buren

FOR COLORADO STATE MAP SEE PAGES 22-23
FOR NEW MEXICO STATE MAP SEE PAGE 62
FOR UTAH STATE MAP SEE PAGES 80-81
FOR NEVADA STATE MAP SEE PAGE 54

UTAH

NEVADA

ARIZONA

La Sal Jct. La Sal Summit Pt. Eastland Monticello Blanding
Lyman Bicknell Teasdale Torrey Grover Angle Boulder
Hanksville Fry Canyon Bluff Montezuma Creek Aneth
Mexican Hat Teec Nos Pos Rock Point Round Rock
Tsaile Cross Canyon St. Michaels Window Rock Luptton Sanders Navajo Chambers
Henrieville Tropic Escalante Cannonville Kanab Fredonia
Ganado Greasewood (Lower) Holbrook Sun Valley Joseph City
Kayenta Tsegi Chilchinbito Rough Rock Chinle Many Farms
Cow Springs Red Lake Tonalea The Gap Tuba City Cameron
Keams Canyon Polacca Cedar Springs Indian Wells Dilkon
Old Oraibi Second Mesa Seba Dalkai Winslow Leupp Sunrise
Page Marble Canyon Jacob Lake North Rim Grand Canyon
Desert View Gray Mountain Flagstaff Winona Angell Mountainaire Munds Park
Williams Parks Bellemont Pine Springs Ash Fork Sedona Cornville Cottonwood
Clarkdale Jerome Chino Valley Prescott McGuireville Lake Montezuma
Beaver Greenville Circleville Panguitch Hatch Brian Head
Cedar City Hamilton Fort Kanarraville Parowan Paragonah
Adamsville Minersville Lund Zane Beryl Enterprise Newcastle Central
Iron Sprs. Desert Mound Pine Valley Veyo New Harmony Pintura Leeds
Hurricane La Verkin Toquerville Rockville Springdale Glendale
Mt. Carmel Mt. Carmel Jct. Orderville Long Valley Jct. Alton
St. George Washington Santa Clara Shivwits Ivins Gunlock
Colorado City Littlefield Bunkerville Mesquite
Modena Uvada Newcastle Panaca Pioche Caliente Elgin Carp Ursine Alamo
Moapa Logandale Overton Glendale
N. Las Vegas E. Las Vegas Henderson Boulder City
Meadview Temple Bar Dolan Springs Chloride Truxton Valentine Hackberry
Peach Springs Nelson Seligman Yampai
Kingman Goldroad Oatman Yucca Wikieup
Bullhead City Riviera Katherine Cottonwood Cove
Golden Shores Topock Needles Lake Havasu City

Prescott National Forest
Kaibab National Forest
Coconino National Forest
Dixie National Forest
Manti-La Sal National Forest
Glen Canyon National Recreation Area
Lake Mead National Recreational Area
Lake Powell
Hualapai Indian Reservation
Navajo Indian Reservation
Hopi Indian Reservation
Kaibab Indian Reservation
Havasupai Indian Reservation
Canyon de Chelly Nat'l Monument
Petrified Forest National Park
Grand Canyon National Park
Zion National Park
Bryce Canyon Nat'l Park
Canyonlands National Park
Hoover Dam

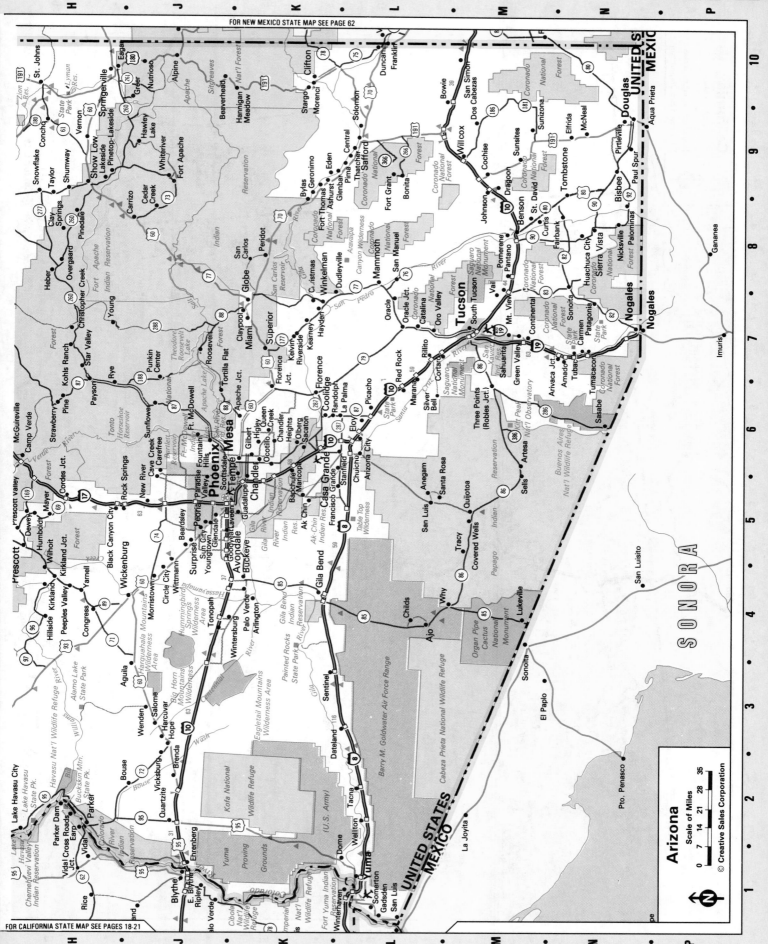

FOR NEW MEXICO STATE MAP SEE PAGE 62

FOR CALIFORNIA STATE MAP SEE PAGES 18-21

Arizona

Scale of Miles

0 7 14 21 28 35

© Creative Sales Corporation

FOR NEVADA STATE MAP SEE PAGE 54
FOR OREGON STATE MAP SEE PAGES 70-71

California

Scale of Miles

0 7 14 21 28 35

© Creative Sales Corporation

N

NEVADA

OREGON

CALIFORNIA

Reno
Sparks
Carson City
Virginia City
Dayton
Silver Springs
Fernley
Fallon
Wabuska
Wadsworth
Nixon
Gerlach
Eagle Picher

Pyramid Lk.
Indian Reservation
Winnemucca Lk.
Honey Lk.

Medford
Ashland
Talent
Jacksonville
Cave Junction
Brookings
Crescent City
Klamath Falls
Lakeview
Merrill
Malin
Tulelake
Newell
Bonanza

Alturas
Canby
Adin
Likely
Madeline
Cedarville
Lake City
Ft. Bidwell
Davis Cr.
Eagleville
Termo
Ravendale
Madeline
Standish
Litchfield
Milford
Herlong
Wendel
Doyle

Susanville
Janesville
Westwood
Chester
Greenville
Taylorsville
Quincy
Portola
Loyalton
Sierraville
Sierra City
Downieville
Truckee
Kings Beach
Tahoe City
Squaw Valley

Weed
Mt. Shasta
McCloud
Dunsmuir
Montague
Yreka
Hornbrook
Hilt
Gazelle
Grenada
Etna
Callahan
Fort Jones
Greenview
Hamburg
Happy Camp
Somes Bar
Forks Of Salmon
Orleans
Weitchpec
Hoopa

Redding
Anderson
Cottonwood
Red Bluff
Corning
Orland
Willows
Williams
Colusa
Maxwell
Chico
Paradise
Oroville
Marysville
Yuba City
Linda
Gridley
Biggs
Durham

Burney
Fall River Mills
McArthur
Bieber
Lookout
Nubieber
Old Sta.
Shingletown
Manton
Mineral
Mill Creek
Belden
Quincy

Weaverville
Junction City
Lewiston
Hayfork
Douglas City
Platina
Ono
Igo
Whiskeytown
French Gulch

Garberville
Redway
Leggett
Laytonville
Willits
Ukiah
Hopland
Boonville
Philo
Navarro
Mendocino
Ft. Bragg
Caspar
Albion
Point Arena
Manchester

Eureka
Arcata
McKinleyville
Trinidad
Blue Lake
Fortuna
Ferndale
Rio Dell
Scotia
Carlotta
Alton
Loleta
Petrolia
Honeydew
Miranda
Redcrest
Weott
Bridgeville

Clearlake
Lakeport
Lucerne
Upper Lake
Potter Valley
Redwood Valley
Kelseyville
Clear Lake

Smith River
Gasquet
Requa
Orick

Nat'l Forest
Modoc Nat'l Forest
Lassen Nat'l Forest
Lassen Volcanic Nat'l Park
Shasta Nat'l Forest
Trinity Nat'l Forest
Klamath Nat'l Forest
Six Rivers Nat'l Forest
Mendocino Nat'l Forest
Plumas Nat'l Forest
Tahoe Nat'l Forest
Redwood Nat'l Park
Prairie Creek Redwoods State Park
Jedediah Smith Redwoods St. Pk.
Humboldt Redwoods St. Pk.

Sacramento R.
Klamath River
Trinity River
Eel River
Pit River
Feather River
Smith River

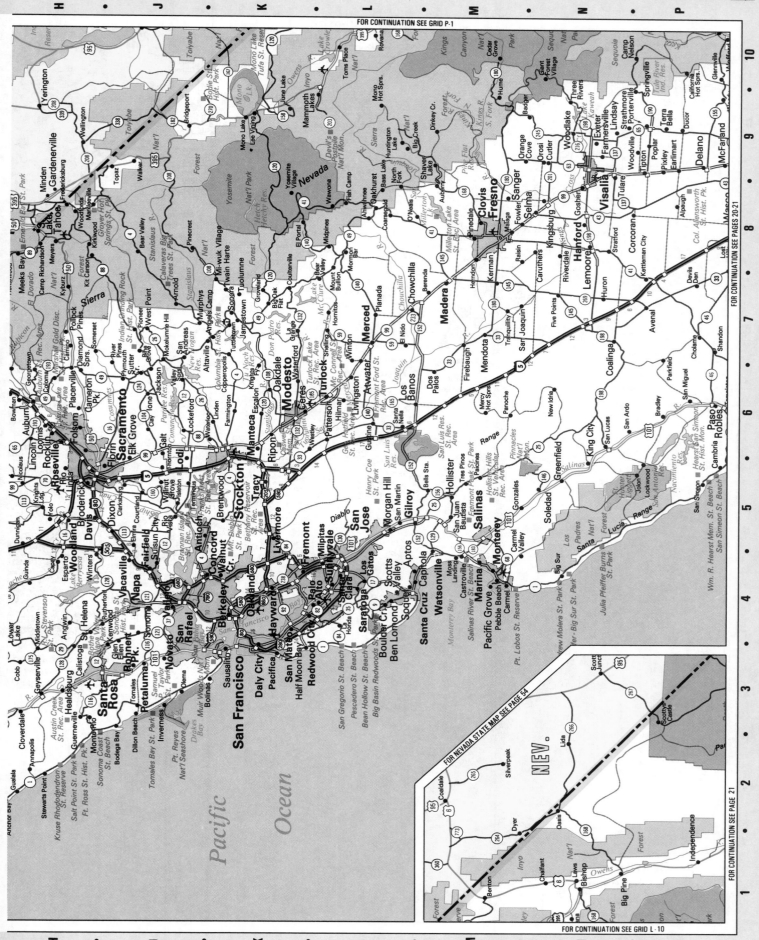

FOR CONTINUATION SEE GRID P-1

FOR CONTINUATION SEE PAGES 20-21

FOR NEVADA STATE MAP SEE PAGE E4

FOR CONTINUATION SEE PAGE 21

FOR CONTINUATION SEE GRID L-10

FOR CONTINUATION SEE PAGES 18-19

Carmel
Pt. Lobos St. Reserve
Carmel Valley
Gonzales
Soledad
Greenfield
Pinnacles Nat'l Mon.
Panoche
Tranquillity
San Joaquin
Raisin
Fowler
Sanger
Malaga
Selma
Orange Cove
Orosi
Cutler
Badger
Giant Forest Village
Sequoia Nat'l Park

Big Sur
Andrew Molera St. Park
Pfeiffer - Big Sur St. Park
Julia Pfeiffer Burns St. Park

Los Padres Nat'l Forest
New Idria
Caruthers
Kingsburg
Riverdale
Goshen
Woodlake
Three Rivers
Kaweah
Sequoia Nat'l Park

King City
San Lucas
San Ardo
Coalinga
Huron
Stratford
Hanford
Lemoore
Visalia
Farmersville
Lindsay
Exeter
Camp Nelson
Forest

Bradley
Parkfield
Avenal
Kettleman City
Corcoran
Tulare
Woodville
Porterville
Strathmore
Tipton
Poplar
Pixley
Earlimart
Terra Bella
Springville
Tule River Ind. Res.
Forest

San Simeon
Wm. R. Hearst Mem. St. Beach
San Simeon St. Beach
Cambria
Paso Robles
Templeton
Atascadero
San Miguel
Cholame
Shandon
Devils Den
Col. Allensworth St. Hist. Pk.
Delano
Ducor
California Hot Sprs.
Kernville
Isabella Res.
Onyx

Cayucos St. Beach
Cayucos
Morro Bay
Morro Bay St. Park
Baywood Pk.
Baa De Oro St. Park
Montana De Oro St. Park
San Luis Obispo
Santa Margarita
Pozo
Simmler
Blackwells Corner
Lost Hills
Wasco
McFarland
Glennville
Woody
Wofford Heights
Bodfish

Pismo Beach
Grover City
Pismo St. Beach
Oceano
Arroyo Grande
Nipomo
Twitchell
Buttonwillow
Shafter
Green Acres
Bakersfield
Edison
Caliente
Keene

Guadalupe
Orcutt
Santa Maria
Sisquoc
New Cuyama
Cuyama
McKittrick
Tule Elk St. Reserve
Fellows
Pumpkin Center
Taft
Ford City
Maricopa
Lamont
Arvin
Tehachapi
Mojave

Casmalia
Los Alamos
La Purisima Mission St. Hist. Park
Los Olivos
Padres
Madre
Los
Mtns.
Frazier Pk.
Ft. Tejon St. Hist. Pk.
Gorman
Willow Sprs.
Rosa

Surf
Vandenberg Air Force Base
Lompoc
Buellton
Solvang
Lake Cachuma
Gaviota
Montecito
Castaic Lake St. Rec. Area
Palmdale

Gaviota St. Park
Refugio St. Beach
El Capitan St. Beach
Goleta
Santa Barbara
Carpenteria St. Beach
Emma Wood St. Beach
Summerland
Carpinteria
Ojai
Fillmore
Santa Paula
Saticoy
Moorpark
Valencia
San Fernando
Acton
Glendale
Pasadena

Ventura
Oxnard
Port Hueneme
Pt. Mugu St. Park
Thousand Oaks
Simi Valley
Agoura Hills
Beverly Hills

San Miguel Is.
San Miguel Passage
Santa Cruz Is.
Leo Carrillo St. Beach
Malibu
Santa Monica Mtns. Nat'l Rec. Area
Santa Monica
Los Angeles
Redondo Beach
Rancho Palos Verdes

Santa Rosa Is.
Santa Cruz Channel
Anacapa Is.
Channel Islands National Park
Santa Monica Bay
Long Beach
Huntington Beach
Newport Beach
Laguna

Pacific

Ocean

Santa Barbara Is.
Channel Islands National Park
San Nicolas Is.
Santa Catalina Is.
Avalon
San Pedro Channel
Outer Santa Barbara Channel
San Clemente
San

San Clemente Is.
Gulf
Santa Cat

California
Scale of Miles
0 7 14 21 28 35
N
© Creative Sales Corporation

11 12 13 14 15 16 17

FOR NEVADA STATE MAP SEE PAGE 54

NEVADA

N P Q R S T U V

Lone Pine
Keeler
136
395
Cartago
190
Olancha
Darwin
Owens Lk.
Haiwee Res.
Little Lake
China Lake
178
Inyokern
Ridgecrest
14
Red Rock Canyon St. Park
Cantil
Randsburg
Red Mountain
Johannesburg
California City
Boron
North Edwards
Edwards Air Force Base
Rodgers Lake
395
58
Hinkley
Lenwood
Barstow
Yermo
Daggett
Helendale
Oro Grande
Adelanto
Pearblossom
Saddleback Butte St. Pk.
Lancaster
18
Phelan
Victorville
Apple Valley
Hesperia
Lucerne Valley
247
31
Newberry Sprs.
12
10

Death Valley
Stovepipe Wells
Panamint Sprs.
190
Furnace Cr. Ranch
Death Valley Jct.
127
Shoshone
178
Tecopa
Panamint Range
Death Valley Nat'l Monument
Salt Cr.
Amargosa R.
Avawatz Mtns.
127
U.S. Naval Weapons Sta.
Ft. Irwin Military Res.
42
15
Cady Mtns.
40
31
Ludlow
31
Amboy
Bullion Mtns.
Twentynine Palms Marine Corps Base

Armagosa Valley
Mercury
Indian Springs
373
160
Pahrump
372
178
Goodsprings
161
Jean
93
168
169
15
Glendale
Overton
North Las Vegas
Las Vegas
Henderson
51.5
146
160
Boulder City
Nelson
165
Cima
East Mohave Nat'l Scenic Area
Kelso
Providence Mtns. St. Rec. Area
Goffs
20
Fenner
Essex
Providence Mtns.
Sacramento Mtns.
Old Woman Mtns.
Needles
95
CALIFORNIA

Mesquite
170
Bunkerville
7
Virgin R.
Temple Bar
Lake Mead Nat'l Rec. Area
Black Mtns.
Willow Beach
Cottonwood Cove
164
Searchlight
Ivanpah
Laughlin
163
Bullhead City
93
Chloride
Kingman
McConnico
Yucca
Hualapai Mtns.
Golden Shores
Topock
ARIZONA
Lake Havasu City
95
Lake Havasu State Pk.
Parker Dam
Buckskin Mtn. State Pk.
Earp
Parker
Poston
Rice
Vidal
62
Big Maria Mtns.
Colorado River Indian Res.
Quartzsite
Bouse
72
95
95
Blythe
Ehrenberg
Ripley
Palo Verde
Cibola Nat'l Wildlife Refuge
Picacho St. Rec. Area
Martinez Lake
Stone Cabin
Imperial Nat'l Wildlife Refuge
Ft. Yuma Ind. Res.
Winterhaven
Dome
Yuma
Wellton
Tacna
San Luis Rio Colorado
Somerton
Algodones
Galeana
2

Wrightwood
2
Glendora
Pomona
Ontario
Fullerton
Anaheim
Santa Ana
El Toro
Dana Pt.
San Clemente
Camp Pendleton
Oceanside
Carlsbad
Vista
San Marcos
Escondido
Leucadia
Encinitas
Del Mar
La Jolla
San Diego
Coronado
Chula Vista
Imperial Beach
Tijuana
Rosarito
Big Bear Lake
San Bernardino
Riverside
Yucaipa
Beaumont
Banning
Cabazon
Morongo Valley
Yucca Valley
Joshua Tree
Twentynine Palms
62
Desert Hot Sprs.
Palm Sprs.
Thousand Palms
Palm Desert
Indio
Coachella
Indian Wells
La Quinta
Mecca
86
195
111
Salton Sea St. Rec. Area
Desert Shores
Salton City
Salton Sea
Niland
Calipatria
Westmorland
Brawley
Imperial
Seeley
El Centro
Calexico
Mexicali
Holtville
Heber
98
115
Alamorio
Glamis
Chocolate Mtns.
Chocolate Mountain Naval Aerial Gunnery Range
Imperial Dam
78
Colonia Progreso
La Rumorosa
Hermosillo
2

Sun City
Hemet
74
Idyllwild
San Jacinto
Romoland
Perris
Corona
Lake Elsinore
Murrieta
Temecula
Fallbrook
Pala
Pauma Valley
Palomar Mtn.
Ramona
Julian
Santa Ysabel
Cuyamaca Rancho St. Park
Mt. Laguna
Pine Valley
Alpine
El Cajon
Jamul
Santee
Poway
San Marcos
Campo
Boulevard
Tecate
U.S. MEXICO
Ocotillo
Ocotillo Wells
Borrego Sprs.
Anza-Borrego Desert St. Park
Ocotillo Wells St. Vehicular Rec. Area
Elmore
Cahuilla Ind. Res.
Santa Rosa Ind. Res.
Cleveland Nat'l Forest
San Bernardino Nat'l Forest

FOR ARIZONA STATE MAP SEE PAGES 16-17

11 12 13 14 15 16 17

FOR WYOMING STATE MAP SEE PAGES 88-89

WYOMING

UTAH

Colorado

Scale of Miles

0 7 14 21 28 35

© Creative Sales Corporation

N

FOR UTAH STATE MAP SEE PAGE 80-81

FOR NEW MEXICO STATE MAP SEE PAGE 62

Saratoga, Medicine Bow, Centennial, Albany, Woods Landing, Mountain Home, Riverside, Encampment, Larmie, Baggs, Dixon, Severy, Cowdrey, Walden, Rustic, Roosevelt National Forest

Carter, Fort Bridger, Lyman, Urie, Mountain View, Robertson, Lonetree, Burntfork, McKinnon, Manila, Green Lake, Hiawatha, Queaty, Green River

Flaming Gorge Res., Flaming Gorge National Recreational Area, Ashley National Forest, High Uintas Wilderness Area, Oak Park Res., Steinaker Res.

Whiterocks, Monarch, Neola, Lapoint, Maeser, Vernal, Naples, Jensen, Bonanza, Bluebell, Cedarview, Gusher, Fort Duchesne, Leota, Ouray, Roosevelt, Altamont, Upalco, Arcadia, Ioka, Bridgeland, Myton, Duchesne

Dinosaur National Monument, Browns Park Nat'l. Wildlife Refuge, Sunbeam, Maybell, Craig, Lay, Elk Springs, Blue Mountain, Dinosaur, Rangely, Colorado Northwestern Community College

Milner, Steamboat Sprs., Hayden, Pagoda, Hamilton, Oak Creek, Phippsburg, Yampa, Toponas, McCoy, Bond, State Bridge, Wolcott, Coalmont, Rand, Gould, Hot Sulphur Springs, Parshall, Kremmling, Tabernash, Fraser, Winter Park, Granby, Nederland, Rollinsville, Georgetown, Silverthorne, Dillon, Frisco, Breckenridge, Blue River, Climax, Leadville, Fairplay, Alma, Como, Garo Park, Granite, Twin Lakes, Buena Vista

Meeker, Buford, Rio Blanco, New Castle, Silt, Rifle, Parachute, DeBeque, Cameo, Collbran, Molina, Mesa, Palisade, Skyway, Glenwood Sprs., Carbondale, Basalt, Snowmass, Woody Creek, Redstone, Aspen, Snowmass Village, Marble, Crested Butte, Redvale, Dotsero, Gypsum, Eagle, Edwards, Avon, Dowd, Gilman, Vail, Red Cliff, Malta

Mack, Loma, Fruita, Grand Junction, Clifton, Whitewater, Orchard City, Delta, Lazear, Austin, Hotchkiss, Paonia, Bowie, Somerset, Cedaredge, Crawford, Maher, Almont, Gunnison, Parlin, Doyleville, Sargents, Poncha Springs, Salida, Coaldale, Howard

Colorado National Monument, Gateway, Uravan, Montrose, Cimarron, Sapinero, Powderhorn, Lake City, Creede, Saguache, Center, Moffat, Villa Grove, Mineral Springs

Paradox, Bedrock, Nucla, Naturita, Vancorum, Redvale, Norwood, Ridgway, Ouray, Telluride, Saw Pit, Placerville, Ophir, Red Mountain, Gladstone, Silverton, Dunton, Rico, Stoner, Rockwood, Hermosa

Moab, La Sal Jct., La Sal, Slick Rock, Egnar, Summit Pt., Dove Creek, Cahone, Pleasant View, Yellow Jacket, Lewis, Arriola, Cortez, Dolores, Lebanon, Mancos, Hesperus, Durango, Bayfield, Ignacio, Arboles, Pagosa Sprs., Chimney Rock, Chromo

Monticello, Eastland, Blanding, Fry Canyon, Bluff, Montezuma Creek, Aneth, Mexican Hat, Shiprock, Beklabito, Flora Vista, Kirtland, Turley, Aztec, Bloomfield, Farmington

Manti-La Sal National Forest, Canyonlands National Park, Arches National Park, Dark Canyon Wilderness Area, Hovenweep Nat'l Monument, Mesa Verde National Park, Ute Mountain Indian Reservation, San Juan National Forest, Navajo Lake State Park

Towaoc, Fort Lewis, Breen, Kline, Marvel, Oxford, Redmesa, Allison, La Plata, Cedar Hill, Dulce, Lumberton, Monero, Chama, Los Ojos, Rutheron, Ensenada, Brazos, Tierra Amarilla, Tres Piedras, Antonito, Conejos, Romeo, La Jara, Sanford, Manassa, San Acacio, Capulin, Platoro, Summitville, Monte Vista, Homelake, Alamosa, Mosca, Hooper, Del Norte, South Fork, Spar City, Wagon Wheel Gap, Great Sand Dunes National Monument, Crestone

Green River, Thompson, Cisco, Crescent Jct., Woodside, Sunnyside, East Carbon City, Moab

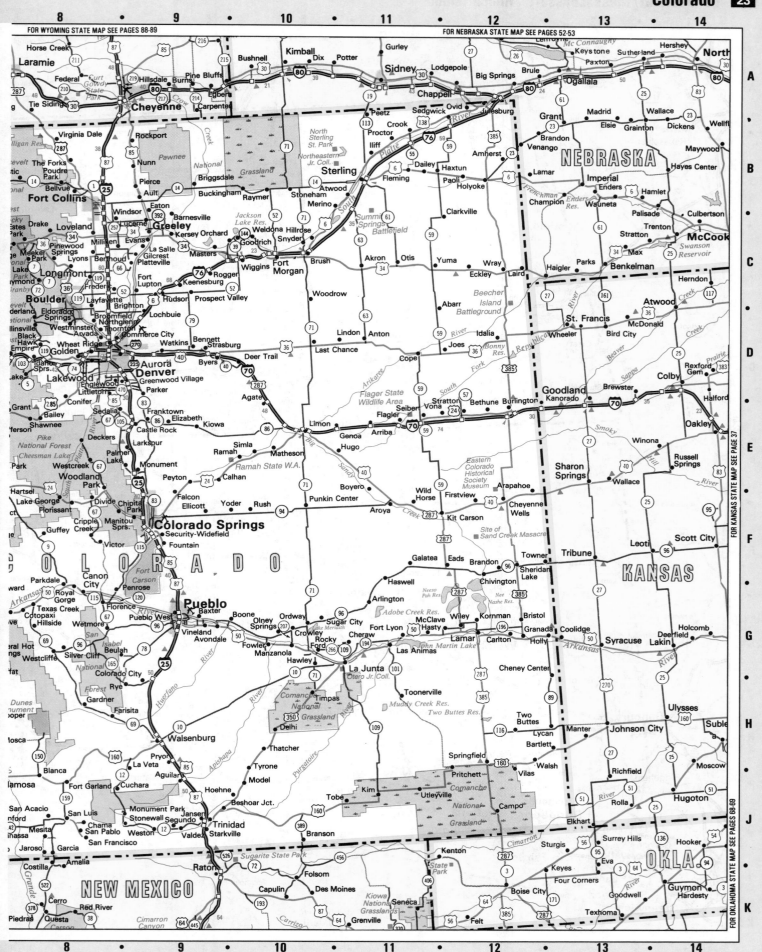

FOR VERMONT STATE MAP SEE PAGE 55

FOR NEW YORK STATE MAP SEE PAGES 58-61

N.H.

VT.

MASS.

N.Y.

CONN.

Troy
Albany
Rensselaer
Nassau
Pittsfield
Hudson
Great Barrington
Hillsdale
Sheffield
Salisbury
Stanfordville
Amenia
Dover Plains
Poughquag
Sherman
Pawling
New Fairfield
Danbury
Brewster
Salem Ctr.
Ridgefield
Cross River
Bedford
Wilton
New Canaan
Norwalk
Darien
Stamford
Greenwich

Williamstown
North Adams
Adams
Cheshire
Dalton
Hinsdale
Lenox
Richmond
Stockbridge
West Stockbridge
Lee
Becket
West Becket
New Marlborough
Sandisfield
Canaan
Norfolk
Colebrook
Winsted
Barkhamsted
New Hartford
Sharon
Cornwall
Cornwall Bridge
Goshen
Torrington
Litchfield
Warren
Kent
Harwinton
Burlington
Farmington
Plymouth
Bristol
Thomaston
Watertown
Morris
Bethlehem
Washington
New Milford
Woodbury
Southbury
Brookfield
Bethel
Newtown
Monroe
Redding
Georgetown
Trumbull
Bridgeport
Stratford
Milford
Weston
Westport
Fairfield

Florida
Charlemont
Buckland
Shelburne Falls
Shelburne
Ashfield
Conway
Whately
Williamsburg
Chesterfield
Worthington
Cummington
Peru
Middlefield
Chester
Westhampton
Easthampton
Northampton
Huntington
Montgomery
Russell
Blandford
Tolland
Granville
Hartland
East Hartland
Granby
East Granby
Simsbury
Canton
Bloomfield
Avon
West Hartford
Newington
Rocky Hill
Southington
Berlin
New Britain
Meriden
Cheshire
Naugatuck
Wallingford
Seymour
Hamden
Woodbridge
North Haven
Ansonia
Derby
Shelton
Orange
West Haven
New Haven
East Haven
Guilford
Madison

Colrain
Heath
Bernardston
Gill
Greenfield
Deerfield
Montague
Sunderland
Leverett
Amherst
Hadley
South Hadley
Belchertown
Granby
Holyoke
Three Rivers
Chicopee
West Springfield
Springfield
Agawam
Longmeadow
East Longmeadow
Suffield
Windsor Locks
Enfield
Somers
Stafford
Windsor
South Windsor
Ellington
Tolland
Vernon
Manchester
East Hartford
Hartford
Glastonbury
Wethersfield
Cromwell
Middletown
East Hampton
Durham
Haddam
Killingworth
North Branford
Branford
Clinton
Westbrook
Old Saybrook
Old Lyme
East Lyme

Wilmington
Whitingham
Readsboro
Stamford
Pownal
Clarksburg
Leyden
Northfield
Warwick
Orange
Athol
Templeton
Petersham
Barre
Hardwick
Ware
Palmer
Monson
Wales
Holland
Brimfield
Sturbridge
Southbridge
Dudley
Webster
Woodstock
Westford
Eastford
Ashford
Willington
Coventry
Mansfield Center
Storrs
Chaplin
Hampton
Brooklyn
Columbia
Hebron
Marlborough
Colchester
Bozrah
Norwich
Franklin
Lebanon
Windham
Scotland
Plainfield
Canterbury
Sterling
Jewett City
Salem
Montville
Oakdale
Chesterfield
Ledyard Ctr.
New London
Groton
Mystic
Stonington
Waterford

Swanzey
Troy
Winchester
Fitzwilliam
Rindge
Jaffrey
Peterborough
Greenville
Ashby
Winchendon
Gardner
Templeton
Westminster
Leominster
Princeton
Holden
Worcester
Leicester
Spencer
West Brookfield
Brookfield
Warren
North Brookfield
Oakham
New Braintree
Gilbertville
Charlton
Oxford

Long Island Sound

Greenport
Southold
Shelter Island
Peconic
Montauk
Gardiners Island
Fishers Island

8 • 9 • 10 • 11 • 12 • 13 • 14 • 15

FOR NEW HAMPSHIRE STATE MAP SEE PAGE 55

A

Wilton Merrimack Derry Hampstead Amesbury Salisbury
Milford Litchfield Londonderry Atkinson Merrimac Salisbury Beach St. Res.
Nashua Windham West Newbury Newburyport
Silver Lake St. Pk. Hudson Salem Haverhill Newbury Parker River Nat'l Wildlife Ref.
Hollis Methuen Groveland Plum Is.
Townsend Tyngsborough Lawrence Georgetown Rowley Plum Is. St. Pk.

B

Pepperell Lowell Dracut Boxford Ipswich Halibut Point State Park
Lunenburg Groton Andover Wenham Essex Rockport
Westford Chelmsford Tewksbury North Reading Danvers Hamilton Gloucester
Shirley Billerica Wilmington Reading Manchester-by-the-Sea
Harvard Littleton Carlisle Lynnfield Beverly Salem
Acton Bedford Wakefield Peabody Marblehead
Boxborough Concord Woburn Saugus Swampscott
Sterling Bolton Maynard Lexington Lynn Nahant
Clinton Stow Lincoln Revere
Boylston Hudson Wayland Cambridge Chelsea Winthrop

C

Northborough Marlborough Cochituate Newton Boston Massachusetts Bay
Shrewsbury Wellesley Hull Atlantic
Westborough Natick Milton Quincy Ocean
Framingham Dedham Hingham Scituate

D

Grafton Hopkinton Westwood Norwood Weymouth Norwell
Millbury Upton Medfield Canton Braintree Randolph
Milford Millis Walpole Holbrook Rockland Hanover Marshfield
Northbridge Medway Sharon Avon Abington Hanson Provincetown
Whitinsville Hopedale Norfolk Stoughton Whitman Pembroke Duxbury Herring Cove Beach
Mendon Wrentham Brockton East Bridgewater Truro

E

Uxbridge Bellingham Foxborough Easton Kingston Wellfleet
Blackstone Mansfield Bridgewater Halifax Plympton Cape Cod
Slatersville N. Attleborough Norton Raynham Plymouth Cape Cod Bay Wellfleet Harbor
Woonsocket Harrisville Ashton Berkley Middleborough Carver Nat'l Eastham
Pascoag Attleboro Taunton Rehoboth Berkley Seashore Orleans

F

Chepachet Esmond Pawtucket Dighton Freetown Buzzards Bay Sagamore Sandwich Brewster
Harmony Providence Seekonk Somerset Wareham Barnstable Dennis Yarmouth
Glocester Cranston East Providence Swansea Bourne Hyannis Harwich Chatham
Foster Center Auburn Fall River Rochester Marion Otis A.F.B. Centerville West Dennis South Dennis

G

West Greenwich Center East Greenwich Barrington Warren Bristol Acushnet Mattapoisett Falmouth Osterville Yarmouth
Nooseneck Warwick Homestead Fairhaven East Falmouth Monomoy Island
Exeter Saunderstown Middletown Westport New Bedford Buzzards Bay
Wickford Portsmouth Dartmouth West Is.

H

Kingston Jamestown Newport Little Compton Naushon Is. Vineyard Haven Oak Bluffs Nantucket Sound
Woodville Wakefield Conanicut Is. Tisbury Edgartown Chappaquiddick Island Muskeget Is.
Wood River Jct. Narragansett Pier West Tisbury Nantucket
Charlestown Gay Head Chilmark Martha's Vineyard Island Tuckernuck Is. Nantucket Island

J

Westerly Block Island Sound Block Island Nat'l W.R. Vineyard Sound
Block Island
Block Island State Beach

N

Connecticut Massachusetts Rhode Island

Scale of Miles
0 3 6 9 12 15

© Creative Sales Corporation

K

8 • 9 • 10 • 11 • 12 • 13 • 14 • 15

Florida

Scale of Miles

0 7 14 21 28 35

N

Atlantic

Ocean

Gulf

of

Mexico

Apalachee Bay

GEORGIA

FOR GEORGIA STATE MAP SEE PAGES 28-29

FOR CONTINUATION SEE PAGE 27, GRID N-6

Donalsonville
Bainbridge · Cairo
Thomasville
Valdosta
Lakeland
Homerville
Quitman
Madison
Greenville
Monticello
Tallahassee
Havana
Quincy
Gretna
Chattahoochee
Bristol
Bloxham
Crawfordville
Sopchoppy
Carrabelle
Woodville
Lloyd
Capps
Perry
Mayo
Day
Live Oak
Jasper
White Springs
Lake City
Watertown
Fort White
Branford
Old Town
Cross City
Steinhatchee
Stewart City
Deckle Beach
Suwanee
Cedar Key
Chiefland
Trenton
Bell
Bronson
Archer
Williston
High Springs
Alachua
Newberry
Lake Butler
Starke
Keystone Heights
Gainesville
Hawthorne
Reddick
Dunnellon
Inglis
Crystal River
Homosassa Springs
Inverness
Citrus Springs
Brooksville
Hudson
New Port Richey
Tarpon Springs
Clearwater
Largo
Treasure Island
St. Petersburg Beach
St. Petersburg
Tampa
Temple Terrace
Plant City
Dover
Brandon
Riverview
Sun City Center
Apollo Beach
Zephyrhills
Dade City
Lacoochee
Bushnell
Webster
Wildwood
Ocala
Belleview
Silver Springs
Palatka
East Palatka
Hastings
Crescent City
Bunnell
Flagler Beach
St. Augustine
St. Augustine Beach
Green Cove Springs
Orange Park
Baldwin
Callahan
Hilliard
Kingsland
Folkston
Fargo
Jacksonville
Atlantic Beach
Neptune Beach
Jacksonville Beach
Fernandina Beach
Saint Marys
Ormand by the Sea
Ormand Beach
Daytona Beach
Port Orange
New Smyrna Beach
Edgewater
Mims
Titusville
Cape Canaveral
Merritt Island
Cocoa Beach
Rockledge
Satellite Beach
Indian Harbour Beach
Melbourne
W. Melbourne
Palm Bay
Sebastian
Gifford
Vero Beach
Fellsmere
Cocoa
St. Cloud
Kissimmee
Orlando
Winter Park
Winter Springs
Casselberry
Sanford
DeBary
Deltona
DeLand
DeLeon Springs
Mt. Dora
Eustis
Apopka
Winter Garden
Lake Buena Vista
Clermont
Polk City
Haines City
Winter Haven
Lake Wales
Lakeland
Plant City
Bartow
Fort Meade
Frostproof
Avon Park
Waverly
Pembroke
Ridge Manor
DeLeon
Umatilla
Paisley

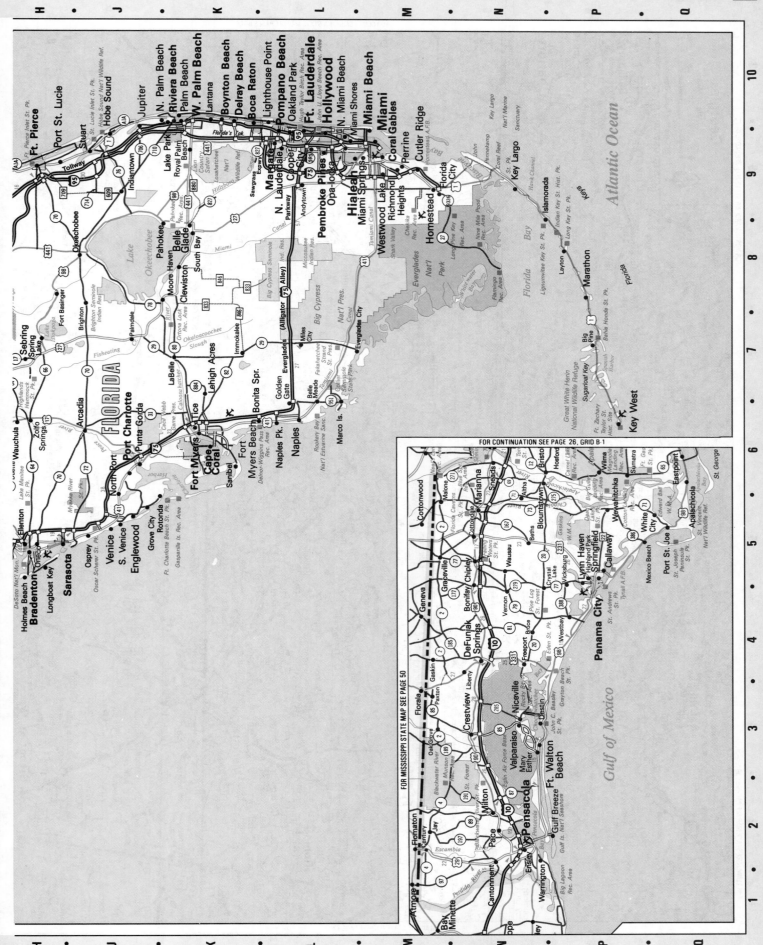

FOR CONTINUATION SEE PAGE 26, GRID B-1

FOR MISSISSIPPI STATE MAP SEE PAGE 50

Atlantic Ocean

Gulf of Mexico

FLORIDA

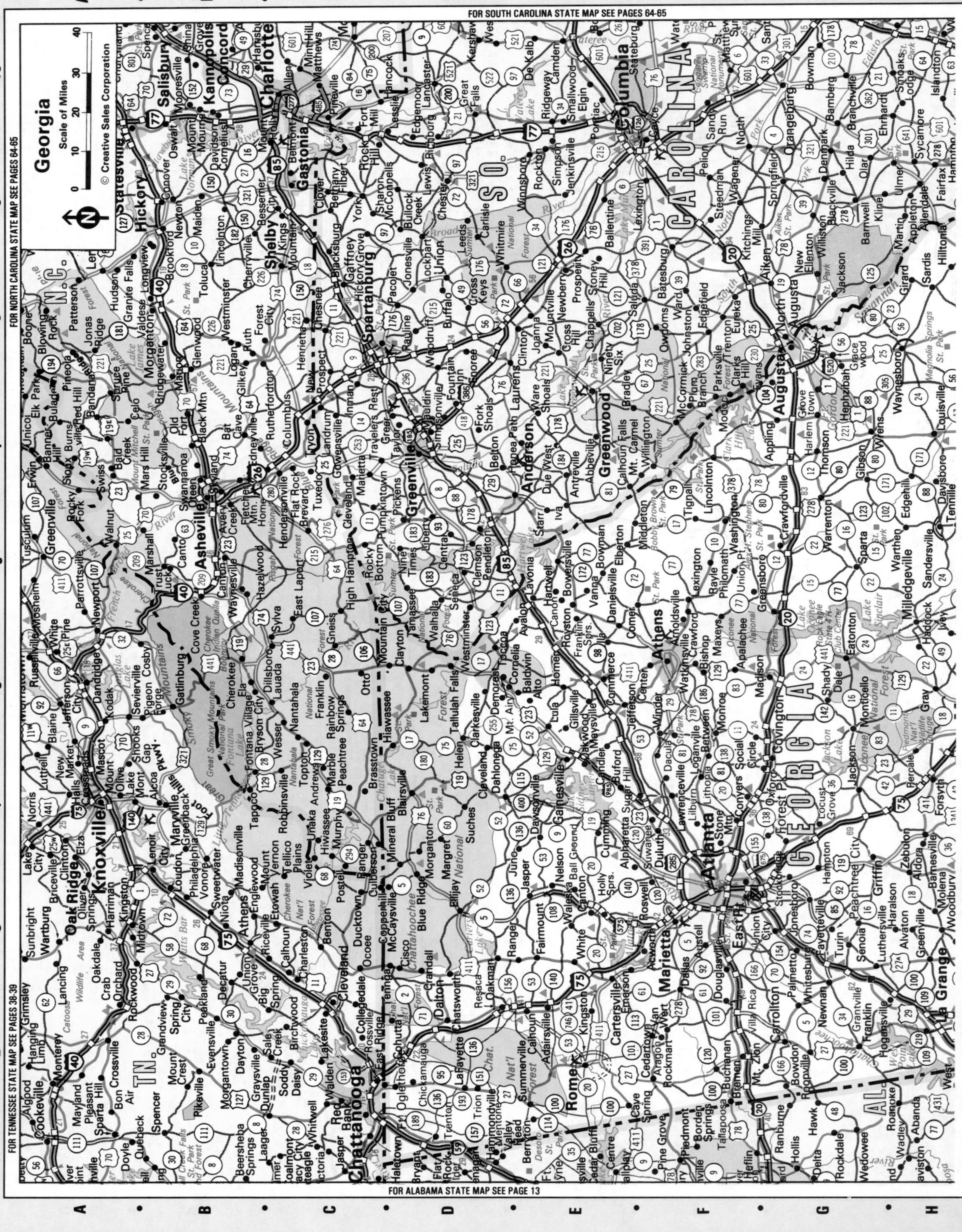

FOR SOUTH CAROLINA STATE MAP SEE PAGES 64-65
FOR NORTH CAROLINA STATE MAP SEE PAGES 64-65
FOR TENNESSEE STATE MAP SEE PAGES 38-39
FOR ALABAMA STATE MAP SEE PAGE 13
Georgia
Scale of Miles
0 10 20 30 40
© Creative Sales Corporation
N.C.
TN.
SO. CAROLINA
GEORGIA
AL.
Atlanta
Athens
Augusta
Columbia
Charlotte
Knoxville
Chattanooga
Asheville
Greenville
Spartanburg
Anderson
Greenwood
Gastonia
Marietta
Rome
Dalton
La Grange
Milledgeville

FOR FLORIDA STATE MAP SEE PAGES 26-27

FOR ALABAMA STATE MAP SEE PAGE 13

A B C D E F G

Hawaii

Scale of Miles

0 4 8 12 16 20

© Creative Sales Corporation

N

Maui

Kalahu Pt.
Moloea Pt.
Hana
Kipahulu
360
Pukuilua Pt.
Waikapuala St. Pk.
Wailua
Kaupo
Apole Pt.
Haleakala Crater
378
Makawao
377
Keokea
37
Haiku
Paia
Spreckelsville
36
Pauwela
Pauwela Pt.
Ulupalakua
Cape Hanamanioa
Keoneoio
Kahului
Puunene
31
Kihei
Natalele Pt.
Kahakuloa Pt.
Waihee Pt.
Waihee
Wailuku
311
Maalaea
Wailea
Makena
340
Iao Valley
30
Kahului Bay
Maalaea Bay
Kamaole Beach Park
Nukuole Pt.
Honokohau
Olowalu Mopua
Hebli Pt.
30
Lahaina
Maui
Miles
0 2 4

Molokai

Lamaloa Head
Halawa
Cape Halawa
Wailua
Pauwalu
Waialua
460
Kalae
Kaluaaha
Pukoo
Ualapue
Kamalo
450
Iliopt.
Laau Pt.
Kalaupapa
Makanalua Pen.
Kaiupua Pt.
Kalae
Kualapuu
Kaunakakai
Kamiloa
Mauna Loa
Kolo
Kalohi Channel
Pailolo Channel
Molokai
Miles
0 2 4

Niihau
(Private)
Puuwai
Kaulakahi Channel

Kauai
Anahola
Lihue
56
Lawai
Haena
50
Mana
Waimea
Kauai
Pacific Ocean

Pacific Ocean

Kauai Co.
Honolulu Co.

Oahu (inset)
Kahuku
83
Kahana
Kaneohe
Kailua
Pearl City
H2
Honolulu
Waikiki
H1
Haleiwa
Makaha
Nanakuli
Oahu
Honolulu Co.
Maui Co.

HAWAII

Molokai
Kaiwi Channel
Auau Channel
Kealaikahiki Channel

Lanai
Kualapuu
450
Kamalo
460
Koele
Lanai City
Keomuku
Mauna Loa
Lanai

Maui (inset)
Hana
360
Haliimaile
Ulupalakua
Honokahua
36
37
Kahului
31
Lahaina
30
Maui

Kahoolawe
Kaka Pt.

Maui Co.
Hawaii Co.

Alenuihaha Channel

Hawaii
Waiakea
Pohoiki
Hilo
130
Pahoa
Kaimu
Kalapana
Honohina
Hakalau
Papaikou
Rainbow Falls
Keaau
Puna Black Sand Beach
Opihikao Beach
Kaena Pt.
Papaaloa
Pepeekeo
19
Paukaa
Kurtistown
Glenwood
Hawaii Volcanoes National Park
Honokaa
Kukuihaele
Waimea
Kailua
Mountain View
200
Honuapo
Mauna Kea 13,796 ft.
Mauna Loa 13,680 ft.
11
Naalehu
Kaaluulu
Hawi
Niulii
250
Waiaka
190
Kalaoa
Kainaliu
Captain Cook
Keokea
Kokee
Pahala
Waiohinu
Waiohukini
Ka Lae
Upolu Pt.
Mahukona
210
Puako
Kawaihae
19
Honokahau
Napoopoo
Honaunau
Hookena
Papa
Milolii
Keahole Pt.
Kauna Pt.
Hanamalo Pt.
Hawaii

Oahu
Kahuku Pt.
Kahuku
Laie
Hauula
Kahana
Kahaluu
Kaneohe
Kailua
Mokapu Pt.
Kaneohe Marine Air Station
Waimanalo
Sea Life Park
Makapuu Pt.
Koko Head
Kailua
Sunset Beach
Polynesian Cultural Center
Sacred Falls
83
Kualoa Pt.
Kaneohe Bay
Waimanalo Bay
Pali Lookout
61
Diamond Head
72
Hawaii Kai
H3
92
Waikiki
Kahana Beach
Kaena Pt.
Haleiwa
Wahiawa
H2
99
78
Honolulu
Pearl City
63
Aiea
Waipahu
99
Mililani Town
Schofield Barracks
Range
750
Waianae
Makakilo City
95
Ewa
H1
Honolulu Airport
Barbers Pt.
Kepuhi Pt.
Makaha
Dillingham Air Force Base
930
Maili
Nanakuli
93
Waianae
780
Barbers Pt.
Oahu
Kaena Pt.
Kauai Channel
Pacific Ocean
Miles
0 2 4

Kauai
Moloaa
Anahola
Kealia
Kapaa
56
Wailua
Hanamaulu
Lihue Airport
Niumalu
580
583
Lihue
Nawiliwili
Puhi
50
Koloa
Kilauea
Hanalei
56
Kalaheo
Lawai
Eleele
Port Allen
Koloa
Makahuena Pt.
Haena Pt.
Haena
Mt. Waialeale 5,148 ft.
Waimea Canyon
Waimea
Hanapepe
Kalaheo
Koheo Pt.
550
Kokee State Park
Kaumakani
Makaha Pt.
Kalalau
550
Waimea
Kekaha
Mana
Kauai
Pacific Ocean
Miles
0 2 4

Pacific Ocean

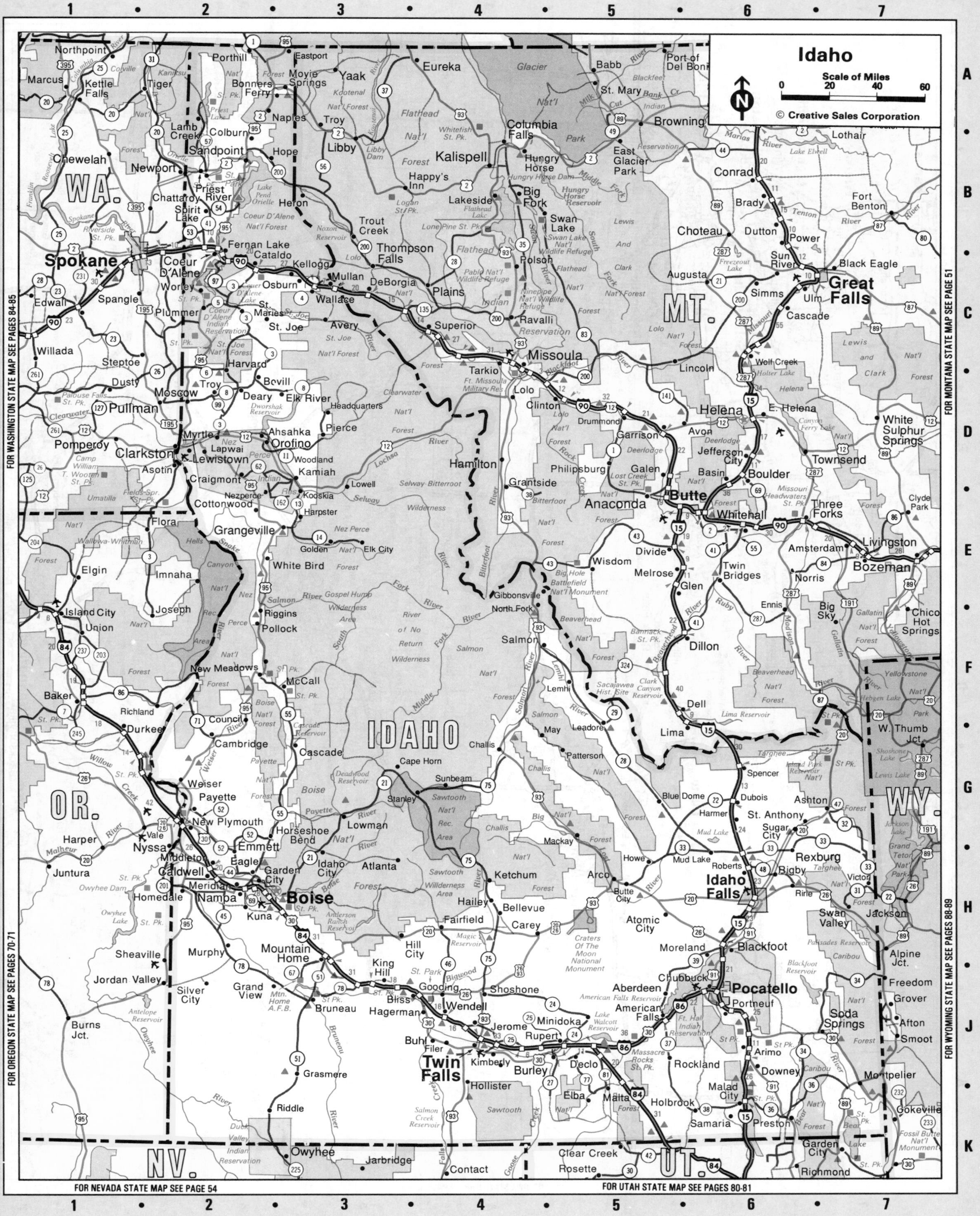

Idaho

Scale of Miles
0   20   40   60

© Creative Sales Corporation

N

FOR WASHINGTON STATE MAP SEE PAGES 84-85
FOR OREGON STATE MAP SEE PAGES 70-71
FOR MONTANA STATE MAP SEE PAGE 51
FOR WYOMING STATE MAP SEE PAGES 88-89
FOR NEVADA STATE MAP SEE PAGE 54
FOR UTAH STATE MAP SEE PAGES 80-81

WA. · OR. · NV. · UT. · MT. · WY. · IDAHO

Spokane · Coeur D'Alene · Sandpoint · Bonners Ferry · Moscow · Lewiston · Clarkston · Grangeville · McCall · New Meadows · Cascade · Boise · Nampa · Caldwell · Meridian · Mountain Home · Twin Falls · Burley · Pocatello · Idaho Falls · Rexburg · Blackfoot · American Falls · Malad City · Soda Springs · Montpelier · Salmon · Challis · Ketchum · Hailey · Shoshone · Gooding · Jerome · Rupert

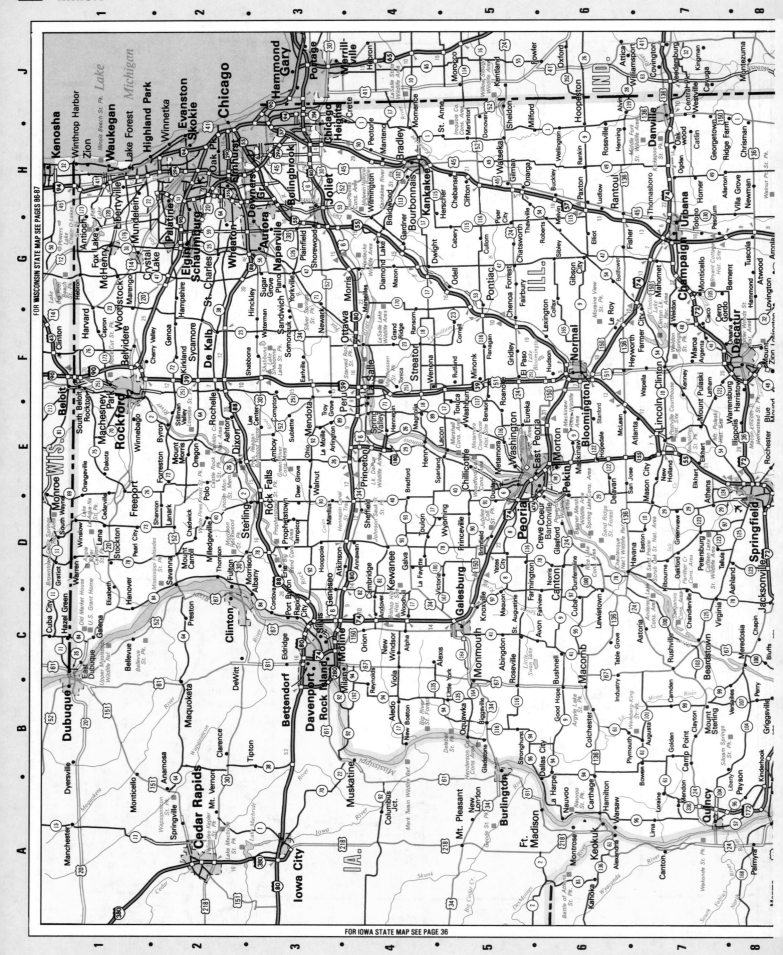

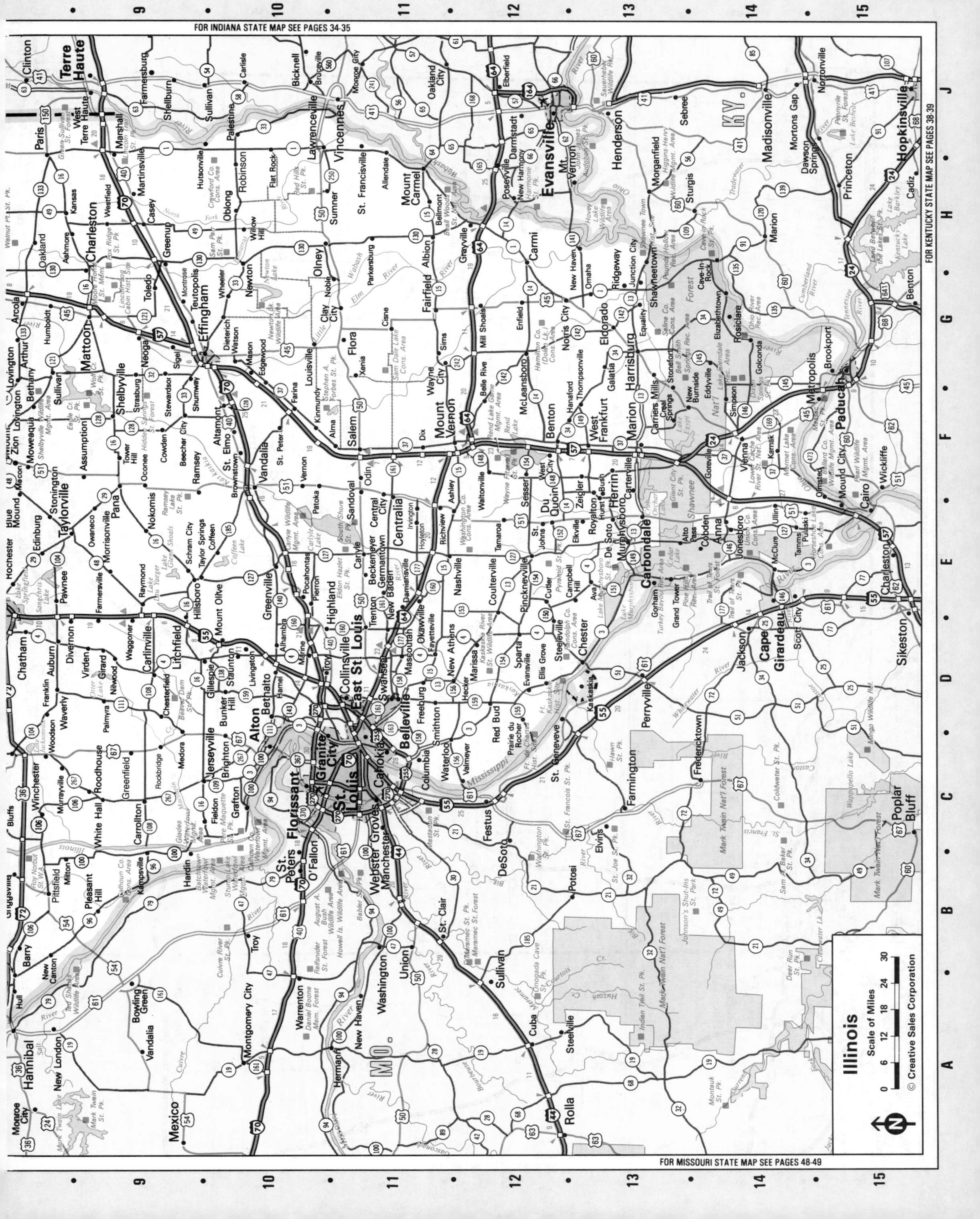

FOR INDIANA STATE MAP SEE PAGES 34-35
FOR KENTUCKY STATE MAP SEE PAGES 38-39
FOR MISSOURI STATE MAP SEE PAGES 48-49
Illinois
Scale of Miles
0 6 12 18 24 30
© Creative Sales Corporation
MO.
KY.
St. Louis
East St. Louis
Evansville
Terre Haute
Paducah
Cape Girardeau
Carbondale
Effingham
Mattoon
Charleston
Centralia
Mount Vernon
Belleville
Alton
Hannibal
Rolla

FOR OHIO STATE MAP SEE PAGES 66-67

FOR MICHIGAN STATE MAP SEE PAGES 44-45

FOR ILLINOIS STATE MAP SEE PAGES 32-33

Chicago **Lake Michigan** **Michigan City** **South Bend** **Elkhart** **Mishawaka** **Gary** **Hammond** **East Chicago** **Valparaiso** **Hobart** **Crown Point** **Merrillville** **Schererville**

Fort Wayne **Muncie** **Anderson** **Marion** **Kokomo** **Lafayette** **W. Lafayette** **Indianapolis** **Carmel** **Richmond** **New Castle** **Peru** **Wabash** **Huntington** **Goshen** **Warsaw** **Plymouth** **La Porte** **Logansport** **Crawfordsville** **Danville**

INDIANA

MI

IL

OH

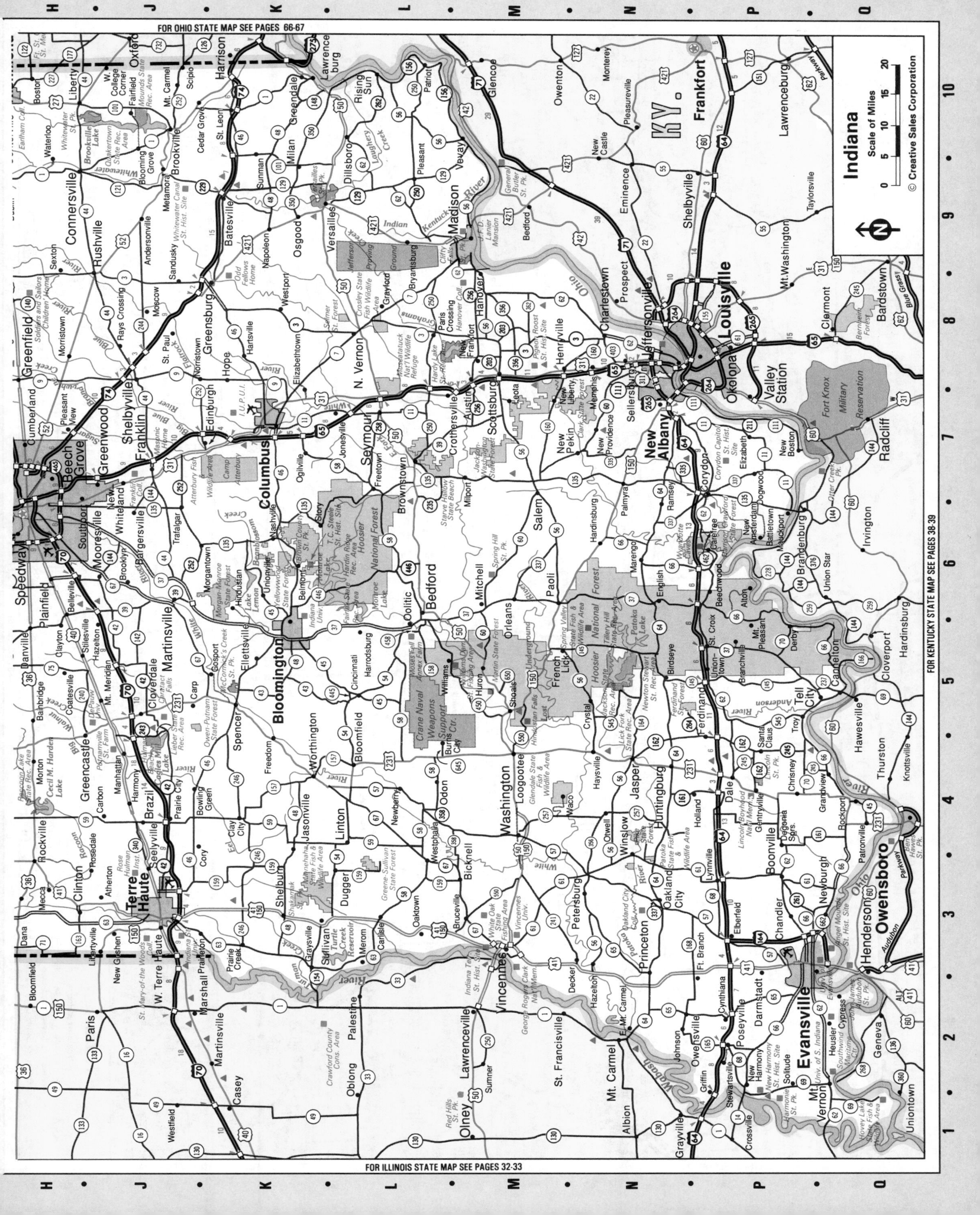

FOR OHIO STATE MAP SEE PAGES 66-67

FOR ILLINOIS STATE MAP SEE PAGES 32-33

FOR KENTUCKY STATE MAP SEE PAGES 38-39

Indiana

Scale of Miles

0 5 10 15 20

© Creative Sales Corporation

KY.

Major cities and towns:

Frankfort, Louisville, Jeffersonville, New Albany, Evansville, Owensboro, Henderson, Terre Haute, Bloomington, Columbus, Bedford, Washington, Vincennes, Seymour, Madison, Greenfield, Greensburg, Connersville, Rushville, Shelbyville, Franklin, Greenwood, Speedway, Beech Grove, Plainfield, Martinsville, Spencer, Linton, Jasper, Huntingburg, Tell City, Corydon, Salem, Paoli, French Lick, Mitchell, Orleans, Boonville, Mt. Vernon, Princeton

Hoosier National Forest
Hoosier National Forest
Fort Knox Military Reservation
Camp Atterbury
Crane Naval Weapons Support Ctr.
Monroe Lake
Patoka Lake
Brookville Lake
Whitewater State Park

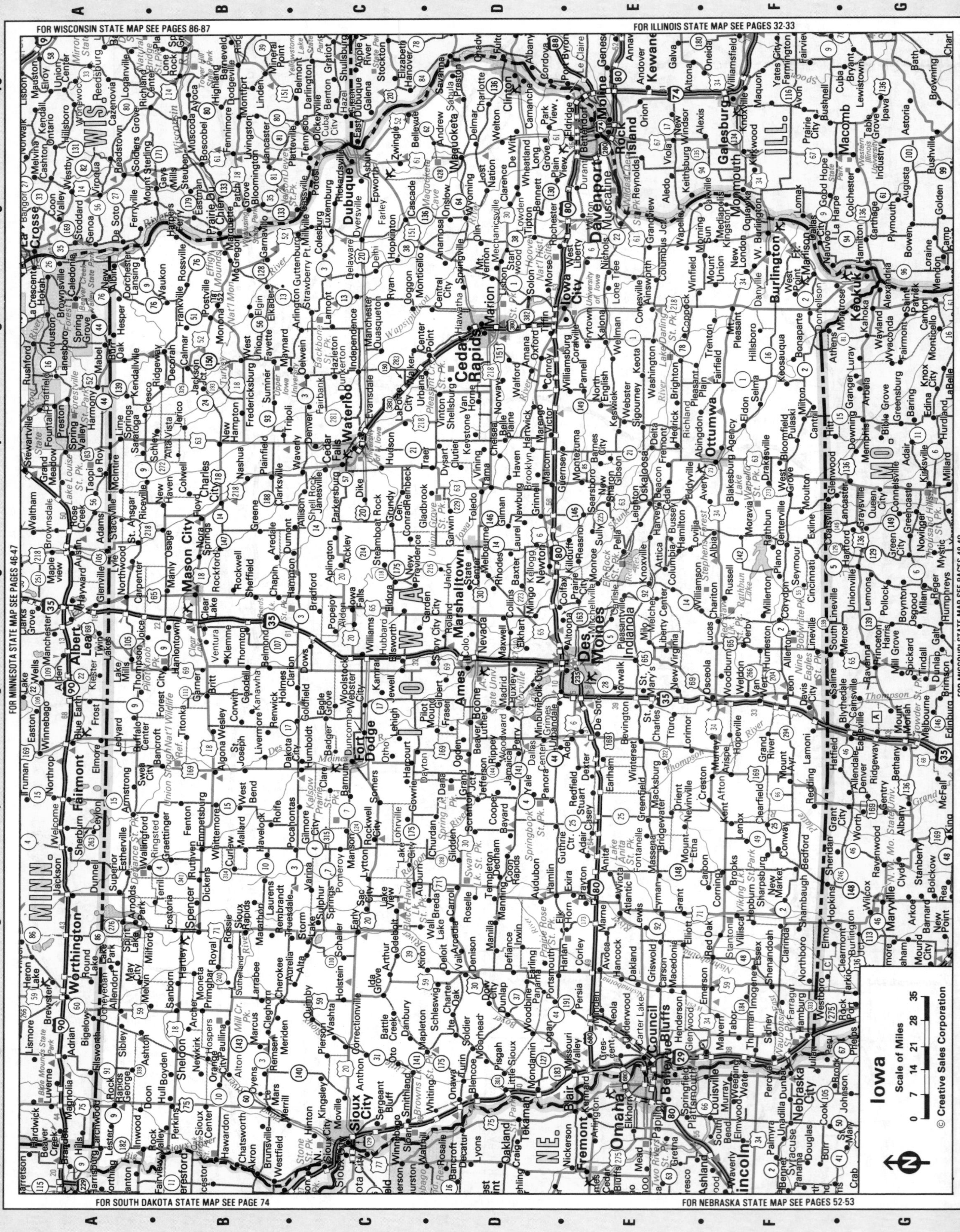

FOR WISCONSIN STATE MAP SEE PAGES 86-87
FOR ILLINOIS STATE MAP SEE PAGES 32-33
FOR MINNESOTA STATE MAP SEE PAGES 46-47
FOR MISSOURI STATE MAP SEE PAGES 48-49
FOR SOUTH DAKOTA STATE MAP SEE PAGE 74
FOR NEBRASKA STATE MAP SEE PAGES 52-53
Iowa
Scale of Miles
0 7 14 21 28 35
© Creative Sales Corporation
IOWA
MINN.
WIS.
ILL.
MO.
NE.
Des Moines
Cedar Rapids
Davenport
Sioux City
Council Bluffs
Waterloo
Dubuque
Iowa City
Omaha

FOR MISSOURI STATE MAP SEE PAGES 48-49

FOR IOWA STATE MAP SEE PAGE 36

FOR NEBRASKA STATE MAP SEE PAGES 52-53

FOR OKLAHOMA STATE MAP SEE PAGES 68-69

FOR COLORADO STATE MAP SEE PAGES 22-23

Kansas

Scale of Miles

0 10 20 30 40 50

© Creative Sales Corporation

IA MO NE CO OK

Council Bluffs · Lincoln · Grand Island · Kearney · St. Joseph · Kansas City · Leavenworth · Lawrence · Topeka · Manhattan · Junction City · Salina · Abilene · Hutchinson · Wichita · McPherson · Newton · El Dorado · Winfield · Arkansas City · Ponca City · Independence · Coffeyville · Bartlesville · Chanute · Emporia · Great Bend · Hays · Dodge City · Garden City · Goodland · Colby

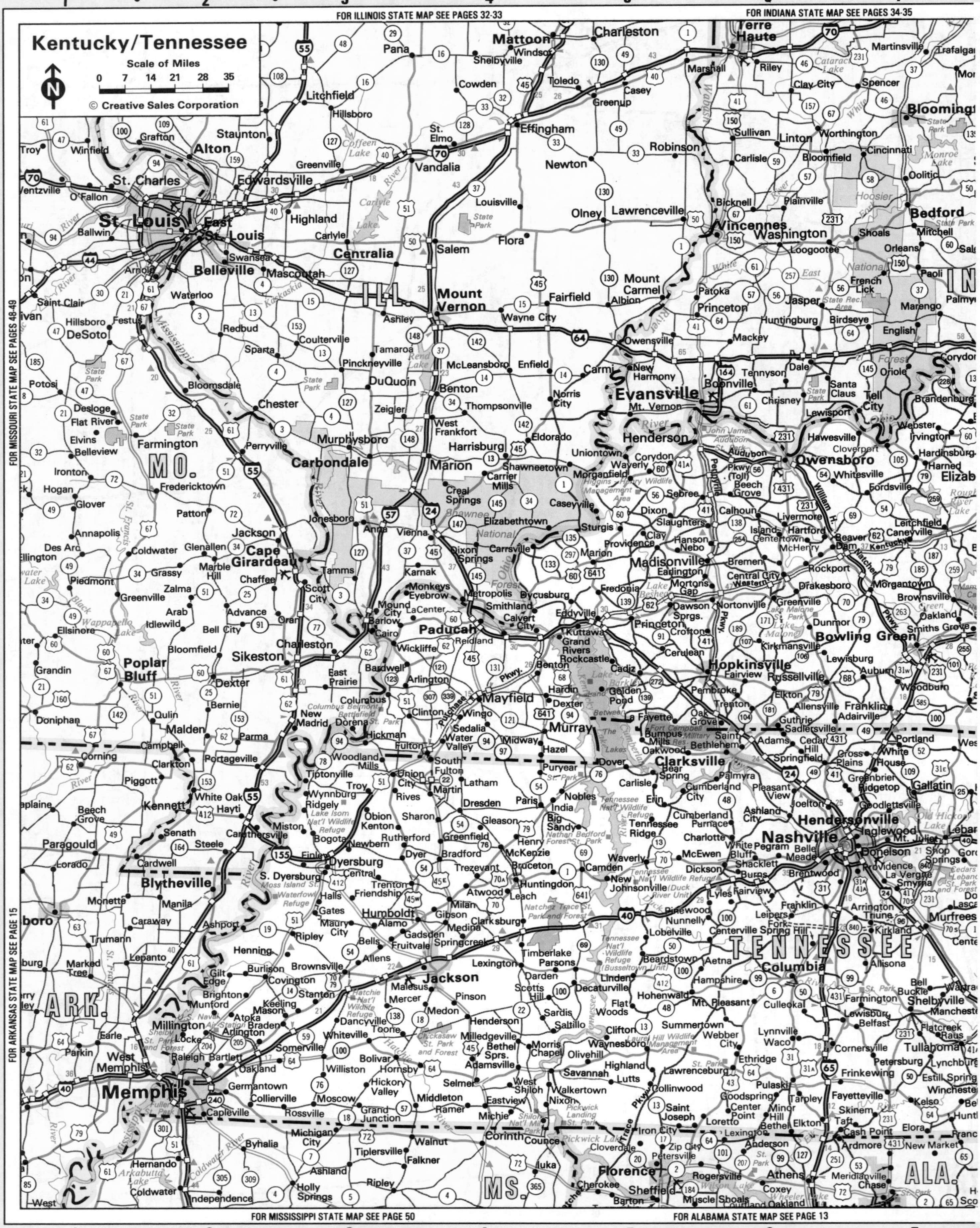

Kentucky/Tennessee

Scale of Miles

0 7 14 21 28 35

© Creative Sales Corporation

N

FOR ILLINOIS STATE MAP SEE PAGES 32-33

FOR INDIANA STATE MAP SEE PAGES 34-35

FOR MISSOURI STATE MAP SEE PAGES 48-49

FOR ARKANSAS STATE MAP SEE PAGE 15

FOR MISSISSIPPI STATE MAP SEE PAGE 50

FOR ALABAMA STATE MAP SEE PAGE 13

MO.

ARK.

MS.

ALA.

TENNESSEE

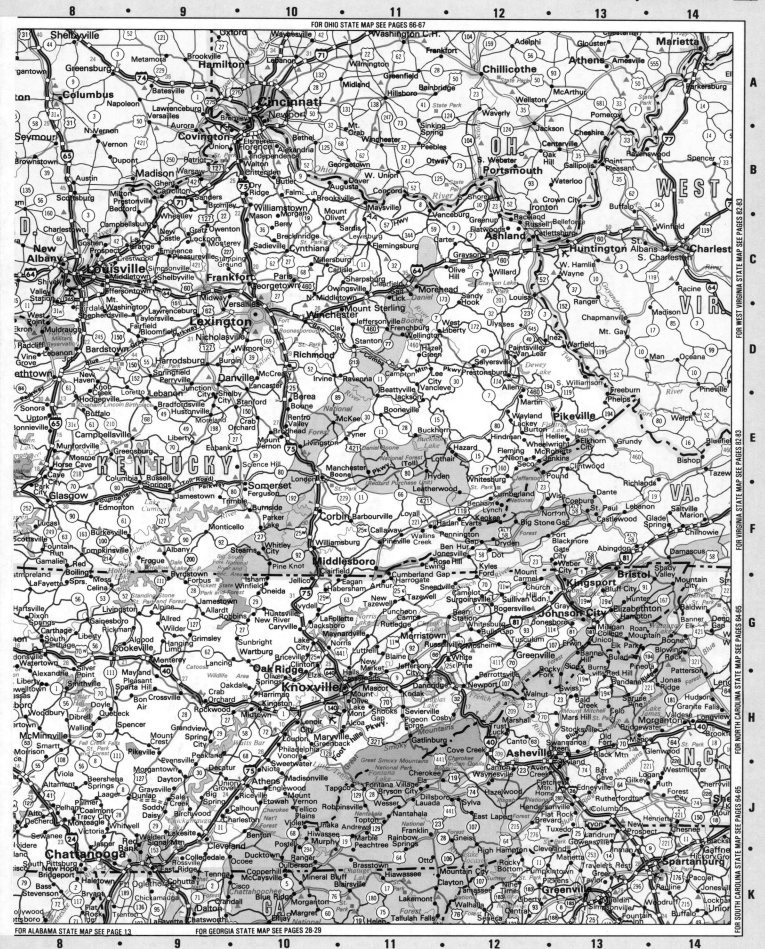

FOR OHIO STATE MAP SEE PAGES 66-67

FOR WEST VIRGINIA STATE MAP SEE PAGES 82-83

FOR VIRGINIA STATE MAP SEE PAGES 82-83

FOR NORTH CAROLINA STATE MAP SEE PAGES 64-65

FOR SOUTH CAROLINA STATE MAP SEE PAGES 64-65

FOR ALABAMA STATE MAP SEE PAGE 13

FOR GEORGIA STATE MAP SEE PAGES 28-29

FOR MISSISSIPPI STATE MAP SEE PAGE 50

Louisiana

Scale of Miles

0 7 14 21 28 35

© Creative Sales Corporation

FOR ARKANSAS STATE MAP SEE PAGE 15

Gulf of Mexico

LOUISIANA

TEXAS

MS

FOR TEXAS STATE MAP SEE PAGES 75-79

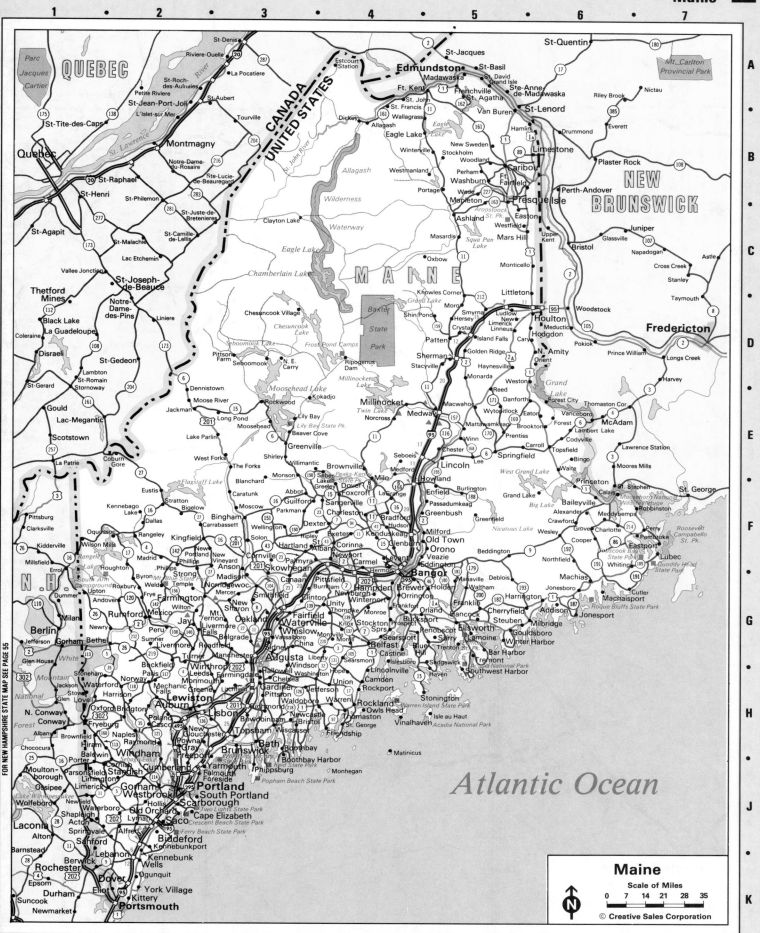

Maine

Scale of Miles

0   7   14   21   28   35

© Creative Sales Corporation

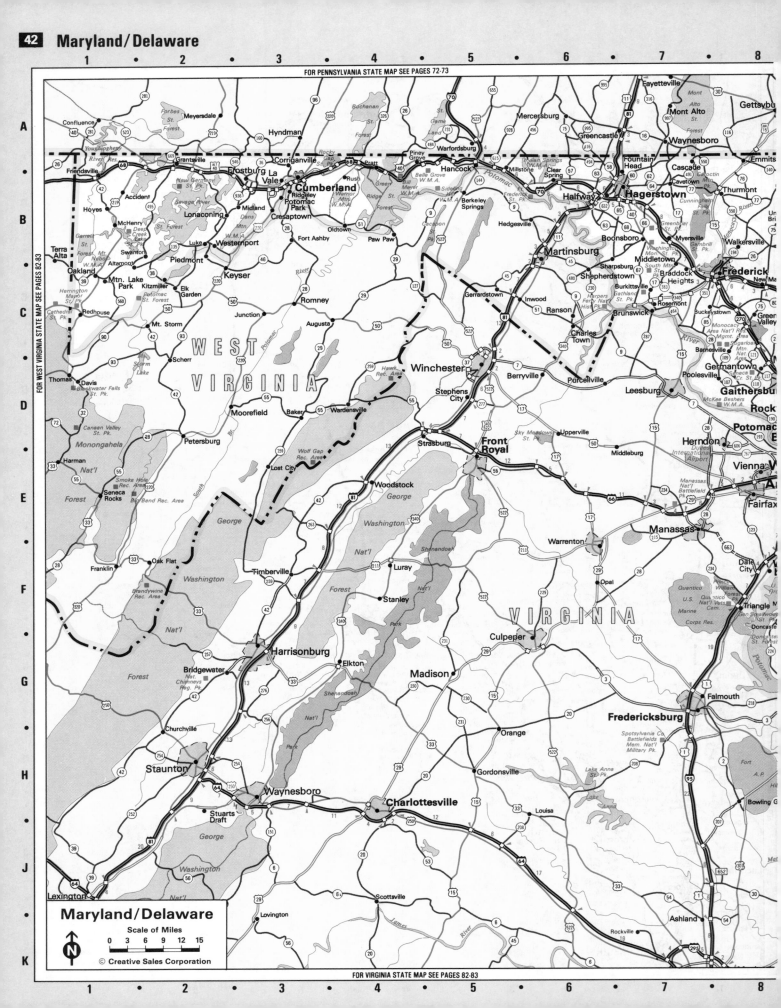

FOR PENNSYLVANIA STATE MAP SEE PAGES 72-73

FOR WEST VIRGINIA STATE MAP SEE PAGES 82-83

WEST VIRGINIA

VIRGINIA

Maryland/Delaware

Scale of Miles

0   3   6   9   12   15

N

© Creative Sales Corporation

FOR VIRGINIA STATE MAP SEE PAGES 82-83

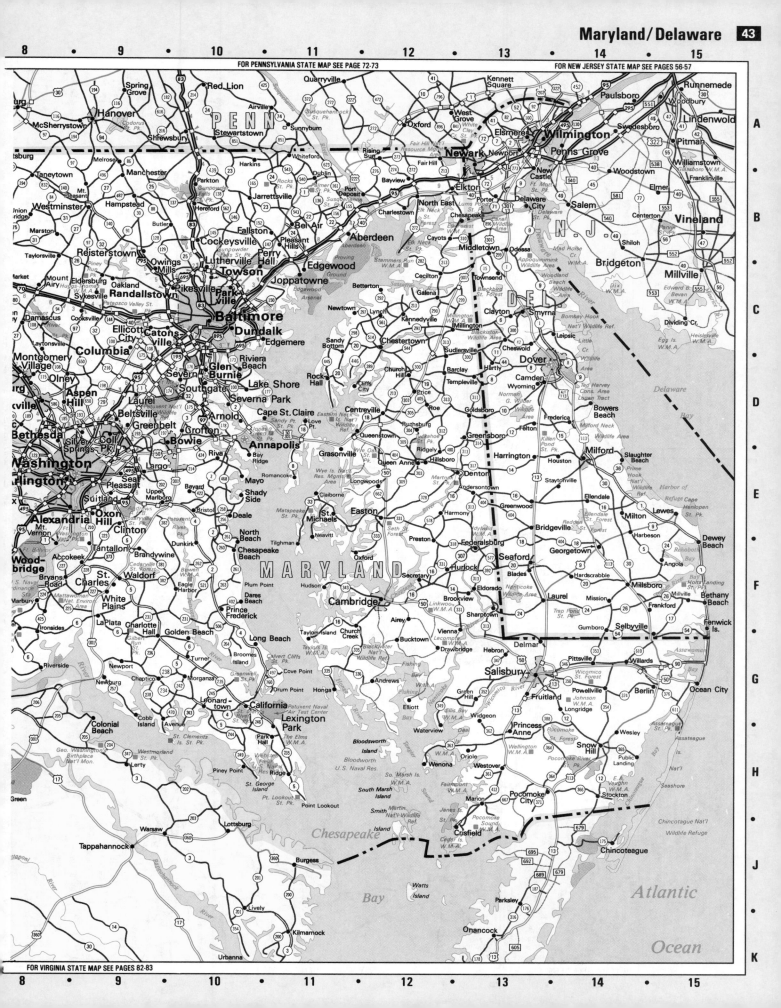

FOR PENNSYLVANIA STATE MAP SEE PAGE 72-73   FOR NEW JERSEY STATE MAP SEE PAGES 56-57

FOR VIRGINIA STATE MAP SEE PAGES 82-83

FOR CONTINUATION SEE GRID B-1

When travelling in wilderness areas or on unfamiliar roads, it is always best to be cautious and particularly attentive to local driving conditions. Be alert at all times and use the designated rest areas as often as necessary.

CANADA
UNITED STATES

ONT.

CANADA
UNITED STATES

MICH.

Lake Superior

Lake Huron

Lake Michigan

Sault Ste. Marie

Marquette

Negaunee **Ishpeming**

Houghton

Escanaba

Petoskey

Alpena

Traverse City

Cadillac

Green Bay

Appleton

Manitowoc

Two Rivers

Oshkosh

Ironwood

FOR CONTINUATION SEE GRID A-10

FOR WISCONSIN STATE MAP SEE PAGES 86-87

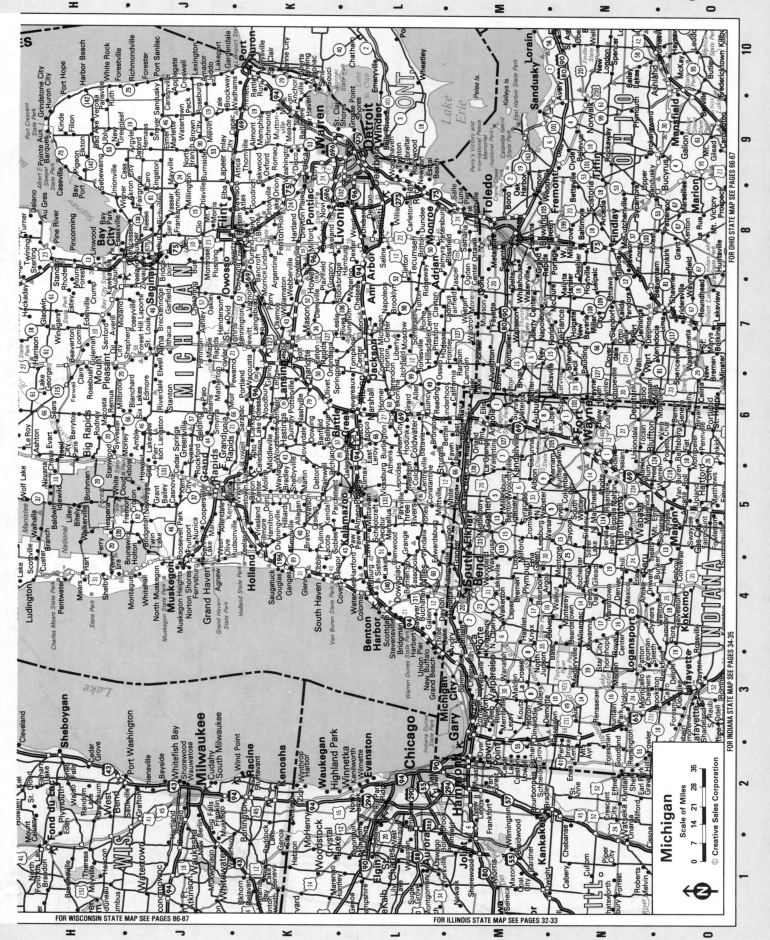

Michigan

Scale of Miles

0 7 14 21 28 35

© Creative Sales Corporation

FOR CONTINUATION SEE GRID A-9
FOR WISCONSIN STATE MAP SEE PAGES 86-87

Grand Portage Indian Res.
Grand Portage State Forest
Hovland
Grand Portage
Judge C. R. Magney State Park
Croftville
Grand Marias
Cascade River St. Pk.
Lutsen

FOR CONTINUATION SEE GRID C-10

Shebandowan
Croftville
Grand Marias
Cascade River St. Park
Lutsen
Schroeder
Taconite Harbor
Little Marais
Silver Bay
Beaver Bay
Two Harbors
Knife River
Larsmont

ONTARIO

Boundary Waters Canoe Area
Superior National Forest
Gunflint Trail

Apostle Islands Nat'l Lakeshore
Madeline Island
Madeline Island State Park
Big Bay

Ashland
Washburn
Bayfield
Red Cliff Indian Res.
Hurley
Montreal
Mellen
Park Falls
Fifield
Phillips
Winter
Radisson

Isabella
Finland
Winton
Ely
Babbitt
Tower
Aurora
Biwabik
Hoyt Lakes
Markham
Virginia
Eveleth
Gilbert
Superior
Duluth
Proctor
Cloquet
Carlton
Iron River
Poplar
Lake Nebagamon
Solon Springs
Minong
Hayward
Cable

Farrington
Flanders
Mine Centre
Buyck
Ash Lake
Orr
Cook
Angora
Britt
Chisholm
Hibbing
Nashwauk
Keewatin
Calumet
Coleraine
Bovey
Grand Rapids
Swan River
Goodland
Warba
Meadow Lands
Floodwood
Brookston
Cotton
Independence
Canyon
Twig
Hermantown
Carlton
Cloquet
Scanlon
Wrenshall
Barnum
Moose Lake
Kettle River
Willow River
Sturgeon Lake
Askov
Bruno
Sandstone
Webster
Siren

Voyageurs National Park
South International Falls
International Falls
Ericsburg
Ray
Littlefork
Loman
Lindford
Grand Falls
Big Falls
Margie
Mizpah
Northome
Funkley
Kelliher

Rainy River
Baudette
Williams
Roosevelt
Waskish
Red Lake Wildlife Area
Upper Red Lake
Lower Red Lake
Red Lake
Redby
Red Lake Indian Reservation

Warroad
Salol
Badger
Greenbush
Middle River
Goodridge
Gatzke
Grygla
Fourtown
Holt
Viking
Newfolden
Thief River Falls
St. Hilaire
Plummer
Oklee
Brooks
Mentor
Erskine
Gully
Trail
Clearbrook
Gonvick
Bagley
Lengby
Fosston
Shevlin
Solway
Bemidji
Wilton
Cass Lake
Bena
Deer River
Ball Club
Boy River
Remer
Longville
Outing
Federal Dam
Walker
Hackensack
Akeley
Nevis
Backus
Pine River
Hill City
Jacobson
Swatara
Palisade
Aitkin
McGregor
Cromwell
Tamarack
McGrath
Finlayson
Hinckley
Mora
Milaca
Foley

Bemidji
Blackduck
Tenstrike
Hines
Turtle River
Pinewood
Leonard
Shevlin
Clearbrook
Gonvick
Bagley
Lengby

Roseau
Strathcona
Strandquist
Middle River
Newfolden
Thief River Falls

Angle Inlet
Lake of the Woods
Red Lake Wildlife Area
Norris Camp
Hayes Lake State Park
Lost River State Forest
Pencer
Wannaska

CANADA
UNITED STATES

Oak Island
Sioux Narrows
Nestor Falls
Bergland
Finland
Pinewood
Pine Island State Forest
Clementson
Birchdale
Baudette

Rosa
Greenbush
Badger
Roseau
Warroad
Salol

Mensino
Piney
Vassar
Boseau
Mensino
Lancaster
Bronson
Karlstad
Lake Bronson State Park
Twin Lakes
Talma
Strandquist
Holt
Viking

Jean Baptiste
St. Vincent
Humboldt
Hallock
Kennedy
Donaldson
Argyle
Stephen
Alvarado
Oslo
Warren
Newfolden
Thief River Falls
St. Hilaire
Red Lake Falls
Crookston
Fisher
Climax
Beltrami
Nielsville
Shelly
Halstad
Ada
Borup
Felton
Georgetown
Hendrum
Perley
Hitterdal

Letellier
Drayton
Oslo
East Grand Forks
Grand Forks
Fisher
Crookston
Mentor
Erskine
Fertile
Winger
Lockhart
McIntosh
Fosston

Twin Valley
Gary
Ulen
Waubun
White Earth
Ogema
Callaway
Mahnomen
Naytahwaush
White Earth Indian Reservation
Tamarac Nat'l Wildlife Ref.
Detroit Lakes
Audubon
Lake Park
Frazee
Vergas
Dent
Perham
New York Mills
Bluffton
Wadena
Sebeka
Menahga
Nimrod
Wolf Lake
Park Rapids
Osage
Two Inlets
Ponsford

Moorhead
Dilworth
Glyndon
Hawley
Felton
Comstock
Sabin
Baker
Barnesville
Wolverton
Kent
Rothsay
Breckenridge
Foxhome
Campbell
Doran
Wheaton
Herman
Norcross
Dumont
Donnelly

Fargo
West Fargo
Kindred
Wahpeton
Abercrombie
Dwight
Great Bend
Colfax
Fairmount
Hankinson
Lidgerwood

MINNESOTA

Brainerd
Baxter
Nisswa
Pequot Lakes
Pine River
Crosby
Ironton
Deerwood
Garrison
Isle
Wahkon
Onamia
Milaca
Princeton
Foley
Rice
Little Falls
Royalton
Swanville
Grey Eagle
Long Prairie
Browerville
Eagle Bend
Clarissa
Bertha
Hewitt
Verndale
Staples
Motley
Randall
Cushing
Pillager

Alexandria
Carlos
Miltona
Parkers Prairie
Henning
Vining
Battle Lake
Clitherall
Underwood
Elizabeth
Erhard
Pelican Rapids
Maplewood St. Pk.
Ottertail
Richville
Dalton
Ashby
Dalton
Fergus Falls
Elbow Lake
Kensington
Barrett
Hoffman
Garfield
Brandon
Evansville
Osakis
Sauk Centre
Melrose
Freeport

Mille Lacs
Mille Lacs Lake
Garrison
Isle
Onamia

Beaver Bay
Tettegouche State Park
Split Rock Lighthouse
Gooseberry Falls State Park

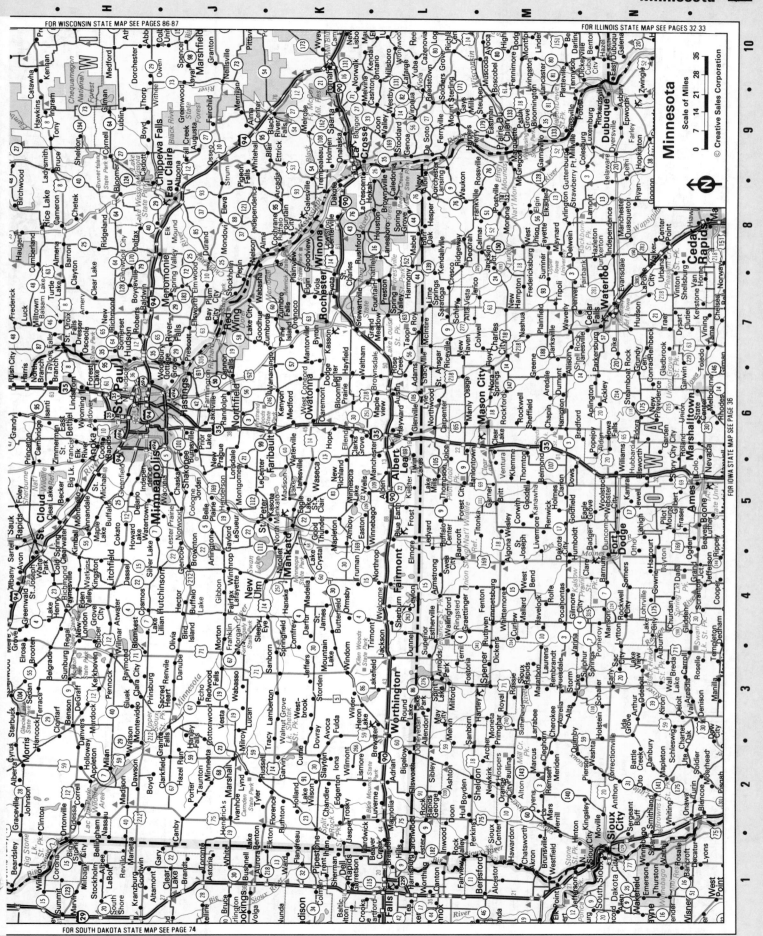

FOR WISCONSIN STATE MAP SEE PAGES 86-87
FOR ILLINOIS STATE MAP SEE PAGES 32 33
FOR SOUTH DAKOTA STATE MAP SEE PAGE 74
FOR IOWA STATE MAP SEE PAGE 36

FOR ILLINOIS STATE MAP SEE PAGES 32-33

FOR CONTINUATION SEE GRID D-1

FOR NEBRASKA STATE MAP SEE PAGES 52-53

FOR CONTINUATION SEE GRID B-3

FOR KANSAS STATE MAP SEE PAGE 37

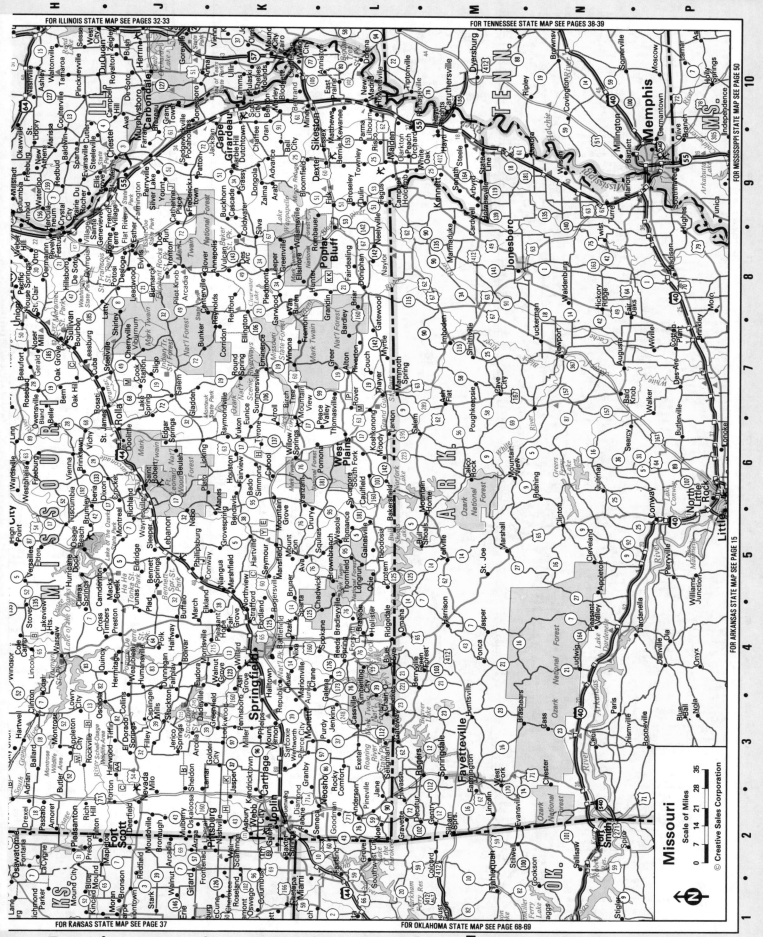

FOR ILLINOIS STATE MAP SEE PAGES 32-33

FOR TENNESSEE STATE MAP SEE PAGES 38-39

FOR MISSISSIPPI STATE MAP SEE PAGE 50

FOR ARKANSAS STATE MAP SEE PAGE 15

FOR KANSAS STATE MAP SEE PAGE 37

FOR OKLAHOMA STATE MAP SEE PAGES 68-69

Missouri

Scale of Miles

0 7 14 21 28 35

© Creative Sales Corporation

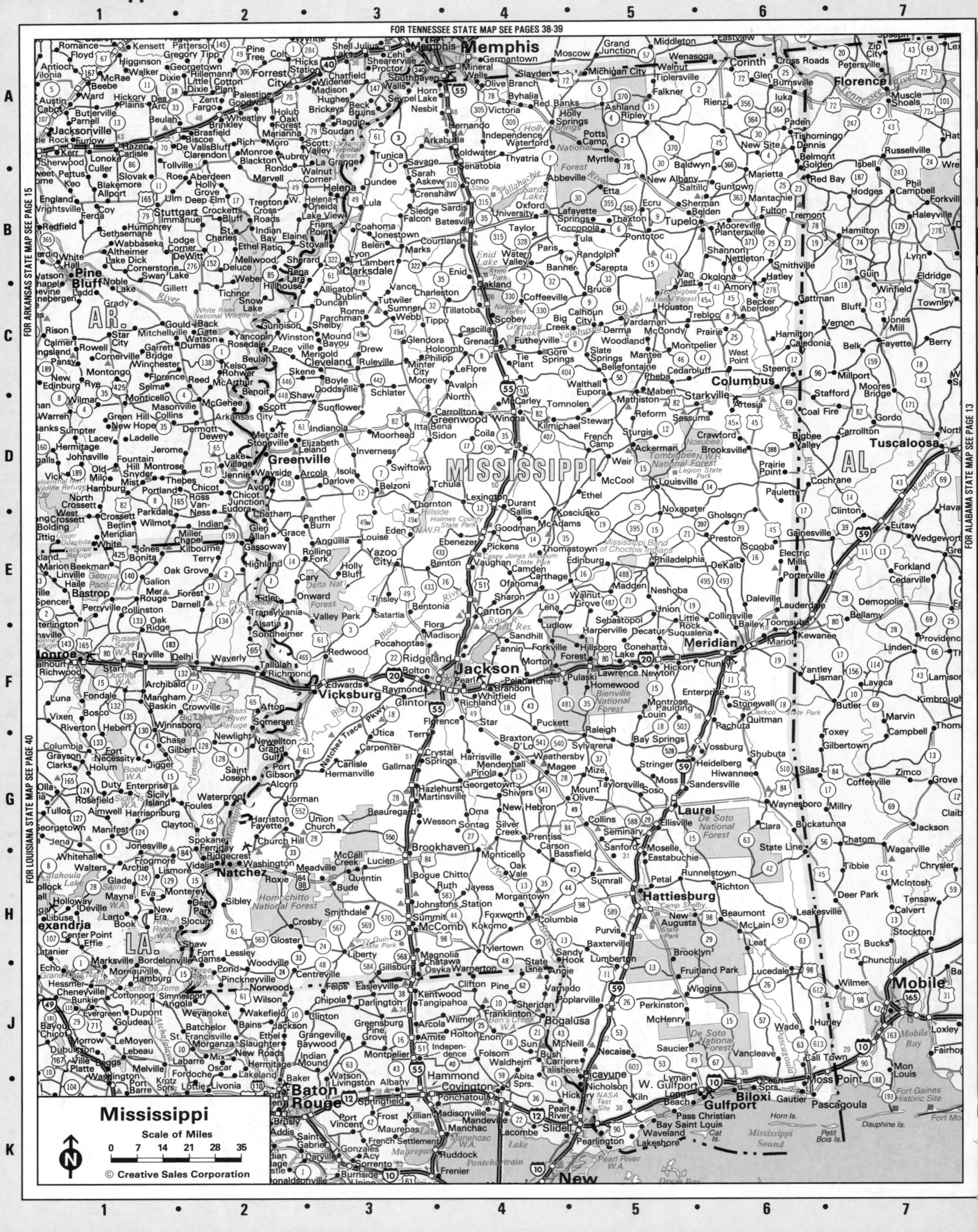

FOR TENNESSEE STATE MAP SEE PAGES 38-39

FOR ARKANSAS STATE MAP SEE PAGE 15

FOR LOUISIANA STATE MAP SEE PAGE 40

FOR ALABAMA STATE MAP SEE PAGE 13

MISSISSIPPI

AR.

LA.

AL.

Memphis

Tuscaloosa

Mobile

Columbus

Meridian

Jackson

Vicksburg

Natchez

Hattiesburg

Laurel

Gulfport

Biloxi

Baton Rouge

New Orleans

Mississippi
Scale of Miles

0 7 14 21 28 35

N

© Creative Sales Corporation

FOR NORTH DAKOTA STATE MAP SEE PAGE 63

FOR SOUTH DAKOTA STATE MAP SEE PAGE 74

FOR WYOMING STATE MAP SEE PAGES 88-89

FOR IDAHO STATE MAP SEE PAGE 31

FOR IDAHO STATE MAP SEE PAGE 31

Montana

Scale of Miles

0 15 30 45 60

© Creative Sales Corporation

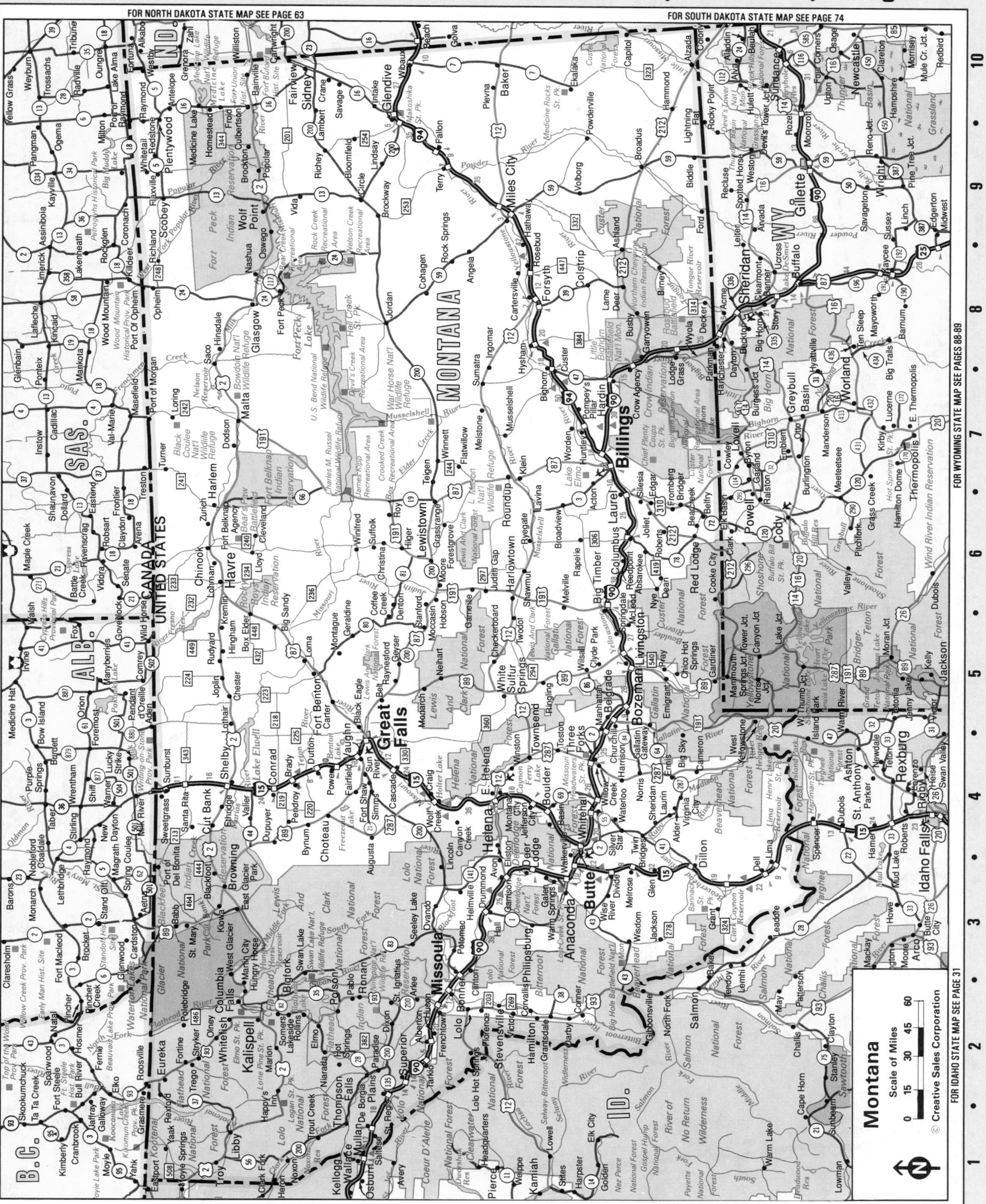

FOR SOUTH DAKOTA STATE MAP SEE PAGE 74

WY

Mule Cr. Jct.
Redbird
Gap
Hot Springs
Edgemont
Cheyenne
Pine Ridge
Kyle
Long Valley
White River
Wood
44
44
73
63
1-83

Lance Creek
Provo
Buffalo Gap National Grassland
Angostura Res.
Oelrichs
Oglala
Indian Reservation
Allen
Parmelee
Okreek Mission
18
85
63

Manville
Lusk
Node
Van Tassell
Oglala National Grasslands
Pine Ridge
Wounded Knee
Wounded Knee Battle Site
Martin
Batesland
Rosebud
Saint Francis
Rosebud Indian Reservation
53
71
71
18
391
73
83

B

Jay Em
Harrison
Whitney
Chadron
Clinton
Gordon
Merriman
Eli
Cody
Nenzel Kilgore
Crookston
Valentine
Sparks
Norder
12

C
Fort Robinson State Park
Crawford
Chandron St. Park
Rushville
Hay Springs
River
Cottonwood Lake St. Pk.
Samuel R. McKelvie Nat'l Forest
Ft. Niobrara Nat'l Wildlife Refuge
Niobr

Nebraska Nat'l Forest
Box Butte Res.
St. Pk.
Walgren Lake St. Pk.
Snake
River
Merritt Res.
Wood Lake
Johnst
85
20
385
87
87
250
61

Fort Laramie
Lingle
Agate Fossil Beds Nat'l Mon.
Marsland
Niobrara
Hemingford
North
Valentine Nat'l Wildlife Ref.
Ainsworth
159
29
71
27
61
97

D
Torrington
North Platte Nat'l Wildlife Ref.
Alliance
Antioch
Lakeside
Brownlee
7
2
2

Huntley
Yoder
Morrill
Mitchell
Scottsbluff
Ellsworth
Bingham
Ashby
Hyannis
Whitman
Mullen
Seneca
Purdum
Elsmere
83
2

E
Hawk Sprs.
Lyman
Terrytown
Minatare
Angora
Gering
Melbeta
McGrew
Bayard
Broadwater
Crescent Lake National Wildlife Refuge
Arthur
Dismal
River
Thedford
Nebraska National Forest
Halsey
Dunning
N E B R
26
385
61
97
91

La Grange
Albin
Harrisburg
Bridgeport
Lisco
North Platte River
Tryon
Loup
151
88
88
92
61
97
2

F
Egbert
Bushnell
Kimball
Dix
Potter
Dalton
Gurley
Oshkosh
Lewellen
Ash Hollow St. Hist. Pk.
Lake McConaughy State Park
Buffalo Bill St. Hist. Pk.
Stapleton
Gandy
Arnold
Arnold Lake St. Pk.
Bro
Bo
Oliver Res. St. Pk.
Sidney
Lodgepole
Chappell
LeMoyne
Keystone
Lake C.W. McConaughy
Brule
Ogallala
Paxton
Sutherland
Callaway
30
80
385
26
92
27
97
40
92

Big Springs
Sedgwick
Ovid
Brule
Hershey
North Platte
Maxwell
Brady
Gothenburg
71
19
43
30
24
80
30
47
40

G
Briggsdale
Buckingham
Raymer
Crook
Julesburg
Grant
Madrid
Elsie
Wallace
Dickens
Wellfleet
Moorefield
Willow Island
Cozad
113
138
76
61
23
25
23
83
60
21

Stoneham
Sterling
Willard
Atwood
Fleming
Haxtun
Paoli
Venango
Brandon
Grainton
Maywood
Curtis
Farnam
Eustis
Elwood
Smi
52
71
59
176
25
23
18
21

H
Jackson Lake Res.
Weldona
Snyder
Log Lane Village
Orchard
Wiggins
Fort Morgan
Brush
Akron
Otis
Yuma
Clarkville
Holyoke
Amherst
Imperial
Champion
Enders
Wauneta
Hamlet
Palisade
Hayes Center
Red Willow St. Pk.
Hugh Butler Lake
Cambridge
Bartley
Indianola
Arapahoe
Edison
Beaver City
Stamfor
23
6
63
59
34
6
61
8
61
18
283
34
6
47

COL.
Woodrow
Eckley
Wray
Max
Stratton
Trenton
Culbertson
McCook
Wilsonville
71
34
61
17
34
47

Laird
Haigler
Parks
Benkelman
Danbury
Lebanon
Swanson Reservoir
Medicine Creek Res. St. Pk.
25
89

J
Last Chance
Lindon
Anton
Cope
Joes
Idalia
St. Francis
Bird City
McDonald
Atwood
Oberlin
Norcatur
Almena
36
27
161
36
117
State Park
3

Wheeler
Herndon
Jennings
Clayton
Keith Sebelius Lake
Edmond
Logan
Norton
Phi
83
36
9

River Bend
Limon
Arriba
Seibert
Vona
Stratton
Burlington
Goodland
Brewster
Colby
Gem
Rexford
Selden
Dresden
Lenora
383
24
35
70
23
283

Hugo
Genoa
Hoxie
Menlo
Halford
Morland
71
24

FOR WYOMING STATE MAP SEE PAGES 88-89

FOR COLORADO STATE MAP SEE PAGES 22-23

FOR SOUTH DAKOTA STATE MAP SEE PAGE 74
FOR MINNESOTA STATE MAP SEE PAGES 46-47

Nebraska

Scale of Miles

0 7 14 21 28 35

N

© Creative Sales Corporation

FOR IOWA STATE MAP SEE PAGE 36
FOR KANSAS STATE MAP SEE PAGE 37

S.D.

Kimball, White Lake, Plankinton, Fulton, Mount Vernon, Mitchell, Stickney, Alexandria, Ethan, Farmer, Salem, Montrose, Canistota, Sioux Falls, Baltic, Dell Rapids, Colton, Crooks, Garretson, Hartford, Harrisburg, Larchwood, Ellsworth, Bigelow, Round Lake

Winner, Dallas, Gregory, Burke, Platte, Corsica, Dimock, Bridgewater, Parkston, Menno, Freeman, Olivet, Parker, Lennox, Canton, Inwood, Worthing, Lester, Rock Rapids, George, Sibley, Ocheyedan, Allendorf, Lake Park, May City, Spirit Lake

Herrick, St. Charles, Fairfax, Ravinia, Wagner, Tripp, Scotland, Viborg, Centerville, Irene, Beresford, Fairview, Rock Valley, Doon, Hull, Boyden, Sheldon, Newkirk, Archer, Moneta, Primghar, Royal, Hartley, Sanborn

Wewela, Mills, Burton, Springview, Naper, Anoka, Butte, Spencer, Bristow, Monowi, Verdel, Lynch, Niobrara, Santee, St. Helena, Crofton, Wynot, Vermillion, Alcester, Hawarden, Chatsworth, Akron, Brunsville, Westfield, Le Mars, Merrill, Remsen, Oyens, Marcus, Cleghorn, Aurelia, Alta, Cherokee, Meriden, Quimby, Washta

Bassett, Newport, Stuart, Atkinson, Emmet, O'Neill, Inman, Amelia, Chambers, Page, Verdigre, Winnetoon, Bazile Mills, Wausa, Creighton, Orchard, Royal, Brunswick, Osmond, Belden, Magnet, Coleridge, Laurel, Concord, Allen, Wakefield, Dakota City, South Sioux City, Sioux City, Moville, Kingsley, Pierson, Holstein, Correctionville, IOWA, Arthur, Battle Creek, Danbury, Schaller

Rose, Amelia, Ewing, Clearwater, Neligh, Foster, Plainview, Pierce, Randolph, Sholes, Carroll, Wayne, Winside, Emerson, Thurston, Winnebago, Sloan, Smithland, Whiting, Onawa, Turin, Soldier, Mapleton, Schleswig, Ute, Charter Oak, Deloit, Kiron, Vail, Denison

Almeria, Taylor, Burwell, Ericson, Bartlett, Elgin, Tilden, Norfolk, Hoskins, Pilger, Wisner, Bancroft, Rosalie, Decatur, Lyons, Beemer, West Point, Oakland, Craig, Tekamah, Herman, Winslow, Nickerson, Blair, Missouri Valley, Logan, Pisgah, Little Sioux, Woodbine, Panama, Portsmouth, Harlan, Persia, Corley, Dunlap, Defiance

Sargent, Elyria, Ord, Comstock, Spalding, Albion, Newman Grove, Humphrey, Clarkson, Leigh, Howells, Dodge, Scribner, Snyder, Uehling, Hooper, North Bend, Fremont, Kennard, Arlington, Ames, Cedar Bluffs, Prague, Malmo, Mead, Elkhorn, Omaha, Council Bluffs, Carter Lake, Crescent, Underwood, Neola, Minden, Avoca, Hancock, Oakland

Westerville, Berwyn, Ansley, Loup City, Ashton, Elba, Palmer, Archer, Clarks, Silver Creek, Fullerton, Genoa, Columbus, Rogers, Schuyler, Richland, Linwood, Octavia, Bruno, Wahoo, Ithaca, Ceresco, Gretna, Papillion, Bellevue, Springfield, Plattsmouth, Glenwood, Griswold, Carson, Macedonia, Henderson

Mason City, Litchfield, Hazard, Rockville, Dannebrog, St. Paul, Boelus, Cairo, Chapman, Central City, Marquette, Benedict, Polk, Stromsburg, Osceola, Shelby, David City, Rising City, Garrison, Ulysses, Dwight, Valparaiso, Ashland, South Bend, Louisville, Murray, Weeping Water, Elmwood, Thurman, Imogene, Essex

Pleasanton, Sumner, Miller, Ravenna, Poole, Grand Island, Wood River, Alda, Phillips, Aurora, Bradshaw, Hampton, York, Waco, Goehner, Seward, Raymond, Greenwood, Waverly, Lincoln, Milford, Denton, Martell, Roca, Bennet, Palmyra, Unadilla, Dunbar, Syracuse, Percival, Sidney, Nebraska City, Hamburg, Northboro, Farragut

Kearney, Shelton, Gibbon, Prosser, Kenesaw, Doniphan, Giltner, Trumbull, Juniata, Harvard, Fairmont, Grafton, Friend, Exeter, Crete, Dorchester, Crab Orchard, Cook, Brock, Julian, Peru, Westboro, Clarinda

Lexington, Overton, Elm Creek, Riverdale, Ocessa, Smithfield, Bertrand, Loomis, Holdrege, Axtell, Minden, Roseland, Glenvil, Clay Center, Sutton, Geneva, Milligan, Ohiowa, Strang, Shickley, Fairfield, Edgar, Davenport, Tobias, Western, DeWitt, Glatonia, Adams, Pickrell, Cortland, Firth, Burr, Douglas, Talmage, Phelps, Johnson, Auburn, Rock Port, Tarkio

Oxford, Funk, Wilcox, Hildreth, Upland, Campbell, Blue Hill, Lawrence, Bladen, Oak, Nelson, Belvidere, Carleton, Daykin, Bruning, Alexandria, Plymouth, Filley, Beatrice, Elk Creek, Lewiston, Tecumseh, Fairfax

Republican City, Alma, Franklin, Naponee, Riverton, Red Cloud, Inavale, Cowles, Guide Rock, Ruskin, Deshler, Hebron, Fairbury, Diller, Wymore, Blue Springs, Burchard, Pawnee City, Table Rock, Dawson, Humboldt, Verdon, Dubois, Falls City, Fortescue, Mound City, Craig

Long Island, Prairie View, Phillipsburg, Kensington, Athol, Lebanon, Esbon, Burr Oak, Webber, Republic, Narka, Superior, Chester, Hollenberg, Hanover, Hardy, Steele City, Odell, Barneston, Oketo, Summerfield, Bern, Sabetha, Morrill, Hamlin, Hiawatha, Highland, Robinson

KANSAS, Kirwin, Agra, Smith Center, Formoso, Jewell, Mankato, Randall, Courtland, Scandia, Cuba, Washington, Belleville, Agenda, Greenleaf, Barnes, Frankfort, Marysville, Beattie, St. Benedict, Seneca, Vermillion, Powhattan, Fairview, Leona, Denton

Gaylord, Cedar, Portis, Downs, Glen Elder, Cawker City, Beloit, Jamestown, Concordia, Clyde, Vining, Palmer, Clifton, Waterville, Blue Rapids, Wheaton, Onaga, Havensville, Wetmore, Netawaka, Circleville, Muscotah, Whiting, Huron, Atchison

Woodston, Stockton, Osborne, Alton, Morganville

FOR KANSAS STATE MAP SEE PAGE 37

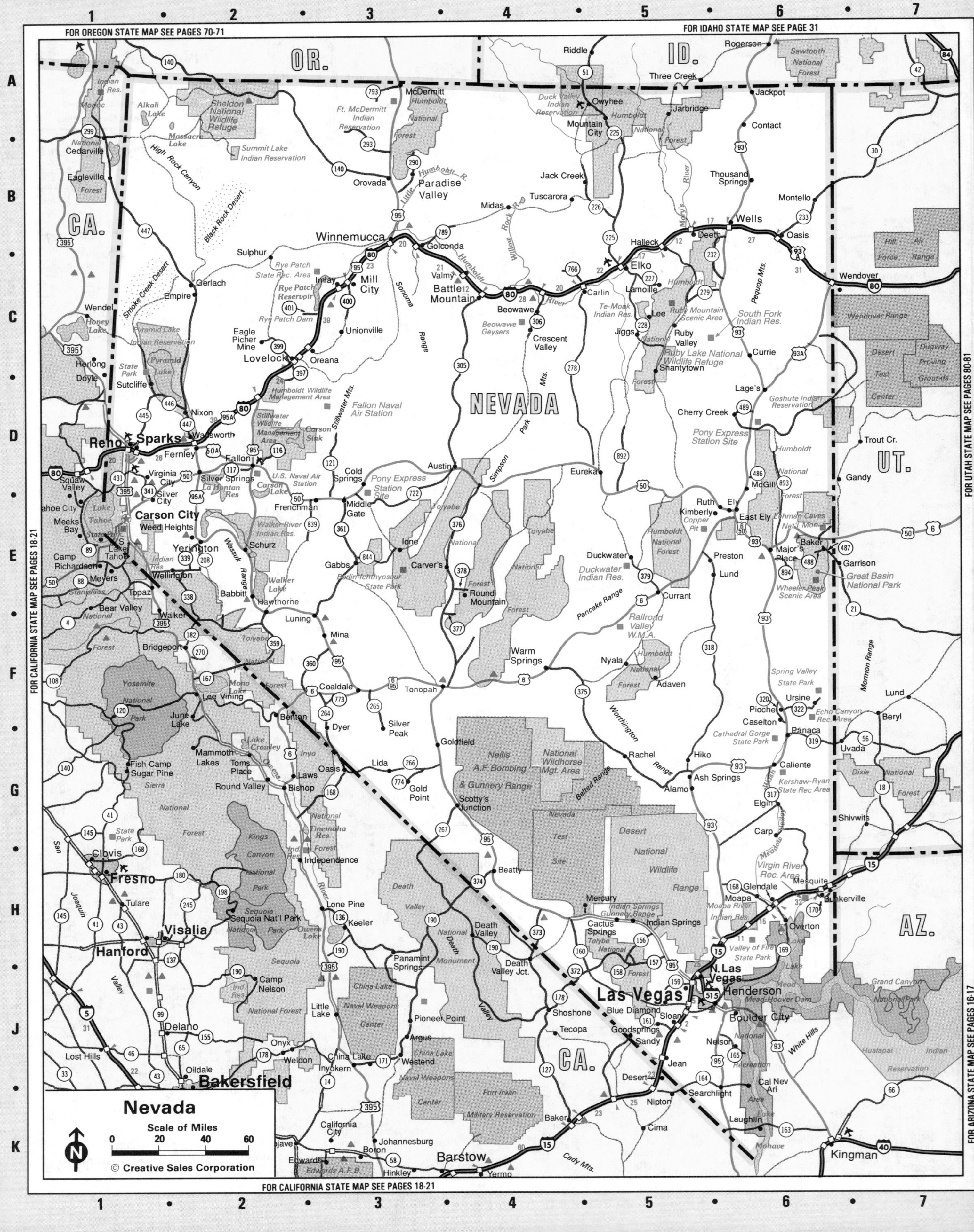

FOR OREGON STATE MAP SEE PAGES 70-71

FOR IDAHO STATE MAP SEE PAGE 31

OR.

ID.

CA.

NEVADA

UT.

AZ.

CA.

FOR CALIFORNIA STATE MAP SEE PAGES 18-21

FOR UTAH STATE MAP SEE PAGES 80-81

FOR ARIZONA STATE MAP SEE PAGES 16-17

Nevada

Scale of Miles

0   20   40   60

© Creative Sales Corporation

N

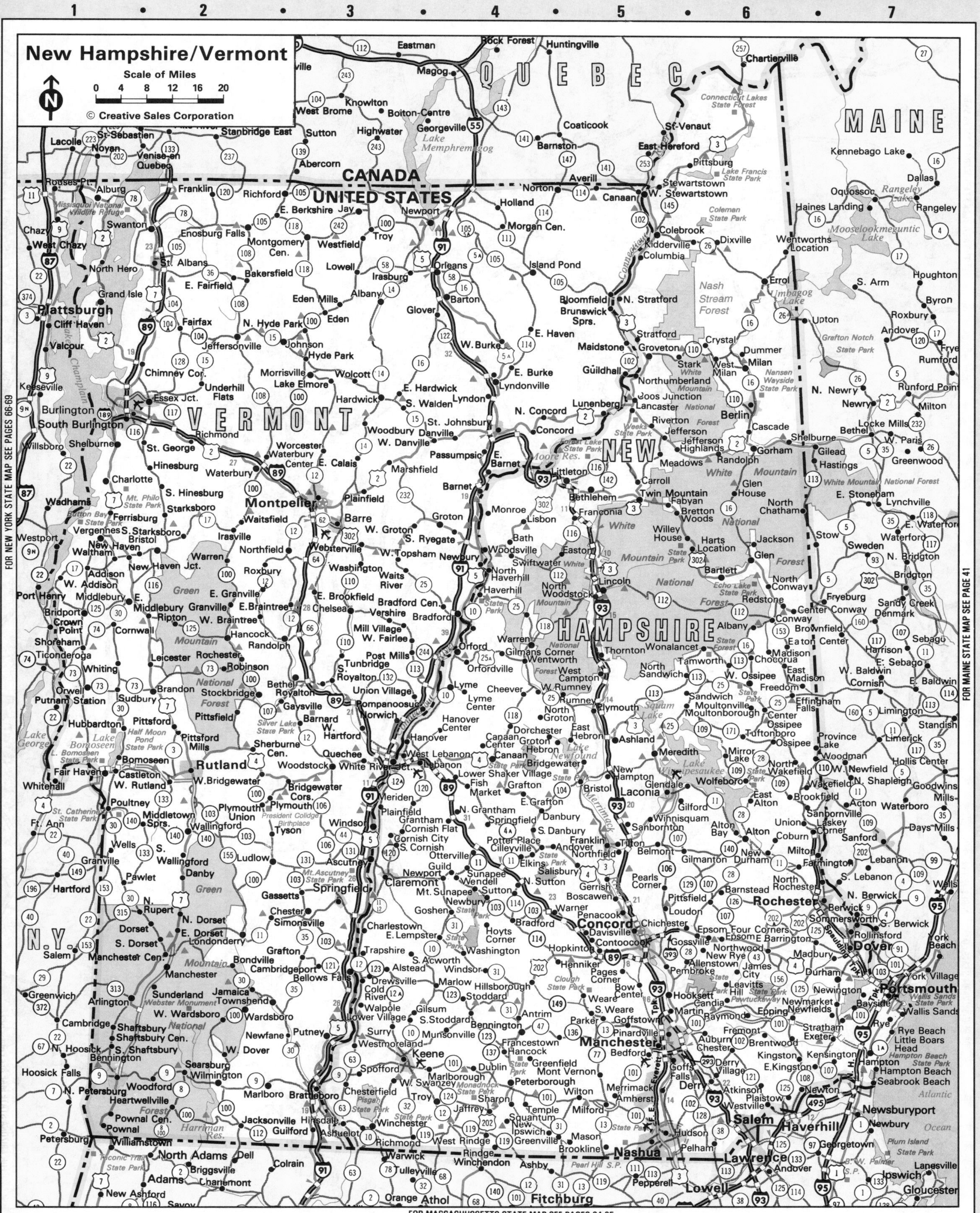

New Hampshire/Vermont

Scale of Miles
0 4 8 12 16 20

© Creative Sales Corporation

N

States / Regions: QUEBEC · MAINE · CANADA · UNITED STATES · VERMONT · NEW HAMPSHIRE · N.Y.

Connecticut Lakes State Forest · Nash Stream Forest · White Mountain National Forest · Green Mountain National Forest · Coleman State Park · Lake Francis State Park · Lake Memphremagog · Umbagog Lake · Mooselookmeguntic Lake · Rangeley Lake · Lake Champlain · Lake Winnipesaukee · Squam Lake · Newfound Lake · Atlantic Ocean

Selected places:
Eastman, Rock Forest, Huntingville, Magog, Georgeville, Coaticook, Chartierville, Knowlton, Bolton-Centre, Sutton, Highwater, St-Venaut, East Hereford, Kennebago Lake, West Brome, Abercorn, Norton, Canaan, Pittsburg, Oquossoc, Dallas, Lacolle, St-Sébastien, Noyan, Stanbridge East, Holland, Morgan Cen., W. Stewartstown, Stewartstown, Rangeley, Alburg, Franklin, Richford, E. Berkshire, Jay, Newport, Island Pond, Colebrook, Dixville, Wentworths Location, Errol, S. Arm, Houghton, Chazy, West Chazy, Swanton, Enosburg Falls, Montgomery Cen., Westfield, Troy, Orleans, Bloomfield, N. Stratford, Kidderville, Columbia, Crystal, Dummer, Milan, Byron, Roxbury, Andover

Plattsburgh, Cliff Haven, Valcour, North Hero, Grand Isle, St. Albans, Bakersfield, Lowell, Irasburg, Albany, Barton, Glover, Brunswick Sprs., E. Haven, Maidstone, Groveton, Stark, West Milan, N. Newry, Newry, Milton, Locke Mills, Bethel, W. Paris, Greenwood

Keeseville, Burlington, South Burlington, Essex Jct., Underhill Flats, Jeffersonville, Johnson, Hyde Park, Morrisville, Lake Elmore, Wolcott, Hardwick, Lyndon, Lyndonville, E. Burke, W. Burke, Guildhall, Northumberland, Lancaster, Jefferson, Riverton, Berlin, Cascade, Shelburne, Gorham, Gilead, Hastings

Willsboro, Shelburne, St. George, Hinesburg, Waterbury, Richmond, Worcester, E. Calais, Woodbury, Danville, St. Johnsbury, Concord, Jefferson Highlands, Randolph, Glen House, North Chatham, E. Stoneham, Lynchville

Charlotte, S. Hinesburg, Starksboro, Montpelier, Barre, Plainfield, Marshfield, Barnet, Monroe, Lisbon, Bethlehem, Franconia, Twin Mountain, Fabyan, Bretton Woods, Bartlett, North Conway, Glen, Jackson, Stow, E. Waterford, Waterford

Westport, Vergennes, S. Starksboro, Bristol, New Haven, Warren, Waitsfield, Northfield, Websterville, W. Groton, S. Ryegate, Bath, Woodsville, Swiftwater, Easton, Lincoln, Willey House, Harts Location, Redstone, Fryeburg, Center Conway, Denmark

Port Henry, Middlebury, Ripton, Roxbury, E. Granville, Washington, Bradford, Haverhill, N. Haverhill, North Woodstock, Albany, Conway, Brownfield, Eaton Center, Madison, Chocorua, Sebago

Crown Point, Shoreham, Whiting, Leicester, Rochester, Randolph, Hancock, Chelsea, Vershire, Mill Village, W. Fairlee, Post Mills, Orford, Warren, Wentworth, W. Campton, Thornton, Wonalancet, Tamworth, Ossipee, Harrison, E. Sebago, W. Baldwin

Ticonderoga, Orwell, Putnam Station, Sudbury, Brandon, Pittsford, Stockbridge, Bethel, Royalton, Gaysville, Barnard, Sherburne Cen., Woodstock, Tunbridge, S. Royalton, Union Village, Lyme, Norwich, Hanover, Dorchester, Groton, E. Hebron, Ashland, Meredith, Moultonville, Moultonborough, Tuftonboro, Ossipee, Province Lake, Cornish, E. Baldwin

Fair Haven, Castleton, W. Rutland, Rutland, Bomoseen, Hubbardton, Pittsford Mills, White River Jct., West Lebanon, Lebanon, Canaan, Groton, East Hebron, Bristol, New Hampton, Sandwich, North Sandwich, Center Ossipee, Effingham Falls, Limington, Standish

Whitehall, Poultney, Middletown Sprs., Wallingford, Ludlow, Plymouth, Tyson, Bridgewater Cors., Meriden, Windsor, Grantham, Cornish Flat, N. Grantham, Springfield, Danbury, Franklin, New Durham, Milton, Farmington, S. Lebanon

Wells, Granville, Pawlet, Danby, Gassetts, Chester, Springfield, Claremont, Newport, Sunapee, Wendell, Sutton, N. Sutton, Salisbury, Northfield, Tilton, Belmont, Gilmanton, Alton, Union, Sanford, Days Mills

Hartford, N. Rupert, Dorset, S. Dorset, E. Dorset, Simonsville, Charlestown, Goshen, Newbury, Bradford, Warner, Penacook, Concord, Davisville, Contoocook, Pittsfield, Loudon, Barnstead, Rochester, Berwick, N. Berwick, Wells

Salem, Manchester Cen., Manchester, Bondville, Grafton, Cambridgeport, Bellows Falls, Alstead, Washington, Hoyts Corner, Hopkinton, Henniker, Chichester, Epsom Four Corners, Epsom, Gossville, Northwood, Barrington, Sommersworth, S. Berwick, Dover, York Beach

Arlington, Sunderland, Shaftsbury, Jamaica, Townshend, W. Wardsboro, Wardsboro, Drewsville, Cold River, Marlow, Hillsborough, Stoddard, Antrim, Bennington, Francestown, Hancock, Weare, Goffstown, Pinardville, Manchester, Bedford, Martin, Raymond, Epping, Newfields, Stratham, Exeter, Portsmouth, Rye, Wallis Sands

N. Hoosick, Bennington, Hoosick Falls, N. Petersburg, Woodford, Heartwellville, Wilmington, Searsburg, W. Dover, Newfane, Putney, Westmoreland, Keene, Marlboro, Dublin, Peterborough, Wilton, Milford, Amherst, Merrimack, Derry, Atkinson, Plaistow, Newton, Seabrook, Hampton Beach, Newburyport, Newbury

Petersburg, Williamstown, North Adams, Briggsville, Adams, Savoy, New Ashford, Pownal, Pownal Cen., Stamford, Jacksonville, Guilford, Hinsdale, Ashuelot, Winchester, Richmond, West Rindge, Rindge, Greenville, Brookline, Pelham, Hudson, Nashua, Lawrence, Salem, Haverhill, Ipswich, Gloucester

Colrain, Warwick, Tulleyville, Winchendon, Ashby, Pepperell, Lowell, Orange, Athol, Fitchburg, Lanesville

FOR NEW YORK STATE MAP SEE PAGES 66-69 · FOR MAINE STATE MAP SEE PAGE 41 · FOR MASSACHUSETTS STATE MAP SEE PAGES 24-25

Grid references: Top/bottom 1 2 3 4 5 6 7 · Side A B C D E F G H J K

FOR NEW YORK STATE MAP SEE PAGES 58-61

FOR PENNSYLVANIA STATE MAP SEE PAGES 72-73

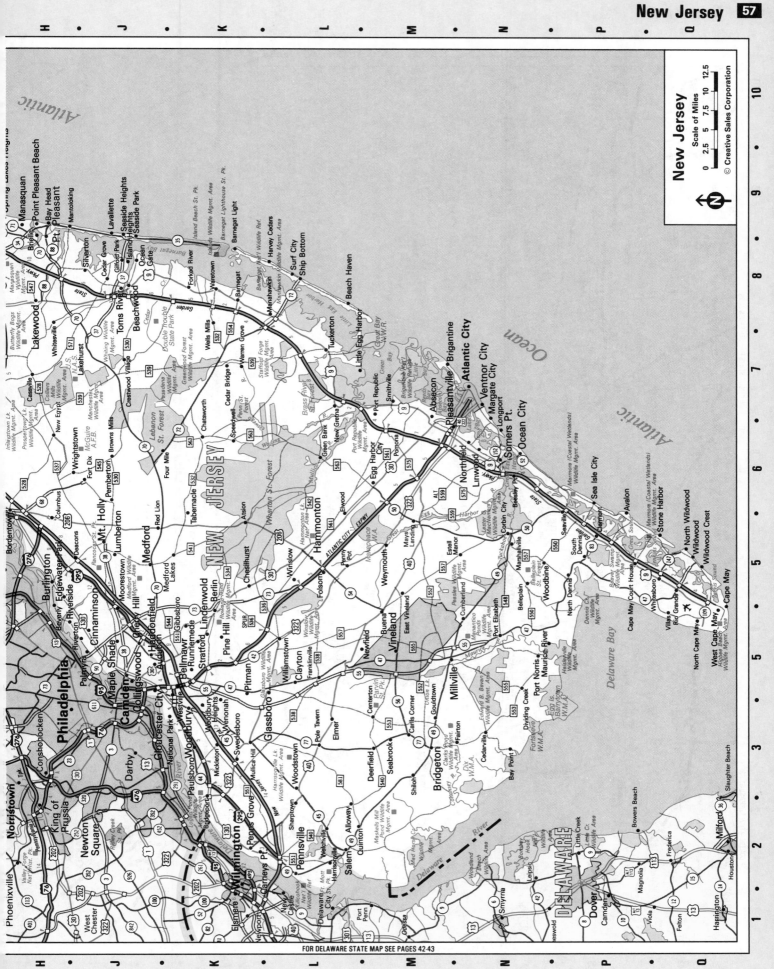

New Jersey

Scale of Miles

0   2.5   5   7.5   10   12.5

© Creative Sales Corporation

N

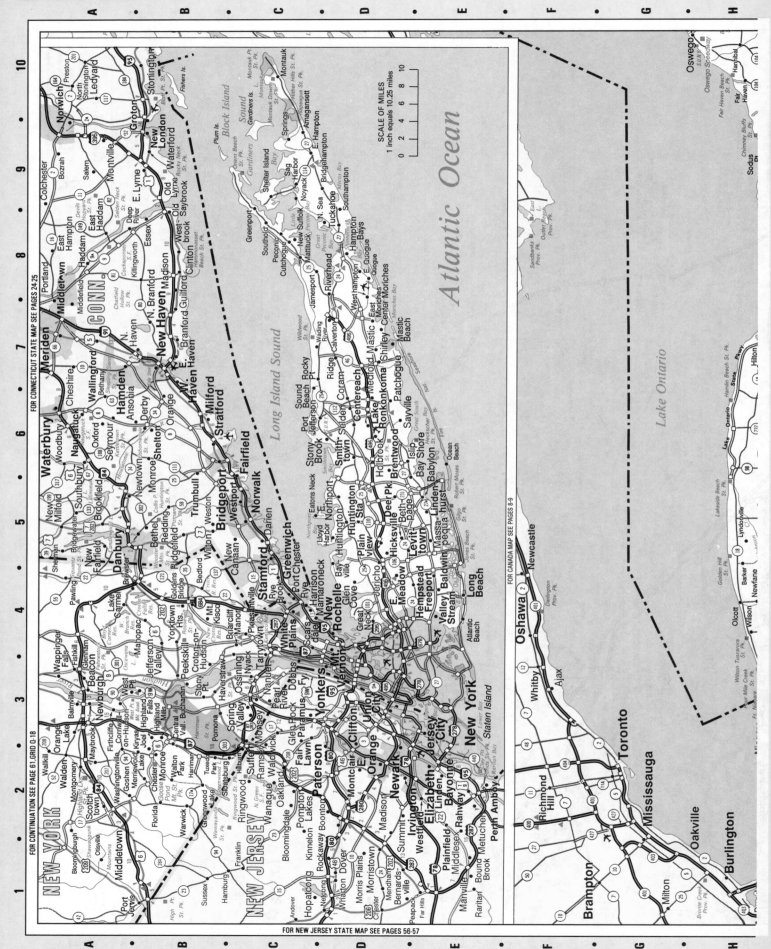

FOR CONTINUATION SEE PAGE 61, GRID Q-18

FOR CONNECTICUT STATE MAP SEE PAGES 24-25

FOR CANADA MAP SEE PAGES 8-9

SCALE OF MILES
1 inch equals 10.25 miles
0 2 4 6 8 10

Atlantic Ocean

Long Island Sound

Block Island Sound

Lake Ontario

NEW YORK

CONN.

NEW JERSEY

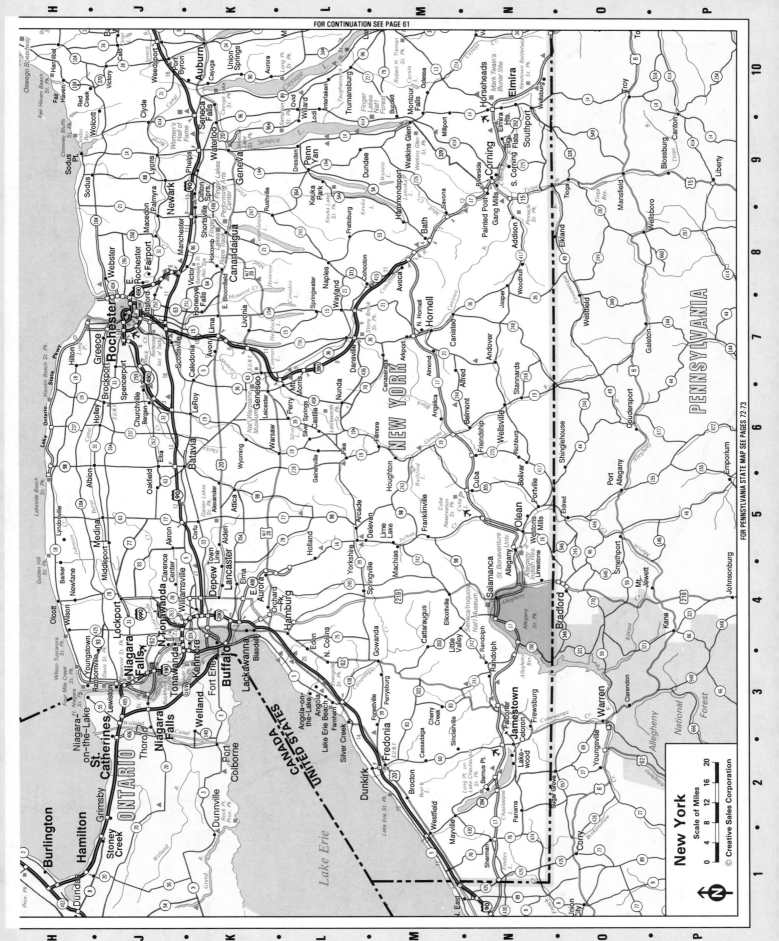

FOR CONTINUATION SEE PAGE 61

New York
Scale of Miles

© Creative Sales Corporation

FOR PENNSYLVANIA STATE MAP SEE PAGES 72-73

FOR VERMONT STATE MAP SEE PAGE 55

QUEBEC · CANADA · UNITED STATES

VERMONT

NEW YORK

ONTARIO

Adirondack Park

New York

Scale of Miles

0 4 8 12 16 20

© Creative Sales Corporation

St. Albans · Swanton · Alburg · Milton · Colchester · Essex Jct. · Winooski · Burlington · South Burlington · Shelburne · Hinesburg · Charlotte · Vergennes · Middlebury · Bristol · New Haven · Ferrisburg

Lacolle · Rouses Pt. · Champlain · Plattsburgh · Peru · Keeseville · Morrisonville · W. Plattsburgh · Dannemora

Barrington · Mooers · Chateaugay · Burke · Malone · Brushton · Bloomingdale · Saranac Lake · Lake Placid · Olympic Site Tour · John Brown · Mt. Marcy Elev. 5344 Highest Pt. in N.Y.

Port Lewis · Huntingdon · Ormstown

Westport · Mineville · Port Henry · Witherbee · Ticonderoga · Lake George · Glens Falls · Hudson Falls · Ft. Edward · Whitehall · Granville · Poultney · Pawlet

Warrensburg · Lake Luzerne · Hadley · Corinth · Northville

Finch · Chesterville · Massena · Cornwall · Barnhart Is. · Eisenhower Lock · Robert Moses St. Pk. · F.D.R. Power Project Visitors Center · Brasher Falls · Winthrop · Norfolk · Norwood · Unionville

Waddington · Morrisburg · Iroquois · Prescott · Ogdensburg · Heuvelton · Canton · Potsdam · Hermon · Edwards · Star Lake · Old Forge · Speculator · Atwell · Raquette Lake · Tupper Lake

Kemptville · Merrickville · Smiths Falls · Brockville · Morristown · Hammond · Alexandria Bay · Theresa · Gouverneur · Antwerp · Philadelphia · Ft. Drum Military Reserve · Carthage · Lowville · Boonville · Camden

Kingston · Gananoque · Cape Vincent · Clayton · Thousand Island Int'l Bridge · St. Lawrence Park · Chaumont · Dexter · Brownville · Watertown · Adams · Sackets Harbor · Henderson · Mannsville · Pulaski · Mexico · Fulton · Central Square · Constantia

Lake Champlain

St. Lawrence River

CANADA

FOR MASSACHUSSETTS STATE MAP SEE PAGES 24-25   FOR CONNECTICUT STATE MAP SEE PAGES 24-25

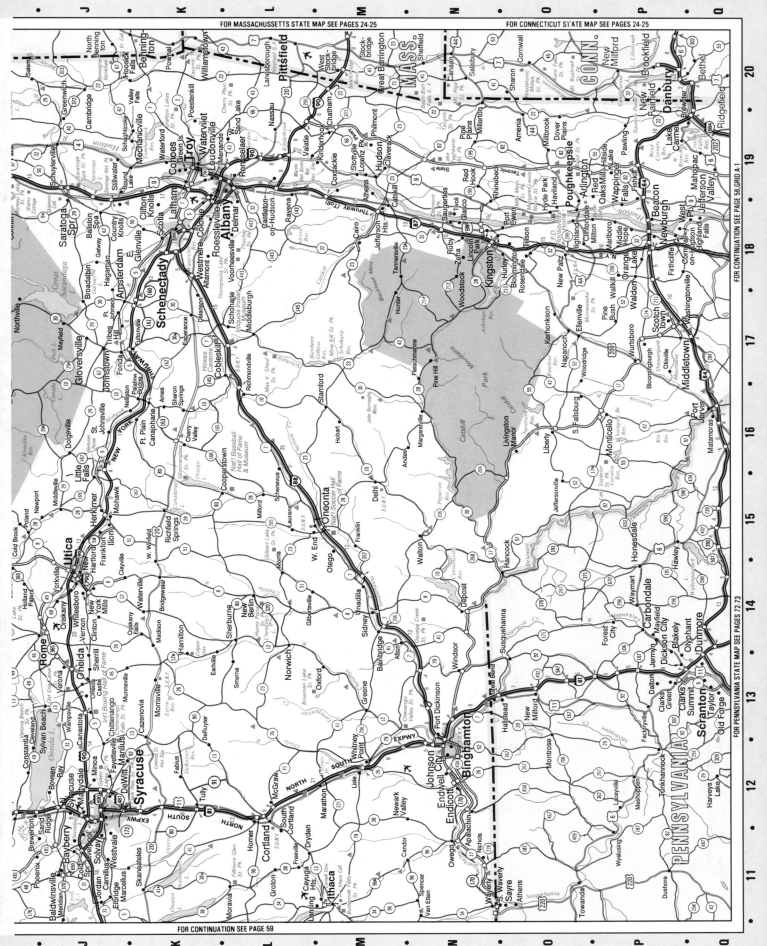

FOR CONTINUATION SEE PAGE 59

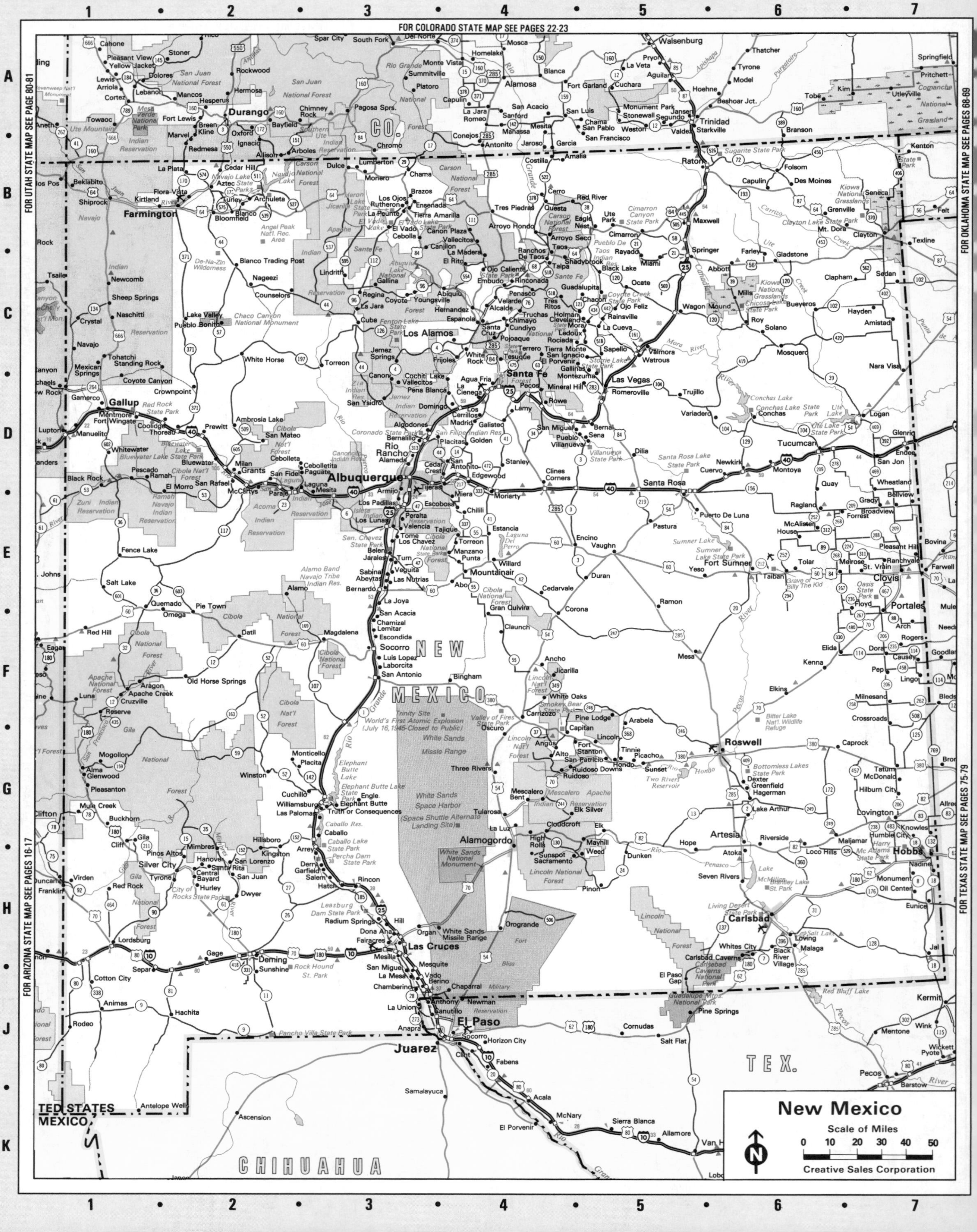

FOR UTAH STATE MAP SEE PAGE 80-81

FOR OKLAHOMA STATE MAP SEE PAGES 68-69

FOR ARIZONA STATE MAP SEE PAGES 16-17

FOR TEXAS STATE MAP SEE PAGES 75-79

NEW MEXICO

CO

TEX.

CHIHUAHUA

UNITED STATES
MEXICO

New Mexico

Scale of Miles

0 10 20 30 40 50

N

Creative Sales Corporation

FOR MINNESOTA STATE MAP SEE PAGES 46-47

FOR MONTANA STATE MAP SEE PAGE 51

FOR SOUTH DAKOTA STATE MAP SEE PAGE 74

North Dakota

Scale of Miles

0 10 20 30 40 50

© Creative Sales Corporation

N

CANADA
UNITED STATES

MAN (Manitoba)
SAS (Saskatchewan)
MN (Minnesota)
MT (Montana)
SD (South Dakota)

NORTH DAKOTA

Selected cities and towns: Williston, Minot, Grand Forks, Fargo, Bismarck, Mandan, Dickinson, Jamestown, Valley City, Devils Lake, Grafton, Langdon, Cavalier, Pembina, Wahpeton, Lisbon, Oakes, Ellendale, Bowman, Hettinger, Mott, New England, Beach, Medora, Watford City, New Town, Stanley, Tioga, Crosby, Bottineau, Rolla, Rugby, Harvey, Carrington, New Rockford, Cooperstown, Hillsboro, Mayville, Larimore, Lakota, Cando, Rock Lake, Bisbee, Kenmare, Garrison, Washburn, Underwood, Turtle Lake, McClusky, Wilton, Hazelton, Linton, Strasburg, Napoleon, Wishek, Ashley, Lehr, Kulm, Edgeley, Forman, Gwinner, Milnor, Wyndmere, Lidgerwood, Hankinson, Casselton, West Fargo, Moorhead

Theodore Roosevelt National Park North Unit, South Unit

Fort Union Nat'l Historic Site

Lake Sakakawea

Fort Berthold Indian Reservation

Standing Rock Indian Reservation

Missouri River
Red River
James River
Sheyenne River
Souris River

Devils Lake

Lake Oahe

FOR KENTUCKY STATE MAP SEE PAGES 38-39
FOR VIRGINIA STATE MAP SEE PAGES 82-83
FOR TENNESSEE STATE MAP SEE PAGES 38-39
FOR GEORGIA STATE MAP SEE PAGES 28-29

8 • 9 • 10 • 11 • 12 • 13 • 14

FOR VIRGINIA STATE MAP SEE PAGES 82-83

A B C D E F G H J K

Chatham • Halifax • Chase City • South Hill • Lawrenceville • Emporia • Franklin
Martinsville • Danville • Clarksville • John H. Kerr Reservoir • Roanoke Rapids • Pleasant Hill • Roduco • Gates • Corapeake • Morgans Corner • Barco
Bethel Hill • Stovall • Wise • Norlina • Garysburg • Murfreesboro • Sunbury • Elizabeth City • Camden • Coinjock • Bertha • Grandy
Yanceyville • Leasburg • Roxboro • Oxford • Henderson • Rheasville • Weldon • Jackson • Conway • Winton • Ahoskie • Hertford • Edenton • Mamie • Jarvisburg • Powells Point • Harbinger
Burlington • Hillsborough • Rocky Mount • Point Harbor • Nags Head • Whalebone • Wanchese
Greensboro • Durham • Raleigh • Wilson • Greenville • Washington • Columbia • East Lake • Manns Harbor • Rodanthe • Waves • Salvo
Asheboro • Chapel Hill • Goldsboro • New Bern • Plymouth • Belhaven • Engelhard • Avon • Buxton • Frisco • Hatteras
Fayetteville • Jacksonville • Morehead City • Beaufort • Ocracoke • Portsmouth
Lumberton • Wilmington • Wrightsville Beach • Carolina Beach • Kure Beach • Southport
Florence • Conway • Myrtle Beach • Surfside Beach • Garden City
Georgetown • Pawleys Island • Debidue Beach
Charleston • Mt. Pleasant • Isle of Palms • Sullivans Island • James Island • Folly Beach

Raleigh Bay

Pamlico Sound

Albemarle Sound

Atlantic Ocean

North Carolina
South Carolina

Scale of Miles
0 7 14 21 28 35

N

© Creative Sales Corporation

FOR PENNSYLVANIA STATE MAP SEE PAGES 72-73

FOR MICHIGAN STATE MAP SEE PAGES 44-45

FOR MICHIGAN STATE MAP SEE PAGES 44-45

FOR INDIANA STATE MAP SEE PAGES 34-35

CANADA
UNITED STATES

Lake Erie

ONTARIO

MICHIGAN

OHIO

Cleveland
Cleveland Hts.
Lakewood
Euclid
Akron
Canton
Youngstown
Warren
Toledo
Sandusky
Lorain
Elyria
Mansfield
Findlay
Lima
Bowling Green
Detroit
Windsor
Ann Arbor
Jackson
Lansing
E. Lansing
Flint
Pontiac
Warren
Sterling Hts.
Livonia
Dearborn
Westland
Port Huron
Sarnia
London
St. Thomas
Chatham
Wallaceburg
Massillon
Wooster
Medina
Brunswick
Strongsville
Parma
Garfield Hts.
Shaker Hts.
Willoughby
Mentor
Ashtabula
Geneva
Conneaut
Painesville
Bucyrus
Galion
Marion
Upper Sandusky
Tiffin
Fremont
Fostoria
Norwalk
Vermilion
Huron
Bellevue
Maumee
Perrysburg
Sylvania
Defiance
Napoleon
Van Wert
Celina
St. Marys
Wapakoneta

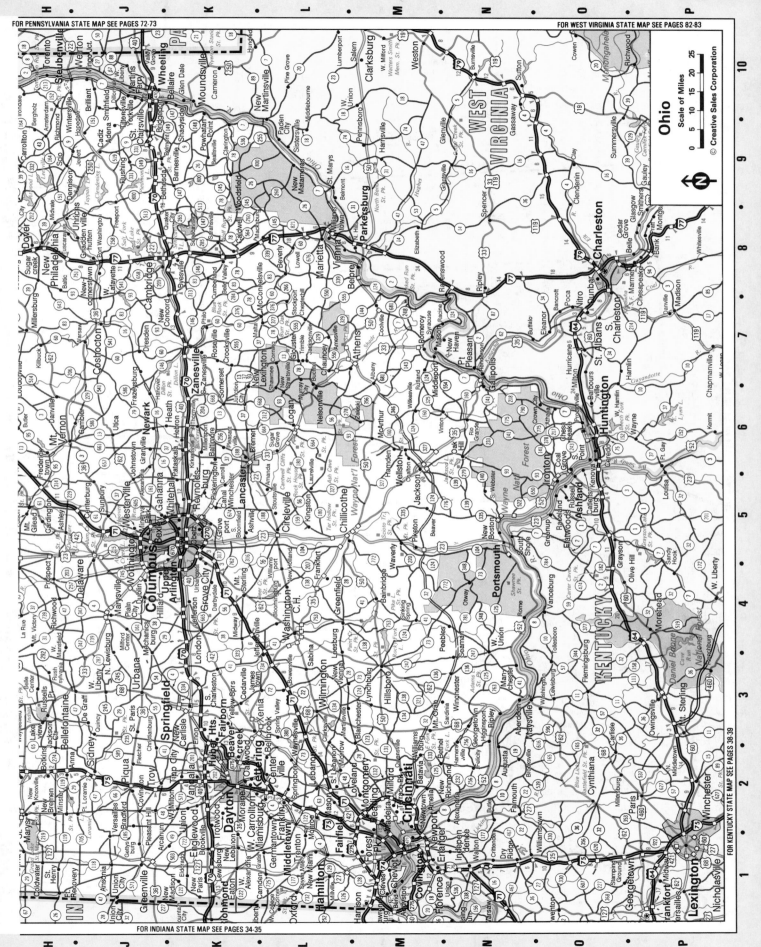

FOR PENNSYLVANIA STATE MAP SEE PAGES 72-73

FOR WEST VIRGINIA STATE MAP SEE PAGES 82-83

FOR INDIANA STATE MAP SEE PAGES 34-35

FOR KENTUCKY STATE MAP SEE PAGES 38-39

Ohio
Scale of Miles
0 5 10 15 20 25

© Creative Sales Corporation

FOR COLORADO STATE MAP SEE PAGES 22-23 FOR KANSAS STATE MAP SEE PAGE 37

COLORADO

KANSAS

Dodge City

Johnson City

Springfield   Bartlett

Pritchett   Vilas

Kim   Utleyville   Campo

Comanche National Grassland

Richfield   Hugoton   Kismet   Meade   Montezuma   Minneola   Greensburg   Bucklin   Cullison

Sublette

Coldwater   Protection   Ashland

Elkhart   Liberal   Tyrone   Floris   Mocane   Knowles   Buffalo   Lookout   Plainview

Beaver St. Pk.   Englewood   Hardtn

Kenton   Sturgis   Surrey Hills   Hough   Hooker   Turpin   Forgan   Laverne   Selman   Edith   Tegarden   Cora   Alv

Black Mesa St. Pk.   Eva   Optima   Bryan's Corner   Boyd   Rosston   Lovedale   Freedom

Wheeless   Boise City   Four Corners   Guymon   Balko   Gray   Slapout   May   Ft. Supply   Brace   Avard   Waynok

Kiowa National Grasslands   Griggs   Goodwell   Hardesty   Balko   Elmwood   Laverne   Catesby   Mooreland   Curtis   Quinlan

Mt. Dora   Felt   Texhoma   Booker   Darrouzett   Tangier   Fargo   Woodward   Belva

Clayton   Rita Blanca   'Nat'l Grassland   Perryton   Follett   Shattuck   Goodwin   Gage   Sharon

Texline   Stratford   Farnsworth   Lipscomb   Higgins   Arnett   Vici   Cestos   Seiling

Sedan   Dalhart   Gruver   Waka   Spearman   Glazier   Durham   Camargo   Taloga   Oakwood

Cactus   Etter   Sunray   Morse   Canadian   Crawford   Angora   Aledo   Putnam   Burmah

Hayden   Amistad   Hartley   Dumas   Stinnett   Roll   Reydon   Strong City   Cheyenne   Hammon   Butler   Custer City   Clinton

Channing   Lake Meredith National Recreation Area   Sanford   Borger   Miami   Durham   Black Kettle Nat'l Grassland   Rankin   Foss St. Pk.   Arapaho

Boys Ranch   Tascosa   Fritch   Phillips   Allison   Dempsey   Weatherfor

Masterson   Bunavista   Pampa   New Mobeetie   Briscoe   Elk City

Skellytown   Skellytown   White Deer   Kings Mill   Mobeetie   Wheeler   Sweetwater   Elk City   Foss   Corn

Adrian   Vega   Amarillo   Wildorado   Bushland   Lark   Groom   McLean   Lela   Twitty   Erick   Texola   Sayre   Doxey   Burns Flat   Forty One   Bessie   Cordell

Glenrio   Conway   Claude   Alanreed   Shamrock   Carter   Dill City   Rocky   Cloud Chief

Canyon   Umbarger   Dawn   Goodnight   Ashtola   Dozier   Samnorwood   Willow   Sentinel   Gotebo   Hobart

Hereford   Summerfield   Black   Friona   Happy   Wayside   Clarendon   Lelia Lake   Hedley   Quail   Lutie   Wellington   Madge   Vinson   Granite   Lone Wolf   Babbs   Roosevelt

Bovina   Dimmitt   Nazareth   Tulia   Silverton   Brice   Memphis   Lakeview   Newlin   Hollis   Gould   Duke   Blair   Martha   Warren   Altus

Hart   Parnell   Estelline   McQueen   Ozark   Headrick   Indiahoma

Clovis   Farwell   Texico   Lariat   Muleshoe   Earth   Springlake   Olton   Edmonson   Kress   Quitaque   Turkey   Tell   Childress   Lincoln   Olustee   Creta   Eldorado   Elmer   Tipton   Manitou   Chattanooga

Portales   Arch   Needmore   Fieldton   Sudan   Amherst   Hale Center   Cotton Center   Aiken   Lockney   Floydada   Matador   Whiteflat   Paducah   Kirkland   Acme   Quanah   Chillicothe   Vernon   Davidson   Hollister   Loveland

Rogers   Circle Back   Littlefield   Spade   Anton   Abernathy   Petersburg   Dougherty   Glenn   Dumont   Crowell   Thalia   Lockett   Oklaunion   Burkburnett

Goodland   Lingo   Maple   Morton   Enochs   Whitharral   Shallowater   Reese Vill.   Idalou   Ralls   McAdoo   Finney   Gilliland   Vera   Red Springs   Dundee

Bledsoe   Lehman   Whiteface   Levelland   Hurlwood   New Deal   Crosbyton   Dickens   Guthrie   Benjamin   Seymour

Bronco   Smyer   Wolfforth   Lubbock   Posey   Slaton   Spur   Girard   Munday   Goree   Bomarton   Westover   Olney

Sundown   New Home   Southland   Wilson   Kalgary   Jayton   Rochester   Weinert   Elbert

Ropesville   Meadow   Tahoka   Post   Clairemont   Old Glory   Haskell   Sagerton   Newcastle

O'Donnell   Grassland   Draw   Justiceburg   Aspermont   Swenson   Old Rule   Throckmorton   Graham

Fluvanna   South Bend

TEXAS

N.M.

Nara Visa

Canadian

Palo Duro Canyon   Caprock Canyons State Park   Buffalo Lake Nat'l Wildlife Refuge   Muleshoe Nat'l Wildlife Refuge   Mackenzie State Park

FOR NEW MEXICO STATE MAP SEE PAGE 62

FOR TEXAS STATE MAP SEE PAGES 75-79

Oklahoma

Scale of Miles

0   7   14   21   28   35

N

© Creative Sales Corporation

FOR KANSAS STATE MAP SEE PAGE 37

When travelling on highways in states where there are long stretches of open space, it is important to watch your speed. The 65 mile per hour speed limit applies only to rural areas where it is clearly marked. Drivers should always observe the posted speed limit. Remember, speed kills, so take it easy.

FOR MISSOURI STATE MAP SEE PAGES 48-49

FOR ARKANSAS STATE MAP SEE PAGE 15

FOR TEXAS STATE MAP SEE PAGES 75-79

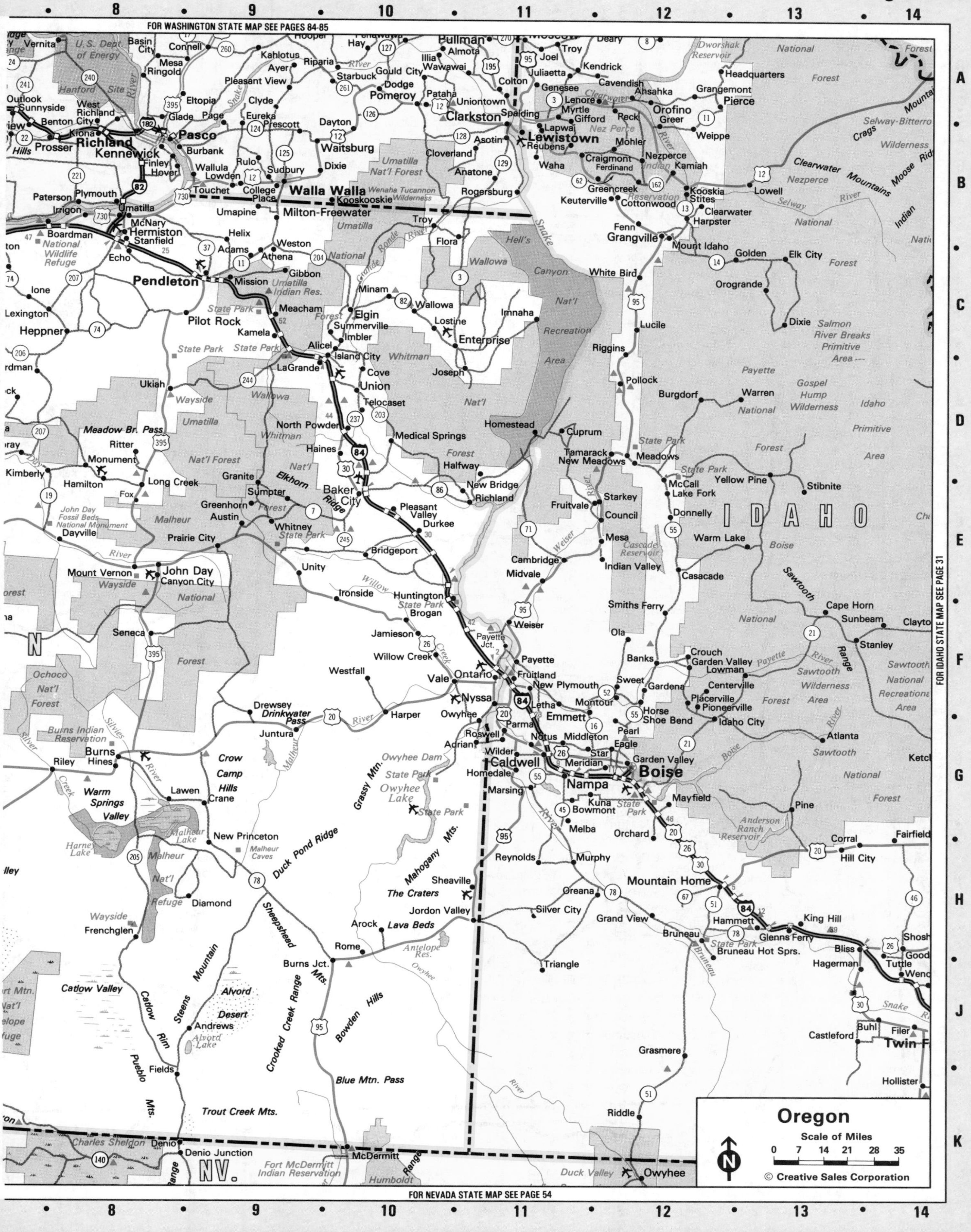

FOR WASHINGTON STATE MAP SEE PAGES 84-85

FOR IDAHO STATE MAP SEE PAGE 31

FOR NEVADA STATE MAP SEE PAGE 54

FOR IDAHO STATE MAP SEE PAGE 31

Oregon

Scale of Miles

0 7 14 21 28 35

N

© Creative Sales Corporation

IDAHO

NV.

1 2 3 4 5 6 7

FOR NEW YORK STATE MAP SEE PAGES 58-61

A B C D E F G H J K

FOR OHIO STATE MAP SEE PAGES 66-67

Lake Erie

Erie

Presque Isle St. Pk.

N. East
Fairview
Lake City
Conneaut
abula
Platea
Cranesville
Girard
McKean
Wattsburg
Wesleyville
Albion
Springboro
Waterford
Edinboro
Union City
Corry
Spartansburg
Gowanda
Fredonia
Brocton
Westfield
Cassadaga
Cherry Creek
Mayville
Chautauqua L.
Sinclairville
Little Valley
Cattaraugus
Springville
Lime Lake
Machias
Franklinville
Houghton
Fillmore
Canaseraga
Arkport
Angelica
Almond
Belmont
Erie
Sherma
Lakewood
Panama
Celoron
Bemus Pt.
Jamestown
Randolph
E. Randolph
Salamanca
Cuba
Friendship
Wellsville
Richburg
Stannards
Andover
Frewsburg
Allegany St. Pk.
Allegany
Olean
Portville
Bolivar

Cambridge Springs
Venango
Saegertown
Blooming Valley
Centerville
Townville
Tidioute
Youngsville
Sugar Grove
Warren
Clarendon
Chapman St. Pk.
Allegheny National Forest
Kinzua Dam Nat'l Rec. Area
Webb's Ferry Nat'l Forest
Willow Bay Nat'l Forest
Bradford
Smethport
Eldred
Shinglehouse
Oswayo
Port Allegany
Coudersport
Walton
Denton Hill St. Pk.

Andover
Linesville
Conneautville
Mill Village
Conneaut Lake
Meadville
Cochranton
Pleasantville
Titusville
Hydetown
Oil Creek St. Pk.
Cooperstown
Rouseville
Tionesta
Minister Creek Nat'l Forest
Beaver Meadows Nat'l Forest
Tionesta Lake Nat'l Rec. Area
Kane
Mt. Jewett
Kinzua Bridge
Elk St. Pk.
Sizerville
Austin
Sizerville St. Pk.
Pymatuning Res.
Pymatuning St. Pk.
Sinnemahoning St. Pk.
Emporium
Ole Bull St. Pk.

Greenville
Jamestown
Goddard St. Pk.
New Lebanon
Sugarcreek
Oil City
Clarion
Ridgway
St. Marys
Johnsonburg
Russell City
Wilcox
Bendigo St. Pk.
Driftwood
Westport
S. Renovo
Renovo
Kettle Creek St. Pk.

Sharon
Hermitage
Farrell
Wheat and
Mercer
Franklin
Sandy Lake
Stoneboro
Jackson Center
Shippenville
Knox
Clarion
State Univ.
Strattanville
Brockway
Falls Creek
Du Bois
Clearfield
Snow Shoe
Bald Eagle St. Pk.
Milesburg
Clear Creek St. Pk.
Parker Dam St. Pk.
S. B. Elliott St. Pk.
Bucktail St. Pk.

PENNSYLVANIA

Youngstown
New Castle
Slippery Rock
State Univ.
New Wilmington
W. Middlesex
Grove City
Harrisville
Eau Claire
St. Petersburg
Callensbur
Parker
Bruin
Petrolia
Karns City
Chicora
E. Butler
Corsica
Sligo
Brookville
Summerville
Reynoldsville
Sykesville
Troutville
Big Run
Grampian
Curwensville
Philipsburg
Osceola Mills
Chester Hill
Bellefonte
Centre Hall
State College

Bessemer
New Beaver
Big Beaver
Ellwood City
Ellport
Butler
Harmony
Zelienople
Connoquenessing
Evans City
Saxonburg
W. Kittanning
Worthington
Dayton
Kittanning
Punxsutawney
Glen Campbell
Marion Center
Cherry Tree
Barnesboro
Spangler
Hastings
Newburg
Lumber City
Glen Hope
Irvona
Coalport
Ramey
Houtzdale
Port Matilda
Penn. St. Univ.
Greenwood Furnace St. Pk.

Beaver Falls
Beaver
New Brighton
Monaca
Conway
Mars
Freeport
Ford Cliff
Ford City
Rural Valley
Creekside
Clymer
Clover
Westover
Patton
Ashville
Bellwood
Altoona
Tyrone
Petersburg
McVeytown

Midland
Baden
Economy
New Kensington
Lower Burrell
Vandergrift
Apollo
Homer City
Indiana
Indiana Univ.
Carrolltown
Ebensburg
Loretto
Gallitzin
Cresson
Hollidaysburg
Williamsburg
Huntingdon
Mt. Union
Shirleysburg

Aliquippa
Ambridge
Corapolis
Franklin Park
Bellevue
Oakmont
Plum
Avonmore
Saltsburg
Nanty-Glo
Portage
Lily
Cassandra
Summerhill
Newry
Duncansville
Marklesburg
Roaring Spring
Martinsburg
Woodbury
Saxton
Dudley
Saltillo
Orbisonia
Three Springs
Shade Gap
Kittatinny Tunnel
Tuscarora Tunnel

Pittsburgh
Wilkinsburg
Murrysville
Monroeville
Blairsville
Bolivar
New Florence
Derry
Brownstown
Westmont
Johnstown
Geistown
Scalp Level
Windber
Blue Knob St. Pk.
Babcock St. Pk.
Trough Creek St. Pk.
Broad Top City

Weirton
Carnegie
Dormont
W. Mifflin
White Oak
McKeesport
Jeanette
Latrobe
Greensburg
Ligonier
Benson
Boswell
Pleasantville
Hooversville
Central City
Stoystown
New Paris
Raystown Nat'l Rec. Area
Mt. Union
Blain

Burgettstown
Bridgeville
Canonsburg
Bethel Park
Jefferson
Clairton
Youngwood
W. Newton
New Stanton
Mt. Pleasant
Donegal
Jennerstown
Laurel Mtn North
Laurel Summit St. Pk.
Linn Run St. Pk.
Laurel Hill St. Pk.
Kooser St. Pk.
Somerset
Bedford
Everett
Breezewood
Chambersburg
Cowans Gap St. Pk.

Washington
E. Washington
Houston
New Eagle
Donora
Monessen
Charleroi
Cokeburg
California
Centerville
W. Brownsville
Scottdale
Everson
Connellsville
S. Connellsville
Dunbar
New Centerville
Rockwood
Garrett
Berlin
Rainsburg
McConnellsburg
Mercersburg
Greencastle

Waynesburg
Marianna
Rices Landing
Carmichaels
New Salem
Brownsville
Uniontown
Fairchance
Smithfield
Masontown
Greensboro
Point Marion
Ohiopyle
Ohiopyle St. Pk.
Ft. Necessity Nat'l Battlefield
Friendship Hill Nat'l Site
Ursina
Meyersdale
Hyndman
Wellersburg
Salisbury
Youghiogheny Lake Nat'l Rec. Area

Cameron
Ryerson Station St. Pk.
Star City
Westover
Morgantown
Coopers Cox S.P.
Friendsville
Grantsville
Addison
Accident
Frostburg
Cumberland
Hancock
Hagerstown

Mannington
Barrackville
Rivesville
Masontown
New Germany Nat'l Forest
Savage River S.F.
Midland
Lonaconing
Warrior Mtn. Wildlife Management Area
Rocky Gap St. Pk.
Green Ridge S.F.
Indian Springs Wildlife Management Area
Williamsport
Funks

OH
WV
MD

FOR WEST VIRGINIA STATE MAP SEE PAGES 82-83
FOR MARYLAND STATE MAP SEE PAGES 42-43

1 2 3 4 5 6 7

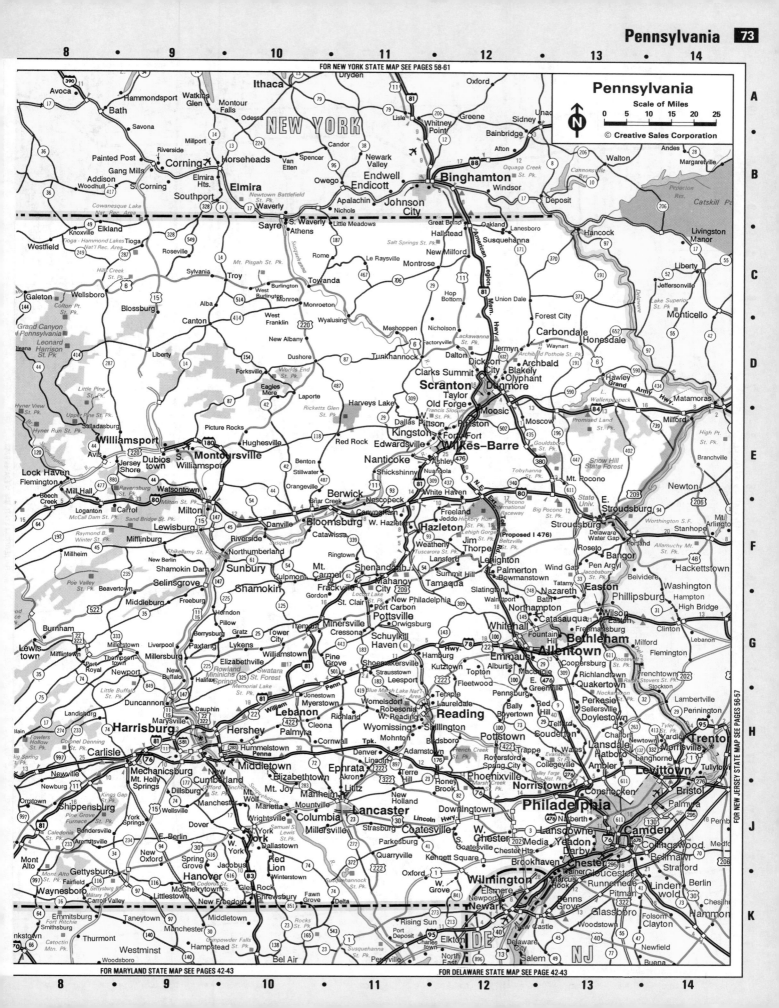

Pennsylvania
Scale of Miles
0 5 10 15 20 25
© Creative Sales Corporation
N

FOR NEW YORK STATE MAP SEE PAGES 58-61

FOR NEW JERSEY STATE MAP SEE PAGES 56-57

FOR MARYLAND STATE MAP SEE PAGES 42-43

FOR DELAWARE STATE MAP SEE PAGE 42-43

FOR MINNESOTA STATE MAP SEE PAGES 46-47

FOR IOWA STATE MAP SEE PAGE 36

South Dakota

Scale of Miles

0 10 20 30 40 50

© Creative Sales Corporation

FOR NORTH DAKOTA STATE MAP SEE PAGE 63

FOR NEBRASKA STATE MAP SEE PAGES 52-53

Texas

Scale of Miles

0 8 16 24 32 40

© Creative Sales Corporation

N

FOR NEW MEXICO STATE MAP SEE PAGE 62

FOR CONTINUATION SEE PAGE 76

FOR CONTINUATION SEE PAGE 78

NEW MEXICO

TEXAS

CHIHUAHUA

UNITED STATES

MEXICO

Ancho
Jicarilla
Lincoln National Forest
White Oaks
Carrizozo
Capitan
Lincoln
Angus
Alto
San Patricio
Ruidoso Downs
Ruidoso
Hondo
Tinnie
Picacho
Sunset
Bent
Mescalero
Elk Silver
Tularosa
La Luz
High Rolls
Cloudcroft
Alamogordo
White Sands Nat'l Mon.
Sacramento
Mayhill
Weed
Elk
Dunken
Hope
Pinon
Seven Rivers
Lincoln National Forest
Three Rivers
Pine Lodge
Arabela
Mesa
Elida
Dora
Pep
Goodland
Lingo
Milnesand
Crossroads
Bledsoe
Lehman
Maple
Morton
Enochs
Bula
Needmore
Circle Back
Littlefield
Sudan
Amherst
Fieldton
Spa
Whitharral
Reese V
Whiteface
Levelland
Smyer
Sundown
Bronco
McDonald
Hilburn City
Lovington
Maljamar
Loco Hills
Humble City
Knowles
Hobbs
Monument
Nadine
Oil Center
Eunice
Jal
Denver City
Wellman
Seagraves
Loop
Welc
Seminole
Meadov
Brownfield
Ropes
Frankel City
Patricia
Gardendale
Midland
Notrees
Odessa
Kermit
Wink
Penwell
Monahans
Pyote
Barstow
Wickett
Royalty
Crane
Grandfalls
Imperial
McCamey
Girvin
Bakersfield
Iraa
Shef
Fort Stockton
Roswell
Dexter
Greenfield
Hagerman
Lake Arthur
Artesia
Riverside
Atoka
Caprock
Carlsbad
Black River Village
Loving
Malaga
Whites City
Carlsbad Caverns
Carlsbad Caverns National Park
El Paso Gap
Dell City
Cornudas
Salt Flat
Guadalupe Mtns. National Park
Red Bull Lake
Orla
Mentone
Pecos
Toyah
Balmorhea State Park
Saragosa
Balmorhea
Coyanosa
Las Cruces
Mesilla
San Miguel
La Mesa
Chamberino
Canutillo
El Paso
Ciudad Juarez
San Elizario
Clint
Fabens
Tornillo
Acala
Fort Hancock
McNary
Sierra Blanca
Allamore
Van Horn
Lobo
Valentine
Davis Mountains State Park
Fort Davis
Alpine
Marfa
Plata
Shafter
Ojinaga
Redford
Fort Leaton State Park
Terlingua
Study Butte
Chisos Basin
Big Bend National Park
Boquillas del Carmen
Sanderson
Dryden
Chihuahua
Fort Bliss
Huencon Tanks State Park
Magoffin House State Park
Horizon City
Socorro
Newman
Anthony
Berino
Chaparral
Mesquite
Dona Ana
Dona Organ
White Sands Missile Range
Orogrande
Fairacres
Hill
Rincon
Engle
Truth or Consequences
Palomas

180
62
20
10
25
54
82
70
380
285
31
18
115
385
349
302
290
67
166
118
90
Rio Grande
Pecos
Alamito
Terlingua Creek
Maravillas Creek
Big Canyon

FOR NEW MEXICO STATE MAP SEE PAGE 62

FOR CONTINUATION SEE PAGE 75

FOR CONTINUATION SEE PAGE 78

NEW MEXICO

TEXAS

Major cities: Amarillo, Lubbock, Midland, Odessa, Big Spring, San Angelo, Abilene, Sweetwater, Snyder, Lamesa, Clovis, Hobbs, Wichita Falls, Lawton, Vernon, Childress, Brownwood

Selected place names:
Grenville, Mt. Dora, Clayton, Texline, Pitta Blanca, Stratford, Griggs, Goodwell, Texhoma, Bryan's Corner, Balko, Hardesty, Elmwood, Slapout, May, Ft. Supply, Woodward, Sedan, Dalhart, Cactus, Etter, Sunray, Morse, Gruver, Waka, Spearman, Perryton, Farnsworth, Booker, Darrouzett, Follett, Catesby, Fargo, Tangier, Hayden, Amistad, Hartley, Channing, Dumas, Stinnett, Canadian, Miami, Durham, Crawford, Nara Visa, Logan, Masterson, Sanford, Borger, Phillips, Bunavista, Pampa, Rampa, Clinton, Elk City, Sayre, Skellytown, White Deer, Panhandle, New Mobeetie, Briscoe, Wheeler, Mayfield, Doxey, Adrian, Vega, Wildorado, Bushland, Amarillo, Conway, Groom, Alanreed, Shamrock, Erick, Texola, Carter, Canyon, Umbarger, Dawn, Happy, Wayside, Goodnight, Clarendon, Lelia Lake, Hedley, Quail, Wellington, Hereford, Summerfield, Black, Friona, Dimmitt, Nazareth, Hart, Tulia, Silverton, Brice, Memphis, Lakeview, Newlin, Estelline, Hollis, Clovis, Farwell, Texico, Lariat, Bovina, Muleshoe, Springlake, Olton, Kress, Planview, South Plains, Flomot, Turkey, Northfield, Tell, Childress, Portales, Arch, Rogers, Needmore, Fieldton, Sudan, Amherst, Hale Center, Cotton Center, Aiken, Lockney, Floydada, Matador, Paducah, Crowell, Thalia, Vernon, Dora, Goodland, Bula, Littlefield, Spade, Anton, Petersburg, Abernathy, Glenn, Dumont, Finney, Guthrie, Benjamin, Seymour, Bledsoe, Lehman, Whiteface, Levelland, Shallowater, Reese Vill., New Deal, Idalou, Ralls, Crosbyton, Dickens, Vera, Red Springs, Munday, Goree, Smyer, Wolfforth, Lubbock, Posey, Slaton, Spur, Kalgary, Girard, Jayton, Knox City, O'Brien, Rochester, Weinert, Sundown, Ropesville, New Home, Southland, Wilson, Meadow, Brownfield, Tahoka, Post, Clairemont, Aspermont, Old Glory, Rule, Haskell, Throckmorton, Newcastle, Bronson, Denver City, Wellman, Seagraves, Loop, Welch, O'Donnell, Grassland, Draw, Fluvanna, Justiceburg, Hamlin, Stamford, Avoca, Lueders, Albany, Humble City, Knowles, Hobbs, Monument, Nadine, Oil Center, Eunice, Seminole, Gail, Snyder, Roby, Anson, Funston, Caddo, Lamesa, Patricia, Ackerly, Vealmoor, Vincent, Dunn, Inadale, Sweetwater, Merkel, Tye, Abilene, Baird, Putnam, Cisco, Eastland, Frankel City, Knott, Tarzan, Lenorah, Fairview, Loraine, Roscoe, Trent, Caps, Clyde, Kermit, Notrees, Gardendale, Midland, Stanton, Big Spring, Coahoma, Colorado City, Silver, Winters, Goldsboro, Cross Plains, Monahans, Pyote, Penwell, Odessa, Garden City, Sterling City, Robert Lee, Bronte, Norton, Hatchel, Ballinger, Brownwood, Wink, Wickett, Royalty, Crane, Grandfalls, Imperial, Rankin, Coyanosa, Water Valley, Carlsbad, Miles, Paint Rock, Rowena, Talpa, Santa Anna, Bangs, Early, San Angelo, Tankersley, Sherwood, Knickerbocker, Mertzon, Wall, Vancourt, Eden, Eola, Millersview, Doole, Lometa, Big Lake, Christoval

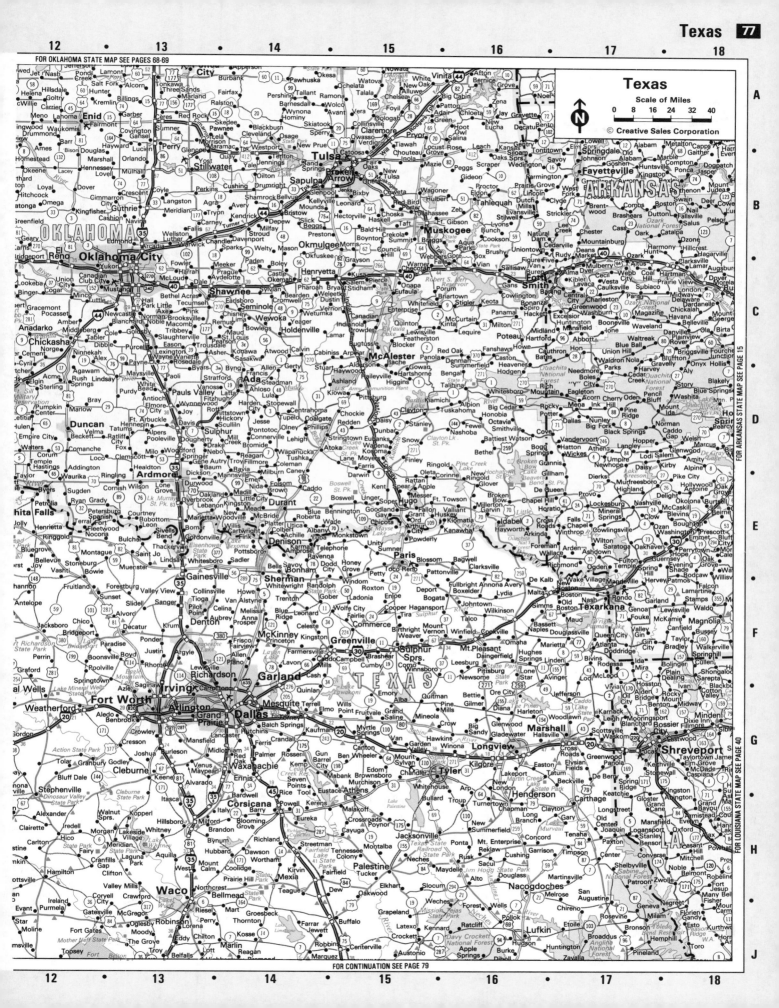

FOR OKLAHOMA STATE MAP SEE PAGES 68-69

FOR ARKANSAS STATE MAP SEE PAGE 15

FOR LOUISIANA STATE MAP SEE PAGE 40

FOR CONTINUATION SEE PAGE 76
FOR CONTINUATION SEE PAGE 75

6　7　8　9　10　11

J

Rankin
Mertzon
Knickerbocker
Eden
Rochelle
Richland Springs
Lometa
Adamsville
Copp
McCamey
Big Lake
Christoval
Melvin
Brady
San Saba
Lampasa
Girvin
Pecos
Barnhart
Calf Creek
Voca
Cherokee

Fort Stockton
Bakersfield
Iraan
Menard
Hext
Katemcy
Pontotoc
Valley Spring
Tow
Buchanan Dam
Fredonia
Bluffton
Buchanan

K

Sheffield
Fort Lancaster State Park
Ozona
Eldorado
Fort McKavett State Park
Fort McKavett
London
Mason
Grit
Llano
Kingsland
Lake Lyndon B. Johnson
Longho
Marble Falls

Sonora
Roosevelt
Junction
Segovia
Doss
Cherry Spring
Willow City
Round Mountain
Spicew
Loyal Valley

Telegraph
Harper
Enchanted Rock State Park
Fredericksburg
Johnson City
Stonewall
Lyndon B. Johnson State Park

L

Sanderson
Juno
Mountain Home
Hunt
Ingram
Kerrville
Center Pt
Sisterdale
Spring Branch
Blanco
Luckenbach
Hye
Stonewall

Dryden
Loma Alta
Rocksprings
Kerrville State Park
Camp Verde
Comfort
Blanco State Park
New Brau

Langtry
Rio Grande
Seminole Canyon State Park
Carta Valley
Barksdale
Camp Wood
Lost Maples State Park
Vanderpool
Medina
Pipecreek
Leon Springs
Conyers
Ne

M

Comstock
Devils Lake
Amistad National Recreation Area
Lake Walk
Garner State Park
Utopia
Bandera
Tarpley
Lake Hills
Mico
Medina Lake
Riomedina
San Antonio
Navarro Hotel
Castroville
Kelly A.F.B.
Universal City
San
Martinez

Basin
Boquillas del Carmen
Del Rio
Ciudad Acuna
Fort Clark Springs
Brackettville
Concan
D'Hanis
Knippa
Sabinal
Hondo
Somerset
Elmer

Spofford
Dabney
Blewett
Uvalde
Frio River
Moore
Natalia
Lytle
Leming

N

Quemado
Normandy
La Pryor
Frio Town
Batesville
Divot
Derby
Bigfoot
Poteet
Jourdanton
Pleasant
Pearsall
Charlotte
Christine

Piedras Negras
Eagle Pass
Crystal City
Dilley
Hindes
Campbellton
Whitsett

Nueva Rosita
Brundage
Big Wells
Woodward
Los Angeles
Tilden
Three Rivers
Carrizo Springs
Asherton
Cotulla
Fowlerton
Calliham
George We

TEXAS

Catarina
Artesia Wells
Nueces

Encinal
Freer
Ora

P

COAHUILA

Freer
San Diego
Ben B

Monclova
Nuevo Laredo
Laredo
Oilton
Bruni
Benavides
Rio
Mirando City
Realitos
Concepcion
Ramirez
Hebbronville

Q

San Ygnacio
Escobas
Randado
Encin

Bustamante

R

Sabinas Hidalgo
Lopeno
Falcon
La Gloria
Santa Elen
San Isidro
Nuevo Guerrero
El Sauz
La Reforma
Falcon State Park

Cd. Mier
Roma
Rio Grande City
Edinbu
Cd. Camargo
La Grulla
La Joya
Mission
Sullivan City

NUEVO LEON

Presa De El Azucar
Bentson Rio Grande Valley State Park
Hidalgo
Reynosa

S

San Pedro de las Colonias
Monterrey

UNITED STATES
MEXICO

6　7　8　9　10　11

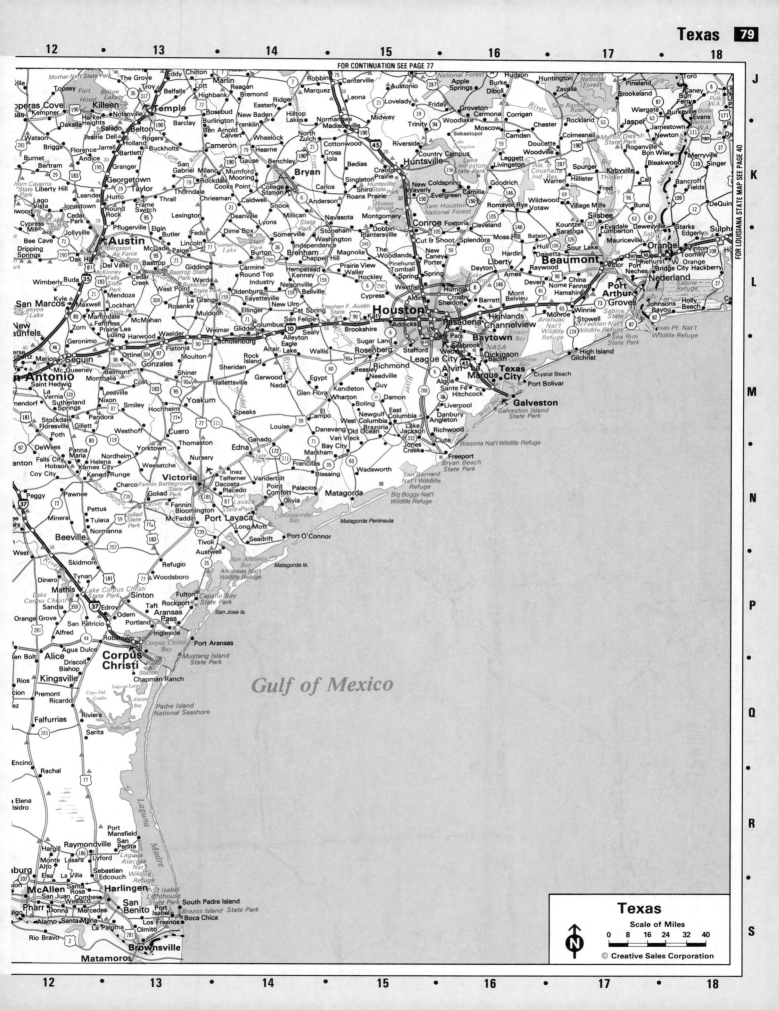

Gulf of Mexico

FOR LOUISIANA STATE MAP SEE PAGE 40

Texas

Scale of Miles

0   8   16   24   32   40

© Creative Sales Corporation

FOR WYOMING STATE MAP SEE PAGES 88-89
FOR COLORADO STATE MAP SEE PAGES 22-23

Utah

Scale of Miles
0 7 14 21 28 35

© Creative Sales Corporation

N

WYOMING

COLO.

IDAHO

NEVADA

Salt Lake City

Pocatello · Blackfoot · Soda Springs · Logan · Ogden · Provo · Orem · Nephi · Tooele · Wendover · Price · Duchesne · Roosevelt · Vernal · Evanston · Rock Springs · Green River

Great Salt Lake

Bonneville Salt Flats · Dugway Proving Grounds · Hill Air Force Range

FOR IDAHO STATE MAP SEE PAGE 31
FOR NEVADA STATE MAP SEE PAGE 54

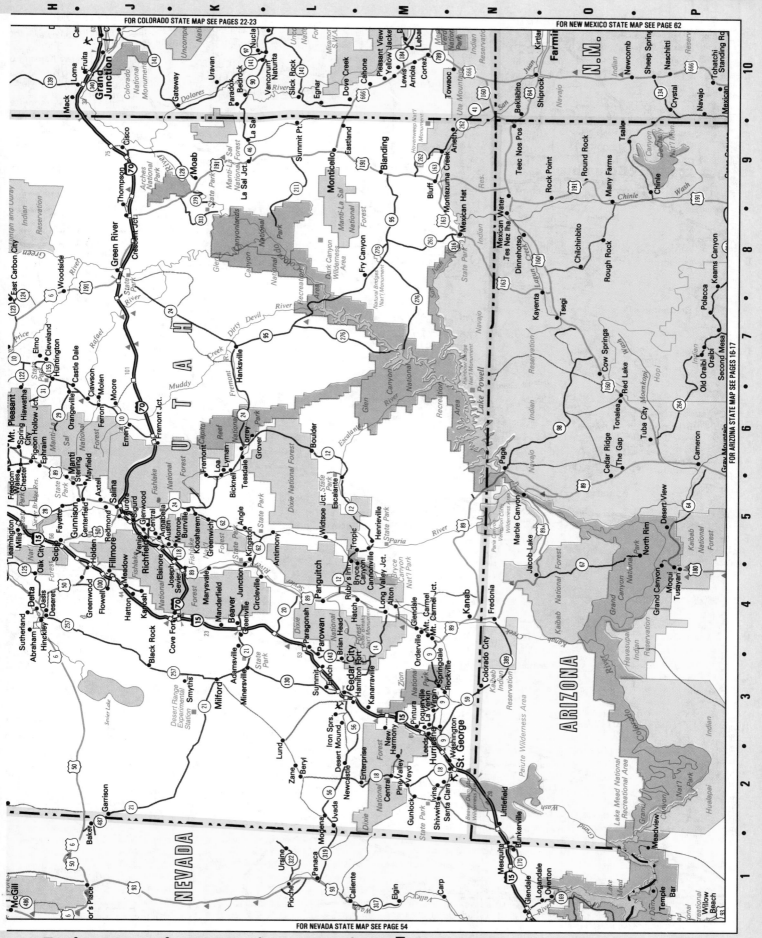

FOR OHIO STATE MAP SEE PAGES 66-67

FOR PENNSYLVANIA STATE MAP SEE PAGES 72-73

FOR OHIO STATE MAP SEE PAGES 66-67

FOR KENTUCKY STATE MAP SEE PAGES 38-39

FOR TENNESSEE STATE MAP SEE PAGES 38-39

FOR NORTH CAROLINA STATE MAP SEE PAGES 64-65

Grid columns: 1 2 3 4 5 6 7
Grid rows: A B C D E F G H J K

OHIO

WEST VIRGINIA

KENTUCKY

TENN.

Kenton, Marion, Richwood, Cardington, Mt. Gilead, Bellville, Butler, Fredericktown, Strasburg, Millersburg, Carrollton, Salineville, E. Liverpool, Chester, Aliquippa, Natrona Hts., Lower, New Kensington, Pittsburgh, Murrysville

Delaware, Centerburg, Mt. Vernon, Danville, Warsaw, Coshocton, New Philadelphia, Uhrichsville, Scio, Wintersville, Cadiz, Weirton, Wheeling, McKeesport, Jeannette, Greensburg, Bethel Park, Washington, Monessen

Columbus, Newark, Cambridge, Zanesville, St. Clairsville, Triadelphia, Bellaire, Moundsville, Morgantown, Uniontown

London, Winchester, Lancaster, Somerset, Crooksville, Caldwell, Woodsfield, New Martinsville, Mannington, Fairmont, Clarksburg, Bridgeport, Masontown, Terra Alta, Oakland

Circleville, Logan, Glouster, Chauncey, Beverly, McConnelsville, Marietta, Parkersburg, Harrisville, Salem, Shinnston, Monongah, Clarksburg, Weston, Buckhannon, Elkins, Parsons, Thomas

Chillicothe, Bainbridge, McArthur, Athens, Williamstown, Vienna, Belpre, Pomeroy, Jackson, Hamden, Vinton, Mason, New Haven, Pt. Pleasant, Gallipolis, Ravenswood, Ripley, Spencer, Gassaway, Sutton, Durbin, Monterey

Portsmouth, Ironton, Ashland, Huntington, Hurricane, Nitro, St. Albans, S. Charleston, Charleston, Dunbar, Clendenin, Clay, Summersville, Richwood, Marlinton, Warm Springs, Clifton Forge

Greenup, Kenova, Milton, Hamlin, Marmet, East Bank, Cedar Grove, Smithers, Gauley Bridge, Montgomery, Fayetteville, Oak Hill, Rainelle, Rupert, White Sulphur Spr., Covington, Lexington

Morehead, Louisa, Wayne, Madison, Chapmanville, Logan, Man, Beckley, Sophia, Mabscott, Alderson, Ronceverte, Lewisburg, Hinton, Union, New Castle, Buchanan

Salyersville, Paintsville, Prestonsburg, Williamson, Matewan, Oceana, Gilbert, Pineville, Mullens, Welch, Princeton, Athens, Peterstown, Pembroke, Hollins, Roanoke, Salem, Vinton

Hazard, Whitesburg, Pikeville, Grundy, War, Bluefield, Narrows, Pearisburg, Blacksburg, Christiansburg, Radford, Rocky Mount, Martinsville

Jonesville, Pennington Gap, Appalachia, Big Stone Gap, Norton, Wise, Coeburn, Lebanon, Honaker, Richlands, Tazewell, Pulaski, Dublin, Wytheville, Marion, Rural Retreat, Hillsville, Bassett, Fieldale

Kingsport, Bristol, Weber City, Gate City, Abingdon, Damascus, Independence, Galax, Mt. Airy, Danville, Eden

FOR TENNESSEE STATE MAP SEE PAGES 38-39

FOR NORTH CAROLINA STATE MAP SEE PAGES 64-65

FOR PENNSYLVANIA STATE MAP SEE PAGES 72-73

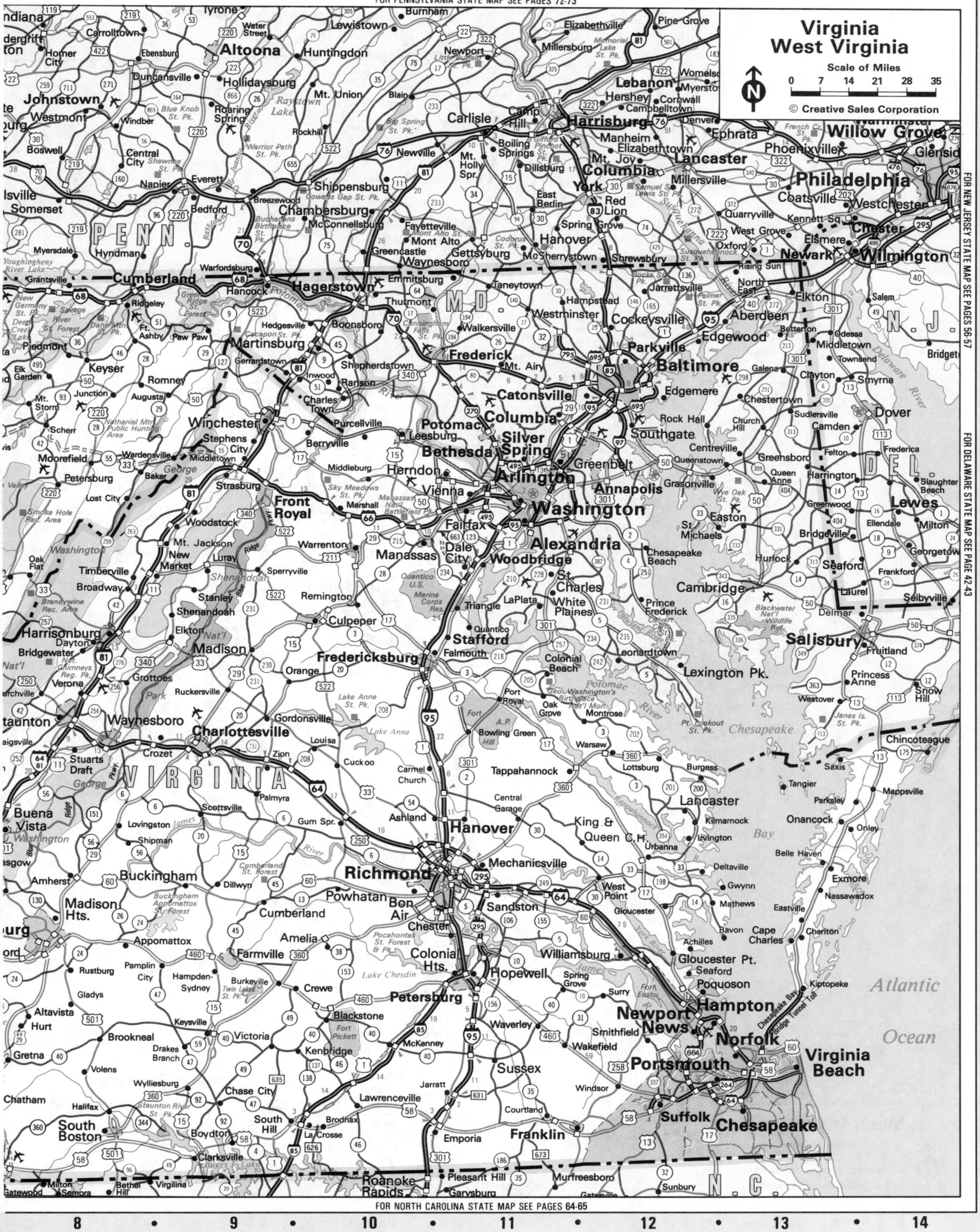

Virginia West Virginia
Scale of Miles
0 7 14 21 28 35
© Creative Sales Corporation
N

FOR NEW JERSEY STATE MAP SEE PAGES 56-57

FOR DELAWARE STATE MAP SEE PAGES 42-43

FOR NORTH CAROLINA STATE MAP SEE PAGES 64-65

Column headers: 8 9 10 11 12 13 14

Row labels: A B C D E F G H J K

Indiana, Tyrone, Water Street, Lewistown, Burnham, Elizabethville, Pine Grove, Lebanon, Womelsdorf, Willow Grove, Glenside

Carrolltown, Altoona, Huntingdon, Newport, Millersburg, Memorial Little Buffalo St. Pk., Hershey, Cornwall, Campbelltown, Ephrata, Phoenixville, Philadelphia

Johnstown, Hollidaysburg, Mt. Union, Blain, Carlisle, Camp Hill, Harrisburg, Manheim, Elizabethtown, Denver, Lancaster, Coatesville, Westchester, Chester, Wilmington

Westmont, Windber, Roaring Spring, Rockhill, Newville, Mt. Holly Spr., Boiling Springs, Mt. Joy, Columbia, York, Millersville, West Grove, Kennett Sq., Elsmere, Newark

Boswell, Central City, Everett, Shippensburg, Chambersburg, Breezewood, McConnellsburg, Fayetteville, East Berlin, Red Lion, Spring Grove, Hanover, Oxford, Rising Sun, North East, Elkton, Salem

Somerset, Bedford, Mont Alto St. Pk., Greencastle, Gettysburg, McSherrystown, Shrewsbury, Susquehanna, Aberdeen, Edgewood, N.J.

Myersdale, Hyndman, Warfordsburg, Hancock, Hagerstown, Emmitsburg, Waynesboro, Taneytown, MD, Hampstead, Westminster, Cockeysville, Parkville, Baltimore, Chestertown, Middletown, Townsend, Odessa

Cumberland, Hedgesville, Boonsboro, Thurmont, Walkersville, Frederick, Mt. Airy, Catonsville, Edgemere, Rock Hall, Galena, Clayton, Smyrna, Dover

Keyser, Romney, Martinsburg, Shepherdstown, Ranson, Charles Town, Columbia, Silver Spring, Bethesda, Southgate, Centreville, Queenstown, Greensboro, Camden, Felton, Frederica

Winchester, Stephens City, Middletown, Berryville, Purcellville, Leesburg, Potomac, Greenbelt, Annapolis, Grasonville, Easton, St. Michaels, Harrington, Greenwood, Bridgeville, Lewes, Milton

Front Royal, Strasburg, Marshall, Middleburg, Herndon, Vienna, Arlington, Washington, Fairfax, Alexandria, Cambridge, Seaford, Georgetown, Frankford

Woodstock, New Market, Mt. Jackson, Luray, Stanley, Shenandoah, Warrenton, Manassas, Dale City, Woodbridge, St. Charles, White Plains, Chesapeake Beach, Prince Frederick, Laurel, Delmar, Selbyville

Harrisonburg, Bridgewater, Dayton, Madison, Culpeper, Remington, Sperryville, Triangle, LaPlata, Leonardtown, Salisbury, Fruitland

Stafford, Falmouth, Fredericksburg, Orange, Gordonsville, Colonial Beach, Oak Grove, Montrose, Lexington Pk., Princess Anne, Snow Hill, Chincoteague

Charlottesville, Crozet, Zion, Louisa, Cuckoo, Port Royal, Bowling Green, Warsaw, Tappahannock, Lancaster, Tangier, Saxis, Parksley, Mappsville, Onancock

Virginia, Waynesboro, Stuarts Draft, Buena Vista, Scottsville, Palmyra, Carmel Church, Central Garage, King & Queen C.H., Urbanna, Kilmarnock, Irvington, Onley, Belle Haven

Staunton, Lovingston, Shipman, Gum Spr., Ashland, Hanover, Mechanicsville, West Point, Gloucester, Deltaville, Gwynn, Mathews, Exmore, Nassawadox

Amherst, Buckingham, Dillwyn, Richmond, Powhatan, Bon Air, Sandston, Gloucester Pt., Achilles, Cape Charles, Cheriton, Eastville

Madison Hts., Cumberland, Amelia, Chester, Colonial Hts., Hopewell, Williamsburg, Surry, Seaford, Poquoson, Kiptopeke

Appomattox, Farmville, Crewe, Blackstone, Petersburg, Colonial Beach, Spring Grove, Newport News, Hampton, Atlantic Ocean

Rustburg, Pamplin City, Hampden-Sydney, Burkeville, Kenbridge, Waverly, Smithfield, Wakefield, Norfolk, Virginia Beach

Altavista, Hurt, Gladys, Brookneal, Drakes Branch, Victoria, Kenbridge, McKenney, Sussex, Windsor, Portsmouth, Suffolk, Chesapeake

Gretna, Volens, Chase City, South Hill, Jarratt, Lawrenceville, Courtland, Franklin, Emporia

Chatham, Halifax, South Boston, Boydton, Clarksville, Brodnax, La Crosse, Bethel, Virgilina, Roanoke Rapids, Pleasant Hill, Murfreesboro, Garysburg, N.C.

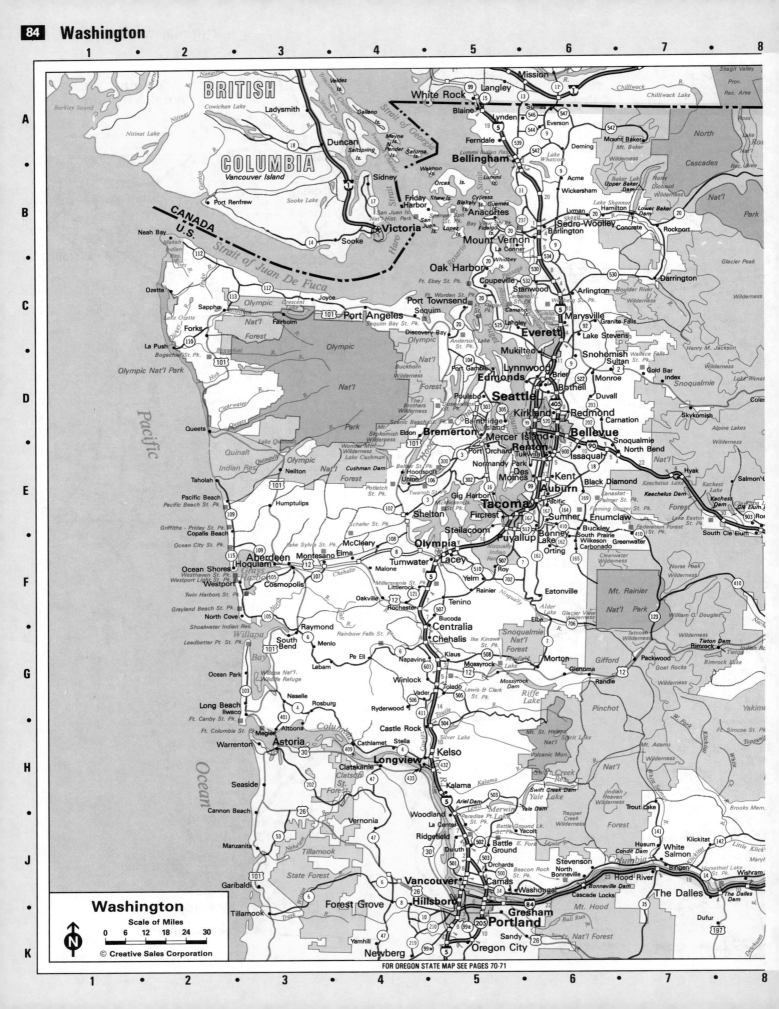

Washington

Scale of Miles

0 6 12 18 24 30

© Creative Sales Corporation

FOR OREGON STATE MAP SEE PAGES 70-71

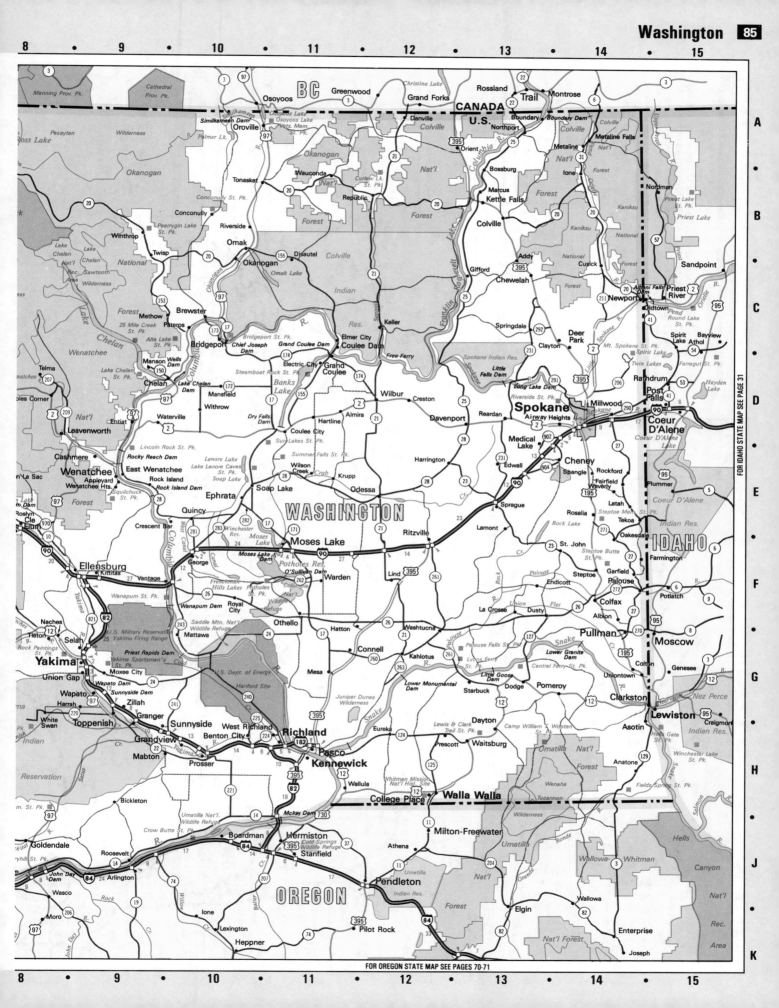

FOR IDAHO STATE MAP SEE PAGE 31

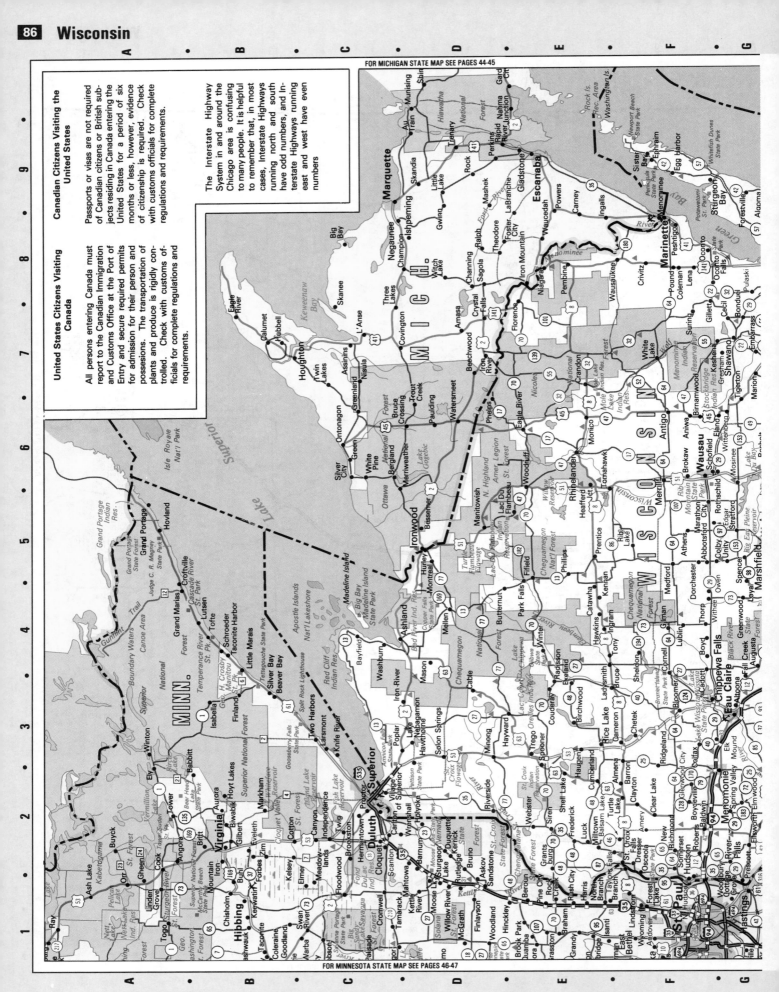

FOR MICHIGAN STATE MAP SEE PAGES 44-45

FOR MINNESOTA STATE MAP SEE PAGES 46-47

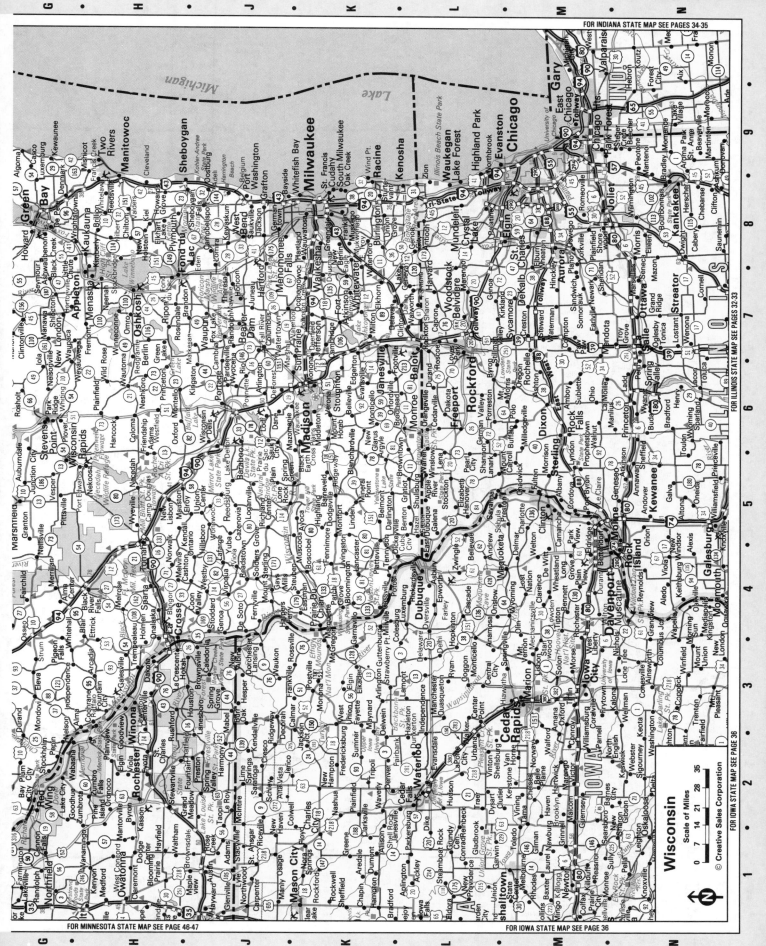

FOR IOWA STATE MAP SEE PAGE 36

FOR ILLINOIS STATE MAP SEE PAGES 32-33

Wisconsin

Scale of Miles

0 7 14 21 28 35

© Creative Sales Corporation

Wyoming

Scale of Miles

0 7 14 21 28 35

© Creative Sales Corporation

N

FOR MONTANA STATE MAP SEE PAGE 51

FOR IDAHO STATE MAP SEE PAGE 31

MT.

IDAHO

WYOM

UTAH

COLORADO

Yellowstone National Park

Grand Teton National Park

Bridger-Teton National Forest

Shoshone National Forest

Targhee National Forest

Caribou National Forest

Wasatch National Forest

Great Salt Lake

Emigrant, Pray, Chico Hot Springs, Cameron, Big Sky, Gardiner, Gallatin National Forest

Nye, Dean, Fishtail, Joliet, Boyd, Edgar, Roberts, Fromberg, Bridger, Belfry, Bearcreek, Red Lodge, Cooke City, Clark, Elk Basin, Frannie, Deaver, Cowley, Powell, Garland, Byron, Lovell, Burlington

Mammouth Springs Jct., Tower Jct., Norris Jct., Canyon Jct., Madison Jct., Lake Jct., Old Faithful, W. Thumb Jct.

Cody, Ralston, Emblem, Greybull, Shell, Basin, Otto, Meeteetse, Manderson, Worland

Grant, Dell, Lima, Lima Reservoir, Spencer, Blue Dome, Dubois, Ashton, St. Anthony, Parker, Chester, Newdale, Sugar City, Teton, Tetonia, Driggs, Rexburg, Lorenzo, Menan, Thornton, Heise, Victor, Moose, Teton Village, Wilson, Jackson, Hoback Jct.

Moran Jct., Jenny Lake, Kelly, Bondurant, Dubois, Burris, Crowheart, Morton, Pavillion, Kinnear, Ethete, Fort Washakie, Riverton, Lander, Hudson, Arapahoe, St. Stephens, Shoshoni, Lysite, Moneta

Grass Creek, Hamilton Dome, Thermopolis, E. Thermopolis, Kirby, Lucerne, Boysen Res., Boysen State Park

Mud Lake, Hamer, Roberts, Lewisville, Rigby, Ririe, Ucon, Idaho Falls, Iona, Ammon, Shelley, Basalt, Firth, Blackfoot, Moreland, Rockford, Pingree, Fort Hall, Chubbuck, Pocatello, Portneuf, Inkom, Bancroft, Conda, Soda Springs

Alpine Jct., Etna, Freedom, Thayne, Bedford, Turnerville, Grover, Auburn, Afton, Fairview, Smoot, Merna, Cora, Pinedale, Daniel, Boulder, Marbleton, Big Piney, Calpet, La Barge, Big Sandy, Farson, Eden, Atlantic City, South Pass City

Rockland, Pauline, Robin, Virginia, Downey, Thatcher, Swanlake, McCammon, Arimo, Lava Hot Springs, Grace, Bennington, Georgetown, Bern, Ovid, Paris, Montpelier, Dingle, Border, Cokeville

Malad City, Holbrook, Samaria, Banida, Clifton, Dayton, Preston, Whitney, Bloomington, Mink Creek, St. Charles, Fish Haven, Garden City, Laketown, Sage, Frontier, Kemmerer, Diamondville, Elkol, Opal, Granger, Superior, Reliance, Rock Springs, Point of Rocks, Table Rock, Red Desert, Wamsutter, Bitter Creek

Snowville, Portage, Clarkston, Lewiston, Richmond, Cove, Cornish, Amalga, Smithfield, Newton, Meadowville, Benson, Hyde Park, Round Valley, Randolph, Sage Jct., Franklin

Plymouth, Fielding, Beaverdam, Riverside, Collinston, Cache Jct., Logan, Hyrum, Wellsville, Paradise, Woodruff, Little America, Green River, Quealy

Cedar Springs, Tremonton, Pentose, Elwood, Bear River City, Corinne, Deweyville, College, Mantua, Brigham City, Perry, Willard, Liberty, Huntsville, Fort Bridger, Carter, Lyman, Mountain View, Urie, Millburne, Robertson, Granger

Hot Sprs, Plain City, N. Ogden, Harrisville, Ogden, Washington Terrace, Wahsatch, Castle Rock, Emory, Evanston, Piedmont, Lonetree, Burntfork, McKinnon, Manila, Green Lake

Roy, Clearfield, Riverdale, Kanesville, Hooper, Clinton, Syracuse, Layton, Kaysville, Centerville, Farmington, Milton, Morgan, Croydon, Henefer, Echo, Coalville, Hoytsville, Devils Slide

Salt Lake City, N. Salt Lake, Bountiful, Woods Cross, Magna, Holladay, Snyderville, Wanship, Peoa, Oakley, Kimball, Marion

Flaming Gorge Reservoir, Flaming Gorge National Recreational Area, Hiawatha, Baggs, Manila, Ashley

Reservation, Wind River Indian Reservation, Ft. Hall Indian Reservation

FOR MONTANA STATE MAP SEE PAGE 51

FOR SOUTH DAKOTA STATE MAP SEE PAGE 74

FOR NEBRASKA STATE MAP SEE PAGES 52-53

FOR COLORADO STATE MAP SEE PAGES 22-23

MT.

SOUTH DAK.

NEBRASKA

CO.

Northern Cheyenne Indian Reservation

Custer National Forest

Belle Fourche Reservoir

Thunder Basin Nat'l Grassland

Black Hills

Devils Tower Nat. Monument

Bighorn National Forest

Medicine Bow National Forest

Pathfinder Reservoir

Seminoe Reservoir

Glendo Res.

Wheatland Res. No. 2

Oglala National Grasslands

Nebraska National Forest

Pine Ridge Indian Reservation

Buffalo Gap National Grassland

Badlands National Park

Wind Cave National Park

Mt. Rushmore Nat'l Mem.

Crazy Horse Mon.

Roosevelt National Forest

Medicine Bow Nat'l Forest

Routt National Forest

Sheridan · Gillette · Buffalo · Casper · Douglas · Glenrock · Rawlins · Laramie · Cheyenne

Rapid City · Sturgis · Deadwood · Lead · Spearfish · Belle Fourche · Newcastle · Hot Springs · Edgemont

Scottsbluff · Gering · Torrington · Chadron · Alliance · Sidney · Kimball · Bridgeport · Bayard

Sterling · Fort Collins

A · B · C · D · E · F · G · H · J · K

8 · 9 · 10 · 11 · 12 · 13

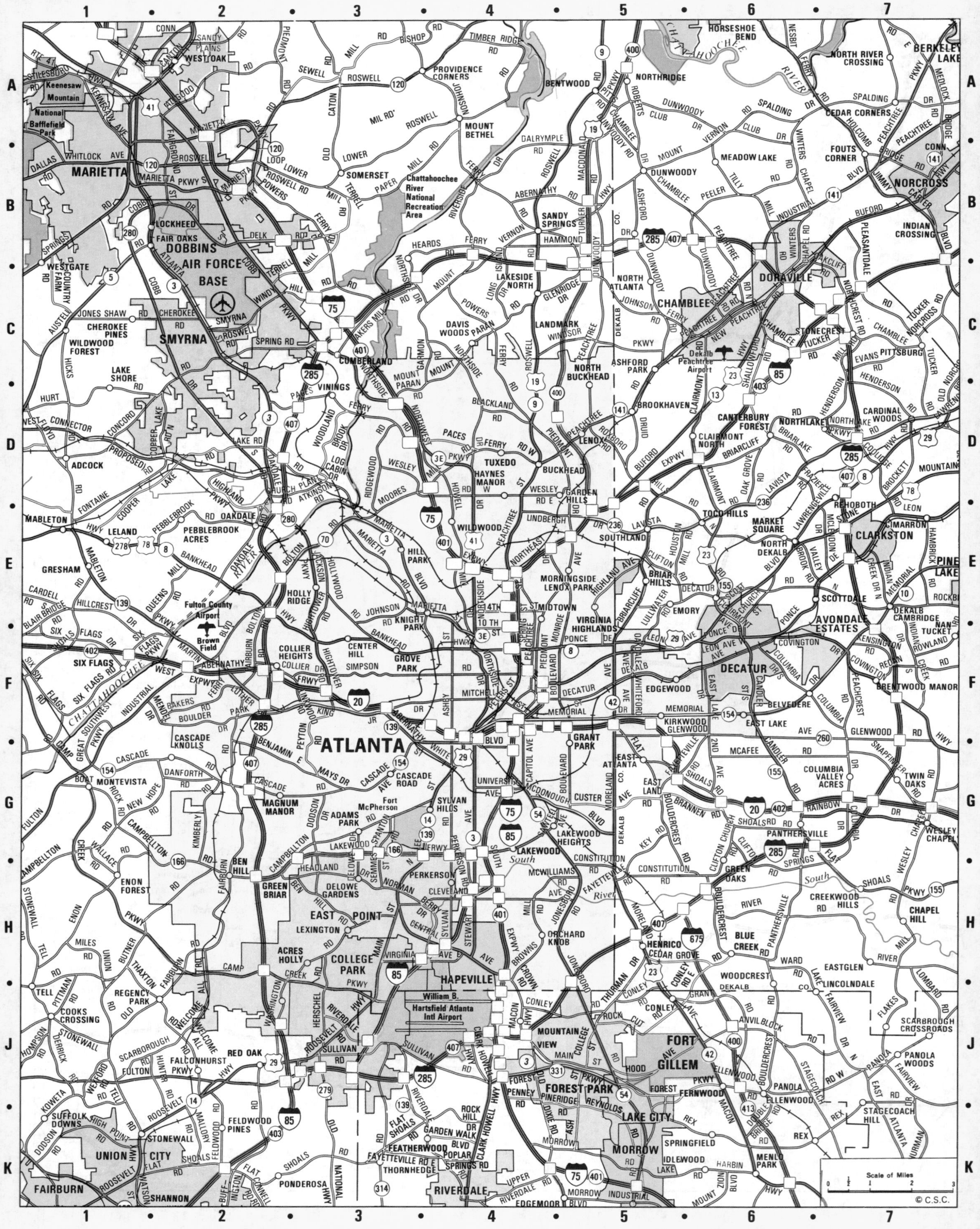

ATLANTA
MARIETTA
SMYRNA
DOBBINS AIR FORCE BASE
Keenesaw Mountain National Battlefield Park
WEST OAK
LOCKHEED
FAIR OAKS
WESTGATE
CHEROKEE PINES
WILDWOOD FOREST
LAKE SHORE
ADCOCK
MABLETON
LELAND
PEBBLEBROOK ACRES
OAKDALE
GRESHAM
SIX FLAGS
Fulton County Airport Brown Field
CASCADE KNOLLS
MONTEVISTA
MAGNUM MANOR
ENON FOREST
BEN HILL
GREEN BRIAR
EAST POINT
LEXINGTON
DELOWE GARDENS
ACRES HOLLY
COLLEGE PARK
HAPEVILLE
William B. Hartsfield Atlanta Intl Airport
REGENCY PARK
COOKS CROSSING
RED OAK
FALCONHURST
SUFFOLK DOWNS
UNION CITY
FAIRBURN
SHANNON
FELDWOOD PINES
PONDEROSA
THORNHEDGE
RIVERDALE
FEATHERWOOD
EDGEMOOR
FOREST PARK
LAKE CITY
MORROW
MOUNTAIN VIEW
FORT GILLEM
FERNWOOD
ELLENWOOD
MENLO PARK
REX
STAGECOACH HILL
PANOLA WOODS
SCARBROUGH CROSSROADS
LINCOLNDALE
WOODCREST
HENRICO
CEDAR GROVE
BLUE CREEK
ORCHARD KNOB
CREEKWOOD HILLS
CHAPEL HILL
PANTHERSVILLE
GREEN OAKS
TWIN OAKS
COLUMBIA VALLEY ACRES
WESLEY CHAPEL
BELVEDERE
EAST LAKE
KIRKWOOD
GLENWOOD
DECATUR
EDGEWOOD
AVONDALE ESTATES
BRENTWOOD MANOR
CLARKSTON
PINE LAKE
CIMARRON
REHOBOTH
NORTH DEKALB
MARKET SQUARE
TOCO HILLS
SOUTHLAND
EMORY
BRIAR HILLS
MORNINGSIDE LENOX PARK
VIRGINIA HIGHLANDS
MIDTOWN
GRANT PARK
EAST ATLANTA
LAKEWOOD HEIGHTS
SYLVAN HILLS
CASCADE ROAD
ADAMS PARK
Fort McPherson
PERKERSON
COLLIER HEIGHTS
CENTER HILL
GROVE PARK
HOLLY RIDGE
KNIGHT PARK
HILL PARK
WILDWOOD
TUXEDO
HAYNES MANOR
BUCKHEAD
GARDEN HILLS
LENOX
NORTH BUCKHEAD
BROOKHAVEN
ASHFORD PARK
CLAIRMONT NORTH
CANTERBURY FOREST
NORTHLAKE
CARDINAL WOODS
STONECREST
CHAMBLEE
Dekalb Peachtree Airport
DORAVILLE
NORTH ATLANTA
LANDMARK
LAKESIDE NORTH
DAVIS WOODS
MOUNT PARAN
SANDY SPRINGS
CUMBERLAND
VININGS
Chattahoochee River National Recreation Area
SOMERSET
MOUNT BETHEL
PROVIDENCE CORNERS
BENTWOOD
NORTHRIDGE
DUNWOODY
MEADOW LAKE
HORSESHOE BEND
NORTH RIVER CROSSING
BERKELEY LAKE
CEDAR CORNERS
FOUTS CORNER
NORCROSS
INDIAN CROSSING
CHATTAHOOCHEE RIVER
South River
Scale of Miles
© C.S.C.

BALTIMORE

REISTERSTOWN
GLYNDON
GLEN MORRIS
SUBURBIA
OWINGS MILLS
RANDALLSTOWN
PIKESVILLE
CATONSVILLE
ELLICOTT CITY
ARBUTUS
COCKEYSVILLE
TIMONIUM
LUTHERVILLE
TOWSON
RUXTON
CARNEY
PARKVILLE
PERRY HALL
WHITE MARSH
ESSEX
DUNDALK
BROOKLYN
GLEN BURNIE
FERNDALE
LINTHICUM
ODENTON

PATAPSCO RIVER

Gunpowder Falls State Park
Patapsco Valley State Park
Druid Lake
Lake Montebello
Loch Raven Reservoir
Curtis Bay
Sparrows Point
Old Road Bay
Back River
Middle River

FORT GEORGE G MEADE MILITARY RESERVATION
PATUXENT WILDLIFE RESEARCH CENTER
Baltimore Washington International Airport
US Coast Guard Yard
US Army General Services Depot

RIVIERA BEACH
BAYSIDE BEACH
PINEHURST ON THE BAY
VENICE ON THE BAY
PASADENA
SEVERNA PARK

Scale of Miles
0   1   2   3

© C.S.C.

This is a map of the Birmingham, Alabama metropolitan area with a coordinate grid (columns 1–7, rows A–K).

Cities, towns, and place names shown on the map include:

SAYRE, KILGORE, LINN CORSSING, BESSIE, GRAYSVILLE, CARDIFF, ALDEN, ADAMSVILLE, LINDBERGH, UNION GROVE, DIVIDE STATION, MT. OLIVE, BROOKSIDE, FIELDSTOWN, MINERAL SPRINGS, REPUBLIC, COALBURG, WALKER CHAPEL, LEWISBURG, GARDENDALE, NEW CASTLE, FULTONDALE, KETONA, TARRANT CITY, GREENS STATION, ROBINWOOD, CHALKVILLE, CENTER POINT, PINSON, ROEBUCK PLAZA, ALTON, BAY VIEW, DOCENA, MULGA, MAYTOWN, SYLVAN SPRINGS, EDGEWATER, BIRMINGHAM, IRONDALE, JEFFERSON PARK, GRANTS MILL, OVERTON, PLEASANT GROVE, FAIRFIELD, ISHKOODA, MIDFIELD, HOMEWOOD, MOUNTAIN BROOK, CAHABA HEIGHTS, HUEYTOWN, BRIGHTON, BROWNSVILLE, WENONAH, OXMOOR, LIPSCOMB, SHANNON, VESTAVIA HILLS, ROCKY RIDGE, BESSEMER, MUSCODA, HOOVER, PATTON CHAPEL, MC CALLA, MORGAN, GREENWOOD, ELVIRA, EASTERN VALLEY, ACTION, NEW HOPE, CHELSEA, GENERY, HELENA, PELHAM

Points of interest: Birmingham Municipal Airport, Southern Museum of Flight, Ruffner Mtn. Nature Ctr., Museum of Art, Civil Rights Inst., University of Alabama Medical Center (U.A.B.), Birmingham Sou. College, Miles College, Samford University, Sloss Furnaces, Vulcan Statue, Civic Center, Oak Mountain State Park, Lake Purdy, Bayview Lake

JEFFERSON CO. / SHELBY CO.

Scale of Miles: 0 1 2 3

N (compass, north arrow)

© C.S.C.

Billerica Wilmington Lynnfield PEABODY SALEM Danversport

BURLINGTON Reading WAKEFIELD LYNN Swampscott

Bedford WOBURN Stoneham SAUGUS NAHANT BAY

LEXINGTON Winchester MELROSE MEDFORD MALDEN REVERE BROAD SOUND Nahant

ARLINGTON SOMERVILLE EVERETT CHELSEA Winthrop MASSACHUSETTS

WALTHAM BELMONT CAMBRIDGE Charlestown LOGAN INTERNATIONAL AIRPORT BAY

Weston WATERTOWN Brighton BOSTON BOSTON HARBOR DEER ISLAND

NEWTON BROOKLINE Roxbury Dorchester THOMPSON ISLAND LONG ISLAND Hull

WELLESLEY NEEDHAM Jamaica Plain SUFFOLK QUINCY BAY Hingham

Roslindale Hyde Park Mattapan QUINCY Hingham

DEDHAM MILTON Weymouth

Dover Westwood BRAINTREE WEYMOUTH

NORWOOD Medfield Walpole CANTON RANDOLPH

Scale of Miles

0 1 2 3

© Arrow Map, Inc.

NIAGARA FALLS
ECHOTA
NIAGARA FALLS
LA SALLE
BERKHOLTZ
Niagara Falls International Airport
Oppenheim Zoo
BEACH RIDGE
PENDLETON
RAPIDS
MILLERSPORT
ST. JOHNSBURG
NASHVILLE
HOFFMAN
WENDELVILLE
ELSERS CORNERS
CHIPPAWA
SANDY BEACH
PEACH HAVEN
EDGEWATER
WURLITZER PARK
SAWYER
MARTINSVILLE
SWORMVILLE
Amherst Airport
Steffen Airport
NORTH TONAWANDA
GETZVILLE
EAST AMHERST
CLARENCE CENTER
S.U.N.Y. Buffalo
Big Six Mile Creek Park
Whitehaven
Grand Island
TONAWANDA
GRANDYLE VILLAGE
KENMORE
NORTH BAILEY
AMHERST
Park C.C.
Buffalo C.C.
HARRIS HILL
SNYDER
Sheridan Park
FERRY VILLAGE
Beaver Island State Park
EGGERTSVILLE
SNYDER
WILLIAMSVILLE
STEVENSVILLE
SNYDER
S.U.N.Y. Buffalo
Buffalo International Airport
BOWMANSVILLE
Fort Erie Airport
FORT ERIE NORTH
SUNY Coll Buffalo
Delaware Park
Buffalo Zoo
DEPEW
LANCASTER
POINT ABINO
RIDGEWAY
CRESCENT PARK
FORT ERIE
ERIE BEACH
Fort Erie Race Track
Buffalo Museum of Science
CHEEKTOWAGA
BELLEVUE
Como Park
THUNDER BAY
CRYSTAL BEACH
Crescent Beach
Waverly Beach
Erie Beach
Airport
War Mem. Stadium
SLOAN
BLOSSOM
ELMA
Buffalo Air Park
GARDENVILLE
Botanical Gardens
Buffalo Harbor
BUFFALO
WEST SENECA
EAST SENECA
ELMA CENTER
EBENEZER
SPRINGBROOK
CANADA
UNITED STATES
ONTARIO
NEW YORK
WELLAND CO.
ERIE CO.
Lake Erie
LACKAWANNA
BLASDELL
WOODLAWN
BAY VIEW
WINDOM
EAST HAMBURG
WEBSTER CORNERS
Orchard Park Airport
Proner Airport
ATHOL SPRINGS
BIG TREE
ORCHARD PARK
LOCKSLEY PARK
South Shore C.C.
MT. VERNON
WANAKAH
CARNEGIE
Orchard Park C.C.
DUELLS CORNERS
Jewett-Holmwood
CLIFTON HEIGHTS
PINEHURST
SCRANTON
ARMOR
Erie Co. Fairgrounds
ELLICOTT
JEWETTVILLE
ELLICOTT HEIGHTS
GRIFFINS MILLS
HIGHLAND-ON-THE-LAKE
LAKE VIEW
HAMBURG
Chestnut Ridge Park
WEST FALLS
WATER VALLEY
Lakeview Airport
Eighteen Mile Creek
NORTH EVANS
JERUSALEM CORNERS
DERBY
EDEN VALLEY
NORTH BOSTON
ANGOLA-ON-THE-LAKE
EVANS
EAST EDEN
PATCHIN

Scale of Miles
0   1   2   3

© C.S.C.

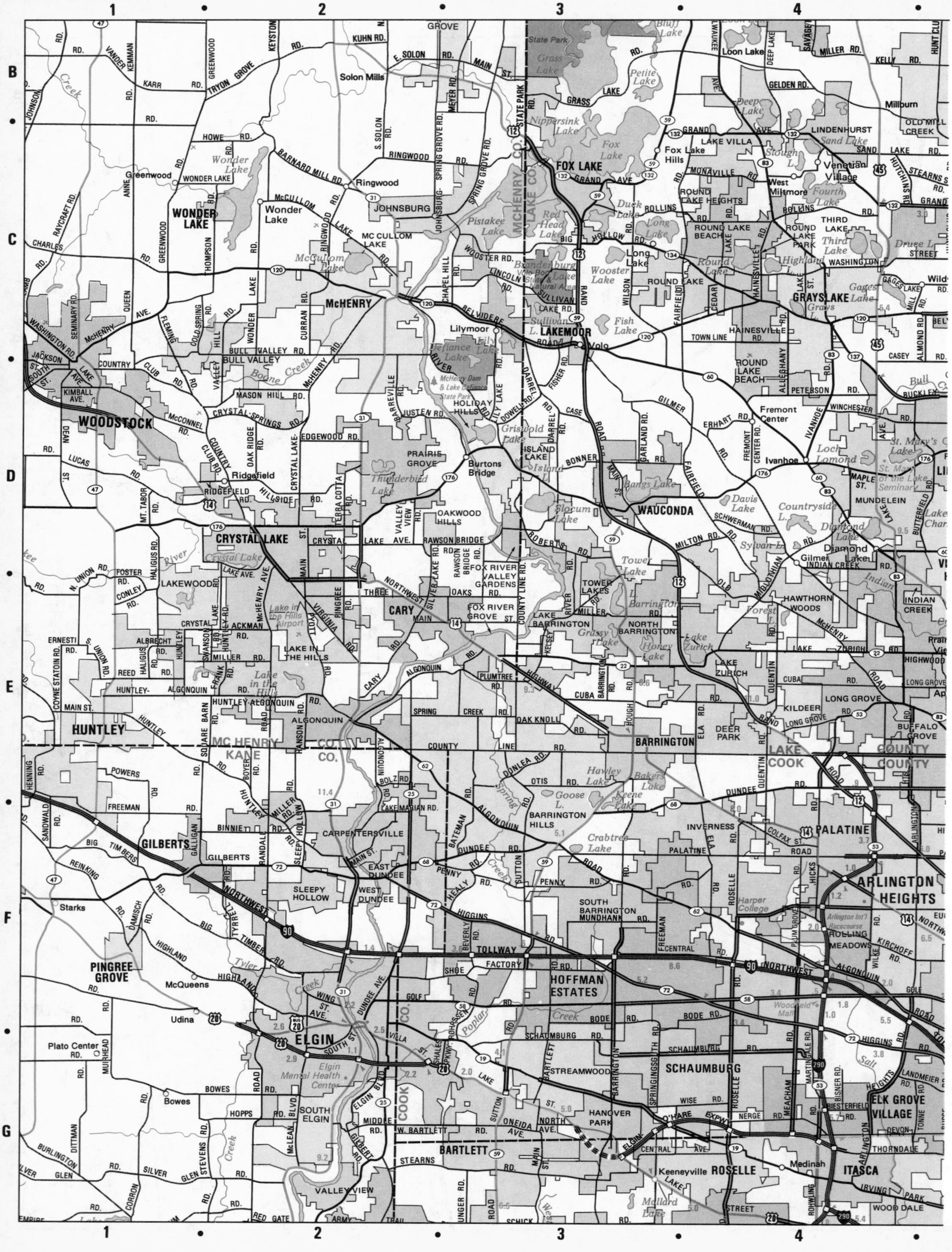

Solon Mills
Fox Lake
Lake Villa
Lindenhurst
Millburn
Loon Lake
Fox Lake Hills
Venetian Village
West Miltmore
Round Lake Heights
Round Lake Beach
Round Lake Park
Round Lake
Third Lake
Grayslake
Hainesville
Greenwood
Ringwood
Wonder Lake
Johnsburg
McCullom Lake
McHenry
Lilymoor
Lakemoor
Volo
Long Lake
Woodstock
Holiday Hills
Round Lake Beach
Fremont Center
Ivanhoe
Ridgefield
Prairie Grove
Burtons Bridge
Oakwood Hills
Wauconda
Mundelein
Crystal Lake
Lakewood
Rawson Bridge
Fox River Valley Gardens
Tower Lakes
Hawthorn Woods
Indian Creek
Lake in the Hills
Cary
Fox River Grove
Lake Barrington
North Barrington
Lake Zurich
Kildeer
Long Grove
Huntley
Algonquin
Deer Park
Barrington
Buffalo Grove
MC HENRY CO.
KANE CO.
LAKE COUNTY
COOK COUNTY
Gilberts
Carpentersville
Barrington Hills
Inverness
Palatine
Arlington Heights
East Dundee
West Dundee
Sleepy Hollow
South Barrington
Rolling Meadows
Starks
Pingree Grove
Hoffman Estates
McQueens
Udina
Elgin
Plato Center
Schaumburg
Streamwood
Bowes
South Elgin
Hanover Park
Elk Grove Village
Bartlett
Keeneyville
Roselle
Medinah
Itasca
Valley View
Wood Dale

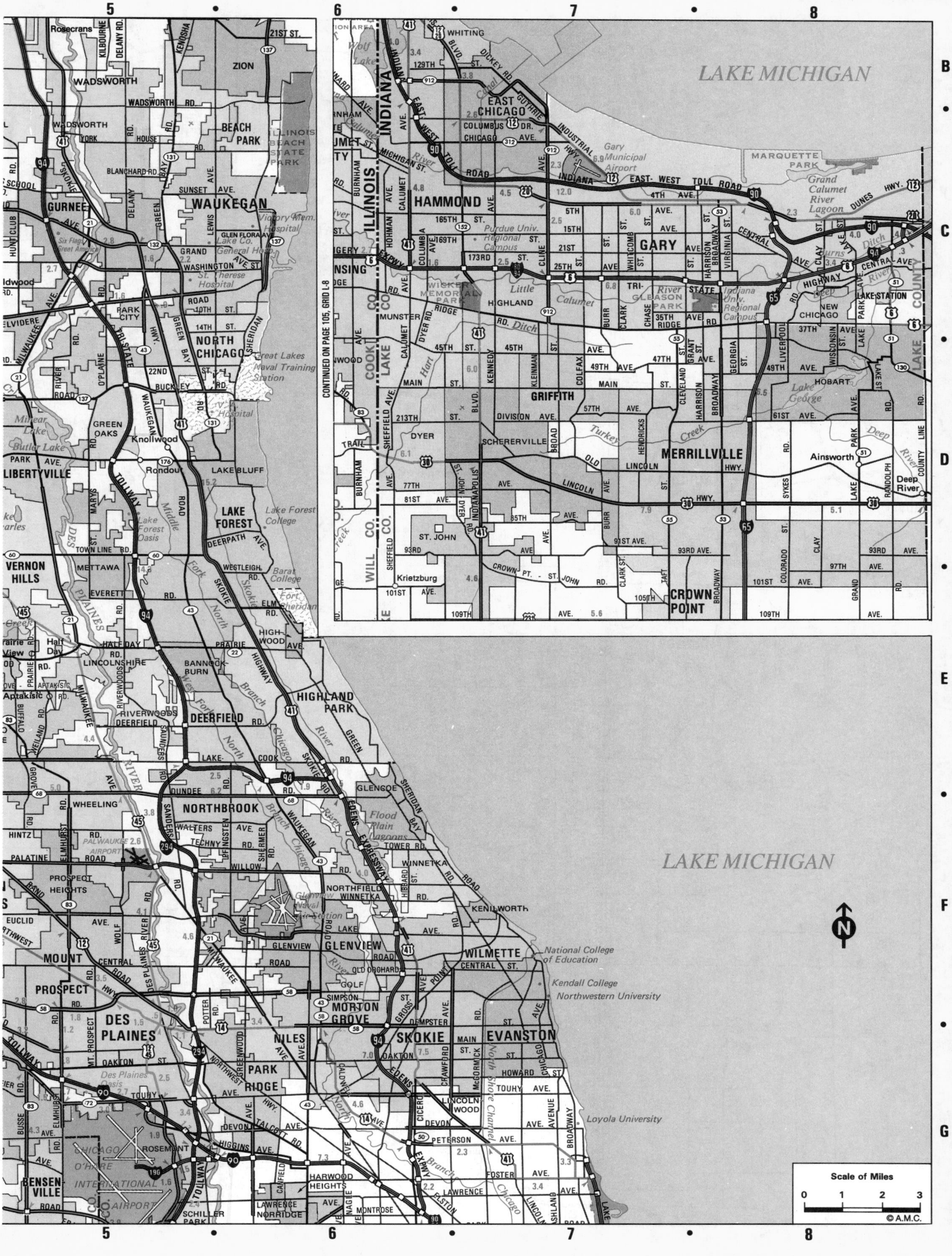
5
6
7
8
B
C
D
E
F
G
LAKE MICHIGAN
LAKE MICHIGAN
CONTINUED ON PAGE 105, GRID L-8
Rosecrans
ZION
WADSWORTH
BEACH PARK
ILLINOIS BEACH STATE PARK
WAUKEGAN
Victory Mem. Hospital
Lake Co. General Hosp.
St. Therese Hospital
GURNEE
Six Flags Great America
PARK CITY
NORTH CHICAGO
Great Lakes Naval Training Station
Hospital
GREEN OAKS
Knollwood
Rondout
LAKE BLUFF
LIBERTYVILLE
LAKE FOREST
Lake Forest College
Lake Forest Oasis
VERNON HILLS
METTAWA
Barat College
Fort Sheridan
HIGHWOOD
Half Day
LINCOLNSHIRE
BANNOCKBURN
Aptakisic
RIVERWOODS
DEERFIELD
HIGHLAND PARK
NORTHBROOK
WHEELING
GLENCOE
Flood Plain Lagoons
PALWAUKEE AIRPORT
PROSPECT HEIGHTS
NORTHFIELD
WINNETKA
KENILWORTH
Glenview Naval Air Station
GLENVIEW
WILMETTE
National College of Education
Kendall College
Northwestern University
MOUNT PROSPECT
DES PLAINES
MORTON GROVE
SKOKIE
EVANSTON
NILES
PARK RIDGE
Des Plaines Oasis
LINCOLNWOOD
Loyola University
ROSEMONT
CHICAGO O'HARE INTERNATIONAL AIRPORT
BENSENVILLE
HARWOOD HEIGHTS
NORRIDGE
SCHILLER PARK
WHITING
EAST CHICAGO
Gary Municipal Airport
MARQUETTE PARK
Grand Calumet River Lagoon
HAMMOND
Purdue Univ. Regional Campus
GARY
INDIANA
ILLINOIS
WICKER MEMORIAL PARK
HIGHLAND
TRI-STATE
GLEASON PARK
Indiana Univ. Regional Campus
LAKE STATION
NEW CHICAGO
MUNSTER
HOBART
Lake George
GRIFFITH
DYER
SCHERERVILLE
MERRILLVILLE
Ainsworth
Deep River
ST. JOHN
Krietzburg
CROWN POINT
COOK CO.
LAKE CO.
WILL CO.
LAKE COUNTY
Scale of Miles
0 1 2 3
© A.M.C.

1   2   3   4

Lake Campton
Empire RD.
Wasco
CORRON RD.
BOLCUM RD.
BURR RD.
OTTER RD.
RANDALL RD.
RED GATE RD.
VALLEY
ARMY TRAIL
COUNTRY CLUB RD.
DUNHAM RD.
WAYNE
MUNGER ROAD
SCHICK
WEBB
Mallard Lake
STREET
290
Wood Dale
BLOOMINGDALE
Cloverdale
DEAN ST.
PRAIRIE ST.
31
SMITH RD.
64
NORTH
INGALTON
ARMY TRAIL ROAD
FAIR OAKS RD.
KUHN RD.
GARY AVE.
CAROL STREAM
GLENDALE HEIGHTS
GLEN ELLYN
355
ADDISON
NORTH
Villa Park

ELBURN
LA FOX
KESLINGER RD.
38
St. CHARLES
KANE CO.
DUPAGE CO.
DuPage County Airport
HAWTHORNE LA.
POWIS RD.
KRESS RD.
PRINCE CROSSING RD.
Prince Crossing
COUNTY FARM RD.
64
GENEVA
JEWELL
PRESIDENT ST.
GENEVA RD.
Wheaton College
3.6
ST. CHARLES
LOMBARD
83
VILLA PARK

HUGHES RD.
POULEY
KANEVILLE RD.
BUNKER RD.
GREEN ST.
GENEVA
KANE COUNTY FAIRGROUNDS
25
WASHINGTON ST.
WEST CHICAGO
ROOSEVELT RD.
6.1 PKWY.
4.0
HIGH LAKE RD.
59
WINFIELD
WHEATON
ROOSEVELT
President St.
38
York Center
Flowerfield
Highland Hills
OAK

Baldmond
KANEVILLE RD.
MAIN ST.
BATAVIA
Mooseheart
WILSON RD.
4.7
KIRK RD.
KRESS CREEK
FERMI LAB
4.3
WINFIELD RD.
BATAVIA RD.
Herrick Lake
NAPERVILLE RD.
56
Morton Arboretum
355
HIGHLAND
BUTTERFIELD
22ND
34
OGDEN AVE.

HEALY RD.
TANNER RD.
OAK
31
56
BUTTERFIELD RD.
FERRY RD.
WARRENVILLE
WARRENVILLE RD.
88
TOLLWAY
6.8
NORTH AURORA
88
Marywood
EAST-
WEST
88
TOLLWAY
LISLE
Illinois Benedictine College
DOWNERS GROVE
55TH
MAPLE

SUGAR GROVE
56
BLISS RD.
WINDSOR
HANKES RD.
DEER PATH
INDIAN TRAIL RD.
AURORA
GALENA BLVD.
Aurora University
5.7
31
FARNSWORTH AVE.
CHURCH RD.
SHEFFER RD.
Eola
N. AURORA RD.
RAYMOND DR.
NAPERVILLE
North Central College
OGDEN
8.3
MAPLE
63RD
WOODRIDGE
PLAINFIELD

Montgomery
5TH AVE.
KAUTZ RD.
OGDEN AVE.
Frontenac
AURORA AVE.
OSWEGO
1.6
75TH
WASHINGTON ST.
HOBSON
NAPER
79TH ST.
75TH

MONTGOMERY
MONTGOMERY RD.
83RD
Wheatland
DU PAGE
WILL
87TH
83RD
55
ARGONNE NATIONAL LABORATORY

NE CO.
DALL CO.
DICKSON RD.
GALENA RD.
MILL RD.
31
25
2.6
OSWEGO
30
34
HAFENRICHTER RD.
NORMANTOWN RD.
91ST ST.
95TH ST.
59
9.7
BOUGHTON RD.
LILY CACHE LN.
BOLINGBROOK
53
JOLIET RD.
LEMONT RD.

YORKVILLE
BRISTOL RIDGE RD.
KENNEDY RD.
71
34
WOLFS CROSSING
Wolfs
30
111TH
244TH ST.
PLAINFIELD RD.
LILY CACHE
NORMANTOWN
9.6
ROMEOVILLE
NEW TOLLWAY
DES PLAINES
LEMONT

VAN EMMON RD.
MINKLER RD.
HILLTOP RD.
126
CHERRY RD.
JOHNSON RD.
WHISKEY RD.
4.0
135TH ST.
126
Lockport
Lake Renwick
Lewis University
AIRPORT RD.
TAYLOR RD.
53
Romeoville
143RD
CREME RD.
Long RD.

AMENT RD.
ASHLEY
WALKER
WHEELER
RESERVATION RD.
126
Renwick
Mink
Creek
STATESVILLE RD.
Stateville Correctional Center
LOCKPORT
167TH
CEDAR RD.
7

47
CATON FARM RD.
GROVE RD.
SCHLAPP
CATON FARM RD.
CATON FARM
DRAUDEN RD.
5.8
Caton Farm
GAYLORD RD.
CATON
3.3 FARM
Bruce RD.
South Lockport
Fairmont
ROSALIND
175TH

IMMANUEL RD.
PENNIMAN RD.
THEODORE
BLACK RD.
59
BRONK RD.
JOLIET RD.
BLACK RD.
CREST HILL
THEODORE ST.
171
Ridgewood
5.0
6
NEW LENOX

PLATTVILLE
CHICAGO RD.
Plattville
VAN DYKE
RIDGE RD.
SHOREWOOD
River
College of St. Francis
52
7
30
WASHINGTON ST.
Ingalls Park
52
SPENCER RD.
LARAWAY RD.

Lisbon Center
52
80
HOLT RD.
COUNTY LINE
80
KENDALL CO.
GRUNDY CO.
MINOOKA
Illinois & Michigan Canal
ROCKDALE
Preston Heights
53
CHERRY RD.
DELANDY RD.

Scale of Miles
0   1   2   3
© A.M.C.

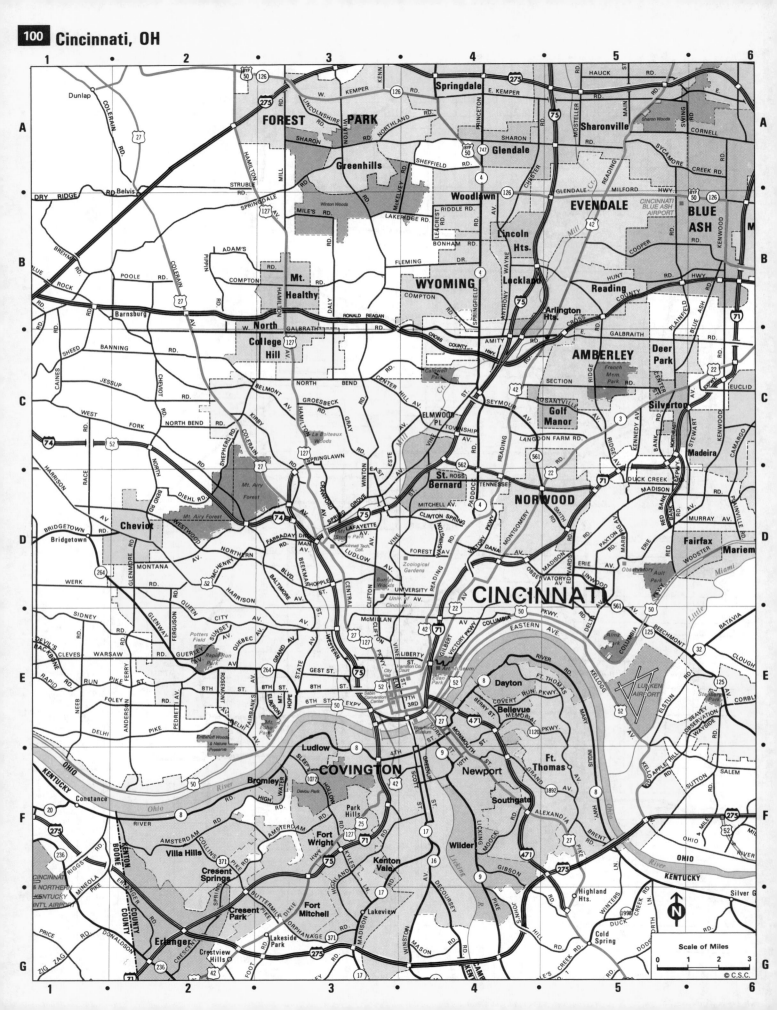

Lake Erie

N

CLEVELAND

LAKEWOOD

ROCKY RIVER

FAIRVIEW PARK

BROOKLYN

BROOK PARK

PARMA HEIGHTS

PARMA

MIDDLEBURG HEIGHTS

BEREA

NORTH ROYALTON

N. ROYALTON

BROADVIEW HEIGHTS

STRONGSVILLE

SEVEN HILLS

INDEPENDENCE

VALLEY VIEW

BRECKSVILLE

SAGAMORE HILLS

NORTHFIELD

MACEDONIA

TWINSBURG

BRUNSWICK

HINCKLEY

RICHFIELD

EVERETT

PENINSULA

BATH

BATH CENTER

GHENT

BOTZUM

ABBEYVILLE

WEYMOUTH

REMSEN CORNERS

GRANGER

BOSTON HEIGHTS

HUDSON

STOW

NEWBURGH HEIGHTS

BROOKLYN HEIGHTS

CUYAHOGA HEIGHTS

GARFIELD HEIGHTS

MAPLE HEIGHTS

NORTH RANDALL

WARRENSVILLE HEIGHTS

BEDFORD

BEDFORD HTS.

WALTON HILLS

OAKWOOD

GLENWILLOW

SOLON

ORANGE

MORELAND HILLS

WOODMERE

PEPPER PIKE

BEACHWOOD

SHAKER HEIGHTS

UNIVERSITY HEIGHTS

CLEVELAND HEIGHTS

EAST CLEVELAND

SOUTH EUCLID

LYNDHURST

MAYFIELD HEIGHTS

RICHMOND HEIGHTS

HIGHLAND HEIGHTS

EUCLID

WICKLIFFE

BRATENAHL

CUYAHOGA CO.
MEDINA CO.

CUYAHOGA CO.
SUMMIT CO.

Lakefront State Park

Burke Lakefront Airport

Gordan Park

Cleveland Municipal Stadium

Edgewater Yacht Club

Institute of Art

Case Western Reserve University

Cleveland State University

John Carroll University

Grace Hosp.

Cleveland Zoological Park

Cuyahoga County Airport

Richmond Mall

Country Club

Pepper Pike Country Club

Ursuline College

Cleveland Hopkins Int'l Airport

Holy Cross Cem.

Cleveland Community College

Parma Comm. Hosp.

Normandy H.S.

Strongsville Airport

Metropolitan Rocky River Reservation

Brecksville V.A. Hosp.

Parkview V.A. Hosp.

Hawthornden St. Hosp.

Northfield Sq. S.C.

Four Points Airport

Bedford Reservation

Tinkers Creek

Cuyahoga Valley National Recreation Area

Furnace Run Park

Brecksville Pkwy. (TOLL)

Briarwood Golf Course

Snowville

Welcome Airport

Macedonia H.S.

Crown Hill Cem.

Cleveland Boys Sch

Hinckley Res.

Virginia Kendall Park

U.S. Military Res.

Scale of Miles
0   1   2   3

© CSC

Moore · Hyatts · HYATTS · Platt · Hollenback · Rome Corners · GALENA · Vans Valley · 605 · 37

Duffy · Home · Shanahan · North · 3 · Trenton · Woodtown

Merchant · Steitz · Rutherford · W. Orange · E. Orange · S. Lackey · LEWIS CENTER · Lewis Center · Jaycox · Big Walnut · CENTER VILLAGE · Center Village

Cook · Harriott · Carriage · Seldom Seen · AFRICA · Africa Rd. · Freeman · HARLEM · Gorsuch · Robins · GreenCook

JEROME · SHAWNEE HILLS · RATHBONE · 745 · 257 · POWELL · 750 · Powell · Polaris Pkwy. · Maxtown · Sunbury · Fancher · Bevelheimer · New Albany-Condit

DUBLIN · DELAWARE · FRANKLIN · MOUNT AIR · Hanawalt · Lazeller Rd. · WESTERVILLE · Smothers · Otterbein College · Walnut St. · Cubbage Rd. · Schrock · Peter Hoover

Plain City · KILEVILLE · 161 · Shier Rings · LINWORTH · WORTHINGTON · Dublin-Granville · RIVERLEA · MINERVA PARK · 3 · HUBER RIDGE · 161 · NEW ALBANY

AMLIN · HAYDEN · CLINTON · Morse · Cooke · Ferris Rd. · GOULD PARK · GAHANNA · Morse

HILLARD · 270 · UPPER ARLINGTON · COLUMBUS · Columbus Park of Roses · Oakland Park · N. Broadway · McCutcheon · BLACKLICK

MUDSOCK · SAN MARGHERITA · MARBLE CLIFF · GRANDVIEW HEIGHTS · Ohio State Univ. · Ohio History Museum · Ohio Dominican College · Port Columbus International Airport · WHITEHALL · 16

NEW ROME · ALTON · VALLEY-VIEW · 670 · State Capital · Broad · Main · BEXLEY · 40 · REYNOLDSBURG · 256 · 70

Galloway · GALLOWAY · BRIGGSDALE · Lou Berliner Park · Livingston · 33 · Capital University · BRICE

GEORGEVILLE · URBANCREST · GROVE CITY · Columbus St. · OBETZ · GROVEPORT · 33 · CANAL WINCHESTER · WATERLOO

DARBYDALE · 665 · PLEASANT CORNERS · London-Groveport · SHADEVILLE · 317 · REESE · Groveport Rd. · 674

HARRISBURG · ORIENT · 762 · FRANKLIN · PICKAWAY · 104 · LOCKBOURNE · U.S. Military Res. · Rickenbacker Air Force Base · LITHOPOLIS

Scale of Miles · 0 1 2 3

©C.S.C.

Scale of Miles
0 1 2 3
© C.S.C.

N

Cities and Places

THORNTON
WESTMINSTER
FEDERAL HEIGHTS
ARVADA
COMMERCE CITY
DUPONT
WELBY
MOUNTAIN VIEW
WHEAT RIDGE
EDGEWATER
LAKEWOOD
GOLDEN
PLEASANT VIEW
EL DORADO ESTATES
IDLEDALE
MORRISON
INDIAN HILLS
TINY TOWN
TWIN FORKS
FENDERS
DENVER
AURORA
GLENDALE
SHERIDAN
ENGLEWOOD
CHERRY HILL VILLAGE
GREENWOOD VILLAGE
LITTLETON
BOW MAR
COLUMBINE VALLEY
GRANDVIEW ESTATES

Counties

ADAMS COUNTY
DENVER COUNTY
JEFFERSON COUNTY
ARAPAHOE COUNTY
DOUGLAS COUNTY

Notable Features

Denver International Airport
Rocky Mountain Arsenal Wildlife Refuge
U.S. Atomic Energy Commission (Rocky Flats Plant)
Standley Lake
Marston Lake
Chatfield Lake
Buckley Air National Guard Base
Lowry Air Force Base
Stapleton International Airport
Cherry Creek Reservoir Park
Centennial Airport
Plains Conservation Center
Federal Correctional Institute
Camp George West (National Guard)
Jefferson Co. Park
Mount Falcon County Park
Red Rocks County Park
Apex County Park
City Park
Denver Botanic Gardens
Denver Zoo
State Capitol
Denver University

Roads/Highways

I-70, I-25, I-225, I-76, I-270, US 6, US 36, US 40, US 85, US 87, US 285, US 287
Pena Blvd., 56th Ave., Tower Rd., 88th Ave., 96th Ave., Proposed I-470, E-470 Toll
Colfax, Broadway, Alameda, Hampden, Havana, Parker Rd., Quincy, Belleview, Bowles
Wadsworth, Kipling, Federal Blvd., Sheridan, Santa Fe Drive, Morrison Rd.

Scale of Miles

0 1 2 3 4 5

© C.S.C.

6 7 8 9 10 11

LEWISVILLE
3040
35E
STEMMONS
Herbon
2281
15TH ST. 544
14TH ST.
MURPHY
PLANO
75
PLANO RD.

121
DENTON TAP RD.
Creek
Elm
Fork
of
the
Trinity
289
RENNER
190
5
SACHSE
A

COLLIN DALLAS
COUNTY COUNTY
TRINITY MILLS RD.
ADDISON
RICHARDSON
RD.
COIT RD.
78

COPPELL
BELT LINE RD.
North Lake
1380
CARROLLTON
ARAPAHO
BELT LINE RD.
BUCKINGHAM
190
GARLAND
NORTHEAST PKWY.

2499
121
114
VALLEY VIEW LN.
ROYAL LN.
FARMERS BRANCH VIEW
635
FOREST LN.
WHITE
LYNDON
75
EXPWY
GREENVILLE
ABRAMS RD.
WALNUT
JOHNSON
FRWY.
JUPITER
FOREST LN.
MILLER
1ST ST.
66
B

DALLAS-FT. WORTH INTERNATIONAL AIRPORT
97
Grapevine
VALLEY VIEW LN.
HARRY
WALNUT
MARSH LN.
INWOOD RD.
288
HILL
HILLCREST
PRESTON RD.
CENTRAL
SKILLMAN ST.
AUDELIA
PLANO RD.
244
GARLAND RD.
78
635
CENTERVILLE RD.
BROADWAY

35E
NORTHWEST
348
12
114
STOREY RD.
482
DENTON DR.
LEMMON
LOVERS LN.
Love Field
HWY.
CEDAR SPRINGS
MAPLE
Southern Methodist Univ. LN.
12
UNIVERSITY PARK
HIGHLAND PARK
NORTH WEST HWY.
BUCKNER BLVD.
White Rock Lake
Mockingbird LN.
12
THOMASSON RD.
BELT LINE RD.
C

Univ. of Dallas
O'CONNER
NURSERY
Texas Stadium
183
77
354
MOCKINGBIRD
BLVD.
OAK LAWN
35E
GREENVILLE AVE.
HASKELL
ABRAMS AVE.
GRAND AVE.
FERGUSON RD.
12
80
THORNTON FRWY.
SUNNYVALE

356
IRVING
SHADY GROVE
356
Trinity River
DALLAS
ROSS AVE.
ELM ST.
78
30
90
MESQUITE

ROY ORR BLVD.
IRVING BLVD.
SINGLETON BLVD.
BLVD.
COMMERCE
Cotton Bowl
SCYENE RD.
352
MILITARY PKWY.
BRUTON RD.
AUGUSTINE
TREE RD.
D

HUNTER FERRELL
BELT LINE
30
DALLAS-FT. WORTH TURNPIKE
12
FT. WORTH AVE.
30
BLVD.
45
342
CEDAR CREST BLVD.
HATCHER
2ND AVE.
175
LAKE JUNE RD.
ELAM ST.
635
BALCH SPRINGS
20

GRAND PRAIRIE
MAIN ST.
DAVIS ST.
180
JEFFERSON BLVD.
COCKRELL HILL
HAMPTON AVE.
ZANG
35E
67
ILLINOIS
CORINTH ST.
SCHEPPS
CENTRAL
310
HAWN FRWY.
MURDOCK RD.
PEACH

JEFFERSON
Naval Air Station
Mountain Creek Lake
WALTON WALKER
WESTMORELAND RD.
ILLINOIS BLVD.
KEIST BLVD.
SUNNYVALE ST.
BONNIE VIEW RD.
12
635
PIONEER PKWY
1382
303
FLORIDA DR.
408
LEDBETTER
12
DR.
SIMPSON STUART RD.
20
HUTCHINS
E

TARRANT DALLAS CO. CO.
POLO RD.
8TH ST.
TOLL BRIDGE
Lake Joe Pool
RED BIRD LN.
20
WISDOM RD.
DUNCANVILLE
CAMP WISDOM RD.
77
CAMP WISDOM RD.
635
342
JOHNSON B.
LANCASTER HUTCHINS RD.
45
DOWDY RD.
POST OAK RD.
Trinity River
SIMMONS RD.

1382
CEDAR HILL
LOVE
DUNCANVILLE RD.
CEDAR HILL RD.
PLEASANT RUN RD.
LANCASTER
PLEASANT RUN RD.
WINTERGREEN RD.
WILMER
F

CEDAR HILL
MANSFIELD RD.
MARVIN
WILSON
BEAR
BELT LINE
DE SOTO
1382
PARKERVILLE RD.
BELT LINE RD.
DALLAS ELLIS COUNTY COUNTY
75
MALLOY
FERRIS

OVILLA
67
JOE POOL
CREEK
Glenn Heights
77
RED OAK
664
342
664
983
45
660
G

6 7 8 9 10 11
© C.S.C

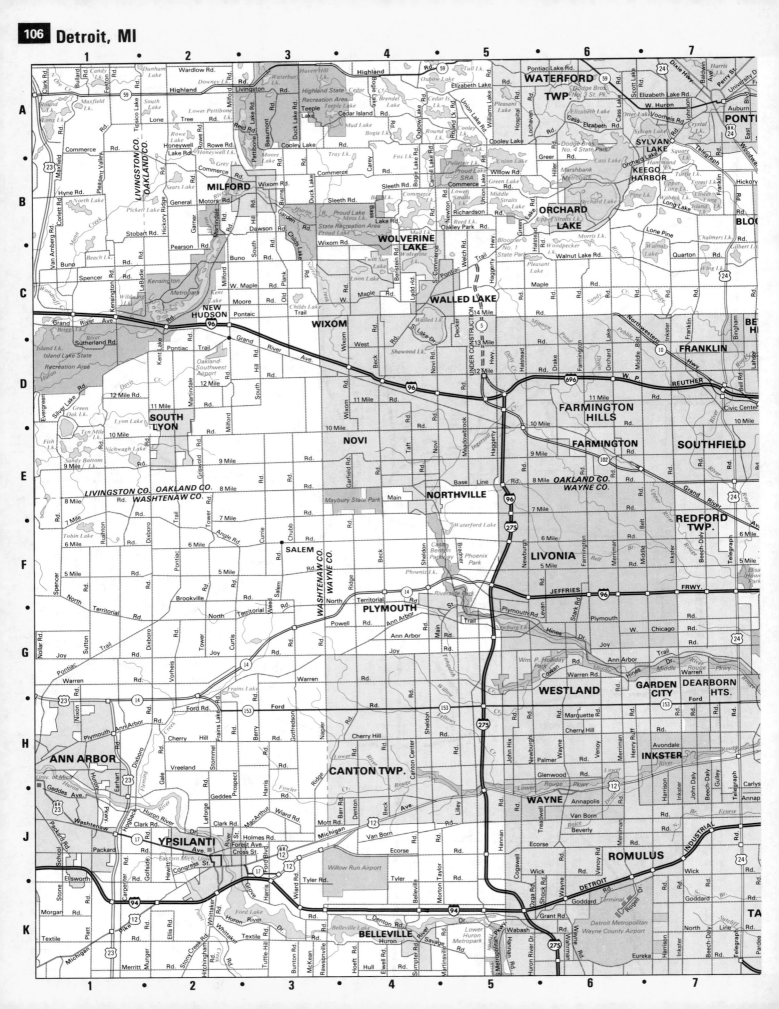

AnchorBay

AUBURN HILLS
ROCHESTER HILLS
UTICA
WALDENBURG Rd.
Berz-Macomb Airport
MOUNT CLEMENS
CLINTON TWP.
PONTIAC
TROY
STERLING HEIGHTS
FRASER
BLOOMFIELD HILLS
BIRMINGHAM
CLAWSON
WARREN
St. Clair Shores
BEVERLY HILLS
ROYAL OAK
MADISON HEIGHTS
ST. CLAIR SHORES
LATHRUP VILLAGE
BERKLEY
HUNTINGTON WOODS
CENTER LINE
ROSEVILLE
HAZEL PARK
EAST DETROIT
OAK PARK
FERNDALE
HARPER WOODS
GROSSE POINTE SHORES
GROSSE POINTE WOODS
Lake St. Claire
HIGHLAND PARK
GROSSE POINT FARMS
DETROIT
HAMTRAMCK
GROSSE POINTE
GROSSE POINTE PARK
U.S.A.
CANADA
Belle Isle Park
WAYNE CO.
ESSEX CO.
DEARBORN
WINDSOR
TECUMSAH
MELVINDALE
RIVER ROUGE
ALLEN PARK
ECORSE
LA SALLE
LINCOLN PARK
TAYLOR
SOUTH GATE
WYANDOTE

Scale of Miles
0   1   2   3

© C.S.C.

LEE COUNTY

CHARLOTTE HARBOR

Cape Coral

Fort Myers

NORTH FORT MYERS

EAST FORT MYERS

FORT MYERS SHORES

BUCKINGHAM

LEHIGH ACRES

ESTERO

BONITA BEACH

FORT MYERS BEACH

ST. JAMES CITY

BOKEELIA

MATLACHA

SANIBEL

CAPTIVA

NORTH CAPTIVA ISLAND

BOCA GRANDE

GULF OF MEXICO

PINE ISLAND

Pine Island Sound

Matlacha Pass

San Carlos Bay

Estero Bay

Caloosahatchee River

CALOOSAHATCHEE NATIONAL WILDLIFE REFUGE

CAPE HAZE-GASPARILLA SOUND AQUATIC PRESERVE

MATLACHA PASS AQUATIC PRESERVE

PINE ISLAND NATIONAL WILDLIFE REFUGE

J.N. "DING" DARLING NATIONAL WILDLIFE REFUGE

ESTERO BAY AQUATIC PRESERVE

KORESHAN STATE PARK

MOUND KEY STATE PARK

BLACK ISLAND

BIG HICKORY ISLAND

SOUTHWEST FLORIDA REGIONAL AIRPORT

FORT MYERS PAGE FIELD

BEAUTIFUL ISLAND

BAYSHORE

SALVISTA

PONDELLA

Cabbage Key

Boca Grande

Useppa Island

York Island

FLAMINGO BAY

Gulf

TAMIAMI TRAIL

IMMOKALEE RD

LEE BLVD

BUCKINGHAM RD

LEONARD RD

NEAL RD

ORANGE RIVER BLVD

PALM BEACH BLVD

ORTIZ AV

CLEVELAND AV

COLONIAL BLVD

DANIELS PKWY

SIX MILE CYPRESS PKWY

METRO PKWY

CYPRESS LAKE DR

COLLEGE PKWY

GLADIOLUS DR

McGREGOR BLVD

SUMMERLIN BLVD

SAN CARLOS BLVD

ESTERO BLVD

SANIBEL-CAPTIVA RD

PERIWINKLE WY

SANIBEL CAUSEWAY (TOLL)

STRINGFELLOW RD

STRINGFELLOW BLVD

PINE ISLAND RD

DEL PRADO BLVD

BURNT STORE RD

SANTA BARBARA BLVD

VETERANS PKWY

ANDERSON AV

BASS RD

BULB RD

TRUCKLAND

CORKSCREW RD

SPRING CREEK RD

COCONUT RD

ALICO RD

LAKE FRONT

ISLAND PARK

NORTH RIVER RD

BAYSHORE RD

SLATER RD

RICH RD

NALLE GRADE RD

DEAL RD

PALM CREEK DR

TICE ST

GUNNERY RD

Scale of Miles

N

© C.S.C.

Scale of Miles
0 1 2 3 4 5

Scale of Miles

© C.S.C.

Scale in Miles
0 2 4
© Trakker Maps, Inc.

N

CALLAHAN
NASSAU COUNTY
ATLANTIC OCEAN

ATLANTIC BEACH
NEPTUNE BEACH
JACKSONVILLE BEACH

JACKSONVILLE

ORANGE PARK

St. Johns River

JACKSONVILLE INTERNATIONAL AIRPORT
JACKSONVILLE NAVAL AIR STATION
JACKSONVILLE HERLONG AIRPORT
CRAIG MUN. AIRPORT
MAYPORT NAVAL STATION

LITTLE TALBOT ISLAND STATE PARK
KINGSLEY PLANTATION STATE HISTORIC SITE
FORT CAROLINE NATIONAL MEMORIAL

NASSAU ST JOHNS RIVER MARSHES AQUATIC PRESERVE
BROWARD ISLANDS

ST JOHNS COUNTY

GUANA RIVER WILDLIFE MANAGEMENT AREA
PINE ISLAND FISH CAMP RD

Ponte Vedra Beach
Palm Valley

TISONIA TOWER
BLACK CREEK TOWER

N

Mosby

Scale of Miles

0 · 1 · 2 · 3 · 4

© C.S.C.

MEXICO CITY AVE.

Kansas City International Airport

Ferrelview

Weatherby Lake

Weatherby

Parkville

Park College

Houston Lake

Riverside

MISSOURI

Gladstone

Oakview

Oakwood Park

Oakwood Oaks

Oakwood Manor

Northmoor

Liberty

William Jewell College

Glenaire

Pleasant Valley

Claycomo

Randolph

Birmingham

Avondale

Fairfax Airport

Douglas Hospital

Downtown Airport

Memorial Park

North Terrace Park

Museum History & Science

Independence

Sugar Creek

Kansas City Kansas

St. Margaret Hosp.

City Hall

Municipal Stadium

General Hosp.

Stock Yards

Blue Summit

Independence

Independence Airport

Lake Quivira

Wyandotte Co.

Johnson Co.

Shawnee

Merriam

Mission

Roeland Park

Fairway

Westwood

Countryside

U. of Kansas Medical Center

Metropolitan Jr. College

Univ. of Mo. at K.C.

Rockhurst College

Nelson Gallery of Art

KANSAS CITY

Kansas City Golf Course

Mission Hills

Indian Hills G.C.

Prairie Village

Baptist Hospital

Milburn Golf Course

Starlight Theatre

Zoo

Swope Park

Ridgeview G.C.

Turners G.C.

Raytown

Stayton Meadows Golf Course

Lenexa

Overland Park

Macklow Brook Golf Course

DeVry Inst. of Tech.

Military Golf Course

Unity Village

Unity Lake

Brookridge Golf Course

Hell Hill G.C.

Leawood

College Blvd.

Greenbriar Golf Course

Avila College

Hillcrest G.C.

Minor Park G.C.

Longview Com. Coll.

Lake Jacomo

Prairie Lee Lake

Lee's Summit

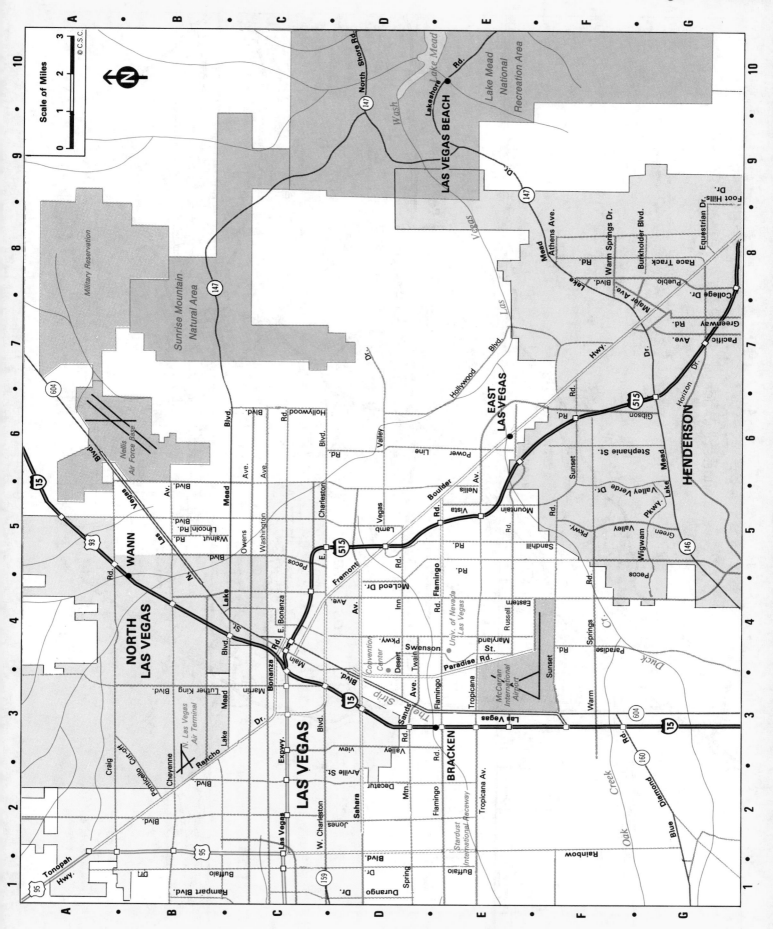

ANGELES NATIONAL FOREST

PACIFIC OCEAN

LOS ANGELES

GLENDALE

BURBANK

PASADENA

SAN FERNANDO

SANTA MONICA

CULVER CITY

BEVERLY HILLS

HOLLYWOOD

SAN GABRIEL

ALHAMBRA

MONTEREY PARK

ROSEMEAD

EL MONTE

TEMPLE CITY

SIERRA MADRE

ALTADENA

SOUTH PASADENA

MONTEBELLO

PICO RIVERA

COMMERCE

BELL GARDENS

HUNTINGTON PARK

MAYWOOD

SOUTH EL MONTE

VERDUGO MOUNTAINS

SANTA MONICA MOUNTAINS

SAN VICENTE MTN.

GRIFFITH PARK

NORTH HOLLYWOOD

STUDIO CITY

SHERMAN OAKS

VAN NUYS

PANORAMA CITY

SUN VALLEY

MISSION HILLS

NORTHRIDGE

RESEDA

TARZANA

ENCINO

CANOGA PARK

WESTWOOD

WEST LOS ANGELES

CENTURY CITY

WEST HOLLYWOOD

PACIFIC PALISADES

VENICE

MARINA DEL REY

ELYSIAN PARK

EAGLE ROCK

BALDWIN HILLS

VETTER PK. 5908

STRAWBERRY PK. 6164

JOSEPHINE PK. 5558

SAN GABRIEL PK. 6161

BROWN MTN. 4484

MT. HARVARD 5440

CONDOR PK. 5439

MT. LUKENS 5074

VERDUGO PK. 3126

Scale of Miles

0 1 2 3

SPRINGS

NORWALK

ARTESIA

CYPRESS

U.S. NAVAL AIR STATION

U.S. NAVAL WEAPONS STATION

SEAL BEACH

DOWNEY

BELLFLOWER

PARAMOUNT

LAKEWOOD

BELL GARDENS

MAYWOOD

SOUTH GATE

CUDAHY

LYNWOOD

LONG BEACH

HUNTINGTON PARK

FLORENCE

COMPTON

CARSON

TERMINAL ISLAND

WATTS

INGLEWOOD

HAWTHORNE

GARDENA

LAWNDALE

TORRANCE

LOMITA

SAN PEDRO

HERMOSA BEACH

REDONDO BEACH

MANHATTAN BEACH

EL SEGUNDO

MARINA DEL REY

PALOS VERDES ESTATES

Rolling Hills

Rolling Hills Estates

Portuguese Bend

Palos Verdes

PT. VINCENTE

LONG PT. of the Pacific

PALOS VERDES PT.

FLATROCK PT.

PT. FERMIN

Venice

N

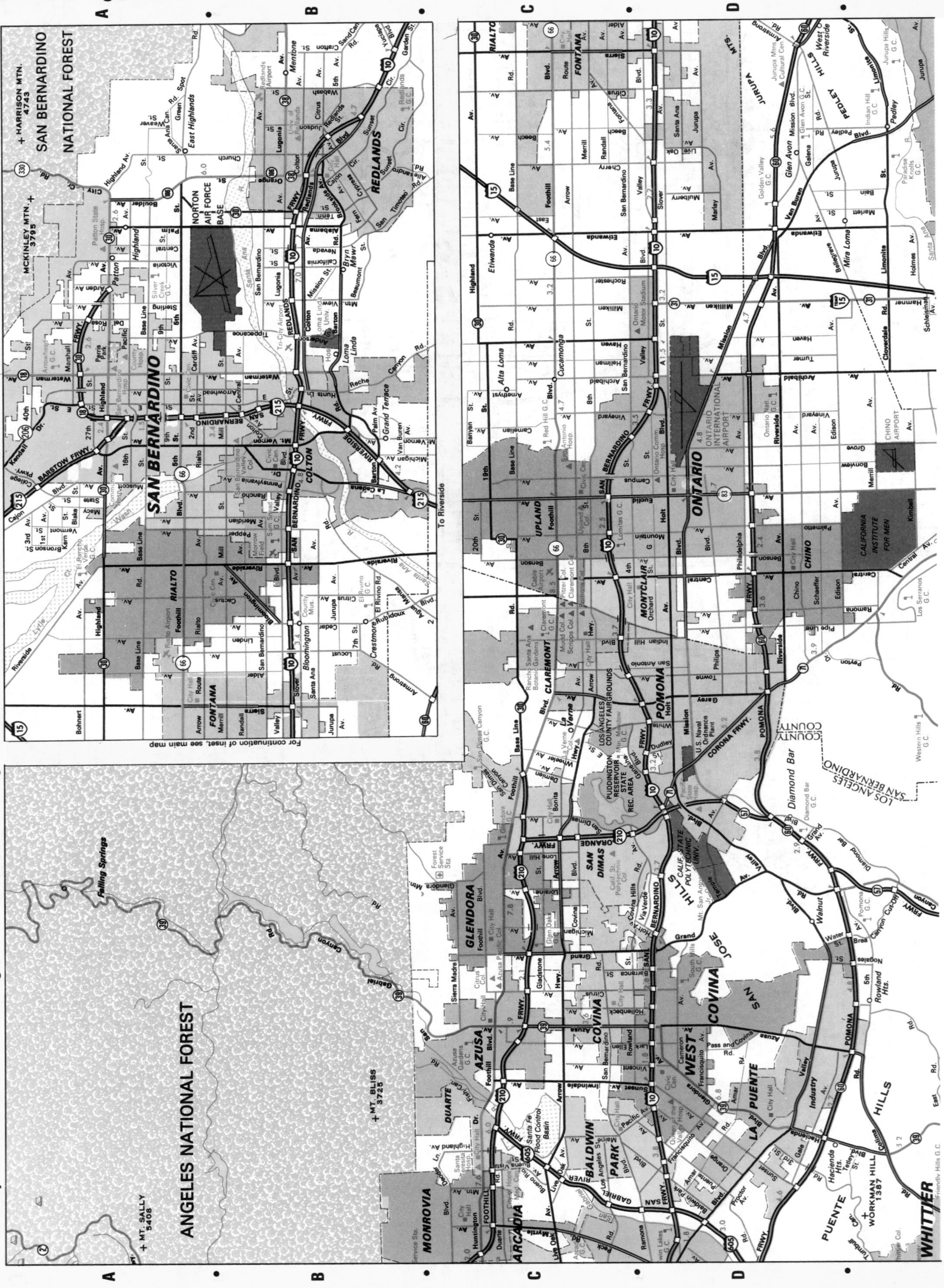
ANGELES NATIONAL FOREST
SAN BERNARDINO NATIONAL FOREST
SAN BERNARDINO
RIALTO
FONTANA
REDLANDS
COLTON
Loma Linda
NORTON AIR FORCE BASE
For continuation of inset, see main map
To Riverside
UPLAND
ONTARIO
ONTARIO INTERNATIONAL AIRPORT
CHINO
CALIFORNIA INSTITUTE FOR MEN
MONTCLAIR
CLAREMONT
POMONA
LA VERNE
SAN DIMAS
GLENDORA
AZUSA
COVINA
WEST COVINA
BALDWIN PARK
LA PUENTE
Industry
ARCADIA
MONROVIA
DUARTE
WHITTIER
PUENTE HILLS
SAN JOSE HILLS
JURUPA MTS.
PEDLEY
Mira Loma
Diamond Bar
LOS ANGELES COUNTY
SAN BERNARDINO COUNTY
MT. SALLY 5408
MT. BLISS 3725
HARRISON MTN. 4743
MCKINLEY MTN. 3795
WORKMAN HILL 1387

Scale of Miles
0 1 2 3

CLEVELAND NATIONAL FOREST

RIVERSIDE

NORCO

CORONA

HOME GARDENS

EL CERRITO

CHINO HILLS

CALIFORNIA INSTITUTE FOR MEN

CALIF. INST. FOR WOMEN

CHINO AIRPORT

U.S. NAVAL RESERVATION

SAN BERNARDINO COUNTY
RIVERSIDE COUNTY

LOS ANGELES COUNTY
ORANGE COUNTY

SAN BERNARDINO COUNTY
ORANGE COUNTY

Silverado

YORBA LINDA

PLACENTIA

BREA

LA HABRA

FULLERTON

ANAHEIM

GARDEN GROVE

BUENA PARK

LA MIRADA

WESTMINSTER

HUNTINGTON BEACH

FOUNTAIN VALLEY

ORANGE

SANTA ANA

TUSTIN

COSTA MESA

NEWPORT BEACH

IRVINE

EL TORO U.S.M.C. AIR STATION

SANTA ANA U.S.M.C. AIR FACILITY

UNIV. OF CALIFORNIA IRVINE CAMPUS

Lake Forest

Trabuco Canyon

DISNEYLAND

WORKMAN HILL 1387

ROWLAND HTS.

DIAMOND BAR

New Albany
Clarksville
Jeffersonville
INDIANA
KENTUCKY
OHIO RIVER
LOUISVILLE
Shively
Matthews
Broadfields
West Buechel
Buechel
Lynnview
Minor Lane Hts

Sherman Minton Bridge
George Rodgers Clark Bridge
J.F. Kennedy Mem. Bridge
Shawnee Park
Commonwealth Park
Gibson
Churchill Downs
Kentucky State Fair & Exposition Center
U.S. Navy Ordinance Plant
Iroquis Park
Ford Car Plant
General Electric Appliance Park
Cherokee Park
Seneca Park
Big Springs G.C.
Bowman Field
Zoological Gardens
Trevilian Park
Audobon Park
Audubon C.C.
Parkway Village
Standford Field
Druid Hills
Rolling Fields
Mockingbird Valley

RIVERSIDE PKWY.
WESTERN PKWY.
PORTLAND ST.
MARKET ST.
MAIN ST.
BROADWAY
KENTUCKY ST.
OAK ST.
HILL ST.
BURNETT
ALGONQUIN PKWY.
WOODLAWN AV.
WINKLER AV.
BERRY BLVD.
LONGFIELD AV.
WATTERSON EXPWY.
KENWOOD DR.
OUTER LOOP
BLUEGRASS AV.
HAZELWOOD AV.
SOUTHERN PKWY.
SOUTHSIDE DR.
STRAWBERRY LA.
CRITTENDEN DR.
PRESTON HWY.
KENTUCKY TURNPIKE
FERN VALLEY RD.
LEVEL RD.
NATIONAL TPK.
GRADE LA.
MINORS LA.
LICK RD.
PARK RD.
SHEPHERDSVILLE RD.
FEGENBUSH LA.
6 MILE LA.
BASHFORD MANOR LA.
GOLDSMITH LA.
HENRY WATTERSON EXPWY.
TYLER AV.
NEWBURGH RD.
GARDINER LA.
BISHOP LA.
JENNINGS LA.
INDIAN TRAIL
POPLAR LEVEL RD.
NORTON AV.
GILMORE LA.
PRESTON HWY.
BROWNSBORO RD.
FRANKFORT AV.
LEXINGTON RD.
GRINSTEAD DR.
STILZ AV.
BAXTER AV.
BARDSTOWN RD.
CHEROKEE PKWY.
RICHMOND DR.
ALTA VISTA RD.
WILLIS AV.
CANNONS LA.
BRECKENRIDGE LN.
CHENOWETH LN.
WESTPORT RD.
HUBBARD LN.
INDIAN HILL TRAIL
MOCKINGBIRD VALLEY RD.
ZORN AV.
STORY AVE.
MELWOOD AV.
PAYNE ST.
LIBERTY ST.
BROADWAY
BRECKENRIDGE ST.
LOGAN ST.
SHELBY ST.
JACKSON ST.
PRESTON ST.
2ND ST.
3RD ST.
7TH ST.
12TH ST.
15TH ST.
21ST ST.
22ND ST.
26TH ST.
34TH ST.
11TH ST.
18TH ST.
RIVER PARK
CHESTNUT ST.
GREENWOOD AVE.
VIRGINIA AVE.
KENTUCKY ST.
SOUTH WESTERN PKWY.
WILSON AVE.
BELLS LN.
CAMP GROUND RD.
CANE RUN RD.
RALPH AV.
DIXIE HWY.
MILLERS LA.
CENTRAL AV.
TAYLOR BLVD.
NEW CUT RD.
MANSLICK RD.
7TH ST. RD.
3RD ST. RD.
ROCKFORD LA.
GAGEL AV.
CRUMS LN.
ST. ANDREWS CHURCH RD.
ST. ANTHONY CHURCH RD.
ARNOLDTOWN RD.
BLANTON RD.
PALATKA RD.
BROWN AVE.
OUTER LOOP
GRAYBROOK RD.
BEECHWOOD AV.
SILVER ST.
EKIN AV.
VINCENNES ST.
8TH ST.
SPRING ST.
MAIN ST.
STATE ST.
GRANT LINE RD.
SLATE RUN RD.
CHARLESTOWN RD.
EMERY CROSSING RD.
McCULLOCH AV.
HARRISON AV.
EASTERN BLVD.
CHARLESTOWN PIKE
HAMBURG PIKE
SPRING ST.
MARKET ST.
PENN ST.
10TH ST.
8TH ST.
MAIN ST.
DUTCH
SPRINGDALE DR.
CHIPPEWA DR.
MULLINS LN.
UTICA PIKE
ALLISON LN.
MIDDLE RD.
SIX MILE LN.
BLANKENBAKER RD.
INDIAN HILLS
Six Mile
Cox Park
Bandman Park

Scale of Miles
0 1 2 3

N

© C.S.C.

Scale of Miles
0 1 2 3
© C.S.C.

N

ARLINGTON
BOLTON
GILDFIELD
BRUNSWICK
BRUNSWICK
Brunswick
Reed Hooker Rd.
George R. Reed Hooker Rd.
PISGAH FISHERVILLE
Peterson Lake Rd.
Shelton
Byhalia
Bray Station
Morning Sun Rd.
LENOW
Berryhill Rd.
Point Rd.
Sanga Rd.
Macon Rd.
Hall Rd.
Houston
Levee Rd.
Frank Rd.
COLLIERVILLE
BAILEY
Bailey Station
Raleigh-LaGrange Rd.
Collierville Rd.
Reynolds St.
CORDOVA
Germantown
GERMANTOWN
Dogwood
Johnson
Forest Hill
FOREST HILL
Irene Rd.
Winchester
Hacks Cross Rd.
Germantown Rd.
Holmes Rd.
TENNESSEE MISSISSIPPI
MINERAL WELLS

SPRING LAKE
ELLENDALE
ELMORE PARK
BARTLETT
Sycamore View Rd.
SHELBY FARMS
Shelby County Penal Farm
Wolf River
Germantown Rd.
Shady Grove Rd.
Kirby Rd.
Poplar Ave.
Quince Rd.
Hickory Hill Rd.
Shelby Dr.
Mendenhall Rd.
CAPLEVILLE
PLUM POINT
Raines Rd.
Getwell Rd.
Perkins Rd.
Winchester Rd.
OAKVILLE
Mt. Moriah Rd.
Clarke Rd.
Quince Rd.
Willow Rd.

LUCY
WOODSTOCK
EGYPT
RALEIGH
Shelby County Airport
Millington Rd.
Coleman Rd.
Stage Rd.
Raleigh-LaGrange Rd.
John F. Kennedy Park
MEMPHIS
Graham St.
Summer Ave.
Macon Rd.
Jackson Ave.
National St.
Highland St.
Walnut Grove Rd.
Getwell Rd.
Perkins Rd.
Goodlett St.
Goodwyn St.
Rhodes College
Southern Ave.
Park Ave.
Sharpe Ave.
Kimball Ave.
Barron Ave.
David Rd.
Airways Blvd.
Memphis International Airport
Tchulahoma Rd.
McKellar Park
McKellar Lake

RAMSEY
BENJESTOWN
Meeman Shelby Forest State Park
Loosahatchie River
Firestone Park
Range Line Rd.
Hollywood St.
James St.
Watkins St.
Wolf River
Chelsea Ave.
Jackson Ave.
Poplar Ave.
Union Ave.
Linden Ave.
Gen. DeWitt Spain Downtown Airport
Firestone Ave.
Thomas St.
Second St.
Third St.
Crump Blvd.
Lamar Ave.
McLemore Ave.
Person Ave.
Cleveland St.
Central Ave.
Cooper St.
McLean Blvd.
Willett St.
Parkway
Lauderdale St.
Latham St.
Mallory Ave.
Florida St.
E. H. Crump Blvd.
S. Pkwy.
Ayers St.
Avalon St.
Vollintine Ave.
Warford St.
Dunn Ave.
Norris Rd.
Perry Rd.
Brooks Rd.
Elvis Presley Blvd.
WHITEHAVEN
Winchester Rd.
Neely Rd.
Levi Rd.
Shelby Dr.
Horn Lake Rd.
Raines Rd.
Holmes Rd.
Weaver Rd.
Mitchell Rd.
Peebles Rd.
Mississippi Park
Coro Lake
Rob-co Lake
Mississippi River
SHELBY CO. CRITTENDEN CO.
Chicken Island
Robinson Crusoe Island
Hopefield Chute
Mississippi River
Presidents Island
McKellar Lake
Fuller State Park
Boxtown Rd.
Sewanee Rd.
North Horn Lake
SHELBY CO. DE SOTO CO.
LAKE VIEW

BEEF ISLAND
REDMAN POINT
ST. CLAIR
MOUND CITY
BLANTON
GAMMON
HARVARD
MARION
WEST MEMPHIS
HULBERT
WYANOKE
Ingram Blvd.
Seventh St.
Missouri St.
N. Avalon St.
Broadway Rd.
TENNESSEE ARKANSAS
Bear Creek

PALM BEACH COUNTY
INDIANTOWN
706
RD
BEE LINE HWY
Jupiter
Jupiter Inlet Colony
Jupiter Inlet
OCEAN ST
To Ft. Pierce
To Stuart
Juno Beach
DONALD ROSS RD
HOOD RD
PROSPERITY FARMS RD
DIXIE HWY
91
P.G.A. BLVD
LOST TREE VILLAGE
Palm Beach Gardens
North Palm Beach
NORTH LAKE BLVD
Lake Park
West
BLUE HERON BLVD
Riviera Beach
Lake Worth Inlet
PARK LAKE RD
MILITARY
95
850
710
702
45 ST
WEST PALM JAI-ALAI
West Palm Beach
Mangonia Park
Palm
Beach
FLAGLER MUSEUM
OKEECHOBEE BLVD
704
PALM BEACH KENNEL CLUB
BELVEDERE RD
PALM BEACH INTERNATIONAL AIRPORT
Glens Ridge
98
Royal Palm Beach
80 SOUTHERN BLVD
441
7
HILL BLVD
882
Greenacres City
Palm Springs
Lake Clarke Shores
10 ST
Lake Worth
South Beach
Wellington
FOREST HILL BLVD
807
802
N Lake
S Lake
1
Atlantis
PALM BEACH CO. AIRPORT
LANTANA RD
Lantana
812
Hypoluxo
Manalapan
HYPOLUXO RD
805
JOG RD
LOXAHATCHEE NATIONAL WILDLIFE REFUGE
BOYNTON WEST RD
804
95
Ocean Ridge
WOOLBRIGHT RD
15 AV
Beynton Beach
Briny Breezes
Gulf Stream
Golf
STARKY RD
ACME DAIRY RD
FLORIDA TURNPIKE
HAGEN RANCH RD
MILITARY
CONGRESS
806
ATLANTIC AVE
Delray Beach
GERMAN TOWN RD
LINTON BLVD
782
Boca Raton
CLINT MOORE RD
YAMATO RD
794
Highland Beach
GLADES RD
BOCA RATON MUNICIPAL AIRPORT
441
7
UNIVERSITY
RANGE LINE
PKWY
EXIT 75
PALMETTO PARK RD
Boca Raton
To Miami
To Ft. Lauderdale
SW 14 ST
BROWARD COUNTY
PALM BEACH COUNTY
Parkland
SAWGRASS EXPY
Deerfield Beach
HILLSBORO BLVD
EXIT 71
SW 10 ST
Coconut Creek
869
818
811
845
Hillsboro Canal

ATLANTIC OCEAN

Map continues on this page A-5

Map continues on this page G-2

Scale of Miles
0 1 2 3
© TRAKKER MAPS INC.

N

Parkland
SAWGRASS EXPY
869
HILLSBORO BLVD
EXIT 71
Coconut Creek
817
Coral Springs
ROYAL PALM BLVD
834
Margate
EXIT 69
SAMPLE RD
DIXIE HWY
FEDERAL HWY
Deerfield Beach
Hillsboro Beach
811
Lighthouse Point
SAMPLE RD
834
COPANS RD
Pompano Beach
POMPANO BEACH AIRPARK
944
McNAB RD
MARGATE BLVD
814
ATLANTIC BLVD
814
North Lauderdale
TPK PLAZA
POMPANO RACE TRACK
95
DIXIE HWY
Sea Ranch Lakes
Tamarac
COMMERCIAL BLVD
CYPRESS CREEK
Fort Lauderdale
COMMERCIAL BLVD
Lauderdale-By-The-Sea
870
EXIT 62
Lauderdale Lakes
Oakland Park
811
816
OAKLAND PARK BLVD
Wilton Manors
OAKLAND PARK BLVD
HUGH TAYLOR BIRCH STATE RECREATION AREA
OAKLAND PARK BLVD
Sunrise
838
Lauderhill
SUNRISE BLVD
816
ANDREWS AVE
842
SUNRISE BLVD
MARKHAM PARK
North New River
75
595
838
Plantation
EXIT 58
BROWARD BLVD
942
BROWARD BLVD
Fort Lauderdale
84
Davie
736
SWIMMING HALL OF FAME
WESTON RD
PINE ISLAND DR
823
817
EXIT 54
FT. LAUDERDALE HOLLYWOOD INTERNATIONAL AIRPORT
595
SW 24 ST
PORT EVERGLADES
CRUISE SHIPS
DAVIE RD
GRIFFIN RD
818
GRIFFIN RD
DANIA JAI-ALAI
Dania
DANIA BEACH BLVD
BEACH STATE RECREATION AREA
South New River Canal
Cooper City
STIRLING RD
822
STIRLING RD
Davie
UNIVERSITY
100 AVE
SHERIDAN ST
SHERIDAN ST
C.B. SMITH PARK
Pembroke Pines
PINES BLVD
820
TAFT ST
Hollywood
JOHNSON ST
Hollywood
HOLLYWOOD BLVD
820
EXIT 49
NORTH PERRY AIRPORT
PEMBROKE RD
Pembroke Park
HOLLYWOOD DOG TRACK
HALLANDALE BEACH BLVD
858
GULFSTREAM PARK
Hallandale
Miramar
MIRAMAR PKWY
HOMESTEAD EXTENSION
EXIT 47
47A
PEMBROKE RD
824
IVES DAIRY RD
Golden Beach
BROWARD COUNTY
DADE COUNTY
FLORIDA TURNPIKE
847
JOE ROBBIE STADIUM
CALDER
826
854
LEHMAN CSWY
Carol City
Miami Gardens
NW 183 ST
860
EXIT 0X
PALMETTO EXPY
North Miami Beach
1
Collins
75
OPA-LOCKA AIRPORT
817
9
826
HAULOVER BEACH PARK
NW 138 ST
816
Opa-locka
135 ST
441
Bal Harbor
Penn-suco
Hialeah Gardens
826
NW 49 ST
959
953
924
125 ST
119 ST
933
North Miami
Bay Harbor Islands
Indian Creek Village
Surfside
27
Medley
MIAMI CANAL
826
932
953
9
103 ST
Biscayne Park
Miami Shores
El Portal
El Portal
Hialeah
LUDLAM RD
PALM AVE
LE JEUNE RD
NW 79 ST
934
North Bay Village
Biscayne Bay
821
PALMETTO EXPY
Miami Springs
Virginia Gardens
944
54 ST
Miami Beach
AIRPORT EXPWY
112
36 ST
27
195
Julia Tuttle CSWY
MIAMI INTERNATIONAL AIRPORT
DOLPHIN EXPY
836
Miami
BAYSIDE MARKETPLACE
VENETIAN CSWY
CONVENTION CENTER
FLAGLER ST
973
FLAGLER ST
ORANGE BOWL
MACARTHUR CSWY
41 CSWY
Sweetwater
SW 8 ST
TAMIAMI
41
PONCE DE LEON
CRUISE SHIPS
Fisher Is.
West Miami
825
CORAL WAY
9
BAYSIDE
RICKENBACKER CSWY
Virginia Key
40 ST
BIRD RD
876
959
Coral Gables
27
DIXIE HWY
1
SCIENCE MUSEUM SPACE TRANSIT PLANETARIUM
VIZCAYA
SEAQUARIUM
MILLER DR
MIAMI MARINE STADIUM
SUNSET DR
117
SNAPPER CREEK EXPY
UNIVERSITY OF MIAMI
South Miami
BRANDON BLVD
Key Biscayne
Kendall
94
KILLIAN DR
MATHESON HAMMOCK PARK
PARROT JUNGLE
CAPE FLORIDA STATE PARK
878
336
LIGHTHOUSE

ATLANTIC OCEAN

MEEKER
GERMANTOWN
MEQUON
COLGATE
MENOMONEE FALLS
WASHINGTON CO.
WAUKESHA CO.
Donges Bay
OZAUKEE CO.
MILWAUKEE CO.
BROWN DEER
RIVER HILLS
BAYSIDE
Schlitz Audubon Ctr.
Plainview
Menomonee
Menominee Co. Park & G.C.
Dretzka Park & G.C.
Brown Deer
Bradley
Dean
Brown Deer Park
FOX POINT
LANNON
Good Hope
Town Hall
Main
SUSSEX
Good Hope
Mill
GLENDALE
Bender
WHITEFISH BAY
W. Mill
W. Mill
Silver Spring
Silver Spring
Villard
Hopkins
Teutonia
Green Bay
SHOREWOOD
PEWAUKEE
BUTLER
Timmerman Airport
Hampton
Capitol
Capitol
Keefe Av.
University of Wisconsin (Milwaukee)
Edgewood
Lake Park
BROOKFIELD
Burleigh
Burleigh
North
North
Brookfield City Park
Sherman
Burleigh St.
McKinley Park
DUPLAINVILLE
Gebhardt
Mayfair
Lisbon
ELM GROVE
WAUWATOSA
Plank
Wisconsin
Blue Mound
MILWAUKEE
City Hall
Milwaukee County Zoo
Vliet
Highland
Wells St.
Marquette Univ.
WAUKESHA
Greenfield
East-West Freeway
State Fair Park
Milwaukee County Stadium
Greenfield
WEST MILWAUKEE
Lake Michigan
NEW BERLIN
Lincoln
Cleveland
Coffee
Lincoln
WEST ALLIS
Jackson Park
SAINT FRANCIS
Lawnsdale
Layton
Beloit
Oklahoma
Howard
Morgan
Holt
Morgan
Superior
Kinnickinnic
CUDAHY
General Mitchell International Airport
Sheridan Park
Calhoun
Airport
GREENFIELD
Edgerton
HALES CORNERS
GREENDALE
Whitnall Park
Root River Pkwy.
Grobschmidt Park
College
OAK CREEK
Grant Park
SOUTH MILWAUKEE
VERNON
MUSKEGO
Little Muskego Lake
W. Janesville
Durham
Drexel
Puetz
Howell
BIG BEND
Big Muskego Lake
Ryan
FRANKLIN
Oakwood
Rainbow Airport
Oakwood G.C.
Bender Park
Muskego Lakes G.C.
WAUSHEKA CO.
RACINE CO.
UNION CHURCH
MILWAUKEE CO.
RACINE CO.
CADDY VISTA
TICHIGAN
Kee Nong Go Mong Lake
Wind Lake
Seven Mile
KNEELAND
Six Mile
Six Mile
HUSHER
TABOR
Waubeesee Lake
Five Mile
RAYMOND
Five and a Half Mile
CALEDONIA
Tichigan Lake
BUENA PARK
NORTH CAPE
THOMPSONVILLE

Scale of Miles
0 1 2 3

© C.S.C.

Plymouth

Brooklyn Park

Brooklyn Center

Fridley

Moore Lake

Long Lake

New Brighton

Arden Hills

Roseville

Crystal

New Hope

Robbinsdale

Columbia Heights

Hilltop

St. Anthony

Lauderdale

Falcon Heights

Golden Valley

Minnetonka

St. Louis Park

MINNEAPOLIS

Hopkins

Edina

Richfield

Mendota

Eden Prairie

Bloomington

Eagan

Burnsville

Medicine Lake

Lake of the Isles

Cedar Lake

Lake Calhoun

Lake Harriet

Lake Nokomis

Diamond Lake

Minnehaha Creek

Wirth Park

Theodore Wirth Park

U.S. Naval Station

Minneapolis St. Paul Intl. Airport

Fort Snelling National Cem.

Fort Snelling State Military Reservation Park

Mall of America

Metro Dome

University of Minn.

Como Park And Golf Course

Braemar Park And Golf Course

Hyland Lake Park Reserve

Staring Lake

Bryant Lake

Glen Lake

Shady Oak Lake

Bass Lake

Eagle Lake

Pine Lake

Twin Lakes

Crystal Airport

Bush Lake

Hyland Lake

Anderson Lakes

Flying Cloud Airport

Blue Lake

Fisher Lake

Rice Lake

Minnesota River

Mississippi River

Va Hospital

Francise Gross Golf Course

Hillside Cem.

United Theological Seminary

La Belle Park

Highland Lake

Silver Lake

Long Lake

Round Lake

Valentine Lake

Lake Johanna

Lake Josephine

Schmidt Lake

Pike Lake

Sandy Lake

Columbia Park

Westwood Hill Park

Phalen Lake

Lake Minnetonka

Walnut Park

Gun Club Lake

Snelling Lake

Pine Island

Mud Lake

Grass Lake

Wood Lake

Richfield Lake

Penn Lake

East Marsh Lake

Long Meadow Lake

Meadow Lake

Black Dog Rd.

Yankee Doodle Rd.

Pilot Knob Rd.

Shepard Rd.

Post Rd.

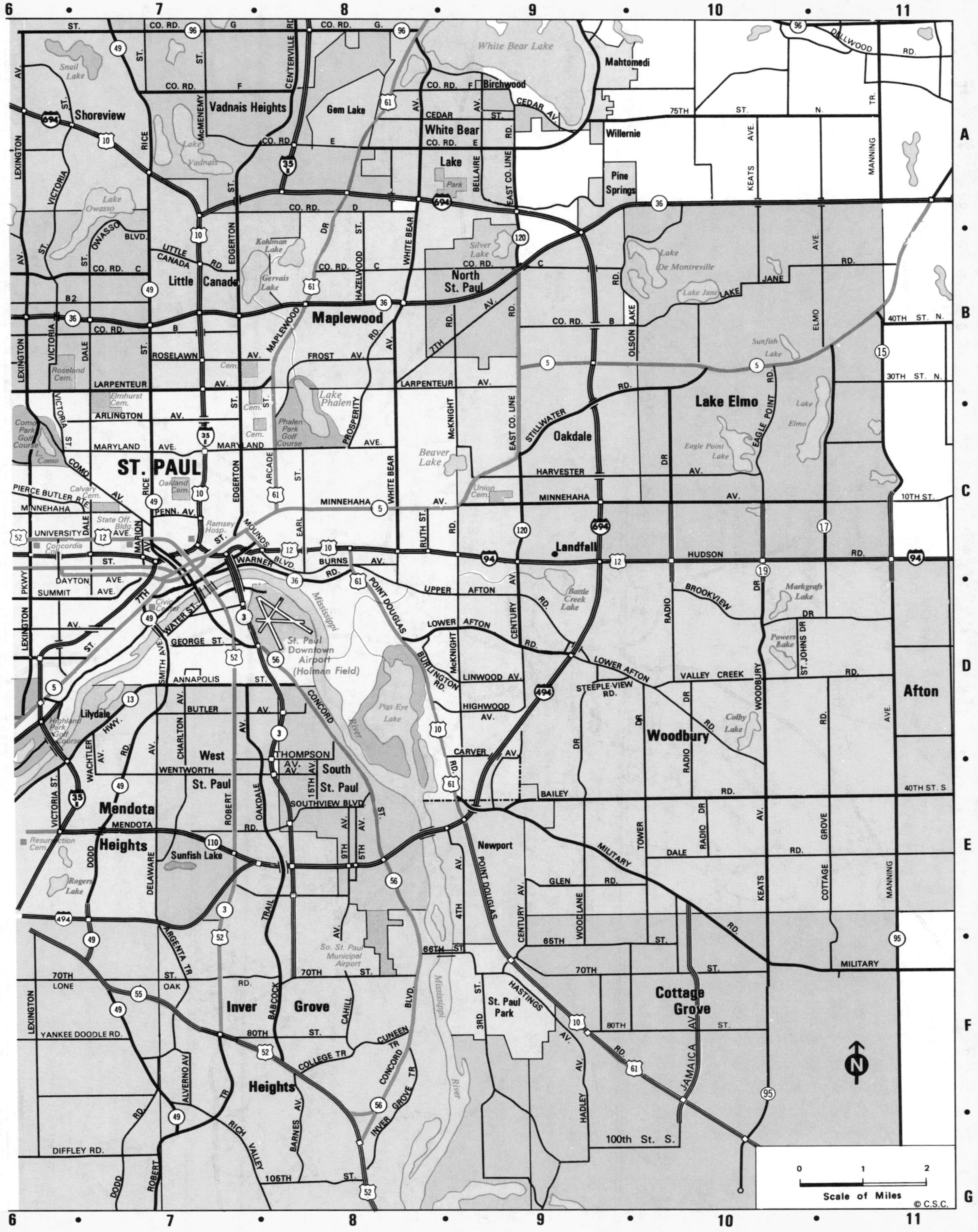

ST. PAUL

Shoreview
Vadnais Heights
Gem Lake
White Bear Lake
Mahtomedi
Birchwood
Willernie
Pine Springs
Little Canada
Maplewood
North St. Paul
Oakdale
Lake Elmo
Landfall
Woodbury
Afton
West St. Paul
South St. Paul
Mendota
Mendota Heights
Sunfish Lake
Lilydale
Newport
Inver Grove Heights
Cottage Grove
St. Paul Park

Snail Lake
Lake Owasso
Lake Vadnais
Kohlman Lake
Gervais Lake
Silver Lake
Lake De Montreville
Lake Jane
Sunfish Lake
Lake Elmo
Eagle Point Lake
Markgrafs Lake
Powers Lake
Colby Lake
Battle Creek Lake
Rogers Lake
Lake Phalen
Beaver Lake
Pigs Eye Lake
Mississippi River

Como Park Golf Course
Phalen Park Golf Course
Highland Park Golf Course
Elmhurst Cem.
Calvary Cem.
Roseland Cem.
Union Cem.
Resurrection Cem.

St. Paul Downtown Airport (Holman Field)
So. St. Paul Municipal Airport
Ramsey Hosp.
State Off. Bldg.
Concordia
Civic Center

Roads / labels:
Lexington, Victoria, Rice, Dale, Marion, Edgerton, White Bear, McKnight, Century, Radio Dr., Woodbury Dr., St. Johns Dr., Keats Ave., Manning Ave., Cottage Grove, Military Rd., Hudson Rd., Stillwater Rd., Minnehaha, Larpenteur, Maryland, Frost, Prosperity, Arlington, Wheelock, Summit, Dayton, University, Pierce Butler Rte., Como, Warner, Burns, Upper Afton, Lower Afton, Valley Creek, Linwood, Highwood, Carver, Bailey, Newport, Glen Rd., Woodlane, Tower Dr., Dale Rd., Jamaica, Hadley, Hastings, Point Douglas, Burlington Rd., Concord, Thompson, Southview Blvd., Wentworth, Butler, Annapolis, George St., Water St., Smith Ave., Robert, Oakdale, Cahill, Babcock, Argenta Tr., Delaware, Dodd, Alverno Av., Rich Valley, Inver Grove Tr., Barnes Av., College Tr., Cuneen Tr., Diffley Rd., Yankee Doodle Rd., Lone Oak, 70th, 80th, 66th, 65th, 70th, 100th St. S., 105th, 75th St., 40th St. N., 30th St. N., 10th St., 40th St. S.

Highways: 694, 35E, 35W, 36, 35, 94, 494, 61, 52, 10, 12, 5, 110, 13, 49, 55, 3, 56, 120, 95, 15, 17, 19, 96, G, F, E, D, C, B

N

Scale of Miles
0   1   2

© C.S.C.

Grid rows: A B C D E F G
Grid columns: 6 7 8 9 10 11

A B C D E F G

10 9 8 7 6 5 4 3 2 1

AVONDALE
SAUNDERSVILLE
HENDERSONVILLE
GREEN MILL
MOUNT JULIET
WILSON
DAVIDSON
CO. CO.
HOPEWELL
HERMITAGE HILLS
LAKEWOOD
SUMNER CO.
DAVIDSON CO.
RAYON CITY
OLD HICKORY
DONELSON
SEVEN POINTS
RUTHERFORD CO.
LA VERGNE
KIMBRO
SMITH SPRINGS
RURAL HILL
FOSTER CORNERS
UNA
BROOKLIN
ANTIOCH
WRENCOE
UNION HILL
GOODLETTSVILLE
MADISON
INGLE-WOOD
NASHVILLE
PARAGON MILL
PROVIDENCE
BEACON
OGLESBY
TUSCULLUM
BERRY HILL
OAK HILL
LICKTON
LITTLE CREEK
WHITES CREEK
BELLE MEADE
WEST MEADE
FOREST HILLS
BRENTWOOD
JOELTON
GERMANTON
RICHLAND
GOWER
VAUGLANS GAP
PASQUO
BELLEVUE
DAVIDSON CO.
WILLIAMSON CO.
MOUNT ZION
MARROWBONE
MOORE
CHEATHAM CO.
DAVIDSON CO.

Briley Parkway
Opryland
Scale of Miles
0 1 2 3
N
© C.S.C.

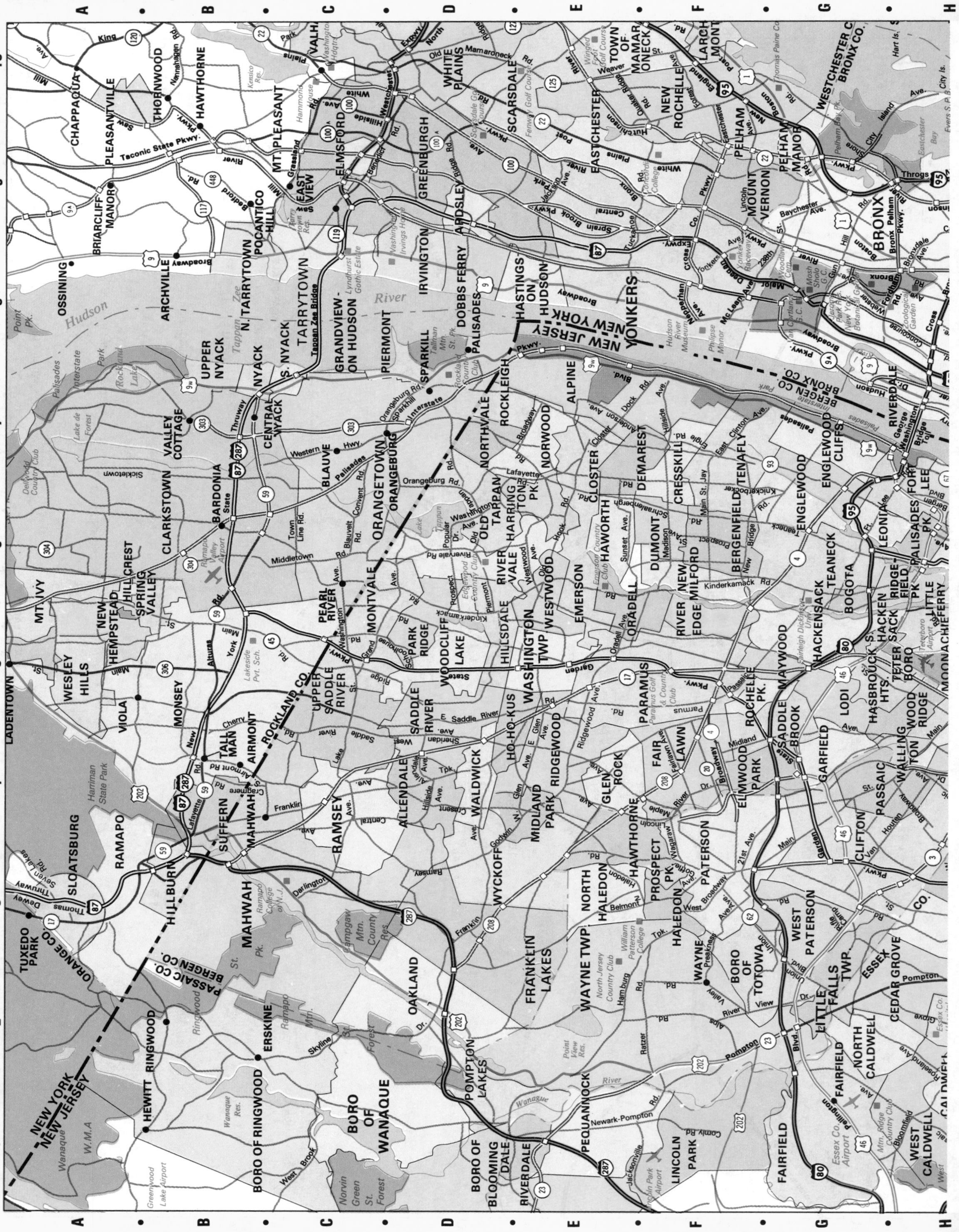
NEW YORK
NEW JERSEY
ROCKLAND CO.
BERGEN CO.
PASSAIC CO.
ORANGE CO.
WESTCHESTER CO.
BRONX CO.
Hudson River
Tappan Zee
Tappan Zee Bridge
OSSINING
BRIARCLIFF MANOR
CHAPPAQUA
PLEASANTVILLE
THORNWOOD
HAWTHORNE
ARCHVILLE
POCANTICO HILL
N. TARRYTOWN
TARRYTOWN
MT. PLEASANT
EAST VIEW
ELMSFORD
VALHALLA
WHITE PLAINS
GREENBURGH
IRVINGTON
ARDSLEY
DOBBS FERRY
HASTINGS ON HUDSON
SCARSDALE
EASTCHESTER
TOWN OF MAMARONECK
LARCHMONT
NEW ROCHELLE
PELHAM
PELHAM MANOR
MOUNT VERNON
YONKERS
BRONX
RIVERDALE
UPPER NYACK
NYACK
S. NYACK
CENTRAL NYACK
GRANDVIEW-ON HUDSON
PIERMONT
SPARKILL
PALISADES
VALLEY COTTAGE
CLARKSTOWN
BARDONIA
BLAUVELT
ORANGETOWN
ORANGEBURG
TAPPAN
NORTHVALE
ROCKLEIGH
ALPINE
NORWOOD
CLOSTER
DEMAREST
CRESSKILL
TENAFLY
ENGLEWOOD
ENGLEWOOD CLIFFS
FORT LEE
LEONIA
PALISADES PK.
HARRINGTON PK.
OLD TAPPAN
HAWORTH
DUMONT
BERGENFIELD
NEW MILFORD
TEANECK
BOGOTA
RIDGEFIELD PK
LITTLE FERRY
HACKENSACK
RIVER EDGE
ORADELL
EMERSON
WESTWOOD
RIVER VALE
HILLSDALE
WASHINGTON TWP
PARAMUS
MONTVALE
PEARL RIVER
PARK RIDGE
WOODCLIFF LAKE
UPPER SADDLE RIVER
SADDLE RIVER
HO-HO-KUS
RIDGEWOOD
GLEN ROCK
FAIR LAWN
ELMWOOD PARK
ROCHELLE PK.
SADDLE BROOK
MAYWOOD
LODI
HASBROUCK HTS.
S. HACKENSACK
TETERBORO
WOOD RIDGE
MOONACHIE
GARFIELD
WALLINGTON
PASSAIC
CLIFTON
ALLENDALE
WALDWICK
MIDLAND PARK
WYCKOFF
FRANKLIN LAKES
RAMSEY
MAHWAH
SUFFERN
AIRMONT
TALLMAN
MONSEY
VIOLA
WESLEY HILLS
NEW HEMPSTEAD
HILLCREST
SPRING VALLEY
MT. IVY
LADENTOWN
RAMAPO
SLOATSBURG
HILLBURN
TUXEDO PARK
RINGWOOD
HEWITT
ERSKINE
BORO OF RINGWOOD
OAKLAND
BORO OF WANAQUE
POMPTON LAKES
BORO OF BLOOMINGDALE
RIVERDALE
PEQUANNOCK
WAYNE TWP.
NORTH HALEDON
HALEDON
HAWTHORNE
PROSPECT PK.
PATERSON
WEST PATERSON
WAYNE
BORO OF TOTOWA
LITTLE FALLS TWP.
LINCOLN PARK
FAIRFIELD
NORTH CALDWELL
CEDAR GROVE
ESSEX
WEST CALDWELL
Harriman State Park
Wanaque W.M.A.

Sound

Island

Long

Long Island

TRUMBULL
BRIDGEPORT
STRATFIED
MELVILLE
VILLAGE
EASTON
PLATTSVILLE
ASPETUCK
GREENFIELD HILL
FAIRFIELD
MILL PLAIN
SOUTHPORT
FAIRFIELD
WESTPORT
WESTON
LYON PLAIN
WILTON
SOUTH WILTON
CRANBURY
WESTPORT
EAST NORWALK
SOUTH NORWALK
CANNONDALE
NORTH WILTON
GILBERT CORNERS
WINNIPAUK
NORWALK
WEST NORWALK
ROWAYTON
TONEKENE
RIDGEFIELD
NEW CANAAN
Mansfield
DARIEN
NOROTON
NORTON HEIGHTS
GLEN BROOK
BOUTONVILLE
LEWISBORO
SCOTTS CORNER
POUND RIDGE
HORSESHOES HILL
SARIES CORNERS
LONG RIDGE
NORTH STAMFORD
SPRINGDALE
STAMFORD
MIANUS
OLD GREENWICH
RIVERSIDE
COS COB
BYRAM
STANWICH
ROUND HILL
GREENWICH
GLENVILLE
PEMERWICK
PORT CHESTER
RYE BROOK
RYE
BEDFORD CENTER
BEDFORD
WINDMILL FARM
NORTH GREENWICH
RIVERSVILLE
HARRISON
MAMARONECK
VILLAGE OF MAMARONECK
BEDFORD HILLS
MOUNT KISCO
ARMONK
VALHALLA
HARRISON
LARCHMONT

NEW YORK
CONNECTICUT
FAIRFIELD CO.
WESTCHESTER CO.
SUFFOLK CO.
NASSAU CO.

FT. SALONGA
ASHAROKEN
EATONS NECK
LLOYD NECK
Crab Meadow Pk.
Sunken Meadow St. Pk.
Caumsett St. Pk.
Lloyd Pt.
Eatons Neck Pt.
Lloyd Harbor

Greenwich Pt.
Greenwich Point Park
Stamford Harbor
Westcott Cove
Cove Harbor
Scott's Cove
Chimmons Island
Sheffield Island
Shea Is.
Bridgeport Harbor
Seaside Park
Southport Harbor
Sherwood Island State Park

Saugatuck River
Mianus River
Cross River Res.
New Croton Res.
Bryam Lake Res.
Laurel Reservoir
North Stamford Reservoir
Putnam Lake
Round Lake
Rockwood Lake

95
15
7
1
136
123
124
137
104
106
22
684
287
120
127
121
172
117
128
100
53
57
58
59
33
8
25
111
135

Scale of Miles

0 1 2 3

© C.S.C.

SAN REMO
VILLAGE OF THE BRANCH
SMITHTOWN
SMITHTOWN TWP.
HAUPPAUGE
VILLAGE OF ISLANDIA
CENTRAL ISLIP
ISLIP TWP.
EAST ISLIP
BAY SHORE
N.Y. Inst. of Tech.
Carleton
Islip

KINGS PARK
MIDDLEVILLE
VERNON VALLEY
EAST NORTHPORT
COMMACK
EAST BRENTWOOD
BRENTWOOD
NORTH BAY SHORE
WEST BAY SHORE
BRIGHT WATERS

V.A. Hospital
Lakefield
Brentwood
Wicks
Crooked Hill

HUNTINGTON
HUNTINGTON BAY
HALESITE
CENTERPORT
EAST NORTHPORT
GREEN LAWN
ELWOOD
HUNTINGTON TWP.
SOUTH HUNTINGTON
DEER PARK
BABYLON TWP.
WEST BABYLON
BABYLON
WEST BABYLON

LLOYD HARBOR
COLD SPRING HARBOR
HUNTINGTON STATION
MELVILLE
WYANDANCH
FARMINGDALE
SOUTH FARMINGDALE
NORTH AMITYVILLE
AMITYVILLE
COPIAGUE
LINDENHURST

Republic Airport

OYSTER BAY COVE
COVE NECK
LAUREL HOLLOW
WOODBURY
PLAINVIEW
OLD BETHPAGE
BETHPAGE
MASSAPEQUA
MASSAPEQUA PK.
SEAFORD

SYOSSET
LOCUST GROVE
HICKSVILLE
LEVITTOWN
WANTAGH
BELLMORE
MERRICK

OYSTER BAY
NORWICH
MUTTONTOWN
BROOKVILLE
JERICHO
WESTBURY
NEW CASSEL
EAST MEADOW
UNIONDALE
ROOSEVELT
FREEPORT
BALDWIN
OCEANSIDE

BAYVILLE
MILL NECK
MATINECOCK
UPPER BROOKVILLE
OLD WESTBURY
EAST HILLS
OLD BROOKVILLE

LATTINGTOWN
LOCUST VALLEY
GLEN HEAD
ROSLYN HARBOR
ROSLYN HTS.
MINEOLA
HEMPSTEAD
ROCKVILLE CENTRE
LYNBROOK
EAST ROCKAWAY
HEWLETT BAY PARK

GLEN COVE
SEA CLIFF
GLEN HEAD
FLOWER HILL
ROSLYN
SEARINGTOWN
GARDEN CITY
MALVERNE
HEWLETT HARBOR
WOODS BURG
HEWLETT

SANDS POINT
MANOR HAVEN
PORT WASHINGTON NORTH
MANHASSET
NORTH HILLS
WILLISTON PK.
NEW HYDE PARK
ELMONT
VALLEY STREAM
WOODMERE
CEDARHURST
LAWRENCE

U.S. Naval Reservation

KINGS POINTS
GREAT NECK ESTATES
SADDLE ROCK
GREAT NECK
PLANDOME MANOR
KENSINGTON
LAKE SUCCESS
FLORAL PARK
NASSAU CO.
QUEENS CO.
ELMONT
ROSEDALE

BAYSIDE
QUEENS VILLAGE
JAMAICA
SPRINGFIELD GDNS.
EDGEMERE
ATLANTIC BEACH

JONES IS.
LIDO BEACH
POINT LOOKOUT
LONG BEACH
ATLANTIC BEACH
BARNUM IS.
ISLAND PK.

OAK BEACH
DUNEWOOD
SALTAIRE
Fire Island
Robert Moses State Park
Captree State Park

Great South Bay
Atlantic Ocean

H J K L M N P Q

Scale of Miles
0 1 2 3
© ADC of Alexandria

N

POQUOSON

Plum Tree Island Wildlife Refuge
Plumtree Point
Grandview Park

NEWPORT NEWS

NASA
LANGLEY AIR FORCE BASE

HAMPTON

HAMPTON ROADS

CHESAPEAKE BAY

Salt Ponds

Walker Airfield
Fort Monroe

JAMES RIVER

Fishing Point
Ragged Island Creek
Batten Bay
Lake Maury

Newport News Point

HAMPTON ROADS

Fort Wool

WILLOUGHBY
Willoughby Bay
BELLINGER
OCEAN VIEW

Norfolk Naval Air Station

INT'L TERMINAL BLVD

LYNNHAVEN ROADS
Lynnhaven Inlet
Lynnhaven Bay

NORFOLK

CRITTENDEN

Craney Island Supply Depot

NANSEMOND RIVER

LAFAYETTE RIVER

Norfolk International Airport

USN Little Creek Amphibious Base

Little Neck
KINGS GRANT

CRANEY HEDGEROW
TWIN PINES

CHURCHLAND

Little Creek Reservoir

ELIZABETH RIVER

PORTSMOUTH

SAINT MICHAEL RIVER

EASTERN BRANCH ELIZABETH RIVER

SUFFOLK

INDIAN RIVER

COLLEGE PARK

VIRGINIA BEACH

BOWERS HILL

CRADDOCK

PORTLOCK

Stumpy Lake

Portsmouth Chesapeake Airport

South Norfolk Airport

GREEN RUN

DEEP CREEK

Mill Creek

SOUTHERN BRANCH ELIZABETH RIVER

CHESAPEAKE

GREAT BRIDGE

FENTRESS

US Naval Airfield Fentress Station

GREAT DISMAL SWAMP
NATIONAL WILDLIFE REFUGE

ARCADIA

EDMOND

Central State Univ.

Edmond Mem. Hosp.

Okla. Christian College

Turner Turnpike

JONES

Mercy Hospital

Quail Creek C.C.

Quail Creek Sch.

Heritage Hall Sch.

Lone Star Sch.

Eisenhower J.H.S.

THE VILLAGE

Okla. City Art Museum

Midwest Christian College

Stinchcomb Wildlife Refuge

Wiley Post Airport

YUKON

WARR ACRES

BETHANY

Deaconess Hosp.

NICHOLS HILLS

National Cowboy Hall of Fame

Remington Pk. Race Track

Expressway Junction Airport

LAKE ALUMA

Lake Hefner

Lake Hefner G.C.

Oklahoma City G.C.

Belle Isle Lake

Lincoln Park

FOREST PARK

SPENCER

Twin Hills C.C.

NICOMA PARK

WOODLAWN PARK

Lake Overholser

Bethany Gen. Hosp.

Will Rogers Park

OKLAHOMA CITY

Okla. City Univ.

State Capitol

Univ. of Okla. Med. Center

CHOCTAW

O.S.U. Tech.

Civic Center

MIDWEST CITY

Midwest City Mem. Hosp.

Downtown Airport

SMITH VILLAGE

DEL CITY

Rose State College

Pleasant Valley Sch.

Western Heights H.S.

Airport

South Comm. Hosp.

Tinker Air Force Base

Oklahoma City Air Force Station

MUSTANG

FIREWORKS CITY

F.A.A. Ctr.

Will Rogers World Airport

Okla. City Comm. College

VALLEY BROOK

OKLAHOMA CO. / CLEVELAND CO.

Stanley Draper Lake

CLEVELAND CO. / MC CLAIN CO.

GRADY CO.

TUTTLE

MOORE

Canadian River

NEWCASTLE

Max Westheimer Field

NORMAN

Lake Thunderbird

HALL PARK

Scale of Miles
0   1   2   3

© C.S.C.

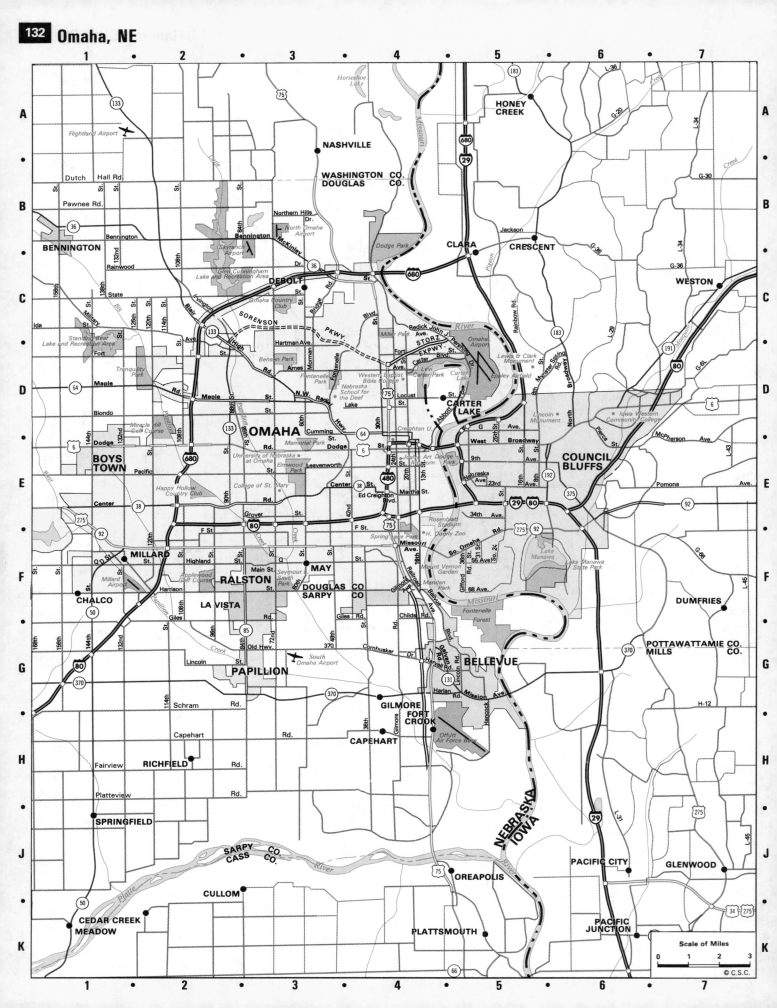

Scale of Miles
0 1 2 3

© C.S.C.

ORLANDO

KISSIMMEE

WALT DISNEY WORLD

LAKE APOPKA

EAST LAKE TOHOPEKALIGA

APOPKA

WINTER PARK

WINTER GARDEN

OCOEE

WINDERMERE

EDGEWOOD

PINE CASTLE

BELLE ISLE

LAKE BUENA VISTA

ALTAMONTE SPRINGS

LONGWOOD

WINTER SPRINGS

CASSELBERRY

MAITLAND

EATONVILLE

FOREST CITY

SANLANDO SPRINGS

MIDWAY PARK

CHASE

SEMINOLE COUNTY

ORANGE COUNTY

OSCEOLA COUNTY

WAKIWA SPRINGS STATE PARK

ZELLWOOD

PLYMOUTH

MCDONALD

POKAN

YOTHERS

HOOPER FARMS

ZELLWOOD FARMS RD

SOUTH APOPKA

KEENE RD

TAFT

INTERCESSION CITY

CAMPBELL

ST. CLOUD

DAVENPORT

ORLANDO INTERNATIONAL AIRPORT

EXECUTIVE AIRPORT

KISSIMMEE MUNICIPAL AIRPORT

ST. CLOUD AIRPARK

UNIVERSAL STUDIOS

MARRIOTT WORLD RESORT

GATORLAND

CITRUS BOWL

CHURCH STREET STATION

MEDICAL CENTER

MERCY MEDICAL CENTER

ORLANDO NAVAL TRAINING CTR

ORLANDO SPORTS STADIUM

BEN WHITE RACEWAY

MARTIN MARIETTA CORP.

O.N.T.C. HOSP.

MEAD BOTANICAL GARDENS

BAY HILL COUNTRY CLUB

ORLANDO CENTRAL PARK

Bull Slough

Boggy Creek Swamp

Lake Nona

Mud Lake

Lake Conway

Little Conway

Lake Jessamine

Lake Holden

Clear Lake

Lake Mann

Turkey Lake

Lake Down

Lake Butler

Lake Tibet

Big Sand Lake

Little Sand Lake

Lake Sheen

Lake Mabel

Bay Lake

South Lake

Seven Seas Lagoon

Reedy Lake

Lake Willis

Lake Bryan

Lake Ruby

Lake Olivia

Lake Whitney

Lake Roberts

Lake Crescent

Lake Roper

Lake Speer

Little Lake Sawyer

Lake Sawyer

Lake Hancock

Lake Hartley

Huckleberry Lake

Lake Needham

Lake Aldrich

Black Lake

Deer Is.

Johns Lake

Marl Bed Flats

Eureka Hammock

Moses E. Levy Grant

Philip R. Young Grant

Triplet Lake

Little Howell Lake

Lake Howell

Bear Gully Lake

Lake Phillips

Lake Pearl

Lake Irma

Bear Lake

Lake Brantley

The Springs

Lake Lotus

Lake Destiny

Lake Maitland

Minnehaha Lake

Lake Osceola

Lake Virginia

Lake Killarney

Lake Fairview

Lake Wekiva

Crooked Lake

Lake Prairie

Lake Stanley

Silver Lake

Lake Olympia

Starke Lake

Trout Lake

Lake Marden

Lake Sims

Lake Alpharetta

Long Lake

Lockhart Lake

Lake Hill

Lake Coroni

Lake McCoy

Lake Alma

Lake Alden

Lake Standish

Lake Francis

Marshall Lake

Lake Fuller

Semmes Lake

Crown Point

Gator Island

Hull Island

Lake Avalon

Lake Apopka

Little Lake Sawyer

Bay Lake

Tub Lake

Reams Lake

Shingle Creek

Reedy Creek

Boggy Creek

Shingle Creek

EAST LAKE TOHOPEKALIGA

Fells Cove

Hillard Isle

Runnymeade Lake

Live Oak

Paradise Island

Makinson Island

Grass Island

Cypress Cove

Fish Lake

Wilson Cove

Buenaventure Lakes

CO CO (ORANGE CO / OSCEOLA CO)

Scale of Miles
0   1   2   3

© TRAKKER MAPS INC.

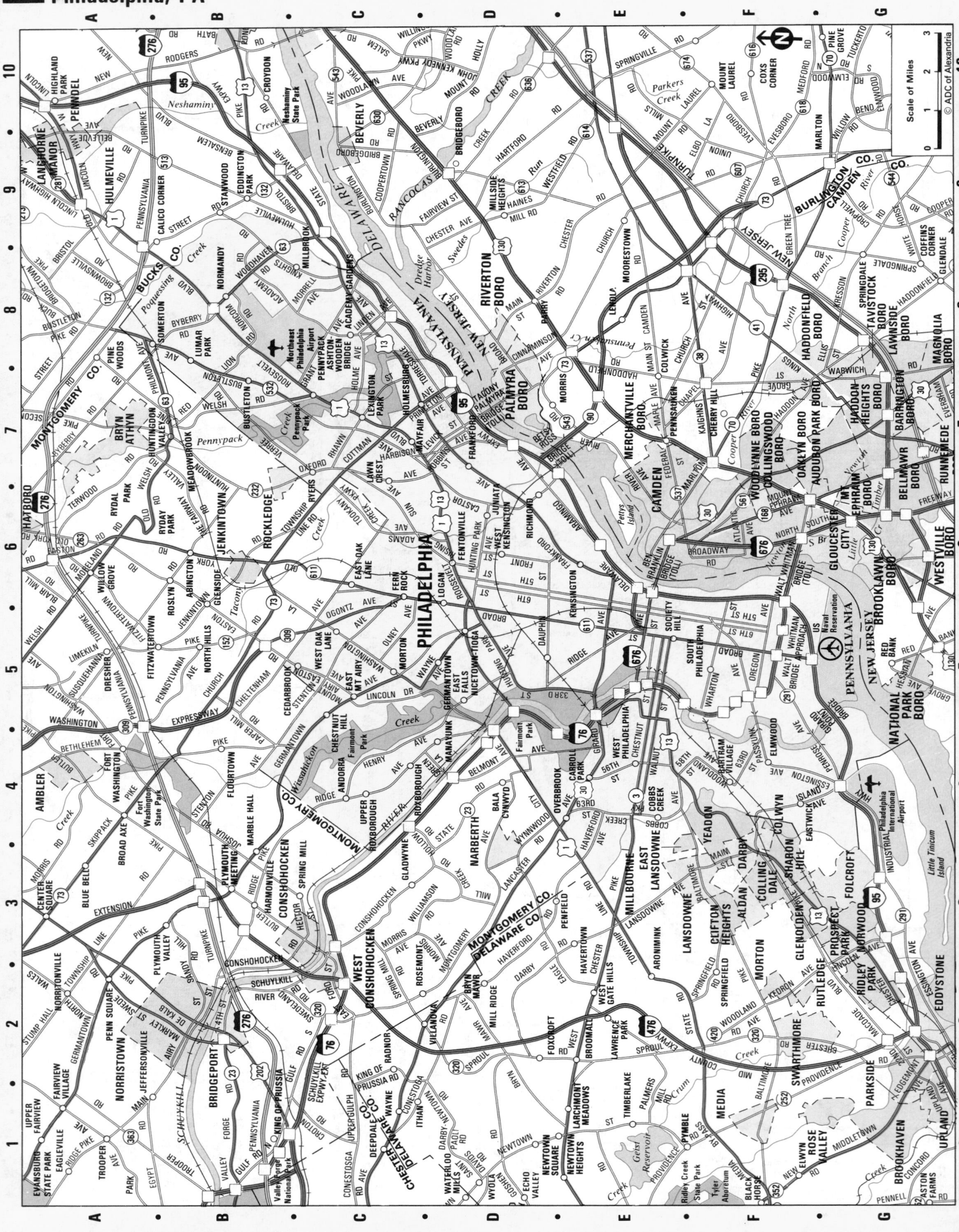

N

Scale of Miles

0 1 2 3

© ADC of Alexandria

PHILADELPHIA

CAMDEN

NEW JERSEY

PENNSYLVANIA

BUCKS CO.

MONTGOMERY CO.

DELAWARE CO.

CHESTER CO.

BURLINGTON CO.

CAMDEN CO.

Northeast Philadelphia Airport

Philadelphia International Airport

Pennypack Park

Fairmount Park

Neshaminy State Park

Fort Washington State Park

Valley Forge National Park

Ridley Creek State Park

Delaware River

Schuylkill River

Wissahickon Creek

Pennypack Creek

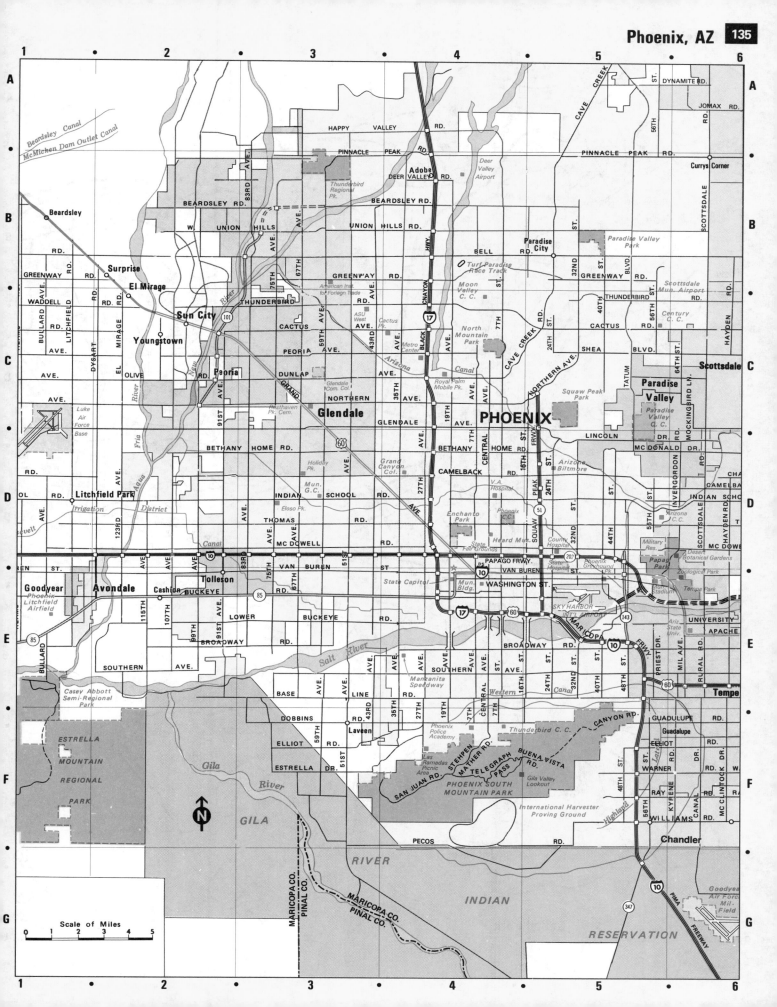

Scale of Miles
0   1   2   3   4   5

Scale of Miles
0 .25 .5 .75 1 1.25

Grid columns: 1 2 3 4 5 6
Grid rows: A B C D E F G

VANCOUVER
E. MILL PLAIN BLVD.
Pearson Field
WASHINGTON
OREGON

SKYLINE BLVD.
NEWBERRY RD.
N.W. SKYLINE BLVD.
GERMANTOWN RD.
SLAVE ISLAND RD.
GILLIMAN
LOOP
MARINE DR.
Multnomah Channel
Columbia Slough
COLUMBIA BLVD.
Hayden Island
MULTNOMAH COUNTY
CLARK COUNTY
Columbia River

N. FESSENDEN ST.
N. PORTSMITH AVE.
N. LOMBARD ST.
N. WILLAMETTE BLVD.
WILLIS BLVD.
N. COLUMBIA
N. PENINSULAR AVE.
N. PORTLAND RD.
N. DENVER AVE.
Exposition Center
Delta Park
Portland Yacht Club
Tomahawk Island
Portland G.C.
Tyee Yacht Club
Rose City Yacht Club
Columbia River Yacht Club
N.E. MARINE RD.
Portland Int'l Airport
Portland Air Force Base
Colwood G.C.

LOMBARD ST.
N. WILLAMETTE
Columbia Park
Univ. of Portland
Swan Island
Willamette River
Forest Park
N. PORTLAND AVE.
N. INTERSTATE AVE.
GREELEY AVE.
N. UNION AVE.
Peninsula Park
N.E. COLUMBIA BLVD.
N.E. LOMBARD ST.
N.E. SUNDERLAND AVE.
Riverside G.C.
Broadmoor G.C.
Columbia Edgewater G.C.
Alberta Park
KILLINGSWORTH ST.
N.E. 42ND AVE.
N.E. CULLY RD.

YEON AVE.
N.W. VAUGHN ST.
MacLeay Park
N.W. CORNELL RD.
SKYLINE RD.
PORTLAND
N.E. FREMONT ST.
N.E. 33RD AVE.
N.E. 39TH AVE.
THE ALAMEDA
N. 5TH
Rose City G.C.
Broadway Bridge
Memorial Coliseum
N.E. BROADWAY
N.E. HALSEY ST.
SANDY
N.E. GLISAN ST.
BURNSIDE

BRONSON RD.
CORNELL RD.
WALKER RD.
174TH AVE.
170TH AVE.
N.W. 23RD AVE.
N.W. 19TH AVE.
FREMONT BRIDGE
Portland State Univ.
Zoological Gardens and Museum
W. HUMPHREY
BARNES RD.
S.W. VISTA AVE.
S.W. BROADWAY DR.
S.W. FAIRMONT BLVD.
MARKET
Laurelhurst Park
S.E. STARK ST.
S.E. MORRISON ST.
S.E. BELMONT ST.
S.E. HAWTHORNE BLVD.
S.E. DIVISION ST.
Mt. Tabor Park

WALKER RD.
JENKINS RD.
MURRAY
CEDAR HILLS BLVD.
West Slope
CANYON RD.
S.W. FATTON RD.
Council Crest
Univ of Oregon Med. Sch.
HAMILTON ST.
DOSCH RD.
SUNSET BLVD.
TERWILLIGER BLVD.
Ross Is. Bridge
Ross Island
McLOUGHLIN BLVD.
S.E. 26TH AVE.
39TH
POWELL
Warner Pacific College
82ND
71ST
FOSTER RD.
S.E. HOLGATE BLVD.
S.E. HAROLD

FARMINGTON RD.
Raleigh Hills
BEAVERTON-HILLSDALE HWY.
WESTERN AVE.
FERRY RD.
SHATTUCK RD.
S.W. CAMERON RD.
Hillsdale
S.W. VERMONT ST.
Gabriel Park
30TH AVE.
S.W. MULTNOMAH BLVD.
Multnomah
BALDOCK FWY.
Harstack Island
Pioneer Park
S.E. 13TH AVE.
S.E. 28TH AVE.
Reed College
WOODSTOCK BLVD.
Eastmoreland Golf Course
S.E. TOLMAN ST.
S.E. FLAVEL DR.
72ND ST.

ALLEN BLVD.
DENNEY RD.
170TH RD.
HART RD.
MURRAY BLVD.
WEIR RD.
HALL BLVD.
SCHOLLS FERRY RD.
OLESON RD.
GARDEN HOME RD.
TAYLORS FERRY RD.
45TH
S.W. BARBUR BLVD.
S.W. 35TH AVE.
STEPHENSON ST.
TACOMA AVE.
S.E. 17TH AVE.
Bybee Blvd.
Waverly C.C.
RIVERSIDE DR.
32ND AVE.
MILWAUKIE
KING RD.
ALBERTA ST.
BELL AVE.
Kendall
STROW BRIDGE
LINWOOD
Creek

BEAVERTON
Metzger
80TH AVE.
OAK ST.
CAPITAL HWY.
Portland Comm. College
KERR
BOONES FERRY RD.
Lewis & Clark College
Tryon Creek State Park
TERWILLIGER BLVD.
Riverside C.C.
Willamette River
JOHNSON CREEK BLVD.
HARRISON ST.
RAILROAD AVE.
WILLAMETTE
LAKE RD.
99E
99W

TIGARD
217
210
REUSSER RD.
OLD SCHOLLS FERRY RD.
PACIFIC HWY.
MULTNOMAH CO.
WASHINGTON CO.
LAKE OSWEGO
KRUSE WAY
COUNTRY CLUB RD.
Lake Oswego C.C.
Oswego Lake
Oak Grove
OAK GROVE BLVD.
OATFIELD RD.
N. Clackamas Central Park
HILL RD.
WEBSTER RD.
HARMONY RD.
ALDERCREST
LAKE EXPWY.
224

KING CITY
BONITA RD.
CARMEN DR.
Waluga Park
Lake Grove
DURHAM RD.
BEEF BEND RD.
CONCORD RD.
THIESSEN RD.
RIVER RD.
RIVER RD.

DURHAM
TUALATIN
CLACKAMAS CO.
STAFFORD RD.
ROSEMONT RD.
WEST LINN
Maryhurst College
PORTLAND AVE.
43

Scale of Miles
0   .5   1   1.5

© C.S.C.

Raleigh, NC

DURHAM

SPRING HILL
PARKWOOD
GENLEE
DURHAM WAKE
MORRISVILLE
RESEARCH TRIANGLE PARK
NELSON
RALEIGH
RALEIGH-DURHAM INTERNATIONAL AIRPORT
WILLIAM B UMSTEAD STATE PARK
Lake Crabtree
LAKE CRABTREE COUNTY PK
WAKE COUNTY
COUNTY
LYNN CROSSROADS
LEESVILLE
STONEBRIDGE
BRANDON STATION
SIX FORKS
BAYLEAF
Falls Lake Dam
FALLS
WAKE FOREST
WALKERS CROSSROADS
WAKE CROSSROADS
SIX FORKS CROSSROAD
NEUSE
NEW HOPE
MILBURNIE
BARCLAY DOWNS
PARKSIDE
KNIGHTDALE
RALEIGH
Meredith Coll
St Marys Coll
Peace Coll
Saint Augustines Coll
NC State University
State Capitol
Shaw Univ
Dorthea Dix State Hospital
Raleigh Comm Hospital
Wake Memorial Hospital
Rex Hospital
GREEN LEVEL
CARY
MACGREGOR DOWNS
APEX
Luther Airstrip
Western Wake Hospital
Med Ctr
BEDFORD VIL
FRIENDSHIP
CHATHAM WAKE
GREENBRIER ESTATES
GARNER
CLOVERDALE
EMERALD VILLAGE
Lake Johnson
Lake Raleigh

Scale of Miles
0 1 2 3
© ADC of Alexandria

Rochester, NY

Lake Ontario
GRAND VIEW HEIGHTS
CRESCENT BEACH
RIGNEY BLUFF
HILTON
PARMA CENTER
NORTH GREECE
PARMA CORNERS
WEST GREECE
GREECE
SOUTH GREECE
SPENCERPORT
OGDEN CENTER
GATE
NORTH CHILI
CHILI CENTER
WEST CHILI
CRITTENDEN
BRIGHTON
ROCHESTER
IRONDEQUOIT
FOREST LAWN
OKLAHOMA BEACH
Durand Eastman Park
WEST WEBSTER
WEBSTER
UNION HILL
ROSELAND
PENFIELD CENTER
WEST WALWORTH
EAST PENFIELD
PENFIELD
EAST ROCHESTER
FAIRPORT
WAYNEPORT
PITTSFORD
Irondequoit Bay
Rochester-Monroe Co Airport
Univ of Rochester
Nazareth Coll of Rochester
Intl. Mus. of Photography
Susan B. Anthony House
St. Marys Hosp.

Scale of Miles
0 1 2 3
© C.S.C.

RICHMOND

Scale of Miles
0 1 2 3

© ADC of Alexandria

Scale of Miles

0 1 2 3 4

© C.S.C.

N

ST. CHARLES COUNTY
ST. LOUIS COUNTY

MISSOURI
ILLINOIS

Florissant
Black Jack
Hazelwood
Berkeley
Ferguson
Delwood
Bellefontaine Neighbors
Bridgeton
Kinloch
Riverview
Moline Acres
St. Ann
Woodson Terr.
Cool Valley
Jennings
Normandy
Granite City
Breckenridge Hills
St. John
Bel-Ridge
Bellefine
Northwoods
Niedringhaus
Maryland Heights
Bel-Nor
Pine Lawn
Madison
Overland
Hanley Hills
Pagedale
Venice
Olivette
University City
Wellston
Madison County
St. Clair County
Creve Coeur
Brooklyn
Clayton
Forest Park
National City
Frontenac
Ladue
Brentwood
Richmond Heights
St. Louis Univ.
East St. Louis
Des Peres
Huntleigh
Rock Hill
Maplewood
Oakland
ST. LOUIS
Town and Country
Warson Woods
Webster Groves
Sauget
Kirkwood
Glendale
Shrewsbury
Eichelberger
Cahokia
Crestwood
Marlborough
Grantwood Village
North Dupo
Fenton
Sunset Hills
Lakeshire
East Carondelet
Dupo
St. George Village
Bella Villa
Columbia
Sugar Loaf Heights
ST. LOUIS CO.
JEFFERSON CO.
ST. LOUIS COUNTY
JEFFERSON COUNTY
MISSOURI
ILLINOIS
ST. CLAIR COUNTY
MONROE COUNTY
Oakville
Columbia

Mississippi River
Missouri River
Meramec River

Lambert-St. Louis International Airport
Washington University
Forest Park
The Gateway Arch
Jefferson Barracks

Sacramento, CA

1 2 3 4 5 6 7

A
Sacramento Municipal Airport
Elkhorn
RIO LINDA
NORTH HIGHLANDS
Elkhorn Rd.
FOOTHILL FARMS
ORANGEVALE
Ave.
Greenback
Del Paso
Centro
VALLEY VIEW ACRES
Main Ave.
ROBLA
McClellan Air Force Base
Roseville
Auburn
Madison Ave.
FAIR OAK
Northridge C.C.
Sunset
Hazel
Main Ave.
Madison
Bell Ave.
Manzanita
Winding Way
Fair Oaks Blvd.
Winding Way
ALDER CREEK

B
Tule Canal
San Juan
Rd.
Truxel Rd.
Carl Johnston Park
Del Paso
Northgate
Rio Linda Blvd.
Norwood Ave.
Auburn
Haggin Oaks G.C.
CARMICHAEL
Robertson
Del Paso Country Club
Marconi
El Camino
Arden
Garfield
Walnut
Ancil Hoffman Park
Coloma
Rd.
El Dorado
NIMBUS
CITRUS

C
Highway
Discovery Park
Old Sacramento St. Hist. Park
Sacramento
Capitol Ave.
WEST SACRAMENTO
9th St.
16th St.
21st St.
C St.
E St.
J St.
H St.
Exposition Blvd.
California Exposition
SACRAMENTO
Elvas Ave.
Fulton Ave.
Eastern Ave.
Oaks
Fair
Watt Ave.
Arden Way
C.M. Goethe Park
American River
Folsom
RANCHO CORDOVA
Sunrise
White Rock Rd.
Douglas Rd.

D
Greens Lake
ARLINGTON OAKS
Linden Rd.
Broadway
Sutterville
Land Park
Fairy Tale Town
12th Ave.
Sacramento Rd.
14th Ave.
Broadway
99
PERKINS
Power Inn Rd.
Florin
50 Blvd.
South Watt Ave.
ROSEMONT
Kiefer
Bradshaw
Jackson
Old Placerville Rd.
Mather Air Force Base
Excelsior Rd.
Eagles Nest Rd.
16

E
RIVERVIEW
Jefferson Blvd.
Gregory
S. River Rd.
Riverside
Sacramento Executive Airport
Freeport Blvd.
24th St.
Franklin Blvd.
Fruitridge
Stockton Blvd.
Sacramento Expressway
Sacramento Army Depot
Elder Creek
Perkins Rd.
FLORIN
Florin Rd.
Gerber Rd.
Mack Rd.
Elk Grove-Florin Rd.
SOUTH PORT
Meadowview Rd.

Scale of Miles
0   1   2   3

N

Salt Lake City, UT

F
Antelope Island
WOODS CROSS
NORTH SALT LAKE
BOUNTIFUL
68
15
106
Orchard Dr.
Wasatch Bountiful Nat'l Forest

G
DAVIS COUNTY
SALT LAKE COUNTY
Great Salt Lake
Googin
N. Point
Consolidated Drain
Canal
Salt Lake City International Airport
215
2400
DAVIS CO.
SALT LAKE CO.
Beck St.
Victory Rd.
City Creek Canyon Rd.
SALT LAKE CITY

H
80
North Temple
West Valley Freeway
Surplus Canal
4000 W. St.
80
4th St.
3rd St.
6th. N. St.
Riverside Park
State Fair Grounds
Salt Palace
Utah State Capitol
South Temple St.
University of Utah
Fort Douglas Military Res.
Pioneer Trail State Park
Hogle Zoo
Foothill Dr.

J
80
202
N
SALT LAKE CITY
172
13th South St.
21st South
ALT 50
201
154
2700 South
215
Jordan Park
9th St.
3rd St.
Liberty Park
California Ave.
71
11th East
21st South
Mount Olivet Cemetery
Bonneville Golf Course
186
Wasatch Blvd.
Parley's Way
80

K
MAGNA
8000 W.
7200 W.
111
3500 South
4100 South
171
56th South
West St.
4700 South
WEST VALLEY CITY
3100 South
68
171
266
SOUTH SALT LAKE
Fairmont Park
Sugarhouse Park
Forest Dale Golf Course
Salt Lake Country Club Golf Course
53rd South
39th South
45th South
9th East
13th East
23rd East
VAN
181
EAST MILLCREEK
HOLLADAY
215

Scale of Miles
0   1   2   3
© C.S.C.

1   2   3   4   5   6   7

GREY FOREST

SHAVANO PARK

HOLLYWOOD PARK

HILL COUNTY VILLAGE

BRACKEN

SELMA

LIVE OAK

CONVERSE

HELOTES

Univ. of Texas at San Antonio

Camp Bullis Military Reservation

CASTLE HILLS

San Antonio International Airport

WINDCREST

S. Texas Medical Center

LEON VALLEY

Texas Dept. of Trans. Dist. Office

BALCONES HEIGHTS

OLMOS PARK

ALAMO HEIGHTS

TERRELL HILLS

KIRBY

St. Mary's Seminary

Assumption Seminary

Alamo Stadium

Alamo University

Brooke Army Medical Center Fort Sam Houston

Culebra

SAN ANTONIO

Our Lady of the Lake College

The Alamo

City Hall

San Fernando Cem.

Joe Freeman Coliseum

Martindale Army Airfield

MARTINEZ

GARDENDALE

Lackland AFB

Kelly AFB

East Kelly AFB

Billy Mitchell Dr.

Lions Park

CHINA GROVE

Lackland Training Annex

Pecan Valley G.C.

San Antonio State Hospital

Aerospace Med. Center Brooks AFB

Stinson Field

Mission

Calaveras Lake

MACDONA

SOUTHTON

MANGUS CORNER

VON ORMY

BUENA VISTA

Mitchell Lake

CASSIN

Blue Wing Lake

ELMENDORF

Braunig Lake

LOSOYA

SOMERSET

THELMA

BEXAR CO.
ATASCOSA CO.

N

Scale of Miles
0 1 2 3

©C.S.C.

Grid columns: 1 2 3 4 5 6 7
Grid rows: A B C D E F G H J K

Major place labels:

SOLANA BEACH
DEL MAR
SORRENTO
LA JOLLA
MISSION BEACH
PACIFIC BEACH
OCEAN BEACH
CORONADO
IMPERIAL BEACH
SAN DIEGO
MIRAMAR
POWAY
FERNBROOK
EUCALYPTUS HILLS
MORENO
LAKESIDE
LAKEVIEW
JOHNSTOWN
SANTEE
WINTER GARDENS
GLENVIEW
EL CAJON
LA MESA
JAMACHA JUNCTION
JAMACHA
SPRING VALLEY
LEMON GROVE
DICTIONARY HILL
LA PRESA
SUNNYSIDE
BALBOA PARK
NATIONAL CITY
LINCOLN ACRES
LYNWOOD HILLS
CHULA VISTA
HARBOR SIDE
OTAY MESA

Water / natural features:

Pacific Ocean
San Diego Bay
Mission Bay
Torrey Pines State Park
Miramar Reservoir
San Vicente Reservoir
Murray Reservoir
Sweetwater Reservoir
Upper Otay Reservoir
Lower Otay Reservoir
Cabrillo Nat'l. Mon.
Silver Strand State Beach

Military / institutions:

University of California San Diego Campus
Scripps Institute of Oceanography
Scripps Hospital
Miramar Naval Air Station
U.S. Air Force Reservation
Camp Elliott
U.S. Naval Recreational Facilities
San Diego State Univ.
Univ. of San Diego
San Diego Mesa Coll.
Clairemont General Hosp.
Sea World Aquatic Park
North Island Naval Air Station
Naval Training Center
U.S.M.C. Base
U.S. International Univ.
Pointe Loma Coll.
San Diego International Airport
U.S. Military Reservation
U.S. Naval Amphibious Base
San Diego Naval Station
Southwestern College
Imperial Beach Naval Air Station
Imperial Beach Naval Radio Station
Brown Field
U.S. Immigration Detention Facility
Montgomery Field

Highways:
5, 805, 15, 163, 8, 52, 67, 54, 94, 75, 282, 209, 109, 274, 905, 8a

Scale of Miles: 0 1 2 3

© C.S.C.

N (compass, pointing up)

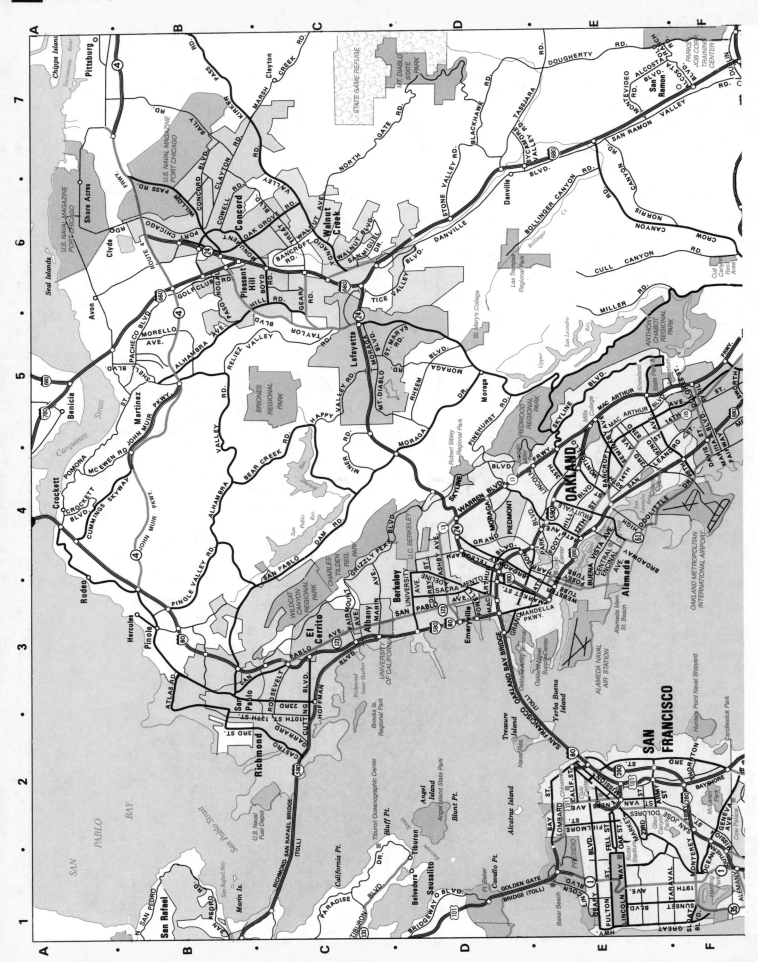

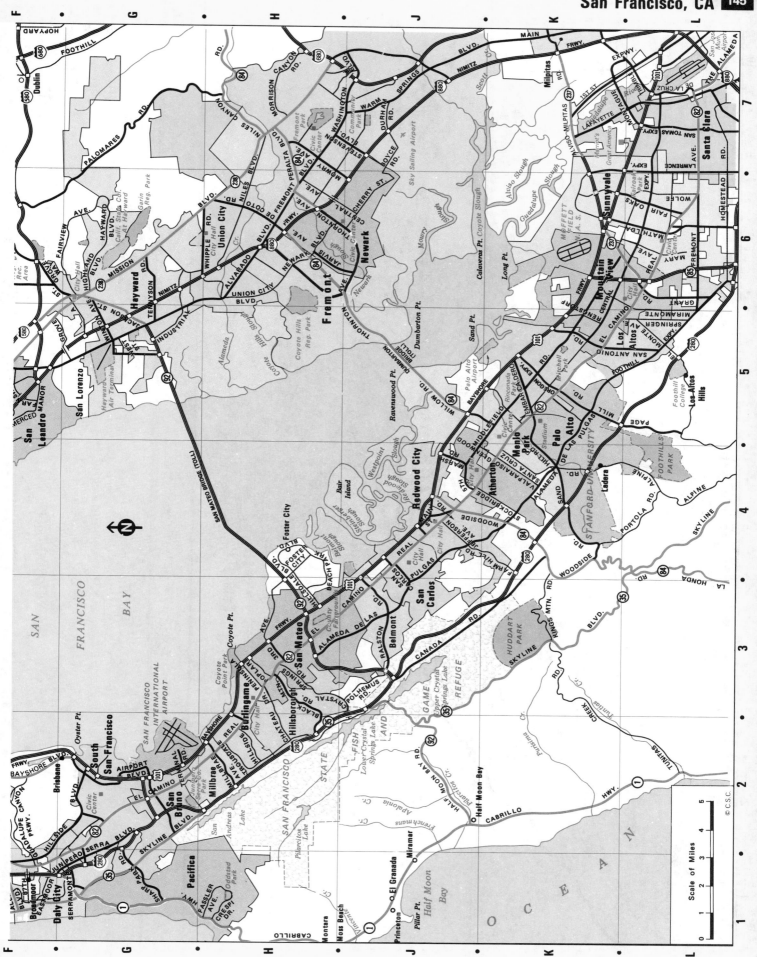

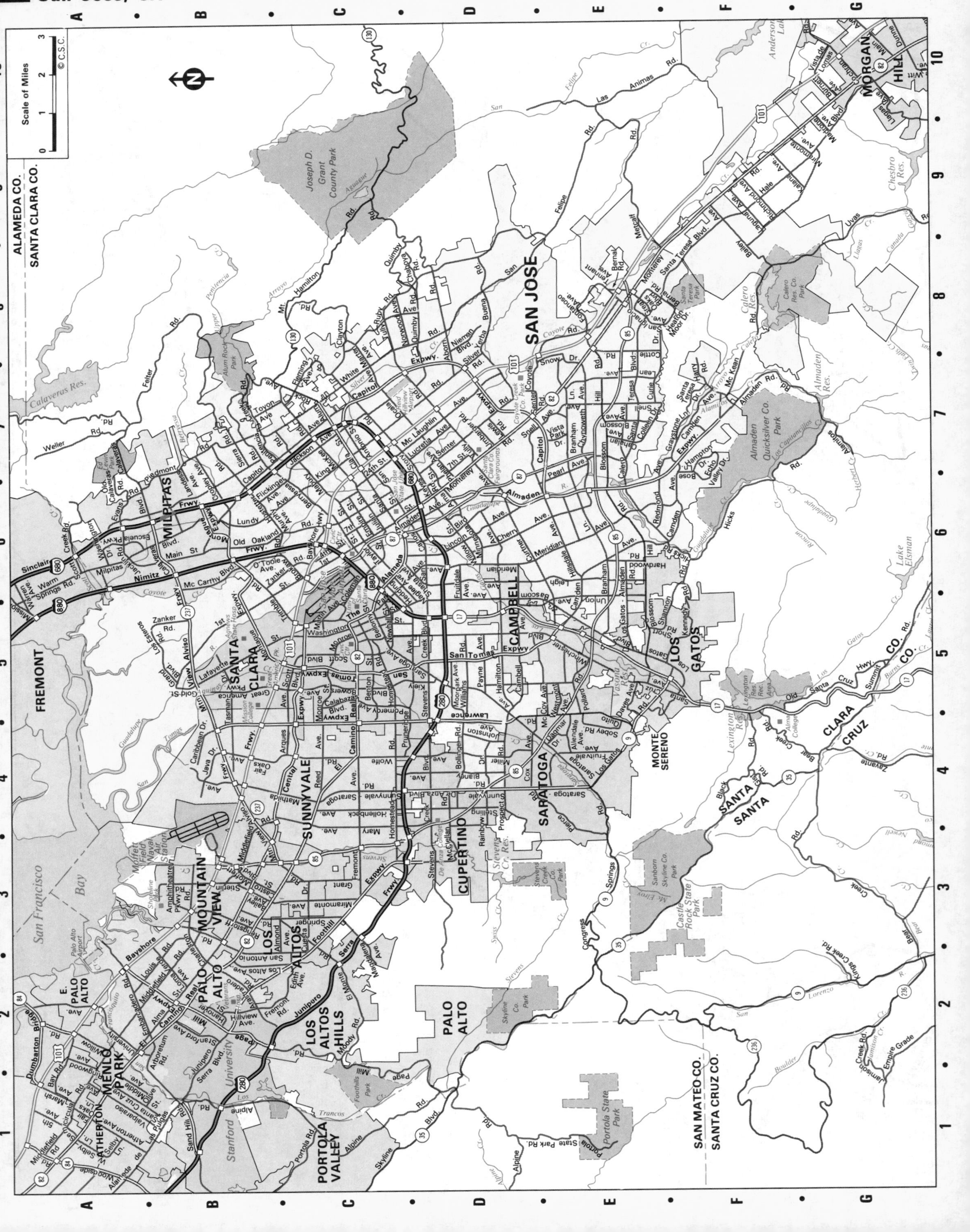

SAN JOSE
MILPITAS
SANTA CLARA
SUNNYVALE
MOUNTAIN VIEW
LOS ALTOS
LOS ALTOS HILLS
PALO ALTO
E. PALO ALTO
MENLO PARK
ATHERTON
PORTOLA VALLEY
CUPERTINO
SARATOGA
CAMPBELL
LOS GATOS
MONTE SERENO
MORGAN HILL
FREMONT
ALAMEDA CO.
SANTA CLARA CO.
SAN MATEO CO.
SANTA CRUZ CO.
San Francisco Bay
Joseph D. Grant County Park
Almaden Quicksilver Co. Park
Calero Res. Co. Park
Santa Teresa Park
Sanborn Skyline Co. Park
Castle Rock State Park
Portola State Park
Foothills Park
Skyline Co. Park
Stevens Creek Co. Park
Moffett Field Naval Air Station
Stanford University
Calaveras Res.
Lake Elsman
Anderson Lake
Chesbro Res.
Almaden Res.
Lexington Res.
Vasona Res.
Scale of Miles
0
1
2
3
© C.S.C.

Scale of Miles
0 1 2 3
© C.S.C.

Column numbers: 1 2 3 4 5 6 7

Row letters: A B C D E F G H J K

EDMONDS
LYNNWOOD
196th Ave. S.W.
Filbert Rd.
527
Main St.
212th Ave. S.W.
Larch Way
9
Maltby Rd.
MALTBY
Echo Lake Rd.
Lost Lake Rd.
Fales Rd.
Welch Rd.
522
Paradise Lake Rd.
KINGSTON
104
220th St.
SEATTLE HEIGHTS
99
5
405
Cedar Way
Larch
228th St. S.W.
Canyon Park Rd.
228th St.
45th Ave. N.E.
Bostian Rd.
175th Ave.
SNOHOMISH CO.
KING CO.
Appletree Cove
WOODWAY
9th Ave.
MOUNTLAKE TERRACE
BRIER
Brier Rd.
Locust Way
Swamp Creek
Pt. Rd.
Tulin Rd.
84th Ave.
RICHMOND BEACH
Ballinger Way
N.E.
Woodinville Rd.
Woodinville Duvall Rd.
RICHLAND HIGHLANDS
Richmond
Beach Rd.
N. 175th St.
522
KENMORE
170th St.
522
BOTHELL
WOODINVILLE
Cottage Lake
Puget Sound
LAKE FOREST PARK
Simonds Rd. N.E.
100th Ave. N.E.
Juanita Woodinville Rd. N.E.
175th Ave.
Bear Creek Rd.
Carkeek Park
N. 145th St.
N. 130th St.
513
St. Edwards State Park
N.E. 132nd St.
N.E. 124th St.
202
116th Ave.
Novelty Hill Rd.
N. 105th St.
Holman Rd. N.W.
North Ave.
Lake City Way
Holmes Pt. Dr. N.E.
JUANITA
N.E. 116th St.
Market St.
KIRKLAND
REDMOND
Avondale
ROLLINGBAY
Golden Gardens Park
N. 85th St.
15th Ave. N.E.
N.E. 65th St.
Magnusson Park
908
Union Hill Rd.
196th Ave. N.E.
208th Ave. N.E.
228th Ave. N.E.
Murden Cove
Shilshole Bay
65th St.
Greenwood Ave.
North
Roosevelt Way
35th Ave. N.E.
99
Green Lake
Green Lake Park
Sand Point Way
132nd Ave. N.E.
140th Ave. N.E.
148th Ave. N.E.
405
901
202
Hill Rd.
Discovery Park
Market St.
N. 45th
N.E. Pacific St.
University of Washington
Montlake Blvd.
Union Bay
HUNTS PT.
Evergreen Point Floating Bridge (Toll)
520
134th Ave. N.E.
Northrup Rd.
Inglewood Hill Rd.
Seattle-Victoria Ferry
Gilman Ave. W.
15th Ave. W.
Elliot Ave.
Queen Anne Ave.
10th Ave.
Madison
Aurora
Lake Union
Lake Washington Blvd.
Hunts Pt.
76th Ave.
84th Ave.
92nd Ave.
104th Ave. N.E.
Bellevue Redmond Rd.
N.E. 8th St.
Lake Sammamish
U.S. Naval Supply Depot
Thorndyke Ave. W.
Seattle-Winslow Ferry
E. Yesler Way
Lake Washington
MEDINA
CLYDE HILL
N.E. 1st St.
BELLEVUE
Lake Sammamish Blvd.
S.E. 24th St.
Pine Lake
Eagle Harbor
Sherwood Forest
Country Club Rd.
SEATTLE
Elliott Bay
E. Empire
23rd
Lake Washington Floating Bridge
90
BEAUX ARTS
Kathber Rd.
Phantom Lake
S.E. 24th St.
Bremerton-Seattle Ferry
Alki Beach Park
S.W. Admiral Way
California Ave. S.W.
Fauntleroy Way S.W.
Chilberg Ave. S.W.
West Seattle Freeway
4th Ave. S.
99
15th Ave.
Rainier Ave.
900
MERCER ISLAND
Seward Park
East Mercer Way
West Mercer Way
Mercer Way
S.E. 40th St.
405
EASTGATE
Newport Way
168th Ave. S.E.
S.E. 60th St.
S.E. 60th St.
90
Lincoln Park
Puget Sound
Delridge Way S.W.
5
King Co. Airport
167
NEWCASTLE
New Castle Rd.
N. 30th St.
S.E. 38th Ave.
ISSAQUAH
SOUTH-WORTH
Vashon-Southworth Ferry
Fauntleroy-Vashon Ferry
VASHON HEIGHTS
35th Ave. S.W.
16th Ave. S.W.
S.W. Holden
S.W. Barton
S.W. Henderson
599
BURIEN
1st Ave. S.
Military Rd.
BRYN MAWR
Renton-Issaquah Rd.
148th Ave. S.E.
COALFIELD
Coalfield Way
Issaquah-Hobart Rd.
Coalfield Issaqua Rd.
Ambaum Blvd. S.W.
S.W. 152nd St.
518
99
W. Valley Hwy.
RENTON
MAPLEWOOD
169
128th St.
164th Ave. S.E.
Creek
S.W. 168th St.
S.W. 176th St.
Maple Wild Ave. S.W.
Sylvester Rd. S.W.
Des Moines
509
Seattle Tacoma Intl. Airport
S. 176th St.
S. 188th St.
180th St.
S.E. 192nd St.
140th Ave. S.E.
Petroviteky Rd.
Lake Desire
Otter Lake
Cedar Grove Rd.
NORMANDY PARK
S.W. 196th St.
91st Ave. S.W.
204th St. S.W.
509
S. 200th St.
5
181
KENT
Pacific Hwy.
116th Ave. S.E.
132nd Ave. S.E.
148th Ave. S.E.
Lake Youngs
Crosson-Sweeney Rd.
18
PORTAGE
220th St. S.W.
Vashon Island
S. 212th St.
S.E. 208th St.
S.E. 240th St.
VASHON ISLAND
131st
S.W. 232nd St.
DES MOINES
516
S. 216th St.
228th St.
167
228th S.E.
S.E. 224th St.
S.E. 240th St.
Kent Black Rd.
Kent North Rd.
248th St. S.W.
MAURY ISLAND
S.E. 240th St.
169
Tramp Harbor
Weitzel Rd.
Wick Rd.

Grid columns: 1 2 3 4 5 6 7
Grid rows: A B C D E F G H J K

TARPON SPRINGS
CRYSTAL BEACH
PALM HARBOR
OZONA
CITRUS PARK
LUTZ
TAMPA
HONEYMOON ISLAND
PINELLAS COUNTY STATE AQUATIC PRESERVE
GARDEN IS. Boggy Bayou
St. Joseph Sound
Sutherland Bayou
Lake Tarpon
CALADESI ISLAND STATE PARK
CALADESI ISLAND
CLEARWATER BEACH IS.
CLEARWATER BEACH
DUNEDIN
MALONE IS.
CORE IS.
MOONSHINE IS.
SAFETY HARBOR
OLDSMAR
Safety Harbor
Mobly Bay
Double Branch
Rocky Creek
Double Bayou
OLD MEMORIAL HWY
CLEARWATER
GULF-TO-BAY BLVD.
 st. clearwater
exec. airport
DREW
COURTNEY CAMPBELL PKWY
ROCKY PT.
TAMPA INTERNATIONAL AIRPORT
BELLEAIR
BELLEAIR BEACH
BELLEAIR BLUFFS
BELLEAIR SHORES
LARGO
Largo Inlet
OLD TAMPA BAY
HOWARD FRANKLIN BRIDGE
ST. PETERSBURG-CLEARWATER INT'L AIRPORT
BIG IS.
INDIAN ROCKS BEACH
INDIAN SHORES
GANDY BLVD
BALLAST PT.
HILLSBOROUGH BAY
PINELLAS PARK
SEMINOLE
KENNETH CITY
Masters Bayou
MUD HOLE IS.
PORT TAMPA
WEEDON IS.
SNAKE IS.
CHRISTMAS IS.
ROSS IS.
Riviera Bay
MACDILL AIR FORCE BASE
CATFISH PT.
SUNKEN ISLAND
REDINGTON SHORES
NORTH REDINGTON BEACH
REDINGTON BEACH
MADEIRA BEACH
CONCH KEY
TRIPOD KEY
BAY PINES
CRYSTAL IS.
Boca Ciega Bay
Placido Bayou
Smacks Bayou
SNELL ISLE
Coffee Pot Bayou
GADSDEN PT.
PINE KEY
TREASURE ISLAND
CAPRI ISLE
North Yacht Basin
CENTRAL AV
ST. PETERSBURG
SOUTH PASADENA
GULFPORT
ALBERT WHITTED MUNICIPAL AIRPORT
Bayboro Harbor
MANGROVE PT.
RUSKIN
Lake Maggiore
COQUINA KEY IS.
Big Bayou
Little Bayou
TAMPA BAY
TROPICAL ISL
SHELL PT
SAND PT
ST. PETERSBURG BEACH
BOCA CIEGA ISLE
MUD KEY
INDIAN KEY
Maximo Channel
PINELLAS COUNTY STATE AQUATIC PRESERVE
LITTLE COCKROACH ISLAND
NEGRO ISL
GULF CITY RD
BIG PASS KEY
CAMP KEY
GOAT ISL
PINELLAS COUNTY BAYWAY
PARDEE KEY
SHELL KEY
South Channel
TARPON KEY
WHALE IS.
SNAKE KEY
BEACON KEY
COCKROACH BAY RD
SUN CITY
North Channel
CABBAGE KEY
SAWYER KEY
CUNNIGHAM KEY
MADELAINE KEY
BONNE FORTUNE KEY
SUNSHINE SKYWAY BRIDGE
SOUTHERN
HILLSBOROUGH CO.
ST. JEAN KEY
FT. DESOTO CO. PARK
HILLSBOROUGH COUNTY
MANATEE COUNTY
BUSCH GARDENS
DAVIS ISLAND
PETER O KNIGHT AIRPORT
HOOKER PT.
SEDDON ISL
BLACK PT.
McKAY BAY

Scale of Miles
0 1 2 3
© C.S.C.

N

Left inset map (Temple Terrace / Tampa area):

MILLS
581
275
93
75
93
BRUCE B DOWNS BLVD
Clay Gully
Hillsboro
UNIV. OF SOUTH FLORIDA
582
582 A
595
582
MAIN ST
TEMPLE TERRACE
580 HWY
TEMPLE TER
43
WILL
HARNEY
VANDEN-BURG AIRPORT
River
56
599
583
Bellow
301
574
MA
599
400
7
BROADWAY AV
FRANK ADAMO DR
James Byrass
618
60
599
45
573
676
41
TAMPA
MADISON AV
676 A
PROGRESS BLVD
RIVERVIEW AIRPORT
RIVERVIEW DR
43
78 ST
BIRD ISLAND
GIBSONTON RD
Bullfrog Creek
SYMMES RD
GIBSONTON
WHISKY STUMP KEY
The Kitchen
75
93
301
DEMBROOKE RD
COWLEY RD
LINCOLN RD
672
BIG
SHONUM
BULLFROG
BEACH BLVD
APOLLO BEACH
45
Bullfrog
43
THE AV NE
POINT RD
Cypress
674
SUN CITY CENTER
SUNCITY CENTER AIRPARK (PVT)
24 ST
TECO RD
BISHOP RD
BONITA DR
301
Little Manatee

Main map (Tucson):

Airport
Big
Hwy
Tucson Florence
Coronado National Forest
Camino De Oeste
Naranja Dr
Thornydale Rd
Magee
Lambert Ln
La-Cholla
Linda Vista Blvd.
Overton
Romero Rd
Hardy Rd
Sage St
Northernau Rd
Cortaro Farms Rd
Magee
Casa Grande Hwy
Ina Rd
10
Orange Grove Dr
Shannon Rd
La-Cholla
La-Canada
Skyline Dr
Alvernon Way
Sunrise Rd
Kolb Rd
Snyder
JAYNES
77
Campbell Ave
Hacienda Del Sol
Pontatoc Rd
Sunset Rd
Silverbell Rd
Camino Del Cerro
Ruthrauff Rd
Wetmore Rd
Rillito
River Rd
Swan Rd
Craycroft
Sabino Canyon Rd
Cloud Rd
Bear Canyon Rd
El Camino Del Oeste
Freeway Airport
Roger Rd
Oracle Rd
1st Ave
River Rd
Sweet Water Dr
Flowing Wells
Eastview
Prince Rd
El Morago
Goret Rd
Miracle Mile
Ft. Lowell Rd
Ft. Lowell Rd
Dodge Blvd
Ft. Lowell Rd
Verde
Wrightstown
Tanque
77
Stone Ave
Ironwood Hill Dr
Grant Rd
Santa Cruz
Grant Rd
Miracle Mile
Grant Rd
TUCSON
Pantano
W. Anklam
W. Speedway Blvd.
Speedway
Campbell
Club
Alvernon
Speedway Blvd.
Greasewood Rd
Marys Rd
University of Arizona
Broadway
Randolph Park Municipal Golf Course
Swan Rd
Wilmot Rd
Bantano
Camino Seco
Shannon Rd
W. Congress
22nd St.
22nd
22nd
Aviation Way
Davis-Monthan Air Force Base
22nd
San Juan Trail
36th St.
10
Silver Lake Rd.
36th
Fairfield Strav
Golf
Links Rd
Escalante
Irvington
John F. Kennedy
Lachola Park
Ajo Hwy
Downtown Airport
Country Club Blvd
Verde
86
Tucson Ajo Hwy
Veterans Hospital
SOUTH TUCSON
Irvington Rd
Tucson-Benson Hwy.
10
De Oeste
Dakota Ave
Valley Rd.
Drexel Rd
S. Park Ave.
Palo Verde Way
Alverson
Valencia Blvd.
LITTLETOWN
Valen
Valencia Rd.
EMERY PARK
12th Ave
Missiondale
Cardinal
Valencia
Tucson International Airport
Los Reales Rd.
Wilmot
Kolb
Vail Rd
19
6th Ave
Mission Rd
Los Nogales
Access Rd
Hughes
PIO
19
San Xavier Indian Reservation
10
Rita Rd
Tucson
19

Scale of Miles

© ADC of Alexandria

INDEX

To The United States

Index to Canadian Cities and Towns on Pages 8-9.
Index to Mexican Cities and Towns on Page 11.

ALABAMA
Page 13

Population: 3,893,888
Capital: Montgomery
Land Area: 50,767 sq. mi.

Abanda E-6
Abbeville H-6
Action Pg. 92, J-4
Ada G-5
Adamsville Pg. 92, C-2
Addison B-4
Akron E-3
Alabaster D-4
Albertville B-5
Alden Pg. 92, C-2
Aldrich D-4
Alexander City E-5
Aliceville E-2
Allgood C-5
Almond E-6
Altoona C-5
Andalusia H-4
Anderson A-4
Anniston C-5
Arab B-5
Arcus H-5
Ardilla H-6
Ardmore A-4
Argo D-5
Arkadelphia C-4
Arley C-4
Ashbury C-6
Ashford H-7
Ashland D-6
Ashville C-5
Athens A-4
Atmore J-3
Attalla C-5
Auburn F-6
Awin G-4
Axis J-2
Babbie H-5
Bailyton B-4
Bakerhill G-6
Ballplay C-6
Bangor C-4
Banks G-6
Bankston C-3
Barfield D-6
Barton A-3
Bass A-6
Batesville G-7
Bay Minette J-3
Bay View Pg. 92, D-2
Bayou LaBatre K-2
Bear Creek B-3
Beatrice G-3
Belgreen B-3
Belk D-3
Bellamy F-2
Belleville H-4
Benton F-4
Berry C-3
Bessemer D-4
Vicinity Pg. 92, H-2
Bessie Pg. 92, C-1
Big Cove B-5
Billingsley E-4
Birmingham D-4
Vicinity Pg. 92
Blacksher H-3
Blount Springs C-4
Blountsville C-4
Blue Mountain D-5
Bluff C-3
Boaz C-5
Bolinger G-2
Bon Secour K-3
Borden Springs C-6
Boyd F-2
Braggs G-4
Brantley H-5
Bremen C-4
Brent E-4
Brewton J-4
Bridgeport A-6
Brighton Pg. 92, G-2
Brilliant C-3
Brinn B-3
Brooklyn H-4
Brookside Pg. 92, C-3
Brooksville C-5
Brookwood D-3
Browns F-4
Brownsville Pg. 92, G-3
Brundidge G-6
Bryant A-6
Butler G-2
Bynum D-5
Cahaba Heights Pg. 92, G-6
Calera E-4
Calvert H-2
Camden G-4
Campbell G-3
Camphill E-6
Carbon Hill C-3
Cardiff Pg. 92, C-2
Carrollton D-2
Carrville F-6
Castleberry H-4
Catalpa G-6
Catherine F-3
Cedar Bluff B-6
Center Point Pg. 92, C-6
Centre C-6
Centreville E-4
Chalkville Pg. 92, B-7
Chapel Pg. 92, H-5
Chastang J-2
Chatom H-2
Chelsea D-5
Vicinity Pg. 92, J-7
Cherokee A-3
Chickasaw J-2
Childersburg D-5
Chrysler H-3
Citronelle H-2
Claiborne H-3
Clanton E-4
Claud F-5
Clayton G-6
Cleveland C-5
Clinton E-2
Clio G-6
Clopton H-6
Cloverdale A-3
Coalburg Pg. 92, D-3
Cochrane E-2
Coden K-2
Coffeeville G-2
Collinsville B-6
Columbia H-7
Columbiana D-5
Consul F-3
Cooper E-5
Cordova C-4
Cottonwood J-6
Courtland B-4
Coxey A-4
Creola J-2
Crossville B-6
Cuba F-2
Cullman C-4
Cullomburg G-2
Dadeville E-6
Daleville H-6
Damascus H-4
Dancy E-2
Danville B-4
Daphne J-3
Dauphin Island K-2
Davenport G-5
Daviston E-6
Davisville F-6
Dawes J-2
Dayton F-3
Deans H-4
Deatsville F-5
Decatur B-4
Deer Park H-2
Dees K-2
Delta D-6
Demopolis F-3
Dill H-6
Divide Station Pg. 92, B-3
Dixie J-4
Dixons Mill G-2
Dixonville J-4
Docena Pg. 92, E-2
Dolomite Pg. 92, G-2
Dora C-4
Dothan H-7
Double Springs C-3
Dry Forks G-3
Dublin G-5
Duke C-6
Duncanville E-3
E. Brewton J-4
Eastern Valley Pg. 92, J-2
Easton E-6
Echola D-3
Eclectic F-6
Edgewater Pg. 92, E-2
Edwin G-6
Eight Mile J-2
Elamville H-6
Elba H-5
Elberta K-3
Elias E-5
Eliska H-3
Elmore F-5
Elrod D-3
Elvira Pg. 92, K-3
Emelle E-2
Enterprise H-5
Eoline E-4
Epes E-2
Equality E-5
Ethelsville D-2
Eufaula G-7
Eunola J-6
Eutaw E-3
Evergreen H-4
Ewell H-6
Fairfax E-7
Fairfield D-4
Vicinity Pg. 92, F-2
Fairhope K-2
Falkville B-4
Fatama G-4
Fayette D-3
Fieldstown Pg. 92, C-4
Flat Rock A-6
Flint City B-4
Flomaton J-4
Florala J-5
Florence A-3
Foley K-3
Forkland F-2
Forkville B-3
Fort Mitchell F-7
Fort Payne B-6
Fountain H-3
Francisco A-5
Frisco City H-3
Fruitdale H-2
Fulton G-3
Fultondale D-4
Vicinity Pg. 92, C-4
Gadsden C-6
Gainesville E-2
Gallant C-5
Gallion F-3
Gantt H-5
Gardendale C-4
Vicinity Pg. 92, B-5
Geiger E-2
Genery Pg. 92, K-3
Geneva J-5
Georgiana G-4
Geraldine B-5
Glencoe C-6
Goodwater E-5
Gordo D-3
Grand Bay K-2
Grants Mille Pg. 92, F-7
Graysville Pg. 92, C-2
Green Bay H-5
Green Pond D-4
Greens Station Pg. 92, C-6
Greensboro E-3
Greenville G-5
Greenwood Pg. 92, K-2
Grove Hill G-3
Guin C-2
Gulf Shores K-3
Guntersville B-5
Gurly B-5
Hackleburg B-3
Haleyville B-3
Halsell F-2
Halsos Mill G-5
Hamilton B-2
Hammondville B-6
Hanceville C-4
Harpersville D-5
Harrisburg E-3
Hartford J-6
Hartselle B-4
Hatton B-3
Havana E-3
Hawk D-6
Hayneville F-4
Hazel Green A-5
Hazen F-4
Headland H-7
Helena D-4
Vicinity Pg. 92, K-4
Henagar B-6
Hobson City D-6
Hodges B-3
Hokes Bluff C-6
Hollis D-6
Hollywood A-6
Holt D-3
Holy Trinity F-7
Homewood D-4
Vicinity Pg. 92, F-4
Hoover Pg. 92, H-4
Hueytown D-4
Vicinity Pg. 92, G-1
Hulaco B-4
Hunter F-5
Huntsville A-5
Hurtsboro F-6
Huxford H-3
Hybart G-3
Ider B-6
Ino H-5
Intercourse F-2
Irondale D-4
Vicinity Pg. 92, E-7
Ishkooda Pg. 92, G-3
Isney G-2
Jachin F-2
Jack H-5
Jackson H-3
Jacksonville C-6
Jasper C-4
Jefferson F-2
Jefferson Park Pg. 92, E-7
Jemison E-4
Jenkins Crossroads G-6
Jones F-4
Jones Chapel C-4
Kellerman D-4
Kelly's Crossroads E-5
Kellyton E-5
Kennedy D-2
Ketona Pg. 92, D-5
Kilgore Pg. 92, B-1
Kimberly C-4
Kimbrough G-3
Kinsey H-6
Kinston H-5
Knoxville E-3
Koenton H-2
La Place F-6
Lafayette E-6
Lanett E-6
Langdale E-7
Lawrenceville H-6
Leeds D-5
Leighton A-3
Letohatchee G-4
Lewisburg Pg. 92, D-4
Lexington A-3
Lillian K-3
Lin Crossing Pg. 92, B-2
Lincoln D-5
Lindbergh Pg. 92, C-1
Linden F-3
Lineville D-6
Lipscomb Pg. 92, H-3
Littleville B-3
Livingston F-3
Lockhart J-5
Lottie H-3
Louisville G-6
Lowndesboro F-5
Loxley K-3
Luverne G-5
Lyefflon H-4
Lynn C-3
Magnolia F-3
Malvern J-6
Maplesville E-4
Marbury E-5
Marion E-3
Marvyn F-6
Maytown Pg. 92, E-2
McCalla Pg. 92, J-1
McDade F-5
McIntosh H-2
McKenzie H-5
Mentone B-6
Meridianville A-5
Midfield Pg. 92, G-3
Midland City H-6
Midway G-4
Midway G-5
Millerville E-5
Millport D-2
Millry G-2
Mineral Springs Pg. 92, C-3
Mitchell F-6
Mobile J-2
Monroeville H-4
Monrovia A-4
Montevallo E-4
Montgomery F-5
Montrose K-2
Mooresville B-4
Morgan Pg. 92, J-3
Morgan City B-5
Morris C-4
Morvin G-3
Moulton B-4
Moundville E-3
Mount Andrew G-6
Mount Olive E-5
Vicinity Pg. 92, B-4
Mount Vernon J-2
Mount Willing G-4
Mountain Brook D-4
Vicinity Pg. 92, F-5
Mulberry F-4
Mulga Pg. 92, E-1
Munford D-6
Muscle Shoals A-3
Muscoda Pg. 92, H-2
Nanafalia G-2
Natural Bridge C-3
New Brockton H-5
New Castle Pg. 92, B-5
New Hope B-5
Vicinity Pg. 92, J-6
New Lexington D-3
New Market A-5
Newburg B-3
Newsite E-6
Newton H-6
Newtonville D-3
Newville H-6
Northport D-3
Oak Grove D-4
Oakland B-4
Oakman C-3
Oakwood F-5
Odenville D-5
Ohatchee C-5
Omaha G-7
Oneonta C-5
Opelika E-6
Opp H-5
Overton Pg. 92, F-6
Owens Crossroads B-5
Oxford D-6
Oxmoor Pg. 92, G-3
Ozark H-6
Palmerdale C-4
Vicinity Pg. 92, A-7
Parrish C-4
Pelham Pg. 92, D-4
Pell City D-5
Pennington F-2
Perdido J-3
Peterman H-3
Peterson D-3
Petersville A-3
Phenix City F-7
Phil Campbell B-3
Pickensville D-2
Piedmont C-6
Pine Apple G-4
Pine Grove C-6
Pine Hill G-3
Pinson Pg. 92, B-6
Pisgah B-6
Plantersville F-4
Pleasant Grove D-2
Vicinity Pg. 92, F-1
Prattville F-5
Priceville B-4
Prichard J-2
Pt. Clear K-2
Rabun J-3
Rainbow City C-5
Rainsville B-6
Ranburne D-6
Range H-3
Red Bay B-2
Red Level H-4
Reece City C-5
Reform D-3
Repton H-3
Republic Pg. 92, D-3
Riley G-4
River Falls H-5
River View J-4
Roanoke E-6
Robertsdale K-3
Robinwood Pg. 92, C-5
Rockdale D-6
Rockford E-5
Rocky Ridge Pg. 92, H-5
Roebuck Plaza Pg. 92, D-7
Rogersville A-3
Rome H-5
Romulus E-3
Russellville B-3
Rutledge G-5
Saco G-6
Safford F-3
Saint Elmo K-2
Salitpa G-2
Samson H-5
Sanford H-5
Santuck E-5
Saraland J-2
Sardis F-4
Satsuma J-2
Sayre Pg. 92, A-2
Scottsboro B-5
Seale F-7
Section B-5
Selma F-4
Shannon Pg. 92, H-3
Shawmut E-7
Sheffield A-3
Shelby E-5
Shepardville G-4
Shorter F-6
Silver Hill K-3
Simcoe B-4
Sipsey C-4
Sledge F-3
Slocomb J-6
Smut Eye G-6
Snead C-5
Snowdoun F-5
Somerville B-4
Southside C-5
Spring Hill H-6
Springville C-5
Sprott E-3
Spruce Pine B-3
Stafford D-2
Steele C-5
Stevenson A-6
Stewartville E-5
Stockton J-3
Sulligent C-2
Sumiton C-4
Summerdale K-3
Sunflower H-2
Suttle F-4
Sweet Water G-3
Sylacauga E-5
Sylvan Springs Pg. 92, E-1
Sylvania B-6
Talladega D-5
Tallassee F-6
Tarrant City Pg. 92, D-5
Tensaw H-3
Terese G-7
Theodore K-2
Thomaston F-3
Thomasville G-3
Thorsby E-4
Three Notch G-6
Tibbie H-2
Town Creek B-4
Toxey G-2
Trinity B-4
Troy G-5
Trussville D-5
Tuscaloosa D-3
Tuscumbia A-3
Tuskegee F-6
Union Grove E-5
Vicinity Pg. 92, D-1
Union Springs G-6
Uniontown F-3
Uriah H-3
Valley Head B-6
Vance E-3
Vernon C-2
Vestavia Hills D-4
Vicinity Pg. 92, G-5
Victoria H-6
Vidette G-5
Village Springs C-5
Vineland G-3
Vinemont B-4
Wadley E-6
Wagarville H-2
Walker Chapel Pg. 92, C-4
Walnut Grove C-5
Walnut Hill E-6
Warrior C-4
Weaver C-6
Wedowee D-6
Wenonah Pg. 92, G-3
West Blockton D-4
West Point B-4
Wetumpka F-5
Whatley G-3
Whiteoak B-2
Whitson D-3
Wicksburg H-6
Wilburn C-4
Wilmer J-2
Wilton E-4
Windham Springs D-3
Winfield C-3
Wing J-4
Winterboro D-5
Woodville B-5
Wren B-3
Yantley F-2
Yarbo H-2
York F-2
Zip City A-3

ALASKA
Page 14

Population: 401,851
Capital: Juneau
Land Area: 570,883 sq. mi.

Akhiok F-5
Akolmiut D-4
Akulurak D-4
Akutan F-2
Alakanuk C-4
Alaktak A-7
Aleknagik E-4
Alice Arm H-10
Allakaket C-6
Ambler B-6
Anartuvuk Pass B-7
Anchorage E-6
Inset Map B-2
Anderson D-7
Angoon G-9
Aniak D-4
Anvik D-5
Arctic Village C-8
Atka H-8
Atkasuk A-6
Attu H-5
Baranof G-9
Barrow A-7
Beaver C-7
Beechey Pt A-7
Bethel D-4
Bettles C-7
Big Delta D-7
Big Port Walter G-9
Black D-4
Brevig Mission B-4
Buckland C-5
Candle C-5
Cantwell D-7
Cape Romanzof D-3
Cape Yakataga F-8
Caro C-7
Chalkyitsik C-8
Chatanika D-7
Chenik F-5
Chevak D-4
Chickaloon E-7
Inset Map A-2
Chicken D-8
Chignik F-4
Chitina E-7
Christian C-8
Christochina E-7
Chugiak B-2
Circle C-8
Circle Hot Springs D-8
Clarks Pt E-5
College D-7
Copper Center E-7
Cordova E-7
Craig H-9
Crooked Creek D-5
Deadhorse B-7
Deering B-5
Delta Junction D-7
Dillingham E-4
Donnelly D-7
Dot Lake D-8
Douglas G-9
Dutch Harbor F-2
Eagle D-8
Eagle River E-6
Inset Map B-2
Edna Bay H-9
Eek E-4
Egavic C-5
Elfin Cove G-9
Emmonak C-4
English Bay F-6
Eureka D-7
Fairbanks D-7
False Pass F-3
Farewell D-6
Flat D-5
Fort Yukon C-8
Gakona E-7
Galena C-6
Gambell C-3
Glen Alps E-6
Glennallen E-7
Golovin C-5
Goodnews Bay E-4
Gordon B-8
Grayling D-5
Gulkana E-7
Gustavus G-9
Haines F-9
Hawk Inlet G-9
Healy D-7
Homer E-6
Inset Map C-1
Hoonah G-9
Hooper Bay D-3
Hope E-6
Inset Map B-2
Houston A-2
Hughes C-6
Huslia C-6
Hydaburg H-9
Itulilick E-5
Juneau G-9
Kachemak E-6
Kake G-9
Kaktovik B-8
Kalla C-6
Kaltag C-5
Karluk F-5
Kashegelok E-5
Kasilof E-6
Inset Map B-1
Kaskanak E-5
Katalla F-7
Kenai B-1
Ketchikan H-10
Kiana B-5
Kinegnak E-4
King Cove F-3
King Salmon F-5
Kipnuk E-4
Kivalina B-5
Klawock H-9
Knik B-2
Kobuk C-6
Kodiak F-6
Kokrines C-6
Koliganek E-5
Kotlick C-4
Kotzebue B-5
Koyuk C-5
Koyukuk C-5
Kuliuk F-5
Kwethluk D-4
Kwigillingok E-4
Larsen Bay F-5
Latouche F-7
Levelock E-5
Lime Village E-5
Livengood C-7
Long D-6
Lower Tonsina E-7
Manley Hot Springs D-6
Manokotak E-4
McCarthy E-8
McGrath D-5
McKinley Park D-7
Medfra D-6
Mekoryuk D-3
Mentasta Lake E-7
Metlakata H-10
Minto D-7
Moose Pass B-2
Mount Edgecumber G-9
Mountain Village D-4
Naknek F-5
Napakiak D-4
Napaskiak E-4
Nenana D-7
New Stuyahok E-5
Newhalen E-5
Nikolai D-6
Nikolski F-1
Noatak B-5
Nogamut E-5
Nome C-4
Nondalton E-5
Noorvik B-5
North Pole D-7
Northeast Cape C-4
Northway E-8
Nulato C-5
Old Harbor F-5
Ooliktok A-7
Ouzinkie F-6
Palmer E-7
Inset Map A-2
Pedro Bay E-5
Pelican G-9
Perryville F-4
Petersburg E-6
Pilgrim Springs C-4
Pilot Point F-4
Inset Map D-4
Platinum E-4
Point Hope A-5
Point Lay A-5
Porcupine F-9
Port Alexander G-9
Port Lions F-5
Portlock F-6
Prudhoe Bay B-8
Quinhagak E-4
Rampart C-7
Rampart House C-8
Richardson D-7
Ruby C-6
Russian Mission D-4
Sagwon B-7
Salchaket D-7
Sand Pt F-4
Saroonga C-3
Selawik B-5
Seward E-6
Inset Map C-2
Shageluk D-5
Shaktoolik C-5
Shishmaref B-4
Shungnak B-6
Sinuk C-4
Sitka G-9
Skagway F-9
Sleetmute D-5
Soldotna E-6
Inset Map B-1
Squaw Harbor G-3
St. George E-2
St. Marys D-4
St. Michael C-5
St. Paul E-2
Stebbins C-4
Stevens Village C-7
Stony River D-5
Stuyahok D-5
Susitna B-2
Takotna D-5
Talkeetna E-7
Inset Map A-1
Tanalian Pt E-5
Tanana C-6
Tatitlek E-7
Teller C-4
Tetlin E-8
Tetlin Junction E-8
Togiak E-4
Tok D-8
Toksook Bay D-4
Tonsina E-7
Tuluksak D-4
Tununak D-4
Tyonek E-6
Inset Map B-1
Ugashik F-5
Umiat B-7
Unalakleet C-5
Unalaska F-2
Valdez E-7
Venetie C-8
Wainwright A-6
Wales B-4
Wasila A-2
Wasilla E-7
White Mountain C-5

ALASKA

Whittier B-2
Willow E-6
Inset Map A-1
Wiseman C-7
Wrangell G-10
Yakutat F-8

ARIZONA
Pages 16-17

Population: 2,718,215
Capital: Phoenix
Land Area: 113,508 sq. mi.

Adobe Pg. 135, B-4
Aguila J-3
Ajo L-4
Ak Chin K-5
Alpine J-10
Amado N-7
Anegam L-5
Angell F-7
Apache Jct. K-6
Arivaca Jct. N-7
Arizona City L-6
Arlington K-4
Artesa M-6
Ash Fork F-5
Ashurst K-9
Avondale K-5
Vicinity Pg. 135, E-2
Bagdad G-4
Bapchule K-6
Beaverhead J-10
Bellemont F-6
Benson M-8
Bisbee N-9
Black Canyon City H-5
Bonita L-9
Bouse J-2
Bowie M-10
Brenda J-2
Buckeye K-5
Bullhead City F-2
Bylas K-9
Cameron E-7
Camp Verde H-6
Carefree J-6
Carmen N-7
Carrizo J-8
Casa Grande K-6
Vicinity Pg. 135, E-2
Catalina L-7
Cave Creek J-6
Cedar Creek J-9
Cedar Ridge D-7
Cedar Springs F-8
Central L-9
Chambers F-9
Chandler K-6
Vicinity Pg. 135, F-7
Chandler Heights K-6
Chilchinbito D-9
Childs L-4
Chinle E-10
Chino Valley G-5
Chloride F-2
Christmas K-8
Christopher Creek H-7
Chuichu L-6
Circle City J-4
Clarkdale G-5
Clay Spring H-8
Claypool K-7
Clifton K-10
Cochise M-9
Colorado City C-4
Concho H-9
Congress H-4
Continental M-7
Coolidge K-6
Cordes Jct. H-5
Cornville G-6
Cortaro L-7
Cottonwood G-6
Covered Wells M-5
Cow Springs D-8
Cross Canyon E-10
Currys Corner Pg. 135, B-6
Curtis M-8
Dateland K-3
Desert View E-6
Dewey H-5
Dilkon F-8
Dinnehotso D-9
Dolan Springs F-2
Dome L-2
Dos Cabezas M-10
Douglas N-10
Dragoon M-9
Dudleyville L-8
Duncan L-10
Eager H-10
Eden K-9
Ehrenberg J-2
Elfrida N-9
Eloy L-6
Emery Park Pg. 149, H-3
Fairbank N-8
Flagstaff F-6
Florence K-7
Florence Jct. K-7
Fort Apache J-9
Fort Defiance E-10
Fort Grant L-9
Fort McDowell J-6
Fort Thomas K-8
Fountain Hills J-6
Francisco Grande K-5
Franklin L-10
Fredonia C-5
Gadsden L-1
Ganado F-9
Gila Bend K-4
Gilbert K-6
Glendale J-5
Vicinity Pg. 135, C-3
Globe K-8
Golden Shores G-2
Goldroad F-2
Goodyear K-5
Vicinity Pg. 135, E-1
Grand Canyon E-5
Gray Mountain E-7
Greasewood (Lower) F-9
Green Valley M-7
Greer J-10
Guadalupe K-5
Vicinity Pg. 135, F-5
Hackberry F-3
Hannigan Meadow K-10
Harcuvar J-3
Hawley Lake J-9
Hayden K-7
Heber H-8
Higley K-6
Hillside H-4
Holbrook G-8
Hope J-3
Hotevilla E-8
Houck F-10
Huachuca City N-8
Humboldt H-5
Indian Wells F-8
Jacob Lake D-5
Jaynes Pg. 149, D-2
Jerome G-5
Johnson M-8
Joseph City G-8
Katherine F-2
Kayenta D-8
Keams Canyon E-9
Kearney K-7
Kelvin K-7
Kingman F-2
Kirkland H-4
Kirkland Jct. H-5
Kohls Ranch H-7
Kyrene Pg. 135, F-6
La Palma L-6
Lake Havasu City G-2
Lake Montezuma G-6
Lakeside H-9
Laveen Pg. 135, E-3
Leupp F-7
Litchfield J-5
Littlefield C-3
Littletown Pg. 149, H-5
Lukeville M-4
Lupton F-10
Mammoth L-8
Many Farms D-10
Marana L-6
Marble Canyon D-6
Maricopa K-5
Mayer H-5
McGuireville G-6
McNeal N-9
Meadview E-2
Mesa J-6
Mexican Water C-9
Miami K-7
Moenkopi E-7
Moqui E-5
Morenci K-10
Morristown J-4
Mountainaire G-6
Mt. View M-7
Munds Park G-6
Naco N-9
Navajo G-10
Nelson F-3
New River J-5
Nicksville N-8
Nogales N-7
North Rim E-6
Nutrioso J-10
Oatman G-2
Ocotillo K-6
Olberg K-6
Old Oraibi E-8
Oracle L-7
Oracle Jct. L-7
Oraibi E-8
Oro Valley L-7
Overgaard H-8
Page C-7
Palm Springs K-6
Palo Verde K-4
Palominas N-8
Pantano M-8
Paradise City Pg. 135, B-5
Paradise Valley J-5
Parker H-2
Parks F-6
Patagonia N-7
Paul Spur N-9
Paulden G-5
Payson H-6
Peach Springs F-4
Peeples Valley H-4
Peoria J-5
Vicinity Pg. 135, C-3
Peridot K-8
Phoenix J-6
Vicinity Pg. 135
Picacho L-6
Pima L-9
Pine H-6
Pine Springs F-5
Pinedale H-8
Pinetop H-9
Pirtleville N-9
Polacca E-8
Pomerene M-8
Prescott G-5
Prescott Valley G-5
Punkin Center J-7
Quartzite J-2
Queen Creek K-6
Quijotoa M-5
Randolph K-6
Red Lake D-7
Red Rock L-7
Rillito L-7
Riverside K-7
Riviera F-2
Rock Point D-10
Rock Springs J-5
Roosevelt J-7
Rough Rock D-9
Round Rock D-10
Rye H-7
Sacaton K-6
Safford L-9
Sahuarita M-7
Saint David M-9
Saint Johns H-10
Saint Michaels F-10
Salome J-3
San Carlos K-8
San Luis L-1
San Luis L-5
San Manuel L-8
San Simon M-10
Sanders F-10
Sasabe N-6
Scottsdale J-6
Vicinity Pg. 135, D-6
Seba Dalkai F-8
Second Mesa E-8
Sedona G-6
Seligman F-4
Sells M-5
Sentinel K-3
Shonto D-8
Show Low H-9
Shumway H-9
Sierra Vista N-8
Silver Bell N-6
Snowflake H-9
Solomon L-9
Somerton L-1
Sonoita N-7
South Tuscon M-7
Vicinity Pg. 149, G-2
Springerville H-10
Stanfield L-6
Star Valley H-7
Stargo K-10
Strawberry H-6
Sun City J-5
Vicinity Pg. 135, C-2
Sun City West J-5
Sun Lake K-6
Sun Valley G-9
Sunflower J-6
Sunizona M-9
Sunrise F-7
Sunsites M-9
Superior K-7
Suprise J-5
Tacna L-2
Taylor H-9
Teec Nos Pas D-10
Tempe K-6
Vicinity Pg. 135, E-6
Tes Nez Iha C-9
Thatcher L-9
The Gap D-7
Three Points (Robles) M-6
Tolleson K-5
Vicinity Pg. 135, E-2
Tombstone N-9
Tonalea D-7
Tonopah J-4
Topock G-2
Tortilla Flat J-7
Tracy M-5
Truxton F-3
Tsaile D-10
Tsegi D-8
Tuba City E-7
Tubac N-7
Tucson M-7
Vicinity Pg. 149
Tumacacori N-7
Tusayan E-5
Vail M-8
Valentine F-3
Valle F-5
Vernon H-9
Vicksburg J-2
Wellton L-2
Wenden J-3
Whiteriver J-9
Why M-4
Wickenburg J-4
Wikieup G-3
Wilhoit H-5
Willcox M-9
Williams F-5
Window Rock F-10
Winkelman K-8
Winona F-7
Winslow H-7
Wintersburg K-4
Wittmann J-4
Yampai F-4
Yarnell H-4
Young H-7
Youngtown J-5
Vicinity Pg. 135, C-2
Yucca G-2
Yuma L-1

ARKANSAS
Page 15

Population: 2,286,435
Capital: Little Rock
Land Area: 52,078 sq. mi.

Alpena A-4
Altheimer E-6
Amity E-4
Arkadelphia E-4
Arkansas City F-7
Ash Flat A-7
Ashdown F-3
Athens E-3
Atkins C-4
Augusta C-7
Bald Knob C-7
Banks F-5
Barling C-2
Batesville B-6
Bay B-8
Bearden F-5
Beebe D-6
Benton D-5
Bentonville A-3
Bergman A-4
Berryville A-3
Bismark E-4
Black Rock B-7
Blue Springs D-4
Bluff City F-4
Blytheville B-9
Booneville C-3
Boxley B-4
Bradley G-3
Brashears B-3
Brinkley D-7
Bryant D-5
Bull Shoals A-5
Cabot D-6
Calico Rock B-6
Calion F-5
Camden F-4
Carlisle D-6
Carthage E-5
Cash B-8
Caulksville C-3
Cave City B-7
Cedarville C-2
Centerville C-4
Charleston C-3
Cherry Valley C-8
Clarksville C-4
Clinton C-5
Conway C-5
Corning A-8
Cotton Plant D-7
Cove E-2
Crossett G-6
Crossroads E-7
Crows D-5
Cushman B-6
Dalark E-4
Damascus C-5
Danville D-4
Dardanelle C-4
DeQueen E-2
DeWitt E-7
Decatur A-2
Delight E-3
Deluce E-3
Dermott F-7
Des Arc D-7
Dierks E-3
Dodridge G-3
Dover C-4
Dumas F-7
Earle C-8
El Dorado G-5
Elaine E-8
Emerson G-4
England D-6
Eudora G-8
Eureka Springs A-3
Falcon F-4
Fallsville B-4
Farmington B-2
Fayetteville B-3
Fisher C-7
Flippin A-5
Florence F-6
Fordyce F-5
Foreman F-2
Forrest City D-8
Fouke G-3
Fountain Hill F-6
Ft. Smith C-2
Garland G-3
Gentry A-2
Gillett E-7
Gilmore C-8
Glenwood E-3
Gosnell B-9
Gould E-7
Grady E-6
Grapevine E-5
Gravette A-2
Green Forest A-4
Greenbrier C-5
Greenwood C-2
Greers Ferry C-6
Gurdon E-4
Hackett C-2
Hagarville C-4
Hamburg G-6
Hampton F-5
Hardy A-7
Harrisburg C-8
Harrison A-4
Hartford D-2
Haskell E-5
Hazen D-7
Heber Springs C-6
Helena D-8
Hermitage F-6
Holly Grove D-7
Hope F-3
Horatio E-2
Horseshoe Bend A-6
Hot Springs D-4
Hoxie B-7
Hughes D-8
Humnoke E-7
Humphrey E-6
Huntsville B-3
Huttig G-6
Jacksonville D-6
Jasper B-4
Jonesboro B-8
Judsonia C-6
Junction City G-5
Keiser B-9
Kensett C-7
Kingsland F-5
Lake City B-8
Lake Village F-7
Lavaca C-3
LePanto C-9
Lead Hill E-5
Leslie B-5
Lewisville F-3
Lincoln B-2
Little Rock D-5
Lockesburg E-3
Lonoke D-6
Lowell A-3
Luxora B-9
Madison D-8
Magnolia G-4
Malvern E-5
Mammoth Spring A-7
Manila B-9
Mansfield C-2
Marianna D-8
Marion C-9
Marked Tree C-8
Marmaduke B-8
Marshall B-5
Marvell D-8
Maumelle D-5
Maynard A-7
McCrory C-7
McGehee F-7
Melbourne B-6
Mena D-2
Mineral Springs F-3
Monette B-8
Monticello F-6
Montrose G-8
Morrilton C-5
Mountain Home A-5
Mountain View B-6
Mt. Ida D-3
Mt. Pleasant B-6
Murfreesboro E-3
N. Little Rock D-5
Nashville E-3
Needmore D-3
Newport C-7
Nola D-3
Norman E-3
Oark B-3
Ola D-4
Onyx D-4
Osceola B-9
Oxford B-6
Ozark C-3
Pansy F-6
Paragould B-8
Paris C-3
Parkdale G-8
Parkin C-8
Pea Ridge A-3
Pelsor B-4
Perryville D-5
Piggott A-9
Pine Bluff E-6
Pleasant Plains C-7
Pocahontas A-7
Pollard A-9
Ponca B-4
Portland G-8
Poughke B-7
Prairie Grove B-2
Prattsville E-5
Prescott F-4
Princeton E-5
Quitman C-6
Rector A-8
Reed F-7
Rison E-6
Rogers A-3
Rose Bud C-6
Rosston F-4
Rushing B-6
Russelville C-4
Salem A-6
Salesville A-6
Scranton C-4
Searcy C-6
Sherdian E-5
Shirley B-5
Siloam Springs A-2
Smackover F-5
Snow Lake E-7
Springdale A-2
St. Francis G-4
Star City E-6
Stephens F-4
Story D-3
Strawberry B-7
Strong G-5
Stuggart D-7
Success A-8
Taylor G-4
Texarkana F-3
Timbo B-5
Trumann B-8
Tupelo C-7
Turrell C-9
VanBuren C-2
Vilonia C-6
Waldo F-4
Waldron D-2
Walker C-6
Walnut Ridge B-8
Warren F-6
Washington F-3
Watson F-7
West Fork B-2
West Helena D-8
West Memphis C-9
Western Grove B-4
White Hall E-6
Wickes E-2
Williams Jct. D-5
Willisville F-4
Wilmar F-6
Wilmot G-8
Wilson C-9
Winslow B-3
Witt Springs B-4
Wynne C-8
Y City D-3
Yellville B-5

CALIFORNIA
Pages 18-21

Population: 23,667,902
Capital: Sacramento
Land Area: 156,299 sq. mi.

Acton S-10
Adelanto S-11
Adin C-7
Agoura Hills S-9
Ahwahnee L-8
Alameda Pg. 144, E-3
Alamorio V-15
Albany Pg. 144, C-3
Albion G-2
Alder Creek Pg. 141, B-7
Alder Springs F-3
Alderpoint E-2
Alhambra Pg. 114, C-5
Alleghany F-6
Almanor E-6
Alpaugh P-8
Alpine V-12
Alta Loma Pg. 116, C-11
Altadena Pg. 114, B-6
Altaville J-6
Alton D-1
Alturas C-7
Amboy S-15
Anaheim T-11
Vicinity Pg. 117, G-7
Anderson D-4
Angels Camp J-7
Angwin H-3
Annapolis H-2
Antioch J-4
Apple Valley S-12
Aptos L-4
Arbuckle G-4
Arcadia Pg. 116, C-7
Arcata C-1
Arlington Oaks Pg. 141, D-1
Arnold J-7
Arroyo Grande Q-6
Artesia Pg. 115, F-6
Artois F-4
Arvin Q-9
Atascadero P-6
Atherton Pg. 146, A-1
Atwater L-6
Auberry L-8
Auburn H-6
Avalon U-10
Avenal N-7
Avon Pg. 144, A-6
Azusa Pg. 116, C-8
Badger M-9
Bakersfield Q-9
Balboa Park Pg. 143, F-3
Baldwin Park Pg. 116, C-7
Banning T-13
Barstow R-12
Bartlett Sprs. G-3
Bass Lake L-8
Baxter G-6
Baywood Park Q-5
Bear Valley K-7
Beaumont T-12
Beckwourth F-7
Bel Air Pg. 114, C-2
Belden E-6
Bell Pg. 115, E-5
Bella Vista D-4
Bellflower Pg. 115, F-6
Bells Station L-5
Belmont Pg. 145, J-3
Belvedere Pg. 144, D-1
Ben Lomond L-4
Bend E-4
Benicia Pg. 144, A-5
Benton K-10
Berenda L-7
Berkeley J-4
Vicinity Pg. 144, D-3
Berry Creek F-6
Bertsch Terr. A-1
Beverly Hills S-10
Vicinity Pg. 114, D-3
Bieber C-6
Big Bar D-3
Big Bear Lake S-13
Big Bend C-5
Big Creek L-9
Big Oak Flat K-7
Big Pine L-10
Big Sur N-4
Biggs G-5
Bishop L-10
Blackwells Corner P-7
Blairsden F-7
Bloomington Pg. 116, B-10
Blue Lake C-2
Blythe U-16
Bodega Bay H-2
Bodfish P-10
Bolinas J-3
Bonita Pg. 143, H-5
Boonville G-2
Boron R-11
Borrego Springs U-13
Boulder Creek L-4
Boulevard V-13
Bowman G-6
Bradley P-6
Brawley V-15
Brea Pg. 117, E-8
Brentwood J-5
Bridgeport J-9
Bridgeville D-2
Broderick H-5
Browns Valley G-5
Brownsville G-6
Bryn Mawr Pg. 116, B-12
Buellton R-6
Buena Park Pg. 117, F-7
Burbank Pg. 114, B-4
Burlingame Pg. 145, H-2
Burney D-5
Burnt Ranch C-3
Butte City F-4
Butte Meadows E-5
Buttonwillow Q-8
Cabazon T-13
Cahuilla U-13
Calexico V-15
Caliente Q-10
California City Q-11
California Hot Sprs. P-9
Calipatria V-15
Calistoga H-3
Callahan C-4
Calpella G-2
Calpine F-7
Cambria P-5
Cameron Park H-6
Camino H-7
Camp Nelson N-10
Camp Richardson H-8
Campbell Pg. 146, E-6
Campo V-13
Camptonville G-6
Canby C-7
Canoga Park Pg. 114, B-1
Cantil Q-10
Canyon Dam E-6
Capay H-4
Capetown D-1
Capitola L-4
Carlotta D-1
Carlsbad U-11
Carmel Valley M-4
Carmichael Pg. 141, B-5
Carnelian Bay G-8
Carpinteria S-8
Carson Pg. 115, F-4
Carson Hill - Cartago N-11
Caruthers M-7
Casmalia R-6
Caspar F-1
Castaic S-9
Castella C-4
Castroville M-4
Cayucos P-5
Cedar Grove M-10
Cedarville C-8
Century City Pg. 114, D-3
Ceres K-6
Chalfant L-10
Challenge F-6
Chatsworth Pg. 114, B-1
Chester E-6
Chico F-5
China Lake P-11
Chino Pg. 116, D-10
Cholame P-7
Chowchilla L-7
Chula Vista V-12
Cima Q-15
Citrus Pg. 141, B-6
Claremont Pg. 116, C-10
Clarksburg H-5
Clay J-6
Clayton Pg. 144, C-7
Clearlake G-3
Clovis M-8
Clyde Pg. 144, A-6
Coachella U-14
Coalinga N-6
Coarsegold L-8
Cobb G-3
Colfax G-6
Coloma H-6
Colton Pg. 116, B-11
Colusa G-4
Commerce Pg. 114, D-5
Compton Pg. 115, F-4
Concord J-4
Vicinity Pg. 144, B-6
Copperopolis J-6
Corcoran N-8
Corning E-4
Corona Pg. 117, F-11
Coronado V-12
Costa Mesa Pg. 117, H-8
Cottonwood D-4
Coulterville K-7
Courtland J-5
Covelo E-3
Covina Pg. 116, C-8
Crannell C-1
Crescent City B-1
Crescent Mills E-6
Crestmore Pg. 116, B-10
Crockett Pg. 144, A-4
Cucamonga Pg. 116, C-11
Cudahy Pg. 115, E-5
Culver City Pg. 114, D-3
Cummings E-2
Cupertino Pg. 146, D-4
Cutler N-9
Cutten C-1
Cuyama R-8
Cypress Pg. 115, G-6
Daggett R-12
Dairyville E-4
Dales E-4
Daly City K-3
Vicinity Pg. 145, G-1
Dana Point U-10
Danville Pg. 144, D-6
Darwin N-11
Davis H-5
Davis Creek B-8
Death Valley Jct. N-13
Del Mar V-11
Vicinity Pg. 143, B-1
Delano P-9
Desert Center T-15
Desert Hot Springs T-13
Desert Shores U-14
Devils Den P-7
Diamond Bar Pg. 116, D-8
Diamond Sprs. H-6
Dictionary Hill Pg. 143, G-6
Dillon Beach J-2
Dinkey Creek L-9
Dixon H-5
Dobbins G-6
Dominguez Pg. 115, F-5
Dorris B-5
Dos Palos L-6
Dos Rios F-2
Douglas City D-3
Downey Pg. 115, E-5
Doyle F-8
Duarte Pg. 116, C-7
Ducor P-9
Dulzura V-12
Dunsmuir C-4
Durham F-5
Eagle Rock Pg. 114, C-5
Eagleville C-8
Earlimart P-9
Earp T-17
East Highlands Pg. 116, A-12
East Los Angeles Pg. 114, D-5
East Palo Alto Pg. 146, A-2
Edison Q-9
El Cajon V-12
Vicinity Pg. 143, E-5
El Centro V-15
El Cerrito Pg. 144, C-3
El Granada Pg. 145, J-1
El Monte Pg. 114, C-6
El Nido L-7
El Portal K-8
El Segundo Pg. 115, F-3
El Toro T-11
Elk Creek F-4
Elk Grove J-5
Elmira J-4
Elmore V-14
Emeryville Pg. 144, D-3
Encinitas V-11
Encino Pg. 114, C-2
Enterprise D-4
Escalon K-6
Escondido U-11
Esparto H-4
Essex R-15
Etiwanda Pg. 116, C-12
Etna B-4
Eucalyptus Hills Pg. 143, C-6
Eureka C-1
Exeter N-9
Fair Oak Pg. 141, A-6
Fairfield J-4
Fall River Mills C-6
Fallbrook U-12
Farmersville N-9
Farmington J-6
Fawnskin S-12
Feather Falls F-6
Fellows Q-8
Fenner R-15
Ferndale D-1
Fields Landing D-1
Fillmore S-9
Firebaugh M-6
Fish Camp L-8
Fish Rock G-2
Five Points N-7
Flint Ridge Pg. 114, B-5
Florence Pg. 115, G-6
Florin H-5
Vicinity Pg. 141, E-4
Floriston G-8
Flournoy E-4
Folsom H-6

CALIFORNIA

COLORADO

Fontana . . . . . Pg. 116, C-12
Foothill Farms . Pg. 141, A-5
Forbestown F-5
Ford City Q-8
Forest Glen . . . D-3
Forest Ranch . . . F-5
Foresthill G-6
Fortuna D-1
Foster City . . Pg. 145, H-4
Fountain Valley . Pg. 117, H-7
Fowler M-8
Frazier Park . . . R-9
Fredericksburg . . H-8
Fremont K-4
Vicinity . . . Pg. 145, A-5
Frenbrook . . Pg. 143, B-7
French Gulch . . D-4
Fresno M-8
Ft. Bidwell . . . B-8
Ft. Bragg F-1
Ft. Dick A-1
Ft. Jones B-4
Fullerton T-11
Vicinity . . . Pg. 117, F-7
Furnace Creek Ranch . N-13
Galt J-5
Garberville . . . E-2
Garden Grove . Pg. 117, G-7
Gardena . . . Pg. 115, F-4
Gasquet A-2
Gaviota R-7
Gazelle B-4
Georgetown . . H-6
Gerber E-4
Geyserville . . H-3
Giant Forest Village . N-10
Gilroy L-5
Glamis V-16
Glen Avon . . Pg. 116, D-12
Glen Ellen . . . H-3
Glendale . . . S-10
Glendora . . . S-11
Vicinity . . . Pg. 116, C-8
Glenn F-4
Glennville . . . P-10
Glenview . . Pg. 143, E-7
Goffs R-16
Goleta S-7
Gonzales . . . M-5
Gorman R-9
Goshen N-8
Graeagle . . . F-7
Granada Hills . Pg. 114, A-1
Grand Terrace Pg. 116, B-11
Graniteville . . G-7
Grass Valley . . G-6
Green Acres . . Q-9
Greenfield . . . N-5
Greenview . . . B-4
Greenville . . . E-6
Grenada B-4
Gridley G-5
Grimes G-4
Grossmont . Pg. 143, F-6
Groveland . . . K-7
Grover City . . Q-6
Guadalupe . . . Q-6
Gualala H-2
Guerneville . . H-2
Guinda H-4
Gustine L-6
Hacienda Hts . Pg. 116, D-7
Half Moon Bay . K-3
Hallelujah Jct. . F-8
Hamburg . . . B-3
Hamilton City . F-4
Hanford N-8
Happy Camp . . B-3
Harbor Side . Pg. 143, J-4
Harden Flat . . K-7
Hawaiian Gdns . Pg. 115, G-6
Hawthorne . . Pg. 115, F-3
Hayfork D-3
Hayward K-4
Vicinity . . . Pg. 145, G-6
Healdsburg . . H-3
Heber V-15
Helena D-3
Helendale . . . R-12
Hemet T-12
Hercules . . . Pg. 144, B-3
Herlong E-8
Hermosa Beach Pg. 115, F-3
Herndon M-7
Hesperia . . . S-12
Highland . . Pg. 116, A-12
Highland Park . Pg. 114, C-5
Hillsborough . Pg. 145, H-2
Hilmar L-6
Hilt A-4
Hinkley R-12
Hobart Mills . . G-7
Hollister . . . M-5
Hollywood . . Pg. 114, C-3
Holtville . . . V-15
Homewood . . . G-7
Honcut G-5
Honeydew . . . D-1
Hoopa C-2
Hopland G-3
Hornbrook . . . B-4
Hornitos . . . K-6
Hume M-9
Huntington Beach . T-10
Vicinity . . . Pg. 117, H-7
Huntington Park Pg. 114, E-5
Huron N-7
Idyllwild . . . T-13
Igo D-4
Imperial . . . V-15

Imperial Beach . . . V-12
Vicinity . . . Pg. 143, K-3
Independence . . M-10
Indio T-14
Industry . . Pg. 116, D-7
Inglewood . . Pg. 115, E-3
Ingot D-5
Inverness . . . J-3
Inyokern . . . P-11
Ione J-6
Irvine . . . Pg. 117, H-9
Isleton J-5
Ivanpah . . . Q-15
Jackson . . . J-6
Jamacha . . Pg. 143, F-7
Jamacha Jct . Pg. 143, F-6
Jamestown . . . K-7
Jamul V-12
Janesville . . . E-7
Johannesburg . Q-11
Johnstonville . . E-7
Johnstown . . Pg. 143, D-7
Jolon N-5
Joshua Tree . . S-13
Julian V-13
Junction City . . D-3
June Lake . . . K-9
Keddie E-6
Keeler N-11
Keene Q-10
Kelseyville . . . G-3
Kelso R-15
Kenwood . . . H-3
Kerman M-7
Kernville . . . P-10
Kettleman City . N-7
King City . . . N-5
Kings Beach . . G-8
Kingsburg . . . N-8
Kirkwood . . . H-8
Kit Carson . . . H-7
Klamath Glen . . B-2
Klamath River . . B-4
Kneeland . . . D-2
Knights Ferry . . K-6
Knights Landing . H-5
Kyburz H-7
La Canada . . Pg. 114, B-4
La Crescenta . Pg. 114, B-4
La Grange . . . K-6
La Habra . . Pg. 117, E-7
La Honda . . . L-3
La Jolla . . . V-11
La Jolla Mesa . Pg. 143, D-1
La Mesa . . Pg. 143, E-6
La Mirada . . Pg. 117, F-7
La Palma . . Pg. 115, F-6
La Presa . . Pg. 143, G-6
La Puente . . Pg. 116, D-7
La Quinta . . . T-13
Lafayette . . Pg. 144, C-5
Laguna Beach . . U-10
Laguna Hills . . Pg. 143, D-1
Lake City . . . B-8
Lake Elsinore . . T-12
Lakehead . . . D-4
Lakeport . . . G-3
Lakeside . . Pg. 143, D-7
Lakewood . . Pg. 115, F-5
Lamont Q-9
Lancaster . . . R-10
Lawndale . . Pg. 115, F-3
Laytonville . . . F-2
Lee Vining . . . K-9
Leggett E-2
Lemon Grove . Pg. 143, G-6
Lemoore . . . N-7
Lenwood . . . R-12
Leucadia . . . V-11
Lewiston . . . D-3
Likely C-7
Lincoln H-5
Lincoln Acres . Pg. 143, H-4
Linda G-5
Linden J-6
Lindsay N-9
Litchfield . . . E-7
Little Lake . . . P-11
Live Oak . . . G-5
Livermore . . . K-4
Livingston . . . L-6
Lockeford . . . J-6
Lockwood . . . N-5
Lodi J-5
Loleta D-1
Loma Linda . . Pg. 116, B-11
Lomita . . . Pg. 115, G-4
Lompoc R-6
Lone Pine . . . N-10
Long Beach . . T-10
Vicinity . . . Pg. 115, G-6
Longvale . . . F-2
Lookout C-6
Loomis H-6
Los Alamos . . R-7
Los Altos . . Pg. 145, C-3
Los Altos Hills . Pg. 146, C-2
Los Angeles . . T-11
Vic. . . . . Pg. 114-117
Los Banos . . . L-6
Los Gatos . . . L-4
Los Molinos . . E-4
Los Olivos . . R-7
Lost Hills . . . P-8
Lower Lake . . G-3
Loyalton . . . F-7
Lucerne G-3
Lucerne Valley . S-12
Ludlow R-14
Lynwood . . Pg. 115, F-4
Lynwood Hills . Pg. 143, J-5
Macdoel B-5
Mad River . . . D-2

Madeline D-7
Madera M-7
Malaga M-8
Malibu S-9
Mammoth Lakes . K-9
Manchester . . G-2
Manhattan Beach Pg. 115, F-3
Manteca . . . K-5
Manton D-5
Maricopa . . . Q-8
Marina M-4
Markleeville . . H-8
Martinez . . Pg. 143, D-1
Marysville . . . G-5
Maxwell . . . G-4
Maywood . . Pg. 114, E-5
McArthur . . . C-6
McCloud . . . C-5
McFarland . . . P-9
McKinleyville . C-1
McKittrick . . . Q-8
Meadow Valley . F-6
Meadow Vista . G-6
Mecca U-14
Meeks Bay . . H-6
Mendocino . . F-2
Mendota . . . M-7
Menlo Park . . Pg. 146, A-2
Merced L-7
Mercy Hot Springs M-6
Meridian . . . G-5
Meyers H-8
Mi-wuk Village . K-7
Middletown . . H-3
Midpines . . . K-8
Milford E-7
Millbrae . . . Pg. 145, H-2
Millville D-4
Milpitas K-4
Vicinity . . . Pg. 146, B-6
Mineral E-5
Mira Loma . Pg. 116, D-12
Miramar . . Pg. 145, J-1
Miranda . . . E-2
Mission Beach Pg. 143, F-1
Mission Hills . Pg. 114, B-2
Mission Viejo . T-11
Modesto . . Pg. 114, C-7
Mojave R-10
Mokelumne Hill . J-7
Mono Hot Springs L-9
Mono Lake . . K-9
Monrovia . . Pg. 116, C-7
Montague . . . B-4
Montara . . Pg. 145, H-1
Montclair . . Pg. 116, D-10
Monte Rio . . H-2
Monte Serona . Pg. 146, E-4
Montebello . . Pg. 114, D-6
Montecito . . . R-7
Monterey . . . M-4
Monterey Park . Pg. 114, C-5
Montgomery Creek C-5
Montrose . . Pg. 114, B-5
Moorpark . . . S-9
Moraga . . . Pg. 144, D-5
Moreno . . . Pg. 143, C-7
Morgan . . . Pg. 146, G-10
Morgan Hill . . L-5
Mormon Bar . . L-8
Morongo Valley . T-13
Morro Bay . . Q-5
Moss Beach . Pg. 145, J-1
Moss Landing . M-4
Mountain View . Pg. 146, B-4
Mt. Bullion . . K-7
Mt. Helix . . Pg. 143, F-6
Mt. Laguna . . V-13
Mt. Shasta . . C-4
Mugginsville . . B-4
Murphys . . . J-7
Murrieta . . . U-12
Napa J-4
National City . Pg. 143, H-4
Navarro . . . G-2
Needles . . . R-16
Nevada City . . H-5
New Cuyama . . R-7
New Idria . . . N-6
Newark . . . Pg. 145, K-4
Newberry Springs R-13
Newell B-6
Newport Beach . T-10
Vicinity . . . Pg. 117, H-8
Nice G-3
Niland U-15
Nimbus . . . Pg. 141, B-7
Nipomo Q-6
Nipton Q-15
Norco . . . Pg. 117, E-11
Nord F-5
North Edwards . R-11
North Fork . . L-8
North Highlands Pg. 141, A-4
North Hollywood Pg. 114, A-3
Northridge . . Pg. 114, B-1
Norwalk . . . Pg. 115, F-6
Novato J-3
Noyo F-2
Nubieber . . . C-6
O'Neals . . . L-8
Oakdale . . . K-6
Oakhurst . . . L-8
Oakland . . . K-4
Vicinity . . . Pg. 144, C-4
Oasis L-11
Oceano . . . Q-6
Oceanside . . U-11
Ocotillo . . . V-14
Ocotillo Wells . V-14
Ojai S-8
Olancha . . . N-11

Old Station . . . D-6
Olema J-3
Olinda D-4
Ono D-4
Ontario . . . T-11
Vicinity . . . Pg. 116, D-10
Onyx P-10
Orange . . . Pg. 117, G-8
Orange Cove . . M-9
Orangevale . . Pg. 141, A-6
Orcutt R-6
Ordbend . . . F-5
Orick B-1
Orland F-4
Orleans . . . C-2
Oro Grande . . R-12
Orosi N-9
Oroville . . . F-5
Otay . . . . Pg. 143, K-5
Otay Mesa . . Pg. 143, K-7
Oxnard S-8
Pacific Grove . . M-4
Pacific Palisades Pg. 114, D-1
Pacifica . . . K-3
Vicinity . . . Pg. 145, G-1
Paicines . . . M-5
Pala U-12
Palermo . . . G-5
Palm Desert . . T-13
Palm Springs . T-13
Palmdale . . . R-10
Palms . . . . Pg. 114, D-3
Palo Alto . . . K-4
Vicinity . . . Pg. 146, B-2
Palo Verde . . U-16
Palomar Mountain U-13
Palos Verdes Estates Pg. 115, G-3
Panamint Sprs. . N-12
Panoche . . . M-6
Panorama City . Pg. 114, B-2
Paradise . . . E-5
Paramount . . Pg. 115, F-5
Parker Dam . . S-17
Parkfield . . . P-6
Pasadena . . . S-10
Vicinity . . . Pg. 114, C-5
Paskenta . . . E-4
Paso Robles . . P-6
Patterson . . . L-5
Patton . . . Pg. 116, A-12
Pearblossom . . S-11
Pebble Beach . M-4
Pedley . . . Pg. 117, G-6
Penn Valley . . G-6
Perkins . . . Pg. 141, D-4
Perris T-12
Petrolia . . . D-1
Phelan S-11
Philo G-2
Pico Rivera . . Pg. 114, E-6
Piedmont . . Pg. 144, D-4
Piercy E-2
Pine Grove . . J-6
Pine Valley . . V-13
Pinecrest . . . J-8
Pinedale . . . M-8
Pinole . . . Pg. 144, B-3
Pioneer Station . J-7
Pismo Beach . . Q-6
Pittsburg . . Pg. 144, A-7
Pixley P-9
Placentia . . Pg. 117, F-8
Placerville . . H-6
Planada . . . L-7
Pleasant Hill . Pg. 144, B-6
Plymouth . . . H-6
Point Arena . . G-2
Pollock Pines . H-7
Pomona . . . T-11
Vicinity . . . Pg. 116, D-9
Pondosa . . . C-5
Poplar P-9
Port Hueneme . S-8
Portola . . . F-7
Portola Valley . Pg. 146, A-2
Portuguese Bend Pg. 115, H-3
Potter Valley . F-3
Poway V-12
Vicinity . . . Pg. 143, B-5
Pozo Q-6
Princeton . . . G-4
Project City . . D-4
Pulga F-6
Pumpkin Center . Q-9
Quincy F-6
Raisin M-7
Ramona . . . V-13
Rancho Cordova Pg. 141, C-6
Rancho Palos Verdes T-9
Randsburg . . Q-11
Ravendale . . D-7
Red Bluff . . . E-4
Red Mountain . Q-11
Redcrest . . . D-1
Redding . . . D-4
Redlands . . Pg. 116, B-11
Redondo Beach . T-9
Redway E-2
Redwood City . Pg. 145, J-4
Redwood Valley . G-2
Requa B-1
Reseda S-9
Richgrove . . . P-9
Richmond . . Pg. 144, C-2
Richvale . . . F-5
Rio Dell . . . D-1

Rio Linda H-5
Vicinity . . . Pg. 141, A-3
Rio Oso . . . G-5
Rio Vista . . . J-5
Ripley U-16
Ripon K-5
River Pines . . H-6
Riverdale . . . N-7
Riverside . . . T-12
Vicinity . . . Pg. 117, E-12
Riverview . . Pg. 141, E-1
Robla . . . . Pg. 141, A-3
Rocklin . . . H-5
Rockport . . . F-2
Rodeo . . . Pg. 144, A-3
Rohnert Park . J-3
Rolling Hills . Pg. 115, G-3
Rolling Hills Estate Pg. 115, G-4
Romoland . . . T-12
Rosamond . . . R-10
Rosemead . . Pg. 114, D-6
Rosemont . . Pg. 141, D-5
Roseville . . . H-5
Rough And Ready G-6
Round Mountain . D-5
Rovana L-10
Rowland Heights Pg. 116, E-8
Rutherford . . . H-4
Sacramento . . H-5
Vicinity . . . Pg. 141
Salinas M-5
Salton City . . U-14
Salyer C-2
San Andreas . . J-7
San Ardo . . . N-6
San Bernardino . T-12
Vicinity . . . Pg. 116, A-11
San Carlos . . Pg. 145, J-3
San Clemente . U-11
San Diego . . . V-12
Vicinity . . . Pg. 143
San Dimas . . Pg. 116, C-9
San Fernando . Pg. 114, A-2
San Francisco . K-3
Vicinity . . . Pg. 145
San Gabriel . . Pg. 114, C-6
San Jacinto . . T-12
San Joaquin . . M-7
San Jose . . . L-5
Vicinity . . . Pg. 146, D-8
San Juan Bautista M-5
San Juan Capistrano U-11
San Leandro . . Pg. 145, F-5
San Lorenzo . . Pg. 145, F-5
San Lucas . . . N-5
San Luis Obispo . Q-6
San Marcos . . V-12
San Marino . . Pg. 114, C-6
San Martin . . L-5
San Mateo . . K-3
Vicinity . . . Pg. 145, H-3
San Miguel . . P-6
San Pablo . . Pg. 144, B-3
San Pedro . . Pg. 115, H-4
San Rafael . . J-3
Vicinity . . . Pg. 144, B-1
San Simeon . . P-5
Sanger M-8
Santa Ana . . . T-11
Vicinity . . . Pg. 117, H-8
Santa Barbara . S-7
Santa Clara . . L-4
Vicinity . . . Pg. 146, C-5
Santa Cruz . . L-4
Santa Fe Springs Pg. 115, E-6
Santa Margarita . Q-6
Santa Maria . . Q-6
Santa Monica . T-9
Vicinity . . . Pg. 114, C-2
Santa Nella . . L-6
Santa Paula . . S-8
Santa Rosa . . H-3
Santa Ysabel . V-13
Santee V-12
Vicinity . . . Pg. 143, D-7
Saratoga . . . L-4
Vicinity . . . Pg. 146, E-4
Saticoy . . . S-9
Sattley F-7
Sausalito . . . J-3
Vicinity . . . Pg. 144, D-1
Sawyers Bar . . C-3
Scotia D-1
Scotts Valley . L-4
Scottys Castle . M-12
Seeley V-14
Selma M-8
Shafter Q-8
Shandon . . . P-6
Shasta D-4
Shaver Lake . . L-8
Shelter Cove . E-1
Shingletown . . D-5
Short Acres . . Pg. 144, A-6
Shoshone . . . P-14
Sierra City . . F-7
Sierraville . . F-7
Signal Hill . . Pg. 115, G-5
Simi Valley . . S-9
Simmler . . . Q-7
Sisquoc . . . R-7
Sites G-4
Sloat F-7
Smith River . . A-2
Snelling . . . K-7
Soda Springs . H-7
Solana Beach . Pg. 143, A-1
Soledad . . . N-5
Solvang . . . R-7
Somerset . . . H-7

Somes Bar . . . B-3
Sonoma . . . J-3
Sonora . . . K-7
Soquel L-4
Sorrento . . Pg. 143, C-1
South El Monte Pg. 114, D-6
South Gate . . Pg. 115, E-5
South Lake Tahoe . H-8
South Pasadena Pg. 114, C-5
South Port . . Pg. 141, D-1
South San Francisco
 . . . . . Pg. 145, G-2
Spring Valley . Pg. 143, H-6
Springville . . N-9
Squaw Valley . G-7
St. Helena . . H-3
Standish . . . E-7
Stanton . . Pg. 117, G-7
Stewarts Point . H-2
Stirling City . . F-5
Stockton . . . K-5
Stonyford . . . F-4
Stratford . . . N-8
Strathmore . . N-9
Studio City . . Pg. 114, C-3
Suisun City . . J-4
Sun City . . . T-12
Sun Valley . . Pg. 114, B-3
Sunland . . . Pg. 114, A-4
Sunnyside . . Pg. 143, H-6
Sunnyvale . . K-5
Vicinity . . . Pg. 146, C-4
Surf R-6
Susanville . . E-7
Sutter G-5
Sutter Creek . J-6
Taft Q-8
Tahoe City . . G-7
Talmage . . . G-3
Tarzana . . . Pg. 114, C-1
Taylorsville . . E-6
Tecopa . . . P-14
Tehachapi . . . Q-10
Temecula . . . U-12
Temple City . . Pg. 114, C-6
Templeton . . . P-6
Terminous . . . J-5
Termo D-7
Terra Bella . . P-8
Thornton . . . J-5
Thousand Oaks . S-9
Thousand Palms T-13
Three Rivers . . N-9
Tiburon . . . Pg. 144, D-1
Tipton N-8
Tomales . . . J-3
Toms Place . . L-10
Topanga . . Pg. 114, D-1
Topanga Beach Pg. 114, D-1
Topaz H-8
Torrance . . Pg. 115, F-3
Tracy K-5
Tranquillity . . M-7
Tres Pinos . . M-5
Trinidad . . . C-1
Trinity Center . C-3
Trona P-12
Truckee . . . G-7
Tujunga . . . Pg. 114, A-4
Tulare N-8
Tulelake . . . B-6
Tuolumne . . . K-7
Turlock K-6
Tustin . . . Pg. 117, G-9
Tuttletown . . K-7
Twain F-6
Twain Harte . . K-7
Twentynine Palms S-14
Ukiah G-2
Union City . . Pg. 145, H-6
Universal City . Pg. 114, C-3
Upland . . . Pg. 116, C-10
Upper Lake . . G-3
Vacaville . . . H-4
Valencia . . . S-9
Vallejo J-4
Valley Springs . J-6
Valley View Acres Pg. 141, A-2
Van Nuys . . Pg. 114, B-2
Venice . . . Pg. 114, E-2
Ventura . . . S-8
Vicinity . . . Pg. 144, D-1
Victorville . . S-12
Vidal T-17
Vina E-4
Vinton F-8
Visalia N-8
Vista U-12
Walker J-8
Walnut . . . Pg. 116, D-8
Walnut Creek . K-4
Vicinity . . . Pg. 144, C-6
Walnut Grove . J-5
Wasco P-8
Washington . . G-7
Waterford . . . K-6
Waterloo . . . J-5
Watsonville . . L-4
Watts . . . Pg. 115, E-4
Wawona . . . L-8
Weaverville . . D-3
Weed C-4
Weitchpec . . . C-2
Weott D-1
West Covina . Pg. 116, D-8
West Hollywood Pg. 114, D-3
West Los Angeles
 . . . . . Pg. 114, D-2
West Point . . J-7
West Riverside Pg. 116, D-12

West Sacramento
 . . . . . Pg. 141, C-1
Westley . . . K-5
Westminister . Pg. 117, G-7
Westmorland . V-14
Westport . . . F-2
Westwood . . . E-6
Wheatland . . G-5
Whitmore . . . D-5
Whittier . . Pg. 117, E-7
Williams . . . G-4
Willits F-2
Willow Creek . C-2
Willow Ranch . B-8
Willow Springs . R-10
Willows . . . F-4
Wilmington . Pg. 115, G-4
Winter Gardens Pg. 143, D-6
Winterhaven . V-16
Winters . . . H-4
Winton . . . L-6
Wofford Heights P-10
Woodfords . . H-8
Woodlake . . . N-9
Woodland . . . H-4
Woodville . . . N-9
Woody P-9
Wrightwood . . S-11
Yermo R-12
Yolo H-5
Yorba Linda . Pg. 117, F-9
Yorkville . . . G-2
Yosemite Village K-8
Yreka B-4
Yuba City . . G-5
Yucaipa . . . T-12
Yucca Valley . S-13

COLORADO
Pages 22-23

Population: 2,889,964
Capital: Denver
Land Area: 103,595 sq. mi.

Abarr C-12
Agate D-10
Aguilar . . . J-9
Akron C-11
Alamosa . . . J-7
Allison . . . J-5
Alma E-7
Almont . . . F-6
Amherst . . . B-12
Antero Jct. . E-7
Anton D-11
Antonito . . J-7
Arapahoe . . E-12
Arboles . . . J-5
Arlington . . G-11
Aroya F-11
Arriba D-11
Arriola . . . J-3
Arvada . . . Pg. 103, C-3
Vicinity . . Pg. 103, C-3
Aspen E-6
Atwood . . . B-11
Ault B-9
Aurora . . . D-9
Vicinity . . Pg. 103, E-7
Austin F-5
Avon D-7
Avondale . . G-9
Bailey D-8
Barnesville . B-9
Bartlett . . . H-12
Basalt . . . E-6
Baxter . . . G-9
Bayfield . . . J-5
Bedrock . . . F-4
Bellvue . . . B-8
Bennett . . . D-9
Berthoud . . B-8
Beshoar Jct. . J-10
Bethune . . . D-12
Black Hawk . D-8
Blanca . . . J-7
Blue Mountain C-3
Blue River . . E-7
Bond D-7
Boone G-9
Boulder . . . C-8
Bowie F-5
Boyero . . . E-11
Brandon . . . F-12
Branson . . . J-10
Breckenridge . D-7
Breen J-4
Briggsdale . . B-9
Brighton . . . C-9
Bristol . . . G-12
Broomfield . C-8
Vicinity . . Pg. 103, A-3
Brush C-10
Buckingham . B-9
Buena Vista . F-7
Buford . . . D-5
Burlington . . D-12
Byers D-9
Cahone . . . H-3
Calhan . . . E-10
Cameo . . . E-4
Campo . . . J-11
Canon City . F-8
Capulin . . . J-7
Carbondale . E-6
Carlton . . . G-12
Castle Rock . D-9
Cedaredge . . F-4
Center . . . H-7

Chama J-8
Chatfield Acres . Pg. 103, K-4
Cheney Center . G-12
Cheraw . . . G-11
Cherry Hill Village
 . . . . . Pg. 103, G-5
Cheyenne Wells . D-12
Chimney Rock . J-5
Chipita Park . F-9
Chivington . F-12
Chromo . . . J-6
Cimarron . . G-5
Clarkville . . B-12
Clifton . . . E-4
Climax . . . E-7
Coaldale . . G-7
Coalmont . . C-6
Collbran . . E-4
Colorado City . G-8
Colorado Springs F-9
Columbine . Pg. 103, J-3
Commerce City . D-9
Vicinity . . Pg. 103, D-6
Como E-7
Conejos . . . J-7
Conifer . . . D-8
Cope D-11
Cortez . . . J-3
Cotopaxi . . G-8
Cowdrey . . B-6
Craig B-5
Crawford . . F-5
Creede . . . H-6
Crested Butte . F-6
Cripple Creek . F-8
Critchell . . Pg. 103, K-1
Crook B-11
Crowley . . . G-10
Cuchara . . . J-9
Dailey B-11
DeBeque . . . E-4
Deckers . . . E-8
Deer Ridge . C-7
Deer Trail . . D-10
Deermont . . Pg. 103, K-2
Del Norte . . H-7
Delhi H-10
Delta F-4
Denver . . . D-9
Vicinity . . Pg. 103
Dillon D-7
Dinosaur . . C-3
Divide F-8
Dolores . . . H-4
Dotsero . . . D-5
Dove Creek . H-3
Dowd D-6
Doyleville . . F-6
Drake C-8
Dunton . . . H-4
Dupont . . . Pg. 103, C-6
Durango . . . J-5
Eads F-12
Eagle D-6
Eastlake . . Pg. 103, A-5
Eaton B-9
Echo Lake . . D-7
Eckley . . . C-12
Edgewater . Pg. 103, E-3
Edwards . . . D-6
Egnar H-3
El Dorado Estates
 . . . . . Pg. 103, C-1
Eldorado Springs E-8
Elizabeth . . E-9
Elk Springs . C-4
Ellicott . . . F-9
Empire . . . D-7
Englewood . . D-8
Vicinity . . Pg. 103, G-4
Estes Park . . C-7
Evans C-9
Fairplay . . . E-7
Falcon . . . F-9
Farisita . . . H-8
Federal Heights Pg. 103, B-4
Fenders . . . Pg. 103, J-1
Firstview . . F-12
Flagler . . . D-11
Fleming . . . B-11
Florence . . . G-8
Florissant . . F-8
Fort Collins . B-8
Fort Garland . J-8
Fort Lewis . . J-4
Fort Lupton . C-9
Fort Lyon . . G-11
Fort Morgan . C-10
Fountain . . . F-9
Fowler . . . G-10
Franktown . . E-9
Fraser . . . D-7
Frederick . . C-8
Frisco . . . D-7
Fruita E-3
Galatea . . . F-11
Garcia . . . J-8
Gardner . . . H-8
Garo Park . . E-7
Gateway . . . F-3
Genoa E-11
Georgetown . D-7
Gilcrest . . . C-9
Gilman . . . D-7
Gladstone . . H-5
Glendale . . Pg. 103, F-5
Glenwood Springs D-5
Golden . . . D-8
Vicinity . . Pg. 103, E-1

COLORADO

Goodrich C-10
Gould B-7
Granada G-12
Granby C-7
Grand Junction E-3
Grand Lake C-7
Grandview Estates
. . . . Pg. 103, J-7
Granite E-7
Grant E-7
Greeley C-9
Greenwood Village . . . D-8
. . Vicinity . . . . Pg. 103, H-5
Guffey F-8
Gunnison E-6
Gypsum D-6
Hamilton C-5
Hartsel E-7
Hasty G-11
Haswell F-11
Hawley G-11
Haxtun B-12
Hayden B-5
Henderson . . . . Pg. 103, A-6
Hermosa J-5
Hesperus J-4
Hiawatha B-3
Hillrose C-10
Hillside G-8
Hoehne J-9
Holly G-12
Holyoke B-12
Homelake H-7
Homewood Park Pg. 103, K-1
Hooper H-7
Hot Sulphur Springs . . C-7
Hotchkiss F-5
Howard F-7
Hudson C-9
Hugo E-11
Idaho Sprs. D-8
Idalia D-12
Idledale . . . . . Pg. 103, G-1
Ignacio J-5
Iliff B-11
Indian Hills . . . Pg. 103, H-1
Jansen J-9
Jaroso J-8
Jefferson E-7
Joes D-12
Johnson Village E-7
Julesburg A-12
Keenesburg C-9
Kersey C-9
Kim J-11
Kiowa E-9
Kit Carson F-12
Kline J-4
Komman G-12
Kremmling C-7
La Jara J-7
La Junta G-11
La Salle C-9
La Veta H-9
Lafayette C-8
Laird C-12
Lake City G-5
Lake George F-8
Lakewood D-8
. . Vicinity . . . . Pg. 103, F-12
Lamar G-12
Larkspur E-8
Las Animas G-11
Last Chance D-10
Lay C-4
Lazear F-5
Leadville E-7
Lebanon J-4
Lewis J-3
Limon E-10
Lindon D-11
Littleton D-8
. . Vicinity . . . . Pg. 103, H-4
Lochbuie C-9
Log Lane Village C-10
Loma E-3
Longmont C-8
Loveland C-8
Lucerne C-9
Lycan H-12
Lyons C-8
Mack E-3
Maher F-5
Malta E-6
Manassa J-7
Mancos J-4
Manitou Springs F-8
Manzanola G-10
Marble E-6
Marshall . . . . . Pg. 103, A-1
Marvel J-4
Masters C-9
Matheson E-10
Maybell B-4
McClave G-11
McCoy D-6
Meeker C-4
Meeker Park B-10
Merino B-10
Mesa E-4
Mesita J-8
Milliken C-8
Milner B-5
Mineral Hot Springs . . G-7
Minturn D-6
Model J-10
Moffat G-7
Molina E-4
Monte Vista H-7
Monarch F-7
Montrose G-4
Monument E-9
Monument Park J-9

Morrison . . . . . Pg. 103, G-2
Mosca H-7
Mount Princeton Hot Spr. F-7
Mountain View . Pg. 103, D-3
Nathrop F-7
Naturita G-3
Nederland D-7
New Castle D-5
Northglenn D-8
. . Vicinity . . . . Pg. 103, B-5
Norwood G-4
Nucla G-4
Nunn B-9
Oak Creek C-6
Olathe F-4
Olney Springs G-10
Ophir H-4
Orchard C-9
Orchard City F-4
Ordway G-10
Otis C-11
Ouray G-5
Ovid A-12
Oxford J-5
Pagosa Sprs. J-6
Palisade E-4
Palmer Lake E-8
Paoli B-12
Paonia F-5
Parachute E-4
Paradox G-3
Park F-9
Parkdale F-8
Parker D-9
Parlin F-6
Parshall C-7
Peetz A-11
Penrose F-9
Peyton E-9
Phillipsburg . . . Pg. 103, K-2
Phippsburg B-6
Pierce B-9
Pinewood Springs C-8
Placerville H-4
Platoro J-6
Platteville C-9
Pleasant View J-3
. . Vicinity . . . . Pg. 103, E-1
Poncha Springs F-7
Poudre Park B-8
Powderhorn G-6
Pritchett H-12
Proctor B-11
Prospect Valley C-9
Pryor H-9
Pueblo G-9
Pueblo West G-9
Punkin Center F-10
Ramah E-9
Rand C-7
Rangely C-3
Raymer B-10
Raymond C-8
Red Mountain H-5
Redcliff E-6
Redmesa J-4
Redstone E-5
Redvale G-4
Rico H-4
Ridgway G-4
Rifle D-4
Rio Blanco D-4
Riverside . . . . . Pg. 103, K-3
Rockport B-9
Rockwood H-5
Rocky G-10
Roggen C-9
Rollinsville D-7
Romeo J-7
Royal Gorge G-8
Rush F-10
Rustic B-7
Rye G-9
Saguache G-7
Salida F-7
San Acacio J-7
San Francisco J-8
San Luis J-8
San Pablo J-8
Sanford J-7
Sapinero G-5
Sargents G-7
Saw Pit G-4
Security-Widefield F-9
Sedalia D-8
Sedgwick A-11
Segundo J-9
Seibert E-11
Shawnee E-8
Sheridan . . . . . Pg. 103, F-12
. . Vicinity . . . . Pg. 103, G-4
Sheridan Lake F-12
Silt D-5
Silver Cliff G-8
Silverthorne D-7
Silverton H-5
Simla E-10
Skyway E-4
Slick Rock H-3
Snow Mass E-6
Snow Mass Village . . . E-6
Snyder C-10
Somerset F-5
South Fork H-6
Spar City H-6
Springfield H-12
Starkville J-9
State Bridge D-6
Steamboat Springs . . . B-6
Sterling B-11
Stoneham B-10
Stoner J-4

Stonewall J-9
Strasburg D-9
Stratton D-12
Sugar City G-11
Summitville H-6
Sunbeam B-4
Superior . . . . . Pg. 103, A-2
Swink G-11
Tabernash D-7
Telluride H-5
Texas Creek G-8
Thatcher J-9
The Forks B-8
Thornton D-8
. . Vicinity . . . . Pg. 103, B-5
Timpas H-10
Tiny Town . . . . Pg. 103, H-1
Tobe J-10
Toonerville H-11
Toponas C-6
Towaoc J-3
Towner F-12
Trinidad J-9
Twin Forks . . . . Pg. 103, H-1
Twinlakes E-6
Two Buttes H-12
Tyrone H-10
Uravan G-3
Utleyville J-11
Vail D-7
Valdez J-9
Vancorum G-4
Victor F-8
Vilas H-12
Villa Grove G-7
Vineland G-9
Vona E-11
Wagon Wheel Gap . . . H-6
Walden B-6
Walsenburg H-9
Walsh H-12
Watkins D-9
Welby . . . . Pg. 103, C-5
Weldona C-10
Westcliffe G-8
Westcreek E-8
Westminster D-8
. . Vicinity . . . . Pg. 103, B-3
Weston J-9
Wetmore G-8
Wheat Ridge D-8
. . Vicinity . . . . Pg. 103, E-3
Whitewater F-4
Wiggins C-10
Wild Horse F-11
Wiley G-12
Windsor B-8
Winter Park D-7
Wolcott D-6
Woodland Park E-8
Woodrow C-10
Woody Creek E-6
Wray C-12
Yampa C-6
Yellow Jacket H-3
Yoder F-9
Yuma C-11

CONNECTICUT
Page 24

Population: 3,107,576
Capital: Hartford
Land Area: 4,872 sq. mi.

Andover F-6
Ansonia H-3
Ashford F-7
Avon F-4
Barkhamsted E-4
Berlin G-4
Bethel H-2
Bethlehem G-3
Bloomfield F-4
Branford J-4
Bridgeport J-2
. . Vicinity . . . . Pg. 128, A-19
Bristol G-4
Brookfield G-2
Brooklyn F-7
Burlington F-4
Byram . . . . Pg. 128, F-13
Canaan E-2
Cannondale . . . Pg. 128, B-16
Canterbury F-7
Canton F-4
Chaplin F-7
Cheshire H-4
Chester H-6
Clinton H-5
Colchester G-6
Colebrook E-3
Columbia F-6
Cornwall F-2
Cornwall Bridge F-2
Cos Cob . . . . . Pg. 128, E-13
Coventry F-6
Cranbury . . . . . Pg. 128, C-17
Cromwell G-5
Danbury H-1
Darien J-2
. . Vicinity . . . . Pg. 128, A-20
Dayville F-8
Deep River H-6
Derby H-3
Durham H-5
E. Hartland E-4
East Granby F-5
East Hampton G-6
East Hartford F-5
East Haven J-4

East Lyme H-3
East Norwalk . . Pg. 128, D-16
Eastford E-7
Easton . . . . . . Pg. 128, A-18
Ellington E-5
Enfield E-5
Essex H-6
Fairfield J-2
. . Vicinity . . . . Pg. 128, B-18
Falls Vill. E-2
Farmington F-4
Franklin G-7
Georgetown J-2
Glastonbury F-5
Glen Brook . . . Pg. 128, D-15
Glenville . . . . . Pg. 128, E-12
Goshen E-4
Granby E-4
Greenfield Hill Pg. 128, B-18
Greenwich K-1
. . Vicinity . . . . Pg. 128, E-12
Groton H-7
Guilford J-5
Haddam H-5
Hamden H-4
Hampton F-7
Hartford F-4
Harwinton F-3
Hebron G-6
Kent F-2
Killingworth H-5
Lebanon G-7
Ledyard Ctr. H-7
Litchfield F-3
Long Ridge . . . Pg. 128, C-13
Madison H-5
Manchester F-5
Marlborough G-6
Melrose E-5
Meriden G-4
Mianus . . . . . . Pg. 128, E-14
Middlefield G-5
Middletown G-5
Milford J-3
Mill Plain . . . . . Pg. 128, C-18
Monroe H-2
Morris G-3
N. Canton E-4
Naugatuck G-3
New Britain G-4
New Canaan J-1
. . Vicinity . . . . Pg. 128, C-15
New Fairfield H-2
New Hartford F-3
New Haven H-4
New London H-7
New Milford G-2
Newington F-4
Newtown H-2
No. Stonington H-8
Norfolk E-3
Noroton Heights
. . . . Pg. 128, E-15
North Branford H-4
North Haven H-4
North Stamford Pg. 128, C-14
North Wilton . . Pg. 128, B-15
Norwalk J-1
. . Vicinity . . . . Pg. 128, D-16
Norwich G-7
Old Saybrook J-6
Plainfield F-7
Plymouth F-3
Pomfret E-7
Prospect H-3
Putnam E-7
Redding H-2
Ridgefield H-1
. . Vicinity . . . . Pg. 140, A-15
Riverside . . . . . Pg. 128, F-14
Rocky Hill G-5
Round Hill . . . . Pg. 128, D-12
Rowayton . . . . Pg. 128, D-16
Salem G-6
Salisbury E-2
Scotland F-7
Seymour H-3
Sharon E-2
Shelton H-3
Silvermine . . . . Pg. 128, B-16
Simsbury F-4
Somers E-6
South Norwalk . Pg. 128, D-16
South Wilton . . Pg. 128, B-16
South Windsor F-5
Southbury G-2
Southington G-4
Southport . . . . Pg. 128, C-18
Springdale . . . . Pg. 128, C-14
Stafford E-6
Stamford K-1
. . Vicinity . . . . Pg. 128, C-14
Sterling F-8
Stratford J-3
Suffield E-5
Thomaston G-3
Thompson E-8
Tolland F-6
Torrington F-3
Trumbull J-2
. . Vicinity . . . . Pg. 128, A-20
Union E-6
Vernon F-6
Voluntown G-8
Wallingford H-4
Warren F-2
Washington G-3
Waterbury G-3
Waterford H-7
Watertown G-3

DELAWARE
Page 43

Population: 594,338
Capital: Dover
Land Area: 1,932 sq. mi.

Angola F-15
Bethany Beach F-15
Blades F-13
Bowers Beach D-14
Bridgeville E-14
Camden D-13
Cheswold C-13
Clayton C-13
Delaware City B-13
Dewey Beach E-15
Dover C-13
Ellendale E-14
Elsmere A-13
Felton D-13
Fenwick Is. F-15
Frankford F-15
Frederica D-14
Georgetown E-14
Greenwood E-13
Gumboro F-14
Harbeson E-14
Hardscrabble F-14
Harrington D-13
Hartly D-13
Houston D-13
Laurel F-14
Leipsic C-14
Lewes E-15
Middletown B-13
Milford D-14
Millsboro F-15
Millville F-15
Milton E-14
Mission A-13
New Castle A-13
Newark A-13
Newport B-13
Odessa B-13
Porter B-13
Seaford F-13
Selbyville F-15
Slaughter Beach E-14
Smyrna C-14
Staytonville D-14
Townsend B-13
Wilmington A-14
Wyoming D-13

DIST. OF COLUMBIA
Page 43

Population: 638,333
Capital: Washington
Land Area: 63 sq. mi.

Washington E-8
. . Vicinity . . . . Pg. 150

FLORIDA
Pages 26-27

Population: 9,746,324
Capital: Tallahassee
Land Area: 58,560 sq. mi.

Alachua C-5
Altamonte Springs
. . . . Pg. 133, B-4
Apalachicola Q-6
Apollo Beach H-5
. . Vicinity . . . . Pg. 148, N-8
Apopka F-7
. . Vicinity . . . . Pg. 133, A-3
Arcadia J-6
Archer D-5
Atlantic Beach B-7
Avon Pk. H-7
Bal Harbor . . . . Pg. 120, B-6
Baldwin B-6
Bartow H-7
Bay Harbor Is. . Pg. 120, B-6
Bay Pines . . . . Pg. 148, G-2
Bellair . . . . Pg. 111, H-2
Bellair Beach . . Pg. 148, E-1
Belle Isle . . . . . Pg. 133, C-5
Belleair K-9
Belleair Beach . Pg. 148, E-1
Belleair Bluffs . . Pg. 148, E-1
Belleair Shores . Pg. 148, E-1
Belleview E-6
Biscayne Park . . Pg. 120, E-5

Blacks Ford . . . . Pg. 111, K-4
Blountstown P-6
Bloxham B-1
Boca Grande . . Pg. 108, A-1
Boca Raton L-10
. . Vicinity . . . . Pg. 120, C-5
Bokeelia . . . . . Pg. 108, B-3
Bonifay N-5
Bonita Spr. L-6
Boynton Beach K-10
. . Vicinity . . . . Pg. 120, D-5
Bradenton H-5
Brandon G-5
Branford C-4
Briny Breezes . . Pg. 120, E-3
Bristol P-6
Brooksville F-5
Buenaventura Lakes
. . . . Pg. 133, D-1
Bunnell D-7
Bushnell F-6
Callahan B-6
Callaway P-5
Campbell . . . . . Pg. 133, K-4
Cantonment N-2
Cape Coral . . . . Pg. 108, C-5
. . Vicinity . . . . Pg. 108, C-5
Captiva . . . . . . Pg. 108, A-2
Carrabelle C-6
Casselberry E-7
. . Vicinity . . . . Pg. 133, B-6
Cedar Key E-4
Chattahoochee A-1
Chiefland D-4
Chipley N-5
Citrus Park . . . . Pg. 148, B-5
Citrus Spr. E-5
Clearwater . . . . Pg. 148, D-2
Clearwater Beach Is.
. . . . Pg. 148, D-1
Clermont F-6
Clewiston K-8
Cocoa Beach C-6
Coconut Creek . Pg. 120, G-2
Cooper City . . . Pg. 111, J-7
. . Vicinity . . . . Pg. 120, F-4
Coral Gables M-9
. . Vicinity . . . . Pg. 120, F-4
Coral Springs . . Pg. 120, A-4
Crawfordville C-2
Crescent City D-7
Crestview N-3
Cross City D-4
Crown Point . . . Pg. 133, C-2
Crystal Beach . . Pg. 148, K-2
Crystal River E-5
Cutler Ridge M-9
Dade City F-5
Davie . . . . Pg. 120, D-5
Daytona Beach E-8
DeBary E-7
DeFuniak Springs N-4
DeLeon Springs E-7
Deer Island . . . Pg. 133, D-1
Deerfield Beach . Pg. 120, G-2
Delray Beach K-10

Deltona . . . . . . Pg. 133, A-6
Doctors Inlet . . . Pg. 111, J-1
Dover H-4
Dunedin . . . . . Pg. 148, C-2
. . Vicinity . . . . Pg. 148, C-2
Dunnellon E-5
Durbin . . . . Pg. 111, J-6
East Palatka D-7
Eastpoint Q-6
Eatonville . . . . . Pg. 133, C-5
Edgewater E-8
Edgewood . . . . Pg. 133, E-5
El Portal . . . . . Pg. 120, E-5
Ellenton H-5
Englewood J-5
Ensley N-2
Eustis E-6
Everglades City M-7
Fellowship Park . Pg. 111, K-4
Fellsmere H-9
Fernandina Beach B-7
Flagler Beach D-7
Fleming . . . . . . Pg. 111, J-4
Florida City M-9
Forest City . . . . Pg. 133, B-5
Fort Basinger H-8
Fort Lauderdale L-9
. . Vicinity . . . . Pg. 120, C-6
Fort Myers . . . . Pg. 108, C-8
Fort Myers Beach K-6
. . Vicinity . . . . Pg. 108, F-6
Fort Pierce H-9
Fort Walton Beach N-3
Fort White C-5
Freeport N-4
Frost Proof H-7
Fruit Cove . . . . Pg. 111, J-3
Gainesville D-5
Gardenia . . . . . Pg. 133, A-7
Gator Island . . . Pg. 133, C-2
Gifford H-9
Golden Beach . . Pg. 120, B-6
Golf . . . . Pg. 120, E-2
Graceville M-5
Green Cove Spr. C-6
Greenacres City Pg. 120, D-3
Greenville B-3
Gretna B-1
Grove City J-5
Gulf Stream . . . Pg. 120, E-3
Gulfport . . . . . . Pg. 148, H-3
Haines City G-7
. . Vicinity . . . . Pg. 133, B-6
Hallandale . . . . Pg. 120, D-6
Hastings D-7

Havana B-2
Hawthorne D-6
Hialeah Gardens Pg. 120, E-3
High Springs C-5
Highland Beach . Pg. 120, F-3
Hilden . . . . Pg. 111, K-6
Hilliard A-6
Hillsboro Beach Pg. 120, A-6
Hobe Sound J-10
Hollywood L-9
. . Vicinity . . . . Pg. 120, D-5
Holmes Beach H-5
Homestead M-9
Homosassa E-5
Hosford P-6
Hudson F-5
Hull Island . . . . Pg. 133, D-1
Hypoluxo . . . . . Pg. 120, D-3
Indian Creek Village
. . . . Pg. 120, E-5
Indian Harbour Beach . . G-8
Indian Rocks Beach
. . . . Pg. 148, F-1
Indian Shores . . Pg. 148, F-1
Indiantown J-9
Inglis E-5
Intercession City Pg. 133, K-4
Inverness E-5
Islamorada . . . . Pg. 111, H-7
Jacksonville B-7
Jacksonville Beach B-7
Jasper B-4
Jay N-2
Juno Beach . . . Pg. 120, B-2
Jupiter . . . . . . Pg. 120, A-2
Jupiter Inlet Colony
. . . . Pg. 120, A-3
Kenneth City . . Pg. 148, G-3
Key Biscayne . . Pg. 120, G-5
Key Largo N-9
Key West H-5
Keystone Hts. C-6
Kissimmee F-7
. . Vicinity . . . . Pg. 133, D-2
LaBelle K-7
Lacoochee F-6
Lake Asbury . . . Pg. 111, K-1
Lake Buena Vista Pg. 133, F-2
Lake City C-5
Lake Park K-9
. . Vicinity . . . . Pg. 120, B-3
Lake Wales G-7
Lake Worth K-10
. . Vicinity . . . . Pg. 120, D-3
Lakeland G-6
Lantana K-10
Largo G-4
. . Vicinity . . . . Pg. 148, E-2
Lauderdale Lakes Pg. 120, B-5
Lauderdale-By-The-Sea
. . . . Pg. 120, B-6
Lauderhill . . . . . Pg. 120, B-5
Leesburg F-6
Lehigh Acres K-7
Lighthouse Pt. L-10
Live Oak B-4
Longboat Key H-5
Longwood . . . . Pg. 133, A-6
Lutz . . . . Pg. 148, A-7
Lynn Haven P-5
Macclenny B-6
Madeira Beach . Pg. 148, G-1
Madison B-3
Makinson Island Pg. 133, K-5
Maitland . . . . . Pg. 133, C-6
Manalapan . . . . Pg. 120, E-3
Mangonia Park . Pg. 120, C-3
Marathon P-8
Marco Is. L-6
Margate . . . . . . Pg. 120, B-5
Marianna N-5
Matlacha . . . . . Pg. 108, C-4
Mayo C-4
McDonald . . . . . Pg. 133, A-2
Medley . . . . . . Pg. 120, E-4
Melbourne G-9
Merritt Is. F-8
Miami M-9
. . Vicinity . . . . Pg. 120, E-5
Miami Beach M-10
. . Vicinity . . . . Pg. 120, D-4
Miami Gardens . Pg. 120, D-4
Miami Shores . . Pg. 120, E-5
Miami Springs M-9
Mickler Landing . Pg. 111, H-7
Midway Park . . . Pg. 133, A-7
Milton N-2
Mims F-8
Miramar . . . . . . Pg. 120, D-5
Monticello B-3
Moore Haven K-8
Mount Dora E-7
Naples L-6
Naples Pk. L-6
Neptune Beach B-7
New Port Richey F-5
New Smyrna Beach . . . E-8
Niceville N-4
North Bay Village Pg. 120, E-5
North Fort Myers
. . . . Pg. 108, C-8
North Lauderdale L-9
. . Vicinity . . . . Pg. 120, B-5
North Miami . . . Pg. 120, E-5
North Miami Beach
. . . . Pg. 120, D-5
North Palm Beach K-10
. . Vicinity . . . . Pg. 120, B-3
North Port J-6

North Redington Beach
. . . . Pg. 148, G-1
Oakland . . . . . . Pg. 133, D-1
Oakland Park L-10
. . Vicinity . . . . Pg. 120, B-5
Ocala E-6
Ocean Ridge . . Pg. 120, E-3
Ocoee . . . . Pg. 133, D-2
Okeechobee J-8
Oldsmar . . . . . Pg. 148, C-4
Opa-Locka L-9
Orange . . . . . . Pg. 111, H-2
Orange Pk. C-6
Orlando F-7
. . Vicinity . . . . Pg. 133
Ormond by the Sea . . . D-8
Ormond Beach D-8
Osceola . . . . . . Pg. 133, H-3
Osprey J-5
Ozona . . . . Pg. 148, C-3
Pace N-2
Palatka D-6
Palm Bay G-9
Palm Beach Gardens
. . . . Pg. 120, B-2
Palm Harbor . . . Pg. 148, B-2
Palm Springs . . Pg. 120, D-2
Palm Valley . . . . Pg. 111, H-7
Palm Valley Landing
. . . . Pg. 111, H-7
Panama City P-5
Parkland . . . . . Pg. 120, G-1
Pembroke G-6
Pembroke Park . Pg. 120, D-5
Pembroke Pines Pg. 120, D-5
. . Vicinity . . . . Pg. 120, D-3
Pensacola N-2
Perrine M-9
Perry C-3
Pine Castle . . . . Pg. 133, F-5
Pineland . . . . . Pg. 108, B-3
Pinellas Park . . . Pg. 148, F-3
Plant City G-6
Plantation . . . . Pg. 120, C-5
Plymouth . . . . . Pg. 133, A-2
Pompano Beach L-10
. . Vicinity . . . . Pg. 120, B-5
Ponte Vedra Beach
. . . . Pg. 111, G-7
Port Charlotte J-6
Port St. Joe Q-5
Port St. Lucie H-9
Punta Gorda L-6
Quincy B-1
Reddick D-5
Redington Beach Pg. 148, G-1
Redington Shores
. . . . Pg. 148, G-1
Remington Park Pg. 111, K-3
Richmond Hts. M-9
Rideout . . . . . . Pg. 111, J-1
Ridge Manor F-6
Ridgewood . . . . Pg. 111, H-1
Riviera Beach K-10
. . Vicinity . . . . Pg. 120, B-3
Rockledge F-8
Rotonda K-6
Royal Palm Beach
. . . . Pg. 120, C-1
Ruskin . . . . Pg. 148, J-7
Russell . . . . . . Pg. 111, K-2
Russell Landing . Pg. 111, J-2
Safety Harbor . . Pg. 148, C-4
Sampson . . . . . Pg. 111, K-5
Sanford E-7
Sanibel K-6
Sanlando Springs Pg. 133, A-5
Sarasota J-5
Satellite Beach G-8
Sea Ranch Lakes Pg. 120, B-6
Sebastian H-9
Sebring H-7
Seminole . . . . . Pg. 148, F-2
Sneads N-6
Sopchoppy C-1
South Apopka . . Pg. 133, B-3
South Bay K-8
South Beach . . . Pg. 120, D-3
South Daytona E-8
South Miami . . . Pg. 120, G-4
South Pasadena Pg. 148, H-3
South Venice J-5
Spanish Landing Pg. 111, K-6
Spring Lake H-7
Springfield P-5
St. Augustine C-7
St. Augustine Beach . . . C-7
St. Cloud G-7
St. James City . Pg. 108, E-4
St. Petersburg G-4
. . Vicinity . . . . Pg. 148, H-5
St. Petersburg Beach . . H-4
Stuart J-10
Sun City . . . . . Pg. 148, K-7
Sun City Ctr. H-5
Sunrise . . . . . . Pg. 120, B-4
Surfside . . . . . . Pg. 120, D-5
Sweetwater . . . Pg. 120, F-3
Switzerland . . . . Pg. 111, J-3
Taft . . . . Pg. 133, G-5
Tallahassee B-2
Tamarac . . . . . Pg. 120, B-4
Tampa G-5
. . Vicinity . . . . Pg. 148, C-7
Tarpon Spr. G-4
. . Vicinity . . . . Pg. 148, A-2

FLORIDA

Temple Terrace G-5
  Vicinity .. Pg. 148, C-8
Tennille C-3
The Springs Pg. 133, A-5
Thomas City B-2
Tice K-6
Titusville F-8
Treasure Island K-6
  Vicinity .. Pg. 148, K-8
Trenton D-4
Truckland .. Pg. 108, E-6
Twenty Mile .. Pg. 111, J-6
Umitilla E-6
Valparaiso N-3
Venice J-5
Vero Beach E-4
Virginia Gardens ... Pg. 120, F-4
Virginia Key .. Pg. 120, F-6
Warrington N-2
Watertown C-5
Wauchula H-6
Wausau N-5
Waverly G-7
Wellington .. Pg. 120, D-1
West Melbourne G-8
West Miami .. Pg. 120, F-4
West Palm Beach ... Pg. 120, C-2
Westwood Lake M-9
Wewahitchka P-5
White City Q-5
Whites Ford Pg. 111, K-5
Wildwood E-6
Williston D-5
Wilma P-6
Wilton Manors ..... Pg. 120, B-6
Windermere .. Pg. 133, E-3
Winter Garden F-7
  Vicinity .. Pg. 133, D-2
Winter Park F-7
  Vicinity .. Pg. 133, C-6
Winter Springs
  Vicinity .. Pg. 133, A-2
Woodville B-2
Zellwood .. Pg. 133, A-2
Zephyrhills G-5
Zolfo Spr. H-6

GEORGIA
Pages 28-29
Population: 6,478,216
Capital: Atlanta
Land Area: 54,153 sq. mi.

Abbeville K-5
Acworth F-3
Adairsville E-2
Adams Park . Pg. 90, G-3
Adcock ..... Pg. 90, D-1
Adel M-5
Adrian J-7
Alamo K-6
Alapaha L-5
Albany L-3
Aldora H-4
Allentown J-5
Alma L-6
Alpharetta E-4
Alston J-6
Alto E-5
Alvaton H-3
Ambrose L-6
Americus K-3
Amsterdam N-3
Andersonville K-3
Apalachee F-5
Appling G-7
Arabi K-4
Aragon F-2
Arlington L-3
Arnoldsville F-5
Ashburn L-4
Ashford Park . Pg. 90, C-5
Athens F-4
Atlanta F-4
  Vicinity Pg. 90
Attapulgus N-3
Augusta G-7
Austell F-3
Avalon E-6
Avondale Estates .. Pg. 90, E-7
Axson M-7
Baconton M-4
Bainbridge N-3
Baldwin E-5
Ball Ground E-3
Barnesville H-4
Barney N-5
Barwick N-5
Baxley L-7
Bellview L-2
Belvedere .. Pg. 90, F-6
Benevolence K-3
Bentwood .. Pg. 90, A-5
Berkeley Lake Pg. 90, A-7
Berlin M-5
Berryton E-1
Between F-5
Bishop F-5
Blackshear L-8
Blakely L-2
Blue Creek . Pg. 90, H-6
Blue Ridge D-3
Bluffton L-2
Bonaire J-5
Boston N-4
Bowden G-2
Bowersville E-6
Bowman E-6

Boykin M-3
Brant Park .. Pg. 90, F-5
Bremen F-2
Brentwood Manor .. Pg. 90, F-7
Briar Hills .. Pg. 90, E-5
Bridgeboro L-4
Bristol L-7
Bronwood L-3
Brookhaven . Pg. 90, D-5
Broxton L-6
Brunswick M-9
Buchanan F-2
Buckhead .. Pg. 90, D-5
Buena Vista J-3
Buford E-4
Butler J-3
Byron J-4
Cadwell J-6
Cairo N-4
Calhoun E-2
Calvary N-3
Camilla M-3
Candler E-4
Canon E-6
Canoochee H-7
Canterbury Forest .. Pg. 90, B-2
Canton E-3
Cardinal Woods ... Pg. 90, D-7
Carnegie L-2
Carrollton G-2
Cartersville E-2
Cascade Knolls ... Pg. 90, G-2
Cave Spring E-2
Cecil M-5
Cedar Corners Pg. 90, A-7
Cedar Springs M-2
Cedartown F-2
Center F-5
Center Hill .. Pg. 90, F-5
Centerville M-2
Chamblee .. Pg. 90, C-5
Chapel Hill . Pg. 90, H-7
Chatsworth D-2
Chauncey K-5
Cherokee Pines ... Pg. 90, C-1
Chester J-6
Chickamauga D-2
Cisco D-3
Clairmont North ... Pg. 90, D-6
Clarkesville D-5
Clarkston .. Pg. 90, E-7
Claxton K-8
Clayton D-5
Cleveland D-4
Climax N-3
Club Candlewood .. Pg. 90, J-2
Clyattville N-5
Clyo J-9
Cobbtown J-8
Cochran J-5
Cogdell M-6
Cohutta D-2
Colemans Lake H-7
College Park Pg. 90, H-3
Collier Heights ... Pg. 90, F-3
Colquitt N-3
Columbia Valley Acres .. Pg. 90, G-7
Columbus J-2
Comer E-6
Commerce E-5
Conley ..... Pg. 90, J-5
Conyers F-5
Cooks Crossing ... Pg. 90, J-1
Coolidge M-4
Cordele K-4
Cornelia E-5
Cotton M-4
Covena J-7
Covington G-5
Crandall D-3
Crawford F-5
Crawfordville G-6
Creekwood Hills ... Pg. 90, H-7
Culloden H-4
Cumming E-4
Cusseta J-2
Cuthbert L-2
Dacula F-4
Dahlonega D-4
Dallas F-3
Dalton D-2
Damascus M-3
Danielsville E-6
Darien L-9
Dasher N-6
Davis Woods Pg. 90, C-4
Davisboro H-7
Dawson L-3
Dawsonville E-4
DeKalb Cambridge .. Pg. 90, B-7
Decatur .... Pg. 90, F-6
Delowe Gardens ... Pg. 90, H-3
Demorest D-5
Dexter J-6
Doerun M-4
Donalsonville M-2
Doraville .. Pg. 90, C-6
Douglas L-6
Douglasville F-3
Dublin J-6
Duluth F-4
Dunwoody .. Pg. 90, B-5

Dupont M-6
East Atlanta . Pg. 90, G-5
East Dublin J-6
East Lake .. Pg. 90, F-6
East Point F-3
  Vicinity .. Pg. 90, H-3
Eastglen ... Pg. 90, H-7
Eastman J-5
Eatonton H-5
Edgehill H-7
Edgemoor .. Pg. 90, K-4
Edgewood .. Pg. 90, F-5
Edison L-3
Elberton E-6
Elko J-5
Ellaville K-3
Ellenton M-5
Ellenwood .. Pg. 90, J-6
Ellijay D-3
Emerson E-3
Emory ..... Pg. 90, E-6
Empire J-6
Enigma L-6
Enon Forest . Pg. 90, H-1
Evans F-8
Faceville N-3
Fair Oaks .. Pg. 90, B-2
Fairburn ... Pg. 90, K-1
Fairmount E-3
Falconhurst . Pg. 90, J-2
Fargo N-7
Fayetteville G-3
Featherwood Pg. 90, K-3
Feldwood Pines ... Pg. 90, K-2
Fernandina Beach .. N-9
Fernwood .. Pg. 90, J-6
Finleyson J-5
Fitzgerald K-5
Flairsville D-4
Flemington K-9
Folkston N-8
Forest Park .. Pg. 90, J-4
  Vicinity .. Pg. 90, J-5
Forsyth H-4
Fort Gaines L-2
Fort Gillem . Pg. 90, J-5
Fort Ogelthorp D-2
Fort Valley J-4
Fouts Corner Pg. 90, B-7
Franklin F-2
Franklin Springs ... E-6
Gainesville E-4
Garden City K-9
Garden Hills Pg. 90, D-5
Geneva J-3
Georgetown K-2
Gibson H-7
Gillsville E-5
Girard H-9
Glennville K-8
Glenwood K-7
Gordon J-5
Gracewood G-8
Grantville G-2
Gray H-5
Green Oaks . Pg. 90, K-5
Greensboro F-6
Greenville H-3
Gresham ... Pg. 90, E-1
Griffin H-4
Grovania J-5
Grove Park . Pg. 90, F-3
Grove Town F-8
Haddock H-5
Hagan K-8
Hahira M-5
Hamilton H-2
Hampton G-4
Hapeville .. Pg. 90, H-4
Haralson H-3
Harlem G-7
Harrison J-7
Hartwell E-6
Hawkinsville K-5
Haynes Manor Pg. 90, E-4
Hazelhurst K-6
Helen D-5
Helena K-6
Henrico L-3
Hephzibah H-8
Herod L-3
Hiawassee D-5
Hickox M-8
Hill Park .. Pg. 90, E-3
Hilltonia H-8
Hilton M-2
Hinesville K-8
Hoboken M-8
Hogansville G-2
Holly Ridge . Pg. 90, M-4
Holly Springs E-3
Homeland M-8
Homer E-5
Homerville M-7
Horseshoe Bend ... Pg. 90, A-6
Ideal J-4
Idlewood .. Pg. 90, E-2
Ila E-6
Indian Crossing ... Pg. 90, B-7
Irwinton J-6
Irwinville L-5
Ivey J-6
Jackson G-4
Jacksonville L-6
Jasper E-3
Jefferson E-5
Jeffersonville J-5
Jesup L-8
Jonesboro G-3
Juno J-6
Kingsland N-9
Kingston E-2

Kirkwood ... Pg. 90, F-5
Kite H-7
Knight Park . Pg. 90, F-3
Knoxville H-4
La Grange H-2
LaFayette D-2
Lake City .. Pg. 90, K-5
Lake Park N-6
Lake Shore . Pg. 90, C-1
Lakeland M-6
Lakemont D-5
Lakeside North ... Pg. 90, C-4
Lakewood .. Pg. 90, H-4
Lakewood Heights .. Pg. 90, G-5
Landmark .. Pg. 90, G-5
Lavonia E-6
Lawrenceville F-4
Leary L-3
Leesburg L-4
Leland ..... Pg. 90, E-1
Lenox M-5
Leslie K-4
Lexington F-6
  Vicinity .. Pg. 90, H-3
Lilburn F-4
Lilly K-4
Lincoldale . Pg. 90, H-7
Lincolnton F-7
Lithonia F-4
Lockheed .. Pg. 90, B-2
Locust Grove G-4
Loganville F-5
Louisville H-7
Lovett H-6
Ludowici L-8
Lula E-5
Lumber City K-6
Lumpkin K-3
Luthersville G-3
Lyons J-7
Mableton .. Pg. 90, E-1
Macon H-5
Madison F-5
Manchester H-3
Manor M-7
Margret D-4
Marietta F-3
  Vicinity .. Pg. 90, B-1
Marron .... Pg. 90, E-7
Marshallville J-4
Maxeys F-5
Maysville E-5
McCaysville D-3
McIntire H-6
McRae K-6
Meadow Lake Pg. 90, M-4
Meigs M-4
Menlo Park D-2
Merrillville M-4
Metcalf N-4
Metter J-8
Middleton F-6
Midtown ... Pg. 90, E-4
Midville H-7
Milan K-6
Milledgeville H-6
Millen H-8
Mineral Bluff D-4
Modoc H-7
Molena H-3
Moncrief N-4
Monroe F-5
Montevista . Pg. 90, G-1
Montezuma J-4
Monticello G-5
Morgan L-3
Morganton D-4
Morningside Pg. 90, E-5
Morris K-2
Morrow .... Pg. 90, K-5
Morven M-5
Moultrie M-4
Mountain City D-5
Mountain View Pg. 90, J-4
Mt. Airy D-5
Mt. Bethel . Pg. 90, A-4
Mt. Vernon K-7
Mt. Zion F-2
Nahunta M-8
Nantucket . Pg. 90, F-7
Nashville M-6
Naylor N-6
Nelson E-4
Newington J-9
Newnan G-2
Newton M-3
Nicholls L-7
Norcross ... Pg. 90, B-5
Norman Park M-4
Norristown J-7
North Atlanta Pg. 90, C-5
North DeKalb Pg. 90, E-6
North River Crossing .. Pg. 90, A-7
Northridge . Pg. 90, A-5
Oak Park J-7
Oakdale .. Pg. 90, E-2
Oakfield L-4
Oakman D-3
Oakwood E-5
Ochlocknee M-4
Ocilla L-6
Odum L-8
Offerman L-8
Oglethorpe J-4
Ohoopee K-7
Oliver J-9
Omaha K-2
Omega L-5
Orchard Knob Pg. 90, H-5
Oxford F-5
Palmetto G-3
Panola Woods Pg. 90, J-7

Panthersville Pg. 90, G-6
Parrott K-3
Patterson L-8
Pavo M-4
Peachtree City G-3
Pearson M-6
Pebblebrook Acres .. Pg. 90, E-2
Pelman ... Pg. 90, M-4
Pembroke K-9
Percale H-4
Perkerson . Pg. 90, H-4
Perry J-5
Philomath F-6
Pine Park N-4
Pinehurst K-5
Pineview K-5
Pitts K-5
Pittsburg .. Pg. 90, C-7
Plains K-3
Ponderosa K-3
Pooler K-9
Portal J-8
Poulan L-5
Preston K-3
Providence Corners .. Pg. 90, A-4
Pulaski J-8
Quitman N-5
Radium Springs L-4
Raleigh H-3
Ranger D-3
Ray City M-6
Rayle F-6
Red Oak ... Pg. 90, J-2
Regency Park Pg. 90, J-1
Rehoboth .. Pg. 90, E-7
Reidsville K-8
Resaca D-2
Revecca K-5
Rex K-9
Reynolds J-4
Richland K-3
Richmond Hill K-9
Rincon J-9
Riverdale H-4
Roberta H-4
Robins J-5
Rochelle K-5
Rockmart F-2
Rocky Ford H-8
Rome E-2
Roopville G-2
Roswell F-3
Saffold M-2
Sale City M-4
Sandersville H-6
Sandy Springs Pg. 90, B-4
Sardis H-9
Sasser L-3
Savannah K-10
Scarbrough Crossroads .. Pg. 90, J-7
Scottdale .. Pg. 90, E-7
Screven L-8
Senoia G-3
Seville K-5
Shady Dale G-5
Shellman L-3
Shiloh H-3
Smithville K-4
Smyrna ... Pg. 90, C-2
Social Circle F-5
Somerset .. Pg. 90, B-3
Soperton J-7
Southland . Pg. 90, E-5
Southwest . Pg. 90, G-2
Sparks M-5
Sparta H-6
Springfield J-9
  Vicinity .. Pg. 90, K-5
St. George N-8
St. Marys N-9
St. Simons Island .. M-9
Stagecoach Hill ... Pg. 90, K-7
Statenville N-6
Statesboro J-8
Stillmore K-7
Stockbridge G-4
Stockton M-6
Stone Mountain F-4
  Vicinity .. Pg. 90, C-6
Stonecrest . Pg. 90, K-2
Stonewall .. Pg. 90, K-2
Suches D-4
Suffolk Downs Pg. 90, K-1
Sugar Hill E-4
Summertown H-7
Summerville E-2
Sumner L-4
Surrency K-7
Suwanee E-4
Swainsboro J-7
Sycamore L-4
Sylvan Hills Pg. 90, A-7
Sylvania H-9
Sylvester L-4
Talbotton J-3
Tallulah Falls D-5
Talmo E-5
Tarrytown N-6
Tarver N-6
Tarversville J-3
Tazewell J-3
Tell ...... Pg. 90, J-1
Tenille H-7
Tennga D-2
Thomaston H-4
Thomasville N-4
Thomson G-7
Thornhedge Pg. 90, A-5
Thunderbolt K-10
Tifton L-5
Tignall F-7
Toccoa D-5

Toco Hill .. Pg. 90, E-6
Toombsboro H-6
Towns K-6
Toyston E-6
Trenton D-1
Trion D-2
Turin G-3
Twin City J-8
Twin Oaks . Pg. 90, G-7
Ty Ty L-5
Unadilla K-5
Union City F-3
  Vicinity .. Pg. 90, K-1
Union Point F-6
Uvalda K-7
Van Wert F-2
Vanna E-6
Vidalia J-7
Vienna K-4
Villa Rica F-2
Vinings ... Pg. 90, D-2
Wadley H-7
Waleska E-3
Waresboro M-7
Warner H-5
Warrenton G-6
Warthen H-6
Warwick K-4
Washington F-6
Watkinsville F-5
Waycross M-7
Waynesboro H-8
Wesley Chapel ... Pg. 90, G-7
West Oak .. Pg. 90, A-2
West Point H-2
Westgate .. Pg. 90, C-1
Whigham N-3
White E-3
Whitesburg G-2
Wildwood .. Pg. 90, E-4
Wildwood Forest ... Pg. 90, C-1
Willacoochee L-6
Winder F-5
Woodbine M-8
Woodbury H-3
Woodcrest . Pg. 90, H-6
Woodland H-3
Wrens G-7
Wrightsville J-6
Zebulon H-4

HAWAII
Page 30
Population: 964,691
Capital: Honolulu
Land Area: 6,425 sq. mi.

Aiea G-6
Anahola D-3
Apole Pt C-9
Apua Pt G-10
Barbers Pt G-4
Cape Halawa A-6
Cape Hanamanioa .. C-8
Captain Cook F-9
Eleele F-2
Ewa G-5
Glenwood F-9
Haena D-2
Haena Pt D-2
Haiku A-9
Hakalau F-10
Halawa A-6
Haleiwa F-4
Hana B-10
Hanalei D-2
Hanamalo Pt G-8
Hanamaulu E-3
Hanapepe F-1
Hauula F-6
Hawaii Kai G-6
Hawi E-9
Hekili Pt B-7
Hilo F-10
Honaunau F-9
Honohina E-10
Honokaa E-9
Honokahau A-7
Honokahua A-7
Honolulu G-5
Honuapo G-9
Hookena F-8
Ka Lae G-9
Kaalualu G-9
Kaena Pt G-10
Kahakuloa Pt A-8
Kahaluu F-6
Kahana F-6
Kahlu Pt A-6
Kahuku F-5
Kahuku Pt E-5
Kahului A-8
Kailua (Hawaii) F-8
Kailua (Oahu) G-6
Kaimu F-10
Kainaliu F-8
Kaka Pt E-7
Kalae A-5
Kalaheo F-2
Kalahu Pt B-10
Kalalau D-2
Kalaoa F-8
Kalapana F-10
Kamalo A-5
Kamiloloa A-5
Kaneohe G-6
Kapaa E-3
Kaumakani F-1
Kauna Pt G-8

Kaunakakai A-5
Kaupo B-9
Kawahae E-8
Keaau F-10
Keahole Pt F-8
Kealia E-3
Keauhou F-8
Kekaha E-1
Keokea B-8
Keomuku D-7
Kepuhi Pt F-4
Kihei B-8
Kikipua Pt A-5
Kilauea D-2
Kipahulu B-10
Koele D-6
Koheo Pt F-2
Koko Head G-7
Kolo A-4
Koloa F-2
Kualapapa A-4
Kualapuu A-4
Kualoa Pt F-6
Kukaiau E-9
Kukuihaele E-9
Kurtistown F-10
Laau Pt A-4
Lahaina A-7
Laie F-5
Lamaloa Head A-6
Lanai City D-6
Lawai F-2
Lihue E-3
Lilo Pt A-3
Maalaea B-8
Mahukona E-8
Maili G-4
Makaha F-4
Makaha Pt D-1
Makahuena Pt F-2
Makakilo City G-4
Makalua Pen A-5
Makapuu Pt F-6
Makawao A-9
Makena B-8
Mana E-1
Mauna Loa A-4
Mililani Town G-5
Mililii G-8
Mokapuu Pt B-10
Moloaa D-3
Mopua B-7
Mountain View F-9
Muolea Pt B-10
Naalehu G-9
Nakalele Pt A-8
Nanakuli G-4
Napoopoo F-8
Nawiliwili E-3
Ninini Pt E-3
Niulii E-9
Nukuele Pt C-8
Olowalu B-7
Opihikao F-10
Pahala G-9
Pahoa F-10
Paia A-8
Papa G-9
Papaaloa E-10
Papaikou F-10
Paukaa F-10
Pauwalu A-6
Pauwela A-8
Pearl City F-5
Pearl Harbor G-6
Pepeekeo F-9
Pepeekeo Pt F-10
Pohoiki F-10
Port Allen F-2
Puako E-8
Puhi E-3
Pukaulua Pt A-10
Pukoo A-8
Puunene A-8
Puuwai B-1
Spreckelsville A-8
Sunset Beach E-5
Ulapue A-8
Ulupalakua B-9
Upola Pt F-5
Wahiawa F-5
Waiahukini G-9
Waiaka E-9
Waiakea F-5
Waialua (Molokai) .. A-6
Waialua (Oahu) F-5
Waianae G-4
Waihee Pt A-8
Waikiki G-6
Wailea E-3
Wailua (Kauai) E-3
Wailua (Maui) A-9
Wailuku A-8
Waimanalo G-7
Waimea (Hawaii) .. E-8
Waimea (Kauai) ... E-1
Waiohinu G-9
Walpahu G-5

IDAHO
Page 31
Population: 943,935
Capital: Boise
Land Area: 82,413 sq. mi.

Ahsahka D-2
American Falls H-5
Arco G-5
Ashton G-7
Atlanta H-3

Atomic City H-5
Avery C-3
Bellevue H-4
Bigby H-6
Blackfoot H-6
Bliss J-4
Blue Dome G-5
Boise H-3
Bonners Ferry A-2
Bovill D-2
Bruneau J-3
Burley J-4
Butte City H-5
Caldwell H-2
Cambridge G-2
Cape Horn G-3
Carey H-4
Cascade G-3
Cataldo C-2
Challis G-4
Chubbuck J-6
Coeur D'Alene C-2
Colburn B-2
Cottonwood D-2
Craigmont D-2
Deary D-2
Declo J-5
Downey J-6
Dubois G-6
Eagle H-2
Eastport A-3
Elba K-5
Elk City E-3
Elk River D-3
Emmett H-2
Fairfield H-4
Fernan Lake B-2
Garden City H-2
Gibbonsville E-3
Golden E-3
Gooding J-4
Grand View J-2
Grangeville E-3
Hagerman J-4
Hailey H-4
Hamer G-6
Harpster E-3
Harvard C-2
Headquarters D-3
Hill City H-3
Holbrook K-6
Hollister J-4
Homedale H-2
Hope B-3
Horseshoe Bend .. G-2
Howe H-5
Idaho City H-3
Idaho Falls H-6
Jerome J-4
Kamiah D-3
Kellogg C-3
Ketchum H-4
King Hill J-3
Kooskia E-3
Kuna H-2
Lamb Creek A-2
Leadore F-5
Lemhi F-5
Lewiston D-2
Lowell D-3
Lowman G-3
Mackay G-5
Malad City K-6
Malta K-5
May G-4
McCall F-3
Meridian H-2
Middleton H-2
Minidoka J-4
Montpelier J-7
Moreland H-6
Moscow D-2
Mountain Home ... H-3
Moyie Springs A-3
Mud Lake H-6
Mullan C-3
Murphy H-2
Myrtle E-3
Nampa H-2
Naples A-3
New Meadows F-2
New Plymouth G-2
North Fork E-4
Orofino D-2
Osburn C-3
Patterson G-5
Payette G-2
Pierce D-2
Plummer C-2
Pocatello J-6
Pollock F-2
Porthill A-2
Portneuf J-6
Preston J-7
Rexburg H-6
Ririe H-6
Roberts H-6
Arimo J-6
Rock Creek J-4
Rockland J-5
Salmon F-4
Samaria J-6
Sandpoint B-2
Shoshone J-4
Silver City J-2
Soda Springs J-7
Spencer G-6
Spirit Lake B-2
Springfield B-2
St. Joe C-3

IDAHO

Sugar City G6
Sunbeam D-2
Troy D-2
Twin Falls J-4
Victor H-7
Wallace C-3
Weiser G-2
Wendell J4
White Bird E-2
Woodland D-3
Worley C-2

ILLINOIS
Page 32-33

Population: 11,426,518
Capital: Springfield
Land Area: 55,645 sq. mi.

Abingdon C-5
Addison . . . . Pg. 98, H-4
Albany D-3
Albion H-11
Aledo B-4
Alexis C-4
Algonquin . . . . . Pg. 96, G-2
Alhambra D-10
Allendale H-11
Allerton H-7
Alma F-11
Alorton . . . . Pg. 140, G-7
Alpha C-4
Alpine . . . . Pg. 99, L-5
Altamont F-10
Alto Pass E-14
Alton D-10
Alvin J-6
Amboy E-3
Andover C-4
Anna E-14
Annawan D-4
Antioch H-1
Aptakisik . . . . . . Pg. 96, E-5
Arcola G-7
Argenta F-7
Arlington E-3

Arlington Heights
. . . . Pg. 96, F-4
Arthur G-8
Ashland D-8
Ashley F-12
Ashmore H-8
Ashton E-2
Assumption F-9
Astoria C-7
Athens D-7
Atkinson D-3
Atlanta E-7
Atwood G-8
Auburn D-8
Aubury Hills . . . . Pg. 99, M-6
Augusta B-7
Aurora F-3
  Vicinity . . . . . Pg. 98, J-2
Ava E-13
Avon C-6
Baldmon D-6
Bannockburn . . . Pg. 97, E-5
Barrington . . . . . Pg. 96, E-3
Barrington Hills . . Pg. 96, F-3
Barry B-8
Bartlett . . . . Pg. 96, G-3
Bartonville E-6
Batavia . . . . Pg. 98, H-2
Beardstown C-7
Beckemeyer E-11
Bedford Park . . . . Pg. 99, J-6
Beecher City F-9
Belle Rive F-12
Belleville D-11
Bellflower G-6
Bellmont H-11
Bellwood . . . . . . Pg. 99, H-5
Belvidere F-1
Bement G-7
Bensenville . . . . . Pg. 96, G-5
Benson E-5
Benton F-12
Berkeley . . . . . . Pg. 99, H-5
Berwyn H-2
  Vicinity . . . . . Pg. 99, H-6
Bethalto D-10
Bethany F-8
Biggsville B-6
Bloomingdale . . . Pg. 96, G-4
Bloomington E-6
Blue Island . . . . . Pg. 99, K-7
Blue Mound E-8
Bluffs C-8
Bolingbrook H-2
  Vicinity . . . . . Pg. 98, K-4
Bourbonnais H-4
Bowen B-7
Bradford E-4
Bradley H-4
Braidwood H-4
Bridgeview . . . . . Pg. 99, J-6
Brighton C-10
Brimfield D-5
Broadview . . . . . Pg. 99, H-6
Brookfield . . . . . Pg. 99, H-6
Brookport G-15
Brownstown F-9
Buckley H-6
Buffalo Grove . . . Pg. 96, E-4
Bull Valley D-2
Bunker Hill C-9
Burbank . . . . . . Pg. 99, K-6
Burnham . . . . . . Pg. 99, L-8
Burr Ridge . . . . . Pg. 98, J-5

Burtons Bridge
. . . . Pg. 96, D-3
Bush F-13
Bushnell C-6
Byron E-2
Cabery G-5
Cahokia C-11
  Vicinity . . . . . Pg. 140, E-7
Cairo F-15
Calumet City . . . . Pg. 99, L-8
Calumet Park . . . . Pg. 99, H-6
Cambridge C-4
Camden B-7
Camp Point B-7
Campbell Hill E-13
Canton D-6
Capron F-1
Carbondale E-13
Carlinville D-9
Carlyle E-11
Carmi G-12
Carol Stream . . . . Pg. 98, H-3
Carpentersville . . Pg. 96, F-2
Carriers Mills F-13
Carrollton C-9
Carterville F-13
Carthage A-6
Cary . . . . Pg. 96, E-2
Casey H-9
Caton Farm . . . . . Pg. 98, L-3
Cave-In-Rock H-14
Cedarville D-1
Central City F-11
Centralia E-11
Cerro Gordo F-7
Chadwick D-2
Champaign G-7
Chandlerville C-7
Channel Lake B-3
Chapin C-8
Charleston H-9
Chatham D-8
Chatsworth G-5
Chebanse H-5
Chenoa F-5
Cherry Valley F-1
Chester D-13
Chesterfield D-9
Chicago J-2
  Vicinity . . . . Pg. 96
Chicago Heights J-3
  Vicinity . . . . Pg. 99, M-7
Chicago Ridge . . . Pg. 99, K-6
Chillicothe E-5
Chrisman H-8
Cicero . . . . Pg. 99, H-6
Cisco F-7
Cisne G-11
Clarendon Hills . . Pg. 98, J-5
Clay City G-11
Clayton B-7
Clifton H-5
Clinton F-7
Cloverdale . . . . . Pg. 98, F-2
Cobden E-14
Coffeen E-10
Colchester B-6
Colfax G-6
Collinsville D-11
Columbia C-11
  Vicinity . . . . . Pg. 140, J-5
Compton E-3
Cordova C-3
Cornell F-5
Coulterville E-12
Country Club Hills
. . . . Pg. 99, L-6
Countryside . . . . Pg. 99, J-6
Cowden F-9
Creal Springs F-13
Crest Hill . . . . . . Pg. 98, L-3
Crestwood . . . . . Pg. 99, L-7
Crete J-3
  Vicinity . . . . Pg. 99, M-7
Creve Coeur E-6
Crystal Lake G-1
  Vicinity . . . . . Pg. 96, D-2
Cuba C-6
Cullom G-5
Cutler E-12
Dakota E-1
Dallas City B-6
Damiansville E-11
Danville J-7
Darien . . . . Pg. 98, J-5
De Kalb F-2
De Soto E-13
Decatur F-8
Deer Grove E-3
Deer Park . . . . . . Pg. 96, E-4
Deerfield . . . . . . Pg. 97, E-5
Delavan E-6
Des Plaines . . . . . Pg. 97, F-5
Diamond Lake G-4
  Vicinity . . . . . Pg. 96, D-4
Dieterich G-10
Divernon E-9
Dix F-11
Dixmoor . . . . . . Pg. 99, L-7
Dixon E-3
Dolton . . . . Pg. 99, L-7
Donovan H-5
Downers Grove H-3
  Vicinity . . . . . Pg. 98, J-4
Du Quoin E-12
Dunfermline D-6
Dunlap D-5
Dupo . . . . Pg. 140, H-6
Dwight G-4
Earlville F-3
East Carondelet
. . . . Pg. 140, H-5
East Chicago Heights
. . . . Pg. 99, K-7
East Dubuque C-1

East Dundee . . . . Pg. 96, F-2
East Hazelcrest . . Pg. 99, L-7
East Peoria E-5
East St. Louis D-11
  Vicinity . . . . Pg. 140, E-7
Easton D-7
Eddyville G-14
Edgewood G-10
Edinburg E-8
Effingham G-10
El Paso F-5
Elburn . . . . Pg. 98, H-1
Eldorado G-13
Elgin G-2
  Vicinity . . . . . Pg. 96, F-2
Elizabeth C-1
Elizabethtown G-14
Elk Grove Village
. . . . Pg. 96, G-4
Elkhart E-7
Elkville E-13
Elliot H-6
Ellis Grove D-12
Elmhurst H-1
  Vicinity . . . . . Pg. 98, H-5
Elmwood Park . . . Pg. 99, H-6
Enfield G-12
Eola . . . . Pg. 98, J-3
Equality G-13
Erie D-3
Eureka E-5
Evanston J-2
  Vicinity . . . . Pg. 97, G-7
Evansville D-12
Evergreen Park
. . . . Pg. 99, K-7
Fairbury G-5
Fairfield G-11
Fairmont . . . . . . Pg. 98, L-4
Fairview C-6
Farina F-10
Farmer City F-7
Farmersville E-9
Farmington D-5
Fayetteville D-11
Fieldon C-10
Fisher G-6
Flanagan F-5
Flat Rock H-10
Flora G-11
Flossmoor . . . . . Pg. 99, M-7
Flowerfield . . . . . Pg. 98, H-4
Forest Park . . . . . Pg. 99, H-6
Forest View . . . . Pg. 99, J-6
Forrest G-5
Forreston E-2
Fox Lake G-1
  Vicinity . . . . . Pg. 96, C-3
Fox Lake Hills . . . Pg. 96, C-3
Fox River Grove
. . . . Pg. 96, E-3
Fox River Valley Gardens
. . . . Pg. 96, C-3
Frankfort . . . . . . Pg. 99, M-5
Franklin D-8
Franklin Park . . . . Pg. 99, H-5
Freeburg D-11
Freeport D-1
Fremont Center
. . . . Pg. 96, D-4
Frontenac . . . . . . Pg. 96, K-3
Fulton D-2
Gages Lake . . . . . Pg. 96, C-4
Galatia B-9
Galena C-1
Galesburg C-5
Galva C-4
Gardner G-4
Geneseo C-3
Geneva . . . . Pg. 96, G-3
  Vicinity . . . . . Pg. 98, H-2
Genoa F-2
Georgetown J-7
Germantown E-11
Gibson City G-6
Gilberts . . . . Pg. 96, F-1
Gillespie D-10
Gilman H-5
Gilmer . . . . Pg. 96, D-4
Girard D-9
Gladstone B-5
Glasford D-6
Glen Ellyn . . . . . Pg. 98, H-4
Glencoe . . . . . . Pg. 97, E-6
Glendale Heights
. . . . Pg. 98, H-4
Glenview . . . . . . Pg. 97, F-6
Glenwood . . . . . Pg. 99, M-7
Golconda G-14
Golden B-7
Golf . . . . Pg. 97, F-6
Good Hope B-6
Goodings Grove
. . . . Pg. 98, L-5
Goreville F-14
Gorham E-13
Grafton C-10
Grand Ridge F-4
Grand Tower E-13
Granite City D-11
  Vicinity . . . . Pg. 140, C-7
Grayslake . . . . . . Pg. 96, C-4
Grayville H-12
Green Oaks . . . . Pg. 96, D-5
Greenfield C-9
Greenup H-9
Greenview D-7
Greenville E-10
Greenwood . . . . Pg. 96, C-1
Gridley F-5
Griggsville B-8
Gurnee . . . . . . Pg. 97, C-5
Hainesville . . . . . Pg. 96, C-3
Half Day . . . . . . Pg. 97, E-5
Hamel D-10

Hamilton A-6
Hammond G-8
Hampshire G-2
Hanaford F-13
Hanover C-1
Hanover Park . . . Pg. 96, G-3
Hardin B-9
Harrisburg G-13
Harristown F-8
Harvard F-1
Harvey . . . . Pg. 99, L-7
Harwood Heights
. . . . Pg. 97, G-6
Hastings . . . . . . Pg. 98, K-5
Havana D-6
Hawthorn Woods
. . . . Pg. 96, E-4
Hazel Crest . . . . Pg. 99, L-7
Hebron G-1
Hecker D-12
Hennepin E-4
Henning H-6
Henry E-4
Herrin F-13
Herscher H-5
Heyworth F-6
Hickory Hills . . . . Pg. 99, K-6
Highland E-11
Highland Hills . . . Pg. 98, H-4
Highland Park H-1
  Vicinity . . . . Pg. 97, E-6
Highwood . . . . . Pg. 97, E-6
Hillsboro E-9
Hillside . . . . Pg. 99, H-5
Hinckley G-3
Hinsdale . . . . . . Pg. 98, J-5
Hodgkins . . . . . . Pg. 99, J-5
Hoffman Estates
. . . . Pg. 96, F-3
Holiday Hills . . . . Pg. 96, D-3
Homer H-7
Hometown . . . . . Pg. 99, K-6
Homewood . . . . . Pg. 99, L-7
Hoopeston J-6
Hoopole D-3
Hopedale E-6
Hoyleton E-11
Hudson F-6
Hull A-8
Humboldt G-8
Huntley . . . . Pg. 96, E-1
Hurst E-13
Hutsonville H-10
Illiopolis E-8
Imbs Station . . . . Pg. 140, H-7
Indian Creek . . . . Pg. 96, E-4
Indian Head Park
. . . . Pg. 99, J-5
Industry B-6
Ingalls Park . . . . Pg. 98, M-4
Inverness . . . . . . Pg. 96, F-4
Irvington F-11
Island Lake . . . . . Pg. 96, D-3
Itasca . . . . Pg. 96, G-4
Ivanhoe . . . . Pg. 96, D-4
Jacksonville C-8
Jerseyville C-9
Johnsburg . . . . . Pg. 96, C-2
Johnston City F-13
Joliet H-3
  Vicinity . . . . Pg. 98, M-4
Jonesboro E-14
Junction City H-13
Justice . . . . Pg. 99, J-6
Kampsville B-9
Kankakee H-4
Kansas H-8
Kaskaskia D-13
Keeneyville . . . . Pg. 96, G-3
Kenilworth . . . . . Pg. 97, F-7
Kenney F-7
Kewanee D-4
Kilbourne D-7
Kildeer . . . . Pg. 96, E-4
Kinderhook B-8
Kingston F-2
Kinmundy F-10
Kirkland F-2
Knollwood . . . . . Pg. 97, D-5
Knoxville C-5
La Fayette D-4
La Fox . . . . Pg. 98, H-1
La Grange . . . . . Pg. 99, G-4
La Grange Park
. . . . Pg. 99, J-5
La Harpe A-6
La Moille E-3
La Salle F-4
Lacon E-5
Lake Barrington
. . . . Pg. 96, E-3
Lake Bluff . . . . . . Pg. 97, D-6
Lake Forest H-1
  Vicinity . . . . Pg. 97, D-6
Lake Villa . . . . . . Pg. 96, C-4
Lake Zurich . . . . Pg. 96, E-3
Lake in the Hills . . Pg. 96, E-2
Lakemoor . . . . . Pg. 96, D-4
Lakewood . . . . . Pg. 96, E-1
Lanark D-2
Lansing . . . . Pg. 99, L-8
Latham E-7
Lawrenceville J-10
Le Roy F-6
Lee Center E-3
Lemont . . . . Pg. 98, K-4
Lena D-1
Lewistown C-6
Lexington F-6
Liberty A-8
Libertyville H-1
  Vicinity . . . . Pg. 96, D-5
Lilymoor . . . . . . Pg. 96, D-3
Lima A-7
Lincoln E-7

Lincoln Estates
. . . . Pg. 99, M-6
Lincolnshire . . . . Pg. 97, E-5
Lincolnwood . . . . Pg. 97, G-6
Lindenhurst . . . . Pg. 96, C-4
Lisbon Center . . . Pg. 98, J-4
Lisle . . . . Pg. 98, J-4
Litchfield D-9
Little York B-5
Livingston D-10
Lockport . . . . . . Pg. 98, L-4
Lombard . . . . . . Pg. 98, H-4
Long Grove . . . . Pg. 96, E-4
Long Lake . . . . . Pg. 96, C-3
Loon Lake . . . . . Pg. 96, B-4
Loraine A-7
Louisville G-10
Lovington F-8
Ludlow H-6
Lynwood . . . . . . Pg. 99, M-8
Lyons . . . . Pg. 99, J-6
Machesney Park E-1
Mackinaw E-6
Macomb B-6
Madison . . . . . . Pg. 140, D-6
Magnolia E-4
Mahomet G-7
Manlius D-3
Manteno H-4
Maquon C-5
Marengo G-1
Marine D-10
Marion F-13
Marissa D-12
Markham . . . . . . Pg. 99, L-7
Marley . . . . Pg. 98, M-5
Maroa F-7
Marseilles G-4
Marshall J-9
Martinsville H-9
Martinton H-5
Marywood . . . . . Pg. 98, J-2
Mascoutah D-11
Mason G-10
Mason City D-7
Matteson . . . . . . Pg. 99, M-6
Mattoon G-9
Maywood . . . . . Pg. 99, H-6
Mazon H-5
McClure E-14
McCook . . . . . . Pg. 99, J-6
McCullom Lake . . Pg. 96, C-2
McHenry G-1
  Vicinity . . . . Pg. 96, C-3
McHenry Shores
. . . . Pg. 96, B-1
McLean E-6
McLeansboro G-12
McQueens . . . . . Pg. 96, F-1
Medinah . . . . . . Pg. 96, G-4
Medora C-9
Melrose Park . . . . Pg. 99, H-5
Melvin G-6
Mendon A-7
Mendota E-3
Meredosia C-8
Merrionette Park
. . . . Pg. 99, K-7
Metamora E-5
Metropolis G-15
Mettawa . . . . . . Pg. 97, D-5
Midlothian . . . . . Pg. 99, M-7
Milan B-4
Milford J-5
Mill Shoals G-12
Milledgeville D-2
Milton B-8
Minonk F-5
Minooka . . . . . . Pg. 98, M-2
Mokena . . . . Pg. 99, M-5
Moline C-3
Momence J-4
Monmouth B-5
Montgomery . . . . Pg. 98, K-2
Monticello F-7
Montrose G-9
Mooseheart . . . . Pg. 98, J-2
Morris G-4
Morrison D-2
Morrisonville E-9
Morristown F-2
Morton E-6
Morton Grove . . . Pg. 97, F-6
Mound City F-15
Mount Carmel H-11
Mount Carroll D-2
Mount Morris E-2
Mount Olive D-10
Mount Prospect
. . . . Pg. 96, F-5
Mount Pulaski E-7
Mount Sterling B-7
Mount Vernon F-12
Mount Zion F-8
Moweaqua F-8
Mundelein G-1
  Vicinity . . . . Pg. 96, D-4
Murphysboro E-13
Murrayville C-8
Naperville G-3
  Vicinity . . . . Pg. 98, J-3
Nashville E-12
National City . . . . Pg. 140, E-7
Nauvoo A-6
Neoga G-9
New Athens D-12
New Baden E-11
New Boston B-4
New Burnside F-14
New Canton A-8
New Haven H-13
New Holland D-7
New Lenox . . . . . Pg. 98, M-5
New Windsor C-4

Newark F-3
Newman H-8
Newton H-9
Ridge Farm H-7
Niles . . . . Pg. 97, G-6
Nilwood D-9
Noble G-11
Nokomis E-9
Normal F-6
Normantown . . . Pg. 98, K-2
Norridge . . . . . . Pg. 97, G-6
Norris D-7
Norris City G-13
North Aurora . . . Pg. 98, J-2
North Barrington
. . . . Pg. 96, E-3
North Chicago . . Pg. 97, D-5
North Dupo . . . . Pg. 140, G-7
North Riverside
. . . . Pg. 99, H-6
North Wood River
. . . . Pg. 140, A-7
Northbrook E-9
  Vicinity . . . . Pg. 97, E-6
Northfield . . . . . . Pg. 97, F-6
Northlake . . . . . . Pg. 99, H-5
Oak Brook . . . . . Pg. 98, J-5
Oak Forest . . . . . Pg. 99, L-6
Oak Lawn . . . . . Pg. 99, K-6
Oak Park . . . . . . Pg. 99, H-6
Oakbrook Terrace
. . . . Pg. 98, H-5
Oakford D-7
Oakland H-8
Oakwood H-7
Oakwood Hills . . Pg. 96, D-3
Oblong H-10
Oconee F-9
Odell G-5
Odin F-11
Ogden H-7
Ohio E-3
Okawville D-11
Old Mill Creek . . Pg. 96, B-4
Olmsted F-15
Olney H-10
Olympia Fields
. . . . Pg. 99, M-7
Omaha G-13
Onarga H-5
Oquawka B-5
Orangeville E-1
Oreana F-7
Oregon E-2
Orion C-4
Orland Hills . . . . Pg. 99, L-6
Orland Park . . . . Pg. 99, L-5
Oswego F-8
  Vicinity . . . . Pg. 98, K-2
Ottawa F-3
Owaneco F-9
Palatine G-2
  Vicinity . . . . Pg. 96, F-4
Palestine J-10
Palmyra D-9
Palos Heights . . . Pg. 99, K-6
Palos Hills . . . . . Pg. 99, K-6
Palos Park . . . . . Pg. 99, K-6
Pana E-9
Paris J-8
Park City . . . . . . Pg. 97, C-5
Park Forest J-3
Park Ridge . . . . . Pg. 97, G-6
Parkersburg H-11
Patoka F-10
Pawnee E-8
Paxton H-6
Payson A-8
Pearl City D-1
Pekin D-6
Peoria D-5
Peotone H-4
Perry B-8
Pesotum G-7
Petersburg D-7
Phoenix . . . . Pg. 99, L-7
Pierron E-10
Pinckneyville E-12
Pingree Grove . . Pg. 96, F-1
Piper City G-5
Pittsfield B-8
Plainfield G-3
  Vicinity . . . . Pg. 98, L-3
Plano . . . . Pg. 98, J-1
Plato Center . . . . Pg. 96, G-1
Platteville . . . . . . Pg. 98, M-1
Pleasant Hill B-9
Plymouth B-6
Pocahontas E-10
Pontiac G-5
Port Byron C-3
Posen . . . . Pg. 99, L-7
Prairie Grove . . . Pg. 96, D-3
Prairie View . . . . Pg. 96, E-5
Prairie du Rocher F-12
Preston Heights
. . . . Pg. 98, M-4
Prince Crossing
. . . . Pg. 98, H-3
Princeton E-4
Princeville D-5
Prophetstown D-3
Prospect Heights
. . . . Pg. 96, F-5
Pulaski E-15
Quincy A-7
Ramsey F-9
Rankin H-6
Ransom G-4
Rantoul H-6
Rapids City C-3
Raymond E-9
Red Bud D-12
Reynolds C-4

Richton Park . . . . Pg. 99, M-6
Richview E-11
Ridgefield . . . . . Pg. 96, D-2
Ridgeway G-13
Ridgewood . . . . Pg. 98, M-4
Ringwood . . . . . Pg. 96, C-2
River Forest . . . . Pg. 99, H-6
River Grove . . . . Pg. 99, H-6
Riverdale . . . . . . Pg. 99, L-8
Riverside . . . . . . Pg. 99, J-6
Riverwoods . . . . Pg. 97, E-5
Roanoke F-5
Robbins . . . . Pg. 99, L-7
Roberts G-6
Robinson H-10
Rochelle E-2
Rochester E-8
Rock Falls D-3
Rock Island B-3
Rockbridge C-9
Rockdale . . . . . . Pg. 98, M-3
Rockford D-1
Rockton E-1
Rolling Meadows
. . . . Pg. 96, F-4
Romeoville F-8
  Vicinity . . . . Pg. 98, K-4
Rondout . . . . . . Pg. 97, D-5
Roodhouse C-9
Roselle . . . . Pg. 96, G-4
Rosemont . . . . . Pg. 97, G-5
Roseville C-5
Rosiclare G-14
Rossville J-6
Round Lake . . . . Pg. 96, C-3
Round Lake Beach
. . . . Pg. 96, D-4
Round Lake Heights
. . . . Pg. 96, C-4
Round Lake Park
. . . . Pg. 96, C-4
Royalton E-13
Rushville C-7
Rutland F-5
Sag Bridge . . . . . Pg. 98, K-5
Salem F-11
San Jose E-6
Sandoval E-11
Sandwich F-3
Sauget . . . . Pg. 140, E-6
Sauk Village . . . . Pg. 99, M-8
Savanna D-2
Schaumburg G-3
  Vicinity . . . . Pg. 96, G-4
Schiller Park . . . . Pg. 97, G-5
Schram City E-9
Sesser F-12
Shabbona F-2
Shannon D-2
Shawneetown G-13
Sheffield D-4
Shelbyville F-9
Sheldon J-5
Shorewood G-3
  Vicinity . . . . Pg. 98, M-3
Shumway G-9
Sibley G-6
Sigel G-9
Silvis C-3
Simpson F-14
Sims G-11
Skokie H-2
  Vicinity . . . . Pg. 97, F-6
Sleepy Hollow . . Pg. 96, F-2
Smithton D-11
Solon Mills . . . . . Pg. 96, B-2
Somonauk F-3
South Barrington
. . . . Pg. 96, F-3
South Beloit E-1
South Chicago Hts.
. . . . Pg. 99, M-7
South Elgin . . . . . Pg. 96, G-2
South Holland . . . Pg. 99, L-8
South Lockport . . Pg. 98, L-4
Sparland E-4
Sparta D-12
Spencer . . . . . . Pg. 98, H-4
Spring Grove . . . Pg. 96, B-2
Spring Valley E-4
Springfield D-8
St. Anne H-4
St. Augustine C-5
St. Charles G-3
  Vicinity . . . . Pg. 98, H-2
St. Elmo F-9
St. Francisville H-11
St. Johns E-12
St. Peter F-9
Stanford E-6
Stanton F-6
Starks . . . . Pg. 96, F-1
Staunton D-10
Steeleville D-12
Steger F-9
Sterling D-3
Stewardson G-9
Stickney . . . . . . Pg. 99, J-6
Stillman Valley E-2
Stockton C-1
Stolle . . . . Pg. 140, F-7
Stone Park . . . . . Pg. 99, H-5
Stonefort G-13
Stonington F-8
Strasburg G-9
Streamwood . . . . Pg. 96, G-3
Streator F-4
Stronghurst B-5
Sublette E-3
Sugar Grove . . . . Pg. 98, J-1
Sugarloaf Hts. . . . Pg. 140, G-7
Sullivan G-8
Summit . . . . Pg. 99, J-6
Sumner H-11

Sunnyside . . . . . Pg. 96, A-2
Sunrise Ridge . . . Pg. 96, A-1
Swansea D-11
Sycamore G-2
Table Grove C-6
Tallula D-7
Tamaroa E-12
Tamms E-14
Tampico D-3
Taylor Springs E-9
Taylorville F-8
Teutopolis G-9
Thawville G-5
Third Lake . . . . . Pg. 96, C-4
Thompsonville G-13
Thomson D-2
Thornton . . . . . . Pg. 99, L-7
Tinley Park . . . . . Pg. 99, L-6
Toledo G-9
Tolono G-7
Toluca E-5
Tonica F-4
Tower Hill F-9
Tower Lakes . . . . Pg. 96, E-3
Trenton E-11
Troy D-11
Troy Grove E-3
Tuscola G-8
Udina . . . . Pg. 96, F-1
Ullin E-14
University Park
. . . . Pg. 99, M-6
Urbana H-7
Valley View . . . . Pg. 96, G-2
Valmeyer C-12
Vandalia F-10
Venetian Village
. . . . Pg. 96, C-4
Venice . . . . Pg. 140, D-7
Vernon F-10
Vernon Hills . . . . Pg. 96, D-5
Versailles B-8
Victoria D-4
Vienna F-14
Villa Grove H-8
Villa Park . . . . . . Pg. 98, H-5
Viola C-4
Virden D-9
Virginia C-7
Volo . . . . Pg. 96, D-3
Wadsworth D-8
  Vicinity . . . . Pg. 96, B-5
Waggoner D-9
Walnut E-3
Waltonville F-12
Wapella F-7
Warren D-1
Warrensburg F-7
Warrenville . . . . . Pg. 98, J-3
Warsaw A-6
Wasco . . . . Pg. 98, G-1
Washburn E-5
Washington E-5
Waterloo C-12
Waterman F-3
Watseka H-5
Watson G-9
Wauconda . . . . . Pg. 96, D-3
Waukegan H-1
  Vicinity . . . . Pg. 96, C-6
Waverly D-8
Wayne . . . . Pg. 96, G-3
Wayne City G-11
Weldon F-7
Wellington J-6
Wenona F-4
West Chicago . . . Pg. 98, H-3
West City F-12
West Dundee . . . Pg. 96, F-2
West Frankfort F-13
West Miltmore . . Pg. 96, C-4
Westchester . . . . Pg. 98, H-5
Western Springs
. . . . Pg. 98, J-5
Westfield H-9
Westmont . . . . . Pg. 98, J-5
Westville J-7
Wheaton G-3
  Vicinity . . . . Pg. 98, H-3
Wheeler G-10
Wheeling . . . . . . Pg. 96, F-5
White Hall C-9
Wildwood . . . . . Pg. 96, C-5
Willow Hill H-10
Willow Springs . . Pg. 98, K-5
Willowbrook . . . . Pg. 98, J-5
Wilmette . . . . . . Pg. 97, F-6
Wilmington H-4
Winchester C-8
Winfield . . . . . . Pg. 98, H-3
Winnebago E-1
Winnetka H-2
  Vicinity . . . . Pg. 97, F-6
Winslow D-1
Winthrop Harbor
. . . . H-1
Wolfs . . . . Pg. 98, K-2
Wonder Lake . . . Pg. 96, C-2
Wood Dale . . . . . Pg. 96, G-4
Wood River . . . . Pg. 140, B-7
Woodhull C-4
Woodridge . . . . . Pg. 98, K-4
Woodson C-8
Woodstock . . . . Pg. 96, D-1
Worth . . . . Pg. 99, K-6
Wyoming D-5
Xenia G-11
Yates City C-5
York Center . . . . Pg. 96, H-4
Yorkville . . . . . . Pg. 96, K-1
Zeigler F-13
Zion . . . . Pg. 97, B-6

INDIANA

Place	Ref.	Place	Ref.
Bennett Switch	E-7	Five Points	Pg. 110, E-5
Berne	E-10	Flora	E-6
Beverly Shores	B-4	Fort Branch	P-2
Bicknell	M-3	Fort Wayne	C-9
Birdseye	N-5	Fortville	H-7
Bloomfield	L-4	Foster	G-6
Blooming Grove	J-9	Fountain City	G-10
Bloomington	K-5	Fowler	E-3
Bluffton	E-9	Francesville	D-4
Boonville	P-3	Frankfort	F-6
Boston	H-10	Franklin	J-7
Boswell	E-3	Frankton	G-7
Bourbon	C-6	Freedom	K-4
Bowling Green	K-4	Freetown	L-6
Branchville	P-5	Fremont	A-10
Brazil	J-4	French Lick	M-5
Bremen	B-6	Fulton	D-6
Bristol	A-7	Galveston	E-6
Brook	D-3	Garrett	B-9
Brooklyn	K-5	Gary	B-3
Brookston	E-5	Vicinity	Pg. 97, B-6
Brookville	J-10	Gas City	E-8
Brownsburg	H-6	Gentryville	P-4
Brownstown	L-6	Glenns Valley	Pg. 110, E-3
Bruceville	M-3	Goodland	E-3
Bryant	E-10	Goshen	B-7
Bryantsburg	L-8	Gosport	K-5
Burlington	F-6	Grandview	Q-4
Burnettsville	E-5	Grass Creek	D-6
Burns City	M-5	Grayford	M-8
Burns City	L-4	Graysville	K-3
Butler	B-10	Greencastle	H-4
Cadiz	G-8	Greendale	K-10
Cambridge City	H-10	Greenfield	H-7
Camby	Pg. 110, F-1	Greensburg	K-8
Cannelton	Q-5	Greentown	E-7
Carbon	J-4	Greenwood	J-7
Carbondale	F-3	Griffin	P-2
Carefree	P-6	Griffith	Pg. 97, B-6
Carlisle	L-3	Grovertown	B-5
Carmel	G-6	Hagerstown	H-9
Carp	J-5	Hammond	B-3
Castleton	G-7	Vicinity	Pg. 97, A-5
Vicinity	Pg. 110, B-5	Hanna	B-5
Cayuga	H-3	Hanover	M-8
Cedar Grove	J-10	Harlan	C-10
Cedar Lake	B-3	Harmony	J-4
Centerville	H-10	Harrodsburg	L-5
Chalmers	E-4	Hartford City	F-9
Chandler	P-3	Hartsville	K-8
Charlestown	N-8	Haysville	N-4
Chester	H-10	Hazleton	N-2
Chesterfield	G-8	Hebron	C-4
Chesterton	B-4	Hedrick	F-3
Chrisney	P-4	Hemlock	F-7
Churubusco	C-9	Henryville	M-8
Cicero	G-7	Heusler	Q-2
Cincinnati	L-5	Highland	Pg. 97, B-6
Clarks Hill	F-5	Highwoods	Pg. 110, C-3
Clarksville	G-7	Hillsboro	G-4
Vicinity	Pg. 118, C-2	Hindustan	K-5
Clay City	K-4	Hobart	B-3
Clayton	H-5	Vicinity	Pg. 97, B-6
Clermont	Pg. 110, C-1	Hobbs	F-7
Clinton	H-3	Holland	P-3
Cloverdale	J-5	Homecroft	Pg. 110, F-4
Coatesville	H-5	Hope	K-7
Collegeville	D-4	Hudson	B-9
Columbia City	C-8	Hudson Lake	A-5
Columbus	K-7	Huntertown	C-9
Connersville	H-9	Huntingburg	N-4
Converse	E-7	Huntington	D-8
Cory	J-3	Huron	M-5
Corydon	P-7	Indianapolis	H-6
Covington	G-3	Vicinity	Pg. 122
Crawfordsville	G-4	Jamestown	H-5
Crothersville	M-7	Jasonville	K-3
Crown Point	B-3	Jasper	N-4
Crystal	N-5	Johnson	N-2
Cumberland	H-7	Jonesboro	F-8
Cynthiana	P-2	Jonesville	L-7
Cypress	Q-2	Kempton	F-6
Dale	P-4	Kendallville	B-9
Dana	H-1	Kentland	D-3
Danville	H-5	Kewanna	D-6
Darmstadt	P-2	Kingman	G-3
Decatur	D-10	Kingsbury	B-5
Decker	N-3	Kingsford Hts.	B-4
Deerfield	F-10	Knightstown	H-8
Degonia Springs	P-4	Knox	C-5
Delphi	E-5	Kokomo	E-6
Demotte	C-4	Koutz	C-4
Denver	D-7	La Crosse	B-5
Derby	Q-5	La Fontaine	E-8
Dillsboro	L-9	La Grange	A-8
Dogwood	P-7	La Paz	B-6
Dover	G-5	La Porte	B-5
Dublin	H-9	Lafayette	F-5
Dugger	L-3	Lake Station	C-3
Dunfee	C-9	Vicinity	Pg. 97, B-7
Dunkirk	F-9	Lake Villa	C-3
Dunlap	A-7	Lakeville	B-6
E. Mt. Carmel	N-2	Lawrence	H-6
Earl Park	D-3	Lawrenceburg	L-10
East Gary	Pg. 97, B-7	Lebanon	G-6
Economy	G-8	Leota	M-7
Edinburgh	K-7	Leroy	B-3
Effner	E-3	Lewistown	J-8
Elberfeld	P-3	Liberty	H-10
Elizabeth	P-7	Libertyville	J-3
Elizabethtown	K-7	Ligonier	B-8
Elkhart	A-7	Linden	G-5
Elletsville	K-5	Linton	L-4
Elwood	F-7	Lizton	H-5
Emporia	G-8	Logansport	E-6
English	N-6	Loogootee	M-4
Enos	D-3	Lowell	C-3
Evansville	P-2	Luther	D-8
Fairfield	J-10	Lynn	G-10
Fairmount	F-8	Lynnville	P-3
Ferdinand	P-4	Mace	G-5
Fickle	F-5	Madison	L-9

Place	Ref.	Place	Ref.
Majenica	D-8	Pierceton	C-8
Malden	B-4	Pike	G-6
Manhattan	J-4	Pine Village	F-3
Marengo	N-6	Plainfield	H-5
Marion	E-8	Pleasant	L-9
Markle	D-9	Pleasant Mills	D-10
Markleville	G-8	Plymouth	B-6
Mars Hill	Pg. 110, E-2	Point Isabel	F-7
Marshall	H-4	Portage	B-4
Martinsville	J-5	Portland	F-10
Mauckport	P-6	Poseyville	P-2
Maxwell	H-8	Prairie City	J-4
Maywood	Pg. 110, E-3	Prairie Creek	K-3
Mecca	H-3	Prairieton	K-3
Medaryville	C-5	Princeton	N-2
Memphis	N-7	Ramsey	N-6
Mentone	C-7	Raub	E-3
Meridian Hills	Pg. 110, B-5	Ravenswood	Pg. 110, B-4
Merillville	B-3	Rays Crossing	J-8
Vicinity	Pg. 97, B-6	Reiffsburg	E-9
Merom	L-3	Rensselaer	D-4
Merriam	B-8	Reynolds	E-4
Metamora	K-9	Richmond	H-10
Metea	D-6	Rising Sun	L-10
Michiana Shores	A-4	Riverside	F-3
Michigan City	A-4	Roachdale	H-5
Michigantown	F-6	Roann	D-7
Mickeyville	Pg. 110, E-2	Rochester	C-6
Middlebury	A-7	Rockfield	E-5
Middlefork	F-6	Rockport	Q-4
Milan	K-9	Rockville	H-3
Millersburg	B-8	Rocky Ripple	Pg. 110, C-3
Milport	H-8	Rogersville	G-9
Mishawaka	B-7	Rome City	B-9
Mitchell	L-6	Romney	F-4
Monon	D-4	Rosedale	J-3
Monroe	F-5	Roselawn	C-3
Monroeville	D-10	Rosston	G-6
Montezuma	H-3	Rossville	F-5
Monticello	E-5	Royal Center	D-5
Montmorenci	F-4	Royalton	H-6
Montpelier	E-8	Rushville	J-8
Mooresville	J-6	Russellville	H-4
Morgantown	K-6	Salem	M-6
Morocco	D-3	Sandusky	J-8
Morristown	H-8	Santa Claus	P-4
Moscow	J-8	Santa Fe	E-7
Mt. Ayr	D-3	Schererville	B-3
Mt. Carmel	J-10	Vicinity	Pg. 97, C-5
Mt. Comfort	H-7	Schneider	C-3
Mt. Etna	D-8	Scipio	J-10
Mt. Meridian	J-5	Scott	A-8
Mt. Pleasant	H-4	Scottsburg	M-7
Mt. Pleasant	P-5	Seelyville	J-3
Mt. Vernon	Q-2	Sellersburg	N-7
Mt. Zion	E-9	Sexton	H-8
Mulberry	F-5	Seymour	L-7
Muncie	G-9	Shelburn	K-3
Munster	B-3	Shelbyville	J-7
Vicinity	Pg. 109, B-5	Sheridan	G-6
N. Liberty	B-6	Shoals	M-5
N. Manchester	D-7	Shore Acres	Pg. 110, B-4
N. Vernon	L-8	Sidney	C-8
Napoleon	K-9	Silver Lake	C-7
Nappanee	B-7	Solitude	P-2
Nashville	K-6	South Bend	A-6
New Albany	N-7	South Whitley	C-8
Vicinity	Pg. 118, A-1	Southport	H-6
New Amsterdam	P-6	Vicinity	Pg. 110, G-4
New Augusta	Pg. 110, B-2	Speedway	H-6
New Bethel	Pg. 110, B-5	Spencer	K-5
New Boston	F-8	Spice Land	H-8
New Carlisle	A-6	Spring Hills	Pg. 110, C-3
New Castle	G-9	St. Croix	P-5
New Frankfort	J-9	St. Francisville	M-2
New Goshen	J-3	St. Joe	C-10
New Harmony	P-2	St. John	Pg. 99, K-7
New Haven	C-10	St. Paul	J-8
New Liberty	M-7	Stewartsville	P-2
New Market	G-5	Stilesville	H-5
New Pekin	M-7	Story	K-6
New Providence	N-7	Sullivan	K-3
New Richmond	G-4	Sulphur Springs	G-8
New Ross	G-4	Summitville	F-8
New Whiteland	J-6	Sunman	K-9
Newberry	L-4	Swayzee	E-7
Newburgh	Q-3	Syracuse	B-8
Newport	H-3	Tell City	Q-5
Newtown	F-4	Templeton	E-4
Nine Mile	D-9	Terre Haute	J-3
Nobelsville	H-8	Thorntown	G-5
Nora	Pg. 110, B-4	Tipton	F-7
Norristown	K-7	Traders Point	Pg. 110, B-4
North Crows Nest	Pg. 110, B-3	Trafalgar	J-6
North Judson	C-5	Tremont	Pg. 110, G-2
Oakland City	N-3	Troy	P-5
Oaktown	C-3	Union City	G-10
Odell	F-4	Uniondale	D-9
Odon	M-4	Uniontown	Q-1
Ogilville	K-7	Unionville	K-6
Oolitic	L-5	Upland	F-8
Orleans	M-5	Urbana	D-7
Osceola	A-7	Valparaiso	B-4
Osgood	K-9	Van Buren	E-8
Ossian	D-9	Veedersburg	G-3
Otis	A-4	Versailles	L-9
Otwell	N-4	Vevay	M-9
Owensville	P-2	Vincennes	M-3
Oxford	E-3	W. College Corner	J-10
Palmyra	N-6	W. Lebanon	F-3
Paoli	M-6	W. Terre Haute	J-3
Paris Crossing	L-8	Wabash	D-7
Parr	D-4	Waco	M-4
Patriot	L-10	Wakarusa	B-7
Pence	F-3	Walkerton	B-6
Pendleton	G-7	Walton	E-6
Peoria	E-7	Wanatah	B-5
Perrysburg	D-7	Warren	E-8
Perrysville	G-3	Warsaw	C-7
Peru	D-7	Washington	M-4
Petersburg	N-3	Waterford	H-9
		Waterloo	B-10

Place	Ref.
Waterloo	B-10
Waynetown	G-4
Webster	H-10
West Lafayette	F-4
West Newton	Pg. 110, G-2
West Point	G-4
Westfield	G-7
Westphalia	L-3
Westport	K-8
Westville	B-4
Wheatfield	C-4
Whitestown	H-6
Whiting	Pg. 99, H-7
Wilkinson	H-8
Williams	L-5
Williams Creek	Pg. 110, B-4
Williamsport	F-3
Wilmot	C-8
Winamac	D-5
Winchester	F-9
Windfall City	F-7
Wingate	G-4
Winona Lake	C-7
Winslow	N-3
Wolcott	D-4
Woodburn	C-10
Woodstock	Pg. 110, C-3
Worthington	K-4
Wynnedale	Pg. 110, C-3
Yorktown	G-8
Zionsville	G-6
Vicinity	Pg. 110, A-2

IOWA

IOWA
Page 36

Population: 2,913,808
Capital: Des Moines
Land Area: 55,965 sq. mi.

Place	Ref.	Place	Ref.
Abingdon	F-7	Burlington	F-8
Ackley	C-6	Burr Oak	A-8
Adair	E-4	Burt	B-4
Adel	E-4	Bussey	E-6
Afton	F-5	Calmar	B-8
Agency	E-6	Calumet	B-2
Ainsworth	E-7	Camanche	D-9
Akron	C-1	Cantril	F-6
Albia	E-5	Carbon	F-3
Alden	C-5	Carpenter	B-6
Algona	B-4	Carroll	D-3
Allendorf	B-2	Carson	F-3
Allerton	F-5	Carter Lake	E-1
Allison	C-6	Carter Lake	Pg. 132, D-5
Alta	C-3	Cascade	D-9
Alta Vista	A-7	Casey	E-4
Alton	B-1	Cedar	F-7
Altoona	E-5	Cedar Falls	C-7
Amana	D-8	Cedar Rapids	D-8
Ames	D-5	Center Point	D-8
Anamosa	D-8	Centerville	F-6
Anderson	F-3	Central City	D-8
Andrew	D-10	Chapin	C-6
Anita	E-3	Chariton	F-6
Anthon	C-2	Charles City	B-6
Aplington	C-6	Charlotte	D-10
Arcadia	D-3	Charter Oak	D-2
Archer	B-2	Chatsworth	B-1
Aredale	C-6	Chautauqua	Pg. 132, D-9
Arispe	F-4	Chelsea	D-7
Arlington	C-7	Cherokee	C-2
Armstrong	B-4	Churdan	D-4
Arnolds Park	A-3	Cincinnati	F-6
Arthur	D-3	Clara	Pg. 132, C-5
Asbury	D-2	Clare	C-4
Ashton	B-2	Clarence	D-9
Athelstan	F-4	Clarinda	F-3
Atkins	D-7	Clarion	C-5
Atlantic	E-3	Clarksville	C-7
Attica	E-6	Clear Lake	B-6
Auburn	D-3	Clearfield	F-4
Audubon	E-3	Cleghorn	C-3
Aurelia	C-3	Clinton	D-10
Avery	E-5	Clutier	D-7
Avoca	E-3	Coggon	D-8
Badger	C-4	Colesburg	C-9
Baldwin	D-9	Colfax	E-6
Bancroft	B-4	Collins	D-6
Barnes City	E-6	Colo	D-5
Barnum	C-4	Columbia	E-6
Bartlett	F-2	Columbus Jct.	E-8
Battle Creek	D-3	Colwell	B-7
Baxter	D-6	Conesville	E-8
Bayard	E-4	Conrad	D-6
Beacon	E-6	Conroy	E-8
Beaver	D-5	Conway	F-4
Bedford	F-4	Coon Rapids	D-3
Beech	E-6	Cooper	D-4
Belle Plaine	D-7	Coppock	E-8
Bellevue	D-9	Coralville	E-8
Belmond	C-5	Corley	E-2
Bennett	E-9	Corning	F-3
Bettendorf	E-10	Correctionville	C-2
Bevington	E-5	Corwith	B-5
Blakesburg	E-6	Corydon	F-5
Blencoe	D-2	Council Bluffs	F-2
Bloomfield	F-6	Vicinity	Pg. 132, E-6
Bonaparte	F-7	Crescent	E-1
Boone	D-5	Vicinity	Pg. 132, C-4
Boyden	B-2	Cresco	B-7
Bradford	C-6	Creston	F-4
Brayton	E-3	Curlew	B-4
Breda	C-3	Dakota City	C-4
Bridgewater	F-4	Dallas Center	D-4
Brighton	E-7	Dana	D-4
Britt	B-5	Danbury	D-2
Brooklyn	D-7	Danville	F-8
Brooks	F-3	Davenport	E-9
Brunswick	C-1	Davis City	G-5
Bryant	D-10	Dayton	D-4
Buffalo Center	B-5	De Soto	E-4
		De Witt	D-9
		Decorah	B-8
		Dedham	D-3
		Defiance	D-3
		Delhi	C-8
		Delmar	D-9
		Deloit	D-3
		Delta	E-6
		Denison	D-3
		Denver	C-7
		Derby	F-5
		Des Moines	E-5
		Dexter	E-4
		Dickens	B-3
		Dike	C-7
		Dolliver	B-4
		Donnellson	F-8
		Doon	B-1
		Dorchester	A-8
		Dow City	D-2
		Dows	C-5
		Drakesville	F-6
		Dubuque	D-9
		Dumfries	Pg. 132, G-7
		Dumont	C-6
		Duncombe	C-4
		Dunkerton	C-7
		Dunlap	D-2
		Durant	D-9
		Dyersville	C-8
		Dysart	D-7

Place	Ref.	Place	Ref.
Elk Horn	E-3	Kalona	E-8
Elkader	C-8	Kamrar	C-5
Elkhart	D-5	Kanawha	B-4
Elliott	F-3	Kellogg	D-6
Ellsworth	D-5	Kendallville	B-8
Emerson	F-2	Kent	F-4
Emmetsburg	B-4	Keokuk	G-8
Epworth	C-9	Keosauqua	F-8
Essex	F-2	Keota	E-8
Estherville	B-4	Keswick	E-7
Evansdale	C-7	Keystone	D-7
Everly	B-3	Killduff	E-6
Exira	E-3	Kingsley	C-2
Fairbank	B-7	Kirkman	E-3
Fairfield	E-7	Kiron	D-3
Farley	C-8	Klemme	B-5
Farnhamville	D-4	Knoxville	E-6
Farragut	F-2	La Porte City	D-7
Fayette	C-8	Lake City	D-3
Fenton	B-4	Lake Mills	B-5
Floyd	B-6	Lake Park	B-3
Fonda	C-3	Lake View	D-3
Fontanelle	E-4	Lamoni	G-4
Forest City	B-5	Lamont	C-8
Fort Dodge	C-4	Lansing	B-8
Fort Madison	F-9	Larchwood	A-1
Fostoria	B-3	Larrabee	C-2
Frankville	B-8	Laurel	D-6
Fraser	D-5	Laurens	C-3
Fredericksburg	B-7	Le Claire	D-9
Fremont	E-6	Le Mars	C-2
Froelich	B-8	Ledyard	B-4
Frytown	E-8	Lehigh	D-5
Fulton	D-9	Leighton	E-7
Garden City	D-6	Lenox	F-4
Garnavillo	C-8	Lester	B-1
Garner	B-5	Lewis	E-3
Garwin	D-6	Liberty Center	F-6
George	B-2	Lime Springs	B-7
Gibson	E-7	Linderwood	E-2
Gilbert	D-5	Lineville	G-5
Gilman	D-6	Lisbon	D-8
Gilmore City	C-4	Little Rock	B-2
Gladbrook	D-6	Little Sioux	D-2
Glenwood	F-2	Livermore	C-4
Vicinity	Pg. 132, J-7	Logan	E-2
Glidden	D-3	Lohrville	D-3
Goldfield	C-5	Long Grove	D-9
Goodell	B-5	Long Tree	E-8
Gowrie	D-4	Lorimor	F-4
Graettinger	B-4	Lost Nation	D-9
Grafton	B-6	Lovilia	F-6
Grand Jct.	D-4	Lowden	D-9
Grand River	F-4	Lucas	F-5
Grandview	E-8	Luther	D-5
Grant	F-3	Luxemburg	C-9
Green Mountain	D-6	Lyman	F-3
Greene	C-6	Lytton	C-3
Greenfield	E-4	Macedonia	F-3
Grimes	D-4	Macksburg	E-4
Grinnell	D-7	Madrid	D-5
Griswold	F-3	Malcom	E-7
Grundy Center	C-6	Mallard	B-4
Guernsey	D-7	Malvern	F-2
Gunder	B-8	Manchester	C-8
Guthrie Center	E-4	Manilla	D-3
Guttenberg	C-8	Manly	B-6
Hamburg	G-2	Manning	D-3
Hamilton	E-5	Manson	C-4
Hamlin	E-3	Mapleton	D-2
Hampton	C-6	Maquoketa	D-10
Hancock	E-3	Marathon	C-3
Hanlontown	B-5	Marcus	C-2
Harcourt	D-4	Marengo	E-7
Harlan	E-3	Marion	D-8
Harper's Ferry	B-9	Marne	E-3
Hartley	B-3	Marquette	B-9
Hartwick	D-7	Marshalltown	D-6
Harvey	E-6	Mason City	B-6
Havelock	C-4	Massena	E-4
Haven	D-6	Matlock	B-2
Hawarden	B-1	Maxwell	D-5
Hawkeye	C-8	May City	B-3
Hazleton	C-7	Maynard	C-8
Hedrick	E-6	McGregor	B-8
Henderson	F-2	McIntire	B-7
Hepburn	F-3	Mechanicsville	D-8
Hesper	A-8	Mediapolis	F-9
Hiawatha	D-8	Melbourne	D-6
Hillsboro	F-8	Melcher	E-5
Hinton	C-1	Melvin	B-2
Holmes	C-5	Meriden	C-2
Holstein	C-3	Merrill	C-1
Honey Creek	Pg. 132, A-5	Milford	B-3
Hopeville	F-5	Millerton	F-6
Hopkinton	C-8	Millville	C-9
Hospers	B-1	Milo	E-5
Hubbard	C-6	Milton	F-7
Hudson	C-7	Minburn	E-4
Hull	B-1	Minden	E-2
Humboldt	C-4	Mingo	E-6
Humeston	F-5	Missouri Valley	E-2
Huxley	D-5	Mitchellville	E-5
Iconium	F-6	Mondamin	E-2
Ida Grove	D-3	Moneta	B-3
Imogene	F-3	Monona	B-8
Independence	C-8	Monroe	E-6
Indianola	E-5	Montezuma	E-7
Inwood	B-1	Monticello	D-8
Iowa Center	D-6	Montour	D-6
Iowa City	E-8	Montrose	F-8
Iowa Falls	C-6	Moorhead	D-2
Ireton	B-1	Moravia	F-6
Irwin	E-3	Morning Sun	E-8
Jackson Jct.	B-7	Morse	E-8
Jamaica	D-4	Moulton	F-6
Janesville	C-7	Mount Ayr	G-4
Jefferson	D-4	Mount Etna	F-4
Jerico	B-7	Mount Sterling	F-7
Jesup	C-8	Mount Union	F-8
Jewell	C-5	Moville	C-2
Joice	B-5	Mt. Pleasant	F-8

IOWA

Place	Ref
Mt. Vernon	D-8
Murray	F-4
Muscatine	E-9
Nashua	B-7
Neola	E-2
Nevada	D-5
Nevinville	F-4
New Albin	A-8
New Hampton	B-7
New Haven	B-7
New London	F-9
New Market	F-3
New Providence	D-6
New Sharon	E-7
New Virginia	F-5
Newburg	D-7
Newkirk	B-2
Newton	E-6
Nichols	E-9
Nora Springs	B-6
North English	E-7
Northboro	G-3
Northwood	B-6
Norwalk	E-5
Norway	D-7
Oakland	E-3
Ocheyedan	A-2
Odebolt	D-3
Oelwein	C-8
Ogden	D-4
Olin	D-9
Onawa	D-2
Onslow	D-9
Orange City	B-2
Orient	F-4
Osage	B-6
Osceola	F-5
Oskaloosa	E-7
Otho	D-5
Oto	D-2
Ottumwa	F-7
Oxford	E-8
Oyens	C-2
Pacific City	Pg. 132, J-6
Pacific Junction	Pg. 132, K-6
Panama	E-3
Panora	E-4
Park View	E-10
Parkersburg	C-7
Parnell	E-7
Paullina	B-2
Pella	E-6
Percival	F-2
Perkins	B-1
Perry	D-5
Persia	E-2
Pierson	C-2
Pilot Mound	D-5
Pisgah	D-2
Plain View	E-9
Plainfield	C-7
Plano	F-6
Pleasant Plain	F-7
Pleasantville	E-5
Pocahontas	C-4
Polk City	E-5
Pomeroy	C-4
Popejoy	C-6
Portsmouth	E-3
Postville	B-8
Prairie City	E-6
Preston	D-10
Primghar	B-2
Prole	E-5
Pulaski	F-7
Quasqueton	C-8
Quimby	C-2
Rathbun	F-6
Reasnor	E-6
Red Oak	F-3
Redding	G-4
Redfield	E-4
Reinbeck	D-7
Rembrandt	C-3
Remsen	C-2
Renwick	C-5
Rhodes	D-6
Riceville	B-6
Richland	E-7
Rickardsville	C-9
Ridgeway	B-8
Ringsted	A-3
Rippey	D-4
Rochester	E-9
Rock Rapids	B-2
Rock Valley	B-1
Rockford	B-6
Rockwell	B-6
Rockwell City	C-4
Roland	C-5
Rolfe	C-4
Roselle	D-3
Rossie	B-3
Rossville	B-8
Royal	B-3
Russell	F-6
Ruthven	B-3
Ryan	C-8
Sabula	C-10
Sac City	C-3
Sanborn	B-2
Saratoga	B-7
Schaller	C-3
Schleswig	D-2
Schley	B-7
Scranton	D-4
Searsboro	E-7
Selma	F-7
Sergeant Bluff	C-2
Seymour	F-5
Shambaugh	G-3
Sharpsburg	F-3
Sheffield	B-6
Sheldon	B-2
Shell Rock	B-6
Shellsburg	D-8
Shenandoah	F-3
Sibley	A-2
Sidney	F-2
Sigourney	E-7
Sioux Center	B-1
Sioux City	C-1
Sioux Rapids	B-3
Sloan	D-1
Smithland	D-2
Soldier	D-2
Solon	D-8
Somers	C-4
Spencer	B-3
Spirit Lake	A-3
Springville	D-8
St. Ansgar	B-6
St. Charles	E-5
St. Joseph	B-4
St. Marys	E-5
Stacyville	A-6
Stanton	F-3
Stanwood	D-8
State Center	D-6
Steamboat Rock	C-6
Storm Lake	C-3
Story City	D-5
Stout	C-7
Strawberry Point	C-8
Stuart	E-4
Sully	D-6
Sulphur Springs	C-3
Sumner	C-7
Superior	B-3
Sutherland	B-2
Swea City	B-4
Tabor	F-2
Tama	D-7
Templeton	D-3
Terril	B-3
Thompson	B-5
Thornton	B-5
Thurman	F-2
Tiffin	E-8
Tipton	D-9
Titonka	B-5
Toledo	D-7
Traer	D-7
Trenton	F-8
Tripoli	C-7
Truesdale	C-3
Truro	F-5
Turin	D-2
Ulmer	D-3
Underwood	E-2
Union	C-5
Urbana	D-7
Urbandale	E-5
Ute	D-2
Vail	D-3
Valeria	E-5
Van Horne	D-7
Van Wert	F-5
Varina	C-3
Ventura	B-5
Victor	E-7
Villisca	F-3
Vining	D-7
Vinton	D-7
W. Burlington	F-8
Walford	D-8
Walker	D-8
Wall Lake	C-3
Wallingford	B-4
Wapello	F-9
Washington	E-8
Washta	C-2
Waterloo	C-7
Waukee	E-5
Waukon	B-8
Waverly	C-7
Webster	E-7
Webster City	C-5
Weldon	F-5
Wellman	E-8
Welton	D-10
Wesley	B-5
West Bend	B-4
West Des Moines	D-4
West Grove	F-7
West Liberty	E-9
West Point	F-8
West Union	B-8
Westfield	C-1
Weston	Pg. 132
Wheatland	D-9
Whiting	D-2
Whittemore	B-4
Wick	B-3
Willey	D-3
Williams	C-5
Williamsburg	E-8
Williamson	F-6
Wilton	D-9
Winfield	F-8
Winterset	E-4
Wiota	E-3
Woodbine	D-2
Woodburn	F-5
Woodward	D-4
Woolstock	C-5
Wyoming	D-9
Yale	E-4
Zwingle	C-9

KANSAS
Page 37

Population: 2,363,679
Capital: Topeka
Land Area: 81,781 sq. mi.

Place	Ref
Abbeyville	E-5
Abilene	D-7
Admire	D-8
Agenda	C-7
Agra	C-4
Alden	E-5
Alexander	D-4
Allen	D-8
Alma	D-8
Almena	B-4
Alta Vista	D-8
Altamont	F-9
Alton	C-5
Altoona	E-8
Americus	D-8
Andale	E-6
Andover	F-7
Anthony	F-6
Arcadia	E-9
Argonia	F-6
Arkansas City	F-7
Arlington	E-5
Ashland	F-4
Atchison	C-9
Athol	C-5
Atlanta	F-7
Attica	F-5
Atwood	B-2
Augusta	F-7
Axtell	C-8
Baldwin City	D-9
Barnard	D-6
Barnes	C-7
Bartlett	F-9
Basehor	D-9
Bassett	E-9
Baxter Springs	F-9
Bazine	D-4
Beattie	C-8
Belle Plaine	F-7
Belleville	C-6
Beloit	C-6
Belpre	E-4
Belvue	D-8
Benedict	E-8
Bennington	D-6
Bentley	E-6
Benton	E-7
Bern	C-8
Beverly	D-6
Bird City	B-2
Bison	D-4
Blue Mound	E-9
Blue Rapids	C-7
Bluff City	F-6
Bogue	C-4
Brewster	C-2
Bronson	E-9
Brookville	D-6
Brownell	D-4
Bucklin	F-4
Buffalo	F-9
Buhler	E-6
Bunker Hill	D-5
Burden	F-7
Burdett	E-4
Burlingame	D-8
Burlington	D-8
Burns	E-7
Burr Oak	C-5
Burrton	E-6
Bushong	D-8
Bushton	D-5
Byers	E-5
Caldwell	F-6
Cambridge	F-7
Caney	F-8
Canton	E-7
Carbondale	D-9
Carlton	D-7
Cassoday	E-7
Cawker City	C-5
Cedar	C-5
Cedar Point	E-7
Cedar Vale	F-8
Centralia	C-8
Chanute	E-9
Chapman	D-7
Chase	E-5
Chautauqua	F-8
Cherokee	E-9
Cherryvale	F-9
Chetopa	F-9
Cimarron	E-3
Circleville	C-8
Claflin	D-5
Clay Center	C-7
Clayton	B-3
Clearwater	F-6
Clifton	C-7
Climax	E-8
Clyde	C-6
Coats	F-5
Coffeyville	F-9
Colby	C-2
Coldwater	F-4
Collyer	C-3
Colony	E-9
Columbus	F-9
Concordia	C-6
Conway Springs	F-6
Coolidge	E-1
Copeland	F-3
Cottonwood Falls	E-7
Council Grove	D-8
Countryside	Pg. 112, H-2
Courtland	C-7
Cuba	C-6
Cullison	F-5
Culver	D-6
Cunningham	F-5
Damar	C-4
De Soto	D-9
Dearing	F-8
Deerfield	E-2
Delphos	C-6
Denison	C-9
Denton	C-9
Derby	F-7
Dexter	F-7
Dighton	D-3
Dodge City	E-3
Douglass	F-7
Downs	C-5
Dresden	C-3
Dunlap	D-8
Dwight	D-7
Earlton	F-9
Easton	C-9
Edgerton	D-9
Edmond	C-4
Edna	F-9
Effingham	C-9
El Dorado	F-7
Elbing	E-7
Elgin	F-8
Elk City	F-8
Elk Falls	F-8
Elkhart	F-1
Ellinwood	E-5
Ellis	D-4
Ellsworth	D-6
Elmdale	E-7
Emmett	D-8
Emporia	D-8
Englewood	F-3
Ensign	E-3
Enterprise	D-7
Erie	F-9
Esbon	C-5
Eskridge	D-8
Eudora	D-9
Eureka	E-8
Fairview	C-8
Fall River	F-8
Florence	E-7
Fontana	E-9
Ford	F-4
Formoso	C-6
Fort Scott	E-9
Fowler	F-3
Frankfort	C-7
Fredonia	F-8
Freeport	F-6
Frontenac	F-9
Fulton	E-9
Galatia	D-4
Galena	F-9
Galesburg	F-9
Galva	E-6
Garden City	E-2
Garden Plain	F-6
Gardner	D-9
Garfield	E-4
Garnett	E-9
Gaylord	C-5
Gem	C-2
Geneseo	D-5
Girard	E-9
Glade	C-4
Glasco	C-6
Glen Elder	C-5
Goessel	E-6
Goodland	C-1
Gorham	D-5
Gove	D-3
Grainfield	C-3
Grandview Plaza	D-7
Great Bend	E-5
Greenleaf	C-7
Greensburg	F-4
Gridley	E-8
Grinnell	C-2
Halstead	E-6
Hamilton	E-8
Hamlin	C-9
Hanover	C-7
Hanston	E-4
Hardtner	F-5
Harper	F-6
Hartford	E-8
Harveyville	D-8
Havana	F-8
Haven	E-6
Havensville	C-8
Haviland	E-5
Hays	D-4
Haysville	F-6
Hazelton	F-5
Healy	D-3
Herington	D-7
Herndon	B-3
Hesston	E-6
Hiawatha	C-9
Highland	C-9
Hill City	C-3
Hillsboro	E-7
Hoisington	D-5
Holcomb	E-2
Hollenberg	C-7
Holton	D-8
Holyrood	D-5
Hope	D-7
Horton	C-9
Howard	F-8
Hoxie	C-3
Hoyt	C-8
Hudson	E-5
Hugoton	F-2
Humboldt	F-9
Hunter	C-5
Huron	C-9
Hutchinson	E-6
Independence	F-8
Ingalls	E-3
Inman	E-6
Iola	E-9
Isabel	F-5
Jamestown	C-6
Jennings	C-3
Jetmore	E-3
Jewell	C-6
Johnson City	E-1
Junction City	D-7
Kanapolis	D-6
Kansas City	D-9
Vicinity	Pg. 112, E-1
Kensington	C-4
Kincaid	E-9
Kingman	F-5
Kinsley	E-4
Kiowa	F-5
Kirwin	C-4
Kismet	F-2
La Crosse	D-4
La Cygne	E-9
La Harpe	E-9
Lakin	E-2
Lane	E-9
Langdon	E-5
Larned	E-4
Latham	F-7
Latimer	D-7
Lawrence	D-9
Le Roy	E-9
Leavenworth	C-9
Leawood	Pg. 112, K-3
Lebanon	C-5
Lebo	D-8
Lecompton	D-9
Lehigh	E-7
Lenexa	Pg. 112, J-1
Lenora	C-3
Leon	F-7
Leona	C-9
Leonardville	C-7
Leoti	D-2
Lewis	E-4
Liberal	F-2
Lincoln	D-6
Lincolnville	E-7
Lindsborg	D-6
Linn	C-7
Linwood	D-9
Little River	E-6
Logan	C-4
Lone Elm	E-9
Long Island	B-4
Longford	D-7
Longton	F-8
Lorraine	D-5
Lost Springs	D-7
Louisburg	E-9
Louisville	C-8
Lucas	D-5
Luka	F-5
Luray	D-5
Lyndon	D-8
Lyons	E-6
Macksville	E-4
Madison	E-7
Maize	E-6
Manchester	D-7
Manhattan	D-8
Mankato	C-5
Manter	E-1
Maple City	F-7
Mapleton	E-9
Marion	E-7
Marquette	D-6
Marysville	C-7
Matfield Green	E-7
Mayetta	D-8
Mayfield	F-6
McCracken	D-4
McCune	F-9
McDonald	B-2
McFarland	D-8
McPherson	E-6
Meade	F-3
Medicine Lodge	F-5
Melvern	D-8
Meriden	D-8
Merriam	Pg. 112, H-2
Milan	F-6
Mildred	E-9
Milford	D-7
Miltonvale	C-6
Minneapolis	D-6
Minneola	F-3
Mission	Pg. 112, H-2
Mission Hills	Pg. 112, G-3
Moline	F-8
Montezuma	E-3
Moran	E-9
Morganville	C-7
Morland	C-3
Morrill	C-8
Morrowville	C-7
Moscow	F-2
Mound City	E-9
Mound Valley	F-9
Moundridge	E-6
Mount Hope	E-6
Mullinville	F-4
Mulvane	F-7
Munden	C-6
Muscotah	C-9
Narka	C-6
Nashville	F-5
Neodesha	F-8
Neosho Falls	E-8
Netawaka	C-8
New Cambria	D-6
New Strawn	D-8
Nickerson	E-6
Norcatur	C-3
Norton	C-4
Nortonville	C-9
Norwich	F-6
Oak Hill	C-6
Oakley	C-2
Oberlin	C-3
Offerle	E-4
Ogden	D-7
Oketo	C-7
Olmitz	D-5
Olpe	D-8
Olsburg	C-7
Onaga	C-8
Osage City	D-8
Osawatomie	E-9
Osborne	C-5
Oswego	F-9
Otis	D-4
Ottawa	D-9
Overbrook	D-8
Overland Park	Pg. 112, J-2
Oxford	F-7
Palco	C-4
Palmer	C-7
Paola	E-9
Paradise	D-5
Park	C-3
Park City	E-7
Parker	E-9
Parsons	F-9
Pawnee Rock	E-5
Paxico	D-8
Peabody	E-7
Perry	D-9
Peru	F-8
Phillipsburg	C-4
Pittsburg	F-10
Plains	F-3
Plainville	C-4
Pleasanton	E-9
Plevna	E-5
Pomona	D-9
Portis	C-5
Potwin	E-7
Powhattan	C-8
Prairie View	C-4
Prairie Village	Pg. 112, H-3
Prescott	E-9
Preston	F-5
Pretty Prairie	E-6
Princeton	E-9
Protection	F-4
Quenemo	D-9
Quinter	C-3
Ramona	D-7
Randall	C-6
Randolph	C-7
Ransom	D-3
Rantoul	E-9
Raymond	E-5
Reading	D-8
Redfield	E-9
Republic	C-6
Rexford	C-3
Richfield	F-1
Richmond	E-9
Riley	C-7
Robinson	C-9
Roeland Park	F-9
Vicinity	Pg. 112, G-3
Rolla	F-1
Rose Hill	F-7
Rossville	D-8
Rozel	E-4
Rush Center	D-4
Russell	D-5
Russell Springs	C-2
Sabetha	C-8
Salina	D-6
Satanta	F-2
Sawyer	F-5
Scandia	C-6
Schoenchen	D-2
Scott City	D-2
Scottsville	C-6
Sedan	F-8
Sedgwick	E-6
Selden	C-3
Seneca	C-8
Severy	E-8
Seward	E-5
Sharon	F-5
Sharon Springs	D-1
Shawnee	Pg. 112, H-1
Silver Lake	D-8
Simpson	C-6
Smith Center	C-5
Smolan	D-6
Solomon	D-7
South Haven	F-6
Spearville	E-3
Spivey	F-6
Spring Hill	D-9
St. Francis	B-1
St. John	E-5
St. Marys	D-8
St. Paul	F-9
Stafford	E-5
Stark	F-9
Sterling	E-6
Strong City	E-8
Sublette	F-2
Summerfield	C-8
Sun City	F-5
Sylvan Grove	C-5
Sylvia	E-5
Syracuse	E-1
Tampa	E-7
Tescott	D-6
Thayer	F-9
Timken	D-4
Tipton	C-5
Tonganoxie	D-9
Topeka	D-8
Toronto	E-8
Towanda	E-7
Tribune	D-1
Troy	C-9
Turon	E-5
Tyro	F-8
Udall	F-7
Ulysses	E-2
Uniontown	F-9
Utica	D-3
Valley Center	E-6
Valley Falls	C-9
Vermillion	C-8
Victoria	D-4
Vining	C-7
Virgil	D-8
WaKeeney	D-4
Wakefield	C-7
Waldo	D-5
Waldron	F-5
Wallace	D-2
Walnut	F-9
Walton	E-7
Wamego	D-8
Washington	C-6
Waterville	C-7
Wathena	C-9
Waverly	E-9
Webber	C-6
Weir Scammon	F-9
Wellington	F-6
Westmoreland	C-8
Westphalia	E-9
Wetmore	C-8
Wheaton	C-8
White City	D-7
Whitewater	E-7
Whiting	C-9
Wichita	F-7
Williamsburg	D-9
Willowbrook	E-6
Wilmore	F-4
Wilsey	D-7
Wilson	D-5
Winchester	C-9
Windom	E-6
Winfield	F-7
Winona	C-2
Woodbine	D-7
Woodston	C-4
Yates Center	E-8
Zenda	F-5
Zurich	C-4

KENTUCKY

Pages 38-39

Population: 3,660,777
Capital: Frankfort
Land Area: 39,669 sq. mi.

Place	Ref
Adairville	F-5
Albany	F-7
Alexandria	B-10
Allen	D-12
Allensville	F-5
Arlington	E-2
Ashland	C-12
Auburn	F-5
Audubon Park	Pg. 118, C-5
Augusta	B-10
Barbourville	F-11
Bardstown	D-8
Bardwell	E-2
Barlow	E-3
Beattyville	D-11
Beaver Dam	E-6
Bedford	B-8
Beech Grove	D-6
Bellefonte	C-12
Bellevue	Pg. 112, E-4
Benham	E-12
Benton	E-4
Berea	D-10
Berry	B-10
Bloomfield	D-8
Bonnieville	E-7
Boone	D-10
Boonesboro	D-10
Booneville	E-11
Bowling Green	E-6
Bradfordsville	D-9
Brandenburg	C-7
Bremen	E-6
Broadfields	Pg. 118, C-5
Bromley	A-10
Brooksville	B-10
Brownsville	E-7
Buckhorn	E-11
Buffalo	D-8
Burgin	D-9
Burkesville	F-8
Burnside	F-10
Burton	E-12
Butler	B-10
Cadiz	F-5
Calhoun	D-6
Callaway	F-11
Calvert City	E-4
Campbellsburg	B-8
Campbellsville	E-8
Campton	D-11
Caneyville	E-7
Carlisle	C-10
Carrollton	B-9
Carrsville	E-4
Carter	C-11
Caseyville	D-4
Catlettsburg	C-12
Cave City	E-8
Centertown	E-6
Central City	E-6
Cerulean	F-5
Clairfield	F-10
Clay	E-5
Clay City	D-10
Clearfield	C-11
Clinton	F-3
Cloverport	D-7
Cold Spring	Pg. 112, G-5
Columbia	E-8
Columbus	F-3
Concord	B-11
Constance	Pg. 112, F-1
Corbin	F-10
Corydon	D-5
Covington	B-9
Vicinity	Pg. 112, F-3
Crab Orchard	E-9
Crescent Springs	Pg. 112, F-2
Crestview Hills	Pg. 112, G-2
Crestwood	C-8
Crittenden	B-10
Crofton	E-5
Cumberland	E-12
Cynthiana	C-10
Danville	D-9
Dawson Springs	E-5
Dayton	Pg. 112, F-4
Dexter	F-4
Dixon	D-5
Dover	B-11
Drakesboro	E-6
Druid Hills	Pg. 118, B-5
Dry Ridge	B-10
Dunmor	E-6
Dycusburg	E-4
Earlington	E-5
Eddyville	E-4
Edmonton	E-8
Ekron	D-7
Elizabethtown	D-7
Elkhorn City	E-13
Elkton	E-5
Elsmere	B-10
Eminence	C-9
Erlanger	Pg. 112, G-2
Eubank	E-9
Evarts	F-12
Fairdale	C-8
Fairfield	D-9
Fairview	E-5
Falmouth	B-10
Ferguson	E-10
Flatwoods	C-12
Fleming	E-12
Flemingsburg	C-11
Florence	B-10
Fordsville	D-7
Foster	B-10
Fountain Run	F-8
Frankfort	C-9
Franklin	F-6
Fredonia	E-5
Freeburn	D-13
Frenchburg	D-11
Frogue	F-9
Ft. Mitchell	Pg. 112, G-3
Ft. Thomas	Pg. 112, F-5
Ft. Wright	Pg. 112, F-3
Fulton	F-3
Gamaliel	F-8
Georgetown	C-10
Ghent	B-9
Glasgow	F-7
Golden Pond	F-4
Goshen	C-8
Gratz	C-9
Grand Rivers	E-4
Grayson	C-12
Greensburg	E-8
Greenup	B-12
Guthrie	F-5
Hanson	E-5
Hardin	E-4
Hardinsburg	D-7
Hardyville	E-8
Harlan	F-11
Harned	D-7
Harrodsburg	D-9
Hartford	E-6
Hawesville	D-6
Hazard	E-12
Hazel	F-4
Hazel Green	D-11
Heller	E-12
Henderson	D-5
Hickman	F-3
Highland Hts.	Pg. 112, G-5
Hindman	E-12
Hodgenville	D-8
Hopkinsville	F-6
Horse Cave	E-8

KENTUCKY

Hopkinsville F-6
Horse Cave E-8
Hustonville E-9
Hyden E-11
Independence B-10
Inez D-12
Irvine D-10
Irvington D-7
Island E-6
Jackson D-11
Jamestown E-9
Jeffersontown C-8
Jenkins E-12
Junction City D-9
Kenton Vale Pg. 100, G-3
Kirkmansville E-6
Knob Creek D-8
Kuttawa E-4
La Fayette F-5
La Grange C-8
LaCenter E-3
Lackey E-12
Lakeside Park Pg. 100, G-3
Lakeview Pg. 100, G-3
Lancaster D-10
Lawrenceburg C-9
Leatherwood E-11
Lebanon D-9
Lebanon Jct. D-8
Lee City D-11
Leitchfield D-7
Lewisburg C-11
Lewisport D-6
Lexington D-9
Liberty E-9
Livermore D-6
Livingston E-10
Lockport C-9
London E-10
Loretto D-8
Lothair E-11
Louisa C-12
Louisville C-8
Vicinity Pg. 118
Loyall F-11
Lucas F-8
Ludlow Pg. 100, F-3
Lynch F-12
Lynnview Pg. 118, E-4
Madisonville E-5
Manchester E-10
Marion E-5
Martin D-12
Mason B-10
Mayfield F-4
Maysville B-11
McCreary D-10
McHenry E-6
McKee E-10
McRoberts E-12
Middlesboro F-10
Middletown C-8
Midway C-9
Midway F-4
Millersburg C-10
Milton B-8
Mockingbird Valley Pg. 118, B-5
Monkeys Eyebrow E-3
Monroe E-8
Monterey C-9
Monticello F-9
Morehead C-11
Moreland D-9
Morgan B-10
Morganfield D-5
Morgantown E-7
Mortons Gap E-5
Mount Olivet B-10
Mount Sterling C-11
Mount Vernon E-10
Mount Washington C-8
Muldraugh D-8
Munfordville E-8
Murray F-4
Nebo E-5
Neon E-12
New Castle C-9
New Haven D-8
Newport A-10
Vicinity Pg. 100, F-4
Nicholasville D-9
North Middletown C-10
Nortonville E-6
Oak Grove F-5
Oakland E-7
Olive Hill C-11
Owensboro D-6
Owenton C-9
Owingsville C-10
Paducah E-4
Paintsville D-12
Paris C-10
Park City E-8
Park Hills Pg. 100, F-3
Parkers Lake F-10
Parkway Village Pg. 118, D-3
Pembroke F-5
Perryville D-9
Phelps D-13
Pikeville E-13
Pine Knot F-10
Pineville F-11
Pleasureville C-9
Prestonsburg D-12
Prestonville B-8
Princeton E-5
Prospect C-8
Providence E-5
Raceland B-12
Radcliff D-7
Ravenna D-11
Reidland E-4
Renfro Valley E-10
Richmond D-10
Rockcastle F-5
Rockport E-6
Rolling Fields Pg. 118, B-5
Russell B-12
Russell Springs E-9
Russellville F-6
Sadieville C-10
Salt Lick C-11
Salyersville D-12
Sanders B-9
Sandy Hook C-12
Sardis C-11
Science Hill E-9
Scottsville F-7
Sebree D-5
Seco E-12
Sedalia F-4
Sharpsburg C-11
Shelby City D-9
Shelbyville C-9
Shepherdsville C-8
Shively C-8
Vicinity Pg. 118, D-1
Silver Grove Pg. 100, G-6
Simpsonville C-8
Slaughters D-5
Smithland E-4
Smiths Grove E-7
Somerset E-10
Sonora D-7
South Shore B-12
South Williamson D-13
Springfield D-9
Stamping Ground C-9
Stanford D-10
Stanton D-11
Stearns F-9
Sturgis D-5
Taylorsville D-9
Tompkinsville F-8
Trenton F-6
Trimble E-9
Tyner E-11
Union B-9
Uniontown D-5
Upton E-8
Valley Station C-8
Van Lear D-12
Vanceburg B-11
Vancleve D-11
Versailles C-9
Villa Hills Pg. 100, F-2
Vine Grove D-7
Wallins Creek F-11
Walton B-10
Warfield D-13
Warsaw B-9
Washington B-11
Water Valley F-4
Waverly D-5
Wayland E-12
Webster D-7
West Beauchel Pg. 118, D-5
West Liberty D-11
West Point D-8
Wheatley B-9
Wheelwright E-12
Whitesburg E-12
Whitesville D-6
Whitley City F-10
Wickliffe E-3
Wilders Pg. 100, F-4
Willard C-12
Williamsburg F-10
Williamstown B-10
Wilmore D-9
Winchester D-10
Wingo F-4
Woodburn F-7

LOUISIANA

Page 40

Population: 4,205,9000
Capital: Baton Rouge
Land Area: 44,521 sq. mi.

Abbeville F-5
Abington B-2
Abita Springs E-8
Acme D-5
Acy E-7
Ada B-3
Addis E-6
Adeline F-6
Afton B-6
Aimwell C-5
Airline Park Pg. 125, C-4
Ajax C-3
Albany E-7
Alco D-3
Alden Bridge A-2
Alexandria D-4
Alsaita A-6
Alto B-5
Ama Pg. 125, C-2
Amelia G-7
Amite E-8
Anacoco D-3
Angie D-9
Angola D-5
Ansley B-4
Antioch A-3
Arabi F-9
Vicinity Pg. 125, C-8
Archibald B-5
Archie C-5
Arcola D-8
Armistead B-3
Arnaudville E-5
Ashland B-3
Athens A-3
Atlanta C-4
Augusta Pg. 125, F-7
Avery Island F-5
Avondale Pg. 125, D-4
Aycock A-3
Bains D-6
Baker E-6
Baldwin F-6
Ball C-4
Bancroft E-2
Barataria F-8
Basile E-4
Baskin B-5
Bastrop A-5
Batchelor D-6
Baton Rouge E-7
Bayou Cane G-7
Bayou Chicot D-5
Bayou Sorrel F-6
Bayou Vista G-6
Baywood E-7
Beaver E-4
Beekman A-5
Beggs E-5
Bell City F-3
Belle Chasse F-9
Vicinity Pg. 125, E-8
Belle Rose F-7
Bellwood C-3
Belmont C-2
Benson C-2
Bentley C-4
Benton A-2
Bernice A-4
Bertrandville F-9
Vicinity Pg. 125, G-7
Berwick F-6
Bienville B-3
Blackburn A-3
Blanchard A-2
Bogalusa D-9
Bohemia G-9
Bolinger A-2
Bonita A-5
Book D-5
Boothville G-10
Bordelonville D-5
Bosco B-5
Bossier City A-2
Bourg G-8
Boyce D-4
Braithwaite Pg. 125, E-9
Branch E-5
Breaux Bridge E-5
Bridge City Pg. 125, D-4
Broussard F-5
Brusly E-6
Bryceland B-3
Bunkie D-5
Buras G-9
Burnside F-7
Burr Ferry D-2
Bush E-9
Cade F-5
Caernarvon Pg. 125, E-9
Calhoun B-4
Calvin C-4
Cameron F-3
Campti C-3
Caney D-2
Carencro E-5
Carlisle F-9
Carville E-7
Caspiana B-2
Castor B-3
Cedar Grove Pg. 125, F-7
Center Point D-5
Centerville F-6
Chacahoula F-7
Chackbay F-7
Chalmette F-9
Vicinity Pg. 125, D-8
Chase B-5
Chataignier E-4
Chatham B-4
Chauvin G-8
Cheneyville D-5
Chestnut B-3
Chipola D-7
Chopin C-4
Choudrant B-4
Church Point E-5
Clarence C-3
Clarks B-5
Clay B-4
Clayton C-6
Clifton D-8
Clinton D-7
Cloutierville C-4
Cocodrie G-7
Colfax C-4
Collinston A-5
Colquitt A-3
Columbia B-5
Concession Pg. 125, F-8
Convent F-7
Converse C-2
Cotton Valley A-3
Cottonport D-5
Coushatta B-3
Covington E-8
Cravens D-3
Creole F-3
Creston B-3
Crowley F-4
Crown Point Pg. 125, G-6
Crowville B-6
Cullen A-3
Cut Off G-8
Cypress C-3
Dalcour F-9
Vicinity Pg. 125, F-8
Darlington D-7
Darnell A-6
Davant F-9
De Quincy E-3
De Ridder E-3
Deer Park C-6
Delacroix F-9
Delcambre F-5
Delhi A-6
Derry C-3
Des Allemands F-8
Destrehan Pg. 125, D-1
Deville D-5
Diamond G-9
Dixie Inn A-2
Dodson B-4
Donaldsonville F-7
Downsville A-4
Dry Creek E-3
Dry Prong C-4
Dubach A-4
Dubuisson E-5
Dulac G-7
Dupont D-5
Duson F-5
Duty C-5
Easlyville D-7
East End Pg. 125, B-5
Eastwood B-2
Echo D-5
Edgerly F-2
Effie D-5
Elizabeth D-4
Elm Grove B-2
Elton E-4
Empire G-9
Englishturn Pg. 125, E-8
Enon D-8
Enterprise C-5
Erath F-5
Eros B-4
Estelle Pg. 125, E-6
Estherwood F-4
Esto D-2
Ethel E-6
Eunice E-4
Eva C-5
Evangeline E-4
Evans D-3
Evelyn B-2
Evergreen D-5
Farmerville A-4
Felps D-7
Fenton E-3
Ferriday C-5
Fields E-2
Fillmore B-2
Fisher C-3
Flatwoods D-4
Flora C-3
Florien D-2
Folsom E-8
Fondale B-5
Fordoche E-5
Forest A-6
Forest Hill D-4
Fort Jesup C-3
Fort Necessity B-5
Foules C-6
Franklin F-6
Franklinton D-8
French Settlement E-7
Frenier F-8
Frogmore C-5
Frost E-7
Galbraith C-4
Galion A-5
Galliano G-8
Gandy D-2
Gardner D-4
Georgetown C-4
Gheens F-8
Gibsland B-3
Gibson G-7
Gilbert B-6
Gillis E-3
Glade C-5
Glenmora D-4
Gloster B-2
Golden Meadow G-8
Goldonna B-4
Gonzales E-7
Gordon A-3
Gorum C-3
Goudeau D-5
Grambling A-4
Grand Bayou B-3
Grand Cane B-2
Grand Chenier F-4
Grand Coteau E-5
Grand Isle G-9
Grand Lake F-3
Grangeville E-7
Grayson B-5
Greensburg D-7
Gretna F-8
Vicinity Pg. 125, D-7
Grosse Tete E-6
Gueydan F-4
Hackberry F-3
Haile A-5
Hall Summit B-3
Hamburg D-5
Hammond E-8
Hanna C-3
Harahan F-8
Vicinity Pg. 125, D-4
Harrisonburg C-5
Harvey Pg. 125, D-6
Hathaway E-4
Hayes F-4
Haynesville A-3
Hebert B-5
Henderson E-6
Hermitage E-6
Hessmer D-5
Hickory E-9
Hicks D-3
Hico A-4
Highland A-6
Hodge B-4
Holloway D-5
Holly Beach F-2
Holmwood F-3
Holton E-8
Holum B-5
Homer A-3
Hornbeck D-3
Hosston A-2
Hot Wells D-4
Houma G-7
Humphreys G-7
Hutton D-3
Ida A-2
Independence E-8
Indian Mound E-7
Indian Village F-6
Iota F-4
Iowa F-3
Ivan A-2
Jackson D-6
Jamestown B-3
Jean Lafitte F-8
Vicinity Pg. 125, F-5
Jeanerette F-6
Jefferson Hts. Pg. 125, C-4
Jena C-5
Jennings F-4
Jesuit Bend Pg. 125, G-7
Jigger B-5
Johnsons Bayou F-2
Jones A-5
Jonesboro B-4
Jonesville C-5
Kaplan F-4
Keatchie B-2
Keithville B-2
Kenner F-8
Vicinity Pg. 125, B-3
Kentwood D-8
Kilbourne A-6
Killian E-8
Kinder E-4
Kingston B-2
Kisatchie C-3
Krotz Springs E-5
Kurthwood D-3
La Place F-8
Labadieville F-7
Labarre E-6
Lacamp D-3
Lacassine F-4
Lacombe E-8
Lafayette F-5
Lafitte F-8
Lafourche F-7
Lake Arthur F-4
Lake Charles F-3
Lake End C-3
Lake Providence A-6
Lakeland E-6
Larose G-8
Larto D-5
Latanier D-4
Lawtell E-5
Le Blanc E-3
LeMoyen E-5
Leander D-4
Lebeau E-5
Lecompte D-4
Leesville D-3
Leeville G-8
Leonville E-5
Libuse D-5
Lillie A-4
Linville A-5
Lisbon A-3
Lismore C-5
Live Oak Pg. 125, G-7
Live Oak Manor Pg. 125, C-3
Livingston E-7
Livonia E-6
Lockport F-8
Logansport C-2
Lone Star Pg. 125, D-1
Longstreet B-2
Longville E-3
Lottie E-6
Louisa F-6
Lucas B-2
Lucky B-3
Luling Pg. 125, D-1
Luna B-5
Lutcher F-7
Madisonville E-8
Mamou E-4
Manchac E-8
Mandeville E-8
Mangham B-5
Manifest C-5
Mansfield C-2
Many C-3
Maringouin E-6
Marion A-5
Marksville D-5
Marrero Pg. 125, D-6
Marsalis A-3
Martin B-3
Mathews F-8
Maurepas E-7
Maxie E-4
Mayna C-5
McDade B-2
McNary D-4
Melder D-4
Melrose C-3
Melville E-5
Mer Rouge A-5
Meraux Pg. 125, D-9
Mermentau F-4
Merryville E-2
Metairie F-8
Vicinity Pg. 125, C-5
Midland F-4
Midway A-2
Mill B-4
Minden A-3
Mira A-2
Mitchel C-2
Mittie E-4
Mix E-6
Monroe A-5
Montegut G-8
Monterey C-6
Montgomery C-3
Montpelier E-7
Mooringsport A-2
Moreauville D-5
Morgan City F-7
Morganza E-6
Morrow E-5
Mount Carmel C-3
Myrtle Grove G-8
Nairn G-9
Naomi F-8
Napoleonville F-7
Natchez C-3
Natchitoches C-3
Negreet C-2
New Era D-5
New Iberia F-6
New Llano D-3
New Orleans F-8
Vicinity Pg. 125, A-7
New Roads E-6
Newellton B-6
Newlight B-6
Noble C-2
North Hodge B-4
Norwood D-6
Oak Grove F-3
Oak Grove A-6
Oak Ridge A-5
Oakdale E-4
Oakland A-4
Oakville Pg. 125, G-7
Oberlin E-4
Oil City A-2
Olivier F-6
Olla C-4
Opelousas E-5
Oscar E-6
Oxford C-2
Packton C-4
Paincourtville F-7
Parks F-5
Patterson F-6
Pearl River E-9
Pecan Island G-4
Perryville A-5
Phoenix F-9
Pickering D-3
Pierre Part F-6
Pigeon F-6
Pilot Town G-10
Pine D-8
Pine Grove E-7
Pine Prairie E-4
Pineville D-4
Pitkin D-3
Plain Dealing A-2
Plaquemine E-6
Pleasant Hill C-2
Pointe a La Hache G-9
Pollock C-4
Ponchatoula E-8
Port Allen E-6
Port Barre E-5
Port Sulphur G-9
Port Vincent E-7
Powhatan C-3
Poydras Pg. 125, E-10
Provencal C-3
Quitman B-4
Raceland F-7
Ragley E-3
Ramah E-6
Rayne F-5
Rayville A-5
Readhimer B-3
Reddell E-4
Reeves E-3
Reggio F-9
Reserve F-8
Richmond B-6
Richwood B-5
Ridgecrest C-6
Ringgold B-3
Riverton B-5
Robeline C-3
Robert E-8
Rocky Mountain A-2
Rodessa A-1
Rosedale E-6
Rosefield C-5
Rosepine D-3
Ruddock F-8
Ruston B-4
Sailes B-3
Saint Bernard Pg. 125, E-10
Saint Clair Pg. 125, E-8
Saint Francisville E-6
Saint Gabriel E-7
Saint Joseph B-6
Saint Martinville F-6
Saint Rose Pg. 125, D-1
Saline B-3
Sarepta A-3
Scarsdale Pg. 125, E-8
Scott F-5
Shaw D-6
Sheridan D-9
Shongaloo A-3
Shreveport B-2
Sibley A-3
Sicily Island C-5
Sieper D-4
Sikes B-4
Simmesport D-5
Simpson D-3
Singer E-3
Slagle D-3
Slaughter E-6
Slidell E-9
Slocum D-6
Somerset B-6
Sondheimer A-6
Sorrento F-7
Spearsville A-4
Spencer A-5
Spokane C-6
Spring Ridge B-2
Springfield E-7
Springhill A-2
Stanley C-2
Starks F-2
Start B-5
State Line D-9
Stella Pg. 125, F-8
Sterlington A-5
Stonewall B-2
Sugartown E-3
Sulphur F-3
Summerfield A-3
Sun E-9
Sunset E-5
Supreme F-7
Talisheek E-9
Tallulah B-6
Tangipahoa D-8
Tannehill B-4
Taylortown B-2
Terry A-6
Tete E-6
Thibodaux F-7
Tidewater G-9
Tioga D-4
Toomey F-2
Toro D-2
Transylvania A-6
Triumph G-10
Truxno A-4
Tullos C-5
Turkey Creek D-4
Union F-7
Union Hill D-4
Urania C-4
Vacherie F-7
Varnado D-9
Venice G-10
Verda C-4
Vidalia C-6
Vienna A-4
Ville Platte E-5
Vinton F-2
Violet F-9
Vivian A-2
Vixen B-5
Waggaman Pg. 125, D-3
Wakefield D-6
Waldheim E-8
Walters C-5
Warnerton D-8
Washington E-5
Waterproof C-6
Watson E-7
Waverly B-6
Weeks F-6
Welsh F-4
Weston B-4
Westwego F-8
Vicinity Pg. 125, E-4
Weyanoke D-6
White Castle F-7
Whitehall C-5
Williana C-4
Wills Point Pg. 125, G-8
Willswood Pg. 125, D-3
Wilmer D-8
Wilson D-6
Winnfield C-4
Winnsboro B-5
Woodworth D-4
Worden D-6
Wye E-3
Youngsville F-5
Yscloskey F-9
Zenoria C-4
Zwolle C-2

MAINE

Page 41

Population: 1,124,660
Capital: Augusta
Land Area: 30,995 sq. mi.

Acton J-2
Addison F-6
Albion G-3
Alexander E-6
Allagash B-4
Andover G-2
Anson F-3
Appleton G-4
Ashland C-4
Athens F-3
Auburn H-3
Augusta G-3
Avon F-2
Bailey Island H-3
Balleyville E-6
Bangor F-5
Bar Harbor G-5
Baring E-6
Bath H-3
Beddington F-5
Belfast G-4
Belgrade G-3
Benton F-3
Berwick J-2
Bethel G-2
Biddeford J-3
Bigelow F-2
Bingham F-3
Blaine C-5
Blanchard F-3
Blue Hill G-5
Boothbay Harbor H-4
Bradford F-4
Bradley F-5
Brewer F-4
Bridgewater C-5
Bridgton H-2
Brighton F-3
Bristol H-4
Brooks G-4
Brownfield H-2
Brownville E-4
Brownville Jct. E-4
Brunswick H-3
Buckfield G-3
Bucks Harbor F-6
Bucksport G-5
Burlington E-5
Burnham F-4
Buxton J-2
Byron G-2
Calais E-6
Cambridge F-3
Camden G-4
Canton G-2
Cape Elizabeth J-3
Cape Porpoise J-2
Caratunk F-3
Caribou B-5
Carmel F-4
Carrabassett F-3
Carroll E-5
Cary D-5
Casco H-2
Castine G-4
Charleston F-4
Cherryfield G-6
Chester E-5
Chisolm G-2
Clayton Lake C-3
Clinton G-4
Coburn Gore E-2
Colby E-6
Columbia F-6
Conner B-5
Cooper F-6
Corea G-6
Corinna F-4
Cornish H-1
Costigan F-5
Crawford F-6
Crouseville B-5
Cumberland Center H-2
Cutler F-7
Daigle B-4
Dallas F-2
Damariscotta H-4
Danforth D-5
Deblois F-5
Dedham F-4
Deer Isle G-5
Dennistown E-2
Dennysville F-6
Dickey B-4
Dixfield G-2
Dixmont G-4
Dover Foxcroft E-4
Durham H-3
Eagle Lake B-4
East Hampden F-4
East Machias F-6
East Millinocket E-4
East Sumner G-2
East Wilton G-3
Eastbrook F-5
Easton C-5
Eastport F-7
Eaton E-6
Eddington F-4
Ellsworth G-5
Estcourt Sta. A-4
Eustis F-2
Fairfield F-3
Falmouth Foreside J-2
Farmingdale G-3
Farmington G-2
Fort Fairfield B-5
Fort Kent A-4
Franklin G-5
Freeport H-3
Frenchville A-4
Friendship H-3
Frye G-2
Fryeburg H-2
Gardiner G-3
Gilead G-2
Glenburn Center F-4
Gorham J-2
Gouldsboro G-5
Grand Isle A-5
Grand Lake Stream E-5
Gray H-3
Greenville E-3
Grindstone D-4
Grove F-6
Guerette B-4
Guilford F-3
Hallowell G-3
Hamlin B-5
Hampden F-4
Hancock G-5
Hanover G-2
Harrington F-5
Harrison H-2
Hartford Center G-2

MAINE

Hartland ... F-3
Haven ... G-5
Haynesville ... D-5
Hersey ... D-5
Hinckley ... H-2
Hiram ... H-2
Hogdon ... C-5
Houghton ... F-2
Houlton ... D-5
Howland ... E-4
Island Falls ... D-5
Jackman ... E-2
Jay ... G-3
Jefferson ... G-3
Jemtland ... B-5
Jonesboro ... F-6
Jonesport ... G-6
Keegan ... B-5
Kenduskeag ... F-4
Kennebago Lake ... F-2
Kennebunk ... J-2
Kennebunkport ... J-3
Kingfield ... F-2
Kingman ... E-5
Kingsbury ... F-3
Kittery ... K-2
Kittery Point ... K-2
Knowles Corner ... C-4
Kokadjo ... E-4
Lagrange ... F-4
Lake Parlin ... E-2
Lambert Lake ... E-6
Larone ... E-5
Lee ... E-5
Lewiston ... H-2
Liberty ... G-4
Lille ... A-5
Lily Bay ... E-3
Limerick ... J-2
Limestone ... B-5
Limington ... J-2
Lincoln ... E-5
Lincolnville ... G-4
Linneus ... D-5
Lisbon ... H-3
Lisbon Falls ... H-2
Littleton ... C-5
Livermore Falls ... G-3
Long Pond ... E-3
Lovell ... H-2
Lubec ... F-7
Ludlow ... D-5
Lynchville ... G-2
Machias ... F-6
Macwahoc ... D-5
Madawaska ... A-4
Madison ... F-3
Madrid ... F-2
Manchester ... G-3
Mapleton ... B-5
Marion ... F-6
Mars Hill ... C-5
Masardis ... C-4
Mattawamkeag ... D-4
Mayfield ... F-3
Medford ... E-4
Medway ... E-4
Mexico ... G-2
Milbridge ... G-5
Milford ... F-5
Millinocket ... D-4
Milo ... E-4
Molunkus ... E-5
Monarda ... D-5
Monroe ... G-4
Monson ... E-3
Monticello ... C-5
Moose River ... E-2
Morrill ... G-4
Moscow ... F-3
Naples ... H-2
New Gloucester ... H-2
Newcastle ... G-3
Newfield ... J-2
Newport ... F-4
Newry ... G-2
Nobleboro ... G-3
Norcross ... E-4
Norridgewock ... G-3
North Amity ... D-6
North Anson ... F-2
North Berwick ... J-2
North Lovell ... H-2
North Lyndon ... B-5
Northeast Carry ... D-3
Northeast Harbor ... G-5
Northfield ... F-6
Norway ... H-2
Oakland ... G-3
Ogunquit ... J-2
Old Orchard Beach ... J-2
Old Town ... F-5
Oquossoc ... F-2
Orient ... D-5
Orland ... G-4
Orono ... F-5
Orrington ... F-4
Ouelette ... B-4
Oxbow ... C-4
Oxford ... H-2
Palmyra ... F-3
Paris ... G-2
Parkman ... F-3
Patten ... D-4
Pittston ... H-3
Poland ... H-2
Portage ... B-4
Portland ... J-3
Presque Isle ... B-5
Princeton ... E-6
Quimby ... B-5
Randolph ... G-3
Raymond ... H-2
Readfield ... G-3

Red Beach ... E-7
Reed ... D-5
Richmond ... H-3
Ripley ... F-3
Ripogenus Dam ... D-4
Robbinston ... E-7
Robinsons ... C-5
Rockland ... H-4
Rockport ... H-4
Rockwood ... E-3
Rome ... G-3
Roxbury ... G-2
Rumford ... G-2
Sabattus ... H-3
Saco ... J-3
Saint Albans ... F-3
Saint David ... A-5
Saint Francis ... B-4
Saint George ... G-4
Saint John ... B-4
Salem ... F-2
Sanford ... J-2
Sangerville ... F-4
Saponac ... E-5
Scarborough ... J-2
Seal Harbor ... G-5
Searsmont ... G-4
Searsport ... G-4
Sebago ... H-2
Sebec Lake ... E-4
Seboeis ... E-4
Seboomook ... D-3
Sedgewick ... G-5
Selden ... D-5
Sheridan ... B-4
Sherman ... D-4
Sherman Mills ... D-5
Sherman Station ... D-4
Shin Pond ... D-4
Shirley Mills ... E-3
Sidney ... G-3
Skowhegan ... F-3
Smyrna Mills ... C-5
Soldier Pond ... B-4
Solon ... F-3
South Arm ... F-2
South Bancroft ... D-5
South China ... G-4
South Hope ... G-4
South Paris ... H-2
South Portland ... J-3
Southwest Harbor ... G-5
Springfield ... E-5
Springvale ... J-2
Squa Pan ... C-4
Stacyville ... D-4
Standish ... J-2
Starboard ... F-6
Stetson ... F-4
Steuben ... G-5
Stockton Springs ... G-4
Stonington ... G-5
Stow ... H-2
Stratton ... F-2
Strong ... F-2
Sweden ... G-2
The Forks ... E-3
Thomaston ... H-4
Topsfield ... E-6
Topsham ... H-3
Tremont ... G-5
Turner ... G-3
Union ... G-4
Unity ... G-4
Upton ... G-2
Van Buren ... B-5
Vanceboro ... E-6
Vienna ... G-3
Vinalhaven ... G-4
Waite ... E-6
Waldoboro ... H-4
Waltham ... F-5
Warren ... H-4
Washburn ... B-5
Washington ... G-3
Waterboro ... J-2
Waterford ... H-2
Waterville ... G-4
Wells ... J-2
Wesley ... F-6
West Enfield ... E-5
West Forks ... E-3
West Newfield ... J-2
West Paris ... G-2
Westbrook ... J-3
Weston ... D-5
Whiting ... F-6
Williamantic ... E-3
Wilsons Mills ... F-1
Wilton ... G-2
Winn ... E-5
Winslow ... G-3
Winter Harbor ... G-5
Winterport ... G-4
Winterville ... B-4
Winthrop ... G-3
Wiscasset ... H-3
Woodland ... B-5
Woolwich ... H-3
Wytopitlock ... D-5
Yarmouth ... H-3
York Beach ... K-2
York Village ... K-2

MARYLAND
Pages 42-43
Population: 4,216,975
Capital: Annapolis
Land Area: 9,837 sq. mi.

Aberdeen ... B-12
Accident ... B-1

Accokeek ... F-9
Airy ... F-12
Altamont ... B-1
Altoona Beach ... Pg. 91, H-5
Andersontown ... E-13
Andrews ... G-12
Annapolis ... D-11
Arbutus ... Pg. 91, F-3
Arnold ... D-10
Vicinity ... Pg. 91, K-6
Aspen Hill ... D-9
Avenue ... G-10
Baltimore ... C-10
Vicinity ... Pg. 91, D-4
Barclay ... D-13
Barnesville ... C-7
Bay Ridge ... E-11
Bayard ... B-1
Bayview ... B-12
Bel Air ... B-11
Belltown ... Pg. 91, B-1
Benfield ... Pg. 91, J-4
Berlin ... G-15
Berwyn Heights ... Pg. 150, B-8
Bethesda ... C-7
Vicinity ... Pg. 150, C-5
Betterton ... C-12
Bladensburg ... Pg. 150, C-9
Blenheim ... Pg. 91, A-5
Bloomsbury ... Pg. 91, F-2
Bonaparte Estates ... Pg. 91, A-7
Boonsboro ... B-7
Bowie ... D-10
Braddock Heights ... C-7
Brandywine ... F-9
Brentwood ... Pg. 150, D-9
Bristol ... E-10
Brooklyn ... Pg. 91, F-4
Brookview ... F-13
Broomes Island ... G-10
Brunswick ... C-7
Bryans Road ... F-8
Buckeystown ... C-7
Bucktown ... G-12
Burkittsville ... C-7
Butler ... B-10
California ... G-11
Cambridge ... F-12
Cape St. Claire ... D-11
Capitol Heights ... Pg. 150, E-8
Carney ... Pg. 91, C-6
Cascade ... A-7
Catonsville ... C-7
Vicinity ... Pg. 91, F-2
Caves Park ... Pg. 91, B-2
Cavetown ... B-7
Cayots ... A-7
Cecilton ... C-12
Centreville ... C-12
Chadwick ... Pg. 91, D-2
Chaptico ... G-9
Charlestown ... C-12
Charlotte Hall ... F-9
Chattolanee ... Pg. 91, B-2
Chesapeake ... B-13
Chesapeake Beach ... F-10
Chestertown ... C-12
Cheverly ... Pg. 150, D-8
Chevy Chase ... Pg. 150, C-5
Church Creek ... F-12
Church Hill ... D-12
Clear Spring ... B-6
Cliffs City ... E-9
Clinton ... E-9
Vicinity ... Pg. 150, D-9
Cobb Island ... G-9
Cockeysville ... B-10
Vicinity ... Pg. 91, A-4
College Park ... Pg. 150, B-8
Vicinity ... Pg. 150, B-8
Colmar Manor ... Pg. 150, D-7
Columbia ... C-9
Columbia Hills ... Pg. 91, F-1
Cooksville ... C-9
Corriganville ... A-3
Cottage City ... Pg. 150, D-7
Cove Point ... G-11
Cresaptown ... B-3
Crisfield ... J-13
Crofton ... D-11
Cronhardt ... Pg. 91, B-3
Crowder ... Pg. 91, F-1
Cub Hills ... Pg. 91, B-6
Cumberland ... B-3
Damascus ... C-8
Dares Beach ... F-11
Deale ... E-11
Delight ... Pg. 91, B-1
Delmar ... G-13
Denton ... E-13
District Heights ... Pg. 150, E-9
Doncaster ... F-8
Dorsey ... Pg. 91, H-2
Drawbridge ... F-13
Drum Point ... G-11
Dublin ... A-11
Dundalk ... C-10
Vicinity ... Pg. 91, F-6
Dunkirk ... F-10
Dunbrook ... Pg. 91, J-6
Eagle Harbor ... F-10
East Point ... Pg. 91, E-6
Easton ... E-12
Edgemere ... C-11
Vicinity ... Pg. 91, F-7
Edgewood ... C-11
Eldersburg ... C-9
Eldorado ... F-13
Elkridge ... Pg. 91, G-3

Elkton ... B-13
Ellicott City ... C-9
Vicinity ... Pg. 91, F-1
Elliott ... G-12
Emmitsburg ... A-8
Essex ... Pg. 91, E-7
Fair Hill ... A-12
Fairmount Heights ... Pg. 150, D-8
Fallston ... B-11
Federalsburg ... E-13
Ferndale ... Pg. 91, G-4
Fishtown ... Pg. 91, C-2
Font Hill ... Pg. 91, G-2
Foremans Corner ... Pg. 91, G-5
Forest Heights ... Pg. 150, F-7
Fork ... Pg. 91, A-7
Fountain Head ... A-7
Frederick ... C-8
Friendship Heights ... Pg. 150, C-5
Friendsville ... A-1
Frostburg ... B-3
Fruitland ... G-14
Furnace Branch ... Pg. 91, G-4
Gaithersburg ... D-8
Galena ... C-12
Gambrills ... Pg. 91, K-3
Garrett Park ... Pg. 150, A-5
Germantown ... D-8
Vicinity ... Pg. 91, B-7
Gittings ... Pg. 91, B-5
Glen Burnie ... D-10
Vicinity ... Pg. 91, H-4
Glen Morris ... Pg. 91, A-6
Glenarden ... Pg. 150, D-9
Glenarm ... Pg. 91, A-6
Glenmar ... Pg. 91, F-1
Glyndon ... Pg. 91, A-4
Golden Beach ... F-10
Goldsboro ... D-13
Grantsville ... A-2
Grasonville ... E-11
Green Haven ... Pg. 91, H-5
Green Hill ... G-13
Green Valley ... C-8
Green Valley North ... Pg. 91, A-3
Greenbelt ... D-9
Vicinity ... Pg. 150, B-9
Greensboro ... D-13
Guilford ... Pg. 91, H-1
Hagerstown ... B-7
Halethorpe ... Pg. 91, F-3
Halfway ... B-6
Hampstead ... B-9
Hampton ... Pg. 91, B-5
Hancock ... A-5
Hanover ... Pg. 91, G-2
Harkins ... A-11
Harmans ... Pg. 91, H-3
Harmony ... E-13
Harrisonville ... Pg. 91, C-1
Harundale ... Pg. 91, H-4
Harwood Park ... Pg. 91, G-2
Hebbville ... Pg. 91, D-2
Hebron ... G-13
Hereford ... B-10
Hillsboro ... E-13
Hollofield ... Pg. 91, E-1
Honga ... G-11
Hoyes ... B-1
Hurlock ... F-13
Hyattsville ... Pg. 150, C-7
Hyde Park ... Pg. 91, E-7
Hydes ... Pg. 91, A-6
Ilchester ... Pg. 91, F-2
Ivy Hill ... Pg. 91, J-6
Jacobsville ... Pg. 91, J-6
Jarrettsville ... B-11
Jenkins ... Pg. 91, A-7
Joppatowne ... C-11
Josenhans Corner ... Pg. 91, H-7
Kennedyville ... C-12
Kensington ... Pg. 150, B-6
Kenwood ... Pg. 91, E-7
Kingsville ... B-11
Kitzmiller ... C-2
LaPlata ... F-9
LaVale ... B-3
Lake Shore ... Pg. 91, J-7
Landover Hills ... Pg. 150, C-9
Lansdowne ... Pg. 91, F-3
Largo ... E-10
Laytonsville ... C-8
Leonardtown ... G-10
Lexington Park ... G-11
Liberty Manor ... Pg. 91, D-1
Linthicum ... Pg. 91, G-3
Lipins Corner ... Pg. 91, J-5
Lochearn ... Pg. 91, D-2
Lodge Forest ... Pg. 91, F-7
Lonaconing ... B-2
Long Beach ... G-11
Long Green ... Pg. 91, A-6
Longridge ... G-14
Longwoods ... E-12
Luke ... B-2
Lutherville ... Pg. 91, B-4
Lynch ... C-12
Maceys Corner ... Pg. 91, K-6
Manchester ... B-9
Manhattan Beach ... Pg. 91, J-5
Manor Woods ... Pg. 91, A-6
Marbury ... F-8
Marion ... H-13
Marston ... B-8

Maryland City ... Pg. 91, K-1
Mayo ... E-11
McHenry ... B-1
Meadowcliff ... Pg. 91, A-6
Melrose ... A-9
Middle River ... Pg. 91, D-7
Middleboro ... Pg. 91, E-7
Middletown ... B-7
Midland ... B-2
Milford ... Pg. 91, D-2
Millington ... C-13
Millstone ... A-5
Morganza ... G-10
Morningside ... Pg. 150, F-8
Mt. Airy ... C-8
Mt. Pleasant ... B-9
Mt. Rainier ... Pg. 150, C-7
Mtn. Lake Park ... C-1
Myersville ... B-7
New Carrollton ... Pg. 150, C-9
New Market ... C-8
Newburg ... G-9
Newport ... C-11
Newtown ... C-11
Nordeau ... Pg. 91, H-1
North Beach ... E-10
North Brentwood ... Pg. 150, C-7
North Chevy Chase ... Pg. 150, B-5
North East ... B-12
Oakland ... C-1
Oakland ... C-9
Ocean City ... G-15
Odenton ... Pg. 91, K-3
Olde Mill ... Pg. 91, J-4
Olney ... D-9
Orchard Beach ... Pg. 91, H-6
Oriole ... H-13
Overlea ... Pg. 91, D-6
Owings Mills ... C-10
Oxford ... F-12
Oxon Hill ... F-9
Vicinity ... Pg. 150, G-7
Park Hill ... H-11
Parkton ... B-10
Parkville ... C-10
Vicinity ... Pg. 91, C-5
Pasadena ... Pg. 91, J-5
Perry Hall ... B-11
Perryvale ... Pg. 91, C-7
Pikesville ... C-10
Vicinity ... Pg. 91, D-3
Pinehurst ... Pg. 91, J-7
Piney Grove ... A-4
Piney Point ... H-11
Pittsville ... G-14
Pleasant Hills ... B-11
Plum Point ... F-11
Pocomoke City ... H-13
Point Lookout ... H-11
Poolesville ... D-7
Port Deposit ... B-12
Pot Spring ... Pg. 91, B-4
Potomac Park ... B-3
Powellville ... G-14
Pratt ... A-4
Preston ... E-12
Price ... E-12
Prince Frederick ... F-10
Princess Anne ... H-13
Providence ... Pg. 91, B-5
Putty Hill ... Pg. 91, C-6
Queen Anne ... E-12
Queenstown ... D-12
Randallstown ... C-9
Vicinity ... Pg. 91, C-1
Redhouse ... C-1
Reisterstown ... B-9
Vicinity ... Pg. 91, A-1
Relay ... Pg. 91, F-3
Ridge ... H-11
Ridgely ... D-12
Ridgeway ... Pg. 91, J-3
Rising Sun ... A-12
Riva ... E-11
Riverdale ... Pg. 150, C-8
Riverside ... G-8
Riviera Beach ... Pg. 91, H-6
Rock Hall ... C-12
Rockville ... D-8
Vicinity ... Pg. 150, A-4
Rodgers Forge ... Pg. 91, C-4
Roe ... D-12
Rolling Park ... Pg. 91, D-2
Rolling Ridge ... Pg. 91, E-1
Rosedale ... Pg. 91, D-6
Rosemont ... C-7
Rush ... B-4
Ruthsburg ... Pg. 91, C-4
Ruxton ... Pg. 91, C-4
Salisbury ... G-13
Sandy Bottom ... C-11
Savage ... Pg. 91, H-1
Seat Pleasant ... E-9
Vicinity ... Pg. 150, D-9
Secretary ... F-12
Severn ... D-10
Vicinity ... Pg. 91, J-3
Severna Park ... D-10
Shady Side ... E-11
Sharpsburg ... C-6
Sharptown ... F-13
Silver Hill ... Pg. 150, F-8
Silver Spring ... D-9
Vicinity ... Pg. 150, B-6
Snow Hill ... H-14
Solley ... Pg. 91, H-5

Somerset ... Pg. 150, C-5
Southgate ... D-10
Sparrows Point ... Pg. 91, G-5
Springbrook ... Pg. 91, C-2
St. Charles ... F-9
St. Michaels ... E-11
Stevenson ... Pg. 91, B-3
Stockton ... H-14
Stonecrest Hills ... Pg. 91, F-1
Suburbia ... Pg. 91, A-1
Sudlersville ... C-13
Summit Park ... Pg. 91, C-3
Sunrise Beach ... Pg. 91, K-4
Swanton ... B-1
Sykesville ... C-9
Takoma Park ... Pg. 150, C-7
Taneytown ... B-8
Taylors Island ... F-11
Taylorsville ... B-8
Templeville ... D-13
Texas ... Pg. 91, A-4
The Oaks ... Pg. 91, C-1
Thurmont ... B-8
Timonium ... Pg. 91, B-4
Towson ... C-10
Vicinity ... Pg. 91, C-4
Turner ... G-10
Union Bridge ... B-8
University Park ... Pg. 150, C-7
Upper Marlboro ... E-10
Valleywood ... Pg. 91, B-3
Venice on the Bay ... Pg. 91, H-7
Ventnor ... F-13
Vienna ... F-13
Waldorf ... F-9
Walkersville ... B-8
Warren ... Pg. 91, A-4
Waterloo ... Pg. 91, H-2
Waterview ... G-13
Wenona ... H-12
Wesley ... G-14
Westerlee ... Pg. 91, C-2
Westernport ... B-2
Westminster ... B-9
Westover ... H-13
White Marsh Town Ctr. ... Pg. 91, C-7
White Plaines ... F-9
Whiteford ... A-11
Widgeon ... G-13
Willards ... G-15
Windmere ... Pg. 91, A-5
Woodlawn ... Pg. 91, D-2
Woodmoor ... Pg. 91, D-2
Worthington ... Pg. 91, F-1

MASSACHUSETTS

MASSACHUSETTS
Pages 24-25
Population: 5,737,037
Capital: Boston
Land Area: 7,824 sq. mi.

Abington ... D-11
Acton ... B-9
Acushnet ... F-11
Vicinity ... Pg. 93, J-7
Adams ... B-3
Agawam ... E-5
Amesbury ... A-11
Amherst ... C-5
Andover ... A-11
Arlington ... Pg. 93, D-3
Ashburnham ... B-8
Ashby ... B-4
Ashfield ... B-4
Athol ... B-7
Attleboro ... E-10
Auburn ... D-8
Avon ... D-11
Ayer ... B-9
Baldwinville ... B-7
Barnstable ... F-13
Barre ... C-7
Becket ... C-3
Bedford ... B-10
Vicinity ... Pg. 93, B-1
Belchertown ... C-6
Bellingham ... E-9
Belmont ... Pg. 93, D-3
Berkley ... F-11
Bernardston ... B-5
Beverly ... B-12
Billerica ... B-10
Vicinity ... Pg. 93, A-1
Blackstone ... E-9
Blandford ... D-4
Bolton ... C-9
Boston ... C-11
Vicinity ... Pg. 93
Bourne ... F-13
Boxborough ... C-9
Boxford ... B-11
Boylston ... C-8
Braintree ... D-11
Vicinity ... Pg. 93, J-6
Brewster ... F-14
Bridgewater ... E-11
Brimfield ... D-6
Brockton ... E-11
Brookfield ... D-7
Brookline ... Pg. 93, F-3
Buckland ... B-4
Burlington ... B-10
Vicinity ... Pg. 93, A-1
Buzzards Bay ... F-12
Cambridge ... C-11
Vicinity ... Pg. 93
Canton ... D-11
Carlisle ... B-10
Carver ... E-12

Centerville ... G-13
Charlemont ... B-4
Charlton ... D-7
Chatham ... F-15
Vicinity ... Pg. 93, H-4
Chelmsford ... A-9
Chelsea ... C-11
Vicinity ... Pg. 93, E-5
Cheshire ... B-3
Chesterfield ... C-4
Chicopee ... D-5
Chilmark ... H-12
Clarksburg ... A-3
Cliftondale ... Pg. 93, C-6
Clinton ... C-9
Cochituate ... C-9
Colrain ... A-5
Concord ... C-10
Conway ... B-5
Cummington ... C-4
Dalton ... B-3
Danvers ... B-11
Dartmouth ... G-11
Dedham ... Pg. 93, H-3
Deerfield ... B-5
Dennis ... F-14
Dennis Port ... F-14
Dighton ... F-10
Dover ... Pg. 93, J-1
Dracut ... A-10
Dudley ... D-7
Duxbury ... E-12
East Bridgewater ... E-11
East Falmouth ... G-13
East Longmeadow ... E-6
Eastham ... F-15
Easthampton ... C-4
Easton ... E-11
Edgartown ... H-13
Essex ... B-12
Everett ... Pg. 93, D-5
Fairhaven ... G-12
Fall River ... F-10
Falmouth ... G-12
Fitchburg ... B-8
Framingham ... D-9
Freetown ... F-11
Gardner ... B-7
Gay Head ... H-12
Georgetown ... A-11
Gilbertville ... C-6
Gill ... A-5
Gloucester ... B-13
Grafton ... D-9
Granby ... D-5
Granville ... E-4
Great Barrington ... D-2
Greenfield ... B-5
Groton ... B-9
Groveland ... A-11
Hadley ... C-5
Halifax ... E-12
Hamilton ... B-11
Hampden ... E-6
Hanover ... D-12
Hardwick ... C-6
Harvard ... B-9
Harwich ... F-14
Hatfield ... C-5
Haverhill ... A-11
Hawley ... B-4
Heath ... A-4
Hingham ... D-11
Vicinity ... Pg. 93, J-7
Holbrook ... D-11
Holden ... C-8
Holland ... E-7
Holyoke ... D-5
Hopedale ... D-9
Hopkinton ... D-9
Hudson ... C-9
Hull ... C-11
Huntington ... D-4
Hyannis ... F-14
Ipswich ... B-11
Kingston ... E-12
Lee ... C-3
Leicester ... D-8
Lenox ... C-3
Leominster ... B-8
Leverett ... B-5
Lexington ... C-10
Vicinity ... Pg. 93, C-2
Leyden ... A-5
Lincoln ... C-9
Littleton ... B-9
Longmeadow ... D-5
Lowell ... A-10
Lunenburg ... B-8
Lynn ... C-11
Vicinity ... Pg. 93, B-6
Lynnfield ... Pg. 93, A-5
Vicinity ... Pg. 93, A-5
Malden ... Pg. 93, D-4
Manchester ... B-10
Mansfield ... E-10
Marblehead ... C-11
Marion ... F-11
Marlborough ... C-9
Marshfield ... E-12
Mattapoisett ... G-12
Maynard ... C-9
Medfield ... D-10
Vicinity ... Pg. 93, K-1
Medford ... Pg. 93, D-4
Medway ... D-10
Melrose ... Pg. 93, C-5
Mendon ... D-9
Merrimac ... A-11
Methuen ... A-10
Middleborough ... F-11
Middlefield ... C-3
Middleton ... B-11
Milford ... D-9
Millbury ... D-8

Millers Falls ... B-6
Millis ... D-10
Milton ... D-11
Vicinity ... Pg. 93, H-4
Monson ... D-6
Montague ... B-5
Monterey ... D-3
N. Attleborough ... E-10
Nahant ... C-11
Vicinity ... Pg. 93, D-7
Nantucket ... H-14
Natick ... D-10
Needham ... D-11
Vicinity ... Pg. 93, G-2
New Bedford ... G-11
New Braintree ... C-7
New Marlborough ... D-3
Newbury ... A-12
Newton ... B-7
Vicinity ... Pg. 93, F-2
Norfolk ... D-10
North Adams ... A-3
North Brookfield ... C-7
North Reading ... B-11
Northampton ... C-4
Northborough ... C-8
Northbridge ... D-9
Northfield ... A-6
Norton ... E-10
Norwood ... D-10
Vicinity ... Pg. 93, K-2
Oak Bluffs ... H-13
Oakham ... C-7
Orange ... B-6
Orleans ... F-15
Osterville ... G-13
Otis ... D-3
Oxford ... D-7
Palmer ... D-6
Paxton ... C-8
Peabody ... B-11
Vicinity ... Pg. 93, A-7
Pepperell ... B-9
Peru ... C-3
Petersham ... B-7
Pinehurst ... Pg. 93, A-2
Pittsfield ... B-2
Plainfield ... B-4
Plymouth ... E-12
Plympton ... E-12
Princeton ... C-8
Provincetown ... E-14
Quincy ... D-11
Vicinity ... Pg. 93, J-6
Randolph ... D-11
Vicinity ... Pg. 93, K-5
Raynham ... E-11
Reading ... B-11
Vicinity ... Pg. 93, A-4
Rehoboth ... F-10
Revere ... C-11
Vicinity ... Pg. 93, D-5
Richmond ... C-2
Rochester ... F-12
Rockland ... D-11
Rockport ... B-13
Rowley ... A-12
Royalston ... A-7
Rutland ... C-7
Sagamore ... F-13
Salem ... B-11
Vicinity ... Pg. 93, B-7
Salisbury ... A-12
Sandisfield ... D-3
Sandwich ... F-13
Saugus ... C-11
Savoy ... B-4
Scituate ... D-12
Seekonk ... F-10
Sharon ... D-10
Sheffield ... D-2
Shelburne ... B-5
Shirley ... B-9
Shrewsbury ... C-9
So. Yarmouth ... G-14
Somerset ... F-10
Somerville ... Pg. 93, E-4
South Hadley ... C-5
Southbridge ... E-7
Spencer ... D-7
Sterling ... C-8
Stockbridge ... C-2
Stoneham ... Pg. 93, B-4
Stoughton ... D-11
Stow ... C-9
Sturbridge ... D-7
Sunderland ... B-5
Sutton ... D-8
Swampscott ... C-12
Swansea ... F-10
Taunton ... E-10
Templeton ... B-7
Tewksbury ... B-10
Three Rivers ... D-6
Tisbury ... H-12
Topsfield ... B-11
Townsend ... B-9
Truro ... E-15
Tyngsborough ... A-10
Upton ... D-9
Uxbridge ... E-9
Vineyard Haven ... H-13
Wakefield ... C-11
Vicinity ... Pg. 93, B-5
Wales ... D-6
Walpole ... D-10
Vicinity ... Pg. 93, K-1
Waltham ... D-10
Vicinity ... Pg. 93, F-1
Ware ... D-6
Wareham ... F-12
Warren ... D-7
Warwick ... A-6
Washington ... C-3
Watertown ... Pg. 93, E-3

MASSACHUSETTS

MICHIGAN

Stow C-9
Sturbridge D-7
Sunderland C-5
Sutton D-8
Swampscott C-12
  Vicinity .... Pg. 93, B-7
Swansea F-10
Taunton E-10
Templeton B-7
Tewksbury B-10
Three Rivers A-10
Tisbury H-12
Topsfield B-11
Townsend B-9
Truro E-15
Tyngsborough A-10
Upton D-9
Uxbridge E-9
Vineyard Haven H-13
Wakefield C-11
  Vicinity .... Pg. 93, B-5
Wales D-6
Walpole D-10
  Vicinity .... Pg. 93, K-1
Waltham .... Pg. 93, E-2
Ware C-6
Wareham F-12
Warren D-7
Warwick A-6
Washington C-3
Watertown .... Pg. 93, E-3
Wayland C-10
Webster E-7
Wellesley C-10
  Vicinity .... Pg. 93, B-5
Wellfleet E-14
Wendell B-6
Wenham B-11
West Boylston C-8
West Brookfield D-7
West Dennis G-14
West Newbury A-11
West Springfield D-5
West Stockbridge C-2
West Tisbury H-12
Westborough D-8
Westfield D-4
Westford B-9
Westhampton C-4
Westminster B-7
Weston .... Pg. 93, E-1
Westport G-11
Westwood D-10
  Vicinity .... Pg. 93, J-2
Weymouth D-11
  Vicinity .... Pg. 93, J-7
Whately C-5
Whitinsville E-8
Whitman E-11
Wilbraham D-6
Williamstown C-3
Wilmington B-10
  Vicinity .... Pg. 93, A-3
Winchendon A-7
Winchester .... Pg. 93, C-3
Windsor B-3
Winthrop C-11
  Vicinity .... Pg. 93, E-6
Woburn C-10
  Vicinity .... Pg. 93, B-3
Worcester C-7
Worthington C-5
Wrentham D-10
Yarmouth F-14

MICHIGAN
Pages 44-45

Population: 9,262,078
Capital: Lansing
Land Area: 56,954 sq. mi.

Acme F-6
Adamsville L-4
Adrian L-8
Afton E-7
Agnew J-4
Ahmeek A-2
Akron H-8
Alabaster G-8
Alanson E-7
Alaska J-5
Alba F-6
Alberta B-2
Albion L-6
Alcona F-9
Alger G-8
Algonac K-10
Allegan K-5
Allen L-6
Allen Park .... Pg. 107, J-8
Allendale J-5
Allenville D-7
Allouez A-2
Alma J-7
Almena L-5
Almont K-9
Aloha E-7
Alpena F-9
Alpha D-2
Alston B-2
Alto K-6
Alverno J-10
Amador J-10
Amasa C-2
Amble J-6
Anchorville K-10
Ann Arbor L-7
  Vicinity .... Pg. 106, H-1
Antrim F-6
Applegate J-10

Arbutus Beach F-7
Arcadia G-4
Argentine K-7
Argyle H-9
Arnheim B-2
Arnold D-3
Arthur J-8
Ashley J-7
Ashton H-6
Assinins B-2
Athens L-6
Atlanta F-8
Atlantic Mine B-2
Attica J-9
Atwood E-6
Au Gres H-8
Au Sable G-9
Au Train C-4
Auburn H-8
Austin C-3
Averill H-7
Bad Axe H-9
Bailey J-5
Baldwin H-5
Banat D-3
Bancroft K-8
Banfield K-6
Bangor K-4
Baraga B-2
Bark River D-3
Barker Creek F-6
Barryton H-6
Barton City F-8
Batavia L-6
Bates F-6
Bath K-6
Battle Creek K-6
Bay City H-8
Bay Mills C-7
Bay Park H-8
Bay Port H-8
Bay View E-7
Beacon C-2
Bear Lake G-5
Beaverton H-7
Beechwood C-2
Belding J-6
Belleville .... Pg. 106, K-4
Bellevue K-6
Bendon F-5
Bennington J-7
Benton Harbor L-4
Benzonia F-5
Bergland B-1
Berkley .... Pg. 107, D-8
Berrien Sprgs. L-4
Bessemer B-9
Bethel L-6
Beulah F-5
Beverly Hills .... Pg. 106, C-7
Big Bay B-3
Big Rapids H-6
Birch Creek E-3
Birch Run J-8
Birmingham .... Pg. 107, C-8
Bitely H-5
Black River F-9
Blanchard H-6
Blaney Park D-5
Blissfield L-8
Bloomfield Hills .... Pg. 106, B-7
Boyne City E-7
Boyne Falls E-7
Bradley K-5
Brampton D-3
Branch H-5
Bravo K-5
Breckenridge J-7
Brethren G-5
Brevort D-6
Bridgeport J-8
Bridgeton J-5
Bridgman L-4
Brighton K-8
Brimley C-7
Britton L-8
Brockway J-9
Brohman H-5
Bronson L-6
Brooklyn L-7
Brown City J-9
Bruce Crossing C-1
Brunswick H-5
Brutus E-7
Buchanan L-4
Buckley G-5
Burlington L-6
Burnside J-9
Burt J-8
Burton J-8
Byron Center J-5
Cadillac G-6
Cadmus L-7
Caledonia K-6
California L-6
Calumet A-2
Camden M-6
Capac J-9
Carbondale E-3
Carleton L-8
Carney E-3
Caro H-8
Carp Lake E-7
Carsonville J-9
Caseville H-9
Casnovia J-5
Cass City H-9
Cassopolis L-4
Cathro F-9
Cedar F-5
Cedar River E-4
Cedar Springs J-6

Cedarville D-8
Center Line .... Pg. 107, D-11
Centreville L-5
Ceresco L-6
Channing C-2
Charlevoix E-6
Charlotte K-6
Chase H-6
Chatham C-4
Cheboygan E-7
Chelsea L-7
Chesaning J-7
Christmas C-4
Cilo J-8
Clare H-6
Clarendon L-6
Clarion E-7
Clarksville L-6
Clawson .... Pg. 107, C-9
Clayton L-8
Cliff A-2
Climax L-5
Clinton L-8
Cloverdale K-6
Coldwater L-6
Coleman H-7
Coloma L-4
Colon L-5
Comins F-8
Concord L-7
Constantine L-5
Conway E-7
Coopersville J-5
Copemish G-5
Copper Harbor A-3
Cornell D-3
Corunna J-7
Covert K-4
Covington C-2
Cross Village E-7
Croswell J-10
Croton J-5
Crump H-7
Crystal Falls C-2
Cunard D-3
Curran F-8
Curtis D-6
Custer H-4
Dafter C-7
Daggett E-3
Dansville K-7
Darragh F-6
Davison J-8
Dayton L-4
DeTour Village D-8
Dearborn L-9
Dearborn Heights
  .... Pg. 106, G-7
Decatur L-4
Deer Park C-6
Deerton C-4
Deford J-9
Delano E-3
Delton K-5
Denton L-8
Detroit L-9
  Vicinity .... Pg. 107, F-8
Devereaux K-7
Dewitt K-7
Dexter L-7
Dighton G-6
Disco J-8
Dixboro L-8
Donaldson C-8
Donken B-1
Dorr K-5
Douglas K-4
Dowagiac L-4
Dowling K-6
Drayton Plains K-8
Drummond D-8
Dublin G-5
Dundee L-8
Dunningville K-5
Durand K-7
Eagle Habor A-3
Eagle River A-2
East Detroit .... Pg. 107, E-12
East Gilead L-6
East Grand Rapids J-5
East Jordan E-6
East Lake G-5
East Leroy L-6
East Tawas G-8
Eastport E-6
Eaton Rapids K-7
Eckerman D-7
Ecorse .... Pg. 107, J-9
Edenville H-7
Edmore J-6
Edwardsburg L-5
Elba J-8
Elberta F-5
Elk Rapids F-6
Elkton H-9
Elmer J-9
Elmira F-7
Elwell J-7
Emmett K-9
Empire F-5
Engadine D-6
Ensign D-4
Epoufette D-7
Erie M-8
Escanaba D-4
Essexville H-8
Estey H-7
Estral Beach L-9
Evans J-6
Evart H-6
Ewen C-1
Fair Haven K-9

Fairfield L-7
Fairgrove J-8
Fairview F-8
Fairway H-5
Farmington .... Pg. 106, D-5
Farmington Hills .... Pg. 106, D-5
Farwell H-6
Fawn River L-6
Fayette D-4
Felch D-3
Felch Mountain D-3
Fennville K-5
Fenton K-8
Ferndale .... Pg. 107, E-9
Ferry H-5
Ferrysburg J-4
Fibre D-7
Fife Lake G-6
Filer City G-4
Filion H-9
Filmore K-5
Flat Rock L-8
Flint J-8
Flushing J-8
Ford River D-4
Forest Hill J-7
Forest Lake C-4
Forester J-10
Forestville H-10
Foster City D-3
Fouch F-5
Fountain G-5
Fowler J-7
Fowlerville K-8
Frankenmuth J-8
Frankfort F-5
Franklin .... Pg. 106, C-7
Freeland H-7
Freesoil G-5
Fremont H-5
Frontier L-7
Fruitport J-5
Galesburg K-5
Galien L-4
Ganges K-4
Garden D-4
Garden City .... Pg. 106, G-6
Garden Corners D-5
Gardendale J-10
Gardenia H-7
Garfield J-7
Garnet D-6
Gaylord F-7
Gera K-5
Germfask C-5
Gibraltar L-9
Girard L-6
Gladstone D-4
Gladwin H-7
Glen Arbor F-5
Glen Haven F-5
Glenn K-4
Glennie F-8
Glenwood L-5
Gobles K-5
Goetzville D-8
Good Hart E-6
Goodrich K-8
Gould City D-6
Gourley D-3
Grand Beach L-4
Grand Blanc K-8
Grand Haven J-4
Grand Ledge K-6
Grand Marais C-5
Grand Rapids J-5
Grange L-5
Granite Bluff D-2
Grant J-5
Grawn F-6
Grayling F-7
Greenbush G-9
Greenland B-1
Greenville J-6
Gregory K-7
Grindstone City H-9
Gros Cap D-7
Grosse Pointe .... Pg. 107, F-13
Grosse Pointe Farms
  .... Pg. 107, F-13
Grosse Pointe Park
  .... Pg. 107, G-12
Grosse Pointe Shores J-9
  Vicinity .... Pg. 107, E-13
Grosse Pointe Woods
  .... Pg. 107, E-13
Gulliver D-5
Gwinn C-3
Hale G-8
Hamburg K-8
Hamilton K-5
Hamlin Lake G-4
Hamtramck .... Pg. 107, F-10
Hancock B-2
Harbert L-4
Harbor Beach H-10
Harbor Springs E-6
Hardwood D-3
Harper Woods .... Pg. 107, E-12
Harris D-3
Harrison H-7
Harrisville F-8
Hart H-4
Hartford L-4
Hartland K-8
Harvey C-3
Hastings K-6
Hawks E-8
Hazel Park .... Pg. 107, E-9
Helmer C-6
Hemans H-9
Henderson J-7

Hermansville D-3
Herron F-8
Hesperia H-5
Hessel D-7
Higgans Lake G-7
Highland Park .... Pg. 107, F-9
Hilliards K-5
Hillman F-8
Hillsdale L-7
Hockaday G-7
Hodunk L-6
Holland K-4
Holly K-8
Holt K-7
Holton H-5
Homer L-6
Honor F-5
Horton L-7
Houghton B-1
Houghton Heights G-7
Houghton Lake G-7
Howard City J-5
Howell K-8
Hubbard Lake F-8
Hubbell B-2
Hudson L-7
Hudsonville K-5
Huntington Woods
  .... Pg. 107, D-8
Huron Beach E-8
Huron City H-9
Hyde D-4
Idlewild H-5
Imlay City J-9
Ingalls E-3
Inkster .... Pg. 106, H-6
Interlochen F-5
Ionia J-6
Iron Mountain D-2
Iron River C-1
Irons G-5
Ironwood B-9
Isabella D-4
Ishpeming C-3
Ithaca J-7
Jackson L-7
Jamestown K-5
Jasper M-8
Jeddo J-10
Johannesburg F-7
Jones L-5
Jonesville L-7
Joppa L-4
Kalamazoo K-5
Kaleva G-5
Kalkaska F-6
Karlin F-5
Kawkawlin H-8
Kearsarge A-2
Kendall K-5
Kent City J-5
Kenton C-1
Kentwood J-5
Kewadin F-6
Keweenaw Bay B-2
Kibbie K-4
Kinde H-9
Kinderhook L-6
Kingsford D-2
Kingston J-9
Kinross C-7
Kiva C-4
L'Anse B-2
La Salle L-8
LaBranche D-3
Lachine F-8
Lacota K-5
Laingsburg K-7
Lake City G-6
Lake George H-6
Lake Leelanau F-5
Lake Linden A-2
Lake Odessa K-6
Lake Orion K-8
Lake Roland K-8
Lakeland K-8
Lakeport J-10
Lakeview J-6
Lambertville M-8
Langston J-6
Lansing K-7
Lapeer J-9
Laporte C-4
Lathrop C-4
Lathrup Village .... Pg. 107, D-8
Laurium A-2
Lawton L-5
Le Roy H-5
Leland F-5
Leoni L-7
Leonidas L-5
Leslie K-7
Levering E-7
Lexington J-10
Liberty L-7
Lilley H-5
Lincoln F-8
Lincoln Park .... Pg. 107, J-8
Linden K-8
Linwood H-8
Litchfield L-7
Little Lake C-4
Livonia K-8
  Vicinity .... Pg. 106, F-6
Long Lake F-8
Long Rapids F-8
Longrie E-3
Loomis H-7
Loretto D-2
Lowell J-6
Lucas G-6
Ludington G-4

Luna Pier M-8
Lupton G-8
Luzerne G-7
Mackinaw City D-7
Madison Heights .... Pg. 107, D-9
Mancelona F-6
Mandan A-3
Manistee G-4
Manistique D-5
Manton G-6
Maple Rapids J-7
Marcellus L-5
Marenisco B-10
Marine City K-10
Marion G-6
Marlette J-9
Marne J-5
Marquette C-3
Marshall L-6
Martin K-5
Marysville K-10
Mashek D-3
Mason K-7
Masonville D-4
Mass City B-1
Matchwood B-1
Matherton J-6
Mattawan L-5
Mayville J-9
McBain G-6
McFarland C-3
McMillan C-5
Meade K-9
Mears H-4
Mecosta H-6
Melstrand C-5
Melvin J-9
Memphis K-9
Mendon L-5
Menominee E-3
Meredith G-7
Merritt G-6
Merriweather A-10
Mesick G-6
Metz E-8
Michigamme C-3
Michigan Center L-7
Middleville K-6
Midland H-7
Mikado G-8
Milburg L-4
Milford K-8
  Vicinity .... Pg. 106, B-2
Millbrook H-6
Millersburg E-8
Millington J-8
Mineral Hills C-2
Mio F-8
Mohawk A-2
Moline K-5
Monroe L-8
Monroe Center F-6
Montague H-4
Montrose J-8
Moran D-7
Moorestown G-6
Morley H-6
Morneci M-7
Morrice K-7
Moscow L-7
Mottville L-5
Mt. Clemens .... Pg. 107, B-13
Mt. Morris J-8
Mt. Pleasant H-6
Muir J-6
Mullett Lake E-7
Munger H-8
Munising C-5
Muskegon J-4
Muskegon Heights J-4
Muttonville K-9
Napoleon L-7
Nashville K-6
Nathan K-9
Naubinway D-6
Negaunee C-3
New Baltimore K-9
New Buffalo L-4
New Era H-4
New Greenleaf H-9
New Haven K-9
Newaygo J-5
Newberry C-6
Newport L-9
Niles L-4
Nirvana H-5
Nisula B-1
North Branch J-9
North Ironwood A-9
North Muskegon J-4
Northland D-3
Northport E-5
Northville .... Pg. 106, E-4
Norton Shores J-4
Norwalk G-5
Norway D-2
Novi K-8
  Vicinity .... Pg. 106, D-4
Nunica J-5
O'Neil F-6
Oak Grove F-7
Oak Park .... Pg. 107, E-8
Oakland K-8
Oakley J-7
Oakwood K-9
Ocqueoc E-8
Ogden Center M-8
Oil City H-7
Okemos K-7
Olivet K-6
Omena F-6

Onaway E-8
Onekama G-4
Onondaga K-7
Ontonagon B-1
Orchard Lake .... Pg. 106, B-5
Orleans J-6
Ortonville K-8
Oscoda G-9
Oskar A-2
Osseo L-7
Ossineke F-9
Otisville J-8
Otsego K-5
Otsego Lake F-7
Ottawa Lake M-8
Ovid J-7
Owosso J-8
Oxbow H-5
Oxford K-9
Ozark D-7
Painesdale B-2
Palmer C-3
Palmyra L-8
Palo J-6
Paradise C-7
Parchment K-5
Paris H-6
Parisville H-9
Parkdale G-4
Parkville L-5
Paulding C-1
Paw Paw K-5
Peck J-9
Pellston E-7
Pentwater H-4
Perkins D-4
Perrinton J-6
Perronville D-3
Perry K-7
Petersburg L-8
Petoskey E-7
Pewamo J-6
Phoenix A-2
Pickford D-7
Pierson J-6
Pierport G-4
Pigeon H-9
Pine River J-7
Pittsford L-7
Plainfield J-7
Plainwell K-5
Pleasant Ridge .... Pg. 107, D-9
Plymouth .... Pg. 106, F-4
Pointe Aux Barques H-9
Polaski F-8
Pontiac K-8
  Vicinity .... Pg. 106, A-7
Port Hope H-10
Port Huron K-10
Port Sanilac J-10
Portage K-5
Portland J-7
Posen E-8
Poseyville H-7
Potterville K-7
Powers D-3
Prescott G-8
Princeton C-3
Prudenville G-7
Pullman K-5
Quanicassee H-8
Quimby K-6
Quincy L-7
Quinnesec D-3
Raber D-7
Ralph C-3
Ramsay B-9
Randville D-2
Ransom M-7
Rattle Run K-10
Ray L-6
Reading L-6
Redford .... Pg. 106, F-7
Reed City H-6
Reese J-8
Remus H-6
Republic C-2
Rexton D-6
Rhodes H-8
Richland K-5
Richmond K-9
Richmondville H-10
Richville J-8
Ridgeway L-7
River Rouge .... Pg. 107, J-9
Riverdale J-7
Rives Junction K-7
Roberts Landing K-10
Rochester K-8
Rock D-4
Rockford J-5
Rockland B-1
Rockwood L-9
Rodney H-6
Rogers City E-8
Romeo K-9
Romulus .... Pg. 106, J-5
Roosevelt Park J-4
Roscommon G-7
Rose City G-8
Roseburg J-9
Rosebush H-7
Roseville .... Pg. 107, D-12
Rothbury H-4
Royal Oak .... Pg. 107, C-9
Rudyard D-7
Rumely C-4
Ruth H-9

Saline L-8
Samaria M-8
Sand Lake J-6
Sands C-3
Sandusky J-9
Sanford H-7
Sans Souci K-10
Saranac J-6
Saugatuck K-4
Sault Ste. Marie C-8
Sawyer L-4
Schaffer D-3
Schoolcraft L-5
Scottdale L-3
Scottville G-4
Sears H-6
Sebewaing H-9
Seney C-5
Sharon G-6
Shelby H-4
Shepherd H-7
Sherman C-3
Shingleton C-5
Shore E-6
Sidnaw C-2
Sigma F-6
Silver City A-10
Sister Lakes L-4
Six Lakes J-6
Skandia C-3
Skidway Lake G-8
Smithville G-6
Smyrna J-6
Snover J-9
Soo Junction C-6
Somerset L-7
South Boardman G-6
South Branch G-8
South Haven K-4
South Range B-2
Southfield .... Pg. 106, E-7
Southgate .... Pg. 107, K-8
Spratt F-8
Spring Lake J-5
Springport K-7
Spruce F-9
St. Clair K-10
  Vicinity .... Pg. 107, D-13
St. Clair Shores J-9
St. Ignace D-7
St. James D-6
St. Johns J-7
St. Louis J-7
Stager D-2
Stalwart D-7
Standish H-8
Stanton J-6
Stanwood H-6
Stephenson E-3
Sterling G-8
Sterling Hts. .... Pg. 107, B-10
Steuben C-4
Stevensville L-4
Stockbridge K-7
Stronach G-5
Strongs C-7
Sturgis L-5
Stutsmanville E-6
Sundell C-4
Sunfield K-6
Suttons Bay F-6
Swanson E-3
Swartz Creek J-8
Sylvester H-6
Tawas City G-8
Taylor .... Pg. 106, J-7
Tecumseh L-8
Tekonsha L-6
Theodore D-2
Thompson D-5
Thornville J-9
Three Lakes C-2
Three Oaks L-4
Three Rivers L-5
Tiovola B-1
Tipton L-7
Tower E-7
Traunik C-4
Traverse City F-5
Trenary C-4
Trenton L-9
Triangle Ranch C-2
Trout Creek C-1
Trout Lake D-7
Troy K-8
  Vicinity .... Pg. 107, B-9
Turner G-8
Tustin G-6
Twin Lake J-4
Twin Lakes B-2
Twining G-8
Ubly H-9
Union L-5
Union City L-6
Union Pier L-4
Unionville H-9
Utica K-9
Vandalia L-5
Vanderbilt F-7
Vassar J-8
Vernon K-7
Verona H-9
Vicksburg K-5
Vienna F-7
Vogel Center G-6
Vriesland K-5
Vulcan D-3
Wacousta K-7
Wadhams J-9
Wakefield B-10
Waldron M-7

MICHIGAN

Walhalla — G-5
Walkerville — H-5
Wallace — E-3
Walled Lake — Pg. 106, C-4
Walton — G-6
Warren — K-9
  Vicinity — Pg. 107, D-11
Washington — K-9
Waterford — Pg. 106, A-6
Waterloo — K-7
Waters — F-7
Watersmeet — C-1
Watertown — J-9
Watervliet — L-4
Watson — D-3
Watson — K-5
Watton — C-2
Waucedah — D-3
Wayland — K-5
Wayne — Pg. 106, L-8
Webberville — K-7
Wells — D-4
Wellston — G-5
West Branch — G-7
West Olive — J-5
Westland — L-8
  Vicinity — Pg. 106, G-5
Weston — M-7
Wetmore — C-4
White — L-5
White Cloud — J-5
White Pine — A-10
White Rock — H-10
Whitehall — J-4
Whitney — D-3
Whittemore — G-8
Williamston — K-7
Willis — L-8
Windsor (Canada) — Pg. 107, J-11
Winegars — H-7
Winona — B-2
Wisner — H-8
Wixom — Pg. 106, C-3
Wolf Lake — G-5
Wolverine — K-6
Wolverine Lake — Pg. 106, B-4
Woodbury — K-6
Woodhaven — L-9
Woodland — K-6
Wyandotte — Pg. 107, K-8
Wyoming — J-5
Yale — J-9
Yalmer — C-4
Ypsilanti — L-8
  Vicinity — Pg. 106, J-2
Yuma — G-5
Zeeland — J-5
Zilwaukee — J-8

MINNESOTA
Pages 46-47

Population: 4,075,970
Capital: St. Paul
Land Area: 79,548 sq. mi.

Ada — D-2
Adams — L-6
Adrian — L-2
Ah-gwah-ching — E-4
Aitkin — F-5
Akeley — E-4
Albany — G-4
Albert Lea — L-5
Alberta — G-2
Alden — L-5
Alexandria — G-3
Alvarado — C-1
Alvwood — D-5
Amboy — K-5
Andover — H-6
Angle Inlet — A-3
Angora — C-7
Annandale — H-5
Anoka — H-6
Appleton — H-2
Arden Hills — Pg. 122, A-6
Argyle — C-1
Arlington — J-4
Ashby — G-2
Askov — F-7
Atwater — H-4
Audubon — E-2
Aurora — D-7
Austin — L-6
Avoca — K-2
Avon — G-4
Babbitt — D-8
Backus — E-4
Badger — B-2
Bagley — D-3
Ball Club — D-5
Barnesville — F-1
Barnum — F-7
Barrett — G-2
Barry — J-2
Battle Lake — F-3
Baudette — B-4
Baxter — F-4
Beardsley — G-1
Beaver Bay — D-9
Beaver Creek — L-1
Becker — H-5
Bejou — D-2
Belgrade — H-3
Belle Plaine — J-5
Bellingham — H-1
Beltrami — D-1
Bemidji — D-4
Bena — D-5

Benedict — E-4
Benson — H-3
Beroun — G-6
Bertha — F-3
Big Falls — C-5
Big Fork — D-5
Big Lake — H-6
Bigelow — L-2
Birchdale — B-5
Birchwood — Pg. 123, A-9
Bird Island — J-4
Biwabik — D-7
Blackduck — D-4
Blomkest — J-3
Blooming Prairie — K-6
Bloomington — Pg. 122, F-3
Blue Earth — L-5
Bluffton — F-3
Bock — G-5
Borup — D-2
Bovey — D-5
Bowstring — D-5
Boy River — E-5
Boyd — J-2
Braham — G-6
Brainerd — F-4
Branch — H-6
Brandon — G-3
Breckenridge — F-1
Brewster — L-2
Britt — D-7
Brook Park — G-6
Brooklyn Center — Pg. 122, A-4
Brooklyn Park — Pg. 122, A-2
Brooks — C-2
Brookston — D-7
Brooten — H-3
Browerville — F-4
Browns Valley — G-1
Brownsdale — L-6
Brownsville — L-8
Brownton — J-4
Bruno — F-7
Buffalo — H-5
Buffalo Lake — J-4
Buhl — D-6
Burnsville
  Vicinity — Pg. 122, G-4
Burtrum — G-4
Butterfield — L-4
Buyck — C-7
Byron — L-6
Caledonia — L-8
Callaway — E-2
Cambridge — H-6
Campbell — F-2
Canby — J-1
Cannon Falls — J-6
Canyon — D-7
Carlos — G-3
Carlton — E-7
Cass Lake — D-4
Cedar Mills — H-4
Centerville — K-8
Ceylon — L-4
Chandler — K-2
Chaska — J-5
Chatfield — L-7
Chickamaw Beach — E-4
Chisholm — D-6
Clara City — H-3
Claremont — K-6
Clarissa — F-3
Clarkfield — J-2
Clarks Grove — L-6
Clear Lake — H-5
Clearbrook — D-3
Clearwater — H-5
Clementson — B-4
Climax — D-1
Clinton — H-1
Clitherall — H-3
Clontarf — H-3
Cloquet — E-7
Cokato — H-4
Cold Spring — H-4
Coleraine — D-6
Cologne — J-5
Columbia Heights — Pg. 122, A-4
Comfrey — K-4
Comstock — E-1
Cook — C-7
Coon Rapids — H-6
Correll — H-2
Cosmos — J-4
Cottage Grove — K-6
Cotton — D-7
Cottonwood — J-2
Croftville — D-10
Cromwell — E-6
Crookston — C-2
Crosby — F-5
Crystal — Pg. 122, A-3
Currie — K-2
Cushing — F-4
Cuyuna — F-5
Cyrus — G-2
Dakota — K-8
Dalton — G-2
Danube — J-3
Danvers — H-2
Darfur — K-4
Dassel — H-4
Dawson — J-1
De Graff — H-3
Deer River — D-5
Deerwood — F-5
Delano — H-5
Dent — F-2
Detroit Lakes — E-2
Dilworth — E-1

Dodge Center — K-6
Donaldson — B-1
Donnelly — G-2
Doran — F-2
Dovray — K-3
Duluth — E-7
Dumont — G-2
Dunnell — L-4
Duquette — F-7
Eagle Bend — F-3
Eagle Lake — K-5
East Bethel — H-6
East Grand Forks — C-1
East Gull Lake — F-4
Easton — L-5
Echo — J-3
Eden Prairie — Pg. 122, E-1
Eden Valley — H-4
Edgerton — K-2
Edina — Pg. 122, E-3
Effie — C-5
Elbow Lake — G-2
Eldred — D-1
Elgin — K-7
Elizabeth — F-2
Elk River — H-6
Ellendale — K-6
Ellsworth — L-2
Elmer — E-6
Elmore — L-5
Elrosa — G-3
Ely — C-8
Emily — E-5
Erhard — F-2
Ericsburg — B-6
Erskine — D-2
Evansville — G-3
Eveleth — D-7
Eyota — K-7
Fairfax — J-4
Fairibault — K-6
Fairmont — L-4
Falcon Heights — Pg. 122, C-6
Farmington — J-6
Farwell — G-2
Felton — E-2
Fergus Falls — F-2
Fertile — D-2
Finland — D-8
Finlayson — F-6
Fisher — C-1
Flom — E-2
Floodwood — E-6
Florence — K-2
Foley — H-5
Forbes — D-7
Forest Lake — H-6
Fort Ripley — F-4
Fosston — D-3
Fountain — L-7
Fox Home — F-2
Franklin — J-3
Frazee — E-3
Freeport — G-4
Fridley — Pg. 122, A-4
Frost — L-5
Fulda — K-3
Funkley — C-4
Garfield — G-3
Garrison — F-5
Garvin — K-2
Gary — D-2
Gatzke — B-3
Gaylord — J-4
Gem Lake — Pg. 123, A-8
Geneva — L-6
Georgetown — E-1
Gheen — C-7
Gibbon — J-4
Gilbert — D-7
Gilman — G-5
Glencoe — J-4
Glenville — L-6
Glenwood — G-3
Gluek — H-3
Glyndon — E-1
Golden Valley — Pg. 122, B-2
Gonvick — D-3
Good Thunder — K-5
Goodhue — K-7
Goodland — E-6
Goodridge — C-3
Goodview — K-8
Graceton — B-4
Graceville — G-2
Granby — G-6
Grand Falls — C-5
Grand Marais — D-9
Grand Meadow — L-7
Grand Portage — C-10
Grand Rapids — D-5
Granite Falls — J-2
Grasston — G-6
Greenbush — B-2
Greenfield — H-5
Grey Eagle — G-4
Grove City — H-4
Grygla — C-3
Gully — D-3
Guthrie — D-4
Hackensack — E-4
Hallock — B-1
Halma — B-2
Halstad — D-1
Ham Lake — H-6
Hancock — H-2
Hanley Falls — J-3
Hanska — K-4
Harding — F-5
Hardwick — L-1
Harmony — L-7
Harris — H-6

Hastings — J-6
Hawley — E-2
Hayfield — K-7
Hayward — L-6
Hazel Run — J-2
Hector — J-4
Heidelberg — J-5
Henderson — J-5
Hendricks — K-1
Hendrum — D-1
Henning — F-3
Herman — G-2
Hermantown — E-7
Heron Lake — L-3
Hewitt — F-3
Hibbing — D-6
Hill City — E-5
Hills — L-1
Hilltop — Pg. 122, A-4
Hinckley — G-6
Hines — D-4
Hitterdal — E-2
Hoffman — G-2
Hokah — L-8
Holland — K-2
Holloway — H-2
Holt — C-2
Holyoke — F-7
Hope — L-6
Hopkins — Pg. 122, D-2
Houston — L-8
Hovland — C-10
Howard Lake — H-5
Hoyt Lakes — D-7
Humboldt — B-1
Hutchinson — J-4
Ihlen — L-1
Independence — H-5
Indus — B-5
International Falls — B-5
Inver Grove Hts. — Pg. 123, F-8
Iona — K-2
Ironton — F-5
Isabella — D-8
Isanti — H-6
Isle — E-6
Ivanhoe — J-2
Jackson — L-4
Jacobson — E-6
Janesville — K-6
Jasper — K-1
Jeffers — K-3
Jenkins — E-4
Johnson — G-2
Jordan — J-5
Karlstad — B-2
Kasota — K-5
Kasson — K-7
Keewatin — D-6
Kelliher — C-4
Kellogg — K-7
Kelsey — E-7
Kennedy — B-1
Kensington — G-2
Kent — F-1
Kenyon — K-6
Kerkhoven — H-3
Kerrick — F-7
Kettle River — E-7
Kiester — L-5
Kimball — H-4
Kingston — H-4
Knife River — E-8
La Crescent — L-8
La Prairie — E-6
Lafayette — K-4
Lake Benton — K-2
Lake Bronson — B-1
Lake City — J-7
Lake Crystal — K-4
Lake Elmo — Pg. 123, B-10
Lake George — D-4
Lake Henry — H-4
Lake Lillian — J-4
Lake Park — E-2
Lake Shore — E-4
Lake Wilson — K-2
Lakefield — L-3
Lakeville — K-6
Lamberton — K-3
Lancaster — A-1
Lanesboro — L-8
Laporte — D-4
Larsmont — E-8
Lastrup — G-4
Lauderdale — Pg. 122, B-5
Le Center — J-5
LeRoy — L-7
LeSueur — J-5
Lengby — D-3
Leonard — D-4
Lester Prairie — J-4
Lewiston — K-8
Lilydale — Pg. 123, D-6
Linden Grove — C-6
Lindford — C-5
Lindstrom — H-6
Lismore — L-2
Litchfield — H-4
Little Canada — Pg. 123, B-7
Little Falls — G-4
Little Fork — B-5
Little Rock — G-5
Lockhart — D-2
Loman — B-5
Long Lake — H-5
Long Prairie — G-4
Longville — E-4
Lonsdale — J-5
Lowry — G-2
Lucan — J-3
Lutsen — D-9
Luverne — L-2

Lyle — L-6
Lynd — K-2
Mable — L-8
Madelia — K-4
Madison — H-2
Madison Lake — K-5
Magnolia — L-2
Mahnomen — D-2
Mahtomedi — Pg. 123, A-9
Mahtowa — F-6
Malmo — F-6
Manchester — L-5
Mankato — K-4
Mantorville — K-7
Maple Lake — H-5
Mapleton — K-5
Mapleview — L-6
Maplewood — Pg. 123, B-8
Marcell — D-5
Margie — C-5
Marietta — H-1
Markham — D-7
Marshall — J-2
McGrath — F-6
McGregor — F-6
McIntosh — D-2
Meadowlands — E-7
Medford — K-6
Meire Grove — G-3
Melrose — G-4
Menahga — E-3
Mendota — Pg. 122, E-6
Mendota Heights — Pg. 123, E-7
Mentor — D-2
Middle River — B-2
Milaca — G-5
Milan — H-2
Millvoy — K-2
Miltona — G-3
Minneapolis — J-5
  Vicinity — Pg. 122
Minneota — J-2
Minnesota Lake — K-5
Minnetonka — Pg. 122, D-1
Mizpah — C-5
Montevideo — H-3
Montgomery — J-5
Monticello — H-5
Moorhead — E-1
Moose Lake — F-6
Mora — G-6
Morgan — J-3
Morris — G-2
Morton — J-3
Motley — F-4
Mountain Iron — D-7
Mountain Lake — K-3
Murdock — H-3
Myrtle — L-6
Nashua — G-2
Nashwauk — D-6
Nassau — H-1
Nay-Tah-Waush — D-3
Nevis — E-4
New Brighton — Pg. 122, A-5
New Hope — Pg. 122, B-2
New London — H-4
New Prague — J-5
New Richland — K-5
New Ulm — K-4
New York Mills — F-3
Newfolden — B-2
Nicollet — K-4
Nielsville — D-1
Nimrod — F-3
Nisswa — F-4
Norcross — G-2
North Branch — H-6
North Mankato — K-5
North St. Paul — Pg. 123, B-9
Northfield — K-6
Northome — C-5
Northrop — L-4
Norwood — J-5
Noyes — A-1
Oak Island — A-3
Oakdale — Pg. 123, C-9
Odessa — H-1
Ogema — E-2
Ogilvie — G-5
Oklee — C-2
Olivia — J-3
Onamia — G-5
Orleans — A-1
Ormsby — K-4
Oronoco — K-7
Orr — C-6
Ortonville — H-2
Osage — E-3
Osakis — G-3
Oslo — C-1
Ottertail — F-3
Outing — E-5
Owatonna — K-6
Palisade — E-6
Park Rapids — E-3
Parkers Prairie — F-3
Paynesville — H-4
Pelican Rapids — F-2
Pencer — B-3
Pennock — H-3
Perley — D-1
Pierz — G-5
Pine City — G-6
Pine Island — K-7
Pine River — E-4
Pine Springs — Pg. 123, A-9
Pinewood — D-4
Pipestone — K-1
Pitt — B-4
Plainview — K-7
Plummer — C-2

Plymouth — Pg. 122, A-1
Ponemah — C-4
Ponsford — E-3
Porter — J-2
Preston — L-7
Princeton — G-5
Prinsburg — J-3
Prior Lake — J-6
Proctor — E-7
Quamba — G-6
Randall — F-4
Randolph — J-6
Raudette — B-4
Ray — B-6
Raymond — H-3
Red Lake — C-4
Red Lake Falls — C-2
Red Wing — J-7
Redby — D-4
Redwood Falls — J-3
Regal — H-4
Remer — E-5
Renville — J-3
Rice — G-5
Richfield — Pg. 122, E-4
Richmond — H-4
Richville — E-7
Robbinsdale — Pg. 122, B-3
Rochester — K-7
Rock Creek — G-6
Rockford — H-5
Roosevelt — A-3
Rose Creek — L-6
Roseau — B-3
Roseville — Pg. 122, B-5
Ross — B-2
Rothsay — F-1
Round Lake — L-3
Round Prairie — G-4
Royalton — G-4
Rush City — G-6
Rushford — L-8
Rushmore — L-2
Russell — K-2
Ruthton — K-2
Rutledge — F-7
Sabin — E-1
Sacred Heart — J-3
Saint Anthony — Pg. 122, B-5
Saint Charles — K-7
Saint Clair — K-5
Saint Cloud — H-5
Saint Francis — H-6
Saint Hilaire — C-2
Saint James — K-4
Saint Joseph — H-5
Saint Louis Park — Pg. 122, D-2
Saint Michael — H-5
Saint Paul — H-6
  Vicinity — Pg. 123
Saint Paul Park — Pg. 123, F-7
Saint Peter — K-5
Saint Vincent — A-1
Salol — B-3
Sanborn — K-3
Sandstone — G-7
Sartell — G-4
Sauk Centre — G-4
Sauk Rapids — G-5
Saum — C-4
Sawyer — F-7
Scanlon — F-7
Schroeder — D-9
Sebeka — F-3
Sedan — G-3
Shakopee — J-5
Shelly — D-1
Sherburn — L-4
Shevlin — D-3
Shoreview — Pg. 123, A-6
Silver Bay — D-9
Silver Lake — J-4
Slayton — K-2
Sleepy Eye — K-4
Solway — D-3
South International — B-6
South St. Paul — Pg. 123, E-7
Spicer — H-4
Spring Grove — L-8
Spring Lake — D-5
Spring Valley — L-7
Springfield — K-4
Squaw Lake — D-5
Staples — F-4
Starbuck — G-3
Stephen — B-1
Stewartville — K-7
Storden — K-3
Strandquist — B-2
Strathcona — B-2
Sturgeon Lake — F-6
Sunberg — H-3
Sunfish Lake — Pg. 123, E-7
Swan River — E-6
Swanville — G-4
Swatara — E-5
Swift — B-3
Taconite — D-5
Taconite Harbor — D-9
Talmoon — D-5
Tamarack — F-6
Taylors Falls — H-7
Tenney — G-2
Tenstrike — D-4
Terrace — H-4
Thief River Falls — C-2
Togo — D-6
Tommald — F-4
Toopi — L-7
Tower — C-7
Tracy — K-3
Trail — C-2
Trimont — L-4

Trosky — K-2
Truman — L-4
Twig — E-7
Twin Lakes — L-5
Twin Valley — D-2
Two Harbors — E-8
Tyler — K-2
Ulen — E-2
Underwood — F-2
Vadnais Hts. — Pg. 123, A-7
Verdi — K-1
Vergas — E-2
Verndale — F-4
Vesta — J-3
Viking — C-2
Villard — G-3
Vining — F-3
Viola — K-7
Virginia — D-7
Wabasha — K-7
Wabasso — J-3
Waconia — J-5
Wadena — F-3
Wahkon — F-5
Waite Park — H-4
Walker — E-4
Walnut Grove — K-3
Waltham — L-6
Wanamingo — K-6
Warba — E-6
Warraska — B-3
Warren — C-1
Warroad — B-3
Waseca — K-5
Waskish — C-4
Watertown — J-5
Waterville — K-5
Watkins — H-4
Watson — H-2
Waubun — E-2
Wawina — E-6
Welcome — L-4
Wells — L-5
West Concord — K-6
West St. Paul — Pg. 123, E-7
Westbrook — K-3
Wheaton — G-1
Whipholt — E-4
White Bear Lake — Pg. 123, A-9
White Earth — E-2
Wilder — L-3
Willernie — Pg. 123, A-9
Williams — B-4
Willmar — H-4
Willow River — F-6
Wilton — D-3
Windom — K-3
Winger — D-2
Winnebago — L-5
Winona — K-8
Winthrop — J-4
Winton — C-8
Wirt — D-5
Wolf Lake — E-3
Wolverton — F-1
Woodbury — K-7
  Vicinity — Pg. 123, D-10
Woodland — G-6
Worthington — L-3
Wrenshall — F-7
Wyoming — H-6
Zemple — D-5
Zim — D-7
Zimmerman — H-6
Zumbro Falls — K-7
Zumbrota — K-7

MISSISSIPPI

MISSISSIPPI
Page 50

Population: 2,520,638
Capital: Jackson
Land Area: 47,233 sq. mi.

Abbeville — B-5
Aberdeen — C-6
Ackerman — D-5
Alcorn — G-2
Algoma — B-5
Alligator — C-3
Amory — C-6
Anguilla — E-3
Arcola — E-3
Arkabutla — A-4
Artesia — C-6
Ashland — A-5
Askew — B-3
Avalon — C-4
Avon — D-2
Bailey — F-6
Baird — C-3
Baldwyn — B-6
Banner — B-5
Bassfield — H-4
Batesville — B-4
Baxterville — H-4
Bay Saint Louis — K-5
Bay Springs — G-5
Beaumont — H-6
Beauregard — F-4
Becker — C-6
Belden — B-6
Bellefontaine — C-5
Belmont — B-6
Belzoni — D-3
Benoit — D-2
Benton — E-4
Bentonia — E-3
Beulah — C-2

Big Creek — C-4
Bigbee Valley — D-6
Biloxi — K-6
Blue Mountain — A-5
Bogue Chitto — H-3
Bolton — F-3
Booneville — A-6
Boyle — C-3
Braxton — G-4
Brandon — F-4
Brookhaven — H-3
Brooklyn — H-5
Brooksville — D-6
Bruce — C-5
Buckatunna — G-6
Bude — H-3
Burnsville — A-6
Byhalia — A-4
Caledonia — C-6
Calhoun City — C-5
Call Town — J-6
Camden — E-4
Canton — E-4
Carlisle — G-3
Carpenter — G-3
Carriere — J-5
Carrollton — D-4
Carson — H-4
Carthage — F-4
Cary — E-3
Cascilla — C-4
Cedarbluff — C-5
Centreville — J-3
Charleston — C-4
Chatawa — J-3
Chatham — E-2
Church Hill — G-2
Clara — G-6
Clarksdale — B-3
Cleveland — C-3
Cliftonville — D-6
Clinton — F-3
Coahoma — B-3
Coffeeville — C-4
Coila — C-4
Coldwater — A-4
Collins — G-5
Collinsville — E-6
Columbia — H-4
Columbus — C-6
Como — A-4
Conehatta — F-5
Corinth — A-6
Courtland — B-4
Crawford — D-6
Crenshaw — B-3
Crosby — H-2
Cross Roads — A-6
Crowder — B-3
Crystal Springs — G-3
D'Lo — G-4
Daleville — E-6
Darling — B-3
Darlove — D-3
DeKalb — E-6
Decatur — F-5
Dennis — A-6
Derma — C-5
Doddsville — C-3
Dorsey — B-6
Drew — C-3
Dublin — C-3
Duck Hill — C-4
Dumas — A-5
Duncan — C-2
Dundee — B-3
Durant — E-4
Eastabuchie — H-5
Ebenezer — E-4
Ecru — B-5
Eden — E-4
Edinburg — E-5
Edwards — F-3
Electric Mills — E-6
Elizabeth — E-3
Ellisville — G-5
Enid — B-4
Enterprise — F-6
Ethel — D-5
Etta — B-5
Eupora — D-5
Falcon — B-3
Falkner — A-5
Fannin — F-4
Fayette — G-2
Flora — F-4
Florence — F-4
Forest — F-5
Forkville — F-4
Fort Adams — H-2
Foxworth — H-4
French Camp — D-5
Friar's Point — B-3
Fruitland Park — J-5
Fulton — B-6
Gallman — G-3
Gattman — C-6
Gautier — K-6
Georgetown — G-3
Gholson — E-6
Gillsburg — J-3
Glen — A-6
Glen Allan — E-2
Glendora — C-3
Gloster — H-2
Golden — B-6
Goodman — E-4
Gore Springs — C-4
Grace — E-2

MISSISSIPPI

MISSOURI

MISSISSIPPI

Grand Gulf G-2
Greenville D-2
Greenwood D-4
Grenada C-4
Gulfport K-6
Gunnison C-2
Guntown B-6
Hamilton C-6
Harperville F-5
Harriston G-2
Harrisville G-4
Hatley B-6
Hattiesburg H-5
Hazlehurst G-3
Heidelberg G-6
Helena B-3
Hermanville G-3
Hernando A-4
Hickory F-5
Hickory Flat A-5
Hilhouse C-2
Hillsboro F-5
Hiwannee G-6
Holcomb C-4
Hollandale D-3
Holly Bluff E-3
Holly Springs A-5
Homewood F-5
Horn A-3
Houston C-5
Hurley J-6
Independence A-4
Indianola D-3
Inverness D-3
Isola D-3
Itta Bena D-3
Iuka A-6
Jackson F-4
Jayess H-4
Johnstons Station H-4
Jonestown B-3
Kewanee F-6
Kilmichael D-4
Kiln K-5
Kokomo H-4
Kosciusko E-5
Lafayette Springs B-5
Lake F-5
Lake View Pg. 119, G-2
Lakeshore K-5
Lambert B-3
Lauderdale E-6
Laurel G-5
Lawrence F-5
LeFlore C-4
Leaf H-6
Leakesville H-6
Leland D-3
Lena E-4
Lessley H-2
Lexington D-4
Liberty H-3
Little Rock F-5
Long Beach K-5
Lorman G-2
Louin F-5
Louise E-3
Louisville D-5
Lucedale J-6
Lucien H-3
Ludlow F-4
Lula B-3
Lumberton J-5
Lyman K-5
Lyon B-3
Maben D-5
Macon D-6
Madden E-5
Madison F-4
Magee G-4
Magnolia H-3
Mantachie B-6
Mantee C-5
Marietta B-6
Marion F-6
Marks B-3
Martinsville G-3
Mathiston D-5
McAdams E-4
McCall Creek H-3
McCarley D-4
McComb H-3
McCondy C-5
McCool D-5
McHenry J-5
McLain H-6
McNeill J-5
Meadville H-3
Mendenhall G-4
Meridian F-6
Merigold C-3
Metcalfe D-2
Michigan City A-5
Mineral Wells C-3
  Vicinity Pg. 119, G-7
Minter City C-3
Mize G-5
Money G-3
Monticello H-4
Montpelier C-5
Montrose F-5
Mooreville B-6
Moorhead D-3
Morgan City D-3
Morgantown H-4
Morton F-5
Moselle G-5
Moss G-5
Moss Point K-6
Mound Bayou C-3
Mount Olive G-5
Myrtle A-5

Natchez H-2
Necaise J-5
Nesbit A-3
Neshoba E-5
Nettleton B-6
New Albany B-5
New Augusta H-5
New Hebron G-4
New Houlka B-5
New Site A-6
Newton F-5
Nicholson K-5
Nitta Yuma E-3
North Carrollton D-4
Noxapater E-5
Oak Vale H-4
Oakland C-4
Ocean Springs K-6
Ofahoma E-4
Okolona B-6
Olive Branch A-4
Oma G-4
Onward E-3
Osyka H-3
Oxford B-4
Pace C-2
Pachuta F-6
Paden A-6
Panther Burn E-3
Paris E-3
Parchman C-3
Pascagoula K-7
Pass Christian K-6
Paulette D-6
Paulding F-5
Pearl F-4
Pearlington K-5
Pelahatchie F-5
Perkinston J-5
Petal H-5
Pheba C-5
Philadelphia E-5
Philipp C-3
Picayune K-5
Pickens E-4
Pinkneyville J-2
Pinola G-4
Plantersville B-6
Plum Point Pg. 119, B-2
Pocahontas F-4
Pond J-2
Pontotoc A-5
Pope B-4
Poplarville J-5
Port Gibson G-2
Porterville F-6
Potts Camp A-5
Prairie C-6
Prairie Point D-6
Prentiss G-4
Preston E-6
Puckett F-4
Pulaski F-4
Purvis H-5
Quentin H-3
Quitman F-6
Raleigh G-5
Randolph B-5
Raymond F-4
Red Banks A-4
Redwood F-3
Reform D-5
Rena Lara B-2
Richland F-4
Richton H-6
Ridgecrest H-2
Ridgeland F-4
Rienzi A-6
Ripley A-5
Robinsonville A-3
Rolling Fork E-3
Roxie H-3
Rosedale C-2
Ruleville C-3
Runnelstown H-6
Ruth H-4
Sallis E-4
Saltillo B-6
Sandersville G-6
Sandhill F-4
Sandy Hook H-5
Sanford H-5
Sarah B-3
Sardis B-4
Sarepta B-5
Satartia F-3
Saucier J-5
Savage A-3
Schlater D-3
Scobey C-4
Scooba E-6
Scott D-2
Sebastopol F-5
Senatobia A-4
Seminary G-5
Sessums D-6
Seypal Lake A-3
Shannon B-6
Sharon E-4
Shaw D-2
Shelby C-3
Sherard B-3
Sherman B-6
Shivers G-4
Shubuta G-6
Shuqualak D-6
Sibley H-2
Sidon D-3
Silver City E-3
Silver Creek G-4
Skene C-2

Slate Springs C-5
Slayden A-4
Sledge B-3
Smithdale H-3
Smithville B-6
Sontag G-4
Soso G-5
Southaven A-3
Star F-4
Starkville D-6
State Line H-6
Steens C-6
Stewart D-5
Stoneville D-2
Stonewall F-6
Stovall B-3
Stringer G-5
Sturgis D-5
Summit H-3
Sumner C-3
Sumrall H-5
Sunflower D-3
Suqualena F-5
Swan Lake C-3
Swiftown D-4
Sylvarena G-5
Taylor B-4
Taylorsville G-4
Tchula D-4
Terry G-3
Thaxton B-5
Thomastown E-4
Thorn C-5
Thornton D-3
Thyatira A-4
Tie Plant C-4
Tillatoba C-4
Tinsley E-3
Tiplersville A-5
Tippo C-4
Tishomingo A-6
Toccopola B-5
Tomnolen D-5
Toomsuba F-6
Trebloc C-6
Tremont B-6
Tula B-5
Tunica A-3
Tupelo B-5
Tutwiler C-3
Tylertown H-4
Union E-5
Union Church G-3
University B-4
Utica G-3
Vaiden D-4
Valley Park E-3
Van Vleet C-5
Vance C-3
Vancleave J-6
Vardaman C-5
Vaughan E-4
Verona B-5
Vicksburg F-3
Victoria A-4
Vossburg G-6
Wade J-6
Walls A-3
Walnut A-5
Walnut Grove E-5
Walthall D-5
Washington H-2
Water Valley B-4
Waterford A-4
Waveland K-5
Waynesboro H-6
Wayside D-2
Weathersby G-4
Webb C-3
Weir D-5
Wenasoga A-6
Wesson G-3
West Gulfport J-5
West Point C-6
Wheeler A-6
Whitfield F-4
Wiggins J-6
Winona D-4
Winstonville C-3
Woodland C-5
Woodville J-2
Yazoo City E-3

MISSOURI
Pages 48-49

Population: 4,916,686
Capital: Jefferson City
Land Area: 68,945 sq. mi.

MISSOURI

Adair D-5
Adrian H-2
Advance K-9
Agency F-2
Albany D-2
Alexandria D-7
Allendale D-3
Alma G-4
Altamont E-3
Alton L-7
Amoret H-2
Anderson L-2
Annapolis K-8
Anniston K-10
Appleton City H-3
Arab D-6
Arbela D-6
Arbor Terrace Pg. 140, C-4
Arbyrd M-9
Arcadia J-8
Archie H-3

Arcola J-3
Arkoe E-2
Arnold H-8
Arroll K-6
Arrow Rock G-4
Asbury K-2
Ash Grove K-3
Ashland G-6
Ashley F-7
Athens D-6
Atlanta E-5
Aullville G-3
Aurora K-3
Auxvasse F-6
Ava K-5
Avalon E-4
Avondale Pg. 112, E-4
Bado K-6
Bakersfield L-6
Ballard K-3
Bardley L-7
Baring D-6
Barnard E-1
Battlefield K-4
Bay H-7
Beaufort H-7
Bel Nor Pg. 140, C-4
Bel Ridge Pg. 140, C-3
Bell City K-9
Bella Villa Pg. 140, H-4
Bellair H-6
Belle H-6
Bellefontaine Neighbors Pg. 140, B-5
Bellerive Pg. 140, C-4
Belton G-2
Bem H-7
Bendavis K-5
Bennett Springs J-5
Benton K-10
Berkeley Pg. 140, B-3
Bernie L-9
Bertrand K-10
Bethany D-3
Bethel E-6
Beulah J-6
Beverly Hills Pg. 140, D-4
Bevier E-5
Bible Grove D-6
Bigelow E-1
Bigspring G-7
Birch Tree K-7
Birmingham Pg. 112, E-5
Bismark J-8
Bixby J-7
Black Jack Pg. 140, A-5
Blackburn G-4
Blackwater G-4
Blodgett K-10
Bloomfield K-9
Blue Eye L-4
Blue Springs G-3
Blythedale D-3
Bogard F-3
Bolckow E-2
Bolivar J-4
Bonne Terre J-8
Boonesboro G-5
Boonville G-4
Bosworth F-3
Bourbon H-7
Bowling Green F-7
Boynton D-4
Bradleyville L-4
Branson L-4
Braymer F-3
Brazeau J-10
Breckenridge E-3
Breckenridge Hills Pg. 140, C-3
Brentwood Pg. 140, F-3
Briar L-8
Bridgeton Pg. 140, B-2
Brighton K-4
Brimson E-4
Brinktown H-6
Bronaugh J-2
Brookfield E-4
Broseley L-9
Brownbranch L-5
Browning E-4
Brumley H-5
Bruner K-5
Brunswick F-4
Buckhorn K-9
Buckner G-3
Buffalo J-4
Bunker J-7
Burlington Jct. D-1
Butler H-2
Cabool K-6
Cainsville D-3
Cairo F-5
California G-5
Callao E-5
Calverton Park Pg. 140, B-4
Calwood F-6
Camdenton H-5
Cameron E-3
Campbell L-9
Canton D-7
Cape Girardeau K-9
Caplinger Mills J-3
Cardwell M-9
Carrington G-6
Carrollton F-3
Carsonville Pg. 140, C-4
Carthage K-2
Caruthersville M-10
Cascade K-9
Cassville L-3
Catherine Place J-9

Caulfield L-6
Center F-7
Centerville J-8
Centralia F-6
Chadwick K-4
Chaffee K-10
Chain-O-Lakes L-3
Chamois G-6
Champ Pg. 140, B-1
Charlack Pg. 140, C-3
Charleston K-10
Cherryville J-7
Chilhowee G-3
Chillicothe E-4
Chula E-4
Clarence E-6
Clarksdale E-2
Clarksville F-7
Clarkton L-9
Claycomo Pg. 112, D-5
Clayton Pg. 140, E-3
Clearmont D-1
Clever K-4
Clifton City G-4
Climax Springs H-4
Clinton H-3
Clyde D-2
Coal H-3
Coatsville D-5
Coldwater K-8
Cole Camp H-4
Collins J-3
Coloma F-4
Columbia G-6
Concordia G-3
Connelsville D-5
Conway J-5
Cook Station J-7
Cool Valley Pg. 140, C-4
Corning D-1
Corridon K-7
Couch L-7
Country Club Hills Pg. 140, C-5
County Life Acres Pg. 140, E-1
Craig E-1
Crane K-3
Crestwood Pg. 140, G-2
Creve Coeur Pg. 140, E-1
Crocker J-6
Cross Timbers H-4
Crystal Lake Park Pg. 140, E-1
Cuba H-7
Curryville F-7
Cyrene F-7
Dadeville J-3
Dearborn F-2
Deerfield J-2
Defiance H-8
Dellwood Pg. 140, B-4
Denver D-3
Des Arc K-8
Des Peres Pg. 140, F-1
Desloge J-8
Dexter K-9
Diamond K-2
Dixon H-6
Doe Run J-8
Dongola K-9
Doniphan L-8
Doolittle J-6
Dorena L-10
Downing D-5
Drexel H-2
Drury K-5
Duenweg K-2
Duncans Bridge F-5
Dunlap E-4
Dunnegan J-4
Durham E-6
Dutchtown K-9
Eagleville D-3
East Prairie K-10
Edgar Springs J-6
Edgerton F-2
Edina E-6
Edinburg E-3
Edmundson Pg. 140, B-3
El Dorado Springs J-3
Eldon H-4
Eldridge J-5
Elkland J-4
Ellington K-7
Elsinore K-8
Elmira F-3
Elmo D-1
Elsberry F-8
Elvins J-8
Elwood E-2
Emden E-6
Eminence K-7
Eolia F-7
Essex L-9
Esther J-8
Ethel E-5
Eudora J-4
Eureka H-8
Everton K-3
Ewing E-6
Excello F-5
Excelsior Springs F-2
Exeter L-3
Fagus L-9
Fair Grove K-4
Fair Play J-4
Fairdealing L-8
Fairfax D-1
Fairmont D-6
Fairview K-2

Farber F-6
Farley F-2
Farmersville E-4
Farmington J-9
Farrar J-9
Faucett F-2
Fayette F-5
Fayetteville J-3
Fenton Pg. 140, H-1
Ferguson Pg. 140, B-4
Ferrelview Pg. 112, A-2
Festus H-8
Filley J-3
Fillmore E-2
Fisk L-9
Flat River J-8
Flordell Hills Pg. 140, C-5
Florence G-5
Florida F-6
Florissant Pg. 140, A-4
Foley G-8
Forbes E-1
Fordland K-4
Forest City E-1
Forest Green F-5
Foristell G-8
Forsyth L-4
Fortescue E-1
Fortuna H-5
Fountain Grove E-4
Frankford F-7
Fredericktown J-9
Freeburg H-6
Fremont K-7
French Village J-8
Frontenac Pg. 140, E-2
Fulton G-6
Gainesville L-5
Galena L-3
Gallatin E-3
Galt E-4
Garden City H-3
Garwood K-8
Gatewood L-7
Gentry D-2
Gerald H-7
Gilliam F-4
Gladden J-7
Gladstone Pg. 112, C-4
Glasgow F-5
Glen Echo Park Pg. 140, C-4
Glenaire Pg. 112, C-5
Glendale Pg. 140, F-2
Glenwood D-5
Glover J-8
Golden City K-3
Goodfellow Terr. Pg. 140, D-5
Goodman L-2
Gower F-2
Graham D-1
Grain Valley G-3
Granby K-3
Grand Pass F-4
Grandin L-8
Granger D-6
Grant City D-2
Grantwood Village Pg. 140, G-3
Granville F-6
Grassy K-9
Gray Summit H-8
Graysville D-5
Green City D-4
Green Ridge G-4
Greencastle D-5
Greendale Pg. 140, D-4
Greenfield K-3
Greensburg D-6
Greentop D-5
Greenville K-8
Greenwood Pg. 112, C-6
Greer L-7
Grovespring K-5
Halfway J-4
Hallsville F-6
Halltown K-3
Hamilton E-3
Hanley Hills Pg. 140, D-4
Hannibal E-7
Hardin F-3
Harris D-4
Harrisburg G-5
Harrisonville G-3
Hartford D-5
Hartville K-5
Hartwell H-3
Harwood J-3
Hatfield D-3
Hawk Point G-7
Hayti M-9
Hayti Heights M-10
Hazelwood Pg. 140, A-3
Helena E-2
Hermann G-7
Hermitage J-4
Higbee F-5
Higginsville G-3
High Point H-5
Hillsboro H-8
Hinton G-5
Hitt D-5
Holcomb L-9
Holden G-3
Hollister L-4
Holts Summit G-6
Hopkins D-2
Hornersville M-9
House Springs H-8
Houston K-6
Houston Lake Pg. 112, D-2
Houstonia G-4

Humansville J-4
Humphreys E-4
Hunter K-8
Huntleigh Pg. 140, F-2
Huntsdale G-5
Huntsville F-5
Hurdland E-6
Hurricane Deck H-5
Iberia H-6
Idlewild K-9
Independence G-3
  Vicinity Pg. 112, F-6
Ironton J-8
Jackson J-10
Jacksonville E-5
Jameson E-3
Jamesport E-3
Jamestown G-5
Jane L-2
Jasper K-2
Jefferson City H-5
Jenkins L-3
Jennings Pg. 140, C-5
Jerico Springs J-3
Joplin K-2
Kahoka D-6
Kansas City G-2
  Vic. Pg. 124-125
Kearney F-2
Kennett M-9
Keytesville F-5
Kidder E-3
Kimberling City L-4
King City E-2
Kingston E-3
Kinloch Pg. 140, B-3
Kirksville E-5
Kirkwood Pg. 140, F-2
Kliever G-5
Knob Noster G-3
Knox City E-6
Knoxville F-3
Koshkonong L-6
La Grange E-7
La Plata E-5
La Tour G-3
LaBelle E-6
LaMonte G-4
Laddonia F-6
Ladue Pg. 140, E-3
Lake Lotawana G-2
Lake Saint Louis G-8
Lake Spring J-7
Lake Waukomis Pg. 112, D-2
Lakenan F-6
Lakeshire Pg. 140, H-3
Lamar J-3
Lancaster D-5
Lanton L-6
Lathrop F-2
Latty J-8
Lawson F-3
Leadwood J-8
Leasburg H-7
Lebanon J-5
Lee's Summit Pg. 112, K-6
Leeper K-8
Leeton H-3
Lemons D-4
Lentner F-6
Leonard E-5
Lewistown E-6
Lexington G-3
Liberal J-2
Liberty F-2
  Vicinity Pg. 112, C-6
Licking K-6
Lilbourn L-10
Lincoln H-4
Linn H-6
Linneus E-4
Lockwood K-3
Lone Jack G-3
Long Lane J-5
Longrun L-5
Longwood G-4
Louisiana F-7
Lowry City H-3
Ludlow E-3
Luray D-6
Macks Creek J-5
Macon E-5
Madison F-6
Malden L-9
Manchester Pg. 140, F-1
  Vicinity Pg. 140, G-1
Manes K-5
Mansfield K-5
Maplewood Pg. 140, E-3
Marble Hills K-9
Marceline E-4
March H-8
Margona Pg. 140, C-3
Marionville K-3
Marlborough Pg. 140, G-3
Marshall G-4
Marshfield K-5
Marthasville G-7
Martinsburg G-6
Mary Ridge Pg. 140, C-3
Maryland Heights Pg. 140, C-1
Maryville D-1
Matthews L-10
Maysville E-2
McBaine G-5
McFall E-2
Melbourne E-3
Memphis D-5

Mendon F-4
Mercer D-4
Mexico F-6
Miami F-4
Miami Station F-4
Middle Grove F-5
Midway G-5
Milan E-4
Milford J-3
Mill Grove D-4
Millard E-5
Miller K-3
Millersburg G-6
Milo J-2
Mineola G-7
Miner K-10
Mirabile F-3
Moberly F-5
Mokane G-6
Moline Acres Pg. 140, B-5
Monett K-3
Monroe City F-6
Montevallo J-3
Montgomery City G-7
Monticello E-6
Montreal J-5
Montrose H-3
Moody L-6
Morley K-10
Morrisville K-4
Mound City E-1
Moundville J-2
Mount Moriah D-3
Mount Vernon K-3
Mount Zion K-5
Mountain Grove K-5
Mountain View K-7
Myrtle L-7
Mystic E-4
Nashville K-2
Naylor L-8
Nebo J-5
Neelyville L-8
Neosho L-2
Nevada J-2
New Bloomfield G-6
New Boston E-4
New Florence G-7
New Franklin G-5
New Hartford F-7
New Haven H-7
New Hope F-8
New London F-7
New Madrid L-10
New Market F-2
New Melle G-7
New Point E-1
Newburg J-6
Niangua K-5
Nixa K-4
Noel L-2
Norborne F-3
Normandy Pg. 140, C-4
Northmoor Pg. 112, D-4
Northview K-4
Northwoods Pg. 140, C-4
Norwood Court Pg. 140, C-4
Novelty E-5
Novinger E-5
O'Fallon G-8
Oak Grove G-3
Oak Hill H-7
Oakland Pg. 140, G-2
Oaks Pg. 112, D-4
Oakview Pg. 112, D-4
Oakville Pg. 140, H-4
Oakwood Pg. 112, D-4
Oakwood Manor Pg. 112, D-4
Oakwood Park Pg. 112, D-4
Ocie L-5
Odessa G-3
Oermann H-8
Olivette Pg. 140, D-3
Olympian Village H-8
Oran K-10
Orchard Farm G-8
Oregon E-1
Orrick F-3
Osage Beach H-5
Osceola H-3
Osgood E-4
Oskaloosa J-2
Otto H-8
Overland Pg. 140, D-3
Owensville H-6
Ozark K-4
Pacific H-8
  Vicinity Pg. 140, G-1
Pagedale Pg. 140, D-4
Palmyra E-7
Paris F-6
Parkville Pg. 112, D-2
Parma L-9
Pasadena Hills Pg. 140, C-4
Pasadena Park Pg. 140, C-4
Passaic H-2
Patton J-9
Pattonsburg E-2
Peace Valley L-6
Peach Orchard L-9
Peculiar G-2
Pennsboro K-3
Perrin E-2
Perry F-6
Perryville J-9
Pevely H-8
Phelps K-3
Philadelphia E-6
Phillipsburg J-5
Piedmont K-8
Pierce City K-3

MISSOURI

Pilot Grove — G-4
Pilot Knob — J-8
Pine Lawn — Pg. 140, D-5
Pineville — L-2
Plad — J-4
Plato — J-6
Platte Woods — Pg. 112, C-2
Plattsburg — F-2
Pleasant Green — G-5
Pleasant Valley — Pg. 112, C-5
Plevna — E-6
Pocahontas — J-8
Polk — J-4
Pollock — D-4
Polo — F-3
Pomona — L-6
Poplar Bluff — L-8
Portageville — L-10
Potosi — J-8
Prairie Hill — F-5
Prairie Home — G-5
Preston — J-4
Princeton — D-4
Protem — L-5
Purdin — E-4
Purdy — L-3
Puxico — K-9
Queen City — D-5
Quincy — H-4
Qulin — L-9
Racine — K-2
Randolph — Pg. 112, E-5
Ravanna — D-4
Ravenwood — D-2
Raymondville — K-6
Raymore — G-2
Raytown — Pg. 112, H-5
Rea — E-2
Redford — K-8
Reeds Spring — L-4
Regal — F-3
Reger — E-4
Renick — F-5
Rensselaer — K-4
Republic — K-4
Reynolds — K-8
Rhineland — G-7
Rich Hill — H-2
Richland — J-5
Richmond — F-3
Richmond Heights — Pg. 140, E-3
Ridgedale — L-4
Ridgeway — D-3
Risco — L-9
Riverside — Pg. 112, D-2
Riverton — L-7
Riverview — Pg. 140, B-6
Rock Hill — Pg. 140, F-4
Rock Port — D-1
Rockville — H-3
Rocky Comfort — L-3
Rogersville — K-4
Rolla — J-6
Romance — L-5
Rombauer — K-8
Rosati — H-7
Rosebud — H-7
Rosendale — E-2
Rothville — F-4
Round Spring — K-7
Rover — L-5
Rushville — F-1
Saint Ann — Pg. 140, C-2
Saint Charles — G-8
  Vicinity — Pg. 140, C-1
Saint Clair — H-8
Saint Clement — F-7
Saint George Village — Pg. 140, H-4
Saint James — H-6
Saint John — Pg. 140, C-3
Saint Joseph — E-2
Saint Louis — G-8
  Vicinity — Pg. 140
Saint Marys — J-9
Saint Patrick — E-7
Saint Robert — J-6
Sainte Genevieve — H-8
Salem — J-7
Saline — D-3
Salisbury — F-5
Sandy Hook — G-5
Santa Fe — F-6
Sarcoxie — K-3
Savannah — E-2
Schuermann Heights — Pg. 140, C-3
Scott City — K-10
Sedalia — G-4
Sedgewickville — J-9
Seligman — L-3
Senath — M-9
Seneca — L-2
Seymour — K-5
Shannondale — F-5
Shelbina — E-6
Shelbyville — E-6
Sheldon — J-3
Sheridan — D-2
Shirley — J-7
Shrewsbury — Pg. 140, F-3
Sikeston — K-10
Silva — K-8
Silver Lake — K-8
Simmons — K-6
Skidmore — D-1
Slater — F-4
Sleeper — J-6
Sligo — J-7
Smithton — G-4
Smithville — F-2
South Fork — L-6
South Gifford — E-5
South Lineville — D-4
Southwest City — L-2
Sparta — K-4
Spickard — E-4
Spokane — L-4
Springfield — K-4
Squires — L-5
Stanberry — E-2
State Line — M-9
Steele — M-9
Steelville — J-7
Stockton — J-3
Stoutsville — F-6
Stover — H-4
Strafford — K-4
Strasburg — G-3
Sturgeon — F-5
Sugar Creek — Pg. 112, F-5
Sullivan — H-7
Summersville — K-7
Sumner — F-4
Sunset Hills — Pg. 140, H-2
Sweet Springs — G-4
Sycamore — L-6
Sycamore Hills — Pg. 140, C-3
Tarkio — D-1
Tebbetts — G-6
Thayer — L-7
Theodosia — L-5
Thomas Hill — F-5
Thomasville — L-6
Thompson — F-6
Thornfield — L-5
Tiffin — J-3
Tina — F-4
Tindall — E-4
Tipton — G-5
Town & Country — Pg. 140, F-1
Townley — L-9
Trenton — E-4
Troy — G-8
Truesdale — G-7
Truxton — G-7
Tunas — J-4
Turney — F-2
Tuscumbia — H-5
Tyrone — K-6
Union — H-7
Union Star — E-2
Unionville — D-4
Unity Village — Pg. 112, J-6
University City — Pg. 140, D-3
Uplands Park — Pg. 140, D-4
Urich — H-3
Utica — E-3
Van Buren — K-8
Vandalia — F-7
Vanzant — K-6
Velda — Pg. 140, D-4
Velda Village Hills — Pg. 140, D-4
Versailles — H-5
Viburnum — J-7
Vichy — H-6
Vienna — H-6
Vinita Park — Pg. 140, D-3
Vinita Terrace — Pg. 140, D-3
Vulcan — K-8
Wainwright — G-6
Walnut Grove — K-4
Wardsville — H-6
Warren — E-6
Warrensburg — G-3
Warrenton — G-7
Warsaw — H-4
Warson Woods — Pg. 140, F-2
Washington — G-7
Wasola — L-5
Waverly — F-4
Wayland — D-6
Waynesville — J-6
Weatherby Lake — Pg. 112, C-2
Weaubleau — J-4
Webb City — K-2
Weber Hill — H-8
Webster Groves — Pg. 140, F-3
Wellston — Pg. 140, D-4
Wellsville — G-7
Wentworth — K-3
West Plains — L-6
Westboro — D-1
Weston — F-1
Westphalia — H-6
White Oak — Pg. 140, C-3
Wilbur Park — Pg. 140, G-4
Wilcox — D-2
Willard — K-4
Williamsburg — G-6
Williamsville — K-8
Willow Springs — K-6
Wilson City — K-10
Windsor — H-4
Winfield — G-8
Winigan — E-4
Winona — K-7
Winston — E-3
Winthrop — F-1
Woodlawn — J-9
Woods Heights — F-3
Woodson Terrace — Pg. 140, C-4
Wooldridge — G-5
Worth — D-2
Wyaconda — D-6
Yarrow — E-5
Yount — J-9
Yukon — K-6
Zalma — K-9

MONTANA
Page 51

Population: 786,690
Capital: Helena
Land Area: 145,398 sq.mi.

Absarokee — E-6
Acton — E-7
Alberton — D-2
Alder — E-4
Alzada — D-10
Anaconda — E-3
Angela — D-8
Antelope — B-10
Arlee — D-2
Ashland — E-8
Augusta — C-4
Avon — D-3
Babb — B-3
Bainville — B-10
Baker — D-10
Basin — E-4
Bearcreek — F-6
Belfry — F-6
Belgrade — D-1
Belt — C-5
Biddle — E-9
Big Fork — C-2
Big Sandy — C-5
Big Sky — E-4
Big Timber — E-6
Bighorn — E-7
Billings — E-7
Birney — E-8
Black Eagle — C-4
Blackfoot — B-3
Bloomfield — C-9
Bonner — D-2
Boulder — E-4
Box Elder — C-5
Bozeman — E-5
Brady — C-4
Bridger — F-6
Broadus — E-9
Broadview — E-6
Brockton — C-9
Brockway — C-9
Browning — C-3
Busby — E-8
Butte — E-4
Bynum — C-4
Cameron — E-4
Canyon Creek — D-4
Capitol — D-10
Carter — C-5
Cartersville — D-8
Cascade — C-4
Checkerboard — D-5
Chester — D-4
Chico Hot Springs — F-5
Chinook — B-6
Choteau — C-4
Christina — E-4
Churchill — E-4
Circle — C-9
Cleveland — D-4
Clinton — D-2
Clyde Park — E-5
Coffee Creek — C-5
Cohagen — D-8
Colstrip — D-8
Columbia Falls — B-2
Columbus — E-6
Conner — D-2
Conrad — C-4
Cooke City — F-6
Corvallis — D-2
Craig — D-4
Crane — C-10
Crow Agency — E-7
Culbertson — B-9
Custer — E-7
Cut Bank — B-4
Darby — D-2
Dean — E-6
Decker — F-8
Deer Lodge — D-3
Dell — F-3
Denton — C-5
Dillon — E-3
Divide — E-3
Dixon — C-2
Dodson — B-7
Drummond — D-3
Dupuyer — C-4
Dutton — C-4
East Glacier Park — B-3
East Helena — D-4
Edgar — E-6
Ekalaka — D-10
Elliston — D-3
Elmo — C-2
Emigrant — E-5
Ennis — E-4
Ethridge — B-4
Eureka — B-2
Fairfield — C-4
Fairview — C-10
Fallon — D-9
Flatwillow — D-6
Flaxville — B-9
Florence — D-2
Ford — D-2
Forestgrove — D-6
Forsyth — D-8
Fort Belknap Agency — C-6
Fort Benton — C-5
Fort Peck — C-8
Fort Shaw — C-4
Fortine — B-2
Frenchtown — D-2
Froid — C-9
Fromberg — E-6
Galen — D-3
Gallatin Gateway — E-4
Gardiner — F-5
Garneill — D-6
Garrison — D-3
Garryowen — E-8
Geraldine — C-5
Geyser — C-5
Glasgow — C-8
Glen — E-3
Glendive — D-10
Grant — F-3
Grantsdale — D-2
Grassrange — D-6
Great Falls — C-4
Hall — D-3
Hamilton — D-2
Hammond — D-10
Happy's Inn — C-1
Hardin — E-7
Harlem — B-6
Harlowton — D-6
Harrison — E-4
Hathaway — D-9
Havre — B-6
Helena — E-6
Helmville — D-3
Heron — C-1
Hilger — D-6
Hingham — F-4
Hinsdale — B-8
Hobson — D-5
Homestead — B-9
Hot Springs — C-2
Hungry Horse — B-2
Huntley — E-7
Huson — D-2
Hysham — D-8
Ingomar — D-8
Jackson — E-3
Jefferson City — D-4
Joliet — E-6
Joplin — C-4
Jordan — C-8
Judith Gap — D-6
Kalispell — B-2
Kiowa — B-3
Klein — D-7
Kremlin — F-4
Lakeside — C-2
Lambert — C-9
Lame Deer — E-8
Laurel — E-6
Laurin — E-4
Lavina — E-6
Lewistown — D-6
Libby — B-1
Lincoln — D-3
Lindsay — C-9
Livingston — E-5
Lloyd — B-6
Lodge Grass — E-7
Lohman — B-6
Loma — C-5
Loring — B-7
Lothair — F-4
Malta — B-7
Manhattan — E-4
Marion — C-2
Martin City — B-2
McLeod — E-5
Medicine Lake — B-9
Melrose — E-3
Melstone — D-7
Melville — E-6
Miles City — D-9
Missoula — D-2
Moccasin — D-5
Monarch — D-5
Montague — C-5
Montana City — D-4
Moore — D-6
Musselshell — D-7
Nashua — C-8
Neihart — D-5
Niarada — C-2
Norris — E-4
Noxon — C-1
Nye — E-6
Olney — B-2
Opheim — B-8
Oswego — C-9
Ovando — D-3
Pablo — C-2
Paradise — C-2
Pendroy — C-4
Philipsburg — D-3
Plains — C-1
Plentywood — B-9
Plevna — D-10
Polebridge — B-2
Polson — C-2
Pompeys Pillar — E-7
Poplar — C-9
Port of Del Bonita — B-3
Port of Morgan — B-7
Port of Ophiem — B-8
Port of Raymond — B-9
Potomac — D-2
Powderville — E-9
Power — C-4
Pray — E-5
Rapelje — E-6
Raymond — B-9
Raynesford — C-5
Red Lodge — F-6
Redstone — B-9
Reedpoint — E-6
Rexford — B-2
Richey — C-9
Richland — B-8
Ringling — E-5
Roberts — E-6
Rock Springs — C-2
Rollins — C-2
Ronan — C-2
Rosebud — D-8
Roundup — D-6
Roy — D-6
Rudyard — C-4
Ryegate — D-6
Saco — D-7
Saint Ignatius — C-2
Saint Mary — B-3
Saint Regis — C-1
Saltese — C-1
Santa Rita — C-5
Savage — C-10
Scobey — B-9
Seeley Lake — D-3
Shawmut — D-6
Shelby — C-4
Sheridan — E-4
Sidney — C-10
Silesia — E-6
Silver Star — E-4
Simms — C-4
Somers — C-2
Springdale — E-5
Stanford — D-5
Stevensville — D-2
Stryker — B-2
Suffolk — C-6
Sumatra — D-7
Sun River — B-4
Sunburst — B-4
Superior — D-2
Swan Lake — C-2
Sweetgrass — B-4
Tarkio — D-7
Teigen — D-7
Terry — D-9
Thompson Falls — C-1
Three Forks — E-4
Toston — E-4
Townsend — E-4
Trego — B-2
Trout Creek — C-1
Troy — B-1
Turner — B-6
Twin Bridges — E-4
Twodot — D-5
Valier — B-4
Vaughn — C-4
Victor — D-2
Vida — C-9
Virginia City — E-4
Volborg — E-9
Walkerville — E-3
Waterloo — E-4
West Glacier — B-3
West Yellowstone — B-10
White Hall — E-4
White Sulphur Springs — D-5
Whitefish — B-2
Whitetail — B-9
Whitewater — B-7
Wibaux — D-10
Willow Creek — E-4
Wilsall — E-4
Winifred — D-6
Winnett — D-7
Winston — E-4
Wisdom — E-3
Wise River — E-3
Wolf Creek — D-4
Wolf Point — C-9
Worden — E-7
Wyola — F-7
Yaak — B-1
Zurich — B-6

NEBRASKA
Pages 52-53

Population: 1,569,825
Capital: Lincoln
Land Area: 76,664 sq. mi.

Abie — F-11
Adams — H-12
Ainsworth — D-7
Albion — E-10
Alda — G-9
Alexandria — H-11
Allen — D-11
Alliance — D-3
Alma — H-8
Almeria — E-7
Amelia — D-8
Ames — F-12
Amherst — G-8
Angora — D-3
Anoka — C-9
Anselmo — E-7
Ansley — F-8
Antioch — D-3
Arapahoe — H-7
Arcadia — F-8
Archer — G-9
Arlington — F-12
Arnold — E-6
Arthur — E-5
Ashby — D-4
Ashland — G-12
Ashton — F-9
Atkinson — D-9
Atlanta — H-8
Auburn — H-12
Aurora — G-10
Axtell — H-8
Ayr — H-9
Bancroft — E-12
Barneston — J-12
Bartlett — E-9
Bartley — H-6
Bassett — D-8
Battle Creek — E-10
Bayard — E-3
Bazile Mills — D-10
Beatrice — H-11
Beaver City — H-7
Beaver Crossing — G-11
Beemer — E-11
Belden — D-11
Belgrade — F-10
Bellevue — G-12
  Vicinity — Pg. 132, G-5
Belvidere — H-10
Benedict — G-10
Benkelman — H-5
Bennet — G-12
Bertrand — H-7
Berwyn — F-8
Big Springs — F-4
Bingham — D-4
Bladen — H-9
Blair — F-12
Bloomfield — D-10
Blue Hill — H-9
Blue Springs — H-11
Boelus — G-9
Boone — F-10
Boys Town — F-12
  Vicinity — Pg. 132, E-1
Bradshaw — G-10
Brady — F-6
Brandon — G-4
Brewster — E-7
Bridgeport — E-3
Bristow — C-9
Broadwater — E-3
Brock — H-12
Broken Bow — F-7
Brownlee — D-6
Brownville — H-12
Brule — F-4
Bruning — H-10
Bruno — F-11
Brunswick — D-10
Burchard — H-12
Burr — H-12
Burton — C-8
Burwell — E-8
Bushnell — F-2
Butte — C-9
Cairo — G-9
Callaway — F-7
Cambridge — H-6
Campbell — H-8
Capehart — Pg. 132, H-4
Carleton — H-10
Carroll — D-11
Carter Lake — Pg. 132, G-2
Cedar Bluffs — F-12
Cedar Creek — Pg. 132, K-1
Cedar Rapids — F-9
Center — D-10
Central City — G-9
Ceresco — G-12
Chadron — C-3
Chalco — Pg. 132, F-1
Chambers — D-9
Champion — G-5
Chapman — G-9
Chappell — F-4
Chester — J-10
Clarks — F-10
Clarkson — E-11
Clatonia — H-11
Clay Center — H-10
Clearwater — D-10
Clinton — C-4
Cody — C-6
Coleridge — D-11
Columbus — F-11
Comstock — F-8
Concord — D-11
Cook — H-12
Cornlea — F-10
Cortland — H-11
Cotesfield — F-9
Cowles — H-9
Cozad — G-7
Crab Orchard — H-12
Craig — E-12
Crawford — C-3
Creighton — D-10
Creston — E-11
Crete — H-11
Crofton — C-10
Crookston — C-6
Culbertson — H-6
Cullom — Pg. 132, K-2
Curtis — G-6
Dakota City — D-12
Dalton — E-3
Danbury — H-6
Dannebrog — F-9
Davenport — H-10
David City — F-11
Dawson — J-13
Daykin — H-11
Debolt — G-8
Decatur — D-11
Denton — G-11
Deshler — H-10
Dewitt — H-11
Dickens — G-6
Diller — H-11
Dix — F-2
Dodge — E-11
Doniphan — G-9
Dorchester — G-11
Douglas — H-12
DuBois — J-12
Dunbar — G-12
Duncan — F-10
Dunning — E-7
Dwight — G-11
Eddyville — G-7
Edgar — H-10
Edison — H-7
Elba — F-9
Elgin — E-10
Eli — C-5
Elk Creek — H-12
Elkhorn — F-12
Ellsworth — D-4
Elm Creek — G-8
Elmwood — G-12
Elsie — G-5
Elsmere — D-7
Elwood — G-7
Elyria — E-8
Emerson — D-11
Emmet — D-9
Enders — H-5
Endicott — J-11
Ericson — E-9
Eustis — G-7
Exeter — G-10
Fairbury — H-11
Fairfield — H-10
Fairmont — H-10
Falls City — J-13
Farnam — F-9
Farwell — F-9
Filley — H-11
Firth — H-11
Fordyce — C-11
Fort Calhoun — Pg. 132, A-3
Fort Crook — Pg. 132, H-4
Foster — D-11
Franklin — H-8
Fremont — F-12
Friend — G-11
Fullerton — F-10
Funk — H-8
Gandy — F-6
Garrison — F-11
Geneva — H-10
Genoa — F-10
Gering — E-2
Gilmore — Pg. 132, H-4
Giltner — G-10
Glenvil — H-9
Goehner — G-11
Gordon — C-4
Gothenburg — G-7
Grafton — H-10
Grainton — G-5
Grand Island — G-9
Grant — G-4
Greeley — F-9
Greenwood — G-12
Gresham — G-11
Gretna — G-12
Guide Rock — J-9
Gurley — F-3
Hadar — E-11
Haigler — H-4
Hallam — H-11
Halsey — E-7
Hamlet — H-5
Hampton — G-10
Harrisburg — F-2
Harrison — C-2
Hartington — D-11
Harvard — H-9
Hastings — H-9
Hay Springs — C-4
Hayes Center — H-5
Hazard — F-8
Hebron — H-10
Hemingford — D-3
Henderson — H-10
Herman — E-12
Hershey — F-6
Hildreth — H-8
Holdrege — H-8
Holstein — H-9
Hooper — F-12
Hoskins — E-11
Howells — E-11
Humboldt — J-12
Humphrey — F-10
Huntley — H-8
Hyannis — D-5
Imperial — H-5
Inavale — J-9
Indianola — H-6
Inman — D-9
Irvington — Pg. 132, C-2
Ithaca — G-12
Johnson — H-12
Johnstown — D-7
Juniata — H-9
Kearney — G-8
Kenesaw — H-9
Kennard — F-12
Keystone — F-5
Kilgore — C-6
Kimball — F-2
La Vista — Pg. 132, F-3
Lakeside — D-4
Laurel — D-11
Lawrence — H-8
Lebanon — H-7
Leigh — E-11
Lemoyne — E-5
Lewellen — E-4
Lewiston — H-12
Lexington — G-7
Liberty — J-12
Lincoln — G-12
Linwood — F-11
Lisco — E-4
Litchfield — F-8
Lodgepole — D-7
Long Pine — D-7
Loomis — H-7
Loup City — F-8
Louisville — G-12
Lyman — D-2
Lynch — C-9
Lyons — E-12
Madison — E-11
Madrid — G-5
Magnet — D-10
Malmo — F-11
Marquette — G-10
Martell — H-11
Martinsburg — D-11
Mason City — F-8
Max — H-5
Maxwell — F-6
May — Pg. 132, G-3
Maywood — G-6
McCook — H-6
McCool Jct. — G-10
McGrew — E-2
Mead — F-12
Meadow — Pg. 132, K-1
Melbeta — E-2
Memphis — G-12
Merna — F-7
Merriman — C-5
Milford — G-11
Millard — Pg. 132, F-1
Miller — H-8
Milligan — H-10
Mills — C-8
Minden — H-8
Minatare — E-2
Mitchell — D-2
Monowi — C-9
Moorefield — G-6
Morrill — D-2
Mullen — D-6
Murray — G-12
Naper — C-8
Naponee — H-7
Nashville — Pg. 132, B-3
Nebraska City — H-12
Neligh — E-10
Nelson — H-10
Nenzel — C-6
Newman Grove — E-10
Newport — D-8
Nickerson — F-12
Niobrara — C-10
Norden — C-7
Norfolk — E-11
North Bend — F-11
North Loup — F-9
North Platte — F-6
O'Neill — D-9
Oak — H-10
Oakdale — E-10
Oakland — E-12
Obert — D-11
Oconto — F-7
Octavia — F-11
Odell — J-11
Odessa — G-8
Ogallala — F-5
Ohiowa — H-10
Omaha — F-12
  Vicinity — Pg. 132
Ong — H-10
Ord — E-8
Oreapolis — Pg. 132, J-5
Orleans — H-8
Osceola — F-10
Oshkosh — E-4
Osmond — D-10
Overton — G-8
Oxford — H-7
Page — D-9
Palisade — H-5
Palmer — F-9
Palmyra — G-12
Panama — H-12
Papillion — G-12
  Vicinity — Pg. 132, G-3
Parks — H-4
Pawnee City — J-12
Paxton — F-5
Pender — E-12
Petersburg — E-10
Phillips — G-9
Pickrell — H-11
Pierce — D-10
Pilger — E-11
Plainview — D-10
Platte Center — F-10
Plattsmouth — G-12
  Vicinity — Pg. 132, K-5
Pleasanton — G-8
Plymouth — H-11
Polk — G-10
Poole — G-8
Potter — F-3
Prague — F-11
Primrose — E-9
Prosser — G-9
Purdum — D-7
Raeville — E-10
Ragan — H-8
Ralston — Pg. 132, F-2

NEBRASKA

Randolph — D-11
Ravenna — G-9
Raymond — G-11
Red Cloud — H-9
Republican City — H-8
Reynolds — J-11
Richfield — Pg. 132, H-2
Richland — F-11
Rising City — F-11
Riverdale — G-8
Riverton — H-9
Roca — G-11
Rockville — F-9
Rogers — F-11
Rosalie — E-12
Rose — D-8
Roseland — H-9
Rushville — C-4
Ruskin — H-9
Saint Edward — F-10
Saint Helena — C-11
Saint Libory — G-9
Saint Mary — H-12
Saint Paul — F-9
Santee — C-10
Sargent — E-8
Saronville — H-9
Schuyler — F-11
Scotia — F-9
Scottsbluff — D-2
Scribner — F-11
Seneca — D-6
Seward — G-11
Shelby — F-10
Shelton — G-8
Shickley — H-10
Sholes — D-11
Shubert — H-12
Sidney — F-3
Silver Creek — F-10
Smithfield — G-7
Snyder — E-11
South Bend — G-12
South Souix City — D-12
Spalding — E-9
Sparks — C-7
Spencer — C-9
Springfield — G-12
  Vicinity — Pg. 132, J-1
Springview — C-8
Stamford — H-7
Stanton — E-11
Staplehurst — G-11
Stapleton — F-6
Steele City — J-11
Steinauer — H-12
Stockville — G-6
Strang — H-11
Stratton — H-5
Stromsburg — F-10
Stuart — D-8
Summerfield — J-12
Sumner — G-8
Superior — H-9
Surprise — G-10
Sutherland — F-6
Sutton — H-10
Syracuse — H-12
Table Rock — H-12
Tarnov — F-10
Taylor — E-8
Tecumseh — H-12
Tekamah — E-12
Terrytown — D-2
Thayer — G-10
Thedford — E-6
Thurston — E-12
Tilden — E-10
Tobias — H-11
Trenton — H-6
Trumbull — G-9
Tryon — E-6
Uehling — E-12
Ulysses — G-11
Unadilla — G-12
Upland — H-8
Valentine — C-7
Valley — F-12
Valparaiso — G-11
Venango — G-4
Verdel — C-10
Verdigre — D-10
Verdon — J-13
Waco — G-10
Wahoo — F-12
Wakefield — D-11
Wallace — G-5
Walthill — E-12
Wauneta — H-5
Wausa — D-10
Waverly — G-12
Wayne — D-11
Weeping Water — G-12
Weissert — F-8
Wellfleet — G-6
West Point — E-11
Western — H-11
Westerville — F-8
Whitman — D-5
Whitney — C-3
Wilber — H-11
Wilcox — H-8
Willow Island — G-7
Wilsonville — H-7
Winnebago — D-12
Winnetoon — D-9
Winside — E-11
Winslow — F-12
Wisner — E-11
Wolbach — F-9
Wood Lake — C-7
Wood River — G-9
Wymore — J-12
Wynot — C-11
York — G-10

NEVADA
Page 54
Population: 800,493
Capital: Carson City
Land Area: 109,893 sq. mi.

Adaven — F-5
Alamo — G-5
Arden — Pg. 113, G-1
Ash Springs — G-5
Austin — D-4
Babbitt — E-2
Baker — E-6
Battle Mountain — C-4
Beatty — H-4
Beowawe — C-4
Blue Diamond — J-5
Boulder City — J-6
Bracken — Pg. 113, E-3
Bunkerville — H-6
Cactus Springs — H-5
Cal Nev Ari — J-6
Caliente — G-6
Carlin — C-5
Carp — G-6
Carson City — E-1
Carver's — E-3
Caselton — F-6
Cherry Creek — D-6
Coaldale — F-3
Cold Spring — D-3
Contact — A-6
Crescent Valley — C-4
Currant — E-5
Currie — C-6
Deeth — B-5
Duckwater — E-5
Dyer — F-3
Eagle Picher Mine — C-2
East Ely — E-6
East Las Vegas — Pg. 113, E-6
Elko — C-5
Ely — E-6
Empire — C-2
Eureka — D-5
Fallon — D-2
Fernley — D-2
Frenchman — E-3
Gabbs — E-3
Gerlach — C-2
Glendale — H-6
Golconda — B-3
Gold Point — G-3
Goldfield — G-3
Goodsprings — J-5
Halleck — B-5
Hawthorne — E-2
Henderson — J-6
  Vicinity — Pg. 113, G-6
Hiko — G-5
Imlay — C-3
Indian Springs — H-5
Ione — E-3
Jack Creek — B-5
Jackpot — A-6
Jarbridge — A-5
Jean — J-5
Jiggs — C-5
Kimberly — E-5
Lage's — D-6
Lamoille — C-5
Las Vegas — J-6
  Vicinity — Pg. 113
Las Vegas Beach — B-3
  — Pg. 113, E-9
Lee — C-5
Lida — G-3
Lovelock — C-2
Lund — E-6
Luning — E-2
Major's Place — E-6
McDermitt — A-3
McGill — D-6
Mercury — H-5
Mesquite — H-6
Midas — B-4
Middle Gate — E-3
Mill City — C-3
Mina — F-3
Moapa — H-6
Montello — B-6
Mountain City — A-5
Nelson — J-6
Nixon — D-2
North Las Vegas — J-6
  Vicinity — Pg. 113, B-3
Nyala — F-5
Oasis — B-6
Oreana — C-3
Orovada — B-3
Owyhee — A-5
Panaca — G-6
Paradise Valley — B-3
Pioche — F-6
Preston — E-6
Rachel — G-5
Reno — D-2
Round Mt. — E-4
Ruby Valley — C-5
Ruth — E-6
Sandy — J-5
Schurz — E-2
Scotty's Jct. — G-4
Searchlight — K-6
Shantytown — C-5
Silver City — D-2
Silver Peak — F-3
Silver Springs — D-2
Sloan — J-5
Sparks — D-2
Sulphur — B-2
Sutcliffe — D-1
Thousand Springs — B-6
Tonopah — F-3
Tuscarora — B-4
Unionville — C-3
Ursine — F-6
Valmy — C-4
Virginia City — D-2
Wadsworth — D-2
Warm Springs — F-4
Weed Heights — E-2
Wellington — E-2
Wells — B-6
Winnemucca — B-3
Yerington — E-2

NEW HAMPSHIRE
Page 55
Population: 920,610
Capital: Concord
Land Area: 8,993 sq. mi.

Albany — E-6
Allenstown — H-6
Alstead — H-3
Alton — G-6
Alton Bay — G-6
Amherst — J-5
Andover — G-5
Antrim — J-4
Ashland — F-5
Ashuelot — K-3
Atkinson — J-6
Auburn — J-6
Barnstead — H-6
Bartlett — E-6
Bath — E-4
Bayside — J-7
Bedford — J-5
Belmont — G-5
Bennington — J-4
Berlin — D-6
Bethlehem — E-5
Boscawen — H-5
Bow Center — H-5
Bradford — H-4
Brentwood — J-6
Bretton Woods — E-5
Bridgewater — G-5
Bristol — G-5
Brookfield — G-6
Brookline — K-5
Canaan — G-4
Canaan Center — F-4
Candia — J-6
Carroll — D-5
Cascade — D-6
Center Conway — E-6
Center Ossipee — F-6
Charlestown — H-3
Cheever — D-5
Chester — J-6
Chesterfield — J-3
Chichester — H-6
Chocorua — F-6
Cilleyville — G-4
Claremont — H-3
Coburn — J-6
Cold River — H-3
Colebrook — B-5
Columbia — B-5
Concord — H-5
Contoocook — H-5
Conway — E-6
Coos Junction — D-5
Cornish City — G-3
Cornish Flat — G-3
Crystal — C-6
Danbury — G-4
Davisville — H-5
Derry — J-6
Derry Village — J-6
Dixville — C-5
Dorchester — F-4
Dover — H-7
Drewsville — H-3
Dublin — J-3
Dummer — C-6
Durham — H-7
East Alton — G-6
East Barrington — H-6
East Grafton — F-4
East Hebron — F-5
East Kingston — J-6
East Lempster — H-3
East Madison — F-6
Easton — E-5
Eaton Center — F-6
Effingham Falls — F-7
Elkins — G-4
Epping — J-6
Epsom — H-6
Epsom Four Corners — H-6
Errol — C-6
Exeter — J-7
Fabyan — D-5
Farmington — H-6
Fish Market — G-4
Francestown — J-4
Franconia — D-5
Franklin — G-5
Freedom — F-6
Fremont — J-6
Gerrish — H-5
Gilford — G-6
Gilmans Corner — F-4
Gilmanton — G-6
Gilsum — J-4
Glen — E-6
Glen House — D-6
Glendale — G-5
Goffs Falls — J-5
Goffstown — J-5
Gorham — D-6
Goshen — H-4
Gossville — H-6
Grafton — G-4
Grantham — G-3
Greenfield — J-4
Greenville — K-4
Groton — F-4
Groveton — C-5
Guild — G-4
Guildhall — C-5
Hampton — J-7
Hampton Beach — J-7
Hancock — J-4
Hanover — F-4
Hanover Center — F-4
Harts Location — E-6
Haverhill — E-4
Hebron — F-4
Henniker — H-5
Hillsborough — H-4
Hinsdale — J-3
Hooksett — H-6
Hopkinton — H-5
Hoyts Corner — H-4
Hudson — K-6
Jackson — D-6
Jaffrey — K-4
James City — H-6
Jefferson — D-5
Jefferson Highlands — D-5
Keene — J-3
Kensington — J-7
Kidderville — B-5
Kingston — J-6
Laconia — G-5
Lancaster — D-5
Laskey Corner — G-7
Leavitts Hill — H-6
Lebanon — G-4
Lincoln — E-5
Lisbon — E-4
Little Boars Head — J-7
Littleton — D-5
Loudon — H-6
Lower Shaker Village — G-4
Lower Village — J-3
Lyme — F-4
Lyme Center — F-4
Madbury — H-7
Madison — F-6
Manchester — J-5
Marlborough — J-4
Marlow — H-4
Martin — J-6
Mason — K-5
Meadows — D-5
Meredith — F-5
Meriden — G-3
Merrimack — J-5
Milan — C-6
Milford — J-5
Milton — G-6
Mirror Lake — F-6
Monroe — D-4
Mont Vernon — J-5
Moultonborough — F-6
Moultonville — F-6
Mount Sunapee — H-4
Munsonville — J-4
Nashua — K-5
New Durham — G-6
New Hampton — G-5
New Ipswich — K-4
New London — G-4
New Rye — H-6
Newbury — H-4
Newfields — J-7
Newington — H-7
Newmarket — J-7
Newport — H-4
Newton — J-7
North Chatham — D-6
North Conway — E-6
North Grantham — G-4
North Groton — F-5
North Haverhill — E-4
North Rochester — H-6
North Sandwich — F-6
North Stratford — C-5
North Sutton — H-4
North Wakefield — G-6
North Woodstock — E-5
Northfield — H-5
Northumberland — C-5
Northwood — H-6
Orford — F-4
Orfordville — F-4
Ossipee — F-6
Otterville — G-4
Pages Corner — H-5
Parker — J-5
Pearls Corner — H-5
Pelham — K-6
Pembroke — H-6
Penacook — H-5
Peterborough — J-4
Pinardville — J-5
Pittsburg — B-6
Pittsfield — H-6
Plainfield — G-3
Plaistow — J-7
Plymouth — F-5
Portsmouth — H-7
Potter Place — G-4
Province Lake — F-7
Randolph — D-6
Raymond — J-6
Redstone — E-6
Richmond — K-3
Rindge — K-4
Riverton — D-5
Rochester — H-7
Rollinsford — H-7
Rumney — F-5
Rye — J-7
Rye Beach — J-7
Salem — J-6
Salisbury — H-5
Sanbornton — G-5
Sanbornville — G-7
Sandwich — F-6
Seabrook Beach — J-7
Sharon — J-4
Shelburne — D-6
Somersworth — H-7
South Acworth — H-4
South Cornish — G-3
South Danbury — G-4
South Stoddard — J-4
South Weare — J-5
Spofford — J-3
Springfield — H-4
Squantum — M-4
Stark — C-6
Stewartstown — B-6
Stoddard — J-4
Stratford — C-5
Stratham — J-7
Sunapee — G-4
Surry — J-3
Sutton — H-4
Swiftwater — E-4
Tamworth — F-6
Temple — J-4
Thornton — F-5
Tilton — G-5
Trapshire — H-3
Troy — K-4
Tuftonboro — F-6
Twin Mountain — D-5
Union — G-7
Wakefield — G-7
Wallis Sands — J-7
Walpole — J-3
Warner — H-5
Warren — F-4
Washington — H-4
Weare — J-5
Wendell — H-4
Wentworth — F-4
Wentworths Location — B-6
West Campton — F-5
West Lebanon — G-3
West Milan — C-6
West Ossipee — F-6
West Rindge — K-4
West Rumney — F-5
West Stewartstown — B-5
West Swanzey — J-3
Westmoreland — J-3
Westville — J-6
Willey House — E-5
Wilton — J-5
Winchester — J-3
Windsor — H-4
Winnisquam — G-5
Wolfeboro — G-6
Wonalancet — F-6
Woodman — H-7
Woodsville — E-4

NEW JERSEY
Pages 56-57
Population: 7,364,823
Capital: Trenton
Land Area: 7,468 sq. mi.

Absecon — M-6
Adelphia — H-7
Allamuchy — C-5
Allendale — Pg. 126, D-4
Allenton — H-6
Alloway — M-2
Alpha — E-3
Alpine — B-6
  Vicinity — Pg. 126, F-7
Andover — C-5
Asbury Park — G-8
Atlantic City — N-7
Atlantic Highlands — G-8
Atsion — K-5
Audubon — K-3
Audubon Park — Pg. 134, F-7
Avalon — P-5
Avenel — Pg. 127, N-6
Baptistown — E-4
Barnegat — K-8
Barnegat Light — K-8
Barrington — Pg. 134, G-7
Bay Head — J-8
Bay Point — N-3
Bayonne — D-7
  Vicinity — Pg. 127, M-4
Beach Haven — M-7
Beachwood — J-7
Bedminster — E-5
Beesley Pt. — N-5
Belleplain — N-4
Belleville — H-7
  Vicinity — Pg. 127, J-3
Bellmawr — Pg. 134, G-7
Belmar — H-8
  Vicinity — Pg. 126, F-4
Bergenfield — C-8
  Vicinity — Pg. 126, E-6
Berlin — K-4
Bernardsville — D-6
Beverly — H-4
  Vicinity — Pg. 134, C-10
Blairstown — C-4
Blawenburg — F-5
Bloomfield — D-7
  Vicinity — Pg. 127, J-3
Bloomingdale — C-7
Bloomsbury — E-3
Bogota — Pg. 126, G-6
Boonton — C-7
Bordentown — H-5
Bound Brook — F-6
Bradley Beach — H-8
Branchville — B-5
Bridgeboro — Pg. 134, D-9
Bridgeport — K-2
Bridgeton — M-2
Brielle — H-8
Brigantine — N-6
Broadway — D-4
Brooklawn — Pg. 134, G-6
Browns Mills — J-6
Budd Lake — C-5
Buena — M-4
Burlington — H-4
Butler — C-7
Buttzville — D-4
Caldwell — Pg. 127, H-1
Califon — E-5
Camden — J-3
  Vicinity — Pg. 134, G-6
Cape May — Q-4
Cape May Court House — Q-4
Carls Corner — M-3
Carlstadt — Pg. 127, H-5
Carneys Pt. — L-1
Carteret — D-7
  Vicinity — Pg. 127, P-2
Cassville — H-7
Cedar Bridge — K-7
Cedar Grove — J-8
  Vicinity — Pg. 126, G-2
Cedarville — N-3
Centerton — M-3
Chatham — D-6
Chatsworth — K-6
Cherry Hill — J-4
  Vicinity — Pg. 134, F-7
Chesilhurst — K-4
Chester — D-5
Cinnaminson — J-4
Clark — Pg. 127, N-1
Clarksburg — H-6
Clarksville — G-5
Clayton — L-3
Clermont — P-5
Cliffside Park — Pg. 127, J-6
Clinton — E-4
  Vicinity — Pg. 126, H-3
Closter — Pg. 126, E-7
Coffins Corner — Pg. 134, G-9
Colesville — A-5
Collingswood — J-3
  Vicinity — Pg. 134, F-7
Colonia — Pg. 127, P-1
Colts Neck — G-7
Columbus — H-5
Colwick — Pg. 134, G-8
Corbin City — N-5
Coxs Corner — Pg. 134, F-10
Cranbury — G-6
Cranford — Pg. 127, M-1
Cresskill — Pg. 126, E-7
  Vicinity — Pg. 126, F-7
Crestwood Village — J-7
Croton — F-4
Cumberland — N-4
Deacons — J-5
Deerfield — M-3
Delaware — C-3
Demarest — Pg. 126, F-7
Denville — C-6
Dividing Creek — N-3
Dover — C-6
  Vicinity — Pg. 126, F-6
Dumont — Pg. 126, E-6
Dunellen — F-6
East Newark — Pg. 127, K-4
East Orange — D-7
  Vicinity — Pg. 127, J-3
East Rutherford — Pg. 127, H-4
East Vineland — M-4
Eatontown — G-8
Edgewater Park — Pg. 134, C-9
Edinburg — G-5
Edison — F-6
Egg Harbor — M-6
Elizabeth — D-7
  Vicinity — Pg. 127, M-3
Elmer — L-3
Elmwood Park — Pg. 126, G-4
Elwood — M-5
Emerson — Pg. 126, F-1
Englewood — C-8
  Vicinity — Pg. 126, F-6
Englewood Cliffs — A-6
Englishtown — Pg. 126, G-7
Erskine — Pg. 126, B-3
Estell Manor — N-5
Everittstown — E-3
Ewingville — G-5
Fair Haven — Pg. 126, G-8
Fair Lawn — C-8
  Vicinity — Pg. 126, F-4
Fairfield — Pg. 126, G-1
Fairmount — D-5
Fairton — N-3
Farmingdale — H-7
  Vicinity — Pg. 134, G-8
Flemington — E-4
Florham Park — D-6
  Vicinity — Pg. 127, Q-1
Folsom — L-4
Fords — Pg. 127, P-1
Forked River — K-8
Fort Dix — J-6
Fort Lee — D-8
  Vicinity — Pg. 126, H-6
Four Mile — F-6
Franklin — B-6
Franklin Lakes — Pg. 126, D-3
Franklinville — L-3
Fredon — C-5
Freehold — G-7
Freewood Acres — H-7
Frenchtown — F-4
Garfield — C-8
  Vicinity — Pg. 126, G-5
Garwood — Pg. 127, M-1
Gibbsboro — K-4
Gilford Park — J-8
Glassboro — L-3
Glen Gardner — E-4
Glen Ridge — Pg. 127, H-3
Glen Rock — Pg. 126, E-4
Glendale — Pg. 134, G-8
Glenwood — A-6
Gloucester City — K-3
  Vicinity — Pg. 134, G-6
Gouldtown — M-3
Great Meadows — D-4
Green Bank — L-6
Green Village — Pg. 127, J-5
Guttenberg — Pg. 127, J-5
Hackensack — C-8
  Vicinity — Pg. 126, G-6
Hackettstown — D-4
Haddon Heights — Pg. 134, G-7
Haddonfield — K-4
  Vicinity — Pg. 134, F-8
Hainesburg — C-4
Haledon — Pg. 126, F-3
Hamburg — B-6
Hamilton Sq. — G-5
Hammonton — L-5
Hampton — E-4
Hanover — D-6
Harmony — D-4
  Vicinity — Pg. 134, F-7
Harrington Park — Pg. 126, E-6
Harrison — Pg. 127, K-4
Harrisonville — L-1
Harvey Cedars — L-8
Hasbrouck Hts. — Pg. 126, G-5
Haworth — Pg. 126, E-6
Hawthorne — C-7
  Vicinity — Pg. 126, F-3
Helmetta — G-7
Hewitt — A-6
  Vicinity — Pg. 126, B-1
High Bridge — E-4
Highland Park — F-6
Highlands — F-9
Hightstown — G-6
Hillsdale — B-6
  Vicinity — Pg. 126, D-5
Ho-Ho-Kus — Pg. 126, E-4
Hoboken — D-7
  Vicinity — Pg. 127, K-5
Holmdel — G-7
Hopatcong — C-5
Hope — C-4
  Vicinity — Pg. 126, F-9
Hopewell — F-5
Hurdtown — C-6
Irvington — D-7
  Vicinity — Pg. 127, L-2
Iselin — Pg. 127, P-1
Island Heights — J-8
Jamesburg — G-6
Jersey City — D-8
  Vicinity — Pg. 126, D-2
Johnsonburg — C-4
Keansburg — F-8
Kearny — D-7
  Vicinity — Pg. 127, K-4
Kenilworth — Pg. 127, M-1
Keyport — G-7
Kinnelon — C-7
Lafayette — B-5
Lakehurst — J-7
Lakeside — H-7
Lakewood — H-7
Lambertville — G-4
Larisons Cor. — F-5
Laurence Harbor — G-7
Lavallete — J-8
Lawnside — Pg. 134, G-8
Lawrence — G-5
Lebanon — E-5
Lenola — Pg. 134, E-9
Liberty Cor. — E-6
Lincoln Park — C-7
  Vicinity — Pg. 126, F-1
Linden — E-7
  Vicinity — Pg. 127, M-2
Lindenwold — K-4
Linwood — N-6
Little Egg Harbor — M-7
Little Falls — Pg. 126, F-2
Little Ferry — Pg. 126, H-5
Livingston — Pg. 127, J-1
Lodi — Pg. 126, G-4
Long Branch — G-9
Long Valley — D-5
Longport — N-6
Lumberton — J-5
Lyndhurst — Pg. 127, J-4
Madison — D-6
Magnolia — F-4
  Vicinity — Pg. 134, G-8
Mahwah — A-6
  Vicinity — Pg. 126, C-4
Manahawkin — L-7
Manalapan — G-6
Manasquan — H-8
Mantoloking — J-8
Manville — F-6
Maple Shade — J-4
  Vicinity — Pg. 134, F-9
Maplewood — Pg. 127, K-2
Marcella — C-6
Margate City — N-6
Marlboro — G-7
Marlton — K-4
  Vicinity — Pg. 134, G-9
Marshallville — N-5
Matawan — F-7
Maurice River — P-4
Mays Landing — M-5
Maywood — Pg. 126, G-5
McAfee — B-6
Medford — J-5
Medford Lakes — K-5
Merchantville — Pg. 134, E-7
Metuchen — E-7
Mickleton — K-3
Midland Park — Pg. 126, E-4
Milburn — Pg. 127, K-1
Milford — E-3
Millside Heights — Pg. 134, D-9
Millstone — F-6
Milltown — F-6
Millville — N-3
Monmouth Jct. — G-6
Monroe — G-6
Montague — A-5
Montclaire — Pg. 127, H-3
Montvale — Pg. 126, D-5
Montville — C-7
Moorestown — J-4
  Vicinity — Pg. 134, E-8
Morris — Pg. 134, G-7
Morris Plains — D-6
Morristown — D-6
Morrisville — E-3
Mt. Arlington — C-6
Mt. Ephraim — Pg. 134, G-6
Mt. Holly — J-5
Mt. Laurel — Pg. 134, F-10
Mullica Hill — L-3
National Park — K-3
Neptune — H-8
Neshanic — F-5
Netcong — C-5
New Brunswick — F-6
New Egypt — J-6
New Gretna — L-7
New Milford — Pg. 126, F-6
New Providence — E-6
New Rochelle — Pg. 126, G-5
Newark — D-7
  Vicinity — Pg. 127, K-3
Newfield — M-4
Newfoundland — B-6
Newton — B-5
North Arlington — Pg. 127, J-4
North Bergen — Pg. 127, J-6
North Caldwell — Pg. 126, G-2
North Cape May — Q-4
North Dennis — P-4
North Haledon — C-7
  Vicinity — Pg. 126, F-3
North Wildwood — Q-5
Northfield — N-6
Northvale — Pg. 126, D-7
Norwood — C-9
  Vicinity — Pg. 126, D-7
Nutley — D-8
  Vicinity — Pg. 127, H-3
Oakland — Pg. 126, D-2
Oaklyn — Pg. 134, F-7
Ocean City — N-6
Ocean Gate — J-8
Oceanport — G-8
Ogdensburg — B-5
Old Bridge — F-7
Old Tappan — Pg. 126, D-6
Oldwick — E-5
Oradell — Pg. 126, F-6
Orange — D-7
  Vicinity — Pg. 127, K-2
Oxford — D-4
Palisades Park — Pg. 126, H-6
Palmyra — Pg. 134, D-7
Paramus — Pg. 126, F-5
Park Ridge — Pg. 126, D-5
Parry — Pg. 134, D-9
Parsippany-Troy Hill — D-6
Passaic — D-8
  Vicinity — Pg. 126, H-4
Paterson — C-7
  Vicinity — Pg. 126, F-3
Paulsboro — K-2
Peapack — E-5
Pemberton — J-5
Penns Grove — L-2
Pennsauken — Pg. 134, E-7
Pennsville — L-1
Pennville — M-5
Penny Pot — M-5
Pequannock — Pg. 126, F-1
Perth Amboy — F-7
  Vicinity — Pg. 127, Q-2

NEW JERSEY

Phillipsburg E-3
Pine Beach .... Pg. 126, H-1
Pine Grove ... Pg. 134, G-10
Pine Hill K-4
Pitman L-3
Pittstown E-4
Plainfield E-6
Plainsboro F-6
Pleasantville N-6
Pole Tavern L-3
Pomona M-6
Pompton Lakes C-7
  Vicinity .... Pg. 126, D-1
Pompton Plains C-7
  Vicinity .... Pg. 126, E-1
Port Elizabeth N-4
Port Norris P-4
Port Reading .... Pg. 127, P-2
Port Republic M-6
Princeton G-5
Princeton Jct. G-6
Prospect Park C-8
Pt. Pleasant H-8
Pt. Pleasant Beach H-8
Quinton M-2
Rahway E-7
  Vicinity .... Pg. 127, N-2
Ramsey .... Pg. 126, C-4
Raritan E-5
Readington E-5
Reaville F-5
Red Bank G-8
Red Lion K-5
Ridgefield B-7
Ridgefield Park . Pg. 126, H-6
Ridgewood B-7
  Vicinity .... Pg. 126, E-4
Ringwood B-7
  Vicinity .... Pg. 126, B-2
Rio Grande Q-4
River Edge . Pg. 126, F-5
River Vale B-6
  Vicinity .... Pg. 126, E-6
Riverdale C-7
Riverside J-4
Riverton J-4
  Vicinity .... Pg. 134, D-8
Robertsville G-7
Rochelle Park . Pg. 126, F-5
Rockaway C-6
Rockleigh . Pg. 126, E-6
Rocky Hill F-5
Roosevelt F-6
Roseland .... Pg. 127, H-1
Roselle E-7
  Vicinity .... Pg. 127, M-2
Roselle Park E-7
  Vicinity .... Pg. 127, M-2
Ross Corners B-5
Rumson G-8
Runnemede K-4
  Vicinity .... Pg. 134, G-7
Rutherford .... Pg. 127, H-4
Saddle Brook . Pg. 126, G-4
Saddle River C-8
  Vicinity .... Pg. 126, D-5
Salem M-1
Sayreville F-7
Sea Isle City P-5
Seabrook M-3
Seaside Heights J-8
Seaside Park J-8
Seaville P-5
Secaucus .... Pg. 127, J-5
Sewaren .... Pg. 127, P-2
Sharptown L-2
Shiloh M-2
Ship Bottom L-8
Shrewsbury G-8
Silverton J-8
Smithburg H-7
Smithville M-6
Somerdale F-4
Somers Pt. N-6
Somerville F-5
South Amboy F-7
South Brunswick G-6
South Dennis P-5
South Hackensack
  .... Pg. 126, G-5
South Orange . Pg. 127, K-2
South Plainfield F-7
South River F-7
South Toms River J-7
Sparta C-5
Speedwell K-6
Spotswood F-6
Spring Lakes Heights .. H-8
Spring Mills E-3
Springdale J-4
  Vicinity .... Pg. 134, G-8
Springfield . Pg. 127, L-1
Stanhope C-5
Stockholm B-6
Stockton F-4
Stone Harbor Q-5
Stratford K-4
Summit D-7
Surf City L-8
Sussex A-5
Swedesboro K-2
Tabernacle K-5
Tavistock .... Pg. 134, G-8
Teaneck .... Pg. 126, G-6
Tenafly C-8
  Vicinity .... Pg. 126, F-7
Teterboro .... Pg. 126, H-6
Tinton Falls G-8
Toms River J-7
Totowa C-7
  Vicinity .... Pg. 126, G-3
Trenton G-5

Tuckerton L-7
Tuttles Cor. B-5
Union Beach F-8
  Vicinity .... Pg. 127, L-2
Union City D-8
  Vicinity .... Pg. 127, K-5
Upper Saddle River
  .... Pg. 126, C-4
Ventnor City N-6
Vernon B-5
Verona .... Pg. 127, H-2
Villas Q-4
Vineland M-4
Waldwick C-8
  Vicinity .... Pg. 126, D-4
Wallington .... Pg. 126, H-4
Wanaque B-7
  Vicinity .... Pg. 126, D-1
Waretown K-8
Warren E-6
Warren Grove K-7
Washington D-4
Washington Crossing F-4
Watchung E-6
Wayne C-7
  Vicinity .... Pg. 126, F-2
Weehawken . Pg. 127, K-5
Welchville L-2
Wells Mills K-7
Wenonah K-3
West Caldwell . Pg. 126, H-1
West Cape May Q-4
West Long Branch G-8
West Milford B-6
West New York D-8
  Vicinity .... Pg. 127, K-6
West Orange D-7
  Vicinity .... Pg. 127, J-2
West Patterson C-7
  Vicinity .... Pg. 126, G-3
West Portal E-4
Westfield E-7
Westville K-3
  Vicinity .... Pg. 134, G-6
Westwood C-8
  Vicinity .... Pg. 126, E-6
Weymouth M-6
Wharton C-6
White Horse H-5
Whitehouse E-5
Whitesboro Q-5
Whitesville H-7
Wildwood Q-5
Wildwood Crest Q-5
Williamstown L-4
Winslow L-4
Wood Ridge . Pg. 126, H-5
Woodbine P-4
Woodbridge F-7
  Vicinity .... Pg. 127, P-2
Woodbury K-3
Woodbury Heights K-3
Woodcliff Lake . Pg. 126, D-5
Woodlynne .... Pg. 134, F-7
Woods Tavern L-2
Woodstown L-2
Woodsville G-4
Wrightstown J-6
Yardville H-5

NEW MEXICO
Page 62

Population: 1,302,894
Capital: Santa Fe
Land Area: 121,335 sq. mi.

Abbott C-5
Abeytas E-3
Abiquiu C-3
Abo E-4
Alameda D-3
Alamo E-2
Alamogordo G-4
Albuquerque D-3
Alcalde C-3
Algodones D-3
Alma G-1
Alto B-4
Amalia B-4
Ambrosia Lake D-2
Amistad E-7
Anapra J-3
Ancho F-4
Angus G-4
Animas J-1
Antelope Wells J-1
Apache Creek F-1
Aqua Fria E-6
Arabela E-6
Aragon F-1
Arch E-7
Archuleta B-2
Armijo D-3
Arrey H-2
Arroyo Hondo B-4
Arroyo Seco B-4
Artesia G-6
Atoka H-6
Aztec B-2
Bayard H-2
Beklabito B-1
Belen E-3
Bellview D-7
Bent G-4
Berino J-3
Bernal D-4
Bernalillo D-3
Bernardo E-3
Bingham F-4
Black Lake C-5

Black River Village H-6
Black Rock D-2
Blanco B-2
Blanco Trading Post .. C-2
Bloomfield B-2
Bluewater D-2
Bosque Farms E-3
Brazos B-3
Broadview E-7
Buckhorn G-1
Bueyeros C-6
Caballo G-3
Canjilon B-3
Canon C-3
Canon Plaza B-4
Capitan F-4
Caprock F-7
Capulin B-6
Carlsbad H-6
Carlsbad Caverns H-6
Carrizozo F-4
Causey F-7
Cebolla B-3
Cebolleta D-2
Cebolletita D-2
Cedar Crest D-4
Cedar Hill B-2
Cedarvale E-4
Central H-2
Cerro B-4
Chacon C-5
Chama B-3
Chamberino J-3
Chamizal F-3
Chaparral J-4
Chilili D-4
Chimayo C-4
Cimarron B-5
Clapham C-6
Claunch F-4
Clayton B-7
Cleveland C-4
Cliff G-1
Clines Corners D-4
Cloudcroft G-4
Clovis E-7
Cochiti Lake C-3
Columbus J-2
Conchas D-6
Coolidge D-1
Corona E-4
Costilla B-4
Cotton City J-1
Counselors C-2
Coyote C-3
Coyote Canyon C-1
Crossroads F-7
Crownpoint D-1
Cruzville F-1
Crystal C-1
Cuba C-3
Cuchillo G-3
Cuervo D-6
Cundiyo C-4
Datil F-2
Deming H-2
Derry H-3
Des Moines B-6
Dexter G-6
Dilia D-5
Domingo D-3
Dona Ana H-3
Dora F-7
Dulce B-3
Dunken G-5
Duran E-5
Dwyer H-2
Eagle Nest B-5
Edgewood D-4
El Morro D-2
El Paso Gap J-5
El Porvenir C-4
El Rito C-4
El Vado B-3
Elephant Butte G-3
Elida F-6
Elk G-5
Elk Silver G-4
Elkins E-6
Embudo C-4
Encino E-5
Endee D-7
Engle G-3
Ensenada B-3
Escobosa D-4
Escondida F-3
Espanola C-4
Estancia E-4
Eunice H-7
Fairacres H-3
Farley B-6
Farmington B-1
Fence Lake E-1
Flora Vista B-2
Floyd E-7
Folsom B-6
Forrest E-5
Fort Stanton G-4
Fort Sumner E-6
Fort Wingate D-1
Frijoles C-3
Gage H-2
Galisteo D-4
Gallina C-3
Gallinas D-5
Gallup D-1
Gamerco D-1
Garfield H-3
Gila H-1
Gladstone B-6
Glenrio D-7
Glenwood G-1

Golden D-4
Grady D-7
Gran Quivira E-4
Grants D-2
Greenfield G-6
Grenville B-6
Guadalupita C-5
Hachita J-2
Hagerman G-6
Hanover H-2
Hatch H-3
Hayden C-7
Hernandez C-4
High Rolls G-4
Hilburn City G-7
Hillsboro G-2
Hobbs H-7
Holman C-4
Hondo G-5
House E-6
Humble City G-7
Hurley H-2
Jal H-7
Jarales E-3
Jemez Springs C-3
Jicarilla F-4
Kenna E-6
Kingston H-2
Kirtland B-1
Knowles G-7
La Cienega E-6
La Cueva C-5
La Jara C-3
La Joya E-3
La Luz G-4
La Madera C-4
La Mesa J-3
La Mesilla H-3
La Plata B-1
La Puente B-3
La Union J-3
Laborcita G-4
Laguna E-3
Lake Arthur G-6
Lake Valley C-2
Lamy D-4
Las Cruces H-3
Las Nutrias E-3
Las Palomas G-3
Las Vegas C-5
Ledoux C-5
Lemitar F-3
Lincoln G-5
Lindrith C-3
Lingo F-7
Loco Hills G-6
Logan D-7
Lordsburg H-1
Los Alamos C-4
Los Cerrillos D-4
Los Chavez D-3
Los Lunas E-3
Los Ojos B-3
Los Padillas D-3
Loving H-6
Lovington G-7
Luis Lopez F-3
Luna F-1
Madrid D-4
Magdalena F-3
Malaga H-6
Maljamar G-6
Manuelito D-1
Manzano E-4
Maxwell B-5
Mayhill G-5
McAlister E-6
McCartys D-2
McDonald F-6
Melrose E-5
Mentmore D-1
Mesa E-6
Mescalero G-4
Mesita D-3
Mesquite H-3
Mexican Springs C-1
Miami C-5
Miera D-5
Milan D-2
Mills D-6
Milnesand F-7
Mimbres H-2
Mineral Hill D-4
Mogollon G-1
Monero B-3
Montezuma C-5
Monticello G-3
Montoya D-6
Monument H-7
Mora C-5
Moriarty D-4
Mosquero D-6
Mountainair E-4
Mt. Dora B-6
Mule Creek G-1
Nadine H-7
Nageezi C-2
Nara Visa C-7
Naschitti C-1
Navajo D-1
Newcomb C-1
Newkirk D-6
Ocate C-5
Oil Center H-7
Ojo Caliente C-4
Ojo Feliz C-5
Old Horse Springs F-2
Omega E-2

Organ H-3
Orogrande H-4
Oscuro F-4
Paguate D-2
Paraje D-2
Pastura E-5
Pecos D-4
Pena Blanca D-3
Penasco C-4
Pep F-7
Peralta E-3
Pescado D-1
Picacho G-5
Pie Town E-2
Pine Lodge E-6
Pinon H-5
Pinos Altos H-1
Placita G-2
Placitas D-4
Pleasant Hill E-7
Pleasanton G-1
Pojoaque C-4
Portales E-7
Prewitt D-1
Pueblo D-4
Pueblo Bonito C-2
Puerto De Luna E-5
Punta E-4
Quay D-6
Quemado E-1
Questa B-4
Radium Springs H-3
Ragland E-6
Rainsville C-5
Ramah D-1
Ramon E-5
Ranchos De Taos B-4
Ranchvale E-7
Raton B-6
Rayado C-5
Red Hill F-1
Red River B-5
Red Rock H-1
Regina C-3
Reserve F-1
Rincon H-3
Rinconada C-4
Rio Rancho D-3
Riverside G-6
Rociada C-4
Rodeo J-1
Rogers F-7
Romeroville D-5
Roswell E-6
Rowe D-4
Roy C-6
Ruidoso G-4
Ruidoso Downs G-4
Rutherford B-3
Sabinal E-3
Sacramento H-4
Saint Vrain E-7
Salem H-3
Salt Lake E-1
San Acacia E-3
San Antonio F-3
San Antonio D-4
San Fidel D-2
San Ignacio C-4
San Jon D-7
San Juan H-2
San Lorenzo H-2
San Mateo D-2
San Miguel J-3
San Patricio G-4
San Rafael D-2
Santa Cruz C-4
Santa Fe D-4
Santa Rita H-2
Santa Rosa D-5
Sapello C-5
Sedan C-7
Sena D-5
Seneca B-7
Separ H-1
Seven Rivers H-6
Shadybrook C-4
Sheep Springs C-1
Shiprock B-1
Silver City H-2
Socorro F-3
Solano C-6
Springer B-5
Standing Rock D-1
Stanley D-4
Sunset G-5
Sunshine J-2
Sunspot H-4
Taiban E-6
Tajique E-4
Talpa C-4
Taos B-4
Tatum G-7
Terrero C-4
Tesuque C-4
Thoreau D-1
Three Rivers G-4
Tierra Amarilla B-3
Tierra Monte C-5
Tijeras D-3
Tinnie G-5
Tohatchi C-1
Tolar E-6
Tome E-3
Torreon C-3
Torreon E-4
Tres Piedras B-4
Tres Ritos C-5
Truchas C-4
Trujillo D-5
Truth or Consequences .. G-3
Tucumcari D-6

Tularosa G-4
Turley B-2
Turn F-4
Tyrone H-1
Ute Park B-5
Vado J-3
Valencia E-3
Vallecitos C-3
Valmora C-5
Variadero D-5
Vaughn E-5
Veguita E-3
Velarde C-4
Villanueva D-5
Virden H-1
Wagon Mound C-5
Watrous C-5
Weed G-5
Wheatland D-7
White Horse C-2
White Oaks F-4
White Rock C-4
White Sands Missile Range
  .... H-4
Whites City H-6
Whitewater D-1
Willard E-4
Williamsburg G-3
Winston G-2
Yeso E-5
Youngsville C-3

NEW YORK

NEW YORK
Pages 58-61

Population: 17,558,072
Capital: Albany
Land Area: 47,377 sq. mi.

Adams F-12
Addison N-8
Afton M-13
Airmont .... Pg. 126, B-4
Akron K-18
Albany K-18
Albion H-6
Alden K-5
Alexander K-5
Alexandria Bay D-12
Alfred M-7
Allegany M-7
Almond M-7
Altamont K-18
Altmar G-12
Amagansett C-9
Amenia O-19
Ames K-16
Amherst .... Pg. 94, C-5
Amityville .... Pg. 129, N-16
Amsterdam J-18
Andes M-16
Andover N-7
Angelica M-6
Angola L-3
Angola-on-the-Lake L-3
  Vicinity .... Pg. 94, K-1
Antwerp D-13
Apalachin N-12
Arcade L-5
Archville .... Pg. 126, B-8
Ardsley .... Pg. 126, D-9
Argyle H-20
Arkport N-7
Arlington O-19
Armonk .... Pg. 128, C-11
Armor .... Pg. 94, H-4
Asharoken .. Pg. 128, G-17
Astoria .... Pg. 127, J-8
Athens M-19
Athol Springs .. Pg. 94, H-4
Atlantic Beach J-8
  Vicinity .... Pg. 129, Q-11
Attica K-5
Atwell G-15
Auburn K-10
Aurora K-10
Ava M-8
Avoca M-8
Avon E-5
Babylon E-5
  Vicinity .... Pg. 129, P-13
Bainbridge M-13
Baldwin E-5
  Vicinity .... Pg. 129, P-13
Baldwinsville J-11
Ballston Spa J-18
Balmville .... Pg. 126, B-6
Bardonia .... Pg. 126, B-6
Barker H-5
Barneveld H-14
Barnum Island Pg. 129, Q-13
Batavia K-5
Bath M-8
Bay Park .. Pg. 129, P-12
Bay Ridge .. Pg. 127, M-6
Bay Shore E-5
  Vicinity .... Pg. 129, M-19
Bay View .. Pg. 94, H-4
Bayberry J-11
Bayside .. Pg. 129, K-10
Bayville E-5
  Vicinity .... Pg. 129, H-14
Beach Ridge .. Pg. 94, B-1
Beacon A-3
Bedford B-3
  Vicinity .. Pg. 128, B-13
Bedford Hills .. Pg. 128, A-11
Bellevue .. Pg. 94, H-4
Bellmore .. Pg. 129, N-16
Belmont N-6
Bemus Pt. .. Pg. 127, N-2
Benson Hurst .. Pg. 127, N-7

Bergen J-6
Berkholtz .... Pg. 94, A-3
Bethpage D-5
  Vicinity .... Pg. 129, L-15
Big Flats N-9
Big Tree .... Pg. 94, H-5
Binghamton N-12
Black River E-13
Blasdell D-4
  Vicinity .... Pg. 94, G-4
Blauve .... Pg. 126, C-7
Bloomingburgh A-2
Bloomingdale C-18
Bloomington N-18
Blossom .... Pg. 94, F-7
Bolivar N-6
Boonville G-14
Bovson Bay J-11
Bowmansville .. Pg. 94, D-7
Brasher Falls B-16
Brentwood D-6
Brentwood .. Pg. 129, L-19
Brewerton J-11
Brewster B-4
Briarcliff Manor C-4
Bridgehampton C-9
Bridgewater K-14
Brighton .. Pg. 138, K-4
Brightwaters . Pg. 129, M-19
Broadalbin J-18
Brockport J-6
Brocton M-2
Bronx .... Pg. 126, G-9
Brooklyn .. Pg. 127, L-7
Brookville . Pg. 129, K-14
Brownsville E-12
Brushton B-16
Buchanan B-3
Buffalo K-4
  Vicinity .... Pg. 94
Burdett M-10
Burke B-17
Cairo M-18
Caledonia K-7
Calverton D-7
Cambridge J-20
Camden H-13
Camillus J-11
Canajoharie K-16
Canandaigua K-8
Canarsie .. Pg. 127, M-8
Canaseraga M-7
Canastota J-13
Candor M-11
Canisteo M-7
Canton C-14
Cape Vincent C-11
Carnegie .... Pg. 94, H-4
Carthage E-13
Cassadaga M-2
Castile K-13
Castleton Corners
  .... Pg. 127, N-4
Castleton-on-Hudson .. L-18
Castorland F-13
Cato J-10
Catskill M-19
Cattaraugus M-4
Cayuga K-10
Cayuga Heights L-11
Cazenovia K-13
Cedarhurst .. Pg. 129, P-11
Celoron N-2
Center Moriches D-7
Center Port .. Pg. 129, H-17
Centereach D-6
Central Islip . Pg. 129, K-20
Central Nyack .. Pg. 126, C-7
Central Square H-12
Central Valley B-3
Champlain A-19
Chappaqua .. Pg. 126, A-9
Chateaugay A-17
Chatham M-19
Chaumont E-12
Cheektowaga .. Pg. 94, E-6
Chelsea .. Pg. 127, N-3
Cherry Creek M-3
Cherry Valley K-16
Chester B-2
Chili Center .. Pg. 138, K-3
Chippawa (Canada)
Chittenango J-13
Churchville J-7
Clarence Center J-4
Clarkstown .. Pg. 126, B-6
Claverack M-19
Clayton D-12
Clayville J-14
Cleveland H-13
Clifton Heights .. Pg. 94, H-3
Clifton Knolls K-18
Clifton Springs K-9
Clinton J-14
Clintondale O-18
Clyde J-10
Cobleskill K-17
Cochocton L-8
Cohoes K-19
Cold Brook H-15
Cold Spring J-11
Coldspring Harbor
  .... Pg. 129, J-16
College Point .. Pg. 127, J-9
Colonie K-18
Commack .. Pg. 129, K-18
Coney Island .. Pg. 127, N-7
Constableville G-14
Constantia H-12
Cooperstown K-15

Copenhagen F-13
Copiague .... Pg. 129, N-17
Coram D-6
Corfu K-5
Corinth H-18
Corning N-9
Cornwall-on-Hudson .. A-3
Cortland L-11
County Knolls J-18
Cove Neck .. Pg. 129, J-15
Coxsackie M-19
Crescent Beach .. Pg. 138, F-3
Crescent Park (Canada)
  .... Pg. 94, E-2
Crittenden .. Pg. 138, K-3
Croghan F-14
Croton-on-Hudson .. B-3
Crystal Beach (Canada)
  .... Pg. 94, F-1
Cuba N-5
Cutchogue C-8
Dannemora B-18
Dansville L-7
DeRuyter K-13
DeWitt J-11
Deer Park D-5
  Vicinity .... Pg. 129, L-18
Deferiet E-13
Delanson K-17
Delevan L-5
Delmar M-15
Depew K-4
  Vicinity .... Pg. 94, E-6
Deposit N-14
Derby K-2
  Vicinity .. Pg. 94, K-2
Dexter E-12
Dobbs Ferry C-3
  Vicinity .. Pg. 126, D-8
Dolgeville J-16
Dongan Hills .. Pg. 127, N-4
Dover Plains O-19
Dresden L-9
Duells Corners .. Pg. 94, H-6
Dundee L-9
Dunkirk M-2
East Amherst .. Pg. 94, B-2
East Aurora K-4
East Bloomfield K-8
  Vicinity .. Pg. 94, K-5
East Glenville J-18
East Hamburg .. Pg. 94, H-6
East Hampton C-9
East Hills .. Pg. 129, K-13
East Meadow D-4
  Vicinity .. Pg. 129, M-14
East Moriches D-7
East New York .. Pg. 127, M-8
East Northport D-5
  Vicinity .. Pg. 129, J-17
East Penfield .. Pg. 138, J-7
East Quogue D-8
East Randolph N-3
East Rochester J-8
  Vicinity .. Pg. 138, J-6
East Rockaway Pg. 129, P-12
East Seneca .. Pg. 94, F-6
East View .... Pg. 126, C-9
Eastchester .. Pg. 126, E-9
Eatons Neck C-7
Eatons Neck .. Pg. 128, H-17
Ebenezer .. Pg. 94, F-6
Echota .... Pg. 94, A-2
Eden L-4
Eden Valley .. Pg. 94, K-4
Edgemere .. Pg. 129, Q-11
Edgewater .. Pg. 94, B-3
Edwards D-14
Eggertsville .. Pg. 94, C-5
Elba J-6
Elbridge J-11
Ellenville H-17
Ellicott .... Pg. 94, H-2
Ellicott Heights .. Pg. 94, H-7
Ellicottville M-4
Ellisburg F-12
Elma K-4
  Vicinity .. Pg. 94, F-7
Elma Center .... Pg. 94, F-7
Elmira Hts. N-10
Elmont .... Pg. 129, N-12
Elmsford .. Pg. 126, C-9
Elsers Corners .. Pg. 94, A-7
Elwood .... Pg. 129, J-17
Endicott N-12
Endwell N-12
Erie Beach (Canada)
  .... Pg. 94, E-3
Esperance K-17
Evans .... Pg. 94, K-2
Evans Mills E-12
Fabius K-12
Fair Haven H-10
Fairport J-8
  Vicinity .. Pg. 138, K-6
Falconer N-3
Farmingdale .. Pg. 129, M-16
Farnham L-3
Fayetteville J-12
Fernwood H-19
Ferry Village .. Pg. 94, C-3
Fillmore M-6
Firthcliffe A-3
Fishkill A-3
Flatbush .... Pg. 127, M-7
Fleischmanns L-16
Floral Park .. Pg. 129, M-11
Florida B-2
Flower Hill .. Pg. 129, K-12
Flushing .... Pg. 127, K-9
Fonda J-17

NEW YORK

Forest Hills .... Pg. 127, L-9
Forest Lawn .... Pg. 138, F-5
Forestville M-3
Fort Ann G-19
Fort Edward H-19
Fort Erie (Canada) Pg. 94, E-3
Fort Erie North (Canada)
.... Pg. 94, D-3
Fort Johnson J-17
Fort Plain K-16
Fort Salonga ... Pg. 128, H-18
Frankfort J-15
Franklin M-15
Franklinville M-5
Freeport E-4
Vicinity .... Pg. 129, P-14
Frewsburg N-3
Friendship M-6
Fulton H-11
Fultonville K-17
Gainesville L-6
Galway J-18
Gang Mills M-8
Garden City .. Pg. 129, M-12
Gardenville ..... Pg. 94, F-6
Gate .... Pg. 138, J-2
Geneseo K-7
Geneva K-9
Getzville .... Pg. 94, B-6
Gilbertsville L-14
Glasco N-18
Glen Cove D-4
Vicinity .... Pg. 129, J-12
Glen Head .. Pg. 129, K-13
Glen Park E-12
Glenham A-3
Glens Falls H-19
Gloversville J-17
Goldens Bridge B-4
Goshen B-2
Gouverneur D-14
Gowanda M-3
Grand View Heights
.... Pg. 138, F-3
Grandview-on-Hudson
.... Pg. 126, C-8
Grandyle Village . Pg. 94, C-2
Granville G-20
Great Kills .... Pg. 127, P-4
Great Neck D-4
Vicinity .... Pg. 129, K-11
Greece J-7
Vicinity .... Pg. 138, G-2
Green Island K-19
Green Lawn ... Pg. 129, J-17
Green Point ... Pg. 127, K-7
Greenburgh .. Pg. 126, D-9
Greene M-13
Greenport C-9
Greenwich J-20
Greenwood Lake B-2
Griffins Mills .. Pg. 94, J-7
Groton J-11
Hadley H-19
Hagaman J-18
Halesite ..... Pg. 129, H-16
Hamburg L-4
Vicinity .... Pg. 94, J-5
Hamilton K-14
Hammond C-13
Hammondsport M-8
Hampton Bays D-8
Hancock O-15
Hannibal H-10
Harriman B-2
Harris Hill ... Pg. 94, C-7
Harrison C-4
Vicinity .... Pg. 128, F-11
Harrisville E-14
Hastings-On-Hudson
.... Pg. 126, E-8
Hauppage .... Pg. 129, K-19
Haverstraw B-3
Haviland O-19
Hawthorne ... Pg. 126, B-10
Hempstead E-4
Hempstead ... Pg. 129, N-13
Herkimer K-15
Hermon C-14
Herrings E-13
Heuvelton C-14
Hewlett Bay Park
.... Pg. 129, P-12
Hewlett Harbor Pg. 129, P-12
Hicksville D-5
Vicinity .... Pg. 129, L-16
Highland O-18
Highland Falls B-3
Highland Mills B-3
Highland-on-the-Lake
.... Pg. 94, J-2
Hillburn .... Pg. 126, A-6
Hillcrest .... Pg. 126, A-6
Hillside Lake P-19
Hilton H-7
Vicinity .... Pg. 138, F-1
Hobart M-16
Hoffman .... Pg. 94, A-5
Holbrook D-6
Holcomb K-8
Holland L-5
Holland Patent H-14
Holley J-6
Homer L-11
Honeoye Falls K-7
Hoosick Falls J-20
Hornell M-7
Horseheads N-10
Houghton M-6
Hudson M-19
Hudson Falls H-19
Hugenot Park .. Pg. 127, Q-3

Huguenot .... Pg. 127, Q-2
Hunter M-17
Huntington D-5
Vicinity .... Pg. 129, J-16
Huntington Sta. D-5
Hurley O-18
Hyde Park O-18
Ilion J-15
Inwood ...... Pg. 129, P-11
Interlaken L-10
Irondequoit ... Pg. 138, H-4
Irvington .... Pg. 126, D-8
Island Park .. Pg. 129, Q-12
Islip D-6
Ithaca M-11
Jamaica ..... Pg. 129, N-11
Jamesport C-8
Jamestown N-3
Jefferson Hts M-18
Jefferson Valley B-4
Jeffersonville O-15
Jericho D-5
Vicinity .... Pg. 129, L-14
Jerusalem Corners
.... Pg. 94, K-1
Jewittville ... Pg. 94, J-6
Johnson City N-12
Johnstown J-17
Jones Island .. Pg. 129, Q-14
Jordan J-11
Keeseville C-19
Kenmore K-3
Vicinity .... Pg. 94, C-4
Kensington .. Pg. 129, L-12
Kerhonkson O-17
Keuka Park L-9
Kinderhook M-19
Kings Park ... Pg. 129, J-19
Kings Point .. Pg. 129, K-11
Kingston N-18
Kiryas Joel B-2
La Salle ...... Pg. 94, A-2
Lackawanna K-4
Vicinity .... Pg. 94, G-4
Lacona G-12
Ladentown ... Pg. 126, A-5
Lake Carmel A-4
Lake Erie Beach L-3
Lake George G-19
Lake Luzerne H-18
Lake Placid D-18
Lake Ronkonkoma ... D-6
Lakeview .... Pg. 94, J-3
Lakewood N-2
Lancaster L-4
Vicinity .... Pg. 94, E-7
Lansing L-11
Larchmont ... Pg. 126, F-10
Latham K-18
Lattington ... Pg. 129, H-13
Laurel Hollow . Pg. 129, J-15
Laurens L-15
Lawrence ... Pg. 129, Q-11
Leicester K-6
Levittown E-5
Vicinity .... Pg. 129, M-15
Lewiston J-3
Liberty O-16
Lido Beach ... Pg. 129, Q-13
Lima K-7
Lime Lake M-5
Limestone N-4
Lincoln Park N-18
Lindenhurst E-5
Vicinity .... Pg. 129, N-17
Lisle M-12
Little Falls J-16
Little Valley M-4
Liverpool J-11
Livingston Manor ... O-16
Livonia K-7
Lloyd Harbor D-5
Vicinity .... Pg. 129, H-15
Lloyd Neck ... Pg. 128, H-16
Lockport J-4
Locksley Park .. Pg. 94, H-3
Locust Grove . Pg. 129, K-15
Locust Valley Pg. 129, J-13
Lodi L-10
Long Beach E-5
Vicinity .... Pg. 129, Q-12
Long Island City Pg. 127, K-7
Lorenz Pk M-19
Lowville F-14
Lynbrook .... Pg. 129, P-12
Vicinity .... Pg. 94, A-2
Lyndonville H-5
Lyons J-9
Lyons Falls G-14
Macedon J-8
Machias M-5
Madison K-14
Mahopac B-4
Malone A-17
Malverne .... Pg. 129, N-12
Mamaroneck C-4
Vicinity .... Pg. 126, E-10
Manchester J-8
Manhasset ... Pg. 129, K-12
Manhattan ... Pg. 127, J-7
Manlius J-12
Mannsville F-12
Manorhaven .. Pg. 129, K-11
Marathon M-12
Marcellus J-11
Margaretville N-16
Mariboro O-18
Martinsville .. Pg. 94, B-5
Massapequa E-6
Vicinity .... Pg. 129, N-15
Massapequa Park
.... Pg. 129, N-16

Massena B-15
Mastic D-7
Mastic Beach D-7
Matinecock .. Pg. 129, J-14
Mattituck C-8
Mattydale J-11
Maybrook A-2
Mayfield M-2
Mayville M-2
McGraw L-12
Meadow Island Pg. 129, Q-14
Mechanicville K-19
Medford D-6
Medina J-5
Melville .... Pg. 129, L-16
Menands K-19
Meridian J-11
Merrick ..... Pg. 129, P-14
Merriewold Lake B-2
Mexico H-11
Middle Hope P-18
Middleburgh L-17
Middleport J-5
Middletown A-2
Middleville L-15
Milford L-15
Mill Neck .... Pg. 129, H-14
Millbrook O-19
Millersport ... Pg. 94, A-7
Millerton N-19
Millport M-10
Milton O-18
Mineola .... Pg. 129, M-13
Minetto H-11
Mineville E-19
Minoa J-12
Mohawk B-2
Monroe B-2
Monsey C-3
Vicinity .... Pg. 126, B-5
Montauk A-2
Montgomery A-2
Monticello P-16
Montour Falls M-10
Mooers A-19
Moravia L-11
Morris L-15
Morristown C-13
Morrisville K-13
Mount Ivy ... Pg. 126, A-6
Mount Kisco B-4
Vicinity .... Pg. 128, B-11
Mount Morris L-7
Mount Pleasant Pg. 126, C-9
Mount Vernon D-4
Vicinity .... Pg. 126, F-9
Mt. Vernon ... Pg. 94, H-3
Munnsville J-13
Muttontown .. Pg. 129, K-14
Nanuet O-17
Napanoch O-17
Naples L-8
Nashville .... Pg. 94, A-4
Nassau L-19
Nelliston J-16
New Berlin L-14
New Brighton . Pg. 127, M-5
New Cassel ... Pg. 129, M-14
New Dorp .... Pg. 127, P-4
New Dorp Beach Pg. 127, P-4
New Hartford J-14
New Hempstead Pg. 126, A-5
New Hyde Park Pg. 129, M-12
New Paltz O-18
New Rochelle D-4
Vicinity .... Pg. 126, F-10
New Suffolk C-9
New York City E-3
Vic. .... Pg. 126-129
New York Mills J-14
Newark J-9
Newark Valley M-12
Newburgh ... A-3,P-18
Newfane H-4
Newport H-15
Niagara Falls J-3
Vicinity .... Pg. 94, A-2
Niagara Falls (Canada)
.... Pg. 94, A-1
Nichols N-11
Norfolk B-15
North Bailey .. Pg. 94, C-4
North Boston .. Pg. 94, K-6
North Chili .. Pg. 138, J-1
North Collins L-3
North Evans .. Pg. 94, J-3
North Greece Pg. 138, G-2
North Haven C-9
North Hills .. Pg. 129, L-12
North Hornell M-7
North New Hyde Park
.... Pg. 129, M-12
North Sea D-8
North Syracuse J-11
North Tarrytown Pg. 126, B-8
North Tonawanda ... J-4
Vicinity .... Pg. 94, B-4
Northville H-17
Norwich L-13
Norwich .... Pg. 129, J-14
Norwood B-15
Noyack C-9
Nunda L-6
Nyack C-3
Vicinity .... Pg. 126, B-7
Oak Beach ... Pg. 129, P-19
Oakfield J-5
Ocean Beach E-6
Oceanside ... Pg. 129, P-13
Odessa M-10
Ogden Center Pg. 138, H-1
Ogdensburg B-13

Olcott H-4
Old Bethpage Pg. 129, L-16
Old Brookville Pg. 129, K-13
Old Forge M-14
Old Westbury Pg. 129, K-13
Olean N-5
Oneida J-13
Oneida Castle J-13
Oneonta M-15
Orange Lake A-3
Orangeburg .. Pg. 126, D-7
Orangetown .. Pg. 126, C-6
Orchard Park K-4
Vicinity .... Pg. 94, H-6
Oriskany J-14
Oriskany Falls J-14
Ossining C-4
Oswego N-11
Otego M-14
Otisville A-1
Ovid L-10
Oxford M-13
Oyster Bay ... Pg. 129, J-14
Oyster Bay Cove Pg. 129, J-15
Ozone Park .. Pg. 127, L-9
Painted Post N-9
Palatine Bridge K-16
Palisades .... Pg. 126, D-8
Palmyra J-8
Panama N-2
Parish H-12
Parma Center . Pg. 138, F-1
Parma Corners Pg. 138, G-1
Patchin .... Pg. 94, K-6
Patchoque D-6
Pawling B-3
Peach Haven .. Pg. 94, A-3
Pearl River C-3
Vicinity .... Pg. 126, C-6
Peconic C-8
Peekskill B-3
Pelham ..... Pg. 126, F-9
Pelham Manor Pg. 126, G-9
Pendleton .... Pg. 94, A-6
Penfield .... Pg. 138, J-6
Penfield Center Pg. 138, H-7
Penn Yan L-9
Perry L-6
Perrysburg M-3
Peru C-19
Phelps K-9
Philadelphia E-13
Philmont M-19
Phoenix H-11
Piermont .... Pg. 126, C-8
Pike L-6
Pine Bush P-17
Pine Hill N-17
Pine Plains N-19
Pinehurst ... Pg. 94, J-3
Pittsford J-8
Vicinity .... Pg. 138, K-5
Plainview D-5
Plandome Manor
.... Pg. 129, K-11
Plattsburgh B-19
Pleasantville B-4
Pocantico Hill . Pg. 126, B-9
Poestenkill K-20
Point Abino (Canada)
.... Pg. 94, E-1
Poland H-15
Pomona B-3
Port Byron J-10
Port Chester . Pg. 128, F-12
Port Dickinson N-13
Port Ewen N-18
Port Henry E-19
Port Jefferson C-6
Port Jervis B-1
Port Leyden G-14
Port Richmond Pg. 127, M-3
Port Washington
.... Pg. 129, K-12
Port Washington North
.... Pg. 129, K-12
Portville N-5
Potsdam B-15
Poughkeepsie O-19
Pound Ridge ... Pg. 128, B-14
Prospect H-14
Pulaski G-12
Queens ..... Pg. 127, K-9
Queens Village Pg. 129, M-11
Quogue D-8
Ramapo .... Pg. 126, A-3
Randolph N-3
Ransomville J-4
Rapids .... Pg. 94, A-7
Ravena L-18
Red Creek H-10
Red Hook N-19
Red Oaks Mill O-19
Remsen H-15
Rensselaer L-19
Rensselaer Falls C-14
Rhinebeck N-19
Richburg N-6
Richfield Springs ... K-15
Richmond Hill . Pg. 127, L-9
Richmondville L-17
Richville C-14
Ridge D-7
Ridgeway (Canada)
.... Pg. 94, E-1
Rigney Bluff . Pg. 138, K-3
Riverdale ... Pg. 126, H-7
Riverhead D-8
Riverside N-9
Tarrytown B-4
Vicinity .... Pg. 126, C-8
Rochester J-7
Vicinity .... Pg. 138

Rockville Center
.... Pg. 129, N-13
Rocky Pt. C-7
Roessleville K-18
Rome J-13
Roosevelt ... Pg. 129, N-14
Rosendale N-18
Roslyn ..... Pg. 129, K-12
Roslyn Harbor Pg. 129, K-13
Roslyn Hts. .. Pg. 129, L-13
Rossville .... Pg. 127, P-3
Round Lake K-19
Rouses Point A-19
Ruby N-18
Rushville K-9
Rye C-4
Vicinity .... Pg. 128, G-12
Rye Brook ... Pg. 128, F-12
Sackets Harbor F-12
Sag Harbor C-9
Saint Johnsville J-16
Saint Lawrence Park . D-12
Salamanca N-4
Salem H-20
Saltaire .... Pg. 129, P-20
San Remo ... Pg. 129, J-19
Sand Ridge J-11
Sands Point .. Pg. 129, J-11
Sandy Beach .. Pg. 94, B-2
Sandy Creek G-12
Saranac Lake D-18
Saratoga Springs ... J-18
Saugerties N-18
Savona M-9
Sawyer .... Pg. 94, A-4
Sayville D-6
Scarsdale C-4
Vicinity .... Pg. 126, E-10
Schaghticoke K-19
Schenectady K-18
Schenevus L-15
Schoharie L-17
Schuylerville J-19
Scotch Town A-2
Scotia K-18
Scottsville J-7
Scranton ... Pg. 94, H-4
Sea Cliff ... Pg. 129, J-12
Seaford .... Pg. 129, P-15
Searington .. Pg. 129, L-12
Selden D-6
Seneca Falls K-10
Sharon Springs K-16
Shelter Island C-9
Sherburne L-14
Sherman N-1
Sherrill J-13
Shirley D-7
Shortsville K-8
Sidney M-14
Silver Creek L-3
Silver Springs L-6
Sinclairville M-2
Skaneateles K-11
Sloan ...... Pg. 94, E-5
Sloatsburg C-2
Smithtown D-6
Smyrna L-13
Snyder .... Pg. 94, D-5
Snyder (Canada) Pg. 94, D-1
Sodus H-9
Sodus Point H-9
Solvay J-11
Sound Beach N-9
South Corning N-9
South Cortland L-11
South Fallsburg O-16
South Farmingdale
.... Pg. 129, M-16
South Glens Falls ... H-19
South Greece . Pg. 138, H-2
South Nyack .. Pg. 126, C-8
Southampton C-8
Southold C-8
Southport N-10
Sparkill .... Pg. 126, D-7
Speculator G-17
Spencer N-11
Spencerport J-7
Vicinity .... Pg. 138, H-1
Spring Valley C-3
Vicinity .... Pg. 126, B-6
Springbrook .. Pg. 94, G-7
Springfield Gdns.
.... Pg. 127, M-10
Springs C-9
Springville L-4
St. Johnsburg . Pg. 94, A-3
Stamford M-16
Stannards N-6
Star Lake D-15
Staten Island . Pg. 127, N-5
Stevensville (Canada)
.... Pg. 94, D-1
Stillwater K-19
Stony Brook C-6
Vicinity .... Pg. 128, H-20
Stony Pt. B-3
Stottville M-19
Success ..... Pg. 129, L-12
Suffern ..... Pg. 126, A-4
Swormville .. Pg. 94, B-7
Sylvan Beach J-13
Syosset .... Pg. 129, K-15
Syracuse K-12
Tall Man .... Pg. 126, A-5
Tannersville M-18
Tarrytown B-4
Vicinity .... Pg. 126, C-8
Theresa D-13

Thornwood ... Pg. 126, B-10
Thunder Bay (Canada)
.... Pg. 94, F-2
Ticonderoga F-19
Tillson O-18
Tivoli N-18
Tonawanda J-4
Vicinity .... Pg. 94, C-3
Town Line K-5
Tribes Hill J-17
Troy K-19
Trumansburg L-10
Tuckahoe D-8
Tully K-12
Tupper Lake D-17
Turin F-14
Tuxedo Park B-2
Vicinity .... Pg. 126, A-3
Unadilla M-14
Union Hill ... Pg. 138, G-7
Union Springs K-10
Uniondale ... Pg. 129, M-13
Unionville B-15
University Gardens
.... Pg. 129, L-11
Upper Brookville
.... Pg. 129, J-14
Upper Nyack . Pg. 126, B-7
Utica J-15
Valatie M-19
Valhalla .... Pg. 128, E-11
Valley Cottage . Pg. 126, B-7
Valley Falls J-20
Valley Stream . Pg. 129, N-11
Van Etten N-11
Vernon J-14
Verona J-12
Victor K-8
Victory J-10
Village of the Branch
.... Pg. 129, J-20
Viola ...... Pg. 126, A-5
Voorheesville L-18
Waddington B-14
Wading River C-7
Walden A-2
Wallkill A-2
Walton N-15
Walton Park B-2
Wampsville J-13
Wanakah ... Pg. 94, H-3
Wantagh .... Pg. 129, N-15
Wappinger Falls A-3
Warrensburg G-19
Warsaw K-6
Warwick B-2
Washingtonville A-2
Water Valley . Pg. 94, J-4
Waterford K-19
Waterloo K-9
Watertown E-13
Waterville K-14
Watervliet K-19
Watkins Glen M-10
Waverly N-11
Wayland L-7
Wayneport ... Pg. 138, K-7
Webster J-8
Vicinity .... Pg. 138, G-7
Webster Corners Pg. 94, H-6
Weedsport J-10
Wellington N-10
Wellsville N-6
Wendelville .. Pg. 94, A-5
Wesley Hills . Pg. 126, A-5
West Carthage F-13
West Chili ... Pg. 138, K-1
West End L-15
West Falls ... Pg. 94, J-6
West Greece . Pg. 138, G-2
West Plattsburgh ... B-19
West Point B-3
West Sand Lake L-19
West Seneca .. Pg. 94, F-5
West Walworth Pg. 138, J-7
West Webster . Pg. 138, G-5
West Winfield K-15
Westbury ... Pg. 129, M-13
Westfield M-2
Westhampton D-8
Westhampton Beach . D-8
Westmere K-17
Westons Mills N-5
Westport D-19
White Plains C-4
Vicinity .... Pg. 126, D-10
Whitehall G-20
Whitesboro J-14
Whitney Point M-12
Willard L-10
Williamsville K-4
Vicinity .... Pg. 94, D-6
Williston Park Pg. 129, L-13
Willow Brook . Pg. 127, N-4
Wilson H-4
Windom .... Pg. 94, G-5
Windsor N-13
Winthrop B-16
Witherbee E-19
Wolcott H-10
Woodbury .. Pg. 129, K-15
Woodhull N-8
Woodmere ... Pg. 129, P-11
Woodridge O-16
Woodsburg ... Pg. 129, Q-12
Woodstock N-18
Wurlitzer Park . Pg. 94, A-2
Wyadanch ... Pg. 129, L-17
Wyoming K-6
Yonkers D-3
Vicinity .... Pg. 126, E-8

Yorkshire L-5
Yorktown Hts B-4
Yorkville J-13
Youngstown H-3
Zena N-18

NORTH CAROLINA
Pages 64-65

Population: 5,881,766
Capital: Raleigh
Land Area: 48,843 sq. mi.

NORTH CAROLINA

Abbotsville E-10
Aberdeen D-8
Acre C-12
Ahoskie A-12
Albemarle D-7
Alexis ...... Pg. 95, A-1
Allen D-10
Allenton E-9
Andrews D-12
Apex .... Pg. 138, D-2
Arapahoe D-10
Archdale C-7
Arcola B-10
Arlington B-6
Asheboro C-7
Asheville B-4
Ashland B-12
Askin C-6
Aurora C-12
Avery Creek B-4
Avon C-14
Ayden C-11
Badin D-7
Bagley C-12
Bald Creek C-4
Baldwin B-5
Bandana C-4
Banner Elk B-5
Barclay Downs . Pg. 138, D-7
Barco A-13
Bat Cave B-4
Bath C-12
Battleboro B-11
Bayleaf .... Pg. 138, A-5
Bear Creek C-9
Beaufort D-13
Belgrade D-11
Belhaven C-12
Belmont D-6
Vicinity .... Pg. 95, E-2
Benson D-9
Bertha A-13
Bessemer City D-6
Bethel B-11
Bethel Hill A-9
Beulaville D-11
Biscoe D-8
Black Mtn. B-4
Bladenboro E-9
Blowing Rock B-5
Bolton E-10
Boone B-5
Bottom A-4
Bowdens D-10
Brandon Station Pg. 138, A-4
Brasstown D-2
Brevard B-4
Bridgeton D-12
Bridgewater C-5
Brookford C-6
Brooks Cross Roads . B-6
Brooksdale B-9
Browns Summit B-8
Brunswick F-10
Bryson City D-2
Bulade C-4
Bullock A-9
Bunn B-10
Burch B-6
Burgaw D-11
Burlington B-8
Burnsville C-4
Buxton C-14
Calypso D-10
Camden A-13
Cameron D-9
Candor D-8
Canto C-3
Canton B-4
Carolina Beach F-11
Carr B-8
Carrboro B-8
Cary C-9
Vicinity .... Pg. 138, D-3
Casville A-8
Cedar Creek D-10
Celo C-4
Centerville B-10
Chadbourn E-10
Chapel Hill B-8
Charlotte D-7
Vicinity .... Pg. 95
Cherokee C-2
Cherryville D-5
China Grove C-7
Chinquapin D-11
Chocowinity C-12
Churchland C-7
Cid C-7
Clemmons C-6
Clinton D-10
Cloverdale .. Pg. 138, E-5
Coinjock A-13
Colerain A-12
College B-9
Columbia B-13
Columbus C-4
Comfort D-11
Concord D-7

Conover C-6
Conway A-12
Corapeake A-12
Cornelius D-6
Council E-10
Cove Creek C-3
Cramerton . Pg. 95, E-1
Creedmoor B-9
Creswell B-13
Culberson D-1
Currie E-10
Dalton B-7
Darden B-12
Davidson C-6
Deep Gap B-5
Del Mar Beach E-12
Delway D-10
Derita ..... Pg. 95, C-7
Dillsboro D-3
Dixie ...... Pg. 95, F-3
Dobson B-7
Dortches B-10
Dudley D-10
Dunn D-9
Durham B-9
Vicinity .... Pg. 138, A-1
East Lake B-13
East Laport D-3
Eastwood D-8
Eden A-8
Edenhouse B-12
Edenton B-12
Edneyville B-4
Edward C-12
Ela D-3
Eldorado C-7
Elizabeth City A-13
Elizabethtown E-10
Elk Park B-4
Elkin B-6
Emerald Village Pg. 138, E-6
Emery D-8
Enfield B-11
Englehard C-13
Erwin D-9
Essex B-10
Ether C-8
Evergreen E-9
Fair Bluff E-9
Fairmont E-9
Faison D-10
Falls ...... Pg. 138, A-6
Farmville C-11
Fayetteville D-9
Flat Rock B-4
Fletcher B-4
Folkston E-11
Fontana Village D-2
Forest City D-5
Fountain C-11
Franklin D-2
Freeman E-10
Fremont C-10
Friendship .. Pg. 138, E-2
Frisco C-14
Fuquay-Varina C-9
Garner .... Pg. 138, E-5
Garysburg A-11
Gastonia D-6
Vicinity .... Pg. 95, D-1
Gates A-12
Genlee .... Pg. 138, C-3
Gilkey D-5
Glade Valley B-6
Glenview C-5
Glenwood C-5
Gneiss D-3
Godwin D-9
Gold Rock B-11
Goldsboro C-10
Goldston C-8
Gordonton B-9
Graingers C-11
Grandy A-13
Granite Falls C-5
Grantham D-10
Green Level . Pg. 138, D-1
Greenbrier Estates
.... Pg. 138, B-8
Greensboro B-8
Greenville C-11
Grifton C-11
Grissettown F-10
Guilford B-8
Halifax A-11
Hamlet D-8
Hampstead E-11
Harbinger B-14
Harmony B-6
Harrells E-10
Harrisburg D-7
Vicinity .... Pg. 95, C-14
Hatteras C-14
Hazelwood C-3
Heartsease B-11
Henderson B-10
Hendersonville B-4
Henrietta D-5
Hertford B-12
Hester B-9
Hickory C-6
Hickory Grove . Pg. 95, C-8
High Hampton D-3
High Point B-7
Hightowers B-8
Hill Crest B-5
Hillsborough B-9
Hiwassee D-2
Hoffman D-8
Holly Ridge E-11
Hollyville (Cash Corner) D-12

OHIO

Grove City K-4
Vicinity . . . Pg. 102, H-3
Groveport K-5
Vicinity . . . Pg. 102, J-6
Hamden M-6
Hamersville N-3
Hamilton L-1
Hamler F-3
Hanover J-6
Harlem . . . . Pg. 102, B-6
Harrisburg . . Pg. 102, K-1
Harrison M-1
Harrod H-3
Hartville H-8
Hayden . . . . Pg. 102, D-1
Hayesville G-7
Heath K-6
Hebron K-6
Hicksville F-1
Higginsport N-3
Hilliard J-4
Vicinity . . . Pg. 102, E-1
Hillsboro M-3
Hinckley . . . Pg. 101, H-2
Hiram F-9
Holgate F-2
Holland E-3
Hopedale J-9
Hubbard F-10
Huber Heights K-2
Huber Ridge . Pg. 102, C-6
Hudson . . . . Pg. 101, H-7
Huron E-6
Hyatts . . . . . Pg. 102, A-3
Independence
. . . . Pg. 101, F-4
Ironton O-6
Jackson M-5
Jackson Center H-3
Jacksonville L-7
Jamestown L-3
Jefferson E-9
Jeffersonville L-4
Jerome . . . . Pg. 102, B-3
Jeromesville G-7
Jewett J-9
Johnstown J-6
Junction City K-6
Kalida G-2
Kellys Island E-6
Kent F-8
Kenton H-3
Kettering K-2
Kileville . . . Pg. 102, C-1
Killbuck H-7
Kingston L-5
Kirkersville K-6
Kirtland Hills E-9
Lagrange F-7
Lakemore G-8
Lakeview H-3
Lakewood E-7
Vicinity . . . Pg. 101, C-1
Lancaster K-6
Laurelville L-5
Lebanon L-2
Leesburg M-3
Leetonia G-10
Leipsic G-3
Lewis Center Pg. 102, A-4
Lewisburg K-1
Lexington H-6
Liberty Center E-2
Lima G-2
Lincoln Heights
. . . . Pg. 100, B-4
Lindsey F-5
Linworth . . . Pg. 102, C-3
Lisbon G-10
Lithopolis . . Pg. 102, K-7
Lockbourne . . Pg. 102, K-4
Lockland . . . Pg. 100, B-4
Lodi G-7
Logan L-6
London K-4
Lorain E-6
Lordstown F-9
Loudonville H-6
Louisville G-9
Loveland M-2
Lowell L-8
Lowellville G-10
Luckey F-4
Lynchburg M-3
Lyndhurst . . Pg. 101, B-7
Lyons E-2
Macedonia H-8
Vicinity . . . Pg. 100, G-6
Madei . . . . . Pg. 100, C-4
Madeira M-2
Madison E-9
Magnolia H-8
Malta K-7
Malvern H-9
Manchester N-3
Mansfield H-6
Maple Heights
. . . . Pg. 101, E-5
Marble Cliff . Pg. 102, F-3
Marblehead E-5
Marietta L-8
Marimet . . . . Pg. 100, D-6
Marion H-4
Martins Ferry J-10
Martinsville L-3
Marysville J-4
Mason L-2
Massillon G-8
Maumee E-3
Mayfield Heights
. . . . Pg. 101, B-7
McArthur M-6
McClure F-3

McConnelsville L-7
McGuffey H-3
Mechanicsburg J-4
Medina F-7
Vicinity . . . Pg. 101, K-1
Mentor E-8
Mentor-on-the-Lake . . E-8
Metamora E-3
Miamisburg K-2
Middle Point G-2
Middleburg Hts
. . . . Pg. 101, F-2
Middleport M-7
Middletown L-1
Midvale H-8
Midway K-4
Milan F-6
Milford M-2
Milford Center J-4
Millersburg H-7
Millersport K-6
Millville L-1
Mineral City . . . . . . H—8
Minerva G-9
Minerva Park J-5
Vicinity . . . Pg. 102, D-4
Mingo Junction J-10
Minster H-2
Monroe L-2
Monroeville F-6
Montpelier E-1
Moraine K-2
Moreland Hills
. . . . Pg. 101, D-7
Morrow L-2
Mt. Air . . . . Pg. 102, B-3
Mt. Blanchard G-4
Mt. Gilead H-5
Mt. Healthy Pg. 100, B-3
Mt. Orab M-3
Mt. Sterling K-4
Mt. Vernon H-6
Mt. Victory H-4
Mudsock . . . Pg. 102, E-1
Murray City L-7
Napoleon F-2
Navarre G-8
Nelsonville L-6
Nevada H-4
New Albany Pg. 102, C-7
New Boston N-5
New Bremen H-2
New Carlisle K-3
New Concord K-7
New Holland L-4
New Knoxville H-2
New Lebanon K-1
New Lexington L-7
New London G-6
New Madison K-1
New Matamoras L-9
New Miami L-1
New Middletown G-10
New Paris K-1
New Philadelphia H-8
New Richmond N-2
New Rome . . . Pg. 102, F-2
New Straitsville L-7
New Vienna L-3
New Washington G-5
New Waterford G-10
Newark J-6
Newcomerstown J-8
Newton M-2
Newton Falls F-10
Niles F-10
North Baltimore F-3
North Bend M-1
North Canton G-8
North College Hill
. . . . Pg. 100, C-3
North Fairfield F-6
North Kingsville D-10
North Lewisburg J-4
North Olmsted F-7
North Ridgeville F-7
North Royalton
. . . . Pg. 101, F-3
Northwood E-4
Norton G-8
Norwalk F-6
Norwood . . . Pg. 100, D-4
Oak Harbor E-5
Oak Hill N-6
Oakwood F-2
Oakwood G-10
Oberlin F-6
Obetz K-5
Vicinity . . . Pg. 102, H-5
Ohio City G-1
Ontario H-6
Orange . . . . Pg. 101, D-7
Orangeville F-10
Oregon E-4
Orient . . . . . Pg. 102, K-2
Orrville G-7
Orwell E-9
Ottawa G-2
Ottawa Hills E-3
Ottoville G-2
Otway N-4
Owensville M-2
Oxford L-1
Painesville E-9
Pandora G-3
Parma F-8
Vicinity . . . Pg. 101, E-3
Parma Heights
. . . . Pg. 101, E-3
Pataskala K-6
Paulding F-1
Payne G-1
Pemberville F-4
Peninsula . . . Pg. 101, J-5

Pepper Pike . Pg. 101, C-7
Perry E-9
Perrysburg E-4
Perrysville H-6
Philo K-7
Pickerington K-5
Piketon M-5
Pioneer E-2
Piqua J-2
Plain City J-4
Pleasant Corners
. . . . Pg. 102, J-2
Pleasant Hill J-2
Pleasantville K-6
Plymouth G-6
Poland G-10
Pomeroy M-7
Port Clinton E-5
Port Washington J-8
Portsmouth N-5
Powell . . . . . Pg. 102, B-3
Powhatan Point K-9
Proctorville O-6
Prospect H-4
Put-in-Bay E-5
Quaker City K-8
Quincy J-3
Racine M-7
Rathbone . . . Pg. 102, A-2
Ravenna F-9
Reading M-2
Vicinity . . . Pg. 100, B-5
Reese . . . . . Pg. 102, H-5
Remsen Corners
. . . . Pg. 101, K-3
Republic F-5
Reynoldsburg K-6
Vicinity . . . Pg. 102, F-7
Richfield . . . Pg. 101, H-5
Richmond H-9
Richmond Heights
. . . . Pg. 101, A-6
Rio Grande N-6
Ripley N-3
Rising Sun F-4
Rittman G-7
Riverlea . . . . Pg. 102, D-4
Roaming Shores E-10
Rock Creek E-9
Rockford H-1
Rocky River Pg. 101, C-1
Rome N-4
Roseville K-7
Rossford E-4
Rushsylvania H-3
Russells Point H-3
Rutland M-7
Sabina L-3
Sagamore Hills
. . . . Pg. 101, G-5
Saint Bernard
. . . . Pg. 100, D-4
Saint Clairsville J-9
Saint Henry H-1
Saint Marys H-2
Saint Paris J-3
Salem G-9
Salineville H-9
San Margherita
. . . . Pg. 102, F-2
Sandusky E-6
Sarahsville K-8
Sardinia N-3
Scio H-9
Seaman N-4
Sebring G-9
Senecaville K-8
Seven Hills . Pg. 101, E-4
Seven Mile L-1
Seville G-7
Shadeville . . . Pg. 102, J-4
Shadyside K-9
Shaker Heights F-8
Vicinity . . . Pg. 101, C-6
Sharonville . . Pg. 100, A-5
Shawnee L-7
Shawnee Hills
. . . . Pg. 102, B-1
Sheffield Lake E-6
Shelby G-6
Sherwood F-1
Shiloh G-6
Shreve H-7
Sidney J-2
Silverton . . . Pg. 100, C-5
Sinking Spring N-4
Smithfield J-10
Solon . . . . . Pg. 101, E-7
Somerset K-6
South Bloomfield K-5
South Charleston K-3
South Euclid
. . . . Pg. 101, B-6
South Lebanon L-2
South Point O-6
South Russell F-9
South Webster N-5
South Zanesville K-7
Spencer F-7
Spencerville H-2
Spring Valley L-3
Springboro L-2
Springdale . . Pg. 100, A-4
Springfield K-3
Stockport L-7
Stoutsville L-5
Stow . . . . . Pg. 101, K-7
Strasburg H-8
Streetsboro F-9
Strongsville F-7
Vicinity . . . Pg. 101, G-1
Struthers G-10
Stryker E-2

Steubenville H-10
Sugar Grove L-6
Sugarcreek H-8
Sunbury J-5
Swanton E-3
Sycamore G-4
Sylvania E-3
Syracuse M-7
Tallmadge F-8
Terrace Park M-2
Thornville K-6
Tiffin G-5
Tiltonsville J-10
Tipp City K-2
Toledo E-4
Toronto H-10
Trenton L-1
Trimble L-7
Trotwood K-2
Troy J-2
Tuscarawas H-8
Twinsburg . . Pg. 101, G-7
Uhrichsville J-8
Union K-2
Union City J-1
University Heights
. . . . Pg. 101, C-6
Upper Arlington J-4
Vicinity . . . Pg. 102, E-3
Upper Sandusky G-4
Urbana J-3
Urbancrest K-4
Vicinity . . . Pg. 102, H-3
Utica J-6
Valley View . Pg. 101, E-5
Valleyview . . Pg. 102, F-2
Van Wert G-1
Vandalia K-2
Vermilion E-6
Versailles J-2
Vinton M-6
Wadsworth G-7
Wakeman F-6
Walbridge E-4
Wapakoneta H-2
Warren F-10
Warrensville Heights
. . . . Pg. 101, D-6
Warsaw J-7
Washington C.H. L-4
Washingtonville . . . G-10
Waterloo . . . Pg. 102, J-7
Waterville E-3
Wauseon E-2
Waverly M-5
Wayne F-4
Waynesburg G-9
Waynesfield H-3
Waynesville L-3
Wellington F-6
Wellston M-6
Wellsville H-10
West Alexandria K-1
West Carrollton K-2
West Farmington F-9
West Jefferson K-4
West Lafayette J-8
West Liberty J-3
West Mansfield H-4
West Milton K-2
West Richfield
. . . . Pg. 101, H-4
West Salem G-7
West Union N-4
West Unity E-2
Westerville J-5
Vicinity . . . Pg. 102, C-5
Westfield Center G-7
Weston F-3
Whitehall K-5
Vicinity . . . Pg. 102, F-6
Whitehouse E-3
Wickliffe . . . Pg. 101, A-7
Wilkesville M-6
Willard G-5
Williamsburg M-2
Williamsport L-4
Willoughby E-8
Willoughby Hills E-8
Willowick E-8
Willshire H-1
Wilmington L-3
Winchester N-3
Windham F-9
Wintersville H-10
Woodlawn . . Pg. 100, B-4
Woodsfield K-9
Woodville F-4
Wooster G-7
Worthington J-5
Vicinity . . . Pg. 102, D-4
Wyoming . . . Pg. 100, B-4
Xenia K-3
Yellow Springs K-3
Yorkville J-10
Youngstown G-10
Zanesville K-7

OKLAHOMA
Pages 68-69
Population: 3,025,487
Capital: Oklahoma City
Land Area: 68,655 sq. mi.

OKLAHOMA

Achille J-11
Acme G-8
Ada G-10
Adair C-13
Addington H-9
Afton C-13
Agawam F-8

Agra E-10
Ahloso G-11
Albany H-11
Albert F-8
Albion G-13
Alcorn C-9
Alderson G-12
Aledo E-7
Alfalfa F-8
Aline C-8
Allen G-11
Alpers G-9
Altus G-6
Alva C-7
Amber F-9
Ames D-8
Amorita B-8
Anadarko F-8
Angora E-6
Antioch G-9
Apache F-8
Apperson C-10
Apple H-12
Aqua Park E-13
Arapaho E-7
Arcadia E-9
Vicinity . . . Pg. 131, A-7
Ardmore H-10
Arnett D-6
Arpelar F-12
Asher F-10
Ashland G-11
Atoka H-11
Atwood F-11
Avant C-11
Avard C-7
Avery E-10
Aydelotte E-10
Babbs F-7
Bache F-12
Bado D-7
Bald Hill E-12
Balko C-5
Barnsdall C-11
Barr D-8
Bartlesville C-11
Battiest G-13
Baum H-11
Bearden F-11
Beggs E-11
Bellvue H-13
Belva C-7
Bengal G-13
Bennington H-11
Bernice C-13
Bessie F-7
Bethany . . . . Pg. 131, D-2
Bethel H-13
Bethel Acres F-10
Big Cabin C-13
Big Cedar G-13
Bigheart C-11
Billings C-9
Binger F-8
Bison D-9
Bixby D-12
Blackburn D-11
Blackwell C-10
Blair G-6
Blanchard F-9
Blocker F-12
Blue H-11
Boise City H-2
Boley E-11
Bomar J-10
Boswell H-11
Bowlegs F-11
Box E-13
Boyd C-4
Boynton E-12
Brace C-7
Braggs E-12
Braman C-9
Bray G-9
Briartown F-13
Bridgeport E-8
Brinkman F-6
Bristow E-11
Broken Arrow D-11
Broken Bow H-13
Bromide H-11
Brooksville F-10
Brown E-7
Brushy E-13
Bryan's Corner C-4
Bryant F-11
Buffalo C-6
Bugtussle F-12
Bunch E-13
Burbank C-10
Burlington C-8
Burmah E-7
Burns Flat F-7
Butler E-7
Byars G-10
Byng G-10
Byron C-8
Cabiness F-11
Cache G-8
Caddo H-11
Calvin F-11
Camargo D-7
Canadian F-12
Canadian Club City . . H-11
Caney H-11
Canton D-8
Capron C-8
Carleton D-8
Carmen C-8
Carnegie F-8
Carney E-10
Carrier C-8
Carter F-6

Cartwright J-10
Cashion E-9
Castle E-11
Caston F-13
Catesby C-6
Catoosa D-12
Cedar Springs D-8
Cement F-8
Centrahoma G-11
Centralia C-12
Ceres D-10
Cestos D-7
Chandler E-10
Chattanooga G-7
Checotah E-12
Chelsea C-12
Cherokee C-8
Chester D-7
Cheyenne E-6
Chickasha F-8
Childers C-12
Chilocco B-10
Chisney F-10
Chloeta C-13
Chockie G-11
Choska E-12
Chouteau D-12
Cimmarron City E-9
Claremore D-12
Clayton G-12
Clemscott H-9
Cleo Springs D-8
Cleveland D-11
Clinton E-7
Cloud Chief F-7
Coalgate G-11
Cogar F-8
Colbert J-11
Cole F-9
Coleman H-11
Collinsville D-12
Colony F-8
Comanche G-9
Commerce B-13
Connerville G-11
Cookietown H-8
Cookson E-13
Cooperton G-7
Cora C-7
Cordell F-7
Corinne H-13
Corn E-7
Cornish H-9
Corum G-8
Council Hill E-12
Courtney H-9
Covington D-9
Cowden F-8
Cowlington F-13
Coweta D-12
Coyle D-10
Crawford E-6
Crekola E-12
Crescent D-9
Creta G-6
Criner F-9
Cromwell F-11
Crowder F-12
Curtis C-7
Cushing D-10
Custer City E-7
Cyril G-8
Dacoma C-8
Daisy G-12
Dale F-10
Darwin H-12
Davenport E-10
Davidson H-7
Davis G-10
Deer Creek C-9
Del City . . . . Pg. 131, F-5
Delaware C-12
Dempsey E-7
Denman F-13
Depew E-11
Devol H-7
Dewey C-12
Dibble F-9
Dickson H-10
Dill City F-7
Dillworth B-10
Dougherty G-10
Douglas D-9
Dover D-9
Doxey F-6
Drake D-10
Driftwood C-8
Drummond D-8
Drumright D-11
Duke G-7
Dunbar G-12
Duncan G-9
Durant H-11
Durham E-6
Durwood H-10
Dustin F-11
Eagle City E-7
Eakly F-8
Earlsboro F-10
Eason F-10
Eddy D-8
Edith C-7
Edmond . . . . Pg. 131, A-5
El Reno E-9
Eldon D-13
Eldorado G-6
Elgin G-8
Elk City E-6
Elmer G-7
Elmore City G-9
Elmwood C-5
Emet H-10
Empire City G-9
Enid D-9

Enterprise F-12
Erick F-6
Eubanks G-12
Eufaula F-12
Eva C-3
Fair Oaks D-12
Fairfax C-10
Fairland C-13
Fairmont D-9
Fairview D-8
Fallis E-10
Fallon H-12
Fanshawe F-13
Fargo D-6
Farris H-12
Faxon G-8
Fay E-7
Featherston F-12
Felt C-2
Fillmore H-11
Finley H-12
Fittstown G-10
Fitzhugh G-10
Fleetwood H-9
Fletcher G-8
Floris B-5
Folsom H-11
Foraker B-11
Forest Park . Pg. 131, D-5
Forgan B-5
Fort Arbuckle G-9
Fort Cobb F-8
Fort Gibson E-13
Fort Supply C-6
Fort Towson H-13
Forty One F-7
Foss E-7
Four Corners C-3
Fowler E-10
Fox H-9
Foyil C-12
Francis G-10
Frederick G-7
Freedom C-7
Gage D-6
Gans F-13
Gansel D-9
Garber D-9
Garvin H-13
Gate C-6
Gay H-12
Geary E-8
Gene Autry H-10
Gerty G-11
Gibbon B-8
Gideon D-13
Glencoe D-10
Glenpool D-11
Glover H-13
Goldsby F-9
Goltry C-8
Goodland H-12
Goodwell C-3
Goodwin D-6
Gore E-13
Gotebo F-7
Gould G-6
Gowan G-12
Gracemont F-8
Grady H-10
Grainola B-11
Grandfield H-7
Granite F-6
Grant H-12
Gray C-4
Grayson E-12
Green D-13
Greenfield E-8
Griggs C-3
Grove C-13
Guthrie E-9
Guymon C-3
Haileyville G-12
Hall Park F-9
Hammon E-6
Harden City G-10
Hardesty C-4
Hardy B-10
Harmon D-6
Harrah E-10
Hartshorne G-12
Haskell E-12
Hastings H-8
Hayward D-9
Haywood G-12
Hayworth J-13
Headrick G-7
Healdton H-9
Heavener F-13
Hectorville E-12
Helena C-8
Hennepin G-9
Hennessy D-9
Henryetta E-11
Hickory G-10
Higgins C-6
Hillsdale C-8
Hinton E-8
Hitchcock D-8
Hobart F-7
Hodgen G-13
Holdenville F-11
Hollis G-6
Hollister H-7
Hollow C-12
Homestead D-8
Hominy D-11
Honobia G-13
Hooker B-4
Hoot Owl C-13
Hopeton C-7
Hough B-3
Howe F-13

Hucmac D-7
Hugo H-12
Hulah B-11
Hulbert D-13
Hulen G-8
Humphreys G-7
Hunter C-9
Huskey H-12
Hydro E-8
Idabel H-13
Indiahoma G-7
Indianola F-12
Ingersoll C-8
Inola D-12
Isabella D-8
Jay C-13
Jefferson C-9
Jenks D-11
Jennings D-11
Jesse G-11
Jet C-8
Joy G-10
Kansas D-13
Karma J-11
Karns F-11
Kellyville E-11
Kendrick E-10
Kent H-12
Kenton B-2
Keota F-13
Keyes C-3
Kiamichi G-12
Kildare C-10
Kingfisher E-9
Kingston J-11
Kinta F-13
Kiowa G-11
Knowles C-5
Konawa F-10
Kosoma H-12
Kremlin C-9
Kusa E-11
Lacey D-8
Lahoma D-8
Lake Valley F-7
Lamar F-11
Lambert C-8
Lamont C-9
Lane H-11
Langston E-10
Latta G-10
Laverne C-6
Lawton G-8
Leach D-13
Lebanon H-10
Leedey E-6
Lehigh G-11
Lela D-10
Lenapah C-12
Leon H-9
Leonard E-11
Lequire F-13
Letitia G-8
Lewisville F-12
Lexington F-10
Lima F-10
Lincoln G-9
Lindsay G-9
Little Axe F-10
Little City H-10
Loco G-9
Locust Grove D-13
Lone Grove H-10
Lone Wolf F-7
Longdale D-8
Lookeba F-8
Lookout C-7
Lovedale C-6
Loveland H-7
Lovell D-9
Loyal D-8
Lucien D-9
Lugert F-7
Lula G-11
Luther E-10
Lyman C-10
Lyons E-13
Macomb F-10
Madill H-10
Manchester B-9
Mangum F-6
Manitou G-7
Mannsville H-10
Maramac D-10
Marietta H-10
Marland C-10
Marlow G-9
Marshall D-9
Martha G-6
Mason E-11
Maud F-10
May C-6
Mayfield F-6
Maysville G-9
Mazie D-12
McAlester F-12
McBride H-11
McCurtain F-13
McLoud F-10
McQueen G-6
McWillie F-7
Mead H-10
Medford C-9
Meeker E-10
Meers G-8
Meno D-8
Meridian E-10
Messer H-12
Miami C-13
Middleberg F-9
Milburn H-11
Milfay E-11
Mill Creek G-10
Millerton H-12

OKLAHOMA

OREGON
Pages 70-71
Population: 2,633,105
Capital: Salem
Land Area: 98,184 sq. mi.

PENNSYLVANIA
Pages 72-73
Population: 11,863,895
Capital: Harrisburg
Land Area: 44,888 sq. mi.

PENNSYLVANIA

Dayton F-4
Deepdale . . . Pg. 134, C-1
Delaware Water Gap F-13
Delta K-11
Denver H-11
Derry H-4
Dickson City D-12
Dillsburg J-9
Donegal J-4
Donora H-2
Dormont H-2
  Vicinity . . . Pg. 136, E-2
Dover H-9
Downingtown J-12
Doylestown H-13
Dresher . . . Pg. 134, A-5
Driftwood E-6
DuBois E-5
Duboistown E-9
Dudley H-6
Dunbar J-3
Duncannon H-8
Duncansville H-6
Dunmore D-12
Dushore D-10
Eagles Mere D-10
Eagleville . . Pg. 134, A-1
East Berlin J-9
East Brady F-3
East Butler F-3
East Falls . . Pg. 134, D-5
East Greenville . . . H-12
East Lansdowne
  . . . . Pg. 134, D-3
East Mt. Airy . Pg. 134, C-5
East Oak Lane
  . . . . Pg. 134, C-6
East Stroudsburg . . F-13
East Washington . . . H-2
Eastwick . . Pg. 134, F-4
Easton G-13
Eau Claire E-3
Ebensburg G-5
Economy G-2
Eddington Park
  . . . . Pg. 134, B-9
Eddystone . Pg. 134, G-2
Edinboro C-2
Edwardsville E-11
Eldred C-6
Elizabethtown H-10
Elizabethville G-10
Elkland C-8
Ellport F-2
Ellwood City F-2
Elmwood . . Pg. 134, F-4
Elwyn . . . Pg. 134, F-1
Emlenton E-3
Emmaus G-12
Emporium D-6
Ephrata H-11
Erie B-2
Etna . . . . . Pg. 136, B-5
Evans City F-2
Everett J-6
Everson J-3
Factoryville D-12
Fairchance J-3
Fairfield K-8
Fairview B-1
Fairview Village
  . . . . Pg. 134, A-1
Falls Creek E-5
Farrell E-1
Fawn Grove K-10
Fentonville . Pg. 134, D-6
Fern Rock . . Pg. 134, C-6
Fitzwatertown
  . . . . Pg. 134, A-5
Fleetwood G-12
Flemington E-8
Flourtown . Pg. 134, B-4
Folcroft . . . Pg. 134, G-3
Ford City F-3
Ford Cliff F-3
Forest City D-12
Forksville D-10
Fort Washington
  . . . . Pg. 134, A-4
Forty Fort E-12
Fountain Hill G-13
Foxcroft . . Pg. 134, D-2
Frackville F-11
Frankford . . Pg. 134, C-7
Franklin D-3
Franklin Park G-2
Freeburg F-9
Freeland F-12
Freemansburg G-13
Freeport G-3
Galeton C-8
Gallitzin G-5
Garrett J-4
Geistown H-5
Germantown Pg. 134, D-5
Gettysburg K-9
Girard B-2
Gladwyne . . Pg. 134, C-3
Glen Campbell F-5
Glen Hope F-6
Glen Rock K-10
Glenolden . . Pg. 134, G-3
Glenside . . Pg. 134, B-6
Gordon G-11
Grampian F-5
Gratz G-10
Great Bend C-12
Greencastle K-7
Greensboro K-2
Greensburg H-3
Greentree . . Pg. 136, E-2
Greenville D-1
Grove City E-2
Halifax G-9

Hallstead C-12
Hamburg G-11
Hanover K-9
Harmonville Pg. 134, B-3
Harmony F-2
Harrisburg H-9
Harrisville E-2
Harveys Lake D-11
Hastings G-5
Hatboro H-13
Havertown . . Pg. 134, D-3
Hawley D-13
Hawthorn F-4
Hazleton F-11
Heidelberg . . Pg. 136, E-1
Herndon G-9
Hershey H-10
Hollidaysburg H-6
Holmesburg Pg. 134, C-7
Homer City G-4
Homestead . . Pg. 136, E-6
Honesdale D-13
Honey Brook J-12
Hooversville H-5
Hop Bottom C-12
Hopewell H-6
Houston H-2
Houtzdale F-6
Hughesville E-10
Hulmeville . . Pg. 134, A-9
Hummelstown H-10
Huntingdon G-7
Huntingdon Valley
  . . . . Pg. 134, B-7
Hydetown C-3
Hyndman K-5
Indian Lake J-5
Indiana G-4
Industry G-1
Ingram . . . Pg. 136, D-1
Irvona F-5
Ithan . . . . . Pg. 134, C-1
Jackson Center E-2
Jacobus J-10
Jamestown D-1
Jeanette H-3
Jeddo F-12
Jefferson H-2
Jeffersonville Pg. 134, A-2
Jenkintown . . Pg. 134, B-6
Jennerstown H-4
Jersey Shore E-9
Jim Thorpe F-12
Johnsonburg D-5
Johnstown H-5
Jonestown H-10
Juniata . . . Pg. 134, D-6
Kane C-5
Karns City F-3
Kennett Square J-12
Kensington . . Pg. 134, E-6
King of Prussia
  . . . . Pg. 134, B-1
Kingston E-12
Kistler H-7
Kittanning F-3
Knox E-3
Knoxville C-8
Kulpmont F-10
Kutztown G-12
Lake City B-2
Lancaster J-11
Landisburg H-8
Lanesboro C-12
Langhorne H-14
Lansdale H-13
Lansdowne J-13
  Vicinity . . . Pg. 134, F-3
Lansford F-12
Laporte D-10
Larchmont Meadows
  . . . . Pg. 134, E-2
Latrobe H-4
Laureldale H-11
Lawn Crest . . Pg. 134, C-7
Lawrence Park B-2
Le Raysville C-11
Lebanon H-10
Leesport H-11
Lehighton F-12
Lemoyne H-9
Levittown H-14
Lewisburg F-9
Lewistown G-8
Lexington Park
  . . . . Pg. 134, C-7
Liberty D-9
Ligonier H-4
Lilly H-5
Lincoln H-11
Linesville C-1
Lititz H-11
Little Meadows C-11
Littlestown K-9
Liverpool G-9
Lock Haven E-8
Logan . . . . Pg. 134, D-6
Loganton E-8
Loretto G-5
Lower Burrell G-3
Lumar Park Pg. 134, B-8
Lumber City F-5
Lykens G-10
Macungie G-12
Mahanoy City F-11
Manayunk . . Pg. 134, D-4
Manchester H-9
Manheim J-11
Manns Choice J-5
Mansfield C-9
Marble Hall Pg. 134, B-4
Marcus Hook K-13

Vicinity . . . Pg. 146, F-3
Marianna J-2
Marietta J-10
Marion Center F-4
Marklesburg H-6
Mars G-2
Martinsburg H-6
Marysville H-9
Masontown J-2
Matamoras D-14
Mayfair . . . Pg. 134, C-7
McKean . . . Pg. 134, D-3
McKeesport H-2
McSherrytown K-9
McVeytown G-7
Mckee's Rocks
  . . . . Pg. 136, C-2
Meadville D-2
Mechanicsburg H-9
Media . . . . Pg. 134, F-1
Mercer E-2
Mercersburg K-7
Meshoppen D-11
Meyersdale K-4
Middleburg G-9
Middletown H-9
  Vicinity . . . Pg. 147, A-10
Midland G-1
Mifflinburg F-9
Mifflintown G-8
Mifflinville E-11
Milesburg F-7
Milford E-14
Mill Creek H-7
Mill Hall E-8
Mill Village C-2
Millbourne . . Pg. 134, E-3
Millerbrook . Pg. 134, C-8
Millersburg G-9
Millerstown G-8
Millersville J-10
Millheim F-8
Millridge . . Pg. 134, D-2
Milton F-9
Minersville G-11
Mohnton H-11
Monaca G-2
Monessen H-2
Monroe C-10
Monroeville G-3
Mont Alto J-8
Montoursville E-9
Montrose C-12
Moosic D-12
Morrisville H-14
Morton . . . Pg. 134, C-5
Moscow E-12
Mountville J-10
Mt. Carmel F-10
Mt. Holly Springs . . . J-9
Mt. Jewett C-5
Mt. Joy J-10
Mt. Pleasant H-3
Mt. Pocono E-13
Mt. Union H-7
Mt. Wolf J-10
Murrysville G-3
Myerstown H-11
Nanticoke E-11
Nanty-Glo G-5
Narberth F-2
  Vicinity . . . Pg. 134, D-3
Nazareth G-13
Nescopeck F-11
New Albany D-10
New Alexandria H-3
New Beaver F-1
New Berlin F-9
New Bethlehem F-4
New Brighton F-2
New Buffalo G-9
New Castle F-1
New Centerville J-4
  Vicinity . . . Pg. 146, B-9
New Cumberland . . . H-9
New Eagle H-2
New Florence H-4
New Freedom K-10
New Holland J-11
New Kensington G-3
New Lebanon D-2
New Milford C-12
New Oxford J-9
New Paris J-5
New Philadelphia . . . G-11
New Salem J-2
New Stanton H-3
New Wilmington E-1
Newburg F-5
Newburg J-8
Newport G-9
Newry H-6
Newtown Heights
  . . . . Pg. 134, E-1
Newtown Square
  . . . . Pg. 134, D-1
Newville H-8
Nicetown-Tioga
  . . . . Pg. 134, D-5
Nicholson D-12
Normandy . . Pg. 134, B-8
Norristown J-13
  Vicinity . . . Pg. 134, A-2
Norritonville Pg. 134, A-2
North Apollo G-3
North Belle Vernon . . H-3
North East B-3
North Hills . . Pg. 134, B-5
North Wales H-13
North York J-10
Northampton G-12
Northumberland F-9
Norwood . . Pg. 134, G-3
Nuangola E-11
Oakland C-12

Oakmont G-3
  Vicinity . . . Pg. 146, D-4
Ohiopyle J-3
Oil City D-3
Old Forge D-12
Olyphant D-12
Orangeville E-10
Orbisonia H-7
Orrstown J-8
Orwigsburg G-11
Osceola Mills F-6
Oswayo C-7
Overbrook . . Pg. 134, D-4
Oxford K-11
Palmerton F-12
Palmyra H-10
Parker E-3
Parkesburg J-11
Parkside . . Pg. 134, G-2
Patton G-5
Paxton G-9
Pen Argyl F-13
Penfield . . . Pg. 134, D-3
Penn Square Pg. 134, A-2
Pennsburg H-13
Perkasie H-13
Petersburg G-7
Petrolia F-3
Philadelphia
  Vicinity Pg. 134
Philipsburg F-6
Phoenixville H-12
Picture Rocks E-10
Pillow G-9
Pine Grove G-10
Pittsburgh . . Pg-2, 136
Pittston E-12
Platea B-2
Pleasantville D-3
Pleasantville H-5
Plum G-3
Plumville F-4
Plymouth Valley
  . . . . Pg. 134, B-3
Point Marion K-2
Polk D-2
Port Allegany C-6
Port Carbon G-11
Port Matilda F-7
Port Royal G-8
Portage H-5
Portersville F-2
Portland F-13
Pottstown H-12
Pottsville G-11
Prospect Park
  . . . . Pg. 134, G-3
Punxsutawney F-4
Pymble . . . Pg. 134, F-1
Quakertown H-13
Quarryville J-11
Radnor . . . Pg. 134, C-2
Rainsburg J-5
Ramey F-6
Reading H-12
Red Hill H-13
Red Lion J-10
Renovo E-7
Reynoldsville E-5
Rices Landing J-2
Richland H-11
Richlandtown H-13
Richmond . . Pg. 134, D-6
Ridgway D-5
Ridley Park . . Pg. 134, F-3
Rimersburg E-3
Ringtown F-11
Riverside F-10
Roaring Spring H-6
Robesonia H-11
Rockledge . . Pg. 134, B-6
Rockwood J-4
Rome C-11
Rose Valley . . Pg. 134, G-1
Rosemont . . Pg. 134, D-2
Roseto F-13
Roseville C-9
Roslyn . . . Pg. 134, B-6
Rosslyn Farms
  . . . . Pg. 136, D-1
Rouseville D-3
Roxborough Pg. 134, C-4
Royersford H-12
Rural Valley F-4
Rutledge . . Pg. 134, G-2
Saegertown C-2
Saint Clair G-11
  Vicinity . . . Pg. 146, E-4
Saint Marys D-5
Saint Petersburg . . . E-3
Salisbury K-4
Salladasburg E-9
Saltillo H-7
Saltsburg G-3
Sandy Lake D-2
Sankertown G-5
Saxonburg F-3
Saxton H-6
Sayre C-10
Scalp Level H-5
Schuylkill Haven . . . G-11
Scottdale H-3
Scranton D-12
Selinsgrove F-9
Sellersville H-13
Seward H-4
Shade Gap H-7
Shamokin F-10
Shamokin Dam F-9
Sharon E-1
Sharon Hill . Pg. 134, F-3
Sharpsburg . Pg. 136, B-5
Shenandoah F-11
Shickshinny E-11

Shillington H-11
Shinglehouse C-6
Shippensburg J-8
Shippenville E-3
Shirleysburg H-7
Shoemakersville . . . G-11
Shrewsbury K-10
Slatington F-12
Sligo E-3
Slippery Rock E-2
Smethport C-6
Smithfield K-3
Snow Shoe F-7
Society Hill . Pg. 134, E-6
Somerset J-4
Somerton . . Pg. 134, B-8
Souderton H-13
South Bethlehem . . . G-13
South Coatesville . . J-12
South Connellsville . . J-3
South Fork H-5
South Philadelphia
  . . . . Pg. 134, F-5
South Renovo E-7
South Waverly B-10
South Williamsport . . E-9
Spangler G-5
Spartansburg C-3
Spring City H-12
Spring Grove J-9
Spring Mill . Pg. 134, C-3
Springboro C-1
Springfield . . Pg. 134, F-2
Stanwood . . Pg. 134, B-9
State College F-7
Stillwater E-10
Stoneboro D-2
Stoystown J-4
Strasburg J-11
Strattanville E-4
Strausstown G-11
Stroudsburg F-13
Sugar Grove B-4
Sugarcreek D-3
Summerhill H-5
Summerville E-4
Summit Hill F-12
Sunbury F-10
Susquehanna C-12
Swarthmore Pg. 134, F-2
Sykesville B-9
Sylvania B-9
Tamaqua F-12
Tatamy G-13
Taylor D-12
Telford H-13
Temple H-12
Terre Hill H-11
Thompsontown G-9
Thornburg . . Pg. 136, D-1
Three Springs H-7
Tidioute C-4
Timberlake . Pg. 134, E-1
Tioga C-9
Tionesta D-3
Titusville D-3
Topton G-12
Towanda C-10
Tower City G-10
Townville C-3
Trainer J-13
  Vicinity . . . Pg. 146, F-3
Trappe H-12
Tremont G-10
Trevose . . . Pg. 134, A-9
Trooper . . . Pg. 134, A-1
Troutville F-5
Troy C-10
Tullytown H-14
Tunkhannock D-11
Tyrone G-6
Union City C-3
Union Dale C-11
Uniontown J-3
Upland . . . Pg. 134, G-1
Upper Fairview
  . . . . Pg. 134, A-1
Upper Roxborough
  . . . . Pg. 134, C-4
Ursina K-4
Vandergrift G-3
Venango C-2
Villanova . . Pg. 134, D-2
Walnutport G-12
Wampum F-1
Warren C-4
Washington H-2
Waterford C-2
Waterloo Mills
  . . . . Pg. 134, D-1
Watsontown E-9
Wattsburg B-3
Waymart D-13
Wayne . . . . Pg. 134, C-1
Waynesboro K-8
Waynesburg J-2
Weatherly F-12
Wellersburg K-5
Wellsboro C-8
Wellsville J-9
Wesleyville B-2
West Brownsville . . . J-2
West Chester J-12
West Conshohocken
  . . . . Pg. 134, C-2
West Easton G-13
West Gate Hills
  . . . . Pg. 134, D-2
West Grove K-11
West Hazleton F-11
West Homestead
  . . . . Pg. 136, E-5
West Kensington
  . . . . Pg. 134, D-6

West Kittanning F-3
West Liberty F-2
West Middlesex E-1
West Mifflin H-2
  Vicinity . . . Pg. 136, G-5
West Newton H-3
West Oak Lane
  . . . . Pg. 134, C-5
West Philadelphia
  . . . . Pg. 134, D-4
West Pittston E-12
West Reading H-11
West View . . Pg. 136, A-2
West York J-10
Westfield C-8
Westmont H-5
Westover G-5
Wheatland E-1
White Haven E-12
White Marsh Pg. 134, A-6
White Oak H-3
Whitehall H-2
  Vicinity . . . Pg. 136, G-4
Wilkes-Barre E-12
Wilkinsburg G-3
Williamsburg G-6
Williamsport E-9
Williamstown G-10
Willow Grove Pg. 134, A-6
Wilson G-13
Wind Gap F-13
Windber H-5
Winterstown K-10
Womelsdorf H-11
Woodbury H-6
Worthington F-3
Wrightsville J-10
Wyalusing D-11
Wyola . . . . Pg. 134, D-1
Wyomissing H-11
Yardley H-14
Yeadon J-13
  Vicinity . . . Pg. 134, F-4
York J-10
York Springs J-9
Youngsville C-4
Youngwood H-3
Zelienople F-2

RHODE ISLAND
Page 25
Population: 947,154
Capital: Providence
Land Area: 1055 sq. mi.

Ashton E-8
Auburn F-9
Barrington F-10
Berkeley E-9
Bristol G-10
Carolina H-9
Charlestown H-9
Chepachet E-9
Clayville F-8
Cranston F-9
East Greenwich G-9
East Providence . . . F-10
Esmond E-9
Exeter G-9
Fiskeville F-9
Foster Center F-8
Glocester E-8
Harmony E-8
Harrisville E-8
Homestead G-10
Hope F-9
Hope Valley G-8
Jamestown G-10
Lippitt F-9
Little Compton G-10
Mapleville E-8
Middletown G-10
Millville G-8
Narragansett Pier . . H-9
Nasonville E-8
Newport G-10
Nooseneck G-9
North Foster F-8
North Scituate F-9
North Tiverton G-10
Pascoag E-8
Pawtucket F-9
Portsmouth G-10
Providence F-10
Slatersville E-9
Usquepaug G-9
Vernon F-9
Wakefield H-9
Warren G-10
Warwick F-10
Washington F-9
West Greenwich F-8
Westerly H-8
Wickford G-9
Wood River Jct. H-8
Woodville H-8
Woonsocket E-9

SOUTH CAROLINA
Pages 64-65
Population: 3,121,820
Capital: Columbia
Land Area: 30,203 sq. mi.

Abbeville F-4
Adams Run J-7
Aiken G-5
Allendale H-6
Almeda J-6

Anderson F-4
Andrews G-8
Antreville F-4
Appleton H-6
Awendaw H-8
Aynor F-9
Ballentine F-6
Bamberg H-6
Barnwell H-6
Batesburg G-5
Bayboro F-9
Belton F-5
Bennettsville E-8
Bethany D-6
Bethune F-7
Bishopville F-7
Blacksburg D-5
Blackville H-6
Blenheim E-8
Bonneau H-7
Bowman H-7
Boykin F-7
Bradley F-4
Branchville H-6
Brownsville E-8
Buffalo E-5
Bullock Creek E-5
Cades G-8
Cainhoy H-8
Calhoun Falls F-4
Camden F-7
Canadys H-7
Carlisle E-5
Cassatt F-7
Cayce G-6
Centenary F-9
Central E-3
Chappells F-5
Charleston J-8
Chelsea K-7
Cheraw E-7
Chesnee D-5
Chester E-6
Chesterfield E-8
Clarkshill G-5
Clemson E-3
Cleveland D-4
Clinton F-5
Clio E-8
Clover D-6
Columbia F-6
Conway G-9
Cool Spring F-9
Cresent Beach G-10
Cross H-7
Cross Hill F-5
Cross Keys E-5
Dalzell F-7
Darlington F-8
De Kalb F-7
Debidue Beach H-9
Denmark H-6
Dillon E-9
Dovesville E-8
Due West F-4
Edgefield G-5
Edgemoor E-6
Edisto Beach J-8
Edisto Island J-7
Effingham F-8
Ehrhardt H-6
Elgin F-6
Enoree E-5
Estill J-6
Eureka E-8
Evergreen F-8
Fair Bluff F-9
Fairfax J-6
Filbert D-6
Florence F-8
Floydale E-9
Folly Beach J-8
Forest Beach K-7
Foreston G-7
Fork E-9
Fork Shoals E-4
Fort Mill D-6
Fountain Inn E-5
Frogmore K-7
Furman J-6
Gaffney D-5
Galivants Ferry F-9
Garden City G-9
Gardens Corner K-7
Garnett J-6
Georgetown G-8
Givhans H-7
Goose Creek H-8
Gourdin G-8
Gownesville D-4
Grays J-6
Great Falls E-6
Greeleyville G-8
Green Pond J-7
Green Sea F-9
Greenville E-4
Greenwood F-4
Greer E-4
Hampton J-6
Hanahan H-8
Hannah G-8
Hardeeville K-6
Hartsville F-7
Hemingway G-8
Hickory Grove D-5
Hilda H-6
Hilton Head Island . . K-7
Holly Hill H-7
Honea Path F-4
Indiantown G-8
Inman D-4
Islandton H-7
Isle of Palms J-8

Iva F-4
Jackson H-5
Jacksonboro J-7
James Island J-8
Jamestown H-8
Jefferson E-7
Jenkinsville F-6
Joanna F-5
Johnston G-5
Jonesville E-5
Kershaw E-7
Kingsburg F-9
Kingstree G-8
Kitchings Mill G-5
Kline H-6
Lake City G-8
Lamar F-7
Lancaster E-6
Landrum D-4
Latta E-8
Laurens F-4
Leeds E-5
Lena J-6
Lesslie E-6
Lewis E-6
Lexington F-6
Liberty E-4
Litchfield Beach G-9
Little River F-10
Lockhart E-5
Lodge H-6
Loris F-9
Manning G-8
Manville F-7
Marietta D-4
Marion F-9
Martin H-5
Mauldin E-4
Mayesville F-7
McBee E-7
McColl E-8
McConnells E-6
McCormick G-4
Moncks Corner H-8
Mount Pleasant J-8
Mountville F-5
Mt. Carmel F-4
Mullins F-9
Myrtle Beach G-10
New Ellenton H-5
New Prospect D-5
Newberry F-5
Nichols F-9
Nine Times E-3
Ninety Six F-5
Nixonville F-9
North G-6
North Augusta G-5
North Charleston . . . J-8
Oatland J-7
Oats F-8
Olanta F-8
Olar H-6
Orangeburg G-6
Outland G-5
Owdoms F-5
Pacolet E-5
Pageland E-7
Pamplico F-8
Parksville G-5
Patrick E-7
Pauline E-5
Pawleys Island G-9
Pelion G-5
Pendleton E-3
Pickens E-4
Pineland J-6
Pineville H-7
Pinewood G-7
Plum Branch G-4
Pontiac F-6
Prosperity F-5
Pumpkintown E-4
Rantowles J-8
Rhems G-8
Richburg E-6
Ridgeland J-6
Ridgeville H-7
Ridgeway F-6
Rock Hill E-6
Rockton F-6
Rockville J-8
Rocky Bottom E-3
Ruby E-7
Salters G-8
Saluda F-5
Sampit H-9
Sandy Run G-6
Santee G-7
Sardinia G-7
Sardis F-8
Scranton F-8
Seneca E-3
Sharon E-5
Simpson E-4
Simpsonville E-4
Smallwood G-4
Smoaks H-7
Society Hill E-8
Spartanburg E-5
Springfield G-6
St. George H-7
St. Matthews G-7
St. Stephen G-7
Starr F-4
Stateburg F-7
Steedman G-6
Stoney Hill F-5
Stuckey G-8
Sullivans Island J-8
Summerton G-7
Summerville H-7
Sumter G-7
Surfside Beach G-9

SOUTH CAROLINA

Switzerland K-6
Sycamore H-6
Tamassee E-3
Tatum E-8
Taylor E-4
Tillman J-6
Timmonsville F-8
Tradesville E-7
Travelers Rest E-4
Trenton G-5
Ulmer H-6
Union E-5
Varnville J-6
Wagener G-6
Walhalla E-3
Walterboro J-7
Ward G-5
Ware Shoals F-4
Wateree H-7
Wells H-7
Westminster E-3
Westville E-7
Whitehall J-8
Whitmire E-5
Willington H-4
Williston H-5
Winnsboro F-6
Woodruff E-5
Yauhannah G-9
Yemassee J-7
Yonges Island J-8
York D-6

SOUTH DAKOTA
Page 74
Population: 690,768
Capital: Pierre
Land Area: 75,952 sq. mi.

Aberdeen C-8
Agar C-6
Akaska C-10
Albee F-10
Alcester E-8
Alexandria D-10
Alpena D-10
Altamont C-9
Andover C-9
Arlington F-8
Armour E-8
Artas B-6
Artesian D-8
Ashton D-10
Astoria D-10
Aurora E-9
Badger D-9
Bancroft D-9
Batesland F-4
Belle Fourche C-2
Belvidere E-5
Beresford F-10
Bison B-3
Blunt D-6
Bonesteel F-7
Bowdle C-7
Bradley E-10
Brandon E-10
Brandt D-10
Brentford C-8
Bristol C-9
Britton B-9
Broadland D-10
Brookings D-10
Bruce D-10
Bryant D-9
Buffalo B-2
Buffalo Gap E-2
Burke F-7
Bushnell D-10
Butler C-9
Camp Crook B-2
Canova E-9
Canton F-10
Carthage D-9
Castle Rock C-2
Cavour D-8
Centerville F-9
Central City D-2
Chamberlain E-7
Chelsea C-8
Claire City B-9
Clark C-9
Clear Lake D-10
Colman E-10
Colton E-9
Columbia B-8
Conde C-8
Corona C-10
Corsica E-8
Cottonwood E-4
Cresbard C-7
Crooks E-10
Custer E-2
Dallas F-6
Dante F-8
De Smet D-9
Deadwood D-2
Dell Rapids E-10
Delmont F-8
Dimock E-8
Doland C-8
Dolton E-9
Draper E-5
Dupree C-4
Eagle Butte C-5
Eden B-9
Edgemont E-2
Elk Point G-10
Elm Springs D-3
Emery E-9
Enning D-3
Erwin D-9
Estelline D-9
Ethan E-8
Eureka B-7
Fairburn E-2
Fairfax F-7
Fairpoint C-3
Fairview F-10
Faith C-4
Farmer E-9
Farmingdale D-3
Faulkton C-7
Flandreau E-10
Florence C-9
Fort Pierre D-6
Fort Thompson D-7
Frankfort C-8
Frederick B-8
Freeman F-9
Fruitdale C-2
Fulton D-8
Gann Valley D-7
Garden City C-8
Garretson E-10
Gary D-10
Gayville F-9
Geddes E-8
Gettysburg C-6
Glad Valley B-4
Glenham B-6
Goodwin C-10
Greenwood F-8
Gregory F-7
Grenville C-9
Groton C-8
Hammer B-9
Harrisburg F-10
Harrold D-6
Hayti D-9
Hecla B-8
Hermosa E-2
Herreid B-6
Herrick F-7
Highmore D-7
Hill City D-2
Hillsview B-7
Hitchcock D-8
Hosmer B-7
Hot Springs E-2
Houghton B-8
Hoven C-6
Howard E-9
Howes D-4
Huron D-8
Interior E-4
Ipswich C-7
Irene F-9
Iroquois D-9
Isabel B-5
Java B-6
Jefferson G-10
Kadoka E-4
Kennebec E-6
Keystone D-2
Kimball E-7
Kranzburg C-10
Kyle E-4
La Bolt C-10
La Plant C-6
Lake Andes F-8
Lake City B-9
Lake Preston D-9
Lane E-8
Langford B-9
Lead D-2
Lebanon C-6
Lemmon B-4
Lennox F-10
Leola B-7
Letcher E-8
Lily C-9
Little Eagle B-5
Lodgepole B-3
Long Lake B-7
Long Valley E-4
Lowry C-6
Loyalton C-7
Ludlow B-3
Madison E-9
Marion F-9
Martin F-4
Marty F-8
Marvin C-10
Maurine C-3
McIntosh B-5
McLaughlin B-5
Meadow B-4
Mellette C-8
Menno F-9
Midland D-5
Milbank C-10
Miller D-7
Mission F-5
Mitchell E-9
Mobridge B-6
Monroe E-9
Montrose E-9
Morristown B-4
Mound City B-6
Mount Vernon E-8
Mud Butte C-3
Murdo E-5
Naples D-9
New Effington B-10
Newell C-2
Nisland C-2
North Sioux City G-10
Northville C-8
Nunda D-9
Oacoma E-6
Oelrichs E-2
Oglala F-3
Okreek E-5
Oldham D-9
Olivet F-9
Onaka C-7
Onida D-6
Orient C-7
Ortley C-9
Parker F-9
Parkston E-8
Parmelee E-5
Philip D-4
Pierpont C-8
Pierre D-6
Pine Ridge F-3
Plainview C-8
Plankinton E-8
Platte F-7
Pollock B-6
Prairie City B-3
Presho E-6
Pringle E-2
Provo E-1
Pukwana E-6
Quinn D-4
Ramona E-9
Rapid City D-3
Ravinia F-8
Raymond C-9
Redfield C-8
Redig B-2
Ree Heights D-7
Reliance E-6
Revillo C-10
Ridgeview C-5
Rockerville D-2
Rockham C-8
Roscoe C-7
Rosebud F-5
Roslyn C-9
Roswell C-9
Saint Charles F-7
Saint Francis F-5
Saint Lawrence D-7
Salem E-9
Scenic E-3
Scotland F-9
Selby B-6
Seneca C-7
Shadehill B-4
Sherman E-10
Sioux Falls E-9
Sisseton B-10
Sorum B-3
South Shore C-10
Spearfish D-2
Springfield F-8
Stephan D-7
Stickney E-8
Stockholm C-10
Stoneville C-3
Stratford C-8
Sturgis D-2
Summit C-9
Tabor F-9
Tea F-10
Timber Lake C-5
Tolstoy C-7
Toronto D-10
Trail City B-5
Trent E-10
Tripp F-8
Tulare D-8
Turton C-8
Tyndall F-9
Union Center D-3
Veblen B-9
Verdon C-8
Vermillion G-9
Viborg F-9
Vienna D-9
Vilas E-9
Vivian E-6
Wagner F-8
Wakonda F-9
Wall D-4
Wallace C-9
Ward E-10
Wasta D-3
Watertown D-9
Waubay C-9
Webster C-9
Wessington D-7
Wessington Springs E-8
Westport B-8
Wetonka B-8
Wewela F-6
White D-10
White Butte B-4
White Lake E-8
White River E-5
Whitewood D-2
Willow Lake C-9
Wilmot C-10
Winner F-6
Wood F-5
Woonsocket E-8
Worthing F-10
Yale D-9
Yankton F-9
Zeona C-3

TENNESSEE
Pages 38-39
Population: 4,591,120
Capital: Nashville
Land Area: 41,155 sq. mi.

Adams F-6
Adamsville J-4
Aetna H-5
Alamo H-3
Alcoa H-11
Alexandria G-7
Algood G-8
Allardt G-9
Allens H-3
Allisona H-7
Allred G-9
Alpine G-9
Altamont J-8
Alto G-6
Antioch Pg. 124, F-7
Arlington J-2
  Vicinity Pg. 119, A-10
Arrington H-7
Arthur F-11
Ashland City G-6
Ashport H-2
Athens H-10
Atoka H-2
Atwood G-3
Avondale Pg. 124, A-9
Bailey Pg. 119, F-9
Banner Hill G-13
Bartlett J-2
  Vicinity Pg. 119, C-7
Beacon Pg. 124, G-6
Bean Station G-12
Beardstown H-5
Beersheba Springs H-8
Belfast J-7
Bell Buckle H-7
Belle Meade G-6
  Vicinity Pg. 124, E-4
Bellevue Pg. 124, F-2
Bells H-3
Belvidere J-7
Benjestown Pg. 119, B-5
Benton J-10
Berry Hill Pg. 124, E-6
Bethel J-6
Bethel Springs J-4
Big Sandy G-4
Big Springs J-9
Birchwood J-9
Blaine G-11
Bluff City F-13
Bogota G-3
Bolivar J-3
Bolton Pg. 119, A-9
Bon Air H-8
Braden H-2
Bradford G-4
Brentwood G-6
  Vicinity Pg. 124, G-5
Briceville G-10
Brighton H-2
Bristol F-13
Brooklin Pg. 124, B-6
Brownsville H-3
Bruceton G-4
Brunswick Pg. 119, B-8
Bulls Gap G-12
Bumpus Mills F-5
Burlison H-2
Burns G-6
Byrdstown F-9
Calhoun J-9
Camden G-5
Camelot F-12
Capleville J-2
  Vicinity Pg. 119, G-6
Carlisle G-5
Carthage G-8
Caryville G-10
Cash Point J-6
Cedar Hill F-6
Celina G-8
Center Point J-6
Centertown H-7
Centerville H-6
Central G-3
Charleston J-9
Charlotte G-5
Chattanooga J-8
Church Hill F-12
Clarksburg H-4
Clarksville F-5
Cleveland J-9
Clifton J-5
Clinton G-10
Coalmont J-8
Collegedale J-9
Collierville J-2
  Vicinity Pg. 119, F-10
Collinwood J-5
Columbia H-6
Cookeville G-8
Copperhill J-10
Cordova Pg. 119, D-8
Cornersville J-6
Cosby G-11
Covington H-2
Crab Orchard H-9
Cross Plains F-6
Crossville G-9
Culleoka H-6
Cumberland City G-5
Cumberland Furnace G-5
Cumberland Gap F-11
Dancyville H-3
Dandridge G-11
Darden H-4
Dayton H-9
Decatur H-9
Decaturville H-5
Decherd J-8
Dibrell H-8
Dickson G-5
Dixon Springs G-7
Donelson G-7
  Vicinity Pg. 124, D-7
Dover F-5
Dowelltown G-7
Doyle H-8
Dresden G-3
Ducktown J-10
Dunlap J-9
Dyer G-3
Dyersburg G-3
Eads Pg. 119, C-10
Eagan F-10
East Ridge J-9
Eastview J-4
Egypt Pg. 119, B-6
Elizabethton G-13
Elkton J-6
Ellandale Pg. 119, B-7
Elmore Park Pg. 119, C-7
Elora G-6
Elza G-10
Englewood J-10
Erin G-5
Erwin G-13
Estill Springs J-7
Ethridge J-6
Etowah J-10
Evensville H-9
Fairview H-6
Farmington J-6
Fayetteville J-6
Finley G-3
Fisherville Pg. 119, D-10
Flat Woods H-5
Flatcreek J-7
Forbus F-9
Forest Hill Pg. 119, F-8
Forest Hills Pg. 124, F-4
Foster Corners Pg. 124, F-8
Franklin H-6
Friendship G-3
Fruitvale H-3
Gadsden H-3
Gainesboro G-8
Gallatin G-7
Gates H-3
Gatlinburg H-11
Germanton Pg. 124, B-4
Germantown J-2
  Vicinity Pg. 119, E-8
Gibson H-4
Gildfield G-4
Gilt Edge H-2
Gleason G-4
Goodlettsville G-7
  Vicinity Pg. 124, A-6
Goodspring J-6
Gordonsville G-7
Gower Pg. 124, E-3
Grand Junction J-3
Grandview H-9
Gray G-13
Graysville H-9
Green Hill Pg. 124, C-9
Greenback H-10
Greenbrier G-6
Greeneville G-12
Greenfield G-4
Grimsley G-9
Habersham F-10
Haletown J-8
Halls H-3
Halls Crossroads G-11
Hampshire H-5
Hampton G-13
Hanging Limb G-9
Harriman H-10
Harrogate F-11
Hartsville G-7
Henderson H-4
Hendersonville G-7
  Vicinity Pg. 124, A-8
Henning H-2
Henry G-4
Hermitage Hills
  Pg. 124, C-8
Hickory Valley J-3
Highland J-5
Hohenwald H-5
Hopewell Pg. 124, C-8
Hornsby J-3
Humboldt H-3
Hunter G-13
Huntingdon G-4
Huntland J-7
Huntsville G-10
India G-4
Inglewood G-7
  Vicinity Pg. 124, C-6
Iron City J-5
Isham F-10
Ivydell G-10
Jacksboro G-10
Jackson H-3
Jamestown G-9
Jasper J-8
Jefferson City G-11
Jellico F-10
Joelton G-6
  Vicinity Pg. 124, A-4
Johnson City G-13
Jonesboro G-12
Keeling H-2
Kelso J-7
Kenton G-3
Kimbro Pg. 124, G-8
Kingsport F-13
Kingston H-10
Kirkland H-7
Knoxville H-10
Kodak H-11
Kyles Ford F-12
La Vergne G-7
  Vicinity Pg. 124, G-9
LaFollette G-10
Laager J-8
Lafayette F-8
Lake City G-10
Lake Mont H-10
Lakeside J-9
Lancing G-9
Lascassas H-7
Latham G-4
Lawrenceburg J-5
Leach G-4
Lebanon G-7
Leipers Fork H-6
Lenoir City H-10
Lenow Pg. 119, C-9
Lewisburg H-6
Lexington H-4
Liberty G-7
Lickton Pg. 124, A-5
Linden H-5
Little Creek Pg. 124, B-5
Livingston G-8
Lobelville H-5
Locke J-2
Loretto J-5
Loudon H-10
Lucy Pg. 119, A-6
Luttrell G-11
Lutts J-5
Lyles H-6
Lynchburg J-7
Lynnville J-6
Madisonville H-10
Malesus H-3
Manchester H-7
Marrowbone Pg. 124, C-1
Martin G-4
Maryville H-10
Mascot G-11
Mason H-2
Maury City H-3
Mayland G-8
Maynardville G-10
McBurg J-6
McEwen G-5
McKenzie G-4
McMinnville H-8
Medina H-4
Medon H-4
Memphis J-1, Pg. 119
Mercer H-3
Michie J-4
Middleton J-3
Midtown H-10
Milan H-4
  Vicinity Pg. 124, A-6
Milledgeville H-4
Milligan College G-13
Millington J-2
Minor Hill J-6
Miston G-2
Monteagle J-8
Monterey G-9
Morgantown H-9
Morris Chapel J-4
Morrison H-7
Morristown G-11
Moscow J-3
Mosheim G-12
Moss F-8
Mound City Pg. 119, C-9
Mount Carmel F-12
Mount Crest H-9
Mount Juliet G-7
  Vicinity Pg. 124, C-9
Mount Olive H-11
Mount Pleasant H-6
Mount Vernon J-10
Mount Zion Pg. 124, A-2
Mountain City F-14
Munford H-2
Murfreesboro H-7
Nashville G-6
  Vicinity Pg. 124
New Hope K-8
New Johnsonville G-5
New Market G-11
New River G-10
New Tazewell G-11
Newbern G-3
Newport G-12
Niota H-10
Nixon J-4
Nobles G-4
Norris G-10
Nunnelly H-5
Oak Hill Pg. 124, F-6
Oak Ridge G-10
Oakdale G-9
Oakland J-2
  Vicinity Pg. 119, F-6
Oakville Pg. 124, F-7
Oakwood F-5
Obion G-3
Ocoee J-9
Oglesby Pg. 124, G-6
Old Hickory Pg. 124, B-8
Olivehill J-4
Oliver Springs G-10
Oneida F-10
Palmer H-8
Palmyra F-5
Parago Mill Pg. 124, F-7
Paris G-4
Parrottsville G-12
Parsons H-4
Pasqua Pg. 124, F-3
Peakland H-9
Pegram G-6
Pelham J-8
Petersburg J-6
Philadelphia H-10
Pigeon Forge H-11
Pikeville H-9
Pinewood H-5
Pinson H-4
Pisgah Pg. 119, D-10
Pleasant Hill G-9
Pleasant View G-6
Portland F-7
Providence J-10
  Vicinity Pg. 124, F-7
Pulaski J-6
Puncheon Camp G-11
Puryear G-3
Quebeck H-8
Raleigh J-2
  Vicinity Pg. 119, B-6
Ramer J-4
Ramsey Pg. 119, A-4
Raus J-4
Rayon City Pg. 124, B-7
Red Bank J-9
Red Boiling Springs F-8
Riceville J-10
Richland Pg. 124, D-3
Rickman G-9
Ridgely G-3
Ridgetop G-6
Ripley H-2
Rives H-3
Roan Mountain G-13
Robbins G-9
Rockwood H-9
Rocky Fork G-12
Rogersville G-12
Rossville J-2
Rural Hill Pg. 124, F-8
Russellville G-12
Rutherford G-3
Rutledge G-11
Sadlersville F-6
Saint Bethlehem G-5
Saint Joseph J-5
Sale Creek J-9
Saltillo J-4
Sardis H-4
Saundersville
  Pg. 124, A-9
Savannah J-4
Scotts Hill H-4
Selmer J-4
Seven Points Pg. 124, C-9
Sevierville H-11
Sewanee J-8
Shacklett G-6
Shady Valley F-13
Sharon G-3
Shelby Farms Pg. 119, D-7
Shelbyville H-7
Shooks Gap H-11
Shop Springs G-7
Signal Mtn. J-8
Silver Point J-6
Skiem J-6
Smartt H-8
Smith Springs Pg. 124, F-8
Smithville G-8
Smyrna G-7
Sneedville F-11
Soddy-Daisy J-9
Somerville J-2
South Carthage G-8
South Dyersburg G-3
South Fulton G-3
South Pittsburg J-8
Sparta H-8
Spencer H-8
Spring City H-9
Spring Creek H-4
Spring Hill H-6
Spring Lake Pg. 119, B-7
Springfield F-6
Stanton H-3
Sullivan Gdn. F-12
Summertown J-5
Sunbright G-10
Surgoinsville G-12
Sweetwater H-10
Sycamore Pg. 124, A-1
Taft J-6
Tarpley J-6
Tazewell G-11
Tellico Plains J-10
Tennessee Ridge G-5
Timberlake H-4
Tiptonville F-3
Toone J-3
Tracy City J-8
Trenton G-3
Trezevant G-4
Triune H-7
Troy G-3
Tullahoma J-7
Tusculum G-12
  Vicinity Pg. 124, F-6
Una Pg. 124, F-7
Unicoi G-13
Union City G-3
Union Grove J-9
Union Hill Pg. 124, A-5
Victoria J-8
Viola H-8
Violet G-11
Vonore H-10
Waco J-6
Walden J-8
Walkertown J-4
Walling H-8
Wartburg G-10
Wartrace H-7
Watertown G-8
Waverly G-5
Waynesboro J-5
Webber City J-8
West Meade Pg. 124, E-4
West Shiloh J-4
Westmoreland F-7
White Bluff G-6
White House F-7
White Pine G-12
Whites Creek Pg. 124, B-4
Whitesburg G-12
Whiteville J-3
Whitwell J-8
Wilder G-9
Williston J-3
Winchester J-7
Winfield F-10
Woodbury H-8
Woodland Mills F-3
Woodstock Pg. 119, B-5
Wrencoe Pg. 124, G-7
Wyanoke Pg. 119, E-1
Wynnburg G-3

TEXAS

TEXAS
Pages 75-79
Population: 14,229,191
Capital: Austin
Land Area: 262,017 sq. mi.

Abernathy E-7
Abilene G-10
Acala J-2
Ackerly G-7
Acme D-10
Adamsville J-12
Addicks L-15
  Vicinity Pg. 109, D-1
Addison Pg. 105, A-8
Adrian C-7
Agua Dulce P-12
Aiken E-8
Alamo Heights
  Pg. 142, D-5
Alanreed C-9
Alba F-15
Albany G-10
Aldine L-15
Aledo F-12
Alexander H-12
Alfred P-12
Algoa M-16
Alice P-12
Alief Pg. 109, E-2
Allamoore J-3
Allen F-14
Alleyton L-14
Allison B-10
Allred F-6
Almeda Pg. 109, E-4
Alpine K-5
Altair M-14
Alto H-16
Alvarado G-13
Alvin M-16
Alvord E-12
Amarillo C-7
Ambrose E-14
Ames L-16
Amherst E-7
Anderson K-15
Andice K-12
Andrews G-6
Angleton M-16
Anna E-14
Annona F-16
Anson G-10
Antelope F-12
Anthony H-2
Anton E-7
Apple Springs J-16
Aquilla H-13
Aransas Pass P-13
Archer City E-11
Argyle F-13
Arlington G-13
  Vicinity Pg. 104, D-5
Arp H-16
Artesia Wells P-10
Arthur City E-15
Asherton N-10
Ashtola C-8
Aspermont F-9
Athens G-15
Atlanta F-17
Aubrey E-13
Austin L-13
Austonio J-15
Austwell N-14
Avery F-16
Avinger F-17
Avoca G-10
Azle G-13
Bacliff M-16
Bagwell F-16
Baird G-10
Bakersfield K-7
Balch Springs G-14
  Vicinity Pg. 105, E-11
Balcones Heights
  Pg. 142, D-3
Ballinger H-10
Balmorhea J-5
Bammel Pg. 109, A-4
Bandera L-11
Bangs H-11
Barclay J-13
Bardwell H-14
Barksdale L-10
Barnhart J-8
Barrett
  Vicinity Pg. 109, C-10
Barry H-14
Barstow J-5
Bartlett K-13
Bassett F-16
Bastrop L-13
Batesville N-10
Batson L-16
Bay City M-15
Baytown L-16
  Vicinity Pg. 109, D-4
Beasley M-15

TEXAS

Beaumont L-17
  Vicinity .... Pg. 109, C-7
Beckville G-17
Bedias K-15
Bee Cave L-12
Beeville N-12
Belfalls J-13
Bellaire .... Pg. 109, E-3
Bellevue E-12
Bellmead H-13
Bells E-14
Bellville L-14
Belmont M-13
Belton J-13
Ben G-15
Ben Arnold J-14
Ben Bolt P-12
Benavides Q-11
Benchley K-14
Benjamin F-10
Bertram K-12
Bettie G-16
Big Lake J-7
Big Sandy G-16
  Vicinity .... Pg. 105, A-8
Big Spring H-8
Big Wells N-10
Bigfoot M-11
Birthright F-15
Bishop Q-12
Bivins F-17
Black D-7
Blackwell H-9
Blanco L-11
Blanket H-11
Bleakwood K-18
Bledsoe E-6
Blessing N-15
Blewett M-9
Blooming Grove H-14
Bloomington N-13
Blossom E-15
Blue Mound Pg. 104, C-3
Blue Ridge F-14
Bluegrove E-12
Bluff Dale G-12
Bluffton K-11
Boca Chica S-13
Boerne L-11
Bogata F-15
Boling M-14
Bomarton F-10
Bon Wier K-18
Bonham E-14
Booker A-9
Boonsville F-12
Borger B-8
Boston F-17
Bovina D-6
Bowie E-12
Boxelder F-16
Boyd F-12
Boys Ranch Tacosa . B-7
Brackettville M-9
Bradshaw H-10
Brady J-10
Brandon H-14
Brashear F-15
Brazoria M-15
Breckenridge G-11
Bremond J-14
Brenham L-14
Brice D-9
Bridge City L-18
Bridgeport F-12
Briggs K-12
Briscoe B-9
Broaddus J-17
Bronco F-6
Bronson J-17
Bronte H-9
Brookeland J-17
Brooksmith J-11
Brookshire L-15
Brookside Village
  .... Pg. 109, G-6
Brownfield F-7
Brownsboro G-15
Brownsville S-13
Brownwood H-11
Brundage N-10
Bruni Q-11
Bryan K-14
Buchanan Dam K-12
Buckholts K-13
Buda L-12
Buena Vista Pg. 142, H-5
Buffalo J-15
Buffalo Gap G-10
Bula E-6
Bulcher E-13
Bullard H-16
Buna K-17
Bunavista B-8
Bunker Hill . Pg. 109, E-3
Burkburnett E-11
Burke J-16
Burkett H-10
Burkeville J-18
Burleson G-13
  Vicinity .. Pg. 104, G-3
Burlington J-14
Burnet K-12
Burton L-14
Bushland C-7
Bustamanete R-11
Butler K-13
Byers E-12
Bynum H-14
Cactus A-7
Caddo G-11
Caddo Mills F-15
Caldwell K-14

Calf Creek J-10
Call K-18
Calliham N-12
Calvert K-14
Camden K-16
Cameron K-14
Camilla K-16
Camp Verde L-11
Camp Wood L-10
Campbell F-15
Campbellton N-12
Canadian B-9
Canton G-15
Canutillo H-1
Canyon C-7
Caps G-10
Carbon G-11
Carlos K-15
Carlsbad H-9
Carlton H-12
Carmine L-14
Carmona J-16
Carrizo Springs N-10
Carrollton G-13
  Vicinity ... Pg. 104, F-3
Carta Valley L-9
Carthage H-17
Cash F-15
Cassin .... Pg. 142, H-4
Castle Hills M-11
  Vicinity .. Pg. 142, C-4
Castroville M-11
Catarina N-10
Cayuga H-15
Cedar Creek L-13
Cedar Hill . Pg. 105, F-4
Cedar Park K-12
Celeste F-14
Celina F-14
Center H-17
Centerville J-15
Champions . Pg. 109, A-3
Chandler G-15
Channelview L-16
  Vicinity .. Pg. 109, D-8
Channing B-7
Chapman H-16
Chapman Ranch P-13
Chappell Hill L-15
Charco N-13
Charlotte N-11
Cherokee J-11
Cherry Spring K-11
Chester J-17
Chico F-12
Childress D-9
Chillicothe D-10
Chilton J-13
China L-17
China Grove Pg. 142, F-7
Chireno J-17
Chisos Basin M-5
Chriesman K-14
Christine N-11
Christoval J-9
Circle Back E-6
Cisco G-11
Cistern L-13
Clairemont F-9
Clairette H-12
Clarendon C-9
Clarksville E-16
Claude C-8
Clayton H-17
Cleburne G-13
Cleveland K-16
Clifton H-13
Clint H-1
Cloverleaf . Pg. 109, D-8
Clute M-16
Clyde G-10
Coady .... Pg. 109, D-10
Coahoma G-8
Cockrell Hill Pg. 105, D-4
Coffey City H-15
Coldspring K-16
Coleman H-10
College Station K-14
Colleyville . Pg. 104, B-5
Collinsville F-13
Colmesneil K-17
Colorado City G-9
Columbus L-14
Comanche H-11
Combes R-12
Comfort L-11
Commerce F-15
Como F-15
Comstock L-9
Concan M-10
Concepcion Q-12
Concord H-16
Conroe K-16
Converse L-11
Conway C-8
Cooks Point K-14
Cookville F-16
Coolidge H-14
Cooper F-15
Coppell .... Pg. 105, A-7
Copperas Cove J-12
Cornudas H-3
Corpus Christi P-13
Corrigan J-16
Corsicana H-14
Coryell City J-13
Cost M-13
Cotton Center E-7
Cottonwood K-15
Cottonwood G-13
Cotulla N-10
Country Campus K-16
Coy City N-12

Coyanosa J-5
Crabbs Praire K-15
Crandall G-14
Crane J-6
Cranvills Gap H-13
Crawford J-13
Cresson G-13
Crews H-10
Crockett J-15
Crosby L-15
  Vicinity .. Pg. 109, B-9
Crosbyton E-8
Cross K-15
Cross Cut H-11
Cross Plains H-11
Cross Roads H-15
Crow G-16
Crowell E-10
Crowley G-13
  Vicinity ... Pg. 104, F-3
Crystal City N-10
Cuero M-13
Cumby F-14
Cushing H-16
Cut & Shoot K-15
Cypress L-15
Cypress Mill K-12
D'Hanis M-10
Dabney M-9
Dacosta N-14
Daingerfield F-16
Daisetta K-16
Dalhart B-7
Dalingworth Gardens
  .... Pg. 104, E-5
Dallas G-14
  Vicinity Pg. 105
Damon M-15
Danbury M-15
Danevang M-15
Darrouzett A-9
Dawn C-7
Dawson H-14
Dayton L-16
De Berry G-17
De Kalb F-16
De Leon H-11
De Wees M-12
DeSoto .... Pg. 105, F-8
Deanville K-14
Decatur F-13
Deer Park L-16
  Vicinity .. Pg. 109, F-9
Del Rio M-8
Del Valle L-13
Dell City H-3
Denison E-14
Denton F-13
Denver City F-6
Deport F-15
Derby N-11
Desdemona H-12
Devers L-17
Devine M-11
Dew H-15
Deweyville K-18
Diana G-16
Diboll J-16
Dickens E-9
Dickinson L-15
Dilley N-11
Dime Box K-14
Dinero P-12
Divot N-11
Dobbin K-15
Dodd City E-15
Donie J-14
Donna S-12
Doole J-10
Doss K-11
Doucette K-17
Dougherty E-8
Douglass H-16
Douglassville F-17
Dozier C-9
Draw F-8
Dripping Springs L-12
Driscoll P-12
Dryden L-7
Dublin H-12
Dumas B-7
Dumont E-9
Duncanville Pg. 105, F-7
Dundee E-11
Dunlay M-11
Dunn G-9
Dyersdale .. Pg. 109, B-7
Eagle Lake M-14
Eagle Pass N-9
Early H-11
Earth D-7
East Columbia M-15
Easterly J-14
Eastland G-11
Easton G-16
Edcouch R-12
Eddy J-13
Eden J-10
Edgecliff .. Pg. 104, E-3
Edinburg R-12
Edmonson D-7
Edna M-14
Edom G-15
Edroy P-13
Egypt M-14
El Campo M-14
El Lago .. Pg. 109, G-10
El Paso H-2
El Sauz R-10
Eldorado K-9
Elbert F-11
Electra E-11
Elgin K-13

Elkhart H-15
Ellinger L-14
Elmendorf M-12
  Vicinity .. Pg. 142, J-7
Elmo G-15
Elsa R-12
Elysian Fields G-17
Emory F-14
Encinal P-10
Encino Q-12
Energy H-12
Enloe F-15
Ennis G-14
Enochs E-6
Escobas Q-11
Estelline D-9
Etoile J-17
Etter B-7
Euless .... Pg. 104, C-6
Eureka H-14
Eustace G-15
Evadale K-17
Evant J-12
Evergreen H-15
Everman .. Pg. 104, F-3
Fabens H-1
Fairbanks .. Pg. 108, C-2
Fairfield H-15
Fairlie F-15
Fairview F-14
Fairview G-8
Fairy H-12
Falcon R-11
Falfurrias Q-12
Falls City N-12
Fannett L-17
Fannin N-13
Farmers Branch
  .... Pg. 105, B-8
Farmersville F-14
Farnsworth A-9
Farrar J-14
Farwell D-6
Fayetteville L-14
Fedor K-13
Fentress L-13
Ferris G-14
  Vicinity .. Pg. 105, G-10
Fieldton E-7
Fink E-14
Finney E-9
Flatonia M-13
Flomot D-8
Florence J-12
Floresville M-12
Flower Mound
  .... Pg. 104, A-6
Floydada E-8
Fluvanna F-8
Follett A-10
Fomot D-8
Forest Hill Pg. 104, E-4
Forestburg F-13
Forney G-14
Fort Clark Springs . M-9
Fort Davis K-5
Fort Gates J-12
Fort Griffin G-10
Fort Hancock J-2
Fort McKavett K-10
Fort Stockton J-6
Fort Worth G-13
  Vicinity Pg. 104
Fostoria K-16
Four Corners
  .... Pg. 109, D-10
Fowlerton N-11
Frame Switch K-13
Francitas N-14
Frankel City F-6
Franklin J-14
Frankston H-15
Fransworth A-9
Fred K-17
Fredericksburg L-11
Fredonia K-11
Freeport N-16
Freer P-11
Friday J-16
Frio Town M-10
Friona D-6
Frisco F-13
Fritch B-8
Frost H-14
Fruitland F-12
Fruitvale G-15
Fullbright F-16
Fulton P-13
Funston G-10
Gail G-8
Gainesville E-13
Galena Park Pg. 109, E-7
Galveston M-16
Ganado M-14
Garden City H-8
Garden Valley G-15
Gardendale M-7
  Vicinity .. Pg. 142, E-7
Garland G-14
  Vicinity .. Pg. 105, B-10
Garrison H-17
Garwood M-14
Gary H-17
Gatesville J-12
Gause K-14
Geneva J-17
George West N-12
Georgetown K-13
Geronimo L-12
Giddings L-13
Gilchrist M-17
Gillett N-12
Gilliland E-10
Gilmer G-16
Girard F-9

Girvin J-7
Gladewater G-16
Glazier B-9
Glen Cove H-10
Glen Flora M-15
Glen Rose H-13
Glenn E-9
Glenn Heights
  .... Pg. 105, G-8
Glenrio C-6
Glenwood G-16
Glidden L-14
Gober F-15
Godley G-13
  Vicinity .. Pg. 105, E-10
Goldsboro H-10
Goldthwaite J-11
Goliad N-13
Gonzales M-13
Goodland E-6
Goodlett D-10
Goodnight C-8
Goodrich K-16
Gordon G-12
Gordonville E-13
Goree F-10
Gorman H-11
Gouldbusk J-10
Graford F-12
Graham F-11
Granbury G-12
Grand Prairie G-13
  Vicinity .. Pg. 105, D-6
Grand Saline G-15
Grandfalls J-6
Granger K-13
Grapeland J-15
Grapevine . Pg. 104, B-6
Grassland F-8
Grayback E-11
Greenville F-15
Grey Forest Pg. 142, A-1
Grit K-10
Groesbeck J-14
Groom C-8
Groves L-17
Groveton J-16
Gruver A-8
Gun Barrel City . G-14
Gustine H-12
Guthrie E-9
Guy M-15
Hagansport F-15
Hale Center E-7
Halletsville M-14
Hallsville G-16
Haltom City . Pg. 104, C-3
Hamilton H-12
Hamlin G-9
Hamshire L-17
Happy C-7
Hardin L-16
Hargill R-12
Harker Heights . J-13
Harleton G-16
Harlingen S-13
Harper L-10
Harrold E-11
Hart D-6
Hartley B-7
Harwood L-13
Haskell F-10
Haslet .... Pg. 104, A-3
Hatchel H-10
Hawkins G-16
Hawley G-10
Hearne K-14
Hebbronville Q-11
Hebron .... Pg. 105, A-8
Hedley C-9
Hedwig .. Pg. 109, D-3
Helena N-13
Helotes .. Pg. 142, B-1
Hemleigh G-9
Hemphill J-18
Hempstead L-14
Henderson G-16
Henrietta E-12
Hereford C-6
Hext K-10
Hico H-12
Hidalgo S-12
Higgins B-10
Highbank J-14
Highland Park
  .... Pg. 105, C-9
Highlands L-16
  Vicinity .. Pg. 109, D-9
Hill Country Village
  .... Pg. 142, A-5
Hillister K-17
Hillsboro H-13
Hillshire Village
  .... Pg. 109, D-3
Hilltop Lakes J-14
Hindes N-11
Hitchcock M-16
Hobson N-12
Hochheim M-13
Hockley L-15
Holland K-13
Holliday E-11
Hollywood Park
  .... Pg. 142, A-4
Hondo M-11
Honey Grove E-15
Horizon City H-1
Houmont Park
  .... Pg. 109, C-7
Houston L-15
  Vicinity Pg. 109
Howellville Pg. 109, E-1
Hubbard H-14
Huckabay G-12

Hudson J-16
Hughes Springs F-16
Hull K-16
Humble L-16
  Vicinity .. Pg. 109, A-7
Hunt L-10
Hunters Creek
  .... Pg. 109, D-3
Huntington J-17
Huntsville K-15
  Vicinity .. Pg. 105, F-9
Hurlwood E-7
Hurst .... Pg. 104, C-5
  Vicinity .. Pg. 105, E-10
Hutchins G-14
Hutto K-13
Hye L-11
Idalou E-7
Imperial J-6
Inadal G-9
Independence L-14
Indian Gap J-12
Industry L-14
Inez N-14
Ingleside P-13
Ingram L-11
Iola K-15
Iowa Park E-11
Ira G-8
Iraan K-7
Iredell H-12
Ireland J-12
Irving G-13
  Vicinity .. Pg. 105, C-7
Italy G-13
Itasca H-13
Jacinto City . Pg. 109, D-7
Jacksboro F-12
Jacksonville H-15
Jamestown J-18
Jarrell K-13
Jasper J-17
Jayton F-9
Jean F-11
Jefferson G-17
Jermyn F-12
Jersey Village
  .... Pg. 109, C-2
Jewett J-14
Joaquin H-17
Johnson City L-11
Johntown F-16
Jolly E-11
Jollyville K-12
Jones Creek M-15
Jonesboro H-12
Jonestown K-12
Joshua G-13
Jourdanton N-11
Joy E-12
Junction K-10
Juno L-8
Justiceburg F-8
Justin F-13
Kalgary F-8
Kamay E-11
Kanawha G-16
Karnack G-17
Karnes City N-12
Katemcy K-10
Katy L-15
Kaufman G-14
Keene G-13
Keller .... Pg. 104, B-4
Kellerville C-9
Kemp G-14
Kempner J-12
Kendleton M-15
Kenedy N-12
Kennard J-16
Kennedale . Pg. 104, E-4
Kenney L-14
Kent J-4
Kenwood .. Pg. 109, B-6
Kerens H-14
Kermit G-6
Kerrville L-11
Kilgore G-16
Killeen J-13
Kings Mill C-8
Kingsland K-11
Kingston F-14
Kingsville Q-12
Kirby .... Pg. 142, D-6
Kirbyville K-17
Kirkland D-9
Kirvin H-14
Kleburg .. Pg. 105, E-11
Knickerbocker J-9
Knippa M-10
Knott G-7
Knox City F-10
Kopperl H-13
Kosse J-14
Kountze K-17
Kress D-7
Krum F-13
Kyle L-12
La Gloria R-11
La Grange L-13
La Grulla R-11
La Joya S-12
La Marque M-16
La Paloma S-13
La Porte .. Pg. 109, D-8
La Pryor N-10
La Reforma R-11
La Vernia M-12
La Villa R-12
La Ward N-14
Ladonia F-15
Lago Vista K-12
Laguna Park H-13
Lake Hills M-11
Lake Jackson M-15

Lake Worth . Pg. 104, C-2
Lakeport G-16
Lakeside .. Pg. 104, C-1
Lakeside Village .. H-13
Lakeview D-9
Lamesa G-7
Lamkin H-12
Lampasas J-12
Lancaster G-14
  Vicinity .. Pg. 105, F-9
Lane City M-15
Langtry L-7
Laredo Q-10
Lariat D-6
Lark C-8
Larue H-15
Lasara R-12
Latexo J-15
Lavon F-14
Lawn H-10
LeFors C-9
League City L-15
Leakey L-10
Leander K-12
Leesburg F-16
Leesville M-13
Leggett K-16
Lehman E-6
Leigh G-17
Lela C-9
Lelia Lake C-9
Leming M-12
Lenorah G-7
Leon Springs L-11
Leon Valley L-11
  Vicinity .. Pg. 142, C-2
Leona J-15
Leonard F-14
Levelland E-7
Lewisville F-13
  Vicinity .. Pg. 105, A-6
Lexington K-13
Liberty L-16
Liberty Hill K-12
Libscomb A-9
Lincoln L-13
Lincoln City Pg. 108, C-5
Lindale G-15
Linden F-17
Lindsay E-13
Lingleville H-12
Linus .... Pg. 109, D-10
Lipan G-12
Little Elm F-13
Littlefield E-7
Live Oak .. Pg. 142, B-7
Liverpool M-16
Livingston K-16
Llano K-11
Lobo J-3
Lockett E-10
Lockhart L-13
Lockney E-8
Lodi F-17
Loma Alta L-8
Lomax H-8
Lometa J-11
London K-10
Lone Star F-16
Long Branch H-16
Long Mott N-14
Longview G-16
Longworth G-9
Loop F-7
Lopeno R-11
Loraine G-9
Lorena J-13
Lorenzo E-8
Los Angeles N-11
Los Fresnos S-12
Losoya .... Pg. 142, J-5
Lott J-13
Louise M-14
Lovelady J-15
Loving F-11
Loyal Valley K-11
Lubbock F-8
Luckenbach L-11
Lueders G-10
Lufkin J-16
Luling L-13
Lumberton K-17
Lutie C-9
Lydia F-16
Lyford R-12
Lynchburg .. Pg. 109, D-8
Lyons K-14
Lytle M-11
Mabank G-15
Macdona .. Pg. 142, H-2
Madisonville J-15
Magnolia M-15
Malakoff H-15
Malta F-16
Mangus Corner
  .... Pg. 142, H-2
Mankins E-11
Mansfield G-13
  Vicinity .. Pg. 104, F-5
Maple E-6
Marathon K-5
Marble Falls K-12
Marfa K-4
Marietta F-17
Marion M-12
Markham M-15
Marlin J-14
Marquez J-14
Marshall G-16
Mart J-14
Martindale L-13
Martinez H-17
  Vicinity .. Pg. 142, E-7
Martinsville H-17
Maryneal G-9
Mason K-11
Masterson B-7

Matador E-8
Matagorda N-15
Mathis P-12
Maud F-17
Mauriceville L-17
Maxwell L-12
May H-11
Maydelle H-16
Maypearl G-13
McAdoo E-8
McAllen S-12
McCamey J-7
McCauley G-9
McDade L-13
McFaddin N-13
McGregor J-13
McKinney F-14
McLean C-9
McLeod F-17
McMahan L-13
McNair .... Pg. 109, D-9
McNary J-2
McQueeney L-12
Meadow F-7
Medicine Mound .. D-10
Medina L-11
Megargel F-11
Melissa F-14
Melrose H-17
Melvin J-10
Memphis D-9
Menard K-10
Mendoza L-13
Mentone H-5
Mercedes S-12
Meridian H-13
Merkel G-9
Mertzon J-8
Mesquite G-14
  Vicinity .. Pg. 105, C-11
Mexia H-14
Miami B-9
Mico M-11
Midland H-7
Midlothian G-14
Midway K-15
Milam J-18
Milano K-14
Miles H-9
Milford G-13
Millersview J-10
Millican K-14
Mineola G-15
Mineral N-12
Mineral Wells G-12
Mingus G-12
Mirando City Q-11
Mission S-12
Missouri City Pg. 109, G-3
Mobeetie C-9
Moline J-12
Monahans H-6
Monkstown E-15
Monroe L-17
Mont Belvieu L-16
Montague E-12
Montalba H-15
Monte Alto R-12
Montgomery K-15
Monthalia M-13
Moody J-13
Moore M-11
Mooring K-14
Moran G-11
Morgan H-13
Morgan Mill G-12
Morgans Point
  .... Pg. 109, F-10
Morse B-8
Morton E-6
Morton Valley G-11
Moscow J-16
Moss Hill K-16
Moulton M-13
Mount Calm H-14
Mount Enterprise .. H-16
Mount Houston
  .... Pg. 109, C-6
Mount Pleasant F-16
Mount Sylvan G-15
Mount Vernon F-16
Mountain Home L-10
Muenster E-13
Muldoon L-14
Muleshoe D-6
Mullin J-11
Mumford K-14
Munday F-10
Murchison G-15
Murphy .... Pg. 105, A-11
Myrtle Springs G-15
N. Richland Hills
  .... Pg. 104, C-4
Nacogdoches H-16
Nada M-14
Naples F-17
Nash F-17
Natalia M-11
Navasota K-15
Nazareth D-7
Neches H-15
Nederland L-17
Needmore E-6
Needville M-15
Nelsonville L-14
New Baden J-14
New Boston F-17
New Braunfels L-12
  Vicinity .. Pg. 142, E-7
New Caney L-16
New Deal E-7
New Gulf M-15
New Home F-7
New London G-16

TEXAS

New Summerfield .. H-16
New Ulm L-14
New Waverly K-15
Newark ...... Pg. 104, A-1
Newcastle F-11
Newlin D-9
Newman H-2
Newsome F-16
Newton K-18
Nixon M-13
Nocona E-12
Nolan G-9
Nolanville J-13
Nome K-16
Noodle G-10
Nordheim N-13
Normandy N-9
Normangee J-15
Normanna N-13
North Houston
.... Pg. 109, B-3
North Zulch K-14
Northcrest H-13
Northfield D-9
Norton H-9
Notrees H-6
Novice H-10
Nuevo Laredo P-10
Nursery N-13
O'Brien F-10
O'Donnell F-7
Oak Hill L-12
Oakalla J-12
Oakland M-14
Oakwood H-15
Odem P-13
Odessa H-7
Oglesby H-13
Oilton Q-11
Oklaunion E-11
Old Boston F-17
Old Center H-17
Old Glory F-9
Old Ocean M-15
Olden G-11
Oldenburg L-14
Olivia N-14
Olmito S-13
Olmos Park .. Pg. 142, D-4
Olney F-11
Olton E-7
Omaha F-16
Oplin H-10
Orange L-18
Orange Grove .. P-12
Ore City F-16
Orla H-5
Osceola H-13
Ottine M-13
Ovalo H-10
Overton G-16
Ovilla .... Pg. 105, G-8
Ozona K-8
Paducah E-9
Paige L-13
Paint Rock J-10
Painview D-7
Palacios N-14
Palestine ... H-15
Palmer G-14
Palo Pinto .. G-12
Pampa B-8
Pandora M-13
Panhandle .. C-8
Panna Maria . M-12
Panola G-17
Paradise ... F-13
Paris E-15
Parnell D-9
Pasadena .. L-16
Vicinity .. Pg. 109, F-8
Patricia G-7
Patroon H-17
Pattonville .. E-16
Pawnee N-12
Paxton H-17
Pearland .. Pg. 109, G-6
Pearsall ... N-11
Pecos J-5
Peggy N-12
Penwell ... H-6
Perrin H-11
Perry J-13
Perryton ... A-9
Petersburg .. E-8
Petrolia E-12
Pettus N-12
Petty E-15
Pflugerville .. K-13
Phalba G-15
Pharr S-12
Phillips B-7
Pilot Point .. F-13
Pine Mills .. G-16
Pinehurst ... K-17
Pineland ... J-17
Piney Pt. .. Pg. 109, E-3
Pioneer H-11
Pipecreek ... J-11
Pittsburg ... F-16
Placedo N-14
Plains F-6
Plano F-13
Vicinity .. Pg. 105, A-10
Plantersville .. K-15
Plata L-4
Pleasanton ... N-12
Point Comfort .. N-14
Pollok H-16
Ponder F-13
Ponta H-16
Pontotoc ... K-11
Poolville ... F-12
Port Aransas .. P-13

Port Arthur L-17
Port Bolivar L-16
Port Isabel S-13
Port Lavaca N-14
Port Mansfield ... R-13
Port Neches L-17
Port O'Connor ... N-14
Porter J-16
Portland P-13
Posey F-8
Post F-8
Poteet N-11
Poth M-12
Pottsboro E-14
Pottsville H-12
Powderly E-15
Powell H-14
Poynor H-15
Prairie Dell ... K-13
Prairie Hill H-14
Prairie Lea L-13
Prairie View ... L-15
Premont Q-12
Presidio L-4
Priddy H-11
Princeton ... F-14
Pritchett ... G-16
Proctor H-12
Prosper F-13
Purmela J-12
Putnam G-11
Pyote H-5
Quail C-9
Quanah D-10
Queen City .. F-17
Quemado ... N-9
Quinlan G-14
Quitaque ... D-8
Quitman G-15
Rachal R-12
Ralls E-8
Ramirez Q-12
Randado ... Q-11
Randlett Charlie .. E-12
Randolph ... F-14
Ranger G-11
Rankin J-7
Ratcliff J-16
Ravenna ... E-14
Rayland ... E-9
Raymondville .. R-12
Raywood .. L-17
Reagan J-14
Realitos ... Q-11
Red Bluff .. Pg. 109, G-10
Red Oak .. F-14
Vicinity .. Pg. 105, G-9
Red Springs .. E-10
Redford ... M-4
Reese Vill. .. E-7
Refugio ... P-13
Reklaw ... H-16
Reno E-15
Retta .... Pg. 104, G-4
Rhome ... F-13
Ricardo .. Q-12
Rice G-14
Richardson .. F-13
Vicinity .. Pg. 105, A-9
Richland ... G-14
Richland Hills
.... Pg. 104, C-4
Richland Springs .. J-11
Richmond ... L-15
Richwood ... M-16
Ridge J-14
Riesel J-13
Ringgold .. E-12
Rio Grande City .. R-11
Rio Vista .. H-13
Riomendina .. M-11
Rios Q-12
Rising Star .. H-11
River Oaks .. Pg. 104, D-2
Riverside ... K-15
Riviera Q-12
Roans Prairie .. K-15
Robbins ... J-15
Robert Lee .. H-9
Robinson ... H-13
Robstown .. P-13
Roby G-9
Rochelle ... J-11
Rochester .. F-10
Rock Island .. M-14
Rockdale ... K-14
Rockland ... J-17
Rockport ... P-13
Rockspring .. L-9
Rockwood .. J-10
Roganville .. K-17
Rogers ... J-13
Roma R-10
Romayor .. K-16
Roosevelt ... K-9
Ropesville .. F-7
Rosanky ... L-13
Roscoe ... G-9
Rosebud ... J-14
Rosenberg .. M-15
Rosevine .. J-17
Rosser ... G-14
Rotan G-9
Round Mountain .. K-12
Round Rock .. K-13
Round Top .. L-14
Rowena ... H-9
Roxton ... E-15
Royalty .. J-6
Rule F-10
Rusk H-16
Rye K-16

Sacul H-16
Sadler E-14
Sagerton F-10
Saginaw G-13
Vicinity .. Pg. 104, C-2
Saint Hedwig .. M-12
Saint Jo E-13
Salado J-13
Salt Falt H-3
Samnorwood .. C-9
San Angelo .. J-9
San Antonio .. M-12
Vicinity Pg. 142
San Augustine .. H-17
San Benito .. S-13
San Diego .. P-12
San Elizario .. H-1
San Felipe .. L-14
San Gabriel .. K-13
San Isidro .. R-11
San Juan .. R-12
San Marcos .. L-12
San Patricio .. P-12
San Perlita .. R-13
San Saba .. J-11
San Ygnacio .. Q-10
Sanderson .. L-6
Sandia .. P-12
Sanford .. B-8
Sanger .. F-13
Sansom Park
.... Pg. 104, C-2
Santa Anna .. H-11
Santa Elena .. R-12
Santa Fe .. L-15
Santa Maria .. S-12
Santa Rosa .. S-12
Saragosa .. J-5
Saratoga .. K-17
Sarita .. Q-12
Satsuma .. Pg. 109, B-1
Savoy .. E-14
Schertz .. M-12
Schulenburg .. L-14
Scotland .. E-11
Scottsville .. G-17
Scranton .. G-11
Seabrook .. L-16
Vicinity .. Pg. 109, G-10
Seadrift .. N-14
Seagraves .. F-6
Sealy .. L-14
Sebastian .. R-13
Sebastopol .. K-16
Segovia .. K-10
Seguin .. M-12
Seminole .. G-6
Seven Points .. G-14
Seymour .. E-11
Shafter .. L-4
Shallowater .. E-7
Shamrock .. C-9
Shannon .. F-12
Shavano Park
.... Pg. 142, A-4
Sheffield .. K-7
Shelbyville .. H-17
Sheldon .. L-16
Vicinity .. Pg. 109, C-9
Sheridan .. M-14
Sherman .. F-14
Sherwood .. J-9
Shiner .. M-13
Shiro .. K-15
Shoreacres Pg. 109, G-10
Sidney .. H-11
Sierra Blanca .. J-3
Silsbee .. K-17
Silver .. H-9
Silverton .. D-8
Simms .. F-16
Singleton .. K-15
Sinton .. P-13
Sisterdale .. L-11
Sivells Bend .. E-13
Skellytown .. B-8
Skidmore .. P-13
Slaton .. F-8
Slidell .. F-13
Slocum .. H-16
Smiley .. M-13
Smyer .. E-7
Snook .. K-14
Snyder .. G-8
Socorro .. H-1
Somerset .. M-12
Vicinity .. Pg. 142, J-1
Somerville .. K-14
Sonora .. K-9
Sour Lake .. K-17
South Bend .. F-11
South Houston
.... Pg. 109, F-7
South Padre Island .. S-13
South Plains .. D-8
Southlake .. Pg. 104, B-5
Southland .. F-7
Southton .. Pg. 142, H-6
Spade .. D-7
Spanish Fort .. E-12
Speaks .. M-14
Spearman .. B-8
Spicewood .. K-12
Splendora .. L-16
Spofford .. M-9
Spring .. K-16
Spring Branch .. L-11
Spring Valley Pg. 109, D-3
Springlake .. D-7
Springtown .. F-13
Spur .. F-8
Spurger .. K-17
Stafford .. M-15
Vicinity .. Pg. 109, G-2

Stamford F-10
Stanton H-7
Star J-12
Stephenville .. H-12
Sterling City .. H-8
Stinnett B-8
Stockdale .. M-12
Stoneburg .. E-12
Stoneham .. K-15
Stonwall .. L-11
Stowell .. L-16
Stratford .. A-7
Strawn .. G-11
Streetman .. H-14
Study Butte .. M-5
Sudan .. E-7
Sugar Land .. L-15
Vicinity .. Pg. 109, G-1
Sullivan City .. S-11
Sulphur Sprs. .. F-15
Summerfield .. D-6
Sumner .. E-15
Sundown .. F-6
Sunray .. B-8
Sunset .. F-13
Sutherland Springs M-12
Sweeny .. M-15
Sweetwater .. G-9
Swenson .. F-9
Swenson .. F-9
Taft .. P-13
Tahoka .. F-7
Talco .. F-16
Talpa .. H-10
Tankersley .. J-9
Tarpley .. M-10
Tarzan .. G-7
Tatum .. G-17
Taylor .. K-13
Taylor Lake Village
.... Pg. 109, G-9
Teague .. H-14
Telegraph .. K-9
Telephone .. E-15
Telferner .. N-14
Tell .. D-9
Temple .. J-13
Tenaha .. H-17
Tennesee Colony .. H-15
Tennyson .. H-9
Terlingua .. M-5
Terrell .. G-14
Terrell Hills .. Pg. 142, D-5
Texarkana .. F-17
Texas City .. M-16
Texhoma .. A-8
Texico .. D-6
Texline .. A-6
Thackerville .. E-13
Thalia .. E-11
The Grove .. J-13
The Woodlands .. L-16
Thelma .. Pg. 142, K-5
Thomaston .. M-13
Thorndale .. K-13
Thornton .. J-14
Thorp Spring .. G-12
Thrall .. K-13
Three Rivers .. N-12
Throckmorton .. F-10
Tilden .. N-11
Timpson .. H-17
Tioga .. F-13
Tira .. F-15
Tivoli .. N-14
Toco .. E-15
Tolar .. G-12
Tomball .. K-15
Tool .. H-14
Topsey .. J-12
Tornillo .. H-1
Toyah .. J-5
Trent .. G-10
Trenton .. F-14
Trickham .. H-11
Trinidad .. H-15
Trinity .. J-15
Troup .. H-16
Troy .. J-13
Tuleta .. N-13
Tulia .. D-7
Turkey .. D-9
Turnertown .. H-16
Tuscola .. H-10
Twin Sisters .. L-12
Twitty .. C-9
Tye .. G-10
Tyler .. G-16
Tynan .. P-12
Umbarger .. C-7
Unity .. E-15
Universal City .. M-12
University Park
.... Pg. 105, C-9
Utopia .. M-10
Uvalde .. M-10
Valentine .. K-4
Valera .. H-10
Valley Mills .. H-13
Valley Spring .. K-11
Valley View .. F-13
Van .. G-15
Van Alstyne .. F-14
Van Horn .. J-3
Van Vleck .. M-15
Vancourt .. J-9
Vanderbilt .. N-14
Vanderpool .. L-10
Vashti .. E-12
Vealmoor .. G-8
Vega .. C-7
Venus .. G-13
Vera .. E-10

Vernon E-11
Victoria N-13
Vidor L-17
Village Mills .. K-17
Vincent G-8
Voca J-11
Von Ormy .. Pg. 142, J-2
Voss H-10
Votaw K-17
Waco M-13
Wadsworth .. N-15
Waelder .. L-13
Waka .. A-9
Wake Village .. E-17
Wall .. J-9
Waller .. L-15
Wallis .. L-14
Walnut Sprs. .. H-13
Warda .. L-13
Warren .. K-17
Washington .. K-15
Waskom .. G-17
Water Valley .. H-9
Watson .. K-12
Watsonville .. Pg. 104, F-5
Waxahachie .. G-14
Wayside .. D-8
Weatherford .. G-12
Weaver .. F-15
Webster .. M-16
Weches .. J-16
Weesatche .. N-13
Weimar .. L-14
Weinort .. F-10
Welch .. F-7
Wellington .. D-9
Wellman .. F-7
Wells .. J-16
Weslaco .. S-12
West .. H-13
West Columbia .. M-15
West Orange .. K-17
West Point .. L-13
Westbrook .. G-8
Westfield .. L-15
Vicinity .. Pg. 109, A-9
Westhoff .. M-13
Westlake .. Pg. 104, A-4
Westover .. F-11
Westworth .. Pg. 104, D-2
Wharton .. M-15
Wheeler .. C-9
Wheeler .. G-15
Wheelock .. K-14
White Deer .. C-8
Whiteface .. E-6
Whiteflat .. E-9
Whitehouse .. G-15
Whitesboro .. E-13
Whitewright .. F-14
Whitharral .. E-7
Whitney .. H-13
Whittsett .. N-12
Wichita Falls .. E-12
Wickett .. H-5
Wiergate .. J-18
Wildorado .. C-7
Wildwood .. K-17
Wilkinson .. F-16
Willow City .. K-11
Wills Point .. G-15
Wilmer .. Pg. 105, F-10
Wilson .. F-8
Wimberly .. L-12
Winchell .. J-11
Windcrest .. Pg. 142, C-7
Windom .. F-15
Windthorst .. E-12
Winfield .. F-16
Wingate .. H-9
Wink .. H-5
Winnie .. L-17
Winnsboro .. F-15
Winona .. G-16
Winters .. H-9
Wolfe City .. F-15
Wolfforth .. F-7
Woodlake .. J-15
Woodland Hills
.... Pg. 105, F-8
Woodlawn .. G-17
Woodsboro .. P-13
Woodson .. F-11
Woodville .. K-17
Woodward .. N-10
Wortham .. H-14
Yoakum .. M-13
Yorktown .. M-13
Zavalla .. J-17
Zephyr .. H-11
Zorn .. L-12

UTAH
Pages 80-81
Population: 1,461,037
Capital: Salt Lake City
Land Area: 82,073 sq. mi.

Abraham H-4
Adamsville H-4
Alpine F-5
Alta F-6
Altamont F-8
Alton L-4
American Fork .. F-5
Aneth M-9
Angle J-5
Annabella J-5
Antimony J-5
Arcadia F-8
Aurora J-5

Austin J-5
Axtell H-5
Bacchus .. Pg. 141, K-2
Bear River City .. D-5
Beaver K-4
Benjamin F-5
Beryl K-2
Bicknell K-5
Birdseye G-6
Black Rock ... J-4
Blanding L-9
Blue Cr. C-4
Bluebell F-8
Bluff L-9
Bluffdale F-5
Bonanza G-9
Boneta F-7
Boulder K-6
Bountiful E-5
Vicinity .. Pg. 141, K-6
Brian Head ... L-4
Bridgeland ... F-8
Brigham City .. D-5
Bryce Canyon .. L-4
Burmester ... E-4
Burrville J-5
Cannonville .. L-4
Carbonville .. G-7
Castle Dale .. H-7
Castle Rock .. E-6
Cave C-5
Cedar City ... L-3
Cedar Creek .. C-3
Cedar Fort ... F-5
Cedar Springs .. D-4
Cedarview F-8
Center Creek .. F-6
Centerfield .. H-5
Centerville .. E-5
Vicinity .. Pg. 141, K-6
Central J-5
Central L-2
Charleston ... F-6
Chester H-5
Circleville .. K-4
Cisco J-9
Clarkston ... C-5
Clawson H-6
Clear Creek .. C-3
Clearcreek .. G-6
Clearfield ... E-5
Cleveland ... H-7
Clinton D-5
Clover F-4
Coalville E-6
Colton G-7
Corinne D-5
Cornish C-5
Cove Fort ... J-4
Crescent Jct. .. J-8
Croydon E-6
Delle E-4
Delta H-4
Desert Mound .. L-3
Dividend G-5
Draper F-5
Vicinity .. Pg. 141, J-2
Duchesne F-8
Dugway G-3
East Carbon City .. H-8
East Mill Creek
.... Pg. 141, J-7
Eastland L-9
Echo E-6
Elberta G-5
Elmo H-7
Elsinore J-5
Emery J-6
Enoch L-3
Enterprise .. L-2
Ephraim H-6
Escalante ... L-5
Etna D-2
Eureka G-5
Fairfield ... F-5
Fairview ... H-6
Farmington .. E-5
Faust F-4
Fayette H-5
Ferron H-6
Fillmore ... H-5
Fish Springs .. G-3
Flowell H-4
Fort Duchesne .. F-8
Fountain Green .. G-5
Francis F-6
Freedom ... H-6
Fremont ... J-6
Fremont Jct. .. J-6
Fruit Heights .. E-5
Fruitland .. F-7
Fry Canyon .. L-8
Gandy G-2
Garden City .. C-6
Garrison .. H-2
Geneva F-5
Genola G-5
Glendale .. L-4
Glenwood .. J-5
Goshen G-5
Grantsville .. E-4
Green Lake .. E-9
Green River .. H-8
Greenville .. J-4
Greenwich .. J-5
Greenwood .. H-4
Grouse Creek .. C-2
Gunlock ... L-2
Gunnison .. H-5
Hamilton Fort .. L-3
Hanksville .. K-7
Hanna F-7
Harrisville .. D-5
Hatch L-4

Hatton J-4
Heber City F-6
Helper G-7
Henefer E-6
Henrieville ... L-5
Hiawatha H-6
Hinckley H-4
Holden H-5
Holladay E-5
Vicinity .. Pg. 141, K-7
Honeyville ... D-4
Hot Springs .. D-5
Howell C-4
Hoytsville .. E-6
Huntington .. H-7
Huntsville .. D-6
Hurricane ... M-3
Hyde Park ... C-5
Hyrum D-5
Indianola G-6
Vicinity .. Pg. 141, K-6
Ioka F-8
Iron Springs .. L-3
Ivins M-2
Jensen F-9
Jericho G-5
Joseph J-4
Junction ... K-4
Kamas E-6
Kanab M-4
Kanarraville .. L-3
Kanosh J-4
Kaysville .. D-4
Kelton D-3
Kenilworth .. G-7
Kimball Jct. .. E-6
Kingston ... K-5
Knolls E-3
Koosharem .. J-5
La Sal L-9
La Sal Jct. ... K-9
La Verkin ... L-3
Lake Pt. Jct. .. E-5
Lake Shore .. F-6
Lake View ... F-5
Laketown ... C-6
Lapoint F-8
Leamington .. H-5
Leeds L-3
Leeton E-8
Lehi F-5
Leota F-9
Levan G-5
Lewiston ... C-5
Loa J-6
Logan D-5
Long Valley Jct. .. L-4
Low E-3
Lucin D-2
Lund K-3
Lyman K-6
Lynndyl .. G-4
Maeser F-9
Magna F-5
Vicinity .. Pg. 141, J-2
Manderfield .. K-4
Manila E-9
Manti H-6
Mantua D-5
Mapleton ... F-6
Marion E-6
Marysvale .. J-4
Mayfield .. H-6
Meadow J-4
Meadowville .. C-6
Mendon ... D-5
Mexican Hat .. M-8
Midvale ... F-5
Midway ... F-6
Milburn ... G-6
Milford ... J-3
Mills G-5
Minersville .. K-3
Moab J-9
Modena ... K-2
Molen H-5
Mona G-5
Monarch .. F-9
Monroe ... J-5
Montezuma Creek .. M-9
Monticello .. L-9
Moore H-6
Morgan ... E-5
Moroni ... H-5
Mountain Home .. F-7
Mt. Carmel .. L-4
Mt. Carmel Jct. .. L-4
Mt. Emmons .. F-7
Mt. Pleasant .. G-6
Murray ... E-5
Vicinity .. Pg. 141, J-2
Myton ... F-8
N. Logan .. C-6
N. Salt Lake
.... Pg. 141, F-5

Naples F-9
Neola F-8
Nephi G-5
New Harmony .. L-3
Newcastle L-2
Newton C-5
Oak City H-5
Oakley E-6
Oasis H-4
Ogden D-5
Orangeville .. H-6
Orderville .. L-4
Orem F-6
Ouray F-9
Panguitch .. K-4
Paradise ... D-5
Paragonah .. K-4
Park City ... E-6
Park Valley .. C-3
Parowan ... K-4
Payson G-5
Peoa E-6
Perry Willard .. D-5
Pigeon Hollow Jct. .. H-6
Pine Valley .. L-2
Pintura L-3
Plain City ... D-5
Pleasant Grove .. F-6
Pleasant View .. D-5
Plymouth ... C-5
Portage ... C-5
Porterville .. E-6
Price G-7
Providence .. D-5
Provo F-6
Randolph .. D-6
Redmond .. J-5
Richfield .. J-5
Richmond .. C-5
Riverdale .. D-5
Riverton ... E-5
Rockville .. M-3
Roosevelt .. F-8
Rosette ... C-3
Rowley Jct. .. E-4
Roy E-5
Ruby's Inn .. L-4
Saint George .. M-3
Saint John Sta. .. F-4
Salem G-5
Salina H-5
Salt Lake City .. F-4
Vicinity Pg. 141
Sandy F-5
Santa Clara .. M-2
Santaquin .. G-5
Scipio H-5
Scofield .. G-7
Sevier J-4
Shivwits .. M-2
Sigurd J-5
Silver City .. G-5
Smithfield .. C-5
Smyths ... J-3
Snowville .. C-4
Soldier Summit .. G-7
South Jordan .. F-5
South Ogden .. D-5
South Salt Lake .. E-5
Vicinity .. Pg. 141, J-6
Spanish Fork .. F-6
Spring City .. H-6
Spring Lake .. G-5
Springdale .. M-3
Springville .. F-6
Sterling .. H-6
Stockton .. F-4
Summit K-3
Summit Pt. .. K-9
Sunnyside .. G-8
Sunset E-5
Sutherland .. H-4
Syracuse .. E-5
Tabiona ... F-7
Talmage .. F-7
Teasdale .. K-6
Terrace ... D-6
Thistle ... G-6
Thompson .. H-9
Tooele ... F-4
Toquerville .. L-3
Torrey K-6
Tremonton .. D-5
Tropic L-5
Trout Cr. .. G-2
Tucker ... G-6
Upalco ... F-8
Uvada L-2
Venice ... J-5
Vernal ... F-9
Vernon ... F-4
Veyo L-2
Virgin ... M-3
W. Valley City .. E-5
Wahsatch .. D-6
Wales H-5
Wanship .. E-6
Washington .. M-3
Washington Terrace .. D-5
Wellington .. G-7
Wellsville .. D-5
Wendover .. E-2
West Jordan .. F-5
West Point .. D-4
West Valley City .. F-5
Vicinity .. Pg. 141, J-4
Whiterocks .. F-8
Widtsoe Jct. .. K-5
Woodruff .. D-6
Woods Cross .. E-5
Vicinity .. Pg. 141, F-5
Woodside .. H-8
Zane K-2

VERMONT
Page 55
Population: 511,456
Capital: Montpelier
Land Area: 9,273 sq. mi.

Addison E-1
Albany C-3
Alburg B-1
Arlington J-1
Ascutney G-3
Averill B-5
Bakersfield .. B-2
Barnard F-3
Barnet D-4
Barre E-3
Barton C-4
Bellows Falls .. H-3

VERMONT

Bennington J-1
Bethel F-3
Bloomfield C-5
Bomoseen G-1
Bondville H-2
Bradford E-4
Brandon F-2
Brattleboro J-3
Bridgewater Cors. G-3
Bridport E-1
Bristol E-1
Broadford Cen. E-3
Brunswick Sprs. C-5
Burlington D-1
Cambridge C-2
Cambridgeport H-3
Canaan B-5
Castleton G-1
Charlotte D-1
Chelsea E-3
Chester H-3
Chester Depot H-3
Chimney Cor. C-2
Concord D-4
Cornwall E-1
Danby G-2
Dorset H-1
E. Barnet D-4
E. Berkshire B-2
E. Braintree E-3
E. Brookfield E-3
E. Burke C-4
E. Calais D-3
E. Dorset H-2
E. Fairfield C-2
E. Granville E-3
E. Hardwick D-3
E. Haven C-4
Eden C-3
Eden Mills C-3
Enosburg Falls B-2
Essex Jct. C-2
Fair Haven G-1
Fairfax C-2
Ferrisburg E-1
Franklin B-2
Gassetts H-3
Gaysville F-3
Glover C-4
Grafton H-3
Grand Isle C-1
Granville E-2
Groton E-4
Guilford J-3
Hancock F-2
Hardwick D-3
Heartwellville J-2
Hinesburg D-2
Holland B-4
Hubbardton F-1
Hyde Park C-3
Irasburg B-3
Irasville E-2
Island Pond C-4
Jacksonville J-2
Jamaica H-2
Jay B-3
Jeffersonville C-2
Johnson C-3
Lake Elmore C-3
Leicester F-2
Londonderry H-2
Lowell B-3
Ludlow G-2
Lunenberg D-5
Lyndon D-4
Lyndonville C-4
Maidstone C-5
Manchester H-2
Manchester Cen. H-2
Marlboro J-2
Marshfield D-3
Middlebury E-1
Middleton Sprs. G-1
Mill Village E-3
Montgomery Cen. B-3
Montpelier D-3
Morgan Cen. B-4
Morrisville C-3
New Haven E-1
New Haven Jct. E-1
Newbury E-4
Newfane J-2
Newport D-4
North Concord D-4
North Hero C-1
North Dorset H-2
North Hyde Park C-3
North Rupert H-1
Northfield E-2
Norton B-4
Norwich F-3
Orleans B-4
Orwell F-1
Passumpsic D-4
Pawlet H-1
Pittsfield F-2
Pittsford F-2
Pittsford Mills F-2
Plainfield D-3
Plymouth C-2
Plymouth Union G-2
Pompanoosuc F-3
Post Mills F-3
Poultney G-1
Pownal J-1
Pownal Cen. J-1
Putney J-3
Quechee G-3
Randolph E-3
Richford B-2
Richmond D-2
Ripton F-2
Robinson F-2

Rochester F-2
Roxbury E-2
Royalton F-2
Rutland G-2
Saint Albans B-2
Saint George D-2
Saint Johnsbury D-4
Searsburg J-2
Shafsbury J-1
Shafsbury Cen. J-2
Shelburne D-1
Sherburne Cen. D-1
Shoreham F-1
Simonsville H-2
South Burlington D-1
South Dorset H-2
South Hinesburg D-2
South Royalton F-3
South Ryegate E-4
South Shafsbury J-1
South Starksboro E-2
South Walden D-3
South Wallingford G-2
Springfield H-3
Starksboro E-2
Stockbridge F-2
Sudbury F-1
Sunderland J-2
Swanton B-1
Ticonderoga F-1
Townshend J-2
Troy B-3
Tunbridge F-3
Tyson G-2
Underhill Flats D-2
Union Village F-3
Vergennes E-1
Vershire E-3
Waits River E-3
Waitsfield E-2
Wallingford G-2
Waltham E-1
Wardsboro J-2
Warren E-2
Washington E-3
Waterbury D-2
Waterbury Ctr. D-3
Websterville E-3
Wells G-1
West Addison E-1
West Braintree E-2
West Bridgewater G-2
West Burke C-4
West Danville D-3
West Dover J-2
West Fairlee F-3
West Groton E-3
West Hartford F-3
West Rutland G-2
West Topsham E-3
West Wardsboro J-2
Westfield B-3
White River Jct. F-3
Whiting F-1
Wilmington J-2
Windsor G-3
Wolcott C-3
Woodbury D-3
Woodford J-1
Woodstock G-3
Worcester D-3

VIRGINIA
Pages 82-83
Population: 5,346,818
Capital: Richmond
Land Area: 39,703 sq. mi.

Abingdon K-3
Achilles H-12
Alexandria E-12
Vicinity Pg. 150, F-5
Altavista J-8
Amelia H-10
Amherst H-8
Annandale Pg. 150, F-4
Appalachia H-9
Appomattox H-9
Arlington D-12
Vicinity Pg. 150, F-4
Ashcake Pg. 139, A-5
Ashland G-10
Bailey's Crossroads
Pg. 150, E-4
Bassett J-7
Bastian J-5
Bavon H-13
Beach Pg. 139, J-2
Beaties Mill Pg. 139, C-7
Bedford H-8
Belle Haven G-13
Bensley Pg. 139, J-6
Bermuda Gardens
Pg. 139, J-6
Bermuda Hundred
Pg. 139, J-7
Berryville D-10
Beverly Forest
Pg. 150, G-3
Big Island H-8
Big Stone Gap J-4
Blacksburg H-6
Blackstone J-11
Bluefield H-4
Bon Air Pg. 139, J-6
Boones Mill H-7
Bowling Green F-11
Boydton K-9
Bridgewater F-9
Bristol K-3

Broadway E-8
Brodnax J-10
Brookneal J-8
Buchanan H-7
Buckingham G-9
Vicinity Pg. 139, D-1
Buena Vista G-8
Burgess G-12
Burke Pg. 150, G-2
Burkeville H-9
Cape Charles H-13
Carmel Church G-10
Castlewood J-4
Cedarbluff J-4
Central Garage G-11
Centralia Pg. 139, H-6
Chamberlayne Heights
Pg. 139, C-4
Charlottesville F-9
Charlottsville F-9
Chase City J-9
Chatham J-8
Cheriton H-13
Chesapeake J-12
Vicinity Pg. 130, K-4
Chester H-11
Vicinity Pg. 139, J-4
Chesterfield Pg. 139, H-3
Chilhowie K-4
Chincoteague F-14
Christiansburg J-6
Churchville F-8
Clarksville K-9
Claudville K-6
Clifton Forge G-7
Clinchco H-3
Clintwood J-3
Coeburn J-3
Colonial Beach F-11
Colonial Hts. H-11
Courtland J-11
Covington G-6
Craigsville F-8
Crestview Pg. 139, C-3
Crewe H-9
Crittenden Pg. 130, E-1
Crozet G-9
Culpeper E-10
Cumberland H-9
Dale City E-11
Damascus K-4
Dante J-3
Danville K-7
Dayton E-8
Deltaville G-13
Dillwyn H-9
Drakes Branch J-9
Drewrys Bluff
Pg. 139, G-4
Dublin J-5
Dugspur J-6
Dumbarton Pg. 139, C-3
Eagle Rock G-7
Eastville H-13
Edinburg E-10
Elkton G-9
Elmont Pg. 139, A-3
Emporia K-11
Ewing K-1
Exmore H-13
Fairfax F-11
Vicinity Pg. 150, E-1
Falling Creek Farms
Pg. 139, G-2
Falls Church Pg. 150, E-3
Falmouth F-11
Farmville H-9
Fieldale K-7
Five Forks Pg. 139, H-2
Floyd J-6
Fort Lee Pg. 139, K-6
Franconia Pg. 150, G-4
Franklin K-11
Fredericksburg F-10
Fries K-5
Front Royal D-9
Galax K-5
Gate City K-2
Glade Spring J-4
Gladys H-8
Glasgow G-8
Glen Allen Pg. 139, B-3
Gloucester H-12
Gloucester Pt. H-12
Gordonsville F-9
Goshen G-8
Gretna J-8
Grottoes F-8
Groveton Pg. 150, G-5
Grundy H-2
Gum Spring G-10
Gwynn H-13
Halifax J-8
Hampden-Sydney J-10
Hampton J-13
Vicinity Pg. 130, A-2
Hanover G-11
Harrisonburg F-9
Herndon D-10
Hillsville J-6
Hollins H-7
Holts Corner Pg. 139, D-7
Honaker J-4
Hopewell H-11
Vicinity Pg. 139, K-6
Hughes Corner
Pg. 139, B-7
Hurt J-8
Independence K-4
Iron Gate G-7
Irvington G-12
Jarratt J-11
Jonesville K-1
Keene Mill Heights
Pg. 150, G-2
Kenbridge J-10
Keysville J-9
Kilmarnock G-12
King & Queen C.H. G-12
Kingsland Acres
Pg. 139, G-4
Kiptopeke H-13
La Crosse K-10
Lancaster G-12
Langley Pg. 150, C-4
Laurel Pg. 139, B-3
Lawrenceville J-10
Lebanon J-3
Leesburg D-10
Lexington G-7
Linney's Corner
Pg. 139, B-7
Lottsburg G-12
Lovingston G-8
Luray E-9
Lynchburg H-8
Madison Hts. H-8
Manassas E-10
Mappsville G-14
Marion J-4
Marshall E-10
Martinsville K-7
Mathews H-12
McKenney J-10
McLean Pg. 150, D-4
Meadowville Pg. 139, H-6
Mechanicsville G-11
Middleburg D-10
Middletown D-9
Monterey F-8
Montross F-12
Mt. Jackson E-9
Narrows J-5
Nassawadox H-13
New Castle H-7
New Market E-9
Newmans Pg. 139, C-7
Newport News J-12
Vicinity Pg. 130, A-1
Norfolk J-13
Vicinity Pg. 130
Norton J-2
Oak Forest Pg. 139, B-6
Oak Grove F-12
Old Cold Harbor
Pg. 139, C-7
Onancock G-13
Onley G-14
Orange F-10
Palmyra G-9
Pamplin City H-8
Parksley G-13
Patrick Springs K-7
Pearisburg H-6
Pearsons Corner
Pg. 139, A-5
Pembroke H-6
Pen Daw Pg. 150, G-5
Pennington Gap J-2
Petersburg H-11
Pickadat Corner
Pg. 139, K-5
Pimmit Hills Pg. 150, D-3
Pine Knoll Pg. 139, C-7
Poindexters Pg. 139, A-4
Pole Green Pg. 139, B-6
Poquoson H-12
Vicinity Pg. 130, A-3
Port Royal F-11
Portsmouth J-12
Vicinity Pg. 130, F-3
Pound H-3
Powhatan H-10
Prospect Hill Pg. 150, C-2
Pulaski J-5
Purcellville D-10
Quantico E-11
Radford J-6
Raven H-3
Red Ash A-13
Remington E-10
Richlands H-10
Richmond H-10
Ripplemead H-6
Roanoke H-7
Robious Pg. 139, E-1
Rocky Mount H-7
Ruckersville F-9
Rural Point Pg. 139, B-7
Rural Retreat J-5
Rustburg H-8
Salem H-7
Saltville H-4
Sandston G-11
Saxis G-13
Seaford H-12
Shady Oak Pg. 150, B-1
Shenandoah E-9
Shipman H-8
Short Pump Pg. 139, B-1
Simpkins Corner
Pg. 139, C-6
Smithfield J-12
South Boston K-8
Sperryville E-9
Spring Grove H-11
Springfield Pg. 150, G-3
St. Paul J-3
Stafford F-11
Stanley E-9
Stanleytown J-7
Staunton F-8
Stephens City D-9
Strasburg D-9
Stuart K-6
Stuarts Draft F-8
Studley Pg. 139, A-7
Suffolk J-12
Vicinity Pg. 130, H-1
Sugar Grove J-4
Surry H-12
Sussex J-11
Swan Hill Pg. 139, G-1
Sydnorsville J-7
Tangier G-13
Tappahannock G-11
Tazewell H-4
Timberville E-8
Triangle E-11
Vicinity Pg. 147, K-3
Urbanna G-12
Vanderpool F-7
Vansant H-3
Verona F-8
Victoria J-9
Victoria Hills Pg. 139, J-4
Vienna D-11
Vicinity Pg. 150, E-2
Vinton H-7
Virginia Beach J-13
Vicinity Pg. 130, H-9
Volens J-8
Wakefield J-12
Walnut Grove
Pg. 139, C-6
Walthall Pg. 139, K-5
Warm Springs F-7
Warrenton E-10
Warsaw F-12
Waverly J-11
Waynesboro F-8
Weber City K-3
West Point H-12
Williamsburg H-11
Winchester D-9
Windsor J-12
Windsor Park
Pg. 139, C-1
Wise J-2
Woodbridge E-11
Woodlawn K-5
Woodstock E-9
Wylliesburg J-9
Wytheville J-5
Zion G-9

WASHINGTON
Pages 84-85
Population: 4,132,156
Capital: Olympia
Land Area: 66,511 sq. mi.

Aberdeen F-3
Acme B-6
Addy B-13
Airway Heights D-14
Albion J-7
Alderwood Maner
Pg. 147, A-4
Algona E-6
Almira D-11
Altoona H-3
Anacortes B-5
Index D-7
Anatone H-14
Appleyard E-9
Arlington C-6
Asotin H-14
Auburn E-6
Battle Ground J-5
Bellevue D-6
Bellingham A-5
Benton City H-10
Bickleton H-9
Bingen J-7
Black Diamond E-6
Blaine A-5
Bonney Lake E-6
Bossburg B-13
Bothell D-5
Vicinity Pg. 147, B-5
Boundary A-13
Bremerton D-5
Brewster C-10
Bridgeport C-10
Brier D-16
Vicinity Pg. 147, A-4
Bryn Mawr Pg. 147, H-5
Buckley E-6
Bucoda F-5
Burien Pg. 147, H-3
Burlington B-6
Camas J-5
Carbonado F-6
Carnation D-6
Cashmere E-9
Castle Rock H-4
Cathlamet G-4
Centralia G-5
Chehalis G-5
Chelan C-9
Cheney E-14
Chewelah C-13
Clarkston G-14
Clayton C-13
Cle Elum E-8
Coalfield Pg. 147, D-6
Coles Corner D-8
Colfax F-14
College Place H-12
Colton G-14
Colville B-13
Conconully B-10
Concrete B-7
Connell G-12
Copalis Beach E-2
Cosmopolis F-3
Coulee City D-11
Coulee Dam C-11
Coupeville C-5
Crescent Bar E-9
Creston D-12
Cusick C-14
Danville A-12
Darrington C-7
Davenport D-13
Dayton H-13
Deer Park C-14
Deming A-6
Des Moines E-6
Disautel C-11
Discovery Bay C-5
Dodge G-13
Duluth J-5
Dusty F-13
Duvall D-6
East Wenatchee E-9
Eastgate Pg. 147, F-6
Eatonville F-6
Edmonds D-5
Vicinity Pg. 147, A-2
Edwall E-13
Elbe F-6
Eldon F-4
Electric City D-11
Ellensburg F-9
Elma F-4
Elmer City C-11
Endicott F-13
Entiat D-9
Enumclaw E-6
Ephrata E-10
Eureka H-12
Everett C-6
Everson A-6
Fairfield E-14
Fairholm C-3
Farmington F-15
Ferndale A-5
Fircrest E-5
Forks C-2
Friday Harbor B-5
Garfield F-14
George F-10
Gifford C-13
Gig Harbor E-5
Glenoma G-6
Gold Bar D-7
Goldendale J-8
Grand Coulee D-11
Grandview H-9
Granger G-9
Granite Falls C-6
Greenwater F-7
Hamilton B-6
Harrah G-9
Harrington E-12
Hartline D-11
Hatton G-11
Hoodsport E-4
Hoquiam F-3
Humptulips F-3
Husum J-7
Hyak E-7
Ilwaco G-3
Index D-7
Ione B-14
Issaquah E-6
Joyce C-3
Juanita Pg. 147, C-4
Kahlotus G-12
Kalama J-4
Keller C-12
Kelso H-5
Kenmoore Pg. 147, B-4
Kennewick H-11
Kent E-6
Vicinity Pg. 147, J-4
Kettle Falls B-13
Kingston Pg. 147, A-1
Kirkland D-6
Vicinity Pg. 147, B-5
Kittitas F-9
Klaus E-9
Klickitat J-7
Krupp E-11
La Center J-4
La Conner B-5
La Crosse F-13
La Push C-2
Lacey D-5
Lake Stevens C-6
Lamont E-13
Langley C-5
Latah E-14
Leavenworth D-9
Lebam G-3
Lind F-12
Littlerock F-5
Long Beach G-3
Longview H-4
Lyman B-6
Lynden A-5
Lynnwood D-5
Vicinity Pg. 147, A-3
Mabton H-9
Malone F-5
Maltby Pg. 147, A-6
Mansfield D-10
Manson D-9
Maplewood Pg. 147, H-5
Marcus B-13
Marysville C-6
Mattawa G-10
McCleary F-4
Medical Lake E-13
Megler H-3
Menlo G-3
Mercer Island D-5
Vicinity Pg. 147, D-5
Mesa G-11
Metaline A-14
Metaline Falls A-14
Methow C-9
Millwood D-14
Monroe D-6
Montesano F-3
Morton G-6
Moses Lake F-11
Mossyrock G-5
Mount Baker A-7
Mount Vernon B-5
Mountlake Terrace D-5
Vicinity Pg. 147, A-3
Moxee City G-9
Mukilteo D-6
Naches F-8
Napavine G-4
Naselle G-3
Neah Bay B-2
Neilton E-3
Newcastle Pg. 147, G-5
Newport C-14
Normandy Park E-5
Vicinity Pg. 147, G-2
North Bend E-7
North Bonneville J-6
North Cove F-2
Northport A-13
Oak Harbor C-5
Oakesdale F-14
Oakville F-4
Ocean Park G-3
Ocean Shores F-2
Odessa E-12
Okanogan C-10
Olympia B-10
Omak B-10
Orchards J-5
Orient A-13
Oroville A-10
Orting F-6
Othello F-11
Ozette C-2
Pacific E-6
Pacific Beach E-2
Packwood G-7
Palouse F-14
Pasco H-11
Pateros C-10
Pe Ell G-4
Pomeroy G-14
Port Angeles C-4
Port Gamble D-5
Port Orchard E-5
Port Townsend C-5
Poulsbo D-5
Prescott H-12
Prosser H-10
Pullman G-14
Puyallup F-5
Queets D-2
Quincy E-10
Rainier F-5
Randle G-6
Raymond G-3
Reardan D-13
Redmond D-6
Renton E-6
Vicinity Pg. 147, H-4
Republic B-12
Richland H-11
Richland Highlands
Pg. 147, B-3
Richmond Beach
Pg. 147, B-3
Ridgefield J-5
Rimrock G-7
Ritzville F-12
Riverside B-10
Rochester F-4
Rock Island E-9
Rockford E-14
Rockport B-7
Rollingbay Pg. 147, D-1
Roosevelt J-9
Rosalia E-14
Rosburg G-3
Roslyn E-8
Roy F-5
Royal City F-10
Ryderwood G-4
Salmon La Sac E-8
Sappho C-2
Seattle D-5
Vicinity Pg. 147
Sedro Woolley B-6
Selah G-9
Sequim C-4
Shelton E-4
Silver Creek G-5
Skykomish D-7
Snohomish D-6
Snoqualmie E-7
Soap Lake E-10
South Bend G-3
South Cle Elum F-8
South Prairie F-6
Spangle E-14
Spokane D-14
Sprague E-13
Springdale C-13
St. John F-14
Stanwood C-6
Starbuck G-13
Steilacoom E-5
Stella H-4
Steptoe F-14
Stevenson J-6
Sultan D-6
Sumas A-6
Sumner F-5
Sunnyside H-10
Tacoma E-5
Taholah E-2
Tekoa F-14
Telma D-8
Tenino F-5
Tieton G-8
Toledo G-5
Tonasket B-10
Toppenish H-9
Trout Lake H-7
Tukwila E-6
Tumwater F-4
Twisp C-9
Union E-4
Union Gap G-9
Uniontown G-14
Vader F-5
Vancouver J-4
Vicinity Pg. 150, A-9
Vantage F-9
Vashon Heights
Pg. 147, G-1
Vashon Island
Pg. 147, K-1
Waitsburg H-13
Walla Walla H-12
Wallula H-11
Wapato H-9
Warden F-11
Washougal J-5
Washtucna G-12
Waterville C-10
Wauconda B-11
Waverly E-14
Wenatchee E-9
Wenatchee Heights E-9
West Richland H-11
Westport F-2
White Salmon J-7
White Swan H-8
Wickersham B-6
Wilbur D-12
Wilkeson F-6
Wilson Creek E-11
Winlock G-4
Winslow D-5
Winthrop B-9
Wishram Heights J-8
Withrow D-10
Woodinville Pg. 147, B-6
Woodland J-5
Yacolt J-5
Yakima G-9
Yelm F-5
Zillah G-9

WEST VIRGINIA
Pages 82-83
Population: 1,949,644
Capital: Charleston
Land Area: 24,119 sq. mi.

Alderson G-6
Arnoldsburg E-5
Ashton H-5
Athens H-5
Augusta D-8
Baileysville G-4
Baker D-9
Barboursville F-3
Barrackville C-7
Beckley G-5
Belington D-7
Belmont D-5
Bethlehem B-6
Beverly E-7
Big Chimney F-4
Big Otter F-5
Birch River E-6
Blacksville C-6
Bluefield H-5
Bradley G-5
Bramwell H-5
Bridgeport D-7
Buckhannon D-6
Buffalo E-4
Burnsville E-6
Cairo D-5
Camden-on-Gauley F-6
Cameron C-6
Cedar Grove F-5
Center Pt. D-6
Chapmanville F-3
Charles Town D-10
Charleston F-4
Chesapeake F-4
Chester A-6
Clarksburg D-6
Clay E-5
Clendenin F-5
Coxs Mills D-6
Craigsville F-6
Danville F-4
Davis D-8
Delbarton G-3
Dunbar F-4
Dunmore F-7
Durbin E-7
East Bank F-4
Eleanor E-4
Elk Garden C-8
Elkins E-7
Ellenboro D-5
Fairmont C-7
Fairview C-6
Farmington C-6
Fayetteville F-5
Flatwoods E-6
Follansbee A-6
Forest Hill H-5
Friendly C-5
Ft. Ashby C-8
Ft. Gay F-3

WEST VIRGINIA

Gandeeville E-4
Gap Mills H-6
Gary H-4
Gassaway F-5
Gauley Bridge F-5
Gerrardstown C-9
Gilbert H-4
Gilmer E-6
Glen Dale B-6
Glenville D-5
Grantsville D-5
Hambleton D-7
Hamlin F-4
Harman E-8
Harrisville D-5
Hedgesville C-9
Henderson E-3
Hillsboro F-6
Hinton G-5
Hundred C-6
Huntington F-3
Hurricane F-3
Huttonsville E-7
Iaeger H-4
Ingleside H-5
Inwood C-10
Jane Lew D-6
Jolo H-4
Junction C-8
Junior D-7
Kenna E-4
Kenova F-3
Kermit G-3
Keyser C-9
Keystone H-4
Kimball H-4
Kingwood C-7
Leon E-4
Lester G-5
Lewisburg G-5
Liberty E-4
Linn D-6
Logan G-3
Lost City D-8
Lost Cr. D-7
Lumberport D-6
Mabscott G-5
Madison G-4
Man G-4
Mannington C-6
Marlinton F-6
Marmet F-4
Martinsburg C-9
Mason D-4
Masontown C-7
Matewan G-3
Matoaka H-5
Meadow Bridge G-5
Middlebourne C-5
Midkiff F-3
Mill Creek E-7
Milton F-3
Monongah C-6
Montgomery G-5
Montrose D-8
Moorefield D-9
Morgantown C-7
Mossy G-4
Moundsville B-6
Mt. Hope G-5
Mt. Storm D-8
Muddlety F-5
Mullens H-5
Naoma G-4
Neola G-7
Nettie F-5
New Cumberland . . . A-6
New Haven D-4
New Martinsville C-6
Newton E-5
Nitro F-4
Nutter Fort D-6
Oak Flat E-8
Oak Hill G-5
Oceana G-4
Omar G-3
Paden City C-5
Parkersburg D-5
Parsons D-7
Paw Paw C-9
Pennsboro D-5
Petersburg D-8
Peterstown H-5
Philippi D-7
Piedmont C-9
Pine Grove C-6
Pineville H-4
Poca E-4
Pocatalico E-4
Prichard F-3
Princeton H-5
Pt. Pleasant E-3
Racine F-4
Rainelle G-5
Rand F-4
Ranson D-10
Ravenswood D-4
Reedy E-5
Renick G-6
Rhodell H-5
Richwood F-6
Ridgeley C-9
Ripley E-4
Roanoke E-6
Rock Cave E-6
Romney D-9
Ronceverte G-6
Rowlesburg D-7
Rupert G-6
Salem D-6

Scherr D-8
Seneca Rocks E-8
Shepherdstown C-10
Shinnston C-6
Slatyfork F-6
Smithers F-5
Smithfield C-6
Sophia G-5
South Charleston . . . F-4
Spencer E-5
St. Albans F-4
St. Mary's C-5
Star City C-7
Stonewood D-7
Summersville F-5
Sylvester G-4
Terra Alta C-8
Thomas D-7
Thornwood E-7
Triadelphia B-6
Tunnelton D-7
Union H-6
Valley Head E-7
Van G-4
Vienna D-4
War H-4
Wardensville D-8
Wayne F-3
Webster Spr. E-6
Weirton A-6
Welch H-4
Wellsburg A-6
West Hamlin F-3
West Logan G-4
West Union D-5
Weston D-6
Westover C-7
Wheeling B-6
White Sulphur Spr. . . G-6
Whitesville G-4
Williamson G-3
Williamstown D-4
Yawkey F-4

WISCONSIN
Pages 86-87
Population: 4,705,767
Capital: Madison
Land Area: 54,426 sq. mi.

Abbotsford F-5
Adams H-5
Adell J-8
Algoma G-8
Alma G-2
Alma Center G-4
Almena F-2
Altoona G-3
Amery F-2
Aniwa F-6
Antigo F-6
Appleton G-7
Arcadia H-3
Argyle K-5
Arlington J-6
Ashland D-4
Ashwaubenon G-7
Athens F-5
Auburndale G-5
Augusta G-4
Avoca K-5
Baldwin F-2
Balsam Lake E-2
Bangor J-4
Baraboo J-5
Barneveld K-5
Barron F-3
Bay City G-2
Bayfield C-4
Bayside J-8
Vicinity . . . Pg. 121, A-6
Beadstown G-4
Beaver Dam J-7
Belgium J-8
Belleville K-6
Belmont K-5
Beloit L-6
Benton L-5
Berlin J-6
Big Bend . . . Pg. 121, H-1
Birchwood E-3
Birnamwood F-6
Black Creek G-7
Black Earth K-5
Black River Falls H-4
Blair H-3
Blanchardville K-5
Bloomer G-3
Bloomington K-4
Bonduel G-7
Boscobel K-4
Boyceville F-2
Boyd G-3
Brandon J-7
Brillion H-8
Brodhead L-6
Brokaw F-6
Brookfield . . Pg. 121, H-3
Brown Deer . Pg. 121, A-5
Browntown L-6
Bruce F-3
Buena Park . Pg. 121, K-1
Buffalo H-2
Burlington K-7
Butler . . . . . Pg. 121, C-3
Butternut D-5
Cable D-3

Caddy Vista . Pg. 121, J-6
Cadott F-3
Caledonia . . . Pg. 121, K-6
Calhoun . . . Pg. 121, E-3
Cambra J-6
Cambridge K-7
Cameron F-3
Camp Douglas H-5
Campbellsport J-8
Carrollville . . Pg. 121, H-6
Cascade J-8
Casco G-8
Cashton J-4
Cassville K-4
Catawba E-4
Cazenovia J-5
Cecil G-7
Centuria E-1
Chetek F-3
Chilton H-8
Chippewa Falls F-3
Clayton F-2
Clear Lake F-2
Cleveland L-7
Clinton L-7
Clintonville G-7
Cochrane H-3
Colby G-5
Coleman F-8
Colfax F-3
Colgate . . . . Pg. 121, A-1
Coloma H-6
Columbus J-7
Coon Valley J-4
Cornell F-4
Couderay E-3
Crandon E-7
Crivitz F-8
Cross Plains K-6
Cuba City L-4
Cudahy K-7
Vicinity . . . Pg. 121, F-6
Cumberland E-2
Dane J-6
Darien L-7
Darlington K-5
De Pere G-8
De Soto J-4
DeForest J-6
Deerfield K-6
Delavan K-7
Denmark G-8
Dickeyville L-4
Dodgeville K-5
Dorchester F-5
Dousman K-7
Dresser F-1
Duplainville . Pg. 121, D-2
Durand G-2
Durham . . . . Pg. 121, H-3
Eagle K-7
Eagle River E-6
East Troy K-7
Eastman K-4
Eau Claire G-3
Eden J-7
Edgar F-5
Edgerton K-6
Egg Harbor F-9
Elano F-6
Eleva G-3
Elk Mound G-3
Elkhart Lake H-8
Elkhorn K-7
Ellsworth G-2
Elm Grove . Pg. 121, D-3
Elmwood G-2
Elroy J-5
Embarrass G-7
Ephraim F-9
Ettrick H-3
Evansville K-6
Exeland E-3
Fairchild G-4
Fall Creek G-4
Fall River J-7
Fennimore K-4
Ferryville J-4
Fifield E-5
Florence E-7
Fond Du Lac H-7
Fontana L-7
Footville L-6
Forestville G-8
Fort Atkinson K-7
Fountain City H-3
Fox Lake J-7
Fox Point . . Pg. 121, B-6
Francis Creek H-8
Franklin K-7
Vicinity . . . Pg. 121, H-4
Franksville . Pg. 121, K-6
Frederick E-2
Fremont H-7
Friendship H-6
Fussville . . . Pg. 121, B-3
Galesville H-3
Gays Mills J-4
Genoa J-4
Genoa City L-8
Germantown J-8
Vicinity . . . Pg. 121, A-3
Gillett F-7
Gilman F-4
Glen Flora E-4
Glendale . . . Pg. 121, B-6
Glenwood City F-2
Goerkes Corner
. . . . Pg. 121, D-2
Grafton J-8

Granton G-5
Grantsburg E-1
Granville . . . Pg. 121, A-4
Gratiot L-5
Green Bay G-8
Green Lake H-6
Greendale K-8
Vicinity . . . Pg. 121, G-2
Greenfield . . Pg. 121, F-5
Greenwood G-4
Gresham G-7
Hales Corners
. . . . Pg. 121, G-4
Hammond F-2
Hancock H-6
Hartford J-7
Hartland K-8
Haugen E-2
Hawkins E-4
Hawthorne D-3
Hayward E-3
Hazel Green L-4
Heafford Jct. E-5
Highland K-5
Hilbert H-8
Hillsboro J-4
Holmen H-3
Horicon J-7
Hortonville G-7
Howard G-8
Howards Grove H-8
Hudson F-1
Hurley D-5
Husher . . . . . Pg. 121, K-6
Independence G-3
Ingram E-4
Iola G-6
Iron River C-3
Jackson J-8
Janesville K-6
Jefferson K-7
Johnson Creek K-7
Junction City G-5
Juneau J-7
Kaukauna H-8
Kendall H-5
Kennan E-4
Kenosha L-8
Keshena F-7
Kewaskum J-8
Kewaunee G-9
Kiel H-8
Kimberly H-8
Kingston J-6
Kneeland . . Pg. 121, J-6
La Crosse H-3
La Farge J-4
Lac Du Flambeau . . . D-5
Ladysmith F-4
Lake Delton J-5
Lake Geneva L-7
Lake Nebagamon . . . D-3
Lancaster K-4
Lannon . . . . Pg. 121, B-2
Lena F-7
Linden K-5
Little Chute G-7
Livingston K-4
Lodi J-6
Loganville J-5
Lomira J-7
Lone Rock J-5
Loyal G-4
Lublin F-4
Luck F-2
Luxemburg G-8
Madison K-6
Manawa G-7
Manitowish D-5
Manitowoc H-9
Marathon City F-5
Marcy . . . . . Pg. 121, C-2
Marinette F-8
Marion G-7
Markesan J-6
Marshall K-6
Marshfield G-5
Mason D-4
Mauston H-5
Mayville J-7
Mazomanie J-6
Medford F-4
Meeker . . . . Pg. 121, A-2
Mellen D-4
Melrose H-4
Melvina H-4
Menasha H-7
Menomonee Falls . . . J-8
Vicinity . . . Pg. 121, A-2
Menomonie G-2
Mequon . . . . Pg. 121, A-5
Merrill F-5
Merrillan H-4
Middleton K-6
Milltown E-2
Milton K-6
Milwaukee K-8
Vicinity Pg. 121
Mineral Point K-5
Minong D-3
Mishicot H-9
Mondovi G-3
Monico E-6
Monona K-6
Monroe L-5
Montello J-6
Montfort K-5
Monticello K-6
Montreal D-4
Mosinee G-6

Mount Horeb K-6
Mount Sterling J-4
Mukwonago K-7
Muscoda K-5
Muskego K-8
Vicinity . . . Pg. 121, G-2
Necedah H-5
Neenah H-7
Neillsville G-4
Nekoosa G-5
Nelson G-2
Nelsonville G-6
Neshkoro H-6
New Berlin K-8
Vicinity . . . Pg. 121, E-2
New Glarus K-5
New Holstein H-8
New Lisbon H-5
New London G-7
New Richmond F-2
Niagara E-8
North Cape . Pg. 121, K-4
North Fond du Lac . . . H-7
North Hudson F-1
Norwalk H-4
Oak Creek K-8
Vicinity . . . Pg. 121, G-6
Oakwood . . . Pg. 121, H-6
Oconomowoc K-7
Oconto F-8
Oconto Falls F-8
Omro H-7
Onalaska H-3
Ontario J-4
Oostburg J-8
Orfordville K-6
Osceola F-1
Oshkosh H-7
Osseo G-4
Owen F-4
Oxford H-6
Paddock Lake L-8
Palmyra K-7
Pardeeville J-6
Park Falls E-4
Park Ridge G-6
Patch Grove K-4
Paynesville . Pg. 121, H-5
Pembine E-8
Pepin G-2
Peshtigo F-8
Pewaukee . . Pg. 121, C-1
Phelps D-6
Phillips E-5
Pigeon Falls G-3
Pittsville G-5
Plain J-5
Plainfield H-6
Platteville K-4
Plover G-6
Plum City G-2
Plymouth H-8
Poplar C-3
Port Edwards H-5
Port Washington J-8
Portage J-6
Potosi K-4
Pound F-8
Prairie du Chien K-4
Prairie du Sac J-5
Prentice E-5
Prescott G-1
Princeton H-6
Prospect . . . Pg. 121, F-2
Pulaski G-8
Racine K-8
Vicinity . . . Pg. 121, K-6
Radisson E-3
Randolph J-7
Raymond . . Pg. 121, K-4
Redgranite H-6
Reedsburg J-5
Reedsville H-8
Rhinelander E-6
Rib Lake F-5
Rice Lake E-3
Richland Center J-5
Ridgeland F-2
Ridgeway K-5
Rio J-6
Ripon H-7
River Falls F-2
River Hills . . Pg. 121, A-5
Riverside D-2
Roberts F-2
Rosendale H-7
Rosholt G-6
Rothschild G-5
Saint Croix Falls F-2
Saint Francis K-8
Vicinity . . . Pg. 121, F-7
Saint Martins K-8
Vicinity . . . Pg. 121, G-4
Sauk City J-5
Saukville J-8
Schofield F-6
Seymour G-7
Sharon L-7
Shawano G-7
Sheboygan H-9
Sheboygan Falls J-8
Sheldon F-3
Shell Lake E-2
Shiocton G-7
Shorewood . . Pg. 121, C-7
Shullsburg L-5
Siren E-2
Sister Bay F-9
Soldiers Grove J-4
Solon Springs D-3
Somerset F-1

South Milwaukee . . . K-8
Vicinity . . . Pg. 121, G-7
Sparta H-4
Spencer G-4
Spooner E-3
Spring Green J-5
Spring Valley G-2
Stanley F-4
Stevens Point G-5
Stockbridge H-7
Stockholm G-2
Stoddard J-4
Stoughton K-6
Stratford G-5
Strum G-3
Sturgeon Bay F-8
Sturtevant K-8
Sun Prairie K-7
Superior C-2
Suring F-7
Sussex . . . . Pg. 121, B-1
Tabor . . . . . Pg. 121, J-7
Taylors Falls E-1
Tennyson K-4
Tess Corners
. . . . Pg. 121, G-3
Theresa J-7
Thompsonville
. . . . Pg. 121, K-5
Thorp F-4
Tichigan . . . Pg. 121, J-6
Tigerton G-7
Tomah H-4
Tomahawk E-6
Tony F-4
Trego E-3
Trempealeau H-3
Turtle Lake F-2
Two Rivers H-9
Union Center J-5
Union Church
. . . . Pg. 121, J-4
Union Grove K-8
Unity G-5
Valders H-8
Vernon . . . . Pg. 121, G-1
Verona K-6
Vesper G-5
Village of Superior . . . C-2
Viroqua J-4
Walworth L-7
Washburn C-3
Waterford K-7
Vicinity . . . Pg. 121, K-4
Waterloo K-6
Watertown J-7
Waukesha K-7
Vicinity . . . Pg. 121, E-1
Waunakee K-6
Waupaca G-7
Waupun J-7
Wausau F-6
Wausaukee F-8
Wautoma H-6
Wauwatosa K-8
Vicinity . . . Pg. 121, D-4
Webster D-2
West Allis . . Pg. 121, E-4
West Bend J-8
West Granville
. . . . Pg. 121, B-5
West Milwaukee
. . . . Pg. 121, E-5
Westby J-4
Westfield H-6
Weyauwega G-6
White Lake F-7
Whitefish Bay K-8
Vicinity . . . Pg. 121, C-6
Whitehall G-3
Whitelaw H-8
Whitewater K-7
Whiting G-6
Wild Rose H-6
Willow Creek Pg. 121, A-2
Wind Pt. K-8
Winneconne H-7
Winter E-4
Wisconsin Dells J-5
Wisconsin Rapids . . . G-5
Withee F-4
Wittenberg G-6
Wonewoc J-5
Woodruff E-6
Wrightstown G-8
Wyeville H-5
Wyocena J-6
Yuba J-4

WYOMING
Pages 88-89
Population: 469,559
Capital: Cheyenne
Land Area: 96,989 sq. mi.

Acme B-8
Afton F-3
Aladdin B-12
Albany J-9
Albin H-12
Alcova F-9
Alpine Jct. E-3
Alva B-11
Arapahoe F-6
Arlington H-9
Arminto E-8
Arvada B-9

Atlantic City G-6
Auburn F-3
Baggs J-7
Bairoil G-7
Banner B-8
Bar Nunn F-9
Barnum D-8
Basin C-7
Beckton B-8
Bedford F-3
Beulah B-12
Big Horn B-8
Big Piney F-4
Big Sandy F-5
Big Trails D-8
Bill E-10
Bitter Creek H-6
Bondurant E-4
Border G-3
Bosler H-10
Boulder F-5
Boxelder F-10
Buffalo C-8
Burgess Jct. B-7
Burlington C-6
Burns J-12
Burntfork J-4
Burris F-5
Byron B-6
Calpet F-4
Canyon Jct. B-4
Carpenter J-12
Carter J-4
Casper F-9
Centennial J-9
Cheyenne J-11
Chugwater H-11
Clareton D-11
Clark B-5
Clearmont B-9
Cody C-5
Cokeville G-3
Colony B-12
Cora F-4
Cowley B-6
Creston Jct. H-7
Crowheart E-5
Daniel F-4
Dayton B-8
Deaver B-6
Devil's Tower Jct. . . . B-11
Diamondville H-3
Dixon J-7
Douglas F-10
Dubois E-5
East Thermopolis . . . D-7
Eden H-5
Edgerton E-9
Egbert J-12
Elk Basin B-6
Elk Mountain H-9
Elkol H-4
Elmo H-9
Emblem C-6
Encampment J-9
Ethete F-6
Etna E-3
Evanston J-3
Evansville F-9
Fairview F-3
Farson G-5
Federal J-11
Fort Bridger J-4
Fort Laramie G-11
Fort Washakie F-5
Four Corners C-12
Frannie B-6
Freedom F-3
Frontier H-4
Garland B-6
Gillette C-10
Glendo F-11
Glenrock F-10
Granger H-4
Grass Creek D-6
Green River H-5
Greybull C-7
Grover F-3
Guernsey G-11
Hamilton Dome D-6
Hampshire D-11
Hanna H-9
Hartville G-11
Hawk Springs H-12
Hiland E-8
Hillsdale J-12
Hobock Jct. E-3
Horse Creek J-11
Hudson F-6
Hulett B-11
Huntley H-12
Hyattville C-8
Iron Mountain H-11
Jackson E-3
Jay Em G-12
Jeffrey City G-7
Jenny Lake D-3
Kaycee D-9
Keeline F-11
Kelly E-4
Kemmerer H-3
Kinnear E-6
Kirby D-7
La Barge G-4
La Grange H-12
Lake Jct. B-4
Lamont G-8
Lance Creek E-11
Lander F-6
Laramie J-10

Leiter B-9
Lightning Flat B-11
Lisk D-9
Lingle G-12
Little America J-4
Lonetree J-4
Lost Cabin E-8
Lost Springs F-11
Lovell B-6
Lucerne D-7
Lusk F-12
Lyman J-4
Lysite E-7
Madison Jct. B-3
Mammoth Springs Jct. B-3
Manderson C-7
Manville F-11
Marbleton F-4
Mayoworth D-8
McFadden H-10
McKinnon K-4
Medicine Bow H-9
Meeteetse C-6
Merna F-4
Midwest E-9
Millburne J-4
Mills F-9
Moneta E-7
Moorcroft C-11
Moose D-3
Moran Jct. D-4
Morrisey D-11
Morton E-6
Mountain Home J-10
Mountain View J-4
Mule Cr. Jct. E-12
Natrona E-9
New Haven B-11
Newcastle D-12
Node F-12
Norris Jct. B-3
Old Faithful C-3
Opal H-4
Orin F-11
Orpha F-10
Osage D-12
Oshoto B-11
Otto C-7
Parkman B-8
Pavillion E-6
Piedmont J-4
Pine Bluffs J-12
Pine Tree Jct. D-10
Pinedale F-5
Pitchfork D-5
Point of Rocks H-6
Powder River F-8
Powell B-6
Quealy J-5
Ralston B-6
Ranchester B-8
Rawlins H-8
Recluse B-10
Red Desert H-7
Redbird E-12
Reliance H-6
Reno Jct. D-10
Riverside J-9
Riverton F-7
Robertson J-4
Rochelle D-11
Rock River H-10
Rock Springs H-5
Rocky Point B-11
Rozet C-10
Sage H-3
Saint Stephens F-6
Saratoga J-9
Savageton D-10
Savery J-8
Shawnee F-11
Shell C-7
Sheridan B-8
Shirley Basin G-9
Shoshoni E-7
Sinclair H-8
Slater H-11
Smoot F-3
South Pass City G-6
Spotted Horse B-10
Story C-8
Sundance C-12
Sunrise G-11
Superior H-6
Sussex D-9
Table Rock H-7
Ten Sleep C-8
Teton Village D-3
Thayne F-3
Thermopolis D-6
Tie Siding J-10
Torrington G-12
Tower Jct. B-4
Turnerville F-3
Ucross C-9
Upton C-11
Urie J-4
Valley C-5
Van Tassell F-12
Veteran G-12
Walcott H-9
Waltman E-8
Wamsutter H-7
West Thumb Jct. C-4
Weston B-10
Wheatland G-11
Wilson E-3
Woods Landing J-10
Worland D-7
Wright D-10
Yoder H-12